THE BUSINESS TRAVELER'S WORLD GUIDE

PHILIP SELDON

McGraw-Hill
New York • San Francisco • Washington, D.C. • Auckland
Bogotá • Caracas • Lisbon • London • Madrid • Mexico City
Milan • Montreal • New Delhi • San Juan • Singapore
Sydney • Tokyo • Toronto

McGraw-Hill

A Division of The McGraw-Hill Companies

1 2 3 4 5 6 7 8 9 0   DOC/DOC   9 0 3 2 1 0 9 8

ISBN 0-07-061997-2

Printed and bound by R.R. Donnelley & Sons.

NOTE: *The information contained in this edition of* The Business Traveler's World Guide *has been thoroughly researched and was obtained from sources believed to be reliable. Every effort has been made to insure its accuracy, but the publishers cannot accept either responsibility for any errors and omissions nor liability for any consequences arising from the use of the information contained herein. Corrections and suggestions from business travelers should be addressed to the Editorial Department of the Publishers.*

McGraw-Hill books are available at special quantity discounts to use as premiums and sales promotions, or for use in corporate training programs. For more information, please write to the Director of Special Sales, McGraw-Hill, 11 West 19th Street, New York, NY 10011. Or contact your local bookstore.

This book is printed on acid-free stock.

CONTENTS

This book is dedicated to Astrid Heeren
A shining light in the universe

INTRODUCTION

With the globalization of the economy, business travelers are being faced with a sometimes dizzying array of national and regional business, social and cultural customs and behaviors. This book is designed to help you, the traveling business professional, wade through those customs and build professional and social relationships with potential associates.

Business and social protocol will vary wherever you go, but there are certain constants you should adhere to. No matter what country you visit, demonstrating knowledge about and interest in its history, geography, culture, sports and natural resources will help spark mutual interest socially as long as you do so sincerely, modestly and with a positive outlook. Minding basic local manners will make a good impression; for example, by dressing modestly in a Muslim country, attempting chopsticks in China, or agreeing to a nature hike in Estonia. It helps to phone or fax your approximate dates of the trip well before your departure; once you arrive, immediately call to set time and place.

Getting down to business and making decisions will often take longer than in the United States or the most efficient West European countries, so try to give yourself as much time as possible to make the trip and, in some cases, expect to make several trips before a contract is finalized. In developing countries, not only is the pace of business slower but so is the pace of life. Poor infrastructure often holds things up, for example, being unable to get through by telephone to Romania, or waiting for a brown-out to be over in the Philippines, or poor road conditions in the former Soviet Union. Warmer climates often mean that the business day begins early, as in Israel, but they can also mean that people work and socialize late and begin the business day in late morning, as in Spain.

Dinner table rules are also quite variable throughout the world. It's best to follow the lead of your host, but if you feel that using chopsticks will result in food dropping into your lap, ask for a knife and fork, or if you, as an American have trouble figuring out how to eat European-style with knife and fork, it's best to eat your way, as long as you do it neatly. Many poorer countries consider it wasteful to leave food on your plate.

INTRODUCTION

The level of formality varies when it comes to business attire, but you should always come, at least at initial meetings, in a business suit or conservative dress. Better to err on the side of conservatism. In more affluent countries you will be expected to wear well-cut, good materials; in developing economies, however, appearing "too" well-dressed may attract thieves and even resentment from officials. Nevertheless, one should never dress shabbily. Businesswomen often must be more careful than men in how they dress: in some Muslim countries, they must cover their heads, in others, dressing too fashionably will hinder progress.

Correct body language is also important. North and South Americans often put off more reserved West Europeans and Asians by their tendency to gesticulate and speak loudly, and North Americans themselves are put off if you stand too close to them. Muslims have strong taboos against eating with one's left hand only, as that was the hand used, in nomadic times, to take care of toilet activities. In most Buddhist countries, the taboo is against touching one's head, which is considered the repository of the soul. In countries where there is strong social separation of men and women, men should wait to see if the woman offers her hand, and if not, simply nod or bow upon introduction.

Always pack some small, tasteful gifts - check each section for appropriate protocol on what and when to give and how to present them. Although the gifts you bring along just in case might include an "American souvenir", keep in mind that your Western counterparts won't be too impressed with this sort of thing, nor will the more sophisticated associates in developing countries. Flower-giving is important in most European and South American countries but certain flowers can be loaded with symbolism you wouldn't want to insinuate when invited to dinner. In most cases, red or white roses carry romantic/sexual connotations, while chrysanthemums and dahlias are for funerals. In many Asian countries, the taboos are against blue or white wrapping paper, which are funereal. Sometimes items that could be interpreted as lethal - cutting tools like knives and scissors, or even a scarf - are considered bad luck.

Finally, although in many cases one should try to blend in, don't go overboard. Your associates are fully aware that you are, after all, visiting. "Going native" by donning an Arab headdress will be seen as a mocking gesture, while drinking as much as the locals do in Moldova will result in more hangovers than contracts. Though interrupting everyone and speaking loudly in Argentina may be par for the course, or the officials in China may be slow to act, it never does to be rude. Be careful when discussing politics, and remember that what may be a minor faraway border or ethnic conflict to you may be a major issue to your hosts.

Finally, although much of business protocol is about establishing social relationships that will encourage business dealings, one should never forget that friendliness alone does not a reliable business partner make. Do your own meticulous investigation of any company you are considering contracting with.

USEFUL PHRASES - CHINESE

Do you speak English? Ni hwei shwo yingwen hwa ma?
I understand Wo dung
I do not understand Wobu dung
Yes Dwèi
No Bèdwè
Newspaper Bau
Friend. Peng-you
Man. Ren
Speak Shwo
Stay Ju
I Wo
You Nin
He, She Ta
Good morning, Good day Dzau
Good evening Ni hau ma
Good night Dzài jyèn
Good-bye Dzài jyèn
How is it going? Dzemmayaang?
I am well Wo hau.
Thank you Syèsye
Don't mention it bukechi
May I come in? Wo keyi jinlai ma?
Where can I find? Dzai shemma difang?
Post office. Youjengjyu
I need Wo syuyau
Just a second Deng yihwer.
Dining room Fànting
Please Chíng
Look at Kàn
Don't mention it Bù syè
Pardon me, excuse me Dwèibuchi
Gladly Hau
Drugstore Yaufang
What is your name? Nín gwèisying.
What do you want? Ni yau shèmma?
I want Wo yàu
How much is it? Jèide dwosau chyén
Too much Tai gwéi

USEFUL PHRASES - FRENCH

Do you speak English? Parlez-vous anglais?
I understand Je comprends
I do not understand Je ne comprends pas
Yes Oui
No Non
Sir Monsieur
Madam Madame
Miss Madamoiselle
Your name Votre nom?
My name is Je m'appelle
I Je
You Vous
He, She il, elle
Good morning, Good day bonjour
Good evening bonsoir
Good night bonne nuit
Good-bye au revoir
How are you Comment allez-vous?
Well, thanks, and you? Bien, merci, et vous-meme?
Thank you merci
How much is it? A quel prix?
Hurry up Dépêchez-vous
What time is it? Quelle heure est-il?
Breakfast petit déjeuner
Lunch déjeuner
Dinner diner
Dining room salle à manger
Please S'il vous plait
Thanks (a lot) Merci (beaucoup)
Don't mention it Il n'y a pas de quoi
Pardon me, excuse me Pardon
Gladly Avec plaisir
May I introduce my friend? Permettez-moi de vous present-
er mon ami
Delighted, pleased to meet you Enchante!
What do you want? Que voulez-vous?
I should like Je voudrais
It's too much C'est trop!

USEFUL PHRASES - GERMAN

Do you speak English? Sprechen Sie Englisch?
I understand Ich verstehe
I do not understand Ich verstehe nicht.
Yes Ja
No Nein
Sir Herr
Madam Dame
Miss Fraulein
Doctor Herr Doktor
Interpreter einen Dolmetscher
Post office Postamt
I Ich
You Sie
He, She Er, Sie
Good morning, Good day Guten Morgen, Guten Tag
Good evening Guten Abend
Good night Gute Nacht
Good-bye auf Wiedersehen
How are you Wie geht's?
Well, thanks, and you? Danke, gut, und Ihnen?
Thank you Danke
How much is it? Wieviel?
Hurry up Sich beeilen
What time is it?
Breakfast Fruehstueck
Lunch Mittagessen
Dining room Esszimmer
Please Bitte
Thanks (a lot) Danke Schon
Don't mention it Bitte Schon
Pardon me, excuse me Verzeihen Sie
It doesn't matter Es macht nichts aus
I am sorry Es tut mir leid
I wish Ich wuenschte
I should like Ich möchte gern
To buy Kaufen
How Much? Wieviel?
It's too much Zu viel

USEFUL PHRASES - ITALIAN

Do you speak English? Parla inglese?
I understand Capisco
I do not understand Non capisco
Yes Si
No No
Sir Segnore
Madam Segnora
Miss Signorina
Your name Il Suo nome?
My name is Mi Chiamo
I Io
You Lei
He, She Egli, Ella
Good morning, Good day Buongiorno
Good evening Buona sera
Good night Buona notte
Good-bye Arrivederci
How are you Come sta?
Well, thanks, and you? Bene, grazie, e Lei?
Thank you Grazie
How much is it? Quanto costa?
Hurry up Presto!
What time is it? Che ora é?
Breakfast Colazione
Lunch Pranzo
Dinner Cena
Dining room Sala da pranzo
Please Per piacere
Thanks (a lot) Grazie Mille.
Don't mention it Prego
Pardon me, excuse me Scusi
Gladly Volentieri.
Where is? Dove?
Can you tell me? Sa dirmi?
What do you want? Che vuole?
I want Desidero
I should like Vorrei
It's too much È troppo

16

USEFUL PHRASES - JAPANESE

Do you speak English? Eido dekimasu ka?
I understand Hai; wakarimash'ta
I do not understand Lie; Wakarimesen
Yes Hai
No iie
Sir San
Madam Okusan
Miss Ojo-san
Your name Anata-no onamae-wa
My name is Watakusino namae-wa
I Watakushi
You Anata
He, She Kare, Kanojo
Good morning, Good day Ohayo gozaimas, Komishi-wa
Good evening Konban-wa
Good night Oyas'mi-nasai
Good-bye Sayonara
How are you Ikaga des'ka?
Thank you Arigato
How much is it? Ikura des'ka?
Hurry up Hayaku!
What time is it? Nanji des'ka
Doctor Isha
Pharmacy Kusurya
Breakfast Chooshoku
Lunch Hirugohan
Dinner Bangoha
Dining room Syokugita
Please Doozo
Thanks (a lot) Arigato gozaimas
Don't mention it Do itashimashita
Pardon me, excuse me Gomen nasai
Gladly Yrokonde
Where is? Doko des'ka?
What do you want? Nani ka hoshii desu-ka?
What can I do for you? Nan no go yo desu-ka?
I want Hoshi-i
Very much Taihen

USEFUL PHRASES - PORTUGESE

Do you speak English? Fala o senhor português inglês?
Do you understand? Compreende?
I do not understand Eu não compreendo
Yes Sim
No Náo
Sir Sehnor
Madam Sehnora
Miss Sehnorita
Your name Vosso nome?
My name is O meu nome é
I Eu
You Vocé
He, She Ele, Êla
Good morning, Good day Bom dia
Good evening Boa tarde
Good night Boa noite
Good-bye Adeus
How are you? Como está?
Very well, thanks, and you? Muito bem, gracias
Thank you Gracias
How much is it? Quanto custa?
What time is it? Que horas são?
Breakfast Café-da-manhã
Doctor Um medico
Bathroom Quarto de banho
Dining room A sala de jantar
Please Por favor
Thanks (a lot) Obrigado
Don't mention it Não por isso
Pardon me, excuse me Perdão
I am sorry Eu lamento
Gladly Com prazer
May I introduce my friend? Posso apresentar o meu amigo
Delighted, pleased to meet you Muito prazer
What do you want? O que quer o senhor?
I should like Eu quisera
Will you give me Quer me dar?
It's too much E demasiado

USEFUL PHRASES - RUSSIAN

Do you speak English? Vyi szvzryite po ruskii?
I understand Ya panimayu
I do not understand Ya nye panimayu
Yes Da
No Nyet
Sir Gaspadin
Madam Gaspaszha
Your name Washye Imya
My name is Menya zavut
I Ya
You Vyi
He, She On, Ona
Good morning, Good day Dobroye utro, Dobry dyen
Good evening Dobry Vecher
Good night Spoukoinoi nochi
Good-bye Dosvidanya
How are you Kak vyi pazhyvayite?
Well, thanks, and you? Sposibua, Kharasho, a vyi?
Thank you Sposibua
How much is it? Skolko eta stoyit?
Hurry up Byistree
What time is it? Skolko chas?
Automobile Avtomobyil
Bathroom Toalyet
Breakfast Utrenyi Zavtrak
Lunch Zavtrak
Dinner Abyed
Dining room Stalavaya
Please Pazhaluyistya
Thanks (a lot) Sposibo balshoe
Don't mention it Nye za chto
Pardon me, excuse me Izvinyitye menya
Gladly S udovolviem
What do you want? Chto vyi hotitye?
I wish Ya hachu
I should like Ya byi hatyel
Give me Daitye mnye
It's too much Sliskam mnoga

USEFUL PHRASES - SPANISH

Do you speak English? ¿Habla usted inglés?
I understand Entiendo
I do not understand No Entiendo
Yes Sí
No No
Sir Señor
Madam Señora
Miss Señorita
A doctor Un médico
An interpreter Un intérprete
I Yo
You Usted
He, She El, Ella
Good morning, Good day Buenos días
Good evening Buenas Tardes
Good night Buenas Noches
Good-bye Adíos
Hello Hola
How are you ¿Cómo está usted?
Well, thanks, and you? Bien, gracias, ¿y usted?
Thank you Gracias
How much is it? ¿Cuánto?
What do you want ¿Qué desea usted?
Automobile Auto
Breakfast El desayuno
Telephone El telphono
Bathroom El cuarto de baño
Dining room El comedor
Please Por favor
Thanks (a lot) Gracias
Don't mention it De Nada
Pardon me, excuse me Dispense usted
I am sorry Lo siento
Delighted, pleased to meet you ¡Muchisimo, gusto!
What do you want? ¿Que quere usted?
I wish Yo deseo
I should like Quisiera
It's too much Es demaciado

EUROPE

ARMENIA

Official Name: The Republic of Armenia

Government: Constitutional republic

Area: 29,800 sq.km., 11,506 sq.mi.

Population: 3.7 mil

Religion(s): Christianity, Armenian Orthodox, Protestant, Islamic.

Capital City: Yerevan

Major Business Cities: Kirovakan, Gumayri

Time: GMT +3

Currency: 1 Dram = 100 Louma

Business Hours:
- Government: 09.00-18.00 Mon-Fri
- Banks: 09.00-18.00 Mon-Fri
- Shops: 09.00-18.00 Mon-Fri
- Offices: 09.00-18.00 Mon-Fri

Weight and Measures: Metric System

Electric Current: 220/127V. 50c

Suitable Clothing: Because of its dry, mountainous climate, it's worthwhile to bring a light jacket or sweater for evenings in the warmer months, and medium-weight clothing and heavy coat for winter. Above all, however, dress modestly, even when sightseeing.

Automobile Driving License: An International driving license is required.

Tipping: Officially discouraged, but appreciated by small services

Credit Cards Accepted: American Express, Carte Blanche, Diner's Club, Visa

Customary Dining Hours:
Breakfast: 07.00-09.00
Lunch: 12.00-14.30
Dinner: 18.30-22.00

Local Customs, Business Protocol and Courtesies: Armenia is a landlocked C.I.S. republic located northeast of Turkey. Plagued by a struggling, post-Soviet economy, a series of devastating earthquakes, and military and economic conflict with the neighboring republic of Azerbaijan over the region of Nagorny Karabakh, conducting business here is difficult at best. As visa, currency and customs requirements have undergone a number of changes recently, you should consult your country's Armenian embassy or consulate when arranging your trip. Currently, one should obtain an official invitation in order to get a 30-day visa. Vaccinations are not required unless you are arriving from an infected area. Valuables, including foreign currency, must be registered upon arrival, otherwise they may be confiscated upon departure. There are no restrictions on import of foreign currency, but selling personal items may result in your paying duty later at the airport. The best time for business travel is mid-spring to the end of summer. Keeping in mind local business and social protocol, certain body language may appear odd to the Western traveler · standing very close to one another is normal if engaged in conversation and moving away is regarded as a rejection. Another gesture to look out for: narrowing one's eyes will communicate dislike and a desire to cut off contact.

Meals are leisurely; if you are a dinner guest in someone's home, it would be impolite to leave immediately after coffee · stay for about another hour. Dining out with colleagues will usually last an entire evening. Do not over-order your food-it is considered rude and wasteful to leave food on your plate.

ARMENIA

Certain givens apply to many of the former Soviet republics: Both custom and the unstable economy make bribery the name of the game in many situations. Always carry around small gifts of hard-to-find items, and small denominations for tipping. Business travelers can expect frequent delays and service problems, sometimes but not always solvable with a bribe. Long distance calls can be booked and paid for a day in advance at local telephone or post offices (direct dial and international operator assistance is available). Bring your own toiletries, as there is a shortage, at least of quality brands if any at all. Changing money on the street is illegal and will likely result in your being ripped off.

Health: It is recommended to consult your doctor before your journey. Drinking water is safe in most major cities. The medical and dental treatment is free, but the medications must be paid. In emergencies you must contact your embassy or hotel receptionist.

YEREVAN

Country code: 374- City code: 2

Airport: Yerevan

Distance from City: 7 km. (5 mi.) South-West from the city

Transfers: (Minimum Connecting Time):
International to International: 240 min.
International to Domestic: 240 min.
Domestic to International: 240 min.
Domestic to Domestic: 180 min.

Hotels:
Ani, Soyat-Novy 19, 523961
Armenia, King Vramshapouth 1, 525393
Dvin, Paronyuan 40, 536343
Sevan, Shaumyan 10, 535343

Restaurants:
Aragil, Vicory Park
Ararat, Sverdlov 3

Egnik, Spandaryan Square
Iyre Café, Komitas St.
Masis, Krasnoarmenskaya

Places of Interest:
Contemporary Art Museum
Government House
St. Sarkis Church
Swan Lake
Victory Bridge

AUSTRIA

Official Name: Republic of Austria

Location: Western Europe. Austria is surrounded by the Czech Republic, Slovakia, Hungary, Slovenia, Italy, Liechtenstein, Switzerland and Germany.

Government: Democracy

Area: 83,858 sq. km., 32,378 sq. mi.

Population: 8 million

Religion(s): Roman Catholic majority. Protestant minority.

Capital City: Vienna

Major Business Cities: Innsbruck and Salzburg.

Time: GMT +1 (GMT +2 from late March to late October)

Currency: Austrian Schilling (AUS)=100 Groschen

Currency Requirements: There are no restrictions on the export and the import of local and foreign currencies except for the export of more than AUS100,000 in local currency. For this amount it is required to obtain a permit.

Business Hours:
- Banks: 08.00-15.00 Mon-Fri
- Shops: 08.00-18.00 Mon-Fri; 08.00-12.30 Sat
- Offices: 08.00/09.00-16.00/17.00 Mon-Fri

Weight and Measures: Metric System

Electric Current: 220 volts AC. Plugs are of the continental 2-pin type.

Holidays:
New Year's Day - January 1
Epiphany - January 6
Easter Monday – April 13*
National Day - May 1
Ascension Day – May 21*
Whit Monday – June 1*
Corpus Christi – June 11*
Assumption Day - August 15*
All Saints' Day - November 1
Immaculate Conception - December 8
Christmas Day - December 25
St. Stephen's Day - December 26

* Christian Holidays – vary each year.
Holidays falling on a Sunday are not observed on the following Monday.

Suitable Clothing: Dress conservatively at all times, in well-tailored, classic styles. In winter, bring medium weight to heavy clothing and a warm coat. In summer, bring light to medium weight clothing.

Automobile Driving License: A National Driving License held for at least one year is required.

Customs Allowances: Personal items are duty free, but register valuables upon arrival and keep receipts. Duty-free restrictions are 200 or 400 cigarettes, 50 or 200 cigars, respectively, for those traveling from E.U. or non-E.U. countries. Prohibited are weaponry and drugs.

Tipping: Restaurants include a service charge of 10-15% but is accepted to leave another 5%. Taxi drivers expect a 10% tip.

Local Customs, Business Protocol and Courtesies: Business relationships in Austria are marked by extreme formality, although in one setting not as stiff as one would imagine: an afternoon or evening at a wine garden. Your Viennese counterparts will likely invite you to one of these picturesque wine gardens that dot the outskirts of the city, as a way for you to become better acquainted on a social level. Rules and rank are taken seriously in the Austrian business climate: be punctual to all appointments, and, upon entering an office give your business card to the receptionist as well as your counterparts. When meeting with a group of professionals, shake hands with women first, and otherwise in order of rank. Decisions tend to be made at the top of the hierarchy, so it's important not to offend by misplacing rank. One reason it's useful to exchange business cards immediately is that they will help you quickly figure out titles. It is appropriate to address a person by Herr/Frau followed by his or her title and last name, such as Herr Professor Braun or Frau Engineer Schmidt. You are expected to maintain an air of discretion about your business, and pay attention to detail in your presentations. Follow-through is taken very seriously; if you fail to honor an invitation or cancel a meeting at the last minute, it can severely hurt your business relationship.

Your Austrian counterparts will likely invite you out (and don't offer to pay in this case) for dinner or the opera. If you are invited to someone's home, bring chocolate, fine wine or flowers for the hostess but keep in mind that as in many European countries, there are certain taboos on the nature of the bouquet · never bring red (it signifies romantic love), or even numbers of flowers. Table manners are strict, if you want seconds, place your fork and knife apart on the plate, and when finished, place them together on the plate on a diagonal.

Health: There are no vaccinations required. There is a Health Agreement with the EC countries, that allows free emergency treatment at public hospitals. An additional insurance is highly recommended.

Language: German.

VIENNA

Country code: 43 - City code: 1

AUSTRIA

Airport: Schwechat International Airport.

Distance from City: 18km (11 miles) east of city center

Transportation to Center of City:
From International and Domestic Terminals
By Bus AUS80 (cost) Time approx. 25 min.
By Taxi (cost) AUS350-400 Time approx. 20 min.
Tip luggage porters per piece

Automobile Rentals:
Airport car rental desk
Avis - 7007-2700
Europcar Interrent - 7007-3316
Hertz - 7007-2661

Car rental city office
Avis - 587-6241
Europcar Interrent - 7996176
Hertz - 512-8677

Hotels:
Altstadt Vienna Hotel, Kirchengasse 41, 526-3390-0
Astoria Wien Hotel, Kaerntner St., 32-34, 515770
Best Western Hotel Stefanie, Taborstr., 12, 21150-0
Bristol Hotel, Kaerntner Ring 1, 51516-0
Carlton Opera Hotel, Schikanedergasse 4, 587-5302
Europa Wien Hotel, Kaerntner St., 18, 515940
Furst Metternich Hotel, Esterhazygasse 33, 58870
Holiday Inn Crowne Plaza, Handelskai 269, 72777
Holiday Inn Wien, Triesterstr. 72, 60530
Imperial Hotel, Kaerntner Ring 16, 50110-0
K & K Hotel Maria Theresia, Kirchberggasse 6-8, 52123
Mercure Wien Zentrum, Eleischmarkt 1a & 2, 534600
Opernring Hotel, Opernring 11, 587-5518
Prinz Eugen Hotel, Wiedner Gurtel 14, 505-1741
Radisson SAS Palais Hotel Vienna, Parkring 16, 515170
Renaissance Penta Vienna Hotel, Ungargasse 60, 71175-0
Sacher Hotel, 4 Philharmonikerstr., 51456
Triest Hotel, Wiedner Hauptstr. 12, 58918-0
Vienna Hotel, Am Stadtpark, 717000
Vienna Marriott Hotel, parking 12a, 515180

AUSTRIA

Restaurants:
Café Willendorf, 1060 Linke Wienzeile 102, 587-1789
Einstein, 1010 Radhauspl. 4, 422626
Kauzchen, 1070 Gardegasse 8, 526-4866
Ma Pitom, 1010 Seitenstettengasse 5, 535-4313
Mensa der Hochschule fur Musik, 1010 Johannesgasse 8,
    512-9470
Naschmarkt, 1010 Schwarzenbergpl. 16, 505-3115
Pizza-Bizi, 1010 Rotenturmstr. 4, 513-3705
Plutzer Brau, Schrankgasse 2, 526-1215
Vinissimo, 1060 Windmuhlgasse 20a, 586-4888
Noodeles & Company, 1010 Karlspl. 5, 505-3839
Finglmuller, 1010 Wollzaile 5, 512-6177
Vollwert-Restaurant Lebenbauer, 1010 Teinfaltstr. 3, 533-5556
Weibels Wirtshaus, 1010 Kumpfgasse, 2512-3986

Entertainment:
Café Alt Wien, 1010 Backerstr. 9, 5125-2222
Jazzclub Sixth, 1060 Gumpendorfer Str. 9, 586-8710
Jazzland, 1010 Franz-Josefs-Kai 29, 533-2575
Kaktus, 1010 Seitenstettengasse 5, 533-1938
Krah Krah, 1010 Rabensteig 8, 533-8193
Mekka, 1070 Apollogasse 14
P-1, 1010 Rotgasse 9, 535-9995
Roter Engel, Rabensteig 5, 535-4105
Santo Spirito, 1010 Kumpfgasse 7, 512-9998
Thelonious Monk, 1010 Sonnenfelsgasse 13, 512-1631
Titanic, Theobaldgasse 11, 587-4758
Volksgarten, Burgring/Heldenpl., 533-0518

Shops and Stores:

Adlmuller, Kartner Str. 41	Apparel
Carius & Binder, Karntner Str. 17	Jewelry
E. Broun, Graben 8	Apparel
Flamm, Neuer Markt 12,	Apparel
Gerngross, Mariahilfer Str. and Kirchengasse	Dept. Store
Haban, Karntner Str. 2,	Jewelry
Herzmansky, Mariahilfer Str. 26-30	Dept. Store
Lanz, Kartner Str. 10	Apparel
Maldone, Kartner Str. 4	Apparel
Malowan, Opernring 23	Apparel
Ringstrassen Galerie, Karntner Ring 5-7	Shopping Paza

AUSTRIA

Schullin, Kohlmarkt 7	Jewelry
Sir Anthony, Kartner Str. 21-23	Apparel
Souvenir in der Hofburg, Hofburgpassage 1	Gift Shop
Stafa, Mariahilfer Str. 120	Dept. Store
Steffl, Karntner Str. 19	Dept. Store
Venturini, Spiegelgasse 9	Apparel
Wiener Geschenke, Reitschulgasse 4	Gift Shop

Places of Interest:
St. Stephen's Cathedral
Spanish Riding School – horse training
Belvedere Palace - art galleries.
Schonbrunn Palace
Sigmund Freud's Home

AZERBAIJAN

Official Name: The Republic of Azerbaijan

Government: Constitutional Republic

Area: 86,600 sq. km., 33,436 sq. mi.

Population: 7.5 million

Religion(s): Islamic majority. Russian Orthodox minority

Capital City: Baku

Major Business Cities: Gyandzha, Sumgait

Time: GMT + 4 hrs.

Currency: 1 Manat = 100 Gopik

Currency Requirements: The Import of foreign currency is unlimited but must be declared. The export is limited to the amount declared upon arrival. The import and the export of local currency are prohibited.

Business Hours:
- Government: 09.00-18.00 Mon-Fri
- Banks: 09.00-18.00 Mon-Fri
- Shops: 09.00-18.00 Mon-Fri
- Offices: 09.00-18.00 Mon-Fri

Weight and Measures: Metric System

Electric Current: 220/127V, 50c

Automobile Driving License: An International Driving License is required.

Tipping: A tip of 10%-15% is expected in most restaurants.

Hotels usually include a service charge in the bill.

Credit Cards Accepted: American Express, Carte Blanche, Diners Club, Eurocard, Visa.

Customary Dining Hours:
Breakfast: 07.00-09.00
Lunch: 12.00-14.30
Dinner: 18.30-22.00

Local Customs, Business Protocol and Courtesies: As throughout the former East bloc and FSU, nationalism is on the rise in Azerbaijan, so it's best not to get enmeshed in political discussions or mistake its multi-ethnic society as a "Russian" one or ignore the customs and pride of the dominant culture, which is Muslim. The former Soviet republic, which borders the Caspian Sea, has been warring the past few years with neighboring Armenia over the region of Nagorny Karabakh, and this has spilled over into domestic interethnic clashes. The other big issue in Azerbaijan, one which unifies its various cultural groups, is environmentalism. Despite the poor economy, hospitality reigns, and you should reciprocate for the many invitations you will receive with small gifts from your country. Since Azerbaijan is a Muslim country, dress modestly (no shorts), and do not bring alcohol as a gift.

Health: It is recommended to consult your doctor before your journey. Drinking water is safe in most major cities. The medical and dental treatment is free, but the medications must be paid. In emergencies you must contact your embassy or hotel receptionist.

Language: Azerbaijani.

BAKU

Country code: 994 - City code: 12

AZERBAIJAN

Airport: Baku International

Distance from City: 28 km. (18 mi.)

Transfers: (Minimum Connecting Time):
International to International: 240 min.
International to Domestic: 240 min.
Domestic to International: 240 min.
Domestic to Domestic: 180 min.

Hotels:
Azerbajan, Lenin Prospekt 1, 989842
Moscow, 1-A Mekhti Gussein, 392898

Restaurants:
Caravansarai, Bashennaya 11
Metor, Gogol
Shirvan, Kirov Prospekt 15

Places of Interest:
Botanical Garden
History Museum
Kirov Park
Maiden's Tower
Murad Gates
Palace of Khans

BELARUS

Official Name: Republic of Belarus

Location: Eastern Europe. Belarus is bordered by Russia to the north and east, Lithuania and Latvia to the northwest and Poland to the west. Ukraine lies to the south.

Government: Constitutional Republic.

Area: 207,595 sq. km., 80,153 sq. miles.

Population: 10.5 million

Religion(s): Eastern Orthodox and Roman Catholic majority. Jewish and Muslim minorities.

Capital City: Minsk

Major Business Cities: Minsk and Gomel

Time: GMT +2 (GMT +3 March-September)

Currency: Belarussian Ruble (BYB)

Currency Requirements: Import of foreign currency is unlimited but the amount must be declared. The export is limited to the amount declared on import. The import and export of local currency is prohibited. The local currency that was not spent must be reconverted on departure.

Business Hours:
- Government: 09.00-18.00 Mon-Fri
- Banks: 09.00-18.00 Mon-Fri
- Shops: 09.00-19.00/21.00 Mon-Sat
- Offices: 09.00-18.00 Mon-Fri

Weight and Measures: Metric System

Electric Current: 220 volts AC. The plugs are of the Continental 2-pin round type.

Holidays:
New Year's Day - January 1
Orthodox Church Christmas - January 7
National Armed Forces Day - February 23
Women's Day - March 8
Constitution Day - March 15
Easter (Catholic Church) - April 12-13*
Easter (Orthodox Church) - April 27-28*
Labour Day - May 1
Easter of the Dead - May 6*
Victory Day - May 9
Day of Liberation of Belarus from the Nazi invasion - July 3
Independence Day - July 27
Remembrance Day - November 2
Catholic Church Christmas - December 25

*Christian holidays - vary each year

Suitable Clothing: Bring conservative business clothing; light materials and rainwear for summer, heavy clothing and a coat for winter.

Automobile Driving License: An International or a National Driving License with an authorized translation is required.

Customs Allowances: As currency and customs requirements have undergone a number of changes in recent years, one should consult your country's Belarussian embassy or consulate when arranging your trip. Valuables, including foreign currency, must be registered upon arrival, otherwise they may be confiscated upon departure. Although you may bring in unlimited amounts of foreign currency, and take out any you initially declare, you may not import or export Belarussian rubles. Cigarettes are limited to 250 and one liter of wine and a half liter of spirits are permitted.

Tipping: A service charge 10-15% is usually included in the hotel bill. A 10% tip is customary to be left otherwise.

Credit Cards Accepted: American Express, Carte Blanche, EuroCard, Visa

Customary Dining Hours:
Breakfast: 07.00-09.00
Lunch: 12.00-14.30
Dinner: 18.30-22.00

Local Customs, Business Protocol and Courtesies: Many outsiders still find this country's former name more familiar-Beylorussia-but if you are visiting or conducting business in this former Soviet republic, remember that it is now Belarus and that it's best not to get enmeshed in political discussions. The republic's recent independence is a source of great pride, as is its manufacturing industry-mainly in clothing and appliances. The country's agriculture has been severely affected by the Chernobyl nuclear accident in neighboring Ukraine, and is a sensitive subject. Although this small country has big economic and political problems, most businessmen are eager and hopeful for progress, and will treat you, the potential partner, with great hospitality. Officials, too, are generally friendly to visiting businessmen. You should reciprocate for the many invitations you will receive with small souvenirs from your country for your host's family. As in many countries with shortages, it is bad manners to leave food on your plate; although here, leaving a little bit will signify that you are finished.

Health: It is advisable to consult your doctor before your journey. It is required to have vaccination certificates for Cholera and Yellow Fever if travelling from an infected area. For stays longer than three months, an AIDS test is also required. The drinking water should be boiled or bottled water should be used instead. Emergency treatments are free, but longer treatments have to be paid. A health insurance is strongly recommended.

Language: Belarussian and Russian.

BELARUS

MINSK

Country code: 375 - City code: 172 (6 digits); 17 (7 digits)

Airport: Minsk Airport

Distance from City: 44km (27 miles) west of the city.

Transportation to Center of City:
From International and Domestic Terminals
By Bus Time approx. 45 min.
By Taxi Time approx. 40-45 min.

Transfers: (Minimum Connecting Time):
International to International: 120 min.
International to Domestic: 120 min.
Domestic to International: 120 min.
Domestic to Domestic: 60 min.

Automobile Rentals:
Airport car rental desk
Avis - 791486
Europcar Interrent - 791567

Car rental city office
Avis- 200092
Europcar Interrent - 269062

Hotels:
Belarus Hotel, Korov 13, 225981
Minsk Hotel, Lenin Pospekt 11, 292326
Sputnik Hotel, Brilevskaya, 258849
Planeta Intourist, Masherova 31, 238416

Places of Interest:
The Museum for Architecture and Modern Life
The World War 2 Museum
The Museum for History and Culture
The National Gallery
Troitskoye Predmestye – a suburb of Minsk with 19th century
    buildings.
The Holy Trinity Cathedral and St. Catherine's Church

BELGIUM

Official Name: The Kingdom of Belgium

Location: Western Europe. Belgium is bordered by the Nether-lands, Germany, Luxembourg and France. To the northwest lies the North Sea.

Government: Constitutional Monarchy

Area: 30,519 sq. km., 11,783 sq. miles.

Population: 10.1 million

Religion(s): Roman Catholic majority. There are also small Prot-estant and Jewish minorities.

Capital City: Brussels

Major Business Cities: Antwerp and Liege.

Time: GMT +1 (GMT +2 from late March to late October)

Currency: Belgian Franc (BFR)=100 Centimes.

Currency Requirements: There are no restrictions on the im-port and the export of local or foreign currency.

Business Hours:
- Government: 09.00-12.00; 14.00-17.00 Mon-Fri
- Banks: 09.00-13.00; 14.00-15.00 Mon-Fri
- Shops: 09.00-18.30 Mon-Fri
- Offices: 09.00-17.00 Mon-Fri

Weight and Measures: Metric System

Electric Current: 220 volts AC. Plugs are of the 2-pin round type.

Holidays:
New Year's Day - January 1
Easter Monday - April 13*
May Day - May 1
Ascension Day - May 8
Whit Monday - June 1*
National Holiday - July 21
Assumption Day - May 21*
All Saints' Day - November 1
Armistice Day - November 11
King's Birthday - November 15**
Christmas Day - December 25
Boxing Day - December 26**

* Christian Holidays – vary each year
** Only for administrative and public offices, schools etc.

Suitable Clothing: Bring conservative business clothing; heavy clothing and a coat for winter, and medium weight and rainwear for the rest of the year. For a night at the opera or a concert, men should wear a dark suit (sometimes a tuxedo) and women an evening dress.

Automobile Driving License: A National Driving License is required.

Customs Allowances: Personal items are duty free, but register all valuables upon arrival. Non-E.U. members face more restrictions on tobacco and alcohol: 200 cigarettes, 2 liters of wine and one of spirits.

Tipping: A service charge of 14-16% is usually added to the bill by hotel or restaurant. Cloakroom attendants expect a tip of BFr5-10. Tips are usually included in the taxi fare.

Credit Cards Accepted: AmEx, Diner's Club, Eurocard, Visa

Customary Dining Hours:
Breakfast: 07.00-08.30
Lunch: 12.00-14.00
Dinner: 18.00-20.00

BELGIUM

Local Customs, Business Protocol and Courtesies: Given Belgium's role as a major economic and political meeting place, it is not surprising to find that its business environment is highly efficient. Schedule governmental and business meetings in advance, generally between 10 a.m. and 5 p.m., and be on time. Shake hands lightly with your counterpart upon meeting, and be reserved in speech and demeanor. Give detailed presentations and proposals and expect shrewd negotiations. Typically, you should invite your potential partner for drinks and afterwards, lunch. Wine with meals is customary; in fact, if you invite your counterpart for lunch you should offer a toast. If he or she is hosting either at home or in a restaurant, then he or she will give the toast, and you are expected to respond.

If visiting someone's home, send flowers in advance but keep in mind that as in many European countries, there are certain taboos on the nature of the bouquet never bring red (which signifies romantic love), or even numbers of flowers. Bringing gifts for the children is viewed favorably; business gifts with a company logo are not. In any case, business gifts are rare, except at the New Year. At the table, if you want seconds, place your fork and knife apart on the plate, and when finished, place them together on the plate on a diagonal. Although smoking is not unusual in Europe, here it is not customary to smoke at dinner or in the home, unless indicated otherwise that is, if your host puts out an ashtray.

Keep in mind that Belgium is a country divided by French and Flemish (Dutch) speaking areas; assuming that Flemish-speaking businessmen should speak French at a meeting, or vice versa, could kill your dealings with them. Additionally, if you bring representatives from your company, make sure you have two different French and Flemish ones for the two regions. On your trip, however, bring company literature in either language is acceptable.

Health: There are no special vaccinations required. There is a Health Agreement with the UK, which gives them a reimbursement of up to 75% of medical costs. It is recommended that UK citizens obtain an exemption form before

BELGIUM

travelling. Medical treatment is expensive but the standard is very high. A health insurance is recommended.

Language: Dutch in the north part of the country and French in south.

ANTWERP

Country code: 32 - City code: 3

Airport: Deurne Airport.

Distance from City: 4km (2 miles) southeast of the city.

Transportation to Center of City:
From International and Domestic Terminals
By Bus (cost) BFR40. Time approx. 30 min.
By Taxi (cost) BFR400-500. Time approx. 10-15 min.
Tip luggage porters 50 francs per piece

Automobile Rentals:
Airport car rental desk
Avis - 218-9496
Hertz - 3/230-1641

Car rental city office
Avis - 3/829-1000
Europcar Interrent - 3/235-1625
Hertz - 3/233-2992

Hotels:
Alfa Congrees Hotel, Plantin en Moretuslei 136, 235-3000
Alfa De Keyser Hotel, De Keyserlei 66-70, 234-0135
Alfa Empire Hotel, Appelmanstr. 31, 231-4755
Alfa Theater Hotel, Arenbergstr. 30, 231-1720
Antwerp Hilton, Groenplaats 42, 204-1212
Astoria Antwerp Hotel, Korte Harentalsestr. 5-13, 227-3130
Atlanta Hotel, Kon. Astridplein 14, 203-0919
Golden Tulip Hotel Carlton, Quinten Matsijslei 25, 231-1515
Park Lane Hotel Antwerpen, Van Eycklei 34, 285-8585
Plaza Hotel Centre, Charlottelei 43, 218-9240

Residence Hotel, Molenbergstr. 9-11, 232-7675
Switel Moat House International, Copernicuslaan, 231-6780
Waldorf Hotel, Belgielei 36-38, 230-9950

Restaurants:
'T Vermoeid Model, Lijnwaadmarkt 2, 233-5261
De Manie, H. Conscienceplein 3, 232-6438
De Peerdestal, Wijngaardstraat 8, 231-9503
In de Schaduw van de Kathedraal, Hansschoenmarkt 17-21, 232-4014
La Perouse, Porton Steen, Steenplein, 231-7358
Panache, Statiestraat 17, 232-6905
Pottenbrug, Minderbroedersrui 38, 231-5147
Rooden Hoed, Oude Koornmarkt 25, 233-2844
Sir Anthony Van Dyck, Oude Koornmarkt 16, 233-1925
The Hippodroom, Leopold de Waelplaats 10, 238-8936

Entertainment:
Elfde Gebod, Torfbrug
Engel, Grotte Markt
Groote Witte Arend, Reyndersstraat
Kulminator, Vleminckveld 32
Paelgrom, Pelgrimstraat

Places of Interest:
The Cathedral of Our Lady
The Museum of Folk Culture
The Steen – a monument and a museum
Plantin Moretus Museum
The Church of St.Charles Borromeo
The Royal Museum of Fine Arts
Middelheim Park – a museum of sculptures
Antwerp Zoo

BRUSSELS

Country code: 32 - City code: 2

Airport: Brussels National Airport.

BELGIUM

Distance from City: 13km (8 miles) northeast of the city.

Transportation to Center of City:
From International and Domestic Terminals
By Bus (cost) BFR 45-50 Time approx. 30-60 min.
By Taxi (cost) BFR1000-1500. Time approx. 35-45 min.
Tip luggage porters 50 francs per piece

Automobile Rentals:
Airport car rental desk
Avis - 720-0944
Europcar Interrent - 721-0592
Hertz - 720-6044

Car rental city office
Avis - 537-1280
Europcar Interrent - 640-9400
Hertz - 513-2886

Hotels:
Alfa Louise Hotel, Ave. Louise, Louiselaan 212, 644-2929
Alfa Sablon Hotel, Strostr. 2, Rue de la Paille, 513-6040
Arenberg Hotel, Rue d'Assaut 15, 511-0770
Bedford Hotel Brussels, Rue du Midi 135, 512-7840
Bristol Stephanie Hotel, Ave. Louise 91-93, 543-3311
Brussels Hilton, 38 Blvd. De Waterloo, 504-1111
Carrefour de l'Europe, Rue du Marche-aux Herbes 110, 504-9400
Chelton Hotel Brussels, Rue Veronese Str. 48, 735-2032
City Garden Hotel, 59 Rue Joseph II, 282-8282
Clubhouse Hotel Brussels, Rue Blanche 4, 537-9210
Conrad International Brussels, Ave. Louise 71, 542-4242
County House Of Brussels, Square des Heros 2-4, 375-4420
Euroflat Hotel, Blvd. Charlemagne 50, 230-0010
Europa Inter-Continental Brussels, Rue de la Loi 107, 230-1333
Golden Tulip Hotel Musee New Siru, Place Rogier 1, 203-3580
Golden Tulip Palace Hotel, Rue Gineste 3, 203-6200
Holiday Inn Brussels City Centre, Chaussee de Charleroi 38, 533-6666
Le Meridien Brussels, Carrefour de l'Europe 3, 548-4211
Metropole Hotel, 31 Place de Brouckere, 217-2300
Movenpick Cadett, Rue Paul Spaak 15, 645-6111

BELGIUM

Restaurants:
Au stekerlapatte, rue des Pretres 4, 512-8681
Au Trappiste, av. de la Toison-d'Or 7, 511-7839
Auberge des Chapeliers, rue des Chapeliers 1-3, 513-7338
Aux Armes de Bruxelles, rue des Bouchers 13, 511-2118
Barbizon, Welriekenweg 95, 657-0462
Bernard, rue deNamur 93, 512-8821
Brasserie Roue d'Or, rue des Chapeliers 26, 514-2554
Bruneau, av. Broustin 73-75, 4276978
Café Metropole, place de Brouckere 31, 217-2300
Cap de Nuit, place de la Vieille-Halle-aux-Bles 28, 512-9342
Chez Leon, rue des Bouchers 18, 511-1415
Comme Chez Soi, place Rouppe 23, 512-2921
Falstaff, rue Henri-Maus 23-25, 511-9877
L'Alban Chambon Restaurant, place de Brouckere 31, 217-2300
La Maison du Sygne, rue Charles –Buls 2, 511-8244
La Sirene d'Or, place ste-Catherine 1A, 513-5198
La Truit d'Argent Restaurant Hotel, quai au Bois a Bruler 23,
    219-9546
Le Mozart, chaussee d'Alsemberg 541, 344-0809
Les Quatre Saisons (The Four Seasons), rue Duquesnoy 5,
    511-4215
Ravenstein, rue Ravenstein 1, 512-7768
Trente Rue de la Paille, rue de la Paille 30, 512-0715
Villa lorraine, chausee de la Hulpa 28, 374-3163

Entertainment:
T Spinnekopke, place du Jardin-aux-Fleurs 1, 511-8695
A la Morte Subite, rue Montagne-aux-Herbes-Potageres 7,
    513-1318
Chez Flo, rue au Beurre 25, 512-9496
Griffin's Club, rue Duquesnoy 5, 505-5555
La Fleuren Papier Dore, rue des Alexiens 55, 511-1659
Le Garage, rue Duquesnoy 16, 512-6622
Le Huchier, place du Grand-Sablon, 512-2711
Le Machado, rue des Chapeliers 14, 513-3691
Le Pavillon, place Rogier 3, 224-3111
Le Slave, rue Scailquin 22, 217-6656
Les Enfants du Golf Drouot, place de la Chapelle 6,
    502-6817
Moustache, quai au Bois a Bruler 61, 218-5877
Pops Hall, rue Lincoln 53, 345-9581

Show Point, place Stephanie 14, 217-0167
The Brussels Jazz Club, Grand'Place 13, 512-4093

Shops and Stores:

Anspach Center, de la Monnaie	Shopping Mall
Burbries, Avenue Louise	Apparel
Cartier, Avenue Louise	Apparel
City 2, rue Nueve	Dept. Store
Delvaux, galerie de la Reine 31	Leather Goods
Galerie Agora, Grand' Place	Dept. Store
Galeries Saint-Hubert, rue du Marche-aux-Hubert	Jewelry
Valentino, Avenue Louise	Apparel

Places of Interest:

The Grand Place - The 'Manneken Pis' statue
Maison du Roi - a museum of history and archeology.
Parc de Bruxelles and Palais du Roi - Royal office and park.
Musee d'Art Ancien and Musee d'Art Moderne – modern arts museum
Atomium - exhibitions
Saint-Michel Cathedral
Waterloo – a museum

BULGARIA

Official Name: Republic of Bulgaria

Location: Eastern Europe. Bulgaria is bordered by Romania, Serbia, the former Yugoslavian Republic of Macedonia, Greece and Turkey. The Black Sea is situated on its east coast.

Government: Republic

Area: 110,994 sq. km., 42,855 sq. miles

Population: 8.96 million

Religion(s): Eastern Orthodox majority. Muslim and Roman Catholic minorities.

Capital City: Sofia

Major Business Cities: Sofia, Plovdiv, Varna and Burgas

Time: GMT +2 (GMT +3 from late March to late October)

Currency: Lev (BGL)=100 stotinki

Currency Requirements: The import of foreign currency over USD1,000 must be declared on arrival. The export is limited to the amount declared on entry. Import and export of local currency are prohibited.

Business Hours:
- Government: 08.30 or 09.00-12.30; 13.00-17.30
- Banks: 08.00-12.00 Mon-Fri; 8.00-11 Sat
- Shops: 08.00-13.00; 16.00-19.00 Mon-Sat
- Offices: 08.00-18.00 Mon-Fri

Weight and Measures: Metric System

Electric Current: 220 volts AC. Continental 2-pin plugs are used.

Holidays:
New Year's Day - January 1
National Day - March 3
Easter - April 10-13*
Labor Day - May 1
Culture Day - May 24
Day of the Leaders of the Bulgarian National Revival - November 1
Christmas Eve - December 24
Christmas Day - December 25

*Christian Holidays - vary each year

Suitable Clothing: Bring heavy clothing and a coat for winter, and medium weight and rainwear for the rest of the year. Wear a conservative business suit. Formal evening clothing is rarely required.

Automobile Driving License: A foreign driving license can be used for short visits. An International Driving Permit should be obtained for long stays.

Customs Allowances: As currency and customs requirements have undergone a number of changes in recent years, one should consult your country's Bulgarian embassy or consulate when arranging your trip. Personal items are duty free, but register valuables upon arrival or they may be confiscated upon departure. Although you may bring in unlimited amounts of foreign currency, and take out any you initially declare, you may not import or export Lev. You may bring in 200 cigarettes, 2 liters of wine and one of spirits.

Tipping: Tipping is discretionary, but 10-12% is appreciated.

Credit Cards Accepted: American Express, Master Card, Visa

Customary Dining Hours:
Breakfast: 07.00-09.00
Lunch: 12.00-14.00

Dinner: 19.00-22.00

Local Customs, Business Protocol and Courtesies: Although its economy is in havoc and many Bulgarian businessmen are not yet well-versed in Western business practices, it is, at least, no longer necessary to obtain official permission for any business contact. Numerous trade organizations exist which can introduce you to local competition and help you establish more individual business relationships. It will take much patience to fine tune and bargain your way to a successful business contract (particularly regarding credit terms), but most businessmen are eager and hopeful for progress, and will treat you, the potential partner, with great hospitality.

Despite the chaos you may encounter, professionalism is highly appreciated. Schedule appointments at 10 or 11 a.m. and 2 or 3 p.m., and be punctual even if your host isn't. Use titles with your contact's last name. Keep your presentations detailed and precise. Now that the communist-era restrictions on conducting business outside the office are gone, many Bulgarians have enthusiastically taken to conducting business over food and drinks· this is a good opportunity to establish rapport, since the tone invariably becomes more social than businesslike after a shot or two of slivova, the local plum brandy. The latter and Bulgarian yogurt are sources of local pride, and it is rude to refuse. As in many countries with shortages, it is bad manners to leave food on your plate; although here, leaving a little bit will signify that you are finished. Discussion tends to be lively and your hosts will truly want to hear your opinions, although for the sensitivity's sake one should reply with caution on subjects like religion and politics. You should reciprocate for the many invitations you will receive to visit homes, with flowers, candy, wine and small souvenirs from your country. Business gifts are not typical, but a small gift after signing a deal is appropriate.

Health: It is recommended to consult your doctor before your journey. No vaccinations are necessary. It is advisable to use bottled water during your visit. A medical insurance is recommended.

BULGARIA

Language: Bulgarian. English, Russian, German and French are also spoken.

SOFIA

Country code: 359 - City code: 2

Airport: Sofia Airport

Distance from City: 10km (6 miles) east of the city center.

Transportation to Center of City:
From International and Domestic Terminals
By Bus (cost) BGL5. Time approx. 30 min. (every 10 min.)
By Taxi (cost) USD10-15. Time approx. 20 min.
Tip luggage porters BGL 50 per piece

Transfers: (Minimum Connecting Time):
International to International: 60 min.
International to Domestic: 60 min.
Domestic to International: 60 min.
Domestic to Domestic: 60 min.

Automobile Rentals:
Airport car rental desk
Avis - 738023
Europcar Interrent - 720157
Hertz - 796041

Car rental city office
Avis - 873412
Europcar Interrent - 816850
Hertz - 814042

Hotels:
Novotel Evropa, 131 Maria Louisa Blvd., 317151
Sheraton Sofia Hotel Balkan, 5 Sveta Nedelya Sq., 981-6541

Restaurants:

Anna, Tsanko Tserkovski 6
Berlin, blvd. Yanko Sakasov 2
Budapest, Rakovski 145
Caesar, Solunska 16
Club 21, Midzhur 21, 660339
Dama Pika, Hristo Smirnenski 25
Ed's Diner, Vitosha 4
Gradina, Udovo 4
Havana, blvd. Vitosha 27
Kitaiski Restorant, Tsar Samuil 107
Krim, Slavyanska 17, 870131
Maharadja, Serdika 24, 835230
Mexicano, Krakra 11, 446598
Monmartre, Hristo Smirnenski 36, 665521
Pekin, blvd.Totleben 8
Regata, Angel Kantchev & Han Asparuh
SBZh, Graf Ignatiev 4
Sekura, blvd. Anton Ivanov 100
Tai Pan, Alabin 46
Varshava, blvd.Yanko Sakazov 17
Veselo Kebapche, Serdika 28

Entertainment:
ABC, Triaditsa 1A
Angel Club, pl. Narodno Sabranie
Artklub, Ivan Asen II 4
Bordo, Tsar Asen 14
Cocktail Bar Sugar Johnny, Han Asparuh 18
Frankie's Jass Club and Piano Bar, Karnigradska 15
Funky's Pub, Shandor Petyofi 26A
Marta, Patriarh Eftimii 16
Neron, NDK
Orbi Lux, blvd. Dzheims Baucher
Roderik, Tsar Shishman 27
Swingin' Hall, Dragan Tsankov 8
Yalta, ul. Aksakov 31

Shops and Stores:
Bulgarian Assoc. of Craftsmen, bul. Vitosha 14   Gift Shop
Tsum, bul. Maria Luiza   Dept. Store

Places of Interest:
St.George's Rotunda - a late Roman church.
St.Alexander Nevsky Cathedral
Banya Bashi Mosque
The Central Synagogue
The National Museum of History
The Archaeological Museum
The National Museum of Fine Arts

CZECH REPUBLIC

Official Name: Czech Republic

Location: Central Europe. Czech Republic is bordered by Germany, Poland, Slovak Republic and Austria.

Government: Republic

Area: 78,864 sq. km., 30,450 sq. miles.

Population: 10.3 million

Religion(s): 46% Roman Catholic and 15% Protestant.

Capital City: Prague

Major Business Cities: Brno, Ostrava

Time: GMT +1 (GMT +2 from late March to late October)

Currency: Koruna (KCS) or Crown=100 Haleru (single: Heller)

Currency Requirements: The import and the export of local currency is prohibited. There are no restrictions on foreign currency.

Business Hours:
- Government: 08.30-17.00 Mon-Fri
- Banks: 08.00-16.00 Mon-Fri
- Shops: 08.00-18.00 Mon-Fri (Dept. stores open until 19.00);
    08.00-12.00 Saturday (Dept. stores open until 16.00)
- Offices: 08.00-16.00/16.30 Mon-Fri

Weight and Measures: Metric System

Electric Current: Generally the current is 220 volts AC. In some areas of Prague 110 volts is still used. Plugs are of the round 2-

pin type but most major hotels have standard international 2-pin razor plugs.

Holidays:
New Year's Day - January 1
Easter Monday - April 13*
Labor Day - May 1
Prague Uprising - May 5
Liberation Day - May 8
Day of St. Cyril and St. Methodius - July 5
Anniversary of Burning of Jan Hus - July 6
Anniversary of Independence - October 28
Christmas Eve - December 24
Christmas Day - December 25
Boxing Day - December 26

*Christian Holidays - vary each year

Suitable Clothing: Bring heavy clothing and a coat for winter, and medium-to-light clothing and rainwear for the rest of the year. Wear a conservative business suit in most situations. You may need formal clothing for evenings out.

Automobile Driving License: A National Driving License can be used for stays of up to 180 days, if it is held for one year.

Customs Allowances: As currency and customs requirements have undergone a number of changes in recent years, one should consult your country's Czech embassy or consulate when arranging your trip. Personal items are duty free, but register valuables upon arrival or they may be confiscated upon departure. Although you may bring in unlimited amounts of foreign currency, and take out any you initially declare, you may not import or export Czech Crowns. You may bring in 200 cigarettes, 2 liters of wine and one of spirits.

Tipping: Usually it is left to your discretion, but a 15% tip is accepted.

Credit Cards Accepted: American Express, Diner's Club, Eurocard, Visa

Customary Dining Hours:
Breakfast: 07.00-09.00
Lunch: 12.00-14.00
Dinner: 19.00-22.00

Local Customs, Business Protocol and Courtesies: Although Czech Republic was thought to be the most successful economy of the former East bloc, recent allegations of corruption regarding President Klaus and his subsequent resignation have left the state of the economy very uncertain. Nevertheless, the march toward a free market continues and the business climate there still has many attractions and possibilities. Due to its proximity to the German market, its business practices are often more sophisticated than many other former East bloc nations. Set up and formerly tightly controlled under the communist regime, the country's trade organizational infrastructure is now free to help acquaint foreign businesspersons with the local climate and help you establish more individual business relationships. It will take much patience and a number of visits to fine tune your way to a successful business contract (particularly regarding credit terms and pricing), but most Czech businessmen will treat you, the potential partner, with great hospitality. Schedule appointments two or three weeks before your visit to the country; the best times are 10 or 11 am and 2 or 3 pm, avoiding Friday afternoons. Be punctual, and use titles with your contact's last name, although if your relationship progresses your counterpart will start using first names. Give detailed, precise presentations, with the view that much competition already exists in Czech markets. Some Czech customs are common throughout Central-Eastern Europe, such as those regarding flowers, dinner manners and even shoes. Like in neighboring Austria, Czech businessmen rarely entertain at home, but if invited, leave your shoes at the door (you will be given guest slippers) and expect an enormous meal. Bring flowers, and don't forget the traditional European taboos · never bring red (which signifies romantic love), even numbers of flowers, or certain funereal species. Gifts for the children are viewed favorably; business gifts (given at the close of a deal and at Christmas) with a company logo are not. At a meal, if your host offers a toast, you should offer one in return. Your counterparts will likely ask your opinions, but as in any business environment, don't be overly candid. A particularly senstive topic is the 1993 splitup of Czechoslovakia into the Czech or Slovak republics; you'll find that many Czechs and Slovaks regret it. Nevertheless, refer to them as ethnically separate, not "Czechoslovakians."

Health: Polio and tetanus immunizations are recommended as well as a health insurance. It is recommended to drink bottled water. There are International agreements for free health care. Visitors are advised to check with local health authorities before traveling.

Language: Czech. German and English are spoken in commerce and foreign trade.

PRAGUE

Country code: 420 - City code: 2

Airport: Prague Ruzyne International Airport

Distance from City: 16km (9 miles) from the city center.

Transportation to Center of City:
From International and Domestic Terminals
By Bus (cost) CZK175. Time approx. 25-60 min.
By Taxi (cost) CZK300-500. Time approx. 25-35 min.

Transfers: (Minimum Connecting Time):
International to International: 60 min.
International to Domestic: 80 min.
Domestic to International: 80 min.
Domestic to Domestic: 40 min.

Automobile Rentals:
Airport car rental desk
Avis - 322459
Europcar Interrent - 316-7849

CZECH REPUBLIC

Hertz - 312-0717

Car rental city office
Avis - 231-5515
Europcar Interrent - 2481-1290
Hertz - 290122

Hotels:
Adria Hotel, Vaclavske nam 26, 2108-1200
Ambassador Zlata Husa Hotel, 2419-3111
Ametyst Hotel Praha, Jana Masaryka 11, 2425-4185
Belvedere Praha Hotel, Milady Horakove 19, 2010-6111
Bohemia Grand Hotel, Kraladvorska 4, 2480-4111
Casa Marcello, Rasnovka 1, Hastalske namesti, 231-1230
City Hotel Moran, Na Morani 15, 2491-5208
Golden Tulip Hotel Maximilian, Hastalska 14, 2180-6111
Hoffmeister Hotel, Pod Bruskou 9, 561-8155-60
Inter-Continental Praha, Namesti Curieovych 43/5, 2488-1111
Jalta Hotel, Vaclavske nam 45, 2422-9133
Meteor Plaza Hotel, Hybernska 6, 2419-2111
Palace Praha Hotel, Panska 12, 2409-3111
Pariz Hotel, U Obecniho Domu 1, 2422-2151
Prague Hilton Atrium, Pobrezni 1, 2484-1111
Renaissance Prague Hotel, V. Celnici 7, 2182-2100

Restaurants:
Avalon, Malostranske namesti 12, Mala Strana, 53 02 76
Bar Bar, Vsehrdova 17, Mala Strana
Bellevue, Smetanovo nabrezi 18, 235 9599
Kampa Park, Na Kampe 8b, Mala Strana, 53 30 71
Na rybarne, Gorazdova 17, 29 97 95
Nebozizek, Petrinske sady 411, Mala Strana 53 79 05
Pizzeria Rugantino, Dusni 4,
Pizzeria San Pietro, Benediktska 16, 231 57 27
Prnas, Smetanovo nabezi 2, 24 22 76 14
Red,Hot & Blues, Jakubska 12
Reykjavik, Karlova 20
Sate Grill, Pohorelec 3, Hradcany.
U Lorety, Loretanske namesti 8, 53 13 95
U maltezskych rytiru, Prokopska, Mala Strana, 53 63 57
U supa, Seletna 22
U zatizi, Liliova 1, 24 22 89 77
Vltava, Rasinovo nabrezi, 29 49 64

Entertainment:
AghaRTA Jazz Centrum, Krakovska 5, Nove Mesto
Arkadia, Na prikope 22
Bar Club, Hybernska 10, Nove Mesto
Bunkr, Lodecka 2, Nove Mesto
Lucerna, Vodickova 36, Nove Mesto
Malostanska beseda, Mlostranske namesti 21, Mala Strana
Metropolitan Jazz Club, Jungmannova 14, Nove Mesto
Press Jazz Club, Parizska 9, Stare Mesto, 53 18 35
Radhost, Belehradska 120, Vinohradu
Rock Café, Narodni 22, Nove Mesto
Roxy, Dlouha 33, Staremesto
Subway, Na prikope 22, Nove Mesto
Ujezd, Ujezd 18, Mala Strana
Uzi, Legorova 44, Nove Mesto

Places of Interest:
St. Vitus' Cathedral
Mozart Museum
Church of St.Nicholas
Astronomical Clock
Troja Chateau
Goltz-Kinsky Palace
St.Jacob's Cathedral
Josefov - museums, synagogues, historical buildings.
National Gallery of Bohemian Art
The National Museum

DENMARK

Official Name: The Kingdom of Denmark

Location: Western Europe. Denmark is bordered by Germany, Sweden and Norway. Greenland and the Faroe Islands are also a part of Denmark.

Government: Constitutional Monarchy

Area: 43,093 sq. km., 16,638 sq. miles.

Population: 5.17 million

Religion(s): Evangelical Lutheran majority and a small Roman Catholic minority

Capital City: Copenhagen

Major Business Cities: Aarhus and Odense

Time: GMT +1 (GMT +2 from late March to late October)

Currency: Danish Krone DKK= 100 ore

Currency Requirements: There are no restrictions on the import or export of foreign currency, but large amounts should be declared. Export of local currency is limited to the amount declared on import, plus any amount acquired by the conversion of foreign currency.

Business Hours:
- Government: 08.00-16.00 or 17.00 Mon-Thur
- Banks: 09.30-16.00 Mon-Wed, Fri , 09.30-18.00 Thur
- Shops: 08.00-16.00 or 17.00 Mon-Fri , 08.00-13.00 Sat
- Offices: 08.00/09.00 - 16.00/17.00 Mon-Fri

Weight and Measures: Metric System

DENMARK

Electric Current: 220 volts AC - European 2-pin plugs

Holidays:
New Year's Day - January 1
Maundy Thursday - March 27
Good Friday - April 10*
Easter Sunday - April 12*
Easter Monday - April 13*
Great Prayer Day - April 25
Ascension Day - May 21*
Whitsun - May 18
Whit Monday - June 1*
Constitution Day - June 5
Christmas Eve - December 24
Christmas Day - December 25
Boxing Day - December 26

*Christian Holidays - vary each year

Suitable Clothing: Bring very heavy clothing and a coat for winter, and medium clothing and rainwear for the rest of the year. Wear a conservative business suit in most situations. You may need formal clothing for evenings out.

Automobile Driving License: National Driving License can be used if it is held for at least one year.

Customs Allowances: There are no limits on foreign currency, but you may take out a limit of (previously declared) DKK 50,000. Personal items are duty free, but register all valuables upon arrival. Non-E.U. members face more restrictions on tobacco and alcohol: 200 cigarettes, 2 liters of wine and one of spirits. E.U. members can bring in 300 cigarettes, 3 liters of wine and 1.5 liters of spirits.

Tipping: A service charge is included in the hotel, the restaurant and the taxi prices.

Credit Cards Accepted: Access, American Express, Diner's Club, Eurocard, MasterCard, Visa

Customary Dining Hours:

Breakfast: 07.00-09.00
Lunch: 12.00-14.00
Dinner: 19.00-22.00

Local Customs, Business Protocol and Courtesies: The Danish business climate, although the most informal in Scandinavia, requires a certain level of formality and reserve; the most obvious rules are making appointments in advance, being on time, giving detailed, professional presentations, displaying good manners at a meal and avoiding personal questions. In addition, one should show a reserved demeanor and use titles with last names until indicated otherwise by your Danish contemporary. Don't be pushy or aggressive in your proposals; a soft-sell approach is preferred. Although small talk may start a meeting, talk generally gets quickly to business. Business lunches and dinners are considered the norm. You might be invited to a Danish home, either for dinner, which is a sociable, seven-course affair, or just for after-dinner drinks. Wait for your host to offer a toast; you will be expected to offer a "thank you" toast in return at dessert. Regarding gifts, it is okay to give your colleague something upon the close of a successful deal-a company item, or any other small, impersonal gift like a book or fine wine. When a guest in someone's home, bring the hostess a small gift, candy or flowers.

Health: There is a Health Agreement with some EU Countries, which covers state provided emergency treatment only. It may be necessary to pay at the time of treatment; in this case receipts should be kept to facilitate refunds. Applications should be made to the Kommunens Social-og Sundhedsforvaltning before leaving the country. Check details of the agreement with your health authority before departing. Medical facilities are very good. It is recommended to have a private medical insurance. There are no vaccinations required.

Language: Danish. English, German and French are spoken as a second language.

DENMARK

COPENHAGEN

Country code: 45 - City code: none

Airport: Kastrup International Airport

Distance from City: 10km (6 miles) southeast of the city center.

Transportation to Center of City:
From International and Domestic Terminals
By Bus (cost) DKK16. Time approx. 30-40 min.
By Taxi (cost) DKK120. Time approx. 20 min.
Tip luggage porters DDK10 per piece

Transfers: (Minimum Connecting Time):
International to International: 45 min.
International to Domestic: 45 min.
Domestic to International: 45 min.
Domestic to Domestic: 45 min.

Automobile Rentals:
Airport car rental desk
Avis - 31512299
Europcar Interrent - 32503090
Hertz - 32509300

Car rental city office
Avis - 33152299
Europcar Interrent - 33116200
Hertz - 33127700

Hotels:
71 Nyhavn Hotel, Nyhavn 71, 3311-8585
Alexandra Hotel, H.C. Andersens Blvd. 8, 3314-2200
Astoria Hotel, Banegaardspladsen 4, 3314-1419
Christian IV Hotel, Dronningens Tvaegade 45, 3332-1044
Copenhagen Crown Hotel, Vesterbrogade 41, 3121-2166
Copenhagen Star Hotel, Colbjornsensgade 13, 3122-1100
Esplanaden Hotel, Bredgade 78, 3391-3200
Golden Tulip Hotel Imperial, Vester Farimagsgade 9, 3312-8800
Golden Tulip Hotel Kong Arthur, Noerre Soegade 11, 3311-1212
Grand Hotel, Vesterbrogade 9a, 3131-3600

DENMARK

Hebron Hotel, Helgolandsbade 4, 3131-6906
Komfort Hotel Copenhagen, Longangstr. 27, 3312-6570
Kong Frederik Hotel, Vester Voldgade 25, 3312-5902
Mayfair Hotel, Helgolandsgade 3, 3131-4801
Missionshotellet Nebo, Istedgade 6, 3121-1217
Neptun Hotel, Sankt Annae Plads 14-20, 3313-8900
Opera Hotel, Todenskjoldsgade 15, 3312-1519
Palace Hotel, Raadhuspladsen 57, 3314-4050
Phoenix Hotel Copenhagen, Bredgade 37, 3395-9500
Plaza Hotel, Bernstorffsgade 4, 3314-9262
Radisson SAS Falconer Hotel Copenhagen, Falkoner Alle 9,
Frederiksberg, 3119-8001

Restaurants:
Copenhagen Corner, Radhus Pladsen, 91-45-45
El Meson, Hausers Plads 12, 11-91-31
Els, Store Stranderstræde 3, 14-13-41
Flyvefisken, Lars Bjornstræde 18, 14-95-15
Gyldne Fortun's Fiskekældere, Ved Stranden 18, 12-20-11
Havfruen, Nyhavn 39, 11-11-38
Ida Davidsen, Store Kongensgade, 91-36-55
Kasmir, Norrebrogade 35, 37-54-71
Kommandanten, Ny Adelgade 7, 12-09-90
Kong Hans, Vingardstræde 6, 11-68-68
Krogs, Gammel Strand 38, 15-89-15
L'Alsace, Ny Ostergarade 9, 14-57-43
Pakhuskælderen, Nyhavn 71, 11-85-85
Peder Oxe, Grabrodretorv 11, 11-00-77
Quattro Fontane, Guldbergsgade 3, 39-39-31
Riz Raz, Kompagnistræde 20, 15-05-75
Skt. Gertrudes Kloster, Houser Plads, 14-66-30
Victor, Ny Ostergade 8, 13-36-13

Entertainment:
Fellini, 1 Hammerichsgade, 93-32-39
Vin & Olgod, Skindergade 45, 13-26-25
Casino Copenhagen, Amager Boulevarden 70, 11-51-15
Rosie McGees, Vesterbrogade 2A, 32-19-23
La Fontaine, Kompagnistræde 11
Copenhagen Jazz House, Niels Hemmingsensgade 10,
    15-26-00
Pumpehuset, Studiestræde 52, 93-19-60

DENMARK

Rode Pimpernel, Hans Christian Anderson Blvd 7, 12-20-32
Hviids Vinstue, Kongens Nytorv 19, 15-10-64
Exalon, Fredieriksberggade 38, 11-08-66
Woodstock, Vestergade 12, 11-20-71
Peder Oxe's, Grabrodretorv 11, 11-11-93
Café'en Funk, Blegdamsvej 2, 35-17-41
Lades Kaelder, Kattessunder 6, 14-00-67
Jazzhus Slukefter, Vesterbrogade 3, 11-11-13
Sopavillionen, Gyldenlovesgade 24, 15-12-24

Shops and Stores:

Artium, Vesterbrogade 1	Apparel
Bodrene Andersen, Ostergade 7-9	Apparel
Company Store, Frederiksberggade 24	Apparel
Georg Jensen, Amagertorv 4	Jewelry
Illum, Ostergade 52	Dept. Store
Jens Srensen, Vester Volgade 5	Apparel
Lysberg, Hansen and Therp, Bredgade 3	Gift Shop
Magasin, Kongens Nytorv 13	Dept. Store
Met Mari, Vestergade 11	Apparel
Peter Krog, 4 Bedgade	Jewelry
Petitgas Chapeaux, Kobmagergade 5	Apparel
Solvkaelderen, Kompagnistræde 1	Jewelry
Sweater Market, Frederiksberggade 15	Apparel

Places of Interest:

The Tivoli Gardens - an amusement park
The Amalienborg Palace
The National Museet - exhibitions
Carlsberg Brewery
Tuborg Brewery
Nyhavn - statues, memorials, bars and restaurants.
The Little Mermaid - a sculpture
The Parliament

ESTONIA

Official Name: Republic of Estonia

Location: Northern Europe. Estonia is bordered to the east by the Russian Federation and to the south by Latvia. The north and the west coasts are on the Baltic Sea.

Government: Republic

Area: 45,226 sq. km., 17,462 sq. miles.

Population: 1.51 million

Religion(s): Protestant (Lutheran) majority

Capital City: Tallinn

Major Business Cities: Tallinn, Tartu and Narva

Time: GMT +2 (GMT +3 from late March to late October)

Currency: Kroon (EEK)=100 cents

Currency Requirements: It is necessary to declare on arrival and departure foreign currency, Estonian Kroons and travelers cheques equal to or exceeding EEK80,000. For sums exceeding EEK200,000, it is also necessary to indicate the origin of the sum in the declaration and a document proving its legal origin must be enclosed.

Business Hours:
- Government: 09.00-18.00 Mon-Fri
- Banks: 09.00-15.00 Mon-Fri
- Shops: 09.30/10.00-19.00 Mon-Sat
- Offices: 08.30-18.30 Mon-Fri

Weight and Measures: Metric System

ESTONIA

Electric Current: 220 volts - European style two pin plugs are used.

Holidays:
New Year's Day - January 1
Independence Day - February 24
Good Friday - April 10*
Labor Day - May 1
Victory Day - June 23
St John's Day - June 24
Christmas - December 25
Boxing Day - December 26

*Christian Holidays - vary each year

Suitable Clothing: Bring very heavy clothing and a coat for winter, and medium-to-light clothing the rest of the year. You will definitely need rainwear in the summer. Wear a conservative business suit in most situations.

Automobile Driving License: International Driving Permit is required.

Customs Allowances: There are no limits on foreign currency or personal items, but you must declare them upon arrival or they may be confiscated upon departure. Valuables should also be registered. You may bring in one carton of cigarettes, one liter of wine or spirits, and 10 of beer. You may not import or take out Estonian currency.

Tipping: Tipping is customary if it is not already included in the service and is left to the discretion of the individual.

Credit Cards Accepted: Not generally accepted. Access, American Express, Eurocard, MasterCard and Visa are accepted in some hotels.

Customary Dining Hours:
Breakfast: 07.00-09.00
Lunch: 12.00-14.30
Dinner: 18.30-22.00

Local Customs, Business Protocol and Courtesies: The most economically advanced of the three Baltic states, Estonians are also considered highly reputable and hardworking when it comes to business transactions. Your Estonian counterparts take pride in keeping their word, and therefore any commitment, on your part or theirs and no matter how big or small, should be made with great care. Expect detailed negotiations. Given this highly professional view of business, act accordingly: schedule appointments in advance, be neat and punctual and, at least initially, use titles reflecting your contact's highest educational rank. If you have one, it doesn't hurt to let your own advanced degree be known, as this will be highly respected. The tendency towards honesty will knock down many of the usual formal or bureaucratic barriers once you reach agreement on a transaction. Certain issues strongly affecting this former Soviet republic should be treated with sensitivity. A traditionally "clean" culture as well as concerns over Soviet-era pollution make Estonians strong environmentalists. Although there are many ethnic Russians here, do not assume that Russian is the language of choice, and note also that the Estonian language is entirely different (closely related to that of its neighbor, Finland.)

Health: It is advisable to consult your doctor before your journey. In some circumstances immunizations against diphtheria, hepatitis A, hepatitis B, polio, tetanus, typhoid are recommended. All drinking water must be boiled or sterilized.

Language: Estonian

TALLINN

Country code: 372 - City code: 2 (6 digits); none (7 digits)

Airport: Tallinn International Airport

Distance from City: 4km (2 miles) from the city center.

Transportation to Center of City:

ESTONIA

From International and Domestic Terminals
By Bus (cost) EEK12. Time approx. 20 min.
By Taxi (cost) EEK25-30. Time approx. 15 min.

Transfers: (Minimum Connecting Time):
International to International: 60 min.
International to Domestic: 60 min.
Domestic to International: 60 min.
Domestic to Domestic: 30 min.

Automobile Rentals:
Airport car rental desk
Avis - 6215602
Europcar Interrent - 6388031
Hertz - 6388923

Car rental city office
Avis - 6315930
Europcar Interrent - 6388031

Hotels:
Olympia Hotel, 33 Liivalaia St., 631-5333
Palace Hotel Tallinn, Vabaduse Valjak 3, 640-7300
Viru Hotel, 4 Viru Sq., 630-1311

Restaurants:
Controvento, Vene 12, 440 470
Eeslitall, Dunkri 4, 6313 755
Egeri Kelder, Roosikrantsi 6, 448 415
Ervin's Mexican Kitchen, 6312 736
Gloria Restoran, Muurivahe 16, 446 950
Gnoom, Viru 2, 442 488
Grill Mexicana, Pikk 1/3, 6564 006
Kullassepa Kelder, Kullassepa 9, 442 240
Kuller, Piskopi 1, 442 841
Maharaja Restaurant, Raekoja Plats 13, 444 367
Paan, Mere Puiestee 5,
Pizza Americana, Pikk 1, 6564 006
Primavera, 6339 891
Reskina, Filtri tee 5, 424 389
Shalom, 441 195
Sub Monte Restoran, Ruutli 4, 666 871

Taj Mahal, 6410 746
Toomkooli, Toom-Kooli 13, 446 613
Vana Toomas, 445 818
Vanaema Juures, Rataskaevu 12, 6313 927

Entertainment:
Amsterdamas, Parnu maantee 16
Art Cafe Opera and Jazz Cafe, Pikk 11
Bel Air, Vana Viru 14
Bonnie & Clyde, Liivalaia 33
Cafe Amigo, Viru valjak 4
Dekoltee, Ahtri 10
Diesel Boots, Lai 23
George Brownes, Harju 6
Green Spader, Peterburi tee 48
Hell Hunt, Pikk 39
Hollywood Club & Eldorado Bar, Vana Posti 8
Karja Kelder, Vaike Karja 1
Kover korts, Viru 8
Ku-Ku Club, Vabaduse valjak 8
Nimeta Baar, Suur Karja 4/6
Rio, Parnu maantee 59

Shops and Stores:

Aurum, Kullassepa 4	Jewelry
Baltman, Viru 22	Apparel
City Sokos, Viru Valjak 4	Dept. Store
Egiid, Rataskaevu 3	Apparel
Eks Kaubamaja, Mustamae tee 12	Dept. Store
Hellen & Vallen, Regati 1	Apparel
Maksi Market, Tihniku 5	Dept. Store
Mary Gold, Harju 6	Jewelry
Shifara Galerii, Vana Posti 7	Jewelry
Stockman, Liivalaia 53	Apparel

Places of Interest:
The Old Town - a medieval city
The Castle - the Estonian Government
The Cathedral
Museum of Medieval Art
Tallin City Museum
Maritime Museum

FINLAND

Official Name: Republic of Finland

Location: North Europe - Scandinavia. Finland is bordered by Norway, the Russian Federation and Sweden. To the south and the west is the Baltic Sea.

Government: Constitutional Republic

Area: 338,145 sq. km., 130,559 sq. miles.

Population: 5.08 million

Religion(s): Lutheran majority.

Capital City: Helsinki

Major Business Cities: Tampere

Time: GMT +2 (GMT +3 from late March to late October)

Currency: Markka (FIM) = 100 pennia

Currency Requirements: There are no restrictions on the import and export of local or foreign currency.

Business Hours:
- Government: 08.00-16.00 Mon-Fri
- Banks: 09.15-16.15 Mon-Fri
- Shops: 09.00-18.00 Mon-Fri ; 09.00-14.00/15.00 Sat (Dept stores and malls are open until 18.00).
- Offices: 08.00-16.15 Mon-Fri

Weight and Measures: Metric System

Electric Current: 220 volts AC - Continental 2-pin plugs are standard.

FINLAND

Holidays:
New Year's Day - January 1
Epiphany - January 6
Good Friday - April 10*
Easter Monday - April 13*
May Day Eve - April 30
May Day - May 1
Ascension Day - May 21*
Midsummer's Eve - June 20
Midsummer's Day - June 21
All Saints' Day - November 1
Independence Day - December 6
Christmas Eve - December 24
Christmas Day - December 25
Boxing Day - December 26

*Christian Holidays - vary each year

Suitable Clothing: Bring very heavy clothing and a coat for winter, and medium-to-light clothing the rest of the year. Wear a conservative business suit in most situations.

Automobile Driving License: An International Driving License can be used. A National Driving License can also be used if it is held for at least a year.

Customs Allowances: There are no limits on (previously declared) foreign currency, but you may take out a limit of 10,000 Markka. Personal items are duty free, but register all valuables upon arrival. You may bring in 2 cartons of cigarettes, 2 liters of wine or beer and 1 of spirits, if over age 20; there are stricter restrictions for those under age 20, 18 and 16. Ask your Finnish embassy or consulate for guidelines, as penalties can be high.

Tipping: A service charge is included in the hotel, the restaurant and the bar bills. Tipping is discretionary and is not expected or demanded. Doorman and cloakroom fees are usually clearly marked.

Credit Cards Accepted: Access, American Express, Diner's Club, Eurocard, Visa

FINLAND

Customary Dining Hours:
Breakfast: 07.30-09.00
Lunch: 11.30-13.00
Dinner: 19.00-23.30

Local Customs, Business Protocol and Courtesies: Although business deals are traditionally concluded in an office, Finnish business and social protocol brings to mind a very different environment: the sauna. If your contemporary invites you to a steam bath (which was invented here), do accept · it is a national pastime and signals acceptance. Otherwise, the business climate is more cut-and-dry: make prior appointments to meet businessmen and officials, be punctual, and use titles with last names. The word Johtaja means director; if at a loss for your contact's title, try this one. A handshake upon agreement can be taken as a promise, although of course, all deals should be signed. Successful business deals are usually followed by some sort of social event · a lunch, or, as mentioned, the sauna. If invited to a home, bring an odd number of flowers for the hostess, and shake hands with both men and women upon meeting. Finland, though a Western market economy, has faced a perilous economic downturn since the collapse of the Soviet Union. Issues of sensitivity include its tradition of neutrality (it was the only country bordering Russia that did not become a Soviet satellite or republic), and some formerly Finnish territory taken by Stalin. Finland boasts incredible natural beauty, and your hosts will likely want you to experience it.

Health: A Medical insurance is recommended. A Reciprocal Health Agreement exists with most EU countries but charges are made for prescribed medicines, hospital and dental treatment. Partial refunds can be claimed from the Finnish Sickness Insurance Institute before leaving the country.

Language: Finnish, Swedish. Some English and German are also spoken.

FINLAND

HELSINKI

Country code: 358 - City code: 9

Airport: Helsinki Vantaa
Distance from City: 20km (12 miles) north of the city center.

Transportation to Center of City:
From International and Domestic Terminals
By Bus (cost) FIM70-75. Time approx. 35-40 min. (every 20 min.)
By Taxi (cost) FIM170. Time approx. 30-40 min.
Tip luggage porters FIM3-4 per piece

Transfers: (Minimum Connecting Time):
International to International: 35 min.
International to Domestic: 40 min.
Domestic to International: 30 min.
Domestic to Domestic: 20 min.

Automobile Rentals:
Airport car rental desk
Avis - 822833
Europcar Interrent - 826677
Hertz - 1667-1270

Car rental city office
Avis - 441155
Europcar Interrent - 493973
Hertz - 1667-1391

Hotels:
Anna Hotel, Annankatu 1, 616621
Arctia Hotel Marski, Mannerheimintie 10, 68061
Cumulus Kaisaniemi, Kaisaniemenkatu 7, 172881
Inter-Continental Helsinki, Mannerheimintie 46, 40551
Lord Hotel, Lonnrotinkatu 29, 615815
Martta Hotelli, Uudenmaankatu 24, 646211
Olympia Hotel, Laentinen Brahenkatu 2, 69151
Palace Hotel, Etelaranta 10, 134561
Radisson SAS Hotel Helsinki, Runeberginkatu 2, 69580
Ramada Presidentti Hotel Helsinki, Etelainen Rautatiekatu 4,
    6911

FINLAND

Seaside Hotel, Ruoholahdenranta 3, 69360
Seurahuone Hotel, Kaivokatu 12, 69141
Sokos Hotel Helsinki, Yliopistonkatu 12, 131401
Sokos Hotel Hasperia, Mannerheimintie 50, 43101
Sokos Hotel Vantaa, Hertaksentie 2, Vantaa, 857851
Strand Inter-Continental Helsinki, John Stenbergin ranta 4, 39351

Restaurants:
Alexander Nevski, Pohjoisesplanadi 17, 639-610
Amadeus, Sofiankatu 4, 626-676
Bellevue, Rahapajankatu 3, 179-560
Café Raffaello, Alekstanterinkatu 46, 653-930
China, Anankatu 25, 640-258
Galateia, Mannerheimintie 46, 405-5900
Kosmos, Kalevankatu 3, 607-603
Kynsilaukka, Fredrikinkatu 22, 651-939
Nylandska Jaktlubben, Valkosaari Island, 636-047
Omenapuu, Keskuskatu 5, 2nd Floor, 630-205
Palace Gourmet, Etelaranta 10, 134-561
Pamir, John Stenberginranta 4, 39351
Perho Mechelin, Mechelininkatu 7, 493-481
Piekka Finnish Restaurant, Sibeliuksenkatu 2, 493-591
Pikku Satama, Pikku Satamakatu 3, 174-093
Ritarisali, Kalevankatu 5, 131-131
Savoy, Etelaesplanadi 14, 176-571
Sipuli, Kanavaranta 3, 179-900
Troikka, Caloniuksenkatu 3, 445-229
Villa Thai, Bulevardi 28, 680-2778

Entertainment:
Bothnia Club, Museokatu 10, 446-940
Casino Ray, Etelainen Rautatie 4, 694-2900
Cincin Bar, Mannerheimintie 10, 680-647
Fennia, Mikonkatu 17, 666-355
Hasperia Hotel Nightclub, Mannerheimintie 50, 43101
Hot Tomato Jazz Club, Anankatu 6, 612-1851
Jimo Jazzclub, Keskuskatu 6, 171-585
O'Malley's, Yrjonkatu 28, 131-131
Page, Keskuskatu 3, 175-655
Sakkipilli, Kalevankatu 2, 605-607
Socis Pub, Kaivokatu 12, 691-4004
Storyville, Museokatu 8, 408-007
Tavastia, Urho Kekkosenkatu 4-6, 694-3066

FINLAND

Shops and Stores:

Aarikka, Pohjoisesplanadi	Apparel
Alexi 13, Aleksanterinkatu 13	Dept. Store
Arabia, Pohjoisesplanadi	Apparel
Forum, Mannerheimintie and Simonkatu	Shopping Mall
Kaivopiha, Kaivokatu 10	Shopping Mall
Kalevala Koru, Unioninkatu 25	Jewelry
Kaunis Koru, Aleksanterinkatu 28	Jewelry
Kluuvi, Kluuvikatu and Aleksanterinaktu	Shopping Mall
Lapponia Jewelry, Makelankatu 60A	Jewelry
Marimekko, Pohjoisesplanadi 31	Apparel
Stockmann's, Esplanade and Mannerheimintie	Dept. Store

Places of Interest:
Temppeliaukio Church
The National Museum
Ateneum - Finnish art.
Upenski Cathedral

FRANCE

Official Name: French Republic

Government: Republic - 22 administrative regions containing 96 departments

Area: 210,026 sq. mi.

Population: 58.04 million

Major Business Cities: Capital - Paris, Marseille, Lyon, Toulouse, Strasbourg, Nantes, Bordeaux

Time: GMT + 1 hour

Currency: Franc = 100 centimes

Currency Requirements: There are no restrictions on the import or the export of foreign currency.

Business Hours:
- Government: 08:30 - 12:00, 14:00 - 18:00 Mon. - Fri.
- Banks: 09:00 - 16:30 Mon. - Fri.
- Commerce and Industry: 09:00 - 12:00, 14:00 - 18:00 Mon. - Fri.

Weight and Measures: Metric System

Electric Current: A.C. 220 v 50c

Holidays:
New Years Day - January 1
Easter Monday - April 13*
Labor Day - May 1
VE Day - May 8
Ascension Day - May 21
Whit Monday - June 1*
Bastille Day - July 14

Feast of the Assumption - August 15
All Saint's Day - November 1*
Armistice Day - November 11
Christmas Day - December 25

*Christian Holidays - vary each year

Suitable Clothing: Bring a coat in winter, light clothing and umbrella in summer and medium weight clothing and rainwear for the rest of the year. Wear a conservative but well-cut business suit in most situations. Formal clothing is sometimes required for an evening out or fancy business function.

Automobile Driving License: International drivers license - many foreign driver's licenses are valid in France for up to one year

Customs Allowances: There are no import or export limits of French Francs or foreign currency, although you must declare any foreign currency that may be re-exported, and amounts over 50,000 Francs. Personal items are duty free, but register all valuables upon arrival and keep receipts or you may face bureaucratic entanglements later. Tobacco and alcohol restrictions: 2 cartons of cigarettes, two liters of wine and one of spirits.

Tipping: Porters: 6 -10F per piece. Hotel, Restaurants, Nightspots: 15-20% usually included in your bill but an additional 5-10% to service staff is not unusual. Taxis: 15% Chambermaids: 5F per day. Doormen: 5F.

Credit Cards Accepted: Access, American Express, Carte Blanche, Carte Bleue, Diner's Club, Eurocard, Master Card, Visa.

Customary Dining Hours:
- Breakfast: 07:00 - 09:00 hrs.
- Lunch: 12:00 - 14:30 hrs.
- Dinner: 20:00 - 23:30 hrs.

Local Customs, Business Protocol and Courtesies: French cultural knowledge and pride carries over into the business world, and showing a knowledge of France's history and culture will help in your business relationships. The level of formality varies from city to city and region to region, with Paris and the Mediterranean south somewhat more relaxed and international-minded, and the other major cities more formal. Schedule appointments well in advance; the best times are late morning or around 3 p.m. Although kissing the hand of a woman may appear to be the appropriate French gesture, as a foreigner you will be expected to shake hands. Your counterparts, though likely to speak English, will appreciate any business cards or company literature in French. Pay attention to your own language; make sure it is absolutely correct and concise in all verbal and written communication, or you will not be taken seriously. You are expected to maintain discretion about business affairs, and pay attention to detail in your presentations. Intelligence, logic and patience are valued over pushiness.

If invited to a family home, send flowers in advance and follow up with a thank you note the next day. Keep in mind that as in many European countries, there are certain taboos on the nature of the bouquet (against red or white roses signifying, respectively, romantic love and lust), even numbers, or funereal varieties such as chrysanthemums. Table manners are strict, particularly regarding France's two most famous sources of culinary pride: wine and cheese. Do not slice the tip off a wedge of cheese, or cut it on a horizontal. More importantly, do not bring wine if invited to dinner, as you, a foreigner, are not expected to be able to choose a fine French wine better than your hosts. As an empty glass will signal your host to pour more, leave some wine in your glass if you are finished. Unlike in many countries, food can be cut with a fork (but do not cut bread or salad, or leave food on your plate). Although smoking is not unusual in Europe, here it is not customary to smoke at dinner unless indicated otherwise (that is, if your host puts out an ashtray).

Health: No vaccinations are required. Medical insurance is essential. There is a Reciprocal Health Agreement with some European countries which entitles the insured to a 70_80% refund on medical, dental, hospital treatments and prescribed medicines. Visitors from these countries should obtain an exemption form before traveling.

FRANCE

Language: French

BORDEAUX

Country code: 33 - City code: 556

Airport: Merignac Airport.

Distance from City: 12km (7 miles) west of the city

Transportation to Center of City:
From International and Domestic Terminals
By Bus (cost) FFR33.Time approx. 30 min.
By Taxi (cost) FFR100-120 Time approx. 20-25 min.
Tip luggage porters 10 FF per piece

Automobile Rentals:
Airport car rental desk
Avis - 56343822
Europcar Interrent - 56340579
Hertz - 56341887

Car rental city office
Avis - 56343822
Europcar Interrent - 56312030
Hertz - 56910171

Hotels:
Burdigala Hotel, 115 rue Georges Bonnac, 56901616
Grand Hotel Francais, 12 rue du Temple, 56481035
Holiday Inn Garden Court, 28-30 rue de Tauzia, 56922121
Mercure Shateau Chartons Hotel, 28 Court St. Louis, 56431500

Restaurants:
Clavel, 44 rue Charles-Domercq, 929152
La Cafetiere, 14 rue des Faussets, 516655
Ombriere, 14 pl.du Parlement, 448269
Vieux Bordeaux, 27 rue Buhan, 529436

Entertainment:
Au Boy's, 9 pl. des Martyrs de la Resistance 992326

Cabatet Andalucia, 7 quai Bacalan
L'Aztecal, 61 rue du Pas-St-Georges
La Palmeraie, 22 quai de la Monnaie, 940752
Le Blues Pub, 7 rue Teulere, 527737
Le Chat-Bleu, 122 quai Bacalan
Le Plana, 22 pl. de la Victoire
Le Rodes, 22 pl. des Capucins, 914231
Le Victoria, 231 rue Ste-Catherine, 917335
Les Argentiers, 7 rue Teulere
Senechal, 57 bis quai de Pludate

Places of Interest:
Grand Theatre – a monument.
Cite Mondiale du Vin - a museum and an exhibition hall.
Cathedrale St-Andre
Musee des Beaux-Arts- Fine Arts Museum.
Haut-Brion - vineyards.

LYON

Country code: 33 - City code: 7

Airport: Satolas Airport.

Distance from City: 25km (15 miles) east of the city.

Transportation to Center of City:
From International and Domestic Terminals
By Bus (cost) FFR46. Time approx.35-40 min.(every 20 min.)
By Taxi (cost) FFR250 Time approx. 30 min.
Tip luggage porters 10 FF per piece

Automobile Rentals:
Airport car rental desk
Avis - 72227543
Europcar Interrent - 72227528
Hertz - 72227450

Car rental city office
Avis - 78583344

FRANCE

Europcar Interrent - 78371497
Hertz - 78422485

Hotels:
Bristol Hotel, 28 cours de Verdun, 78375655
Grand Hotel Concorde, 11 rue Grolee, 72404545
Holiday Inn Crowne Plaza Lyon City Centre, 29 rue de Bonnel,
    72619090
Phenix Hotel, 7 quai Bondy, 78282424
Royal Hotel, 20 place Bellecour, 78375731
Valrhotel, 1 quai Georges Levy, Givors, 72399540

Restaurants:
Brasserie Georges, 30 cours de Verdun, 04-72-565454
Café des Federations, 8 rue du Major-Martin, 04-78-282600
Chez Sylvain, 4 rue Tupin, 04-78-421198
Hugon, 12 rue Pizay, 04-18-281094
Le Vivarais, 1 pl. du Dr-Gailleton, 04-78-378515
Leon de Lyon, 1 rue Pleney, 04-78-281133
Les Lyonnais, 1 rue Trsmassac, 04-78-376482
Les Muses, Opera de Lyon, 04-72-004558
Orsi, 3 pl. Kleber, 04-79-895768
Paul Bocuse, 50 quai de la Plage, 04-72-278585

Entertainment:
Bouchon a Vin, 64 rue Merciere
Café-Theatre de L'Accessoire, 26 rue de l'Annonciade,
    04-78-278484
Comoedia, 30 rue Neuve
Espace Gerson, 1 pl. Gerson, 04-78-279699
Hot Club, 26 rue Lanterne
Le Club des Iles, 1 Grande Rue des Feuillants
Opera de Lyon, 1 pl. de la Comedie, 04-72-004545
Palace Mobile, 2 rue Rene-Leynaud
Salle Moliere, 18 quai Bondy, 04-78-280311

Shops and Stores:
Clementine, 18 rue Emile-Zola   Apparel
Etincelle, 34 rue St-Jean   Apparel

Places of Interest:
Musee de la Marionette – a museum

FRANCE

Jardin Archeologique - archaeological site
The Basilica of Notre-Dame-de-Fourviere – a church
Jardin des Plantes - botanical gardens
Musee des Beaux-Arts - Fine Arts Museum.
Cathedral St. Jean
Musee Historique des Tissus – museum

MARSEILLE

Country code: 33 - City code: 91

Airport: Provence Airport.

Distance from City: 25km (15 miles) northwest of the city.

Transportation to Center of City:
From International and Domestic Terminals
By Bus (cost) FFR40. Time approx. 30 min. (every 20 min.)
By Taxi (cost) FFR220-250 Time approx. 30 min.
Tip luggage porters 10 FF per piece

Automobile Rentals:
Airport car rental desk
Avis - 42782167
Europcar Interrent - 42782475
Hertz – 42143270

Car rental city office
Avis - 91507011
Europcar Interrent - 91901100
Hertz – 91140424

Hotels:
Concorde Prado Hotel, 11Av. de Mazargues, 91765111
Fimotel Hotel, 23 Blvd. Rabateau, 91256666
De Rome et. St. Pierre Hotel, 7 cours St. Louis, 91541952

Restaurants:
Ches Fonfon, 140 rue du Vallon des Auffes, 521438
Ches Madie, 138 duai du Port, 904087

Chez-Angele, 50 rue Caisserie, 906335
Dar Djerba, 15 cours Julien, 485536

Entertainment:
Au Son des Guitares, 18 rue Corneille
Bistrot Thiars, 38 pl. Thiars, 540394
Jazz Hot, 48 av. La Rose
Le Club 95, 95 rue St-Jacques
Le Pog's, 5 rue du Chantier, 337722
Le Transbordeur, 12 quai de Rive Neueve, 550281
May be Blues, 2 rue Poggioli, 424100
Quai 9, 9 Quai de Rive Neueve, 333420
Trolleybus, 24 quai Neuve, 543045

Places of Interest:
Musee du Vieux Marseille - museum
The Cathedral
Musee de la Vieille-Charite - museum
Basilique St-Victor
Jardin des Vestiges – ruins
Musee d'Histoire de Marseille - museum
Palais Longchamp - Fine Arts Museum.

PARIS

Country code: 33 - City code: 1

Airport: Orly

Distance from City: 9 miles (14 km.)

Transportation to Center of City
From International and Domestic Terminals
By Bus (30 - 60FF) every 15 minutes, time 40 - 50 minutes
By Train (20 - 30FF) every 15 minutes, time 40 -50 minutes
By Taxi (125 - 200FF) time 35 - 45 minutes
Tip luggage porters 10FF per piece

Transfers: (Minimum Connecting Time):
International to International: 60 minutes

FRANCE

International to Domestic: 60 minutes
Domestic to International: 60 minutes
Domestic to Domestic: 50 minutes

Automobile Rentals
Airport car rental desk
Avis - 49754491
Europcar Interrent - Terminal West - 49754747
Europcar Interrent - Terminal South - 49754748
Hertz - 49758484

City offices
Avis - 44181050
Europcar Interrent - 450000806
Hertz - 43225869

Airport: Charles De Gaulle - Roissy

Distance from City: 14 miles (23 km.)

Transportation to Center of City
From International and Domestic Terminals
By Bus (35 - 60FF) every 15 minutes, time 35 - 60 minutes
By Train (25 - 45FF) every 15 minutes, time 35 - 45 minutes
By Taxi (175 - 300FF) time 45 - 60 minutes
Tip luggage porters 10FF per piece

Transfers: (Minimum Connecting Time):
International to International: 60 minutes
International to Domestic: 60 minutes
Domestic to International: 60 minutes
Domestic to Domestic: 60 minutes

Automobile Rentals
Airport car rental desk
Avis - Terminal 1 - 48623434
Avis - Terminal 2 - 48625989
Europcar Interrent - Terminal 1 - 48623333
Europcar Interrent - Terminal 2 - 48625647
Hertz - 48622900

FRANCE

Transportation to Airport from the Center of City

By Bus (30 - 60FF) every 15 minutes from Esplanade des In-valides, Le Meridien Montparnasse and City Terminal. Time 20 - 60 minutes.

By Train (20 - 30FF) every 15 minutes from Gare D'Orsay and Austerlitz. Time 45 - 55 minutes.

By Taxi (125 - 300FF) time 40 - 60 minutes

Hotels

Bristol, 112 Rue du Faubourg St-Honore, 8me, 01 42 66 91 45

Concorde Lafayette, Place du General Koening, 17me,
    01 40 68 50 68

George V, 31 Avenue George V, 8me, 01 47 23 54 00

Grand Hôtel de Champagne, 17 Rue Jean Lantier, 1er,
    01 42   60 30 03

Grand Inter-Continental, 2 Rue Scribe, 9me, 01 40 07 32 32

Hilton, 18 Avenue de Suffren, 15me, 01 42 73 92 00

Holiday Inn Paris, 10 Place de la Republique, 11me,
    01 43 55 44 34

Hôtel de Crillon, 10 Place de la Concorde, 8e, 01 44 71 15 00

Hôtel de L'Espérance, 15 Rue Pascal, 5e, 01 47 07 10 99

Hôtel Meurice, 228 Rue de Rivoli, 1er, 01 44 58 10 10

Hôtel Ritz, 15 Place Vendôme, 1er, 01 43 16 30 30

Hôtel Saint Honoré, 85 Rue Sainte Honoré, 1er, 01 42 36 20 38

Hôtel Saint Jacques 35 Rue des Écoles, 5e 01 43 26 82 53

Inter-Continental, 3 Rue Castiglione, 1er, 01 44 77 11 11

Meridien Montparnasse, 19 Rue du Commandant Mouchotte,
    14me, 01 43 20 15 51

Meridien, 81 Boulevard Gouvion Saint-Cyr, 17me,
    01 40 68 34 34

Nikko, 61 Quai de Grenelle, 15me, 01 40 58 20 00

Plaza Athenee, 25 Avenue Montaigne, 8me, 01 47 23 78 33

Raphael, 17 Avenue Kleber, 16e, 01 44 28 00 28

Scribe, 1 Rue Scribe, 9me 01 44 71 24 24

Sheraton Prince de Galles, 33 Avenue George V, 8me,
    01 47 23 55 11

Sofitel, 8 Rue Louis Armand, 15me, 01 40 60 30 30

Tremoille, 14 Rue de la Tremoille, 8me 01 47 23 34 20

Restaurants

Au Pied de Cochon, 6 Rue Coquillière, 1er, 01 42 36 11 75

Brasserie Paoli, 104 Rue de Rivoli, 1er, 01 42 33 98 53

Brasserie Terminus Nord, 23 Rue de Dunkerque, 10e,

FRANCE

01 42 85 05 15

Fouquet's, 99 Avenue des Champs-Elysée, 8me,
01 47 23 70 60

Guy Savoy, 18 Rue Troyon, 17me, 01 43 80 40 61

Jules Verne, Eiffel Tower, 7me, 01 45 55 61 44

L'Ambroisie, 9 Place des Vossges, 4me, 01 42 78 51 45

L'Arbuci, 25 Rue de Buci, 6e, 01 44 41 14 14

La Cagouille, 10-12 Place Constantin Brancusi, 14e,
01 43 22 09 01

La Coupole, 102 Blvd de Montparnasse, 14e, 01 43 20 14 20

La Maison d'Alsace, 39 Avenue des Champs-Élysées, 8e, 01
43 59 44 24

La Tour d'Argent, 15 Quai Tournelle, 5me, 01 43 54 23 31

Lasserre, 17 Avenue Franklin D. Roosevelt, 8me,
01 43 59 53 43

Laurent, 41 Avenue Gabriel, 8me, 01 42 25 00 39

Le Caméléon, 6 Rue de Chevreuse, 6e, 01 43 20 63 43

Le Grand Véfour, 17 Rue de Beaujolais, 1er, 01 42 96 56 27

Le Petit Montmorency, 5 Rue Rabelais, 8e 01 42 25 11 19

Le Petit Zinc, 11 Rue Saint Benoit, 6e, 01 42 61 20 60

Le Taillevent, 15 Rue Lamennais, 8me, 01 44 95 15 01

Le Train Blue, Gare de Lyon 13me, 01 43 43 09 06

Lucas-Carton, 9 Place de la Madeleine, 8me, 01 42 65 22 90

Maison Prunier, 16 Ave Victor Hugo, 16e, 01 44 17 35 85

Maxim's, 3 Rue Royale, 8me, 01 42 65 27 94

Restaurant La Petit Chose, 41 Rue des Trois Frères, 18e,
01 42 64 49 15

Robuchon, 59 Avenue Raymond Poincaré, 16e, 01 47 27 12 27

Entertainment

Au Duc des Lombards, 42 Rue des Lombards, 1er, 01 42 33 22 88

Calavados, 40 Avenue Pierre-1er-de-Serbie, 8me, 01 47 20 31 39

Castel's, 15 Rue Princess, 16me, 01 43 26 90 22

Conway's, 73 Rue Saint-Denis, 1er, 01 40 266 13 76

Crazy Horse Saloon, 12 Avenue George V, 8me, 01 47 23 32 32

Folies-Bergere, 32 Rue Richer, 9me, 01 42 46 77 11

Harry's, 5 Rue Daunou, 2me, 01 42 61 71 14

La Locomotive, 90 Boulevard de Clichy, 18me, 01 42 57 37 37

La Villa, 29 Rue Jacob, 6e, 01 43 26 60 00

Le Lapin Agile, 22 Rue des Saules, 18e, 01 46 06 85 87

FRANCE

Le Montana, 28 Rue St. Benoit, 6me, 01 45 48 93 08
Lido, 116 Avenue des Champs-Élysées, 8me, 01 40 76 56 10
Lionel Hampton, Hotel Meridien, 81 'Boulevard Gouvion Stl Cyr,
    17me,Moulin Rouge, Place Blanche, 8me, 01 46 06 00 19
Pont Royal, 7 Rue Montalembert, 7me, 01 45 44 38 27
Rosebud, 11 bis, Rue Delambre, 14me, 01 43 35 38 54
Scheherazade, 3 rue de Liege, 9me,
Slow Club, 130 Rue de Rivoli, 1er, 01 42 33 84 30

Shops and Stores

Au Bon Marche, 38 rue Sevres	Dept. Store
Au Printemps, 30 Av. Ternes	Dept. Store
Baccarat, 30 bis de Paradis	China/Crystal
Boucheron, 26 Pl. Vendome	Jewelry
Bulgari, 27 Ave. Montaigne	Jewelry
Cartier, 13 rue de la Paiax	Jewelry
Celine, 24 Rue Francois	Apparel
Cerruti, 15 Madeline	Apparel
Charles Jourdan, 12 F. St-Honore	Shoes
Christian Dior, F. St-Honore	Apparel
Dior, 30 Ave. Montaigne	Apparel
Etienne Levy, 178 F. St-Honore	Antiques
Fauchon, 24 P la Madeleine	Dept. Store
Galeries Lafayette, Haussmann	Dept. Store
Givenchy, 3 George V	Apparel
Guy Laroche 29 Ave. Montaigne	Apparel
Hermes, 24 Rue St. Honore	Leather
Lanvin, 2 Rue Cambon	Apparel
Lalique, 11 Rue Royale	Glass/China
Le Bon Marche, 22 Rue Sevres	Dept. Store
Louis Feraud, 88 R. St. Honore	Apparel
Missoni, 43 Rue du Bac	Apparel
Nina Ricci, 44 Rue Francois	Apparel
Pierre Cardin, 83 F. St-Honore	Apparel
Revillon, 44 Rue du Dragon	Furs
Ted Lapidus, 35 Rue Francois	Apparel
Van Cleef, 22 Pl. Vendome	Jewelry
Yves St-Laurent, 5 Av. Marceau	Apparel

Places of Interest:
Arc de Triomphe de l'Etoile
Champs Elysees

FRANCE

The Pompidou Center
The Sorbonne
Cite des Sciences et de L'Industrie
Musee D"orsay
Musee des Arts de la Mode
Notre-Dame Cathedral
Picasso Museum
Palais de Justice
The Eiffel Tower
The Louvre

GEORGIA

Official Name: Republic of Georgia

Government: Republic

Area: 69,700 sq. km., 26,911 sq. mi.

Population: 6.3 million

Religion(s): Georgian Orthodox, Russian Orthodox, Islamic

Capital City: Tbilisi

Major Business Cities: Tbilisi and Kutaisa

Time: GMT +3

Currency: Georgian Coupon

Currency Requirements: The Import of foreign currency is unlimited but must be declared. The export is limited to the amount declared upon arrival. The import and the export of local currency are prohibited.

Business Hours:
- Government: 09.00-18.00 Mon-Fri
- Banks: 09.00-18.00 Mon-Fri
- Shops: 09.00-18.00 Mon-Fri
- Offices: 09.00-18.00 Mon-Fri

Weight and Measures: Metric System

Electric Current: 220/127V, 50c

Automobile Driving License: An International driving license is required.

Customs Allowances: As currency and customs requirements have undergone a number of changes in recent years, one should consult your country's Georgian embassy or consulate when arranging your trip. Valuables, including foreign currency, must be registered upon arrival, otherwise they may be confiscated upon departure. Although you may bring in unlimited amounts of foreign currency, and take out any you initially declare, you may not import or export Georgian rubles. Limits are stringent on items like cigarettes and alcohol.

Tipping: A tip of 10%-15% is expected in most restaurants. Hotels usually include a service charge in the bill. Taxi drivers expect 10-15% tip.

Credit Cards Accepted: American Express, Visa, EuroCard, Carte Blanche, Diner's Club

Customary Dining Hours:
Breakfast: 07.00-09.00
Lunch: 12.00-14.30
Dinner: 18.30-22.00

Local Customs, Business Protocol and Courtesies: As throughout the former East bloc, nationalism is on the rise in Georgia, so it's best not to get enmeshed in political discussions. Its recent independence from the Soviet Union is a source of great pride. The country's agriculture has been severely affected by the Chernobyl nuclear accident in neighboring Ukraine, but appliance and clothing manufacture are a strong part of the economy and are a source of local pride. Although this small country has big economic and political problems, most businessmen are eager and hopeful for progress, and will treat you, the potential partner, with great hospitality. You should reciprocate for the many invitations you will receive with small souvenirs from your country for your host's family. As in many countries with shortages, it is bad manners to leave food on your plate; although here, leaving a little bit will signify that you are finished.

Health: It is recommended to consult your doctor before your journey. Drinking water is safe in most major cities. The medical and dental treatment is free, but the medications must be paid. In emergencies you must contact your embassy or hotel receptionist.

Language: Georgian

TBILISI

Country code: 995 - City code: 32

Airport: Novo Alexeyevka

Distance from City: 1.6 km. (1 mi.)

Transfers: (Minimum Connecting Time):
International to International: 60 min.
International to Domestic: 60 min.
Domestic to International: 60 min.
Domestic to Domestic: 20 min.

Hotels:
Adiara, Constitution Square 1, 369822
Iveria, Inoshvili 12, 930488
Metechi Palace, Isaani, 744566
Tbilisi, Rustaveli Prospekt 13, 997829
Vshba, Georgian Military Highway, 511681

Restaurants:
Aravgi, Pushkin 29
Darial, Rustaveli 22
Dynamo, Brdzola 2
Gemo, Lenin St.
Isani, Meshkishvili 3

Shops and Stores:
Central Store, Mardzhinishvili 7   Dept. Store
Tbilisi, Victory Square   Dept. Store
Souvenir, Rustaveli 18   Gifts

Places of Interest:
Academy of Art
Botanical Gardens

GEORGIA

Georgian Art Museum - gold icon exhibitions
Kirkov Park
Old Town
Rustaveli Palace
Sioni Cathedral
Sololaksky Citadel

GERMANY

Official Name: The Federal Republic of Germany.

Location: Europe. Germany is bordered by Poland, Czech Republic, Austria, France, Luxembourg, Belgium, Denmark, Switzerland and The Netherlands. A part of its north coast is on the North Sea.

Government: Federation - 16 Lander (states) with their own constitutions and governments.

Area: 356,859 sq. km., 137,783 sq. miles

Population: 80.6 million

Religion(s): Protestant and Catholic majority.

Capital City: Berlin

Major Business Cities: Bonn, Cologne, Dusseldorf, Frankfurt, Hamburg, Hanover, Munich and Stuttgart.

Time: GMT + 1 (GMT +2 from late March to late October).

Currency: Deutsche Mark (DMK) = 100 Pfennigs

Currency Requirements: There are no restrictions on the import and the export of local or foreign currency.

Business Hours:
- Government: Mon-Fri 08.30-17.00
- Banks: Mon-Fri 08.30-1300 (open until 16.00 Tue & Thur)
- Shops: Mon-Fri 09.00-18.00 Sat 09.00-14.00 (open until 20.30 Thur)
- Offices: Mon-Fri 08.00/09.00-16.00 (hours may vary)

Weight and Measures: Metric System

GERMANY

Electric Current: 220 volts AC - round 2-pin plugs are used.

Holidays:
New Year's Day - January 1
Good Friday - April 10*
Easter Monday - April 13*
Labour Day - May 1
Ascension Day - May 21
Whit Monday - June 1*
Corpus Christi - June 11
Day of Unity - October 3
Christmas - December 25-26
New Year's Eve - December 31

*Christian Holidays - vary each year

Suitable Clothing: Light weight clothing is suitable in the summer. Medium weight clothing with an overcoat is suitable in the winter.

Automobile Driving License: International or national driving license is required.

Customs Allowances: Personal items are duty free, but register all valuables upon arrival and keep receipts or you may face bureaucracy later. Tobacco and alcohol restrictions: 200 cigarettes, two liters of wine and one of spirits.

Tipping: A service charge of 10-15% is usually included in all restaurant and hotel bills. Cloakroom attendants and taxi drivers should also be tipped.

Credit Cards Accepted: Access, American Express, Diner's Club, Eurocard, Master Card, Visa

Customary Dining Hours:
Breakfast: 06.30-09.00
Lunch: 12.30–13.30
Dinner: 18.00–21.00

Local Customs, Business Protocol and Courtesies: Above all in Germany, adhere to conservative protocol and traditions in the German business world. Longtime business, social and familiar relationships are held in high regard, as are age, rank and education. This environment, while producing gracious manners, also makes it much harder for women to be taken seriously in business. In any case, it is essential to dress and behave as conservatively as possible. Appointments should be scheduled at 10 am and between 1.30 and 4, generally. As in many European countries, avoid Friday afternoons. Although the increasingly competitive and active role of international commerce dictates a decrease in leisure time even in vacation-conscious Western Europe, try to restrict your business communication, even by telephone, to your counterpart's office and German business hours. Although English is widely and well-spoken, any business cards or company literature in German will be viewed favorably, as is an offer on your part for an interpreter. It's useful to exchange business cards immediately, as this will help you quickly figure out titles. The appropriate address is Herr/Frau/Fraulein (Mr/Mrs/Miss) followed by highest-ranking title and last name, such as Herr Professor Braun or Frau Engineer Schmidt. Wait for your counterpart to move to a first-name basis if the relationship progresses. You are expected to maintain patience and discretion regarding business affairs, and pay attention to detail in your presentations. Your counterpart will usually control the pace of a meeting or presentation, and usually quite efficiently. You, too, should avoid wasting time. Don't expect a quick resolution of proposals and contracts, as German law puts penalties on unfulfilled claims that a contract will be made.

If your relationship progresses so far as to be invited to dine with the family, either send in advance, or bring flowers, avoiding the usual European taboos such as against red or white roses (signifying, respectively, romantic love and lust), even numbers, or funereal varieties. Small, inexpensive but tasteful gifts made outside of Germany are appropriate for the hostess such as a fine book or chocolate. Bringing candy for the children is viewed favorably; gifts made in Germany are not. In any case, business gifts are rare, except at Christmas or perhaps upon the signing of a contract. For dinner invitation to a home or restaurant,

GERMANY

be as punctual as you would for a business meeting, and send a thank-you note the next day. The host or, when dining out, the highest-ranking businessman will offer a toast; you should offer a toast later in the meal. Smoking is considered impolite at the table, particularly at home, though it is not unusual for cigarettes to be passed out after dinner. Wait for the host or hostess to say "Good Appetite" (Guten Appetit), and respond with a thank you before beginning to eat. Although, in the European style, a knife and fork are used to eat, you may use a just fork to cut softer foods like dumplings. When finished, place your fork and knife together on the plate on a diagonal and try not to leave food on your plate.

Health: No special precautions are necessary. There is a Reciprocal Health Agreement with the UK which provides UK citizens with free medical and dental treatment, however hospital treatment must be paid for. UK citizens should obtain an exemption form before traveling. Additional health insurance is recommended.

Language: German

BERLIN

Country code: 49 - City code: 30

Airport: Tegel International Airport

Distance from City: 8km (4 miles) northwest of the city.

Transportation to Center of City:
From International and Domestic Terminals
By Bus (cost) DMK3-10. Time approx. 1-30 min.(every 20 min.)
By Taxi (cost) DMK20-30 . Time approx. 10 min.
Tip luggage porters DMK2 per piece.

Transfers: (Minimum Connecting Time):
International to International: 30 minutes
International to Domestic: 30 minutes

GERMANY

Domestic to International: 30 minutes
Domestic to Domestic: 30 minutes
Automobile Rentals:
Avis - 4101-3148
Europcar Interrent - 4101-3368
Hertz - 4101-3315

Hotels:
Abaacus Tierpark Hotel, Franz Mett Str. 3-9, 5162-333
Berlin Hilton, Mohrenstr. 30, 20230
Forum Hotel Berlin, Alexanderplatz, 2389-0
Golden Tulip Berlin Excelsior Hotel, Hardenbergstr. 14, 3155-0
Golden Tulip Berlin Mark Hotel, Meinekestr. 18-19, 8800-20
Golden Tulip Hotel Berlin, Lutzowplatz 17, 2605-2700
Grand Hotel Esplanade Berlin, Lutzowufer 15, Tiergarten, 254780
Holiday Inn - Berlin Esplanade, Rohrdamm 80, 38389-0
Holiday Inn Berlin, Hochstr. 2-3, 46003-0
Holiday Inn Crowne Plaza Berlin City Center, Nurnberger Str.
    65, 210070
Inter-Continental Berlin, Budapester Str. 2-3, 26020
Kempinski Hotel Adlon Berlin, Unter den Linden 77, 2261-0
Kempinski Hotel Bristol Berlin, Kurfurstendamm 27, 884340
Maritim Pro Arte Hotel, Friedrichstr. 150-153, 2033-5
Palace Hotel, Im Europa-Center, Budapester Str, Europa
    Center, 25020
Radisson SAS Hotel Berlin, Karl-Liebknecht Str. 5, 2382-8
SORAT Hotel Spree-Bogen Berlin, Alt-Moabit 99, 399200
Schweizerhof Inter-Continental Berlin, Budapester Str. 21-31,
    26960

Restaurants:
Alt-Luxenburg, Windscheidstr. 31, 323-8730
Bamberger Reiter, Regensburgerstr. 7, 218-4282
Blockhaus Nikolskoe, Nikolskoer Weg 15, 805-2914
Borchardt, Franzosische Str. 47, 203-97117
Café Oren, Oranienburger Str. 28, 282-8228
Diyar, Dresdner Str. 9, 615-2708
Franzosischer Hof, Jagerstr. 56, 204-3570
Hardtke, Meinekestr. 27, 881-9827
Marz, Schoneberger Ufer 65, 261-3882
Paris Bar, Kantstr. 152, 313-8052

Reinhard's, Poststr. 28, 242-5295
Rockendorf's, Dusterhauptstr. 1, 402-3099
Thurnagel, Gneisenaustr. 57, 691-4800
Turmstuben, Gendarmenmarkt 5, 229-9313
Zitadellen-Schanke, Am Juliusturm, Spandau, 334-2106
Zur Letzten, Waisenstr. 14-16, 242-5528
Zur Rippe, Poststr 17, 242-4248

Entertainment:
90 Grad, Dennewitzstr. 37, 2628-984
Bar am Lutzowplatz, Am Lutzowpl. 7, 2626-807
Champussy, Uhlandstr. 171-172, 8812-220
Far Out, Kurfurstendamm 15 6, 320-007
Harry's New York Bar, Am Lutzowufer 15, 2547-8821
Kumpelnest 3000, Lutzowstr. 23, 2616-918
Metropol, Nolendorfpl. 5, 2162-787
Pleasure Dome, Hasenheide 13, 6934-061
Sophienklub, Sophienstr. 6, 2824-552
Spielbank Berlin, Europa Center, 2500-890

Shops and Stores:

Axel Sedlatzek, Kurfurstendamm 45	Jewelry
Bogner-Shop Zenker, Kurfurstendamm 45	Apparel
Budapester Schuhe, Kurfurstendamm 199	Apparel
Galeries Lafayette, Franzosische Str. 23,	Dept. Store
Granny's Step, Kurfurstendamm 56	Apparel
Kaufhaus des Westens, Tauentzienstr. 21	Dept. Store
Kaufhof, Alexanderpl.	Dept. Store
Kramberg, Kurfurstendamm 56	Apparel
Mientus, Wilmersdorfer Str. 73	Apparel
Nouvelle, Bleibtreustr. 24	Apparel
Peek und Cloppenburg, Tauentzienstr. 19	Apparel
Selbach, Kurfurstendamm 195/196	Apparel
Wertheim, Kurfurstendamm 181	Dept. Store
Wurzbacher, Kurfurstendamm 36	Jewelry

Places of Interest:
The Reichstag
Museum at Checkpoint Charlie
The Brandenburg Gate
Dahlem Museum Center
Schloss Charlottenburg

GERMANY

BONN

Country code: 49 - City code: 228

Airport: Cologne Wahn International Airport serving Cologne and Bonn.

Distance from City: 14km (8 miles) southeast of Cologne and 21km (13 miles) northeast of Bonn.

Transportation to Center of City:
From International and Domestic Terminals
By Bus (cost) DMK8. Time approx. 25-30 min.
By Taxi (cost) DMK60-DMK65. Time approx 20-25 min.
Tip luggage porters DMK2 per piece

Automobile Rentals:
Airport car rental desk
Hertz - 361085

Car rental city office
Avis - 223047
Europcar Interrent - 652961
Hertz - 217041

Hotels:
Best Western Hotel Domicil, Thomas-Mann Str. 24, 729090
Holiday Inn Crowne Plaza, Berliner Freiheit 2, 72690
Maritim Hotel, Gotesberger Allee, 81080
Arcade, Vorgebirgstr. 33, 72660
Consul, Oxfordstr., 12-16, 72920
Kaiserhov Hotel, Moltkestr. 64, 362016
President, Clemens-August 32-36, 694-001
Residence, Am Kaiserplatz 11, 26970

Restaurants:
Em Hottche, Markt 4, 690-009
Haus Daufenbach, Brudergasse 6, 637-944

Entertainment:
Jazz Galerie, Oxfordstr. 24

GERMANY

La Grange, Wesselstr. 5
Lampe, Breitestr. 35
Locke, Prinz-Albertstr. 20
Pinte, Breitestr. 46
Sky, Bonnerstr. 48

Shops and Stores:
Ehlers Antiquitaten, Berliner Freiheit 28, 676-853   Antiques
Paul Schweitzer, Muffendorfer Hauptstr. 37, 362-659   Antiques

Places of Interest:
The Munster – a romanesque cathedral.
The Landesmuseum
The House of Ludwig van Beethoven – a museum
The Botanical Gardens
The Godesburg – a 13th century castle.

COLOGNE

Country code: 49 - City code: 221

Airport: Cologne Wahn International Airport serving Cologne and Bonn.

Distance from City: 14km (8 miles) southwest of Cologne and 21km (13 miles) northeast of Bonn.

Transportation to Center of City:
From International and Domestic Terminals
By Bus (cost) DEM8. Time approx. 15-30 min.
By Taxi (cost) DEM35. Time approx. 15 min.
Tip luggage porters DEM2 per piece

Transfers: (Minimum Connecting Time):
International to International: 30 min.
International to Domestic: 30 min.
Domestic to International: 30 min.
Domestic to Domestic: 30 min.

GERMANY

Automobile Rentals:
Airport car rental desk
Avis - 402343
Europcar Interrent - 955880
Hertz - 61085

Car rental city office
Avis - 234333
Europcar Interrent - 883011
Hertz – 515084

Hotels:
Best Western Ascot Hotel, Hohenzollernring 95-97, 521076
Best Western Hotel Regent International, Melatengurtel 15, 54990
CM City Class Hotel Europa am Dom, Am Hof 38-46, 20580
CM City Class Hotel Residence, Alter Markt 55, 257-6991
Conti Coln Hotel, Brusseler St., 40-42, 252062
Dom Hotel, Domkloster 2a, 20240
Esser Minotel Koln, An der Malzmuehle 4-8, 234141
Euro Plaza Hotel, Breslauer Platz 2, 16510
Excelsior Hotel Ernst, Domplatz, 2701
Holiday Inn Crowne Plaza, Habsburgerring 9-13, 20950
Hyatt Regency Cologne, Kennedy-Ufer 2a, 828-1234
Maritim Hotel, heumarkt 20, 20270
Mercure Severinshof, Severinstr. 199, 20130
Queens Hotel Koeln, Duerener St., 287, 46760
Renaissance Koln Hotel, Magnusstr. 20, 20340
Rheingold Hotel, Engelbertstr. 33-35, 924090
Savoy Hotel, Turiner St. 9, 16230
Viktoria Hotel, Worringer St. 23, 720-0476
Wasserturm Hotel, Kaygasse 2, 20080

Restaurants:
Bado-La Poele d'Or, Komodienstr. 50-52, 134-100
Die Tomate, Aachenerstr. 11, 257-4307
Fruh am Dom, Am Hof 12-14, 258-0389
Haus Toller, Weyerstr. 96, 214-086
Ratskeller, Rathauspl. 1, 257-6929
Weinhaus im Walfisch, Salzgasse13, 258-0397

GERMANY

Entertainment:
Alter Wartesaal, Am Hauptbahnhof, Johannisstr. 11, 912-8856
Das Ding, Hohenstaufenring 30-32, 246-348
Disco 42, Hohenstaufenring 25, 247-971
Papa Joe's Biersalon, Alter Markt 50-52, 258-2132

Stadtgarten, Venloerstr. 40, 516-037
Subway, Aachnerstr. 82, 517-969

Shops and Stores:

Eau de cologne, Clockengasse 4711, 925-0450	Perfumes Shop
Gebruder Grimm, Mauritiusseinweg 110	Toy Store
Hertie, Hohe Strasse	Dept. Store
Karstadt, Hohe Strasse	Dept. Store
Kaufhof, Hohe Strasse	Dept. Store
Offermann's, Breite Str. 48-50, 252-018	Accessories

Places of Interest:
The Dom – a gothic church with a museum.
Wallraf-Richartz/Ludwig Museum - art galleries.
Romisch-Germanisches Museum
Archaeological museum.
The Altstadt - romanesque churches.
The Botanical Gardens
The Zoo and Aquarium
The Grabkammer – a 2nd century burial chamber.

DUSSELDORF

Country code: 49 - City code: 211

Airport: Dusseldorf Airport.

Distance from City: 10km (6 miles) from the city center.

Transportation to Center of City:
From International and Domestic Terminals
By Bus (cost) DMK3. Time approx. 30 min.
By Taxi (cost) DMK20-30. Time approx. 15-25 min.
Tip luggage porters DMK2 per piece

Transfers: (Minimum Connecting Time):
International to International: 35 min.
International to Domestic: 35 min.
Domestic to International: 35 min.
Domestic to Domestic: 35 min.

Automobile Rentals:
Airport car rental desk
Avis - 4216748
Hertz - 411083

Car rental city office
Avis - 329050
Europcar Interrent - 4201266
Hertz – 357025

Hotels:
Best Western Hotel Eden, Adersstr. 29-31, 38970
Best Western Hotel Majestic, Cantadorstr. 4, 367030
Breidenbacher Hof Hotel, Heinrich-Heine-Allee 36, 13030
Cascade Hotel, Kaiserswertherstr. 59, 492200
Dusseldorf Hilton, Georg Glock St. 20, 43770
Holiday Inn – Konigsallee, Graf-Adolf-Plaz 10, 38480
Plaza Hotel Dusseldorf, Karlstr. 4, 365057
Queens Hotel Dusseldorf, Ludwig-Erhard-Allee 3, 77710
Radisson SAS Hotel Dusseldorf, Karl-Arnold-Platz 5, 45530
Rema-Hotel Central, Luisenstr. 42, 379001
Rema-Hotel Concorde, Graf-Adolf-Str. 60, 369825
Rema-Hotel Monopol, Oststr. 135, 84208
Rema-Hotel Savoy, Oststr. 128, 360336
SORAT Hotel Dusseldorf, Volmerswerther Str. 35, 30220
Villa Viktoria, Blumenthalstr. 12, 469000

Restaurants:
Fuchschen, Ratinger Str. 28-30, 84062
Im Schiffchen, Kaiserwerther Markt 9, 401-051
Rottisserie, Corneliuspl. 1, 13810
Weinhaus Tante Anna, Andreasstr. 2, 131-163
Zum Schiffchen, Hafenstr. 5, 132-422

Entertainment:
Bei Tony, Lorettosrt. 12

GERMANY

Front Page, Mannesman Ufer
Sam's West, Ko

Shops and Stores:

Arts Decoratifs, Hohe Str. 28, 324-553	Dept. Store
Ko Center, Konigsallee 30	Apparel
Ko Galerie, Konigsallee 60	Apparel
Schadow Arcade, Konigsallee 65	Mall

Places of Interest:
The Hofgarten - art galleries.
Kunstsammlung Nordrhein-Westfalen – art museum
Schloss Benrath – a monument
Neandertall Valley – a museum

FRANKFURT

Country code: 49 - City code: 69

Airport: Frankfurt Rhein-Main International Airport.

Distance from City: 12km (7 miles) southwest of the city.

Transportation to Center of City:
From International and Domestic Terminals
By Bus (cost) DMK8-DMK10 Time approx. 30 min.
By Taxi (cost) DMK35. Time approx. 20 min.
Tip luggage porters DMK2 per piece

Transfers: (Minimum Connecting Time):
International to International: 45 min.
International to Domestic: 45 min.
Domestic to International: 45 min.
Domestic to Domestic: 45 min.

Automobile Rentals:
Airport car rental desk
Avis - 69027771
Terminal 2 -69072785
Hertz -69050131

GERMANY

Car rental city office
Avis - 730111
Hertz – 24252627

Hotels:
Arabella Hotel am Busing Palais, Berliner St., 111, Offenbach, 82999-754
Bauer Hotel Scala, Scgafergasse 31, 1381110
Best Western Alexander am Zoo, Waldschmidstr. 59-61, 949600
Best Western Bauer Hotel Domicil, Karlstr. 14, 27111-0
Best Western Hotel National, Beseler St. 50, 27394-0
Best Western Imperial Hotel am Palmengarten, Sophienstr. 40, 7930030
Continental Hotel, Baseler St. 56, 230341
Forum Hotel Frankfurt, Wilhelm Leuschner St., 34, 2606-0
Golden Tulip Hotel Offenbacher Hof, Ludwigstr. 33-37, Offenbach, 82982-0
Hessischer Hof Hotel, Friedrich-Ebert-Anlage 40, 7540-0
Holiday Inn Crowne Plaza Frankfurt, Conference Center, 6802-0
Inter-Continental Frankfurt, Wilhelm-Leuschner-Str. 43, 2605-0
Le Meridien Parkhotel, Wiesenhuttenplatz 28-38, 269-7970
Maritim Hotel, Theodor-heuss-Allee 3, 75780
Marriott Hotel Frankfurt, Hamburger Allee 2-10, 79550
Mercure Hotel & Residenz, Voltastr. 29, 79260
Messe Hotel , Westendstr. 104, 747979
Rema-Hotel Bristol, Ludwigstr. 13-17, 24239-0
Rhein Main Hotel, Heidelbergerstr. 3, 250035
Scandic Crown Hotel Savoy, Wiesenhuttenstr. 42, 273960

Restaurants:
Altes Zollhaus, Friedberger Landstr. 531, 472-707
Avocado, Hochstr. 27, 292-867
Bistrot 77, Ziegelhuttenweg 1-3, 614-040
Borsenkeller, Schillersrt. 11, 281-115
Bruckenkeller, Schutzenstr. 6, 284-238
Cafe Gegenwart, Berger Str. 6, 497-0544
Cafe Karin, Grosser Hirschgraben, 295-217
Charlot, Opernpl. 10, 287-007
Erno's Bistro, Liebigsrt. 15, 721-997
Germania, Textorstr. 16, Sachsenhausen, 613-336
Gilde Stuben, Bleichstr. 38, 283-228

Jaspers, Schifferstr. 8, Sachsenhausen, 614-117
Melange, Jordanstr. 19, 701-287
Papillon, Sheraton Hotel, Frankfurt Airport, 6977-1238
Restaurant Francais, Am Kaiserpl., 215-865
Steinernes Haus, Braubachstr. 35, 283-491
Tequila, Weissadlergasse 5, 287-142
Wolkenbruch, Textorstr. 26, 622-612
Zum Gemalten Haus, Schweizerstr. 67, 614-559
Zur Mullerin, Weissfrauenstr. 18, 285-182

Entertainment:
Al Andalus, Affentorpl. 1, 617-032
An Sibin, Wallstr. 9, 603-2159
Casablanka Bar, Parkhotel, Wiesenhuttenpl. 28, 26970
Cooky's, Am Salzhaus 4, 287-662
Der Frankfurter Jazzkeller, Kleine Bockenheimer Str. 18a, 288-537
Dorian Gray, Airport, 690-2212
Dreikoenigskeller, Faerberstr. 71, 629-273
Fantasy Garden, Seilerstr. 34, 285-055
Funkadelic, Broennerstr. 11, 283-808
Jazz-Life Podium, Kleine Rittergasse 22-26, 626-346
Jimmy's Bar, Friedrich-Ebert-Anlage 40, 614-559
Nachtleben, Kurt Schumacher Str. 45, 20650
Sinkkasten, Bronnerstr. 5-9, 280-385

Shops and Stores:

Escada, Goethestr. 31, 287-799	Apparel
Hochester Porzellan Manufactur, Berlinerst. 60,	Dept. Store
Jil Sander, Goethestr. 29, 283-469	Apparel
La Galleria, Berlinerstr. 66, 281-461	Jewelry
Mitsukoshi, Kaiserstr. 13, 293-085	Dept. Store
Schillersrtasse, Borse	Apparel
Zeil Galerie, Zeil 112-114, 9207-3414	Mall

Places of Interest:
Goethe's House and Museum
Old Opera House
Museum of Arts and Crafts
Museum of Modern Art

GERMANY

HAMBURG

Country code: 49 - City code: 40

Airport: Hamburg Fuhlsbuttel International Airport.

Distance from City: 12km (7 miles) northwest of the city center.

Transportation to Center of City:
From International and Domestic Terminals
By Bus (cost) DMK8 Time approx. 20 min.
By Taxi (cost) DMK30-DMK35 Time approx. 20 min.
Tip luggage porters DMK2 per piece

Transfers: (Minimum Connecting Time):
International to International: 35 min.
International to Domestic: 40 min.
Domestic to International: 40 min.
Domestic to Domestic: 40 min.

Automobile Rentals:
Airport car rental desk
Avis - 50752314
Europcar Interrent - 50752812
Hertz - 50752302

Car rental city office
Avis - 8663071
Europcar Interrent - 362221
Hertz – 230045

Hotels:
Bellevue Hotel, Ander Alster 14, 284440
Berlin Hotel, Borgfelder St., 1-9, 251640
Best Western Hotel St. Raphael, Adenauerallee 41, 248200
Carat Hotel, Sieldeich 9-11, 789660
Forum Hotel Hamburg, Billwerder Neuer Deich 14, 788-400
Hamburg Marriott Hotel, ABC St. 52, 35050
Holiday Inn Crowne Plaza Hamburg, Graumannsweg 10, 228060
Inter-Continental Hamburg, Fontenay 10, 41415-0
Kempinski Hotel Atlantic Hamburg, An der Alster 72-79, 28880

GERMANY

Maritim Hotel Reichshof, Kirchenalle 34-36, 24833-0
Plem Hotel, An der Alster 9, 241726
Radisson SAS Hotel Hamburg, Marseiller St., 2, 35020
Rema Hotel Domicil, Stresmannstr. 62, 431-6026
Renaissance Hamburg Hotel, Grosse Bleichen 36, 349180
Vier Jahreszeiten Hotel, Neuer Jungfernstieg 9-14, 3494-0

Restaurants:
Ahrberg, Strandweg 33, 860-438
At Nali, Rutschbahn 11, 410-3810
Avocado, Kanalstr.9, 220-4599
Fischereihafen-Restaurant Hamburg, Grosse Elbestr. 143, 381-816
Fischerhaus, Fischmarkt 14, 314-0535
Il Giardino,Ulmenstr.17-19, 470-147
La Mer, An der Alster 9, 245-454
Landhaus Dill, Elbchaussee 94, 390-5077
Landhaus Scherrer, Elbchaussee 130, 880-1325
Le Canard, Elbchaussee 139, 880-5057
Noblesse, Grosse Bleichen, 349-180
Peter Lambcke, Holzdamm 49, 243-290
Ratsweinkeller, Grosse-Johannisstr.2, 364-153
Restaurant Royal Kopenhagen, Esplanade 31, 343-672

Entertainment:
Birdland, Gertnerstr.122, 405-277
Cotton Club, Alter Steinweg 10, 343-878
Die Insel, Alsterufer 35, 410-6955
Fabrik, Barnerstr.36, 391-079
Gresse Freiheit 36, Grosse Freiheit 36, 420-3282
Mojo Club, Reeperbahn 1, 319-1999
Schmids Tivoli, Spielbudenpl. 27-28, 311-231
Schmidt Theater, Spielbudenpl. 24, 311-231
Skyy, Spielbudenpl.16b, 319-1711
St.Pauli-Theatre, Spielbudenpl.29, 314-344
Top of the Town, Marseiller Str.2, 3502-3210

Shops and Stores:
Alsterhaus, Jungfernstieg 16-20, 359-010   Dept. Store
Binikowski, Lokstedter Weg 68, 462-852   Gift Shop
Brahmfed & Guttruf, Jungfernstieg   Jewelry
Brucke 4, St. Pauli Landungsbrucken, 316-373   Gift Shop

GERMANY

Galleria, Grosse Bleichen	Mall
Gath & Peine, Luisen 109, 213-599	Gift Shop
Hanse-Viertel, Grosse Bleichen	Mall
Hintze, Jungfernstieg	Jewelry
Jager & Kosh, Jungfernstieg	Apparel
Jil Sander, Milchstr. 8, 5530-2173	Apparel
Karstadt, Monckebergstr. 16, 30940	Dept. Store
Kaufhof, Monckebergstr. 3, 333-070	Dept. Store
Kaufmannshaus, Grosse Bleichen	Mall
Linette, Jungfernstieg	Apparel
Seifarth & Company, Robert-Koch-Str. 17,	Gift Shop
Selbach, Jungfernstieg	Apparel
Ursula Aust, Jungfernstieg	Apparel
Wempe, Jungfernstieg	Jewelry
Windmoller, Jungfernstieg	Apparel

Places of Interest:
Kunsthalle – an art gallery
Michaeliskirche – a baroque church.
Museum fur Kunst und Gewerbe - art and industry exhibits.
Rathaus – a 19th century town hall.

HANNOVER

Country code: 49 - City code: 511

Airport: Langenhagen International Airport

Distance from City: 11km (6 miles) north of the city

Transportation to Center of City:
From International and Domestic Terminals
By Bus (cost) DMK8. Time approx. 20 min.
By Taxi (cost) DMK25-DMK30. Time approx. 15 min.
Tip luggage porters DMK2 per piece

Transfers: (Minimum Connecting Time):
International to International: 30 min.
International to Domestic: 30 min.
Domestic to International: 30 min.

Domestic to Domestic: 25 min.

Automobile Rentals:
Airport car rental desk
Avis - 772018
Europcar Interrent - 736098
Hertz - 779041

Car rental city office
Avis - 14441
Europcar Interrent - 358660
Hertz - 314036

Hotels:
Forum Hotel Schweizerhof Hannover, Hinuberstr. 6, 34950
Holiday Inn Crowne Plaza – Airport, Petzelstr. 60, Langenhagen, 77070
Maritim Airport Hotel, Flughafenstr. 5, 9737-0
Maritim Grand Hotel, Friedrichswall 11, 3677-0
Maritim Stadthotel, Hildesheimer Str. 34-40, 9894-0
Sidler Hotel Pelikan, Podbielskistr. 145, 90930

Restaurants:
Grapenkieker, Hauptstr. 56, Isernhagen, 88068

Entertainment:
Casino, Am Maschsee

Places of Interest:
Opera House
Old Town Hall – a monument
The Landesmuseum – a museum
Sprengel Museum
Museum of modern art.

MUNICH

Country code: 49 - City code: 89

Airport: Franz Joseph Strauss International Airport

GERMANY

Distance from City: 28km (17 miles) northeast of the city.

Transportation to Center of City:
From International and Domestic Terminals
By Bus (cost) DMK14. Time approx. 50 min
By Taxi (cost) DMK80-DMK120. Time approx. 50 min
Tip luggage porters DMK2 per piece

Transfers: (Minimum Connecting Time):
International to International: 35 min.
International to Domestic: 35 min.
Domestic to International: 35 min.
Domestic to Domestic: 35 min.

Automobile Rentals:
Airport car rental desk
Avis - 97597600
Europcar Interrent - 97597001
Hertz - 978860

Car rental city office
Avis - 12600020
Europcar Interrent - 6922277
Hertz - 1295001

Hotels:
Admiral Hotel, Kohlstr. 9, 226641
Arabella Central Hotel Munchen, Schwanthaler Str. 111, 51083-140
Best Western Atrium Hotel, Landwehrstr. 59, 51419-0
Best Western Hotel Cristal, Schwanthaler Str. 36, 55111-0
Best Western Hotel Prinzregent, Ismaninger Str. 42-44,
    41605-0
Carlton Hotel, Furstenstr. 12, 282061
Carmen Hotel, Hansastr. 146-148, 760-1099
Eden Hotel Wolff, Arnulfstr. 4, 551150
Excelsior Hotel, Schuetzenstr. 11, 551370
Forum Hotel Munchen, Hochstr. 3, 4803-0
Golden Tulip Hotel Olymp, Wielandstr. 3, Eching, 32710-0
Koningshof Hotel, Karlsplatz 25, 551360
Maritim Hotel, Goethestr. 7, 55235-0
Munich City Hilton, Rosenhimer Str. 15, 480-0

Munich Park Hilton, Am Tucherpark 7, 3845-0
Palace Hotel, Trogerstr. 21, 41971-0
Rafael Hotel, Neuturmstr. 1, 290980
Sol Inn Munchen, Paul-Heyse Str. 24, 514900
Torbrau Hotel, Tal 41, 225016
Transmar Park Hotel, Zschokkestr. 55, 579360

Restaurants:
Altes Hackerhous, Sendlinger-Str. 75, 260-5026
Augustiner Keller, Arnulfstr. 52, 594-393
Austernkeller, Stollbergstr. 11, 298-787
Bamberger Haus, Brunnerstr. 2, 3088966
Bistro Terrine, Amalienstr. 89, 281-780
Brauhaus zum Brez'n, Leopoldstr. 72, 390-092
Durnbrau, Durnbraugasse 2, 222-195
Franziskaner, Perusastr. 5, 231-8120
Friesenstube, Thomas-Wimmer-Ring 16, 294-600
Glockenbach, Kapuzinerstr. 29, 534-043
Gruene Gans, Am Einlass 5, 266-228
Halali, Schonfeldstr. 22, 285-909
Haxnbauer, Munzstr. 2, 221-922
Hofbrauhaus, Am Platzl, 221-676
Hundskugel, Hotterstr. 18, 264-272
James Cafe, Hochbruckenstr. 14, 298-940
Jeeta's, Seitzstr. 13, 223931
Kafers am Odeonsplatz, Odeonspl. 3, 290-7530
Kaferschanke, Schumannstr. 1, 41681
Konigshof, Karlspl. 25, 551-360
Preysing Keller, Innere-Wiener-Str. 6, 481-015
Ratskeller, Marienpl. 8, 220-313
Santa-Fe, Balanstr. 16, 484-736
Spatenhaus, Residenzstr. 12, 227-841
Spockmeier, Rosenstr. 9, 268-088
Tantris, Johann-Fichter-Str. 7, 362-061
Weichandhof, Betzenweg 81, 111-621
Weinhaus Neuner, Herzogspialstr. 8, 260-3958
Welser Kuche, Residenzstr. 2, 296-565
Wirtshaus im Weinstadl, Burgstr. 5, 290-4044

Entertainment:
Albatros, Occamstrasse, 344-972
Alter Simpl, Turkenstr. 57, 272-3083

Ba-Ba-Lu, Leopoldstrasse, 343-535
CD, Ungererstr. 75
Doctor Flotte, Occamstr. 8
Havana, Herrnstr. 3, 291-884
Maximilian's Nightclub, Maximilianpl. 16, 223-252
Nachtcafe, Maximilianpl. 5,n 595-900
Nachtwerk, Landsbergerstr. 185, 570-7390
Night Club, Promenadenpl. 2-6, 21200
Night Flight, Besucherpark station, 9759-7999
O'Reilly's Irish Cellar Pub, Maximilianstrasse, 292-311
Park-Cafe, Sophienstr. 7, 598-313
Peaches, Feilitzstrasse, 348-470
Pl, Prinzregentenstr., 294-252
Pusser's Bar, Falkenturmstr. 9, 220-500
Scala Music Bar, Brienner Str. 20, 285-858
Schumann's, Maximilianstr. 36, 229-268
Skyline, Munchner-Freiheit, 348-470
Unterfahrt, Kirchenstr. 96, 448-279
Vier Jahreszeiten Kempinski, Maximilianstr. 17, 21250
Waldwirtschaft Grosshesselohe, Georg Kalb-Str. 3, 795-088
Wunderbar, Hochbruckenstr. 3, 295-118

Shops and Stores:

Arcade, Neuhauserstr. 5	Mall
Hertie, b/n train station & Karlsplatz, 55120	Dept. Store
Hirmer, Kaufingerstr. 22, 236-830	Dept. Store
K & L Ruppert, Kaufingerstr. 15, 231-1470	Dept. Store
Karstadt, Haus Oberpollinger, 290-230	Dept. Store
Kaufhof, Corner of Marienpl., 231-851	Dept. Store
Kaufhof, Karlsp. 2, 51250	Dept. Store
Kaufinger Tor, Kaufingerstr. 117	Mall
Kunstring Meissen, Briennerstr. 4, 281-532	Gift Shop
Ludwig Beck, Marienpl. 11, 236-910	Dept. Store
Ludwig Mory, Marienpl. 8, 224-542	Gift Shop
Nymphenburg, Odeonspl. & Briennerstr., 282-428	Gift Shop
Obletter's, Karlspl. 8, 231-8601	Gift Shop
Otto Kellberger's Holzhandlung, Heiliggeistr. 7-8, 226-479	Gift Shop
Sebastian Wesely, Peterspl., 264-519	Gift Shop

Places of Interest:
The Deutsches Museum

GERMANY

Olympiapark
The Hofbrauhaus – a traditional beer garden.
Frauenkirche – a Gothic cathedral.
BMW Museum

STUTTSGART

Country code: 49 - City code: 711

Airport: Echterdingen International Airport

Distance from City: 14km (8 miles) south of the city

Transportation to Center of City:
From International and Domestic Terminals
By Bus (cost) DMK4-6. Time approx. 30 min.
By Taxi (cost) DMK40. Time approx. 30 min.
Tip luggage porters DMK2   per piece

Transfers: (Minimum Connecting Time):
International to International: 30 min.
International to Domestic: 30 min.
Domestic to International: 30 min.
Domestic to Domestic: 30 min.

Automobile Rentals:
Airport car rental desk
Avis - 948-4451
Europcar Interrent - 790091
Hertz - 948-4339

Car rental city office
Avis - 241441
Europcar Interrent - 872021
Hertz - 817233

Hotels:
Best Western Hotel Ketterer, Marien Str. 3, 20390
Copthorne Hotel Stuttgart International, Plieninger Str. 100, 7210
Inter-Continental Stuttgart, Willy Brandt-Str. 30, 20200
Maritim Hotel, Forststr. 2, 942-0

GERMANY

Rema Hotel Astoria, Hospitalstr. 29, 299301
Rema-Hotel Ruff, Friedhofstr. 21,25870
Schlossgarten Hotel, Schillerstr. 23, 20260

Restaurants:
Der Zauberlehrling, Rosenstr. 38, 237-7770
Wielandshohe, Alte Weinsteige 71, Degerloch, 640-8848
Zeppelin-Stuble, Arnulf-Klett-Pl. 7, 20480

Shops and Stores:
Breuninger, Marktstr. 1-3, 2110	Dept. Store
Calwer Passage, Calwer Strasse	Mall
Gunter Krauss's, Kronprinzstr. 21, 297-395	Jewelry
Holy's, Konigstr. 54, 221-872	Apparel

Places of Interest:
The Galerie der Stadt Stuttgart – an art gallery.
The Altes Schloss - A fortress
The Stiftskirche – a church
The Planetarium
The Staatgalerie – sculptures gallery
The Linden Museum
The Daimler-Benz Museum
The Porschewerk

GREAT BRITAIN

Official Name: The United Kingdom of Great Britain and Northern Ireland.

Location: Northwest Europe. The United Kingdom consists of England, Scotland, Wales and Northern Ireland. It lies between the North Sea and the Atlantic Ocean.

Government: Constitutional Monarchy

Area: 241,752 sq. km., 93,341 sq. miles.

Population: 57.65 million

Religion(s): Church of England majority; Roman Catholic minority.

Capital City: London

Major Business Cities: Aberdeen, Belfast, Birmingham, Glasgow, Leeds, Manchester, Edinburgh and Bristol.

Time: GMT (GMT +1 from late March to late October)

Currency: British Pound Sterling (UKP) = 100 pence

Currency Requirements: There are no restrictions on the import and export of foreign or local currency.

Business Hours:
- Government: 09.00-17.00 Mon-Fri
- Banks: 09.30-15.30/16.30 Mon-Fri (some are open on Sat mornings)
- Shops: 09.00-17.30/18.00 Mon-Sat (late night shopping Thur until 20.00)
- Offices: 09.30-17.30 Mon-Fri

Weight and Measures: Imperial system and Metric System

Electric Current: 240 volts AC. Square 3-pin plugs are used.

Holidays:
New Year's Day - January 1
Good Friday - April 10*
Easter Monday - April 13*
May Day - May 5
Spring Bank Holiday - May 26
Summer Bank Holiday - August 25
Christmas Day - December 25
Boxing Day - December 26

*Christian Holidays - vary each year

Suitable Clothing: Bring heavy clothing and a coat for winter, and medium and light clothing for the rest of the year. You will definitely need a raincoat and umbrella. Men should wear a conservative, three-piece suit in most situations. Striped ties are associated with the old-boy network of school ties, so don't wear one unless you too were a part of it.

Automobile Driving License: An International or a National Driving License with English translation is required.

Customs Allowances: No limits exist on bringing in foreign currency, or exporting foreign currency if declared. There are no import or export limits on British Pounds if previously declared. Personal items are duty free, but register all valuables upon arrival, including technological objects such as computer and videocameras, and keep receipts. Non-E.U. members face more restrictions on certain items: 200 cigarettes, 2 liters of wine and one of spirits, and 50 ml. of perfume. E.U. members can bring in, duty free, 800 cigarettes, 90 liters of wine, 110 of beer and 10 of spirits. Prohibited items include weaponry, pornographic material, narcotics, agricultural products and animals without a six-month quarantine.

Tipping: A service charge of 10-15% is included in most hotel and restaurant bills, in which case no additional tip is necessary. Taxi drivers are usually tipped 10% of the fare.

Credit Cards Accepted: American Express, Barclay Card, Diner's Club, MasterCard, Visa.

Customary Dining Hours:
Breakfast: 07.30-09.00
Lunch: 12.00-14.00
Dinner: 19.30-21.30

Local Customs, Business Protocol and Courtesies: Tradition, privacy and reserve are mainstays of social and business interactions in Britain, but this does not mean you will enter a cold, unfriendly climate. Rather, you will encounter much friendliness and courtesy, and often be well-entertained by your British counterparts. Longtime business connections, familial relationships, ancestry, and, often quite importantly, childhood school ties, are held in high regard. Titles are important; use title with last name until your counterpart indicates otherwise. Even on a more informal basis, use ancestral titles such as Lord, Sir or Lady with first name. Schedule appointments in advance, keeping in mind that many people take mid-morning and mid-afternoon tea breaks. Although small talk may start a meeting, discussions generally move quickly to business, and should be initiated by your British counterpart. Make your presentations highly formal and detailed, with a view toward the practical execution and economic benefits of a proposed contract. Most decisions are made by the top brass of a company, so patience and a respect for rank is essential. Don't be pushy or aggressive. Exchanging business gifts is rare, but just in case your new partner presents you with one at the signing of a business deal, bring one along in return; a tasteful but impersonal gift like a book, small art object or fine wine.

You will likely be invited to dinner in a restaurant, or lunch and/or drinks in a pub. When invited to dine at home with a family, bring the hostess a small gift, candy or flowers, and send a thank-you note the next day. In any social situation, business topics are avoided. Gin-and-tonic or sherry are often served before meals, beer or wine during, and coffee afterwards. Wait for your host or hostess to begin the meal, and leave a small portion on your plate and place your knife and fork together on a horizontal across the plate to signify that you are finished. As a general rule, though you might encounter more relaxed attitudes in the course of your trip and relationships, it's best not to make fun of certain British traditions, whether they be mannerisms or the Royal Family. The subject of Northern Ireland is very sensitive. Avoid referring to everyone as English, as this will offend those who are Welsh, Scottish or Irish, by sticking to the generic "British".

Health: There are Reciprocal Health Agreements between the UK and many other countries, such as Norway, Australia, Sweden and Hong Kong. The Agreements differ and it is advisable for visitors to seek further advice before traveling. There are no vaccinations required. A vaccination for tetanus is recommended. Immediate emergency treatment is available to all visitors. It is recommended to have a medical insurance.

Language: English

BIRMINGHAM

Country code: 44 - City code: 21

Airport: Birmingham International Airport

Distance from City: 13km (8 miles) southeast of the city.

Transportation to Center of City:
From International and Domestic Terminals
By Bus (cost)   UKP1.50. Time approx. 35 min.
By Taxi (cost)   UKP10-12. Time approx. 25-30 min.
Tip luggage porters 75 Pence per piece

Transfers: (Minimum Connecting Time):
International to International: 45 min.
International to Domestic: 45 min.
Domestic to International: 45 min.
Domestic to Domestic: 30 min.

Automobile Rentals:
Airport car rental desk
Avis - 782-6183
Europcar Interrent - 782-6507
Hertz - 782-5158

Car rental city office
Avis - 632-4361
Europcar Interrent - 622-5311
Hertz - 643-5387

Hotels:
Apollo Hotel, Hagley Rd., Edgbaston, 455-0271
Copthorne Hotel Birmingham, Paradise Circus, 200-2727
Forte Posthouse, Smallbrook, Queensway, 643-8171
Holiday Inn Crowne Plaza Birmingham, Central Sq., 631-2000
Hyatt Regency Birmingham, 2 Bridge St., 643-1234
Forte Posthouse Birmingham Airport, Coventry Rd., 782-8141
Moor Hall Hotel, Moor Hall Dr., Sutton Coldfield, 308-3751
Royal Angus Thistle Hotel, St. Chads, Queensway, 236-4211
St. John's Swallow Hotel, 651 Warwick Rd., Solihull, 711-3000
Strathallan Thistle Hotel, 225 Hagley Rd., Edgbaston, 455-9777
Swallow Hotel Birmingham, 12 Hagley Rd, Five Ways, 452-1144

Restaurants:
Bambos, 61 Station St., 643 5621
Chung Ying, 16 -18 Wrottesley St., 622 1793
Diwan, 3b Alcester Rd,
Punjab Paradise,377 Ladypool Rd, 499 4110
Ronni Scott's Cafe Bar, 258 Broad St.
Royal Naweed, 44 Woodbridge Rd.
San Carlo, 4 Temple St. 633 0251
Shah Faisal, 348-50 Stanford Rd,Sparkhill
Sum Ye, Arcadian Centre, Hurst Street
Teppanyaki, Arcadian Centre Hurst Street, 622 5183
Warehouse Cafe, 54 Allison St, 633 0261

Entertainment:
The Dibliner, 57 Digbeth
Old Contemtibles,   176 Edmund St.
The Old Fox, Arcadian Centre, Hurst St.

Prince of Wales, 118 Alcester Rd., Moseley.
The Victoria, John Bright St.
Baker's, 163 Broad St.
Bobby Brown's, 48 Gas St
The Cave, 516 Moseley Rd.
Molly Malone's, 28 Bristol St.
Moseley Dance Centre,   572 Moseley Rd.
Ronnie Scott's, 258 Broad St.

Places of Interest:
Dudley Zoo and Castle
Weoley Castle Ruins
Birmingham Cathedral
Birmingham Museum and Art Gallery
The Black Country Museum
Birmingham Botanical Gardens and Glasshouses
Cadbury World
Lunt Roman Fort - a monument
West Midlands Safari Park - a theme park and an animal re-
serve
Alton Towers - a theme park.

EDINBURGH

Country code: 44 - City code: 131

Airport: Turnhouse Airport

Distance from City: 11km (6 miles) west of the city.

Transportation to Center of City:
From International and Domestic Terminals
By Bus (cost)   UKP12-15. Time approx. 25 min. (every 30 min.)
By Taxi (cost)   UKP12-UKP15. Time approx. 25 min.
Tip luggage porters 75 Pence per piece

Transfers: (Minimum Connecting Time):
International to International: 45 min.
International to Domestic: 45 min.
Domestic to International: 45 min.

Domestic to Domestic: 30 min.
Automobile Rentals:
Airport car rental desk
Avis - 333-1866
Europcar Interrent- 333-2588
Hertz - 333-1019

Car rental city office
Avis - 337-6363
Europcar Interrent - 557-3456
Hertz - 556-8311

Hotels:
Bruntsfield Hotel, 69 Bruntsfield Pl, Lothian, 229-1393
Forte Grand Balmoral, 1 Princes St., 556-2414
George Inter-Continental Edinburgh, 19-21 George St., 225-1251
Hilton National Edinburgh, 69 Belford Rd., 332-2545
Holiday Inn Crowne Plaza, 80 High St., The Royal Mile,
    557-9797
King James Thistle, 107 Leith St., St. James Center, 556-0111
Maitland Hotel, 25-33 Shandwick Pl., 229-1467
Old Waverley Hotel, 43 Princes St., 556-4648
Osbourne Hotel, 53-59 York Pl., Midlothian, 556-5577
Roxburghe Hotel, Charlotte Sq., 225-3921
Sheraton Grand Hotel, 1 Festival Sq., 229-9131

Restaurants:
Bambos, 61 Station St., 643-5621
Henderson's, 94 Honover St., 225 2131
Howie's, 75 St. Leonard's St., 668 2917
Indian Cavary Club, 3 Atholl Pl., 228 3282
Jackson's, 2 Jackson Close, 209-213 High St., Royal Mile,
    225 7793
Kalpna, 2-3 St. Patrick Sq., 667 9890
L'Auberge, 56-58 St. Mary's St, 556 5888
Le Pompadour, Princes St, 459 9988
Martins, 70 Rose St, 225 3106
Pierre Victorie, 38 Grassmarket, 226 2442
San Carlo, 4 Temple St., 633-0251

Entertainment:
Berkeley Casino Club, 2 Rutland Pl., 228 4446

Buster Browns, 25-27 Market St., 226 4224
Harry's Bar, 7b Randolph Pl., 539 8100
L'Attache, 1 Rutland Pl., 229 3402
Madogs, 38a George St., 225 4308
Red Hot Pepper Club, 3 Sample St., 229 7733
The Cavendish, W.Tollcross, 228 3252
The Lanes, South Charlotte La., 226 6828

Shops and Stores:

Edinburgh Crystal, Eastfield,	Gift Shop
Edinburgh Woolen Mill, 62 Princes St.	Dept. Store
Gleneagles of Scotland, Princes St.	Dept. Store
Jenners, Princes St.	Dept. Store
Mr. Wood's Fossils, Grassmarket	Gift Shop
Something Simple, 10 Williams St.	Apparel
Sprogs, 45 Williams St.	Apparel

Places of Interest:
Edinburgh Castle
The Palace of Holyrood House -viewing rooms and galleries.
King Arthur's Seat
The National Gallery of Scotland - an art gallery.
The Scottish National Portrait Gallery
The Museum of Antiquities
Deep Sea World - an aquarium.
Edinburgh Butterfly and Insect World
Edinburgh Zoo
Scotch Whiskey Heritage Center - displays of whisky making.

GLASGOW

Country code: 44 - City code: 41

Airport: Glasgow International Airport

Distance from City: 15km (9 miles) west of the city.

Transportation to Center of City:
From International and Domestic Terminals
By Bus (cost) UKP2. Time approx. 55 min. (every 10-30 min).

GREAT BRITAIN

By Taxi (cost) UKP12. Time approx. 15-20 min.
Tip luggage porters 75 Pence per piece

Transfers: (Minimum Connecting Time):
International to International: 45 min.
International to Domestic: 45 min.
Domestic to International: 45 min.
Domestic to Domestic: 30 min.

Automobile Rentals:
Airport car rental desk
Avis - 887-2261
Europcar Interrent -887-0414
Hertz - 887-2451

Car rental city office
Avis - 221-2827
Europcar Interrent - 423-5661
Hertz - 248-7736

Hotels:
Ewington Hotel, 132 Queens Dr., Queens Park, 423-1152
Forte Posthouse Glasgow Airport, Abbotsinch, Paisley, 887-1212
Glasgow Hilton, 1 William St., 204-5555
Glasgow Marriott Hotel, 500 Argyle St., 226-5577
Glasgow Thistle, 36 Cambridge St., 332-3311
Quality Central Hotel, Gordon St., 221-9680
Town House Hotel, 4 Nelson Mandela Place, 332-3320

Restaurants:
Ali Baba's Balti Bar, 54 W. Regent St., 332-6289
Ashoka West End, 1284 Argyle St., 339-0936
Buttery, 652 Argyle St., 221-8188
Café Gandilfi, 64 Albion St., 552-6813
CCA Café/Bar, 350 Sauchiehall St., 332-7864
Cottier's, 93 Hyndland St., 357-5825
Drum and Monkey, St. Vincent St., 221-6636
Fazzi Café Bar, 65-67 Cambridge St., 332-0941
Jsanssens Café Restaurant, 1355 Argyle St., 334-9682
Loon Fung, 417 Sauchiehall St., 332-1240
Malmaison Café and Brasserie, 221-6401

Rogano, 11 Exchange Pl., 248-4055
The Bay Tree, 403 Great Western Rd., 334-5898
The Ubiquitous Chip, 12 Ashton La, 334-5007
Two Fat Ladies, 88 Dumbarton Rd., 339-1944

Entertainment:
Bon Accord, 153 North St., 248-4427
Brewery Tap, 1055 Sauchiehall St., 339-8866
Cleopatra's, 508 Great Western Rd., 334-0560
Drum and Monkey, 93 St. Vincent St.
Halt, 106 Woodland Rd., 332-1210
Horse Shoe Bar, 17-21 Drury St., 221-3051
Nico's, 375 Sauchiehall St.
Riverside Club, Fox St., 248-3144
The Tunnel, 84 Mitchell St., 204-1000
Uisge Beatha, 232-246 Woodland Rd., 332-0473
Volcano, Benalder St., 334-8292

Shops and Stores:
Catherine Shaw, 24 Gordon St.   Gift Shop
Debenham's, 97 Argyle St.   Dept. Store
Frasers, 21-45 Buchanan St.   Dept. Store
Katherine Hamnett, Unit 38 Princes St.   Apparel
Princes Square, 48 Buchanan St.   Shopping Center
St. Enoch's, 55 St. Enoch Sq.   Shopping Center
Strawberry Fields, 517 Great Western Rd.   Apparel
Ted Backer, Unit 25 Princes St.   Apparel
The Barras, Scotrail's Argyle St. Station   Jewelry

Places of Interest:
Glasgow Cathedral
People's Palace - a museum
Kelvingrove Museum and Art Gallery
The Museum of Transport
The Botanic Gardens
Glasgow Zoo
The Burrell Collection and Pollock House - art exhibitions

LONDON

GREAT BRITAIN

Country code: 44 - City code: 71 or 81
Airport: London Heathrow International Airport.

Distance from City: 24km (14 miles) west of central London.

Transportation to Center of City:
From International and Domestic Terminals
By Bus (cost) UKP3.50. Time approx. 50 minutes.
By Taxi (cost) UKP28-35, Time approx. 30-45 minutes.
Tip luggage porters 75 Pence per piece

Transfers: (Minimum Connecting Time):
International to International: 45 min.
International to Domestic: 45 min.
Domestic to International: 45 min.
Domestic to Domestic: 45 min.

Automobile Rentals:
Airport car rental desk
Avis - 899-1000
Europcar Interrent - 897-0811
Hertz - 897-2072

Airport: London Gatwick International Airport

Distance from City: 45km (27 miles) south of central London.

Transportation to Center of City:
From International and Domestic Terminals
By Bus (cost) UKP 10-15. Time approx. 90 min. (buses travel to Heathrow airport)
By Taxi (cost) UKP50-60. Time approx. 1 hour 15 min.
Tip luggage porters 75 Pence per piece

Transfers: (Minimum Connecting Time):
International to International: 55 min.
International to Domestic: 60 min.
Domestic to International: 45 min.
Domestic to Domestic: 40 min.

Automobile Rentals:
Airport car rental desk

Avis - 529721
Europcar Interrent - 531062
Hertz - 530555

Airport: Stansted Airport

Distance from City: 55km northeast of city center.

Transportation to Center of City:
From International and Domestic Terminals
By Taxi (cost) UKP40-45. Time approx. 60-90 min.
By Train (cost) UKP10. Time approx. 41 min.
Tip luggage porters 75 Pence per piece

Automobile Rentals:
Airport car rental desk
Avis - 663030

Airport: London City Airport

Distance from City: 10km east of the city of London.

Transportation to Center of City:
From International and Domestic Terminals
By Taxi (cost) UKP15-20. Time approx. 30-45 min.
By Train (cost) UKP3.30-5.
Tip luggage porters 75 Pence per piece

Automobile Rentals:
Airport car rental desk
Europcar Interrent - 608240

Car rental city office
Avis - 917-6700
Europcar Interrent - 834-8484
Hertz - 723-3888

Hotels:
47 Park Street Westin Demeure Hotel, 47 Park St., Mayfair,
491-7282
Adelphi Hotel, 127-129 Cromwell Rd., 373-7177
Bailey's Hotel, 140 Gloucester Rd., 373-6000

GREAT BRITAIN

Barbican Hotel, Central St., Clerkenwell, 251-1565
Bedford Corner Hotel, 11-13 Bayley St., 580-7766
Berkeley Hotel, Wilton Pl. Knightsbridge, 235-6000
Berners Hotel, 10 Berners St., 636-1629
Bloomsbury Park Hotel, 126 Southampton Row, 430-0434
Brown's Hotel, Albemarle St. & Dover St., 493-6020
Cavendish Hotel, 81 Jermyn St., St. James, 930-2111
Charing Cross Hotel, Strand, 839-7282
Chelsea Hotel, 17 Sloane St., 235-4377
Chesterfield Hotel, Mayfair, 35 Charles St., Mayfair, 491-2622
Churchill Inter-Continental London, 30 Portman Sq., 486-5800
Comfort Inn, 22-32 W. Cromwell Rd., 373-3300
Comfort Inn Hyde Park, 18-19 Craven Hill Gardens, 262-6644
Connaught Hotel, Carlos Pl., Mayfair, 499-7070
Cumberland Hotel, Marble Arch, 262-1234
Forte Crest Bloomsbury Hotel, Coram St., 837-1200
Forte Grand Waldorf, Aldwych, 836-2400
Forte Grand Westbury, Bond St. at Conduit St., 629-7755

Restaurants:
Alastair Littel, 49 Frith St, 734 5183
Bentley's, 11-15 Swallow St, 734 4756
Break for the Border, 5 Goslett Yard, 437 8595
Cafe Fish, 39 Panton St, 930 3999
Cafe Pacifico, 5 Langley St, 379 7728
Chez Moi, 1 Addison Ave, 603 8267
Christopher's, 18 Wellington St, 240 4222
Daquise, 20 Thurloe St,
Fung Shing, 15 Lisle St, 437 1539
Gay Hussar, 2 Greek St, 437 0973
Luba's Place, 164 Essex Rd, 704 2775
Mr Kong, 21 Lisle St, 437 7341
Nam Bistro, 326 Upper St, 354 0851
Rotisserie Jules,6-8 Bute St, SW7.
RSJ, 13a Coin St, 928 4554
Sea Shell, 49-51 Lisson Grove, 723 8703
The Criterion, 224 Piccadilly, 925 0909
The Fire Station, 150 Waterloo Rd, 620 2226
Truffe Noire, 29 Tooley St, 378 0621
Wodka, 12 Alban's Grove, 937 6513
Yung's, 23 Wardour St, 437 4986

Entertainment:
100 Club, 100 Oxford St.
606 Club, 90 Lots Rd.
Bar Rumba, 36 Shaftersbury Ave,
Blue Note, 57 Coronet St.
Bull & Gate, 389 Kentish Town Rd.
Cafe de Paris, 3 Covantry St,
Camden Palace, 1 Camden High St.
Cuba, 11 High St Kensington.
Gossips, 69 Dean St.
Iceni, 11 White Horse St.
Jazz Cafe, 5 Parkway.
Maximus, 14 Leicester Square.
Raw, 112a Great Russell St.
The Fridge, Town Hall Parade,Brixton.
The Garage, 20 Highbury Corner,N1
The Grand, Clapham Junction, St John's Hill
The Orange, 3 North End Crescent.
Vox, 9 Brighton Terrace.
Wag, 35 Wardour St.

Shops and Stores:

Fortnum and Mason, 181 Piccadilly, W1	Dept. Store
Garrard, 112 Regent Street	Jewelry
Hamleys, 188-196 Regent Street	Toys Store
Harvey Nichols, Knightsbridge	Apparel
Simpson, 203 Piccadilly	Dept. Store

Places of Interest:
Harrods - a famous department store
Fortnum and Mason - a department store
Buckingham Palace
Residential Palace of the Monarchy
Changing The Guard
Horse Guards Parade
St. Paul's Cathedral
Tower of London
Westminster Abbey
Houses of Parliament
Madame Tussaud's - a waxworks museum.
Tate Gallery

GREAT BRITAIN

MANCHESTER

Country code: 44 - City code: 161

Airport: Manchester International Airport

Distance from City: 16km (9 miles) from the city center.

Transportation to Center of City:
From International and Domestic Terminals
By Bus (cost) UKP2. Time approx. 55 min (every 20-30 min)
By Taxi (cost) UKP10-12. Time approx. 25-30 min
Tip luggage porters 75 Pence per piece

Transfers: (Minimum Connecting Time):
International to International: 40 min.
International to Domestic: 45 min.
Domestic to International: 40 min.
Domestic to Domestic: 30 min.

Automobile Rentals:
Airport car rental desk
Avis - 436-2020
Europcar Interrent - 436-2200
Hertz - 437-8208

Car rental city office
Avis - 236-6716
Europcar Interrent - 834-5842
Hertz - 236-2747

Hotels:
Corthorne Hotel Manchester, Clippers Quay, Salford Quays, 873-7321
Gardens Hotel, 55 Piccadilly, 236-5155
Holiday Inn Crowne Plaza Midland Hotel, Peter St., 236-3333
Jarvis Piccadilly Hotel, Piccadilly Plaza, 236-8414
Manchester Airport Hilton, Outwood Lane, Ringway, 436-4404
Palace Hotel, Oxford St., 288-1111
Pinewood Thistle Hotel, 180 Wilmslow Rd, Handforth,
    1625-529211

Portland Thistle Hotel, Portland St., Piccadilly Gdns., 228-3400
Ramada Hotel Manchester, Blackfriars St., 835-2555

Restaurants:
Beaujolais, 70 Partland St., 236 7260
Cafe Istanbul, 79 Bridge St.
Cafe Yaqoub, 2 Union St.
Cuckoo Chef, 71 Oldham St.
Dimitri's Taverna, 1 Campfield Arcade.
Eastern Touch, 76 Wilmslow Rd.
El Macho, 103 Portland St.
Fallen Angel, 263 Upper Brook St.
Indian Cottage, 501 Claremont Rd. 224 0446
Jade Garden, 54 Faulkner St.
Koreana, 40 King St., 236 9338
Littel Yang Sing, 17 George St., 228 7722
Pujab Sweethouse, 177 Wilmslow Rd., 225 2960
Tandoori Kitchen, 131 Wilmslow Rd.
The Market Restaurant, 104 High St., 834 3743
Yang Sing, 34 Princess St., 236 2200

Entertainment:
Academy, Oxford Road, 275 2930
Band on the Wall, 25 Swan St., 832 6625
Equinox, Bloom St.
Hacienda, 11-13 Whitworth St., 236 5051
Oscar's, Cooper St.
P J Bells, 85 Oldham St., 834 4266
Paradise Factory, 112-16 Princess St., 273 5422
Rockworld, 65a Oxfort St.
Sankey's Soap, Beehive Mill, Jersey Street.
The Boardwalk, 15 Little Peter St., 228 3555
The Brickhouse, 66 Whitworth St, 236 4418
The Ritz, Whitworth St., 236 4355

Shops and Stores:

Aflecks Palace, 52 Church St.	Dept. Store
Manchester Craft Center, 17 Oak St.	Shopping Center
Royal Exchange Center, St. Ann Sq.	Jewelry
Royal Exchange Shopping Center, St. Ann Sq.	Apparel
Whitworth Art Gallery, Oxford Rd.	Gift Shop

GREAT BRITAIN

Places of Interest:
Granada Studios - film and TV tours
City Art Galleries - paintings, sculptures and ceramics
The Museum of Science and Industry
Wythenshawe Hall - a historic house
The Royal Exchange Shopping Center
The Manchester Museum
Manchester Cathedral
St.Ann's Church
The Opera House

GREECE

Official Name: The Hellenic Republic

Location: Southeast Europe - Mediterranean. Greece is bordered by Albania, Macedonia, Bulgaria and Turkey. Its territory includes the mainland and many islands.

Government: Republic

Area: 131,944 sq. km., 50,944 sq. miles.

Population: 10.11 million

Religion(s): Greek Orthodox majority.

Capital City: Athens

Major Business Cities: Corfu, Heraklion and Rhodes.

Time: GMT +2 (GMT +3 from late March to late October).

Currency: Drachma (DRA)

Currency Requirements: There are no restrictions on the import of foreign currency. Amounts over US$1000 must be declared. Export is limited to the amount declared upon arrival. The import of local currency is limited to DRA100,000 and export DRA300,000.

Business Hours:
- Government: 8.30-13.30; 16.00-19.30 Mon-Fri
- Banks: 08.00-14.00 Mon-Fri
- Shops: 09.00-15.30; 16.00-19.30 Mon-Fri.
- Offices: 08.00-16.00 Mon-Fri (some may open until 20.30)

Weight and Measures: Metric System

GREECE

Electric Current: 220 volts AC. Plugs are of the round 2-pin type.

Holidays:
New Year's Day - January 1
Epiphany - January 6*
Shrove Monday - March 10
Independence Day - March 25
Good Friday - April 10*
Easter Sunday - April 12*
Easter Monday - April 13*
Labor Day - May 1
Day of the Holy Spirit - June 16
Assumption - August 15
Ohi Day - October 28
Christmas Day - December 25
Boxing Day - December 26

*Christian Holidays - vary each year

Greek Orthodox Easter is the most important festival in Greece and no business can take place between Good Friday and Easter Monday

Suitable Clothing: Light clothing is important in the summer, while slightly warmer clothing and a lined jacket or not-too-heavy coat will do in winter. Bring a light- or medium-weight suit, depending on time of year.

Automobile Driving License: A National Driving License is acceptable for EU Nationals. Nationals of non-EU countries may need an International Driving License. The documentation should be carried at all times.

Customs Allowances: There are no limits on personal items. Valuables must be registered upon arrival, otherwise they may be confiscated upon departure. No limits exist on most, though not all, foreign currencies, but local currency limits are strict (check with your Greek embassy or consulate). Currently the export limit is 300,000 drachmas. 250 cigarettes are permitted duty free, as are one liter of wine and a half liter of spirits.

Tipping: A service charge of 15% is usually expected everywhere if it is not already included.

Credit Cards Accepted: Access, AmEx, Carte Blanche, Diner's Club, Eurocard, MasterCard, Visa

Customary Dining Hours:
Breakfast:07.30-09.30
Lunch: 12.30-15.00
Dinner: 21.00-24.00

Local Customs, Business Protocol and Courtesies: Despite the comfortable Mediterranean climate which means a frequent lack of punctuality, lightweight business suits, and flexible deadlines, business transactions are taken quite seriously in Greece. At least initially, you should wear business attire and use titles, and view only signed contracts as valid. You will be expected to establish trust before any contracts are inked, which means exhibiting patience and conducting all major business in person. Above all, in this society where family, heritage and friends are most highly valued, the major element in furthering a professional relationship is through personal contact. Greece is a very hospitable country, and you will likely have plenty of chances to get to know your counterpart and his or her family. Shaking hands is standard in more formal relationships, while close family and friends give a quick embrace and kiss. If invited to a home, bring a small gift for the hostess, and avoid expressing potentially offensive political opinions, particularly regarding relations with Cyprus and Turkey. Even in a business context, a good sense of humor is usually appreciated among Greeks. To refuse an invitation to go for a coffee or the national liquor, ouzo, is considered an insult; in any case, much business is conducted in this manner. Schedule appointments in advance, but loosely, within a brief time frame rather than an exact time. Many businesses are closed Wednesday afternoon.

Health: It is advisable to consult your doctor before your journey. No special vaccinations are required. It is mandatory to have a vaccination certificate for yellow fever if traveling from an infected area. A Reciprocal Health Agreement

GREECE

exists with some European countries but it is poorly implemented. It is highly recommended to have an additional insurance. Chemists can diagnose and supply drugs. There are often long waits for treatments at hospitals. It is recommended to drink only bottled water.

Language: Greek.

ATHENS

Country code: 30 - City code: 1

Airport: Hellinikon International Airport.

Distance from City: 10km (6 miles) south of the city.

Transportation to Center of City:
From International and Domestic Terminals
By Bus (cost) DRA160. Time approx. 20-60 min. (every 20-30 min)
By Taxi (cost) DRA2,500. Time approx. 20-60 min
Tip luggage porters 60DRA per piece

Transfers: (Minimum Connecting Time):
International to International: 60 min.
International to Domestic: 90 min.
Domestic to International: 90 min.
Domestic to Domestic: 45 min.

Automobile Rentals:
Airport car rental desk
Avis - 322-4951
Europcar Interrent -
    East Terminal -961-3424
    West Terminal - 982-9565
Hertz - 961-3625

Car rental city office
Avis - 322-4951
Europcar Interrent - 921-5788

GREECE

Hertz - 922-0102

Hotels:
Athens Hilton, 46 Vassilissis Sofias Ave., 725-0201
Best Western Athens Gate Hotel, 10 Syngrou Ave., 923-8302
Divani Caravel Hotel, 2 Vassileos Alexandrou Ave., 725-3725
Divani Palace Acropolis, 19-25 Parthenonos St., 922-2945
Dorian Inn, 17 Pireos St., Omonia Sq., 523-9782
Esperia Palace Hotel, 22 Stadiou St., 323-8001
Grande Bretagne Hotel, Constitution Sq., 333-0000
Holiday Inn Athens, 50 Michalakopoulou St., 724-8322
Ililisia Hotel, 25 Michalakopoulou St., 724-4051-6
King Minos Hotel, 1 Piraeus St., Omonia Sq., 523-1111
Le N.J.V. Meridien Athens, Place de la Constitution, Syntagma
    Sq., 325-5301
Olympic Palace Hotel, 16 Filelinon, 323-7611
Oscar Athens Hotel, Filadelphias 25 & Samoy, 883-4215-19
Park Hotel, 10 Leoforos Alexandras, 883-2711
Plaza Hotel Athens, 78 Acharnon/Katrivanou St., 822-5111
Zafolia, 87-89 Alexandras Ave., 644-9012

Restaurants:
Apotros, Panepistimiou 10, 363 7046
Bajazzo, Anapafseo 14, 921 3013
Boschetto, Alsos Evangelismos, 721 0893
Famagusta, Zagoras 8, 778 5229
Far East, Stadiou 7, 323 4996
Fourtuna, Anapiron Polemou 22, 722 1282
Ideal, Panepistimiou 46, 330 3000
Kaldera, Leoforos Poseidonos 54, 982 9647
Kollias, Stratigou Plastira 3, 462 9620
Kona Kai, Syngrou 115, 934 7711
Kostoyannis, Zisimopoulou 24, 941 3022
Manessis, Markou Moussourou 3, 922 7684
Mavri Gida, Akti Koumoundourou 64, 422 0691
Melrose, Zosimadou 16, 825 1627
Michiko, Kidathineon 27, 322 0980
Pandelis, Naiadon 96, 982 5512
Prunier, Ipsilantou 63, 722 7379
Rose, Kifissias 227, 612 3051
Symposio, Erechthiou 46, 922 5321
Varoulko, Deligeorgi 14, 411 2043
Vitrina, Navarchou Apostoli 7, 321 1200

Entertainment:
Art Cafe, Vassileos Pavlou 61, 413 7896
Balthazar, Tsoha 27, 644 1215
Cafe Asante, Damareos 78, 726 01021
Folie, Eslin 4, 646 9852
Half Note, Trivonianou 17, 923 2460
Klimataria, Klepsidras 5, 324 1809
Lobby, Ermou 110, 323 6975
Memphis Booze, Ventiri 5, 722 4104
Parafono, Asklippiou 130, 644 6512
Posidonio, Posidonios 18, 941 7602
Radon, Marni 24, 524 7427
Stavlos, Irakleidon 10, 345 2502
Strofilia, Karisti Sq.7, 323 4803

Shops and Stores:

Ahtida, Solonos 97, Kolonaki	Jewelry
Eommex, Mitropoleos 9, Syntagma	Handicrafts
George Goutis, Pandrossou 40, Monastiraki	Jewelry
Gold Coin Jewelry, Stadiou 17, Syntagma	Jewelry
Lalaounis, Panepistimiou 6, Syntagma	Jewelry
Mati, Voukourestiou 20, Syntagma	Gift Shop
Pantigri, Kleomenous 23-25, Kolonaki	Gift Shop
Stavros Melissinos, Pandrossou 89, Monastiraki	Apparel
Studio Kostas Sokaras, Adrianou 25, Plaka	Handicrafts
Voula Mitsakou, Mitropoleos 7, Syntagma	Leather
Xanthopoulos, No. 4 Voukourestiou	Jewelry

Places of Interest:
The Acropolis - temples and museums
Benaki Museum
The National Archaeological Museum
Sounion - a temple
Plaka - shops and flea markets
Piraeus - a seaport

HUNGARY

Official Name: Hungarian Republic

Location: Central Europe. Hungary is bordered by Slovakia, Ukraine, Romania, Serbia, Croatia, Austria and Slovenia.

Government: Constitutional Republic

Area: 93,030 sq. km., 35,919 sq. miles.

Population: 10.5 million

Religion(s): Roman Catholic majority and Protestant minority.

Capital City: Budapest

Major Business Cities: Budapest, Debrecen, Miskolc, Szeged

Time: GMT +1 (GMT +2 from late March to late October)

Currency: Forint (Huf)=100 filler

Currency Requirements:
There are no restrictions on the import of foreign currency, but the amount has to be declared on arrival. The export limited to amount declared on arrival. The Import and the export of local currency is limited to Huf10,000. Only the half of the changed money (up US$100) can be re-exchanged.

Business Hours:
- Government: 8.30-17.00 Mon-Fri
- Banks: 09.00-15.00 Mon-Fri
- Shops: 09.00-17.00 Mon-Fri
- Offices: 09.00-17.00 Mon-Fri

Weight and Measures: Metric System

Electric Current: 220 volts AC - Continental 2-pin plugs.

Holidays:
New Year's Day - January 1
1848 Anniversary - March 15
Easter Monday - April 13*
Labor Day - May 1
Whit Monday - June 1*
Constitution Day/Feast of St. Stephen - August 20
Day of Proclamation/Republic Day - October 23**
Christmas - December 25

*Christian Holidays - vary each year

** Holidays falling on the weekend are not normally compensated. When a holiday falls on a Tuesday, the previous Saturday is often worked instead of the Monday. When a holiday falls on a Thursday, the following Sunday is often worked instead of the Friday.

Suitable Clothing: Bring heavy clothing and a coat for winter, and medium-to-light clothing and rainwear or umbrella the rest of the year. Wear a conservative suit in almost all business situations, perhaps something a bit more formal for evenings out.

Automobile Driving License: An International Driving License required.

Customs Allowances: As currency and customs requirements have undergone a number of changes in recent years, one should consult your country's Hungarian embassy or consulate when arranging your trip. Personal items are duty free, but register valuables upon arrival or they may be confiscated upon departure. You may bring in 250 cigarettes and one liter of spirits.

Tipping: A tip of 10-15% is accepted for most services.

Credit Cards Accepted: Access (MasterCard), American Express, Diner's Club, Eurocard, Visa

Customary Dining Hours:
Breakfast: 07.00-09.00

Lunch: 12.00-14.00
Dinner: 18.00-21.00

Local Customs, Business Protocol and Courtesies: Hungary, although it got a headstart on capitalism before the fall of communism in 1989 and has moved to privatize much of its industry in the decade since, is currently facing economic stagnation. Nevertheless, doing business in Hungary still has many attractions and possibilities, and its business environment has become more sophisticated. Set up and formerly tightly controlled under the communist regime, the country's trade organizational infrastructure is now free to help acquaint foreigners with local businesses and help you establish contact on an individual basis. It will take much patience, perhaps a number of visits to fine tune your way to a successful business contract (particularly regarding credit terms and pricing), but most Hungarian businessmen will treat you, the potential partner, with great hospitality. Your opinion on many topics is valued, but maintain reserve in political discussions. Schedule appointments at 10 or 11 am and 2 or 3 pm, avoiding Friday afternoons. Be punctual, and use titles with your contact's last name. Give detailed, precise presentations, with the view that much competition already exists in Hungarian markets. Maintain patience and discretion regarding business affairs, and pay attention to detail in your presentations. Remember that only a signed agreement is valid.

Health: It is advisable to consult your doctor before your journey. There is a Reciprocal Health Agreement with the UK and hospital treatment is free on presentation of a UK passport but charges are made for prescribed medicines, dental and ophthalmic treatment. It is recommended to drink bottled water. An additional health and accident insurance is recommended.

Language: Hungarian. German, English, French and Russian may be spoken within business circles.

HUNGARY

BUDAPEST

Country code: 36 - City code: 1

Airport: Ferihegy International Airport.

Distance from City: 16km (9 miles) southeast of the city center.

Transportation to Center of City:
From International and Domestic Terminals
By Bus (cost) HUF300. Time approx. 40 min.(every 30 min)
By Taxi (cost) HUF3000-4000. Time approx. 20-30 min.
Tip luggage porters HUF40 per piece

Automobile Rentals:
Avis - 157-6421
Europcar Interrent-
   Terminal 1 - 157-6680
   Terminal 2 - 157-6610

Hertz -
   Terminal 1 - 157-8629
   Terminal 2 - 157-8606

Hotels:
Alba Hotel, Budapest, Apot Peter utca 3, 175-9244
Aquincum Hotel, Arpad Fejedelum utja 94, 250-3360
Astoria Hotel, Kossuth Lajos utca 19, 117-3411
Atrium Hyatt Budapest, Roosevelt ter 2, 266-1234
Budapest Hilton, Hess Andras ter 1-3, 214-3000
Budapest Marriott Hotel, Apaczai Csere Janos u. 4, 266-7000
Danubius Thermal Hotel Helia, Karpat u. 62-64, 270-3277
Forum Hotel Budapest, Apaczai Csere Janos u. 12-14, 117-8088
Grand Hotel Hungaria, Rakoczi utca 90, 322-9050
Annside Hotel Art, Kiralyi Pal utca 12, 266-2166
K&K Hotel Opera, Revay utca 24, 269-0222
Kempinski Hotel Corvinus Budapest, Erzsebet ter 7-8, 266-1000
Liget Hotel, Dozsa Gyorgy ut 106, 269-5300
Mercure Korona Hotel, Budapest, Kecskemeti utca 14, 117-4111
Metropol Hotel, Rakoczi utka 58, 342-1175

HUNGARY

Novotel Budapest Centrum, Alkotas u 63-67, 209-1990
Orion Hotel, Dobrentei utca 13, 156-8583

Restaurants:
Acapulco, VII Erzsebet korut 39, 322-6014
Alabardos, I Ortszaghaz utca 2, 156-0851
Aranyszarvas(Golden Stag), I Szarvas ter 1, 175-6451
Bombay Palace, VI Andrassy ut 44, 131-3787
Fatal, V Vaci utca 67, 266-2607
Fausto's, VIII Dohany utca 5, 322-7806
Japan, VIII Luthur utca 4-6, 114-3427
Jardin de Paris, II Fo utca 20, 201-0047
Kacsa, II Fo utka 75, 201-9992
Kehli, III Mokus utca 22, 250-4241
Kilenc Sarkany, Dozsa Gyorgy ut 56, 342-7120
Kisbuda Gyongye, III Kenyeres utca 34, 168-6402
Leroy's Country Pub, XIII Visegradi utca 50/a, 270-3202
Les Amis, II Romer Floris utca 12, 212-3173
Muzeum Resteurant, VIII Muzeum Korut 12, 267-0375
Remiz, II Budakeszi ut 5, 275-1396
Scampi, Vii Dohany utca 10, 269-6026
Seul House, I Fo utca 8, 201-7452
Tabani Kakas, I Attila ut 27, 175-7165
Taverna Ressaikos, I Apor Peter utca 1, 212-1612
Udvarhaz, II Harmashatarhegyi ut 2, 188-8780
Vadrozsa, II Pentelei ut 15, 326-5817
Vegetarium, V Cukor utca 3, 267, 0322

Entertainment:
Big Mambo, VIII Maria utca 48
Café Pierrot, I Fortuna utca 14, 175-6971
Champions Sports Bar, VII Also Erdosor utca 1
Irish Cat, V Muzeum korut 41
Janis Pub, V Kiralyi Pal utca 8
Jazz Café, V Balassi Balint 25, 132-4377
Merlin Jazz Club, V Gerloczy utca 4
Morrison's Music Pub, VI Revay utca 25
Paris Texas, Raday utca 22
Petofi Csarnok, XIV Zichi Mihaly utca 14, 343-4327
Picasso Point, VI Hajos utca 31

HUNGARY

Places of Interest:
Parliament
Royal Palace - a museum
Margaret Island - a park
Citadella
Matthius Church
Hungarian National Museum

IRELAND

Official Name: Republic of Ireland

Location: Western Europe. Ireland is an island in the North Atlantic Ocean. It is situated off the west coast of Britain.

Government: Republic

Area: 70,283 sq. km., 27,136 sq. miles.

Population: 3.54 million

Religion(s): Roman Catholic majority and Protestant minority.

Capital City: Dublin

Major Business Cities: Cork

Time: GMT (GMT +1 from late March to late October)

Currency: Irish Pound (IRP)=100 pence

Currency Requirements: There are no restrictions on the import and export of either local or foreign currency.

Business Hours:
- Government: 09.00-13.00: 14.00-17.00 Mon-Fri
- Banks: 10.00-12.30; 13.30-15.50 Mon-Fri
- Shops: 09.00-17.30/18.00 Mon-Fri (many shops have late night opening Thur until 20.00)
- Offices: 09.00-17.00/18.00 Mon-Fri

Weight and Measures: British Imperial System; Metric System being introduced.

Electric Current: 230 volts AC

Holidays:
New Year's Day - January 1
St. Patrick's Day - March 17
Good Friday - April 10*
Easter Monday - April 13*
May Holiday - May 5
Bank Holiday - June 2
Bank Holiday - August 4
Bank Holiday - October 27
Christmas Day - December 25
St. Stephen's Day - December 26

*Christian Holidays - vary each year

Suitable Clothing: Medium weight clothing will do year round, adding a coat in winter. You will definitely need a raincoat and umbrella. Wear a conservative business suit in most situations. Formal evening clothing is rarely required.

Automobile Driving License: It is required to have an International Driving Permit, an European License or a full National Driving license. The license must be held for at least two years.

Customs Allowances: No limits exist on bringing in foreign currency, or exporting foreign currency if declared. There are no import or export limits on Irish Pounds if previously declared. Personal items are duty free, but register all valuables upon arrival, or risk confiscation. You may bring in, duty free, 400 cigarettes, 2 liters of wine and one of spirits. Prohibited items include military weaponry, narcotics and pornographic matter.

Tipping: A service charge of 15% is included in many of the hotel and the restaurant bills. It is customary to leave a 10-15% tip to the taxi drivers and to tip the porters .

Credit Cards Accepted: Access, American Express, Diner's Club, MasterCard, Visa

Customary Dining Hours:
Breakfast: 08.00-10.00
Lunch: 12.30-14.00
Dinner: 19.00-21.30

Local Customs, Business Protocol and Courtesies: Business and social custom in Ireland is similar to that of neighboring Great Britain; reserved but often even more friendly and hospitable. Nevertheless, keep in mind that Ireland is a Catholic, more religious society, and people are sensitive when it comes to relations with Great Britain, particularly regarding the conflict in Northern Ireland. Business protocol requires a certain level of formality and reserve; the most obvious rules being making appointments in advance, being on time, displaying good manners at a meal and avoiding personal questions. Make your presentations detailed, with a view toward the practical execution and economic benefits of a proposal. Initially, use titles with last names until indicated otherwise by your Irish counterpart. Business cards are usually exchanged after a first meeting. Be prepared for strong, detailed negotiations. Regarding gifts, you may give your colleague something upon the successful close of a deal or at Christmas · an inexpensive but tasteful gift like a book, accessory or fine wine.

Unlike in many countries, it is acceptable to arrange business breakfasts as well as dinners or over a game of golf. Don't insult your Irish contemporaries by refusing an invitation for drinks. You will likely be invited to dinner in a restaurant, or lunch and/or drinks in a pub. When invited to dine at home with a family, bring the hostess a small gift, candy or flowers (avoiding the usual European taboos on red, white or funereal varieties), and send a thank-you note the next day. In any social situation, business topics are avoided. Gin-and-tonic or sherry are often served before meals, beer or wine during, and coffee afterwards. Wait for your host or hostess to begin the meal, and leave a small portion on your plate and place your knife and fork together on a horizontal across the plate to signify that you are finished.

Health: It is advisable for visitors from EU countries to obtain an exemption form before traveling. There is a reciprocal Health Agreement with some European countries. Visitors should mention that they wish to be treated under the EU's social security regulations before treatment. A vaccination for tetanus is recommended. Private Medical insur-

IRELAND

ance is also recommended.

Language: English and Irish (Gaelic).

DUBLIN

Country code: 353 - City code: 1

Airport: Dublin International Airport

Distance from City: 10km (6 miles) north of the city.

Transportation to Center of City:
From International and Domestic Terminals
By Bus (cost) IRP2.50. Time approx. 20-25 min. (every 20 min)
By Taxi (cost) IRP15.00. Time approx. 15 min.
Tip luggage porters 50 Pence per piece

Transfers: (Minimum Connecting Time):
International to International: 45 min.
International to Domestic: 45 min.
Domestic to International: 45 min.
Domestic to Domestic: 45 min.

Automobile Rentals:
Airport car rental desk
Avis - 605-7500
Europcar Interrent - 844-4179
Hertz - 844-5466

Car rental city office
Avis - 605-7500
Europcar Interrent - 668-1777
Hertz - 602660

Hotels:
Blooms Hotel, Anglesea St., Temple Bar, 671-5622
Buswells Hotel, 25 Molesworth St., 676-4013
Central Hotel, 1-5 Exchequer St., 679-7302
Conrad International Dublin, Earlsfort Terr., 676-5555

Davenport Hotel, At Merrion Sq., 661-6800
Forte Grand Shelbourne, 27 St. Stephen's Green, 676-6471
Hibernian Hotel, Eastmoreland Pl., Ballsbridge, 668-7666
Mont Clare Hotel, At Merrion Sq., 661-6799
Quality Court Hotel, Killiney Bay, 285-1622
Temple Bar Hotel, 14-17 Fleet St., 677-3333

Restaurants:
Ayumi-Ya Japanese Steakhouse, 132 Lover Baggot Street, 01 662 2233
Chapter One, 18\19 Parnell Sq., 01 837 2266
Davy Byrnes, 21 Duke Street, 01 677 5217
Dobbin's Vine Bistro, 15 Stephen's Lane 01 661 3321
Eamonn Doran, 3a Crown Alley Temple Bar, 01 679 9114
Elephant & Castle, 18 Temple Bar, 01 679 3121
George's Bistro & Piano Bar, 29 South Frederick Street, 01 679 7000
L'Ecrivain, 109a Lower Baggot Srteet, 01 661 1919
La Mere Zou, 22 St Stephen's Green, 01 661 6669
Le Coq Hardi, 35 Pembroke Road Ballsbridge, 01 668 9070
Les Freres Jacques, 74 Dame Street, 01 679 4555
Locks Restaurant, 1 Windsor Terrace Portobello, 01 454 3391
Old Dublin Restaurant, 90\91 Francis St., 01 454 2028
The Chili Club, 1 Anne's Lane South Anne St., 01 677 3721
The Commons Restaurant, 85\86 St. Stephen's, 01 475 2597
The Courtyard, 1 Belmont Avenue, 01 283 8815
The Old Stand, 37 Exchequer St., 01 677 7220

Entertainment:
Brazen Head, Lr. Bridge St.
International Bar, Wicklow St.
Kehoe's, Sth. Anne St.
La Stampa, 35 Dawson Street, 01 677 8611
Mc.Daid, Harry St.
Neary's, Chatman St.
O'Neills, Pearse St.
Old Stand, Exchequer St.
Pier 32, 23 Upper Pembroke Street, 01 676 1494
Roly's Bistro, 7 Ballsbridge Terrace, 01 668 2611
Shamilar, 17 South Great George's Street, 01 671 0738
The Pembroke, Pembroke St.
Toners Pub, 139 Lower Baggot Street, 01 676 3090

IRELAND

Tosca, 20 Suffolk St., 01 679 6744
Wong's, 436 Clontarf Road, 01 833 4400

Shops and Stores:
Clery's, O'Connell St.   Dept. Store
Kevin and Howlin, Nassau St.   Apparel
Tower Design Craft Center, Pearse St.   Jewelry

Places of Interest:
The Dail - the parliament
Guinness Brewery
Guinness Museum and Hopstore, and Cooper's Museum.
Trinity College
The National Museum
Irish Whiskey Corner

ITALY

Official Name: The Italian Republic

Location: Western Europe. Italy is bordered by France, Switzerland, Austria and Slovenia. The Mediterranean Sea surrounds the lower part of its territory.

Government: Republic

Area: 301,302 sq. km., 116,333 sq. miles.

Population: 57.8 million

Religion(s): Roman Catholic majority.

Capital City: Rome

Major Business Cities: Bologna, Florence, Genoa, Milan, Naples, Palermo, Turin and Venice.

Time: GMT +1 (GMT +2 from late March to late October)

Currency: Italian Lira (LIT)

Currency Requirements: The import and export of foreign and local currency is limited to LIT20,000,000. Greater amounts should be declared.

Business Hours:
- Government: 08.30-13.45 Mon-Fri
- Banks: 08.30-13.30 and 15.00-16.00/16.30 Mon-Fri
- Shops: 09.00-12.30 and 15.00/16.00-19.30 Mon-Sat
- Offices: 08.30-13.00 and 14.00-18.00 Mon-Fri

Weight and Measures: Metric System

Electric Current: 220 volts AC. Continental 2-pin plugs are used.

ITALY

Holidays:
New Year's Day - January 1
Epiphany - January 6*
Easter Monday - April 13*
Liberation Day - April 25
Labor Day - May 1
Assumption - August 15
All Saints' Day - November 1
Immaculate Conception - December 8
Christmas Day - December 25
Boxing Day - December 26

*Christian Holidays - vary each year

Suitable Clothing: Bring a light coat or lined jacket in winter, light clothing and umbrella in summer and medium weight clothing and rainwear for the rest of the year. Wear a conservative but well-cut business suit in most situations.

Automobile Driving License: An International Driving License or an EU Driving License can be used.

Customs Allowances: Personal items are duty free, but register all valuables upon arrival and keep receipts-or you may face bureaucratic entanglements or even confiscation later. There are no import limits on foreign currency, and you may take out any amounts previously declared. Concerning Italian Lire, you are limited to importing or exporting 20,000,000 Lire, and 50,000, and 100,000 Lire banknotes are not legal tender outside the country. Tobacco and alcohol restrictions: 400 cigarettes, two liters of wine and one of spirits.

Tipping: A service charge and a state tax are usually included in all hotel bills. In restaurants it is acceptable to give the waiter an additional 5-10%, but this is discretionary. A tip of 8-10% is expected by the taxi drivers and sometimes it may be included in the visitors fares.

Credit Cards Accepted: Access, American Express, Diner's Club, Eurocard, MasterCard, Visa

ITALY

Customary Dining Hours:
Breakfast: 07.00-08.30
Lunch: 13.00-15.00
Dinner: 20.00-22.00

Local Customs, Business Protocol and Courtesies: Though Rome, Florence and Venice are Italy's best-known cities of art, the country's corporate world is largely headquartered in Milan, followed by Turin and Genoa. Business atmosphere varies from region to region, with Roman, Milanese and southern Italian businessmen being more relaxed and informal and those in Turin and Genoa more conservative. Milan is the only city where business luncheons and dinners are common. Schedule appointments in advance, generally between 9.30 and 11.30 or 2.30 and 4 pm, and expect business to close for the early afternoon siesta although major corporations and executives may keep going after hours. Exchange cards only in a business context such as a formal introduction or meeting. It is a polite gesture to look at a business card upon receiving it; this will also help you in determining titles, which are necessary until your Italian contact indicates otherwise. If still unclear on a title, try "Dottore" (Director). Your contact may listen to you attentively, but this does not mean he or she has been won over. Make sure your proposals are thorough, strongly supported and practical. Many businessmen speak English, but French is much more popular as a second language, so you may need an interpreter.

Italian businessmen generally keep family separate from foreign business relationships, and you are not expected to include wives in your own business-related social functions until you have met them on several previous occasions. After your first few trips to Italy, however, you may be invited to your counterpart's home for dinner. Guests generally arrive about 15 minutes late. Wait for your hostess to begin eating, and use a fork, not a spoon, to roll pasta. Leave wine in your glass if you do not want it refilled. Do not leave food on your plate, and signify that your are finished by placing your fork and knife at a diagonal across your plate. In the spirit of Italy's stunning artistic heritage, business and social gift-giving protocol dictates costlier, higher-quality items. Business gifts are usually exchanged; books or art objects, or finely crafted office accessories are acceptable·even items with a (small) company logo, as long as they are good quality. If invited to a home, you may bring a small, tasteful gift·but chocolates or flowers are acceptable, keeping in mind the usual European taboos regarding certain flowers; no red or white, no even numbers or funereal varieties.

Health: There is a Reciprocal Health Agreement with the rest of the EU. Visitors from these countries are eligible for free dental and medical treatment, but the medicines must be paid for. It is recommended for visitors from EU countries to obtain an exemption form before traveling. It is advisable to drink bottled water. Medical insurance is recommended.

Language: Italian.

MILAN

Country code: 39 - City code: 2

Airport: Linate International Airport

Distance from City: 10km (6 miles) east of the city

Transportation to Center of City:
From International and Domestic Terminals
By Bus (cost) LIT1,400. Time approx. 30 min. (every 15-20 min.)
By Taxi (cost) LIT25,000-30,000. Time approx. 30 min.
Tip luggage porters LIT1500 per piece

Transfers: (Minimum Connecting Time):
International to International: 40 min.
International to Domestic: 50 min.
Domestic to International: 50 min.
Domestic to Domestic: 40 min.

Automobile Rentals:
Airport car rental desk
Avis - 717214

Europcar Interrent - 7611-0258
Hertz - 7020-0256
Airport: Malpensa International Airport

Distance from City: 48km (29 miles) northwest of the city.

Transportation to Center of City:
From International and Domestic Terminals
By Bus (cost) LIT3,000. Time approx. 60-90 min.
By Taxi (cost) LIT 15,000. Time approx. 50-60 min.
Tip luggage porters LIT1500 per piece

Transfers: (Minimum Connecting Time):
International to International: 60 min.
International to Domestic: 60 min.
Domestic to International: 60 min.
Domestic to Domestic: 60 min.

Automobile Rentals:
Airport car rental desk
Avis - 40099375
Europcar Interrent - 40099351
Hertz - 40099000

Car rental city office
Avis - 6610-1647
Europcar Interrent - 66710491
Hertz - 66985151

Hotels:
Century Tower Hotel, Via Fabio Filzi 25/b, 67504
Doria Grang, Viale Andrea Doria 22, 669-6696
Excelsior Hotel Gallia, Piazza Duca d'Aosta 9, 6785
Golden Tulip Crivi's Hotel, Corso di Porta Vigentina 46, 582891
Grand Hotel Duomo, Via S. Raffaele 1, 8833
Grand Hotel Fieramilano, Viale Boenzio 20, 336221
Grand Hotel Puccini, Corso Buenos Aires 33, 952-1344
Grand Hotel et de Milan, Via Manzoni 29, 723141
Hotel Berlino, Via Plana 33, 324141
Hotel Berna, Via Napo Torriani 18
Hotel Brunelleschi, Via Baracchini 12, 8843
Hotel Cavour, Via Fatebenefratelli 21, 657-2051

ITALY

Hotel Centro, Via Broletto 46, 869-2821
Hotel Cervo, Piazzale Principessa, 2900-4031
Hotel Diana Majestic, Viale Piave 42, 2951-3404
Hotel Galles Milano, Via Ozanam 1, 204841

Restaurants:
Aimo e Nadia, V. Montecuccoli 6, 416-886
Al Porto, Piazza Candore, 832-1481
Alfredo Gran San Bernando, V. Borghese 14, 331-9000
Antica Brasera Meneghina, Via Circo 10, 580-8108
Antica Osteria del Ponte, P. Negri 9 in Casinetta di
   Lugagnono, 20081 Abbiategrasso, 942-0034
Antica Trattoria di Domenico e Maria, V. Montevideo 4,
   837-2849
Aurora, Via Sanova 23, 835-4978
Bagutta, Via Bagutta 14, 702-2767
Biffi Scala, Via Filodramatici 2, 866-651
Bistrot di Gualtiero Marchesi, V. Sn Raffaele 2, 877-159
Buriassi da Lino, V. Lecco 15, 2952-3227
Giannino, Via A Sciesa 8, 5519-5020
Il Girarrosto, Corso Venezia 31, 7600-0481
Osteria del Binari, V. Tortona 1, 8940-6753
Quattro Muri, V. San Giovanni 2, 878-483
Santa Luca, Via San Pietro All'Orto 3, 7602-3155
Scaletta, P. Stazione Genova 3, 5810-0290
Suntory, Via Verdi 6, 869-3022

Entertainment:
Angelo Azzurro, Ripa Porta Ticinese 11, 350992
Biblos, Via Madonnina 17, 805-1860
Ca' Bianca Club, Via Lodovica il Moro 117, 813-5260
Cin Cin Bar, Via Felice Casati 45, 650-476
Cristal, Via Ascanio Sforza 11, 835-3951
El Brellin, Vicolo Valandai, 835-1351
Il Banco, Via Pontaccio, 805-3086
Il Patuscino, Via Madonnina 21, 807-264
Il Ragno, Via Madonnina 11, 805-3643
Scimmie, Via Ascanio Sforza 49, 839-1874

Shops and Stores:

Bulgari, Via Spiga	Jewelry
Emporio Armani, Durini 22	Apparel

Etro, Via Montenapoleone 5	Apparel
Faraone, Via Montenapoleone	Jewelry
Ferragamo, Via Montenapoleone	Apparel
Gianni Versace, Via Montenapoleone	Apparel
Gucci, Via Montenapoleone	Apparel
Michela, Corso Venezia 8	Apparel
Navgli district, Via Calatifimi,	Apparel
Shara Pagano, Via Spiga	Jewelry
Valentino, Via Montenapoleone	Apparel

Places of Interest:
The Duomo - a gothic cathedral.
The Duomo Museum
La Scala - an opera house, theatre and a museum.
Civico Museo di Storia Naturale - museum of nature.
Castello Sforzesco - a castle
The Church of Santa Maria delle Grazie
Museo Archeologico - a museum.

ROME

Country code: 39 - City code: 6

Airport: Leonardo da Vinci (Fiumicino) International Airport

Distance from City: 35km (21 miles) southwest of the city.

Transportation to Center of City:
From International and Domestic Terminals
By Bus (cost) LIT5000-10,000. Time approx.45-60 min.
By Taxi (cost) LIT50,000-80,000. Time approx. 45-50 min.
By Train (cost) LIT12,000. Time approx. 25 min. (every 30)
Tip luggage porters LIT1500 per piece

Transfers: (Minimum Connecting Time):
International to International: 45 min.
International to Domestic: 60 min.
Domestic to International: 60 min.
Domestic to Domestic: 45 min.

ITALY

Automobile Rentals:
Airport car rental desk
Avis - 65011531
Europcar Interrent - 65010879
Hertz - 65011553

Car rental city office
Avis - 4701228
Hertz - 3216831

Hotels:
Advanture Hotel, Via Palestro 88, 446-9714
Berlini Bristol Rome, Piazza Barberini 23, 488-3051
De La Ville Inter-Continental Roma, Via Sistina 67-69, 67331
Eden Hotel, Via Ludovisi 49, 474-3551
Excelsior Hotel, Vittorio Veneto 125, 47081
Golden Tulip Ripa Residence All Suites, Via Orti di Trastevere 1, 58611
Holiday Inn Crowne Plaza Minerva, Piazza della Minerva 69, 6994-1888
Holiday Inn St. Peters, Via Aurelia Antica 415, 6642
Hotel Quirinale Roma, Via Nazionale 7, 4707
Hotel Tritone, Via del Tritone 210, 6992-2575
Hotel Valadier, Via della Fontanella 15, 361-1998
Hotel White, Via In Arcione 77, 6991-1242
Le Grand Hotel, Via Vittorio Emanuele, 47091
Regina Hotel Baglioni, Via V. Veneto 72, 476851
Rex Hotel, Via Torino 149, 482-4828

Restaurants:
Agata e Romeo, V. Carlo Alberto 45, 446-5842
Al Moro, Vicolo delle Bollette 13, 678-3495
Alberto Ciarla, Piazza San Cosimato 40, 581-8668
Bacaro, Via delgi Spagnoli 27, 686-4110
Convivio, V. dell'Orso 44, 686-9432
Cornucopia, P. in Pencinula 18, 580-0380
Dal Bolognese, Piazza del Popolo 1, 361-1426
Elefante Bianco, Via Aurora 19, 489-03764
Evangelista, Lungoteveri Vallati 24, 687-5810
Il Cardinale, V. delle Carceri 6, 686-9336
Il Drappe, Vicolo del Malpasse 10, 687-7365
La Rosetta, Via della Rosetta 9, 686-1002

ITALY

Nino, V. Borgognona 11, 679-5676
Papa Giovanni, V. dei Sediari 4, 686-5308
Piccolo Mondo, V. Aurora 39, 481-4595
Relais Le Jardin, V. Notaris 5, 322-0404
Sabatini, Piazza Santa Maria, Trastevere, 582-2026
Taverna Giulia, Vicolo dell'Oro, 686-9768
Toula, Via della Lupa 29, 687-3750
Vecchia Roma, P. Campitelli 18, 686-4604

Entertainment:
Alibi, Via di Monte Testaccio 44, 574-2448
Black Out, Via Saturnia 18, 7049-6791
Blue Zone, Via Campania 37a, 482-1890
Devil's Chair, Via Tripolitana 190, 8620-8785
Gilda Swing, Via Mario de Fiori 97
Jackie-O, Via Boncompagni 11, 488-5457
Pantheon Club, Via Pozzo delle Cornaccie 36, 688-03431
Veleno, Via Sardegna 27, 493-583

Shops and Stores:

Bottega Orafa, V. Pianellari 24	Jewelry
Buccelati, Via Condotti 31	Jewelry
Bulgari, Via Condotti10	Jewelry
Carlo Eleuteri, Via Condotti 69	Antiques
Discount dell'Alta Moda, V. Gesu e Maria 16	Apparel
Giorgio Armani, Via Babuino	Apparel
Krizia, Via Babuino	Apparel
Luna e l'Altra, Via Banchi Nuovi 105	Apparel
Missoni, Via Babuino	Apparel
Rinascente, Corso	Dept. Store

Places of Interest:
The Vatican
The Colosseum
Roman Forum - ruins
Campidoglio Square - palaces, museums, churches etc.
Piazza Navona
The Villa Borghese - a park, galleries and museums.
The Catacombs of San Callisto
Piazza di Spagna
Fontana di Trevi - a fountain

KAZAKSTAN

Official Name: Republic of Kazakstan

Location: Central Asia. Kazakhstan is bordered by Russia, China, Kyrgystan, Uzbekistan and Turkmenistan. To the West lies the Caspian Sea.

Government: Constitutional Republic

Area: 2,717,300 sq. km., 1,049,150 sq. mi.

Population: 17.4 million

Religion(s): Islam (Sunni) majority. Eastern Orthodox minority

Capital City: Almati

Major Business Cities: Almati and Karaguada

Time: GMT +6

Currency: 1 Tenge = 100 Tein

Currency Requirements: The Import of foreign currency is unlimited but must be declared. The export is limited to the amount declared upon arrival. The import and the export of local currency are prohibited.

Business Hours:
- Government: 09.00-18.00 Mon-Fri
- Banks: 09.00-18.00 Mon-Fri
- Shops: 09.00-18.00 Mon-Fri
- Offices: 09.00-18.00 Mon-Fri

Weight and Measures: Metric System

Electric Current: 220/127V, 50c

Automobile Driving License: An International driving license is required.

Tipping: A tip of 10%-15% is expected in most restaurants. Hotels usually include a service charge in the bill. Taxi drivers expect 10%.

Credit Cards Accepted: American Express, EuroCard and Visa

Customary Dining Hours:
Breakfast: 07.00-09.00
Lunch: 12.00-14.30
Dinner: 18.30-22.00

Local Customs, Business Protocol and Courtesies: As throughout the former East bloc and FSU, nationalism is on the rise in Kazakhstan, so it's best not to get enmeshed in political discussions or mistake its multi-ethnic society as a "Russian" one or ignore the customs and pride of the dominant culture. Despite the poor economy, hospitality reigns, and you should reciprocate for the many invitations you will receive with small gifts from your country. Since Kazakhstan is a Muslim country, dress modestly (no shorts), and do not bring alcohol as a gift.

Health: It is recommended to consult your doctor before your journey. Drinking water is safe in most major cities. The medical and dental treatment is free, but the medications must be paid. In emergencies you must contact your embassy or hotel receptionist.

Language: Kazak

ALMATI

Country code: 7 - City code: 327

Airport: Almaty

Distance from City: 15.3 km. (9.5 mi.)

KAZAKSTAN

Hotels:
Otrar, Gogol St. 73, 330026
Turkestan, Pushkin, 333417

Restaurants:
Aral, Gorky Park
Aul, Mt. Kok-Tyube
Dzhaylau, Medeo Highway
Issyk, Panfilov St. 33
Samal, Medeo Highway

Shops and Stores:
Central Store, Komunisticheskaya   Dept. Store
Souvenirs, Furmanova   Gifts

Places of Interest:
Abai Opera
Art Museum
Ascension Cathedral
Eternal Glory Monument
Gorky Park

KYRGYSZSTAN

Official Name: The Kyrgyz Republic

Location: Central Asia. Kyrgystan is bordered by China, Kazakhstan, Uzbekistan and Tajikistan.

Government: Constitutional Republic

Area: 198,500 sq. km., 76,600 sq. mi.

Population: 4.7 million

Religion(s): Islamic majority, Orthodox minority.

Capital City: Bishkek

Major Business Cities: Osh

Time: GMT +5 hrs

Currency: 1 Som = 100 Tyiyn

Currency Requirements: The Import of foreign currency is unlimited but must be declared. The export is limited to the amount declared upon arrival. The import and the export of local currency are prohibited.

Business Hours:
- Government: 09.00-18.00 Mon-Fri
- Banks: 09.00-18.00 Mon-Fri
- Shops: 09.00-18.00 Mon-Fri
- Offices: 09.00-18.00 Mon-Fri

Weight and Measures: Metric System

Electric Current: 220/127V, 50c

KYRGYSZSTAN

Suitable Clothing: Wear light, but modest clothing in the summer, and medium weight clothing the rest of the year, adding a coat in winter.

Automobile Driving License: An International Driving License is required.

Customs Allowances: As currency and customs requirements have undergone a number of changes in recent years, one should consult your country's Kazakh embassy or consulate when arranging your trip. Valuables, including foreign currency, must be registered upon arrival, otherwise they may be confiscated upon departure. Although you may bring in unlimited amounts of foreign currency, and take out any you initially declare, you may not import or export Kazakh Tenge. Cigarettes are limited to 250, and wine and spirits to one liter and a half liter, respectively. Military weaponry, narcotics and pornographic material are prohibited.

Tipping: A tip of 10%-15% is expected in most restaurants. Hotels usually include a service charge in the bill. Taxi drivers expect a 5-10% tip.

Credit Cards Accepted: American Express, Eurocard, Carte Blanche, Diners Club, Visa.

Customary Dining Hours:
Breakfast: 07.00-09.00
Lunch: 12.00-14.30
Dinner: 18.30-22.00

Health: It is recommended to consult your doctor before your journey. Drinking water is safe in most major cities. The medical and dental treatment is free, but the medications must be paid. In emergencies you must contact your embassy or hotel receptionist.

Language: Kyrgyz

KYRGYSZSTAN

BISHKEK

Country code: 996 - City code: 3312

Airport: Bishkek Airport

Distance from City: 30 km. (19 mi.)

Hotels:
Ala-Too, Dzerzhynsky 1, 226041

Restaurants:
Kyrgyzstan, Orozbekova 62
Seyil, Dzerzhindsky 32
Susamyr, Toktogula 257

Shops and Stores:
Central Store, Lenin 52   Dept. Store
Beriozka, Lenin 243   Gifts

LATVIA

Official Name: Republic of Latvia

Location: Northern Europe. Latvia is bordered by Estonia, Lithuania, the Russian Federation and Belarus. To the north lies the Baltic Sea.

Government: Republic

Area: 64,589 sq. km., 24,938 sq. miles.

Population: 2.64 million

Religion(s): Protestant (Lutheran) majority. Roman Catholic and Russian Orthodox minorities.

Capital City: Riga

Major Business Cities:

Time: GMT +2 (GMT +3 from late March to late October)

Currency: Latvian Lat (LVL)=100 santims

Currency Requirements: There are no restrictions on the import and the export of either local or foreign currency. Foreign currency and valuable items should be declared on arrival. The acceptance of credit cards is limited.

Business Hours:
- Government: 09.00-18.00 Mon-Fri
- Banks: 10.00-12.00 Mon-Fri
- Shops: 09.00-18.00 Mon-Fri
- Offices: 08.30/09.00-17.30/18.00 Mon-Fri

Weight and Measures: Metric System

Electric Current: 220V, 50c

LATVIA

Holidays:
New Year's Day - January 1
Good Friday - April 10*
Easter Sunday - April 13*
Labor Day - May 1
Mother's Day - May 11
Whitsun - May 18
Midsummer's Eve - June 23
Jana Day (St. John the Baptist's Day) - June 24
Republic of Latvia Proclamation Day - November 18
Christmas Day - December 25
Boxing Day - December 26*
New Year's Eve - December 31

*Christian Holidays - vary each year

Suitable Clothing: Bring conservative business clothing; light materials and rainwear for summer, heavy clothing and a coat for winter.

Automobile Driving License: A new European Driving License or an International Driving License is required.

Customs Allowances: As currency and customs requirements have undergone a number of changes in recent years, one should consult your country's Latvian embassy or consulate when arranging your trip. Valuables must be registered upon arrival, otherwise they may be confiscated upon departure, and keep all receipts. Although you may bring in unlimited amounts of foreign currency, and take out any you initially declare, you may not import or export Latvian Lats. Cigarettes are limited to 200, and spirits to 2 to 2.5 liters. Weaponry, drugs and pornographic material are prohibited. Due to the illegal market in recent years in antique and art objects, there are strong restrictions and duties on bringing out these items, as well as required permits from the Ministry of Culture.

Tipping: The tip is included in the restaurants bills and the taxis fares. Tipping is usually expected but should be kept small.

Credit Cards Accepted: Access, American Express, Eurocard,

MasterCard and Visa are acceptable with an advance notification.

Customary Dining Hours:
Breakfast: 07.00-09.00
Lunch: 12.00-14.30
Dinner: 18.30-22.30

Local Customs, Business Protocol and Courtesies: Latvians love the outdoors, for their small country is half covered by forest and around 4,000 lakes, and borders the Baltic Sea. Any interest you express in exploring them will be well received, as will an interest in the environment and sports. Given this national preference for outdoor activities, business discussions may even take place at a walk in a park or visit to the zoo, once you and your counterpart become more comfortable. Invitations to visit a home are more rare. Latvian businessmen are generally industrious and take pride in thorough preparation, and expect similar high standards from you. They are not hesitant to ask and learn about business practices unfamiliar to them, so you may hear many questions concerning a proposed deal. Be truly patient in negotiating terms, which are especially necessary in light of the struggling post-Soviet economy. Honesty and candor is admired, and your ability to ask questions will be as valued as your answers. However, avoid asking overly personal questions or enmeshed in political discussions, and remember that Latvia was once an unwilling Soviet republic, and not "Russian."

Health: It is advisable to consult your doctor before your journey. A Yellow Fever certificate is required if arriving from or via an infected area. Immunizations against diphtheria, hepatitis A, hepatitis B, polio, tetanus and typhoid are recommended. All drinking water must be boiled or sterilized. It is recommended to bring your own medical supplies eg. aspirin etc. which you may need because they are not readily available and those which are, are expensive. A reciprocal health agreement exists with the United Kingdom for urgent and emergency medical treatment. Further details are available from the Department of Health.

LATVIA

Language: Latvian.

RIGA

Country code: 371 - City code: none

Airport: Riga International Airport.

Distance from City: 8km (4 miles) west of the city center.

Transportation to Center of City:
From International and Domestic Terminals
By Bus (cost) LVL 0.8. Time approx. 30 min. (every 20-30 min.)
By Taxi (cost) USD10-20. Time approx. 15 min.

Transfers: (Minimum Connecting Time):
International to International: 60 min.
International to Domestic: 60 min.
Domestic to International: 60 min.
Domestic to Domestic: 30 min.

Automobile Rentals:
Airport car rental desk.
Avis - 207353
Hertz - 207980

Car rental city office.
Avis - 225876
Europcar Interrent - 222637

Hotels:
Brigita Hotel, Saulkalnes St., 11, 262-3000
Eurolink Hotel, 3rd Floor Hotel "Riga", 722-0531
Latvija Hotel, Elizabetes iela 55, 722-2211
Metropole Hotel, 36-38 Aspazijas Blvd., 721-6140
Radisson SAS Daugava Hotel Riga, Kugo St. 24, 706-1111
Riga Hotel, Aspazijas Blvd, 22, 721-6285
Victorifa Hotel, 55 A Caka, 227-2305
de Rome, Kalku iela 28, 8220050-56
Hotel Laine, 11 Skolas Street, 287-658

Restaurants:
Arve, 12/14 Aldaru St., 212-414
Astorija, 16 Audeju St., 211-475
Azias Kiniesu, 6/8 Marstalu St., 225-305
Forums, 24 Kalku St., 227-078
Jana, 16 Skunu St., 226-258
Jever Bistro, 6 Kalku St., 227-078
Lido, 6Tirgonu St., 222-431
Livonija, 21 Meistaru St., 227-824
Marschall, 12 Marstalu St., 227-403
Pie Kristapa, 25/29 Jauniela, 226-354
Put Vejini, 18/22 Jauniela, 228-841
Reformatu Muzikas , 10 Marstalu St., 210-027
Sena Riga, 20 Aspazijas Blvd., 216-869
Solo, 10 Marstalu St., 320-831
Tornis, 1 Meistaru St., 216-155
Zilais Putns, 4 Tirgonu St., 228-214
Anre, 13 Merkela St., 226-282
Don Fa, 33 Avotu St., 276-101
Golden Dragon, 232 Brivibas St., 552-142
Kaukazs, 8 Merkela St., 224-528
Riga, 44/46 Bruninieku St., 293-530

Entertainment:
Alutins, 68 Gertrudes St., 285-717
Bravo, 6 A Kalnina St., 217-233
Diana, 89 Elizabetes St., 228-790
Grilbars, 68 Gertrudes St., 287-832
Lolo Pub, 51 Elizabetes St., 281-849
Zem Ozola, 9 Blaumana St., 217-770
Jumis, 103 Brivibas St., 275-108
Preses Bars, 1 Raina Blvd., 229-708
Laura, 15 Smilsu St., 229-273
Casinos Latvija, 24 Kalku St., 212-322
Casino, 22 Aspazijas Blvd., 216-104
Reformatu Muzikas , 10 Marstalu St., 210-027
Marshall, 12 Marstalu St., 227-403

Shops and Stores:
Rigas Porcelans, 163Maskavas St.   Pottery
Centalais Universal Veikals, 6 Audeju St. Dept.Store
Antiques Shop, 13 M. Pils St.   Antiques

Art Salon, 25 Valnu St.	Souvenirs
Curiosity Shop, 46 Brivibas Blvd.	Antiques
Daina, 38 Brivibas Blvd.	Souvenirs
Dzintra, 5 Valnu St.	Souvenirs
Liga, 121 Brivibas St.	Souvenirs
Livs, 15 Ridaba, 62 Gertrudes St.	Souvenirs

Places of Interest:
Freedom Monument
Open Air Museum of Ethnography
St.Peter's Church
History and Maritime Museum
Orthodox Metropolitan Cathedral
Museum of Applied Arts
St. John's Church
The Dome Museum
Latvia's Museun of Foreign Arts
Latvia's Photography Museum
Latvia's War Museum
Latvia's Museum of Fine Arts
Riga's Automobile Museum

LITHUANIA

Official Name: Republic of Lithuania

Location: Northern Europe. Lithuania is bordered by Latvia, Belarus, Kaliningrad, the Russian Federation and Poland.

Government: Parliamentary Republic

Area: 65,300 sq. km., 25,212 sq. miles.

Population: 3.75 million

Religion(s): Roman Catholic majority. Evangelical Lutheran, Evangelical Reformist and Russian Orthodox minorities.

Capital City: Vilnius

Major Business Cities: Kaunas, Palanga

Time: GMT +2 (GMT +3 from late March to late September)

Currency: Litas (LTL)=100 centas

Currency Requirements: There are no restrictions on the import of local and foreign currencies, except that the export of foreign currency is limited to the amount declared on import.

Business Hours:
- Banks: 09.00-17.00 Mon-Fri
- Shops: 10.00-19.00 Mon-Fri; 10.00-16.00 Sat
- Offices: 09.00-18.00 Mon-Fri (lunch 13.00-14.00)

Weight and Measures: Metric system

Electric Current: 220 volts. Plugs are of the European type.

Holidays:
New Year's Day - January 1
Independence Day - February 16
Good Friday – April 10*
Easter Monday – April 13*
International Labor Day - May 1
Mother's Day - May 4
Day of Statehood - July 6
All Saints' Day - November 1
Christmas Day - December 25
Boxing Day - December 26

Suitable Clothing: Wear a business suit or conservative dress, but keep in mind that anything that appears too expensive may be viewed as ostentatious. In the cold winters, bring a heavy coat and warm clothes, and in summer, light clothing and rainwear.

Automobile Driving License: A National License held for one year is accepted. European nationals must have the new European Driving License.

Customs Allowances: As currency and customs requirements have undergone a number of changes in recent years, one should consult your country's Lithuanian embassy or consulate when arranging your trip. Valuables must be registered upon arrival, otherwise they may be confiscated upon departure, and keep all receipts and other forms. Duty-free cigarettes are limited to 250, wine to two liters and spirits to one. Weaponry, drugs and pornographic material are prohibited. Due to the illegal market in recent years in antique and art objects, there are strong restrictions and duties on bringing out these items, as well as required permits from the Ministry of Culture. Prohibited are military weaponry, drugs and pornography.

Tipping: Restaurants usually include a tip in their bills. A tip is included in the taxi fares.

Local Customs, Business Protocol and Courtesies: The desire to make up for its past Soviet-run economy has resulted in an industrious business environment in Lithuania. They will expect absolute professionalism from you:

make your presentations thorough and convincing and make your meeting agendas well thought out and logical. Formal behavior and deferring to one's superiors are important. Because of the developing economy, credit and prices will be important to your counterparts. Once a verbal agreement is reached, you can expect it to be carried out, but of course it should be in ink as well. The country's long history of being alternately dominated by Poland and Russia has left cultural marks of its two large neighbors on Lithuania. Nevertheless, it is important for visitors to treat recently independent Lithuania as a fiercely individual, European entity. Because of Lithuanians' strong national/religious identity, you will encounter much self-assuredness (or sometimes defensive aggressiveness) in your business and social interactions. But you will meet, too, with much friendliness and hospitality. And a little knowledge of Lithuanian history (the positive aspects only) goes a long way.

Health: It is advisable to consult your doctor well before your journey. There are no mandatory vaccinations, but it is recommended to have immunizations against diphtheria, hepatitis A and hepatitis B. There is a Health Agreement with the United Kingdom for urgent medical treatments.

Language: Lithuanian.

VILNIUS

Country code: 370 - City code: 2

Airport: Vilnius Airport..

Distance from City: 10km (6 miles) from the city center

Transportation to Center of City:
From International and Domestic Terminals
By Bus (cost) US$0.50. Time approx.20 min.
By Taxi (cost) US$4-5 Time approx. 15 min.

Automobile Rentals:

LITHUANIA

Airport car rental desk
Avis - 291131
Hertz - 227025

Car rental city office
Avis - 733226
Hertz - 227025

Hotels:
Zvaigzde Hotel, Pylimo 63, 619626
Hotel Gintaras, Sodu 14, 634496
Sportas Hotel, Bystricios 13, 748953
Trinapolis, Verkiu 66, 778913
AAA, Mano Liza Guest House, Ligonines 5, 222225
Mabre Residence Hotel, Maironio 13, 222087
City Park Hotel, Stuokas-Guseviciaus 3, 223515
Stikliai Hotel, Gaono 7, 627971
Leituva Hotel, Ukmerges 20, 726090
Victoria Hotel, Saltoniskiu 56, 724013
Pilaite, Kalvariju 1, 752292

Restaurants:
Ritos Smukle, Zirmunu 68, 770 786
Literatu Svetaine, 611 889
Lokys, 629 046
Medininkai, Ausros Vartu 4
!901 Uzeiga, Ausros Vartu 11
Stikliai Alude, Gaono 7, 222 109
The Pub, Dominikonu 9
Prie Parlamento, Gedimino 46
Savas Kampas, Vokieciu 4
Metaxa, Gedimino 32
Gero ViskioBaras, Pilies 28
Bix, Etmonu 6
Ritos Sleptuve, Gostauto 8
Hotel Stikliai, Gaono 7
Poniu Laime, Gedimino 31
Geltona Upe, Stikliu 18, 222 875
Auksinis Drakonas, Aguonu 11, 262 701
Sidabrinis Drakonas, Didzioji 40, 221 296
Idabasar, Subaciaus 3, 628 484
Trys Draugai, Pilies 25A, 222 455

Vidudienis, Gedimino 5, 628 089
Raudona-Juoda, Gedimino 14, 620 685

Entertainment:
Armadillo, Gedimino 26
Gelezinis Kablys, Kauno 5
Indigo, Traku 3/2
Klibas Ekstra, Laisves 55,
Langas, Asmenos 8
Max Dance World,Justiniskiu 64
Ministerija, Gedimino 46
Naktinis Vilkas, Lukiskiu Aikste 3
Nasa, Laisves 58
Ritos Sleptuve, Gostauto 8
Tobira, Mykolo 4

Shops and Stores:
Sauluva, Pilies 22 Souveniers
Vilnius, Ukmerges 16 Dept. Store
Sentine Gastronomas, Gedimino 24 Dept. Store
Astromine Rologigios Centras, Basanavisiaus 4 Souvenirs

Places of Interest:
Cathedral and Gediminas Square
Castle Hill and Gediminas Tower – a museum
Pushkin Memorial Museum
St.Casimir's Church
Lithuanian Art Museum
Astronomical Observatory
The Bastion Museum
St.Nicholas' Church
University of Vilnius

MOLDOVA

Official Name: The Republic of Moldova

Government: Democratic Republic

Area: 33,700 sq. km., 13,010 sq. mi.

Population: 4.5 million

Religion(s): Christianity, Eastern Orthodox

Capital City: Kishinev

Major Business Cities: Tiraspol, Beltsy, Bender

Time: GMT +2

Currency: 1 Moldovial Leu = 1000 Rubles

Currency Requirements: The Import of foreign currency is unlimited but must be declared. The export is limited to the amount declared upon arrival. The import and the export of local currency are prohibited.

Business Hours:
- Government: 09.00-19.00 Mon-Fri
- Banks: 09.00-19.00 Mon-Fri
- Shops: 09.00-19.00 Mon-Fri
- Offices: 09.00-19.00 Mon-Fri

Weight and Measures: Metric System

Electric Current: 220V/127V, 50c

Automobile Driving License: International driving license is required.

Customs Allowances: As currency and customs requirements have undergone a number of changes in recent years, one should consult your country's embassy or consulate when arranging your trip. Valuables, including foreign currency, must be registered upon arrival, otherwise they may be confiscated upon departure. Although you may bring in unlimited amounts of foreign currency, and take out any you initially declare, you may not import or export local currency. Limits are stringent on items like cigarettes and alcohol.

Tipping: A tip of 10%-15% is expected in most restaurants. Hotels usually include a service charge in the bill. Taxi drivers expect 10-15%.

Credit Cards Accepted: American Express, Carte Blanche, Diner's Club, Eurocard, Visa.

Customary Dining Hours:
Breakfast: 07.00-09.00
Lunch: 12.00-14.30
Dinner: 18.30-22.00

Health: It is recommended to consult your doctor before your journey. Drinking water is safe in most major cities. The medical and dental treatment is free, but the medications must be paid. In emergencies you must contact your embassy or hotel receptionist.

Language: Moldovian.

KISHINEV

Country code: 373 - City code: 2

Airport: Kishinev

Distance from City: 12.8 km. (8 mi.)

Hotels:
Kosmos, Kotovsky Square 2, 265232
Kishinev, Negruzzi Blvd. 7, 31323

MOLDOVA

Moldova, Lenin Prospekt 7a, 22652

Restaurants:
Butoyash, Kuibyshev 251, 19335
Norok, Gorky St. 20, 33609
Plovdiv, Moskovsky Prospekt 6, 40222
Tourist, Molodyozhi 11a, 29468

Shops and Stores:

Central Store, Lenin 136	Dept. Store
Mertsishor, Pr. Lenin 132	Souvenirs
Podarki, Lenin	Gifts

Places of Interest:
Botanical Gardens
Cathedral of the Nativity
Fine Arts Museum
Old Town Hall
Planetarium
Pushkin Park
Victory Arch

NETHERLANDS

Official Name: The Kingdom of The Netherlands

Location: Northwest Europe. Netherlands is bordered by Germany, Belgium. The north and the west coasts are lying on the North Sea.

Government: Constitutional and Hereditary Monarchy

Area: 33,939 sq. km., 13,104 sq. miles.

Population: 15.167 million

Religion(s): 38% of the population is Roman Catholic and 30% is Protestant.

Capital City: Amsterdam

Major Business Cities: Eindhoven, Maastricht, Rotterdam and The Hague.

Time: GMT +1 (GMT +2 from late March to late October)

Currency: Guilder (DFL) = 100 cents

Currency Requirements: There are no restrictions for the import and the export of either foreign or local currency.

Business Hours:
- Government: 8.00-17.00 Mon-Fri
- Banks: 09.00-16.00 or 17.00Mon-Fri
- Shops: 13.00-17.00 Mon- Fri
- Offices: 08.30-17.00 Mon-Fri

Weight and Measures: Metric System

Electric Current: 220 Volts AC. Plugs are of the round 2-pin type.

Holidays:
New Year's Day - January 1
Good Friday - April 10*
Easter Monday - April 13*
Queen's Day - April 30
National Liberation Day - May 5
Ascension Day - May 21
Whit Sunday - May 18
Whit Monday - June 1*
Christmas - December 25-26

*Christian Holidays - vary each year

Suitable Clothing: Bring conservative business clothing, but also casual wear. In the summer, light to medium weight clothing is suitable, and raingear is important year round. Between November and April, bring winter clothing and a warm coat.

Automobile Driving License: An International Driving License or a National Driving License is required.

Customs Allowances: Personal items are duty free, but register all valuables upon arrival or you may face confiscation. Duty free limits include 200 cigarettes, 2 liters of wine or spirits, and 50 grams of perfume. There are no import limits on foreign currency.

Tipping: A service charge of 15% and VAT is included in the hotel and restaurant bills. It is customary to leave a small change when paying the bill. Tipping porters, doormen and taxi drivers is discretionary.

Credit Cards Accepted: American Express, Diner's Club, Eurocard, Visa

Customary Dining Hours:
Breakfast: 07.00-08.00
Lunch: 12.00-13.30
Dinner: 18.00-21.00

Local Customs, Business Protocol and Courtesies: The Netherlands has a well-oiled commerce system, which places value on hard work and on the record of any potential foreign partner. Generally, doing business there is a pleasure; once contracts are reached, fulfillment proceeds smoothly. In addition, unlike in some of its neighboring countries, foreign businesswomen will encounter little discrimination. Adhere to the usual professional rules and formalities: Schedule governmental and business meetings well in advance, trying not to conflict with the usual break times. (coffee breaks around 10 am and 4.30 pm, lunch at noon). Be absolutely on time. Eye contact is important, whether upon acquaintance, when giving a toast, or discussing business. Learn the titles of your contacts, for written communications as well as meetings. Business cards, exchanged at any time during an appointment, help in this matter since the Dutch often give just their last name upon initial contact. Give detailed, factual presentations, prioritizing your projects and needs, as many Dutch companies have a long list of clients and orders. Keep in mind that breaking a business promise, even a small one, could severely hurt any long-term dealings your company has with the Dutch company at hand.

Though meals are full and frequent, you'll more likely be invited to socialize with your Dutch contemporaries over drinks or an evening snack, or for various entertainment. In some cases, you may be invited for drinks to a home, then proceed on to a restaurant. Wine or beer with meals is customary; your host or hostess will offer a toast, and begin the meal with "Eet Smakelijk." Try small servings of every dish before crossing your knife and fork on your plate, which signifies that you would like seconds. If finished, leave a small amout of food on your plate. If visiting someone's home, be on time, bring a small, tasteful gift and send flowers in advance, or the next day as a thank-you gesture. Remember that as in most European countries, there are certain taboos on the nature of the bouquet: never bring red (which signifies romantic love), or even numbers of flowers. Bringing small gifts or candy for the children is viewed favorably; but business gifts are the norm only for long-time, solid connections.

Health: There are no vaccinations required. A vaccination for tetanus is recommended. There is a reciprocal Health Agreement between all EU countries and it is recommended that visitors from these countries obtain an exemption form before traveling. Medical insurance is advised.

Language: Dutch. English is widely spoken as a second language.

AMSTERDAM

Country code: 31 - City code: 20

Airport: Schiphol International Airport

Distance from City: 15km (9 miles) southwest of the city.

Transportation to Center of City:
From International and Domestic Terminals
By Bus (cost) DFL18. Time approx. 25-30 min.
By Taxi (cost) DFL50. Time approx. 25 min.
Tip luggage porters DFL2 per piece

Transfers: (Minimum Connecting Time):
International to International: 50 min.
International to Domestic: 50 min.
Domestic to International: 50 min.
Domestic to Domestic: 25 min.

Automobile Rentals:
Airport car rental desk
Avis - 604-1301
Europcar Interrent - 604-1566
Hertz - 601-5416

Car rental city office
Avis - 564-1611
Europcar Interrent - 683-2123
Hertz - 612-2441

NETHERLANDS

Hotels:
American Hotel, Leidsekade 97, 624-5322
Amstel Inter-Continental Amsterdam, Professor Tulplein 1,
    622-6060
Amsterdam Marriott Hotel, Stadhouderskade 19-21, 607-5555
Apollofirst Hotel, Apllolaan 123-125, 673-0333
Best Western Eden Hotel, Amstel 144, 530-7878
Canal Crown Hotel, Herengracht 519-525, 420-0055
Caransa Hotel, Rembrandtplein 19, 622-9455
Cok City Hotel, Nieuwe Zydssvoorburgwal 50, 422-0011
Doelen Hotel, Nieuwe Doelenstr. 24, 622-0722
Golden Tulip Barbizon Centre, Stadhouderskade 7, 685-1351
Grand Hotel Krasnapolsky Amsterdam, Dam 9, 554-9111
Holiday Inn Crowne Plaza, Nieuwezijds Voorburgwal 5,
    620-0500
Jolly Carlton, Vijzelstr. 2-18, 622-2066
Mercure Arthur Frommer Hotel Amsterdam, Noorderstr. 46,
    622-0328
Okura Hotel Amsterdam, Ferdinand Bolstr. 333, 678-7111
Park Hotel Amsterdam, Stadhouderskade 25, 671-7474
Pulitzer Hotel, Prinsengracht 313-331, 523-5235
Schiller Hotel, Rembrandtplein 26-36, 623-1660

Restaurants:
Bols Tavern, Rozengracht 106, 624 5752
Cafe Tzwaantje, Berenstraat 12, 623 2373
Cafe Von Puffelen, Prinsengracht 377, 624 6270
Casa Tobio, Lindengracht 31, 624 8987
Christoph, Leliegracht 46, 625 0807
D'Theeboom, Singel 210, 623 8420
D'Vijff Vlieghen, Spuistraat 294-302, 624 8369
De Groene Lateerne, Haarlemmerstraat 43, 624 1952
De Kalderhof, Prinsengracht 494, 622 0682
Excelsior, Nieuwe Doelenstraat 2-8, 623 4836
Het Stuivertje, Hazenstraat 58, 623 1349
Lucius Restaurant, Spuistraat 247, 624 1831
Naesje Claes, Spuistraat 275, 624 9998
Oesterbar, Leidseplein 10, 623 2988
Ristorante Mirafiori, Hobbemastraat 2, 662 3013
Sama Sebo, P.C.Hoofstraat 27, 662 8146
The Old Bell, Rembrandtsplein 46, 624 7682

NETHERLANDS

Entertainment:

Alto, Korte Leidedwarsstraat 115, 626 3249

Bamboo Bar, Lenge LeidsedWarsstraat 64, 624 3993

Beerlist Cafe Gollen, Raamsteeg 4, 626 6645

Boston Club, Kattengat 1, 621 2223

Casino 2000, at Max Euweplein 6, 620 1006

Jozeph Lam Jazz Club, Diemenstraat 8, 622 8086

Juliana's, Apollolaan 140, 673 7313

Mazzo, Rozengracht 114, 626 7500

Shops and Stores:

C &A, Damrak and Nieuwendijk	Dept. Store
De Bijenkorf, Dam Sq.	Dept. Store
Dreesmann, Kalverstraat	Dept. Store
Floating Flower Market	Gift Shop
Galerie Ra, Vijzelstraat 90	Jewelry
Peek & Cloppenburg, Dam Sq.	Dept. Store
Topshop, Nieuwendijk 115	Leather

Places of Interest:

Rijksmuseum - a museum

Amsterdam Historic Museum

The Rijksmuseum Vincent Van Gogh - a museum

Portugees Israelitische Synagogue

The Zuiderkerk - a church

The Nieuwekerk - a church

Anne Frankhuis

Heineken Brewery

ROTTERDAM

Country code: 31 - City code: 10

Airport: Rotterdam-Zestienhoven International Airport

Distance from City: 9km (5 miles) south of the city.

Transportation to Center of City:

From International and Domestic Terminals

By Bus (cost) DFL5-7.Time approx. 20 min. (every 15 min.)

By Taxi (cost) DFL35.00. Time approx. 15 min.

Tip luggage porters DFL2 per piece

NETHERLANDS

Transfers: (Minimum Connecting Time):
International to International: 20 min.
International to Domestic: 20 min.
Domestic to International: 20 min.
Domestic to Domestic: 20 min.

Automobile Rentals:
Airport car rental desk
Avis - 415-8842
Europcar Interrent - 437-1826
Hertz - 415-8239

Car rental city office
Avis - 433-2233
Europcar Interrent - 411-4860
Hertz - 404-6088

Hotels:
Best Western Pax Hotel, Schiekade 658, 466-3344
Best Western Rotterdam Airport Hotel, Vliegveldweg 59-61, 462-5566
Bilderberg Parkhotel Westersingel 70, 436-3611
Central Hotel, Kruiskade 12, 414-0744
Holiday Inn Rotterdam City Center, Schouwburgplein 1, 433-3800
Rotterdam Hilton, Weena 10, 414-4044
Scandia Rainbow Hotel, Willemsplein 1, 413-4790

Restaurants:
Brasserie La Vilette, Westblaak 160, 414-8692
De Pijp, Gaffelstraat 90, 436-6896
Le Coq d'Or, Van Vollenhovenstraat 25, 436-6405
Restaurant Engels, Stationsplein 45, 411-9551
The Old Dutch, Rochussenstraat 20, 436-0344

Entertainment:
Holland Casino Rotterdam, Weena 10, 414-7799

Places of Interest:
The Prins Hendrik Maritime Museum
The Boymans-van Beuningen Museum
Het Nederlands Architectuurinstituut
Euromast and Space Tower

NORWAY

Official Name: The Kingdom of Norway

Location: Scandinavia, Northern Europe. Norway is bordered by the CIS, Finland and Sweden. To the north lies the Arctic Ocean. The south coast is separated from Denmark by the Skagerrat.

Government: Constitutional Monarchy

Area: 323,877 sq. km., 125,050 sq. miles

Population: 4.28 million

Religion(s): Lutheran majority. There are also many other Christian denominations.

Capital City: Oslo

Major Business Cities: Bergen, Stavanger and Trondheim

Time: GMT +1 (GMT +2 late March to late October)

Currency: Norwegian Krone (NOK)=100 ore

Currency Requirements: The import and the export of foreign currency is unlimited and must be declared. The import and export of local currency is limited to NOK25,000. There are no restrictions on Travelers Checks.

Business Hours:
- Government: 09.00-16.00 Mon-Fri
- Banks: 08.30-15.30 Mon-Fri (Thu until 17.00)
- Shops: 09.00-16.00/17.00 Mon-Fri
- Offices: 09.00-16.00 Mon-Fri

Weight and Measures: Metric System

NORWAY

Electric Current: 220 volts AC. Plugs are of the round 2-pin type.

Holidays:
New Year's Day - January 1
Maundy Thursday - March 27
Good Friday - April 10*
Easter Monday - April 13*
May Day - May 1
Ascension Day - May 21*
National Day - May 17
Whit Sunday - May 18
Whit Monday - June 1*
Christmas Day - December 25
Boxing Day - December 26

*Christian Holidays - vary each year

Suitable Clothing: Bring conservative business clothing, and semi-formal wear for evenings out. In the summer, medium weight clothing is suitable, and raingear is important year round. Between November and April, bring winter clothing and a warm coat.

Automobile Driving License: A Full Driving License can be used if it is held for at least one year.

Customs Allowances. Personal items are duty free, but register all valuables upon arrival. Non-E.U. members face more restrictions on tobacco and alcohol: 400 cigarettes, 1 liter of wine and 1 of spirits. Weaponry, drugs and certain agricultural products are prohibited.

Tipping: A service charge is usually included in the hotel and restaurant bills, but an additional 5% tip commonly left. It is not customary to tip taxi drivers. Porters at airport and railway stations charge per piece of luggage. Hotel porters are tipped NOK5-10.

Credit Cards Accepted: Access(Master Card), American Express, Diner's Club, Eurocard, Visa

NORWAY

Customary Dining Hours:
Breakfast: 07.30-09.00
Lunch: 11.30-13.00
Dinner: 18.00-22.00

Local Customs, Business Protocol and Courtesies: Doing business in Norway is a mix of tough talk and friendly social activity. It requires a certain level of formality and reserve, but Norwegians are also very hospitable and enjoy lots of entertainment. Schedule appointments in advance; lateness will not be tolerated. Maintain a cool but sincere professional demeanor, as heartiness and a stock "how are you" will be taken as overly familiar or false. Once rapport is established, business meetings will include casual conversation, but remember that despite the friendlier tone, negotiators here are tough and shrewd. Your presentations should be fact-oriented and well laid out.

Business and meals do not generally mix; business breakfasts are unusual, and lunch and dinner conversation is friendly and casual. If visiting someone's home, be on time, bring a small, tasteful gift or send flowers in advance that morning, or the next day as a thank-you gesture. Remember that as in most European countries, there are certain taboos on the nature of the bouquet · never bring red roses or white bouquets or even numbers of flowers. In Norway, do not bring carnations, either. Regarding gifts, it is okay to give your colleague something upon the close of a successful deal · a company item, or any other small, impersonal gift like a book or fine wine.

Health: There are Reciprocal Health Agreements with most of the European countries. The receipts should be presented at the social insurance office (Trygdekasse) of the district where treatment was carried out before leaving Norway. The refund may vary depending on the country of origin. Medical insurance is advised.

Language: Norwegian.

NORWAY

OSLO

Country code: 47 - City code: none

Airport: Fornebu International Airport.

Distance from City: 8km (4 miles) southwest of the city.

Transportation to Center of City:
From International and Domestic Terminals
By Bus (cost) NOK35. Time approx.20 min.(every 10 min.)
By Taxi (cost) NOK100-110. Time approx. 10 min.
Tip luggage porters NOK10 per piece

Transfers: (Minimum Connecting Time):
International to International: 30 min.
International to Domestic: 45 min.
Domestic to International: 45 min.
Domestic to Domestic: 30 min.

Automobile Rentals:
Airport car rental desk.
Avis -67530557
Europcar Interrent - 67532340
Hertz - 67583100

Car rental city office.
Avis - 22835800
Europcar Interrent - 22607440
Hertz - 02656610

Hotels:
Ambassadeur Best Hotels, Camilla Colletts Vei 15, 22441835
Bondeheimen Hotel, Rosenkrantzgt. 8, 22429530
Comfort Hotel Majorstuen, Bogstadveien 64, 22695100
Continental Hotel, Stortingsgaten 24-26, 22824000
Grand Hotel, Karl Jahansgate 31, Sentrum, 22429390
Inter Nor Savoy Hotel, Universitetsgt.11, 22202655
Karl Johan Hotel, Karl Johansgt. 33, 22427480
Radisson SAS Plaza Hotel Oslo, Sonja Hanies Plass 3,
    22171000

NORWAY

Radisson SAS Scandinavia Hotel Oslo, Holbergsgt. 30, 22113000
Rica Triangel Hotel, Holbergs Plass 1, 22208855
West Hotel, Skovveien 15, 22554030

Restaurants:
Ambassadeur, Camilla Collets vei 15, 44-18-35
Babette's Gjestehus, Roald Amundsensgt. 6, 41-64-64
Bagatelle, Bygdoy Alle 3/5, 44-63-97
D'Artagnan, Ovre Slottsgt. 16, 41-50-62
De Fem Stuer, Kongevn. 26, 14-60-90
Det Gamle Raadhus, Nedre Slottsgt. 1, 42-01-07
Dinner, Arbeidergt. 2, 42-68-90
Dionysos Taverna, Calmeyersgt. 11, 60-78-64
Feinschmecker, Balchensgt. 5, 44-17-77
Frognerseteren, Voksenkollen, 14-37-36
Hos Thea, Gabelsgt. 11, 44-68-74
Kaffistova, Rosenkrantz' GT. 8, 42-95-30
Kastanjen, Bygdoy Alle 18, 43-44-67
La Canard, Oscars GT. 81, 43-40-28
Lofotstua, Kirkevn. 40, 46-93-96
Shalimar, Konghellegt. 5, 37-47-68
Theatercaffen, Stortingsgt. 24-26, 33-32-00

Entertainment:
Barbeint, Drammensv. 20, 44-59-74
Churchill Wine Bar, Fr. Nansens Pl. 6, 33-53-43
Fridtjof's, Fr. Nansens Pl. 7, 33-44-88
Gamle Christianania, Grensen 1, 42-74-93
Grotten, Wergalandsvn. 5, 20-96-04
Kristiania, Kristian IV's GT. 12, 42-56-60
Larry, Parkvn. 12, 69-69-04
Oslo Jazzhus, Stockholmsgt. 12, 38-59-63
Oslo Mikrobryggery, Bogstadvn. 6, 56-97-76
Sky Bar, Sonia Henies Pl. 3, 17-10-00
Smuget, Rosenkrantz' GT. 22, 42-52-62
Snorre-Kompagniet, Rosenkrantz' GT. 11, 33-52-60
Stortorvets Gjaestgiveri, Grensen 1, 42-88-63
Studenten Bryggery, Karl Johans Gt. 45, 42-56-80

Shops and Stores:
Cristiania GlasMagasin, Storvet 9   Dept. Store

NORWAY

David-Andersen, Karl Johans Gt. 20	Jewelry
ExpoArte, Drammensvn. 40	Jewelry
Heyerahl, Stortingsgt. 18	Jewelry
Maurtua, Fr. Nansens Pl. 9	Apparel
Oslo Sweater Shop, Tullinsgt. 5	Apparel
Rein og Rose, Ruselokkvn. 3	Apparel
Siril, Rosenkrantz' GT. 23	Apparel
Steen & Strom, Kongens Gt. 23	Dept. Store
William Scmidt, Karl Johans Gt. 41	Apparel

Places of Interest:
The Museum to the Norwegian Resistance Movement
Vigeland Sculpture Park
The Royal Palace
Viking Ship House - a museum
Kon-Tiki Museum
Ski Museum and Jump Tower
Akershus Castle and Fortress

POLAND

Official Name: The Republic of Poland

Location: Central Europe. Poland is bordered by the Russian Federation, Belarus, Ukraine, Lithuania, the Czech Republic, the Slovak Republic and Germany. To the north lies the Baltic Sea.

Government: Republic

Area: 304,465 sq. km., 117,554 sq. miles.

Population: 38.5 million

Religion(s): Roman Catholic majority.

Capital City: Warsaw

Major Business Cities: Krakow

Time: GMT +1 (GMT +2 from late March to late October)

Currency: Zloty (PLZ)=100 groszy

Currency Requirements: The import of foreign currency is unlimited and must be declared. The export is limited to the amount declared on arrival. The import and export of local currency is prohibited.

Business Hours:
- Government: 08.30-16.00 Mon-Fri
- Banks: 08.00-14.00 Mon-Fri
- Shops: 09.00 or 11.00-19.00 Mon-Fri
- Offices: 08.00-16.00 Mon-Fri

Weight and Measures: Metric System

Electric Current: 220 volts AC. Plugs are continental 2-pin type.

Holidays:
New Year's Day - January 1
Easter Monday - April 13*
Labor Day - May 1
Polish National Day - May 3
Corpus Christi - June 11*
Assumption - August 15
All Saints' Day - November 1
Independence Day - November 11
Christmas - December 25
Boxing Day - December 26*

* Christian Holidays - vary each year.
Holidays falling at the weekend are NOT granted a day in lieu to be celebrated the following Monday.

Suitable Clothing: Conservative business clothing should be worn to all meetings. In the summer, light to medium weight clothing is suitable. Between November and April, bring winter clothing and a warm coat.

Automobile Driving License: An International Driving Permit is recommended but not legally required.

Customs Allowances: As currency and customs requirements have undergone a number of changes in recent years, one should consult your country's Polish embassy or consulate when arranging your trip. Personal items are duty free, but register valuables upon arrival or they may be confiscated upon departure. Although you may bring in unlimited amounts of foreign currency, and take out any you initially declare, you may not import or export Zlotys. You may bring in 250 cigarettes, .75 liter of wine, one of spirits and a .25 liter of vodka. Military weaponry, narcotics and pornography are prohibited.

Tipping: Most restaurant bills include a service charge. If the service is not included it is customary to leave a 10% tip.

Credit Cards Accepted: Access, American Express, Diner's Club, Eurocard, Visa

POLAND

Customary Dining Hours:
Breakfast: 07.00-09.30
Lunch: 12.00-14.30
Dinner: 18.00-24.00

Local Customs, Business Protocol and Courtesies: Poland's large market has made it a popular place to do business, though one must have patience in dealing with this new market economy and its slow, bureaucratic holdovers from the past. Polish businessmen tend to be genuinely helpful and cordial, if not fully experienced with foreign trade. Set up and formerly tightly controlled under the communist regime, the country's trade organizational infrastructure is now free to help acquaint foreign businesspersons with the local climate and help you establish more individual business relationships. It will take much patience and a number of visits to fine tune your way to a successful business contract (particularly regarding credit terms and pricing). Make your presentations thoroughly professional and competitive, and expect shrewd bargaining skills from your Polish counterparts.

Sometimes business and other topics are discussed over a friendly, late-afternoon lunch; do not refuse an invitation. Your Polish colleagues will want to hear your opinions, but be careful regarding sensitive subjects like politics and religion. Like in neighboring Austria and the Czech and Slovak Republics, Polish businessmen rarely entertain at home, but if invited, bring a small, tasteful gift, fine wine or liqueur, or flowers. Don't forget the traditional European taboos against red or white bouquets, even numbers of flowers, or certain funereal species. Gifts for the children are viewed favorably; business gifts (given at the close of a deal and at Christmas) with a company logo are not. At a meal, if your host offers a toast, you should offer one in return, with compliments then and later on the meal or home.

Health: It is advisable to consult your doctor before your journey. There are Reciprocal Health Agreements with most EU countries for hospital and medical treatment. No vaccinations are necessary. It is advisable to drink bottled water. Medical insurance recommended.

POLAND

Language: Polish.

WARSAW

Country code: 48 - City code: 22

Airport: Okecie International Airport

Distance from City: 10km (6 miles) southwest of the city.

Transportation to Center of City:
From International and Domestic Terminals
By Bus (cost) PLZ4. Time approx. 30 min. (every 20 min.)
By Taxi (cost) PLZ17-18. Time approx. 15 min.
Tip luggage porters PLZ10 per piece

Transfers: (Minimum Connecting Time):
International to International: 75 min.
International to Domestic: 90 min.
Domestic to International: 90 min.
Domestic to Domestic: 50 min.

Automobile Rentals:
Airport car rental desk
Avis - 650-4872
Europcar Interrent - 650-4454
Hertz - 650-2896

Car rental city office
Avis - 630-7316
Europcar Interrent - 226-3344
Hertz - 621-1360

Hotels:
Bristol Hotel Warsaw, 42-44 Krakowskie Przediscie, 121061
Forum Hotel Warsaw, Nowogrodzka 24-26 St., 621-0271
Holiday Inn Warsaw, 48-54 Zlota St., 620-0341
Mercure Fryderyk Chopin Hotel, Al Jana Pawla II, 22, 620-0201
Orbis Europejski Hotel, Krakowskie Przedmiscie 13, 265051
Orbis Grand Hotel, Ul. Krucza 28, 629-4051

POLAND

Sheraton Warsaw Hotel and Towers, ul. B. Prusa 2, 657-6100Victoria Inter-Continental Warsaw, 11 Krolewska St., 657-8011
Warsaw Marriott Hotel, Al. Jerozolimskie 65/79, 630-6306

Restaurants:
Ambassador, ul.Ujazdowskie 8, 259961
Balzac, ul. Jana Pawla 11, 200201
Bazyliszek, Rynek Starego Miasta, 311841
Belvedere, in Lazienki Park, 414806
Cristal Budapeszt, ul.Marszalkowska 21, 253533
Dong Nam, ul.Marszalkowska 45\49, 213234
El Popo, ul.Senatorska 27, 272340
Foksal, ul.Foksal 3\5, 277225
Fukier, Rynek Starego Miasta 27, 311013
Gessler, ul.Senatorska 37, 270633
Hoang Kim, ul.Freta 18
Maharajah-Thai, ul.Szeroki Dunaj 13, 635-2501
Mekong, ul.Wspolna 35, 211881
Montmartre, Nowy Swiat 7, 628-6315
Parnas, ul.Krakowskie Przedmiescie 4\6, 26 00 71
Rycerska, ul.Szeroki Dunaj 9\11, 313688
Tokio, ul.Dobra 17,
Tsumbame, ul.Folksal 16, 265127
Valencia, ul.Smocza 27, 383217

Entertainment:
Akwarium, ul.Emilii Plater 49, 205072
Alcatraz, pl.Bankowy 1,
Europa Voltaire, ul.Szkolna 2\4,
Fiolka, ul.Pulawska 257, 439822
Fugazi, ul.Leszno 5,
Giovanni, ul.Krakowskie Przedmiescie 26\28
Graund Zero, ul.Wspolna 62, 625-5280
Hybrydy, ul.Zlota 7\9, 273763
Irish Pub, ul.Miodowa 3.
Park, ul.Niepodleglosci 196, 257199
Remont, ul.Warynskiego 12, 257497
Stodola, ul.Batorego 10, 256031
Van Beethoven, ul.Krakowska 17, 460994

Shops and Stores:
Arex Spolcazoo, ul. Chopina 5B   Apparel

POLAND

Moda Polska, ul. Switokrzyska	Dept. Store
Polski Len, ul. Targowa	Apparel
Trzech Krzyzy, al. Ujazdowskie	Dept. Store

Places of Interest:
Zamek Krolewski - a castle with a museum
Lazienki Park - palaces and pavilions
Wilanow Palace
Zelazowa Wola - a museum
Cathedral of St. John
Historical Museum of Warsaw
The Tomb of the Unknown Soldier
The National Museum

PORTUGAL

Official Name: The Portuguese Republic

Location: Western Europe. Portugal is situated on the Iberian Peninsula. It is bordered by Spain to the north and east and the Atlantic Ocean to the west and south.

Government: Republic

Area: 92,389 sq. km., 35,672 sq. miles.

Population: 11 million

Religion(s): Roman Catholic and Protestant.

Capital City: Lisbon

Major Business Cities: Faro and Oporto.

Time: GMT +1 (GMT +2 from late March to late October)

Currency: Escudo (ESC)=100 centavos

Currency Requirements: The import of local or foreign currency is unlimited and must be declared. The export of local currency is limited to ESC100,000. The export of foreign currency is limited to the equivalent of ESC1,000,000. The amount may be exceeded on presentation of a proof that the same amount or more was imported.

Business Hours:
- Government: 09.00-18.00 Mon-Fri
- Banks: 08.30-15.00 Mon-Fri, 09.30-11.30 Sat
- Shops: 09.00-13.00 and 15.00-19.00 Mon-Fri; 09.00-13.00 Sat
- Offices: 9.00-12.30 and 14.00-17.00/18.00 Mon-Fri

Weight and Measures: Metric System

Electric Current: 220 volts AC. Plugs are of the continental 2-pin type.

Holidays:
New Year's Day - January 1
Carnival - February 11
Good Friday - April 10*
Liberty Day - April 25
Labor Day - May 1
Corpus Christi - June 11*
Camoes Day - June 10
St. Antony - June 13
Assumption - August 15
Republic Day - October 5
All Saints' Day - November 1
Restoration Day - December 1
Immaculate Conception - December 8
Christmas Day - December 25

* Christian Holiday - vary each year

Suitable Clothing: Wear a conservative business suit to all meetings. In summer, bring light materials, in winter, medium-weight and a light coat and rainwear. Bring shoes that can navigate Lisbon's cobblestoned streets.

Automobile Driving License: A National or an International Driving License can be used.

Customs Allowances: Personal items are duty free, but register all valuables upon arrival and keep receipts or you may face bureaucratic entanglements or even confiscation later. There are no import limits on foreign currency, and you may take out any amounts previously declared. There is a 50,000 import or export cap on Escudo. Tobacco and alcohol restrictions: 250 cigarettes, two liters of wine and one of spirits.

Tipping: Tipping is optional but is generally not over 10%. Tipping for taxi drivers is discretionary.

Credit Cards Accepted: Access (Master Card), American Express, Diner's Club, Eurocard, Visa

PORTUGAL

Customary Dining Hours:
Breakfast: 07.30-08.30
Lunch: 12.00-14.00
Dinner: 19.30-22.00

Local Customs, Business Protocol and Courtesies: Business in Portugal is often done in a conservative, old world manner, in coffee houses, with a dignified absence of pressure, and careful decision making. Portuguese businessmen initiate discussions in a friendly, casual manner, and also are very serious about their work. In advance of your visit to Portugal, you should send a formal letter requesting a meeting in any business or governmental capacity. Be on time, even though your contact may not be. Upon introduction or at the close of an initial meeting (take your cue from your counterpart), exchange business cards, and use the titles on them unless indicated otherwise. It generally helps to promote your ideas separately (and subtly) with your various contacts before going into a presentation. Your presentations and verbal communication should be detailed and concise, particularly regarding prices and delivery dates. Do not refuse lunch or coffee invitations, as much business is conducted in these settings. Be prepared with business gifts, such as a quality office accessory, book or art object, to be given after a contract has been agreed upon, and at Christmas.

If visiting someone's home, bring a small, tasteful gift or send flowers in advance that morning, or the next day as a thank-you gesture. Remember that as in most European countries, there are certain taboos on the nature of the bouquet; never bring red roses or white bouquets, even numbers of flowers, and avoid funereal varieties like chrysanthemums. If your host or hostess gives a toast in your honor, be sure to give a brief thank-you return. Guests are served first. As fish is a staple in Portuguese cuisine, it comes with its own fork and knife. If you want seconds, place your knife straight on your plate and your fork diagonal from left, and when finished, leave a little food on your plate and place your utensils together on the plate at a diagonal.

PORTUGAL

Health: It is advisable to consult your doctor before your journey. A vaccination certificate for yellow fever is required if you are coming from an infected area. A Reciprocal Health Agreement exists with all other EU countries which covers in-patient treatment, X-rays and dental. The medicines must be paid by the patient. A Vaccination for tetanus is recommended.

Language: Portuguese.

LISBON

Country code: 351 - City code: 1

Airport: Portela de Sacavem

Distance from City: 7km (4 miles) north of the city.

Transportation to Center of City:
From International and Domestic Terminals
By Bus (cost) ESC400. Time approx. 30 min. (every 15 min)
By Taxi (cost) ESC1000. Time approx. 20 min.
Tip luggage porters ESC100 per piece

Transfers: (Minimum Connecting Time):
International to International: 60 min.
International to Domestic: 60 min.
Domestic to International: 60 min.
Domestic to Domestic: 45 min.

Automobile Rentals:
Airport car rental desk
Avis - 849-9947
Europcar Interrent - 801176
Hertz - 849-2722

Car rental city office
Avis - 356-1176
Europcar Interrent - 353-5115
Hertz - 579027

PORTUGAL

Hotels:
AS Janelas Verdes Inn, Rua das Janelas Verdes 47, 396-8143
Alfa Hotel Lisboa, Av. Columbano Bordalo, 726-2121
Britania Hotel, Rua Rodrigues Sampaio 17, 315-5016
Capitol Hotel, Rua Eca de Queroz 24, 353-6811
Eduardo VII - Best Western, Av. Fontes Pereira de Melo 5, 353-0141
Fenix Hotel, Praca Marques de Pombal 8, 386-2121
Florida Hotel, Rua Duque Palmela 32, 357-6145
Golden Tulip Hotel Altis, Rua Castilho 11, 314-2496
Lisboa Hotel, Rua Barata Salgueiro 5, 355-4131
Mundial Hotel, Rua Dom Duarte 4, 886-3101
Quality Hotel, Campo Grande 7, 795-7555
Rex Hotel, Rua Castilho 169, 388-2161
Sofitel Lisboa, Av. Da Liberdade 123-125, 342-9202
Sol Palmeiras, Av. Marginal, Paco de Acros, 441-6621

Restaurants:
Adega da Tia Matilda, Rua de Beneficencia 77, 772 172
Antigua Casa Faz Frio, Rua Dom Pedro V 96, 361 860
Avis, Rua Serpa Pinto,12B, 328 392
Bachus, Largo da Trinidade 9, 321 260
Baralto Bomjardin, Travessa de Santo Antao 11, 342 4389
Bota Alta, Travessa da Queimada 35, 327 959
Casa da Comida, Travessa Das Amoreiras, 685 376
Casa de Lerao, Castelo Sao Jorge, 875 962
Comida de Santo, Calcadas Eng Miguel Pais 39, 396 3339
Gambrinus, Rua Das Portas de Santo Antao 25, 342 1466
Gare Martima Michel, Alcantara, 676 335
Martinho do Arcada, Praco do Comercio, 879 239
Mercado de Santa Clara, Campo do Santa Clara, 873 986
Michel, Largo de Santa Cruz do Castelo 5, 864 338
Pabe, Rua Duque de Palmela 27A, 535 675
Pap'Acorda, Rua da Atalaia 57, 346 4811
Porta Branca, Rua Teixera 35, 321 024
Sua Excelencia, Rua do Code 42, 603 614
Taveres Rico, Rua da Misericordia 37, 321 112
Xele Bananas, Praca das Flores 29, 670 515

Entertainment:
Adega Machado,Rua do Norte 91, 360 995
Alcantara Cafe, Rua da Cozinha Economica, 363 6432

PORTUGAL

Alcantara Mar, Rua da Cozinha Economica, 363 6432
Bipi-Bipi, Rua Oliviera Martin 6, 778 924
Fragil, Rua da Atalia 128, 346 9578
Gafiera, Calcade de Tijolo, 325 953
Hot Clube de Portugal, Praca de Alegria 39, 367 369
Lisboa a Noite, Rua das Gaveas 69, 346 2603
Lontra, Rua San Bento 157, 661 083
Loucurus, Avenida Alvares Cabral 37, 681 117
Mascote de Atalia, Rua da Atalia
Mata Bicho, Rua do Gremio Lusitano 18, 346 8868
Perreirinha de Alfama, Beco do Espirito Santo 1, 868 209
Plateau, Rua das Janelas Verdes, 665 116
Ritz Club, Rua da Gloria 57, 352 4140
Senhor Vinho, Rua Meio a Lapa 1, 672 681
Severa,Rua das Gaveas 51, 328 314
Xafarix, Don Carlos 1, 396 9487

Shops and Stores:

Amoreiras, Avenida Eng. Duarte Pacheco	Shopping Center
Ana Salazar, Rua do Carmo 16e,	Apparel
Centro Colombo, Ave. Lusiada Letras	Shopping Center
Eloy de Jesus, Rua Garrett 45,	Jewelry
Manuel Henriques de Cervalho, Escola Polytechnica 97, Antiques	
Libersil, Ave. da Liberdade 38	Shopping Center
Loja das Meias, Rossio 1,	Apparel
Rosa & Teixeira	Apparel

Places of Interest:
Castelo de Sao Jorge - St. George's Castle
Solar do Vinho do Porto
Gulbenkian Museum
Belem

ROMANIA

Official Name: Romania

Location: South East Europe. Romania is bordered by Moldova, Ukraine, Yugoslavia, Hungary and Bulgaria. To the east lies the Black Sea.

Government: Republic

Area: 237,500 sq. km., 91,700 sq. miles.

Population: 22.76 million

Religion(s): Romanian Orthodox and Roman Catholic.

Capital City: Bucharest

Time: GMT +2 (GMT +3 from late March to late October)

Currency: Leu (plural Lei.)=100 bani

Currency Requirements: There are no restrictions on the import of foreign currency, but it has to be declared. Visitors may export foreign currency up to the declared amount on arrival. The import and the export of local currency are prohibited.

Business Hours:
- Government: 08.00-16.00 Mon-Fri, 08.00-12.30 Sat
- Banks: 09.00-16.00 Mon-Thur; 09.00-13.00 Fri
- Shops: 10.00-18.00 Mon-Fri
- Offices: 08.00-16.00 Mon-Fri

Weight and Measures: Metric System

Electric Current: 220 volts AC. Plugs are of the continental 2-pin type.

Holidays:
New Year - January 1
Orthodox Easter - April 27
Labor Day - May 1
National Day - December 1
Christmas - December 25

Suitable Clothing: Bring heavy clothing and a coat for winter, and medium-to-light clothing and an umbrella the rest of the year. Wear a conservative suit in almost all business situations.

Automobile Driving License: A National or an international Driving License can be used if it is held for at least one year.

Customs Allowances: In recent years, visitors had to exchange a minimum amount of hard currency per day, but these rules have been easing up, so check with your country's Romanian embassy or consulate when arranging your trip. Personal items are duty free, but register valuables upon arrival or they may be confiscated upon departure. Although you may bring in unlimited amounts of foreign currency, and take out any you initially declare, you may not import or export Lei. You may bring in 200 cigarettes, 4 liters of wine and 2 of spirits.

Tipping: A service charge of 12% is added to most restaurant bills. Porters, chamber maids and taxi drivers expect a 10% tip.

Credit Cards Accepted: American Express, Eurocard, Visa

Customary Dining Hours:
Breakfast: 07.00-09.00
Lunch: 12.00-15.00
Dinner: 19.00-22.00

Local Customs, Business Protocol and Courtesies: Western business practices in Romania are still in a fledgling state, and the visiting businessman may encounter many delays and poor quality-products. Nevertheless, the business environment is steadily improving, and Romanians take great pride in the progress they've made in the past several years. Meetings can be lengthy and numerous, but they are a good way for you to find out as much as possible about your potential partners' operations as for them to learn, from you, about what may be unfamiliar Western ones. It will take much patience to fine tune and bargain your way to a successful business contract (particularly regarding credit terms), but despite the chaos you may encounter, professionalism is highly appreciated. Schedule appointments in advance, and be punctual even if your contact isn't. Use titles with your contact's last name. Keep your presentations detailed and precise. Presentations should be factual and highly organized, which may speed up those lengthy negotiations, and keep competition in mind. No agreement is valid until signed. Your Romanian colleagues will warn you often of theft, and for good reason. Though violent crime against Westerners is rare, a well-dressed foreigner's hotel room and back pocket is frequently the target of thieves. Hold on to room keys at all times, and hold on tight to your wallet or purse.

You should reciprocate for invitations you will receive to visit homes, with flowers, fine wine or liqueur or small, tasteful item from your country. Discussions are open and animated, toasts and compliments flow freely after the many shots of plum brandy you will be inevitably offered. With the demise of one of the most repressive regimes in the world, most Romanians are very hospitable and eager to talk, and hear your opinion, on all sorts of subjects.

Health: It is advisable to consult your doctor before your journey. There is a Reciprocal Health Agreement with some EU Countries. Vaccinations for cholera, tphoid, tetanus and polio are recommended. Hepatitis A and hepatitis B vaccinations are also recommended in some instances. It is advisable to drink bottled water.

Language: Romanian.

BUCHAREST

Country code: 40 - City code: 1

Airport: Otopeni International Airport.

ROMANIA

Distance from City: 17km (10 miles) north of the city.

Transportation to Center of City:
From International and Domestic Terminals
By Bus (cost) LEI600. Time approx. 30 min. (every 15 min.)
By Taxi (cost) LEI700. Time approx. 20 min.
Tip luggage porters LEI5 per piece

Transfers: (Minimum Connecting Time):
International to International: 45 min.
International to Domestic: 45 min.
Domestic to International: 45 min.
Domestic to Domestic: 30 min

Automobile Rentals:
Airport car rental desk
Avis - 212-0011
Europcar Interrent -312-7078
Hertz - 212-0040

Car rental city office
Avis - 223-2080
Europcar Interrent - 614-4058
Hertz - 611-4365

Hotels:
Inter-Continental Bucharest, 4 Blvd. Nicolae Balcescu, 210-7330

Places of Interest:
The Royal Palace
The Museum of Music
The Doamnei Church
The National History Museum
The House of the People
Antim Monastery
The Bucharest History Museum
The Botanical Gardens

RUSSIA

Official Name: Russian Federation

Location: Eastern Europe/Asia. The Russian Federation is bordered by Mongolia, China, Korea, Afghanistan and Iraq to the south. The Arctic Ocean lies to the north and the Black Sea in the south. The Bering Strait lies to the west.

Government: Democratic-Federative Republic

Area: 17,075,400 sq. km., 6,592,850 sq. miles.

Population: 148.6 million

Religion(s): Russian Orthodox majority.

Capital City: Moscow

Major Business Cities: St. Petersburg

Time: GMT +2/+10 (GMT +3/+13 from late March to late October)

Currency: Ruble (Rub)=100 kopeks

Currency Requirements: The import of foreign currency is unlimited but must be declared on arrival. The export is limited to the amount declared on arrival. The import and export of local currency is prohibited. The local currency that is not spent must be reconverted on departure.

Business Hours:
- Government: 09.00-18.00 Mon-Fri
- Banks: 09.00/10.00-18.00/19.00 Mon-Fri
- Shops: 09.00/10.00-18.00/19.00 Mon-Sat
- Offices: 09.00/10.00-18.00/19.00 Mon-Fri

Weight and Measures: Metric System

RUSSIA

Electric Current: 220 volts AC. Plugs are of the Continental 2-pin round type.

Holidays:
New Year's Day - January 1
Russian Orthodox Christmas - January 7
International Women's Day - March 8
Russian Orthodox Easter - April 27*
Spring and Labor Day - May 1-2
Victory in Europe Day - May 9
Russian Independence Day - May 12
October Revolution Day - November 7
Constitution Day - December 12

* Christian Holidays - vary each year

Suitable Clothing: Bring very heavy clothing and a coat for winter, and medium clothing and rainwear for the rest of the year. Wear a conservative business suit in most situations.

Automobile Driving License: An International or a National Driving License with an authorized translation is required.

Customs Allowances: As currency and customs requirements have undergone a number of changes in recent years, one should consult your country's Russian embassy or consulate when arranging your trip. Personal items are duty free, but register valuables upon arrival or they will likely be confiscated upon departure. Although you may bring in unlimited amounts of foreign currency, and take out any you initially declare, you may not import or export Rubles. You may bring in 250 cigarettes, 1 liter of wine, and a half-liter of spirits. Military weaponry, narcotics and pornography are prohibited.

Tipping: A service charge of 10-15% is usually included in the bills of most hotels. If not, it is customary to leave a 10% tip.

Credit Cards Accepted: American Express, Carte Blanche, Diner's Card, EuroCard, Visa

Customary Dining Hours:
Breakfast: 07.00-09.00

RUSSIA

Lunch: 12.00-14.30
Dinner: 18.30-22.00

Local Customs, Business Protocol and Courtesies: Patience, careful investigation and a long-term view rather than immediate profit, are key to conducting business successfully in Russia, not to mention wading through chaos of its bureaucracy and transportation. Be prepared for frequent snags and last-minute postponements or cancellations. Russian businessmen behave much more reservedly and formally with foreign counterparts than with their countrymen, and are usually helpful and cordial. Despite the surrounding chaos, they are usually quite professional and well-prepared for meetings. Schedule all business and government appointments in advance. The Ministry of Foreign Trade can be helpful in establishing initial contact with individual companies and their officials. The proper use of titles is essential, and can usually be gleaned from the exchange of business cards with everyone present at the beginning of a meeting. When in doubt, address the person as Gospodin or Gospozha (Mr. or Mrs., respectively.) with his or her last name. Although shaking hands is customary, visiting businesswomen should refrain from this unless a hand is offered. You should also be ready to provide an interpreter when necessary, but do not appear to be speaking to the interpreter rather than the person you are actually holding discussions with. Any knowledge of Russian on your part, or company materials and business cards with Russian, will make a good impression. Decision making often gets bogged down in committees, and it will take much patience and a number of visits to fine tune your way to a successful business contract (particularly regarding credit terms and pricing). Presentations should be factual and highly organized, with knowledge of the competition. Expect shrewd bargaining skills from your Russian counterparts. No agreement is valid until signed.

Russia's highly entrepreneurial society includes much organized crime and many poor credit risks, so it is essential that you investigate your potential partners and their businesses very thoroughly. Your Russian contemporary, too, should expect you to build trust. In this hospitable coun-

RUSSIA

try, you will be offered plenty of opportunity to socialize and be entertained, as well as talk business. These discussion frequently take place in restaurants, over lunch or dinner.

Do not turn down an invitation to dine at home with a family. In this case, be on time and bring flowers (odd numbers only, and not dominated by red or white) chocolates, a nice book or small, inexpensive but tasteful item from your country. The latter is appropriate for business gifts as well, which are given frequently at meetings. Quality items with your company's logo are also acceptable. As in a number of Slavic countries, shoes are removed in the house; you will be given guest slippers at the door. Your host will offer a toast before and/or during the meal, and you should respond with your own immediately. When finished, leave a small amount and place your fork and knife together at a horizontal across the plate. Second helpings will be offered, but remember that shortages are common and do not take too much, or leave over large amounts of food.

Health: It is advisable to consult your doctor before your journey. If intending to stay more than three months, it is necessary to have a certificate confirming that you are HIV negative. It is highly recommended to boil all the drinking water or to use only bottled water. Emergency treatment is free, but longer treatments have to be paid. A health insurance is recommended.

Language: Russian.

MOSCOW

Country code: 7 - City code: 095

Airport: Moscow-Sheremetyevo International Airport

Distance from City: 29km (18 miles) northwest of the city.

RUSSIA

Transportation to Center of City:
From International and Domestic Terminals
By Bus (cost) Rub500. Time approx. 1 hour
By Taxi (cost) USD25-35. Time approx. 40-60 min.
Tip luggage porters 50 kopeks   per piece

Transfers: (Minimum Connecting Time):
International to International: 60 min.
International to Domestic: 150 min.
Domestic to International: 150 min.
Domestic to Domestic: 60 min.

Automobile Rentals:
Airport car rental desk
Avis - 578-5646
Europcar Interrent - 578-3878
Hertz - 578-7532

Car rental city office
Avis - 240-9932
Europcar Interrent - 488-8000
Hertz - 284-4391

Hotels:
Kempinski Hotel Baltschug Moskau, ul. Baltschug 1, 230-9500
Marco Polo Presnja Hotel Moscow, Spiridonjevskij 9, 220-0120
Metropol Hotel Moscow, 1/4 Teatralny Proezd, 927-6000
National Hotel, 14/1 Okhotny Ryad, 258-7000
Palace Hotel, 1 Tverskaja-Yamskaja Str. 19, 956-3152
Renaissance Moscow Hotel, Olympijskij Prospect 18/1,
    223-9000
Tverskaya Hotel, 31 1st Tverskaya-Yamskaya, 258-3000
Aerostar, Leningradsky Prospekt 37, 1555030
Bauschug Kempinski, Ulitsa Bauschug 1, 2309500
Belgrade, Smolenskaya Ploshchad 5, 2481643
Budapest, Petovskye Linii 2/18, 2948820
Cosmos, Prospekt Mira 150, 2170785
Intourist, Tverskaya Ulitsa 3/5, 2031565
Leningradskaya, Kalenchovskaya Ulitsa 21/40, 9753032
Minsk, Tverskaya Ulitsa 22, 2991300
Moscow Palace Hotel, Tverskaya Yamskaya Ulitsa 19, 9563152
Moskva, Okhotny Ryad 7, 2911000
Russya, Ulitsa Varvarka 6, 2985400

Restaurants:
Arlecchino , Ulitsa Drushynovskaya 15 , 2057088
Arkadia Jass Club, Teatralny Proyesd 3
Glazour, Smolensky Bulvar 12, 2484438
Imperial, Ryleyeva Ulitsa 9, 2916063
Kropotkinskaya 36, Ulitsa Prechistenka 36, 2017500
Potel & Chabot, Bolshaya Kommunisticheskaya 2A, 2710707
Swiss Chalet, Korobeynikov Pereulok ½, 2020106
Writers' Union, Ulitsa Vorovskogo 52, 2912169
Aragvi, Ulitsa Tverskaya 6, 2293762
Arbat, Ulitsa Novy Arbat 29, 2911445
Atrium, Leninsky Prospekt 44, 1373008
Delhi Ulitsa Krasnaya Presnya 23b, 2521766
Italia, Ulitsa Arbat 49, 2414342
Pirosmany, Novodyevichy Proezd 4, 2471926
Prague, Ulitsa Arbat 2, 2906171
Sedmoya Nebo, Ostankino TV Tower, 2822293
Slavyansky Bazaar, Ulitsa Nikolskaya 13, 9211872
Golden Dragon, Ulitsa Plushchika 64, 2412299

Entertainment:
Night Flight, Ulitsa Tverskaya 17
Casino Royale, Begovaya Ulitsa 22
Alexander Blok, Krasnopresnenskaya Nebereshnaya 12
Sinyaya Ptiza, Ulitsa Chechova 23
Arkadia Jass Club, Teatralny Proyesd 3
Taganka Bar, Ulitsa Radishchevskaya 15, 2724351

Shops and Stores:

GUM, Red Square	Dept. Store
Moskovsky Univermag, Kalantshevskaya Ploshchad 6	Dept. Store
Petrovsky Passage, Ulitsa Petrovska 10	Dept. Store
Zum, Ulitsa Petrovska 2	Dept. Store
Unisat, Ulitsa Vachtangova 5	Jewelry
Andy's Fashion, Vernatskogo Prospekt 9/10	Apparel
Beneton, Ulitsa Arbat 13	Apparel
Stockmann, Leninsky Prospekt 73	Apparel
Petrovsy Arcade, Ulitsa Petrovska 10	Apparel
Russky Souvenir, Kutusovsky Prospekt 9	Jewelry

Places of Interest:
Red Square
Kremlin - museums.
St.Basil's Cathedral
Pushkin Museum of Fine Arts
Central House of Artists – art exhibitions
Archangel Cathedral
Ul.Krymsky Val 10. M:Oktyabrskaya. – art exhibitions

SPAIN

Official Name: The Kingdom of Spain

Location: Western Europe. Spain is bordered by Portugal and France. The Balearic Islands lie off the east coast of Spain in the Mediterranean Sea. The northwest coastline lies on the North Atlantic Ocean.

Government: Constitutional and Hereditary Monarchy

Area: 504,782 sq. km., 194,897 sq. miles.

Population: 39.1 million

Religion(s): Roman Catholic.

Capital City: Madrid

Major Business Cities: Barcelona, Bilbao, Malaga, Seville and Valencia.

Time: GMT +1 (GMT +2 from late March to late October)

Currency: Peseta (PTS)=100 centimos

Currency Requirements: The import and the export of foreign currency are unlimited but should be declared if it exceeds PTS500,000. The import of local currency must be declared if the amount exceeds PTS1,000,000. The export of local currency must not exceed the imported amount.

Business Hours:
- Government: 09.00-14.00; 16.00-19.00 Mon-Fri
- Banks: 08.30-14.00 Mon-Fri
- Shops: 09.00-14.00; 16.00-19.00 Mon-Fri
- Offices: 09.00-09.30-15.00-17.00

Weight and Measures: Metric System

SPAIN

Electric Current: 220 volts AC. Plugs are generally of the 2-pin type.

Holidays:
New Year - January 1
Epiphany - January 6*
Good Friday - April 10*
Labor Day - May 1
Assumption - August 15
All Saints' Day - November 1
Constitution Day - December 6
Immaculate Conception Day - December 8
Christmas Day - December 25

*Christian Holidays - vary each year

Suitable Clothing: Men should wear a conservative business suit and tie, and black shoes after sundown. Women should wear a conservative dress or suit. In winter in most parts of Spain, wear medium-weight clothing, and light clothing in summer. In southern Spain, have medium to light clothing year round. Bring rainwear.

Automobile Driving License: Either a translation of the National Driving License (available from the Consulate), an International Driving Permit or a New EU Driving License (three-part pink document) is required.

Customs Allowances: Personal items are duty free, but register all valuables upon arrival and keep receipts or you may face bureaucratic entanglements or even confiscation later. Tobacco and alcohol restrictions: 250 cigarettes, and one liter each of wine and spirits.

Tipping: A service charge of 15% is included by law in most cafe, bar, hotel, restaurant and taxi bills. It is customary to tip the waiter, chambermaid and hotel porter. Taxi drivers are tipped 5-10% in general when the vehicles are metered, although it is still discretionary.

Credit Cards Accepted: Access, American Express, Diner's Club, Eurocard, Visa

Customary Dining Hours:
Breakfast: 17.30-09.00
Lunch: 14.00-16.30
Dinner: 20.30-24.00

Local Customs, Business Protocol and Courtesies: The business and social climate are a mix of traditional manners and informal energy. Spanish businessmen tend to initiate discussions in a friendly, casual manner (do not push them into the subject yourself the first time you meet) and also are very serious about their work. Keep in mind when scheduling appointments and accepting social invitations, that Spaniards tend to get going late in the morning (10 or 11 a.m.), take a siesta between 1.30 and 4.30 p.m. and when they get back to the office, work until around 8 p.m. Dinner and entertainment often run very late, too. Make appointments in advance, and be on time, although lateness on the part of your counterpart may not be unusual. Upon introduction, shake hands with everyone, even children. People who have close social relationships will often hug, kiss or pat on the back, but do not do this unless you too have a comfortable social relationship with the person. At initial meetings, business cards are exchanged (you can have Spanish ones printed very quickly), and people will typically address each other using their title and last name. It helps to speak or understand Spanish, of course, but keep in mind that it may be hard to keep up with as people tend to speak all at once, and very quickly and emotionally. In negotiations, be low-key and polite but firm and confident.

Your counterparts may invite you to a bullfight; in this case, don't display emotion or disapproval at all the bloodletting. Do not refuse lunch or coffee invitations, as much business is conducted in these settings. Business gifts are a nice, if unnecessary gesture, such as a quality office accessory, book or art object, to be given after a contract has been agreed upon, and at Christmas. Much entertaining is done in restaurants; however, if you are invited to a home, bring a small, tasteful gift and flowers for the hostess, and send a thank-you note the next day. Remember that as in most European countries, there are certain taboos on the nature of the bouquet · never bring red roses or white bouquets, even numbers of flowers, and avoid funereal varieties like chrysanthemums and dahlias. Wait for your host and hostess to begin eating before you do so yourself. Don't overload your plate, as it is impolite to leave leftovers. When finished, leave a little food on your plate and place your utensils together on the plate at a diagonal. Do not ask for a tour of the home.

Health: There is a Reciprocal Health Agreement with some EU countries, although it is limited. It is advisable to drink bottled water. A health insurance is advised.

Language: Spanish (Primarily Castilian, Catalan, Galician and Basque).

BARCELONA

Country code: 34 - City code: 93

Airport: Barcelona-El Prat International Airport.

Distance from City: 10km (6 miles) southwest of the city.

Transportation to Center of City:
From International and Domestic Terminals
By Bus (cost) PTS500. (every 15 min.)
By Taxi (cost) PTS2,500-3,000. Time approx. 20 min.
Tip luggage porters PTS150 per piece

Transfers: (Minimum Connecting Time):
International to International: 45 min.
International to Domestic: 45 min.
Domestic to International: 45 min
Domestic to Domestic: 30 min.

Automobile Rentals:
Airport car rental desk
Avis - 379-4026
Europcar Interrent - 3/379-9253
Hertz - 370-5811

SPAIN

Car rental city office
Avis - 424-8985
Europcar Interrent - 488-1953
Hertz - 217-8076

Hotels:
Alexandra Hotel, Calle Mallorca 251, 487-2124
Ambassador Hotel Barcelona, Pintor Fortuny 13, 412-0530
Arts Hotel, Barcelona, Carrier de la Marina 19-21, 221-1000
Astoria Hotel, Pairs 203, 209-8311
Avenida Palace Hotel, Gran Via 605-607, 301-9600
Calderon Hotel, Rambla Cataluna 26, 301-0000
Claris Hotel, Pau Claris 150, 487-6262
Colon Hotel, Av. Catedral 7, 301-1404
Condes de Barcelona, Paseo de Gracia 73-75, 484-2200
Derby Hotel, Loreto 21, 322-3215
Fira Palace Hotel, Avda. Rius I Taulet 1-3, 426-2233
Gallery Hotel, Rosellon 249, 415-9911
Golden Tulip Hotel Diplomatic, Pau Claris 122, 488-0200
Gran Derby Hotel, Loreto 28, 322-3062
Le Meridien Barcelona, Ramblas No. 111, 318-6200
Majestic Hotel, Paseo de Gracia 70-72, 488-1717
Melia Barcelona, Avda Sarria 50, 410-6060
Melia Comfort Apolo, Avda. Paralelo 57-59, 443-1122
Reding Hotel, Gravina 5-7, 412-1097
Rivoli Ramblas Hotel, Rambla dels Estudis 128, 302-6643
Wilson Hotel, Diagonal 568, 209-2511

Restaurants:
Agut d'Avignon, Trinitat 3, 302 6034
Arcs de Sant Gervasi, Sandalo 103, 201 9277
Beltxenea, Mallorca 275, 215 3024
Bilbao, Carrer de Perill 33, 458 9624
Botafumiero, Grand de Gracia 81, 218 4230
Can Isidre, Les Flors 12, 441 1139
El Asador de Aranda, Avda.Tibidabo 31, 417 0115
Jaume de Provenca, Provenca 88, 430 0029
Jean Luc Figueras, C.Santa Teresa 10, 415 2877
La Cuineta, Pietat 12, 315 4156
La Dama, Diagonal 423\425, 202 0686
La Odisea, Copons 7, 302 3692
Los Caracoles, Escudellers 14, 302 3185

Niechel, C,Bertran I Rozpide 16 bis, 203 8408
Orotava, Consell de Cent 335, 302 3128
Passadis del Pep, Pla del Palau 2, 310 1021
Quo Vadis, Carme 7, 317 7447
Reno, Tuset 27, 200 1390
Set Portes, Passeig Isabel II 14, 319 3033
TramTram, Major de Sarria 121, 204 8518
Via Veneto, Ganduxer 1012, 200 7024

Entertainment:
Arnau, Paral.lel 60, 242 2804
Bar Pastis, Santa Monica 4, 318 7980
Belle Epoque, Muntaner 246, 209 7711
Blue Note, Maremagnum,Part Vell, 225 8003
Bodega Bohemia, Lancaster 2, 302 5061
El Molino, Vila I Vila 99, 329 8854
L'Autitori, Balmes 245, 310 0755
La Cova del Drac, Vallmaior 33, 200 7032
La Fira, Provenca 171, 323 7271
Lloret del Mar, 366 512
Mas I Mas, Maria Cubi 199, 209 4502
Nick Havanna, Rossello 208,215 6591
Perelada, 538 125
Universal, Maria Cubi 182\184, 200 7470

Shops and Stores:

Adolfo Dominguez, Passeig de Gracia 35	Apparel
El Bulevard Rosa, Passeig de Gracia 53-55	Apparel
El Corte Ingles, el Placa de Catanya 14	Dept. Store
Joaquim Berao, Rosello 277	Jewelry
L'Illa Shopping Mall, Diagonal 545	Dept. Store

Places of Interest:
Picasso Museum
Maritime Museum
Miro Foundation – an art gallery
The Expiatory Church of the Holy Family
Placa de la Sagrada Familia
Gothic Cathedral

SPAIN

MADRID

Country code: 34 - City code: 91

Airport: Madrid Barajas International Airport.
Distance from City: 16km (9 miles) northeast of the city.

Transportation to Center of City:
From International and Domestic Terminals
By Bus (cost) PTS115. Time approx. 30 min.(every 30 min)
By Taxi (cost) PTS1,500-2,000. Time approx. 10-15 min.
Tip luggage porters PTS150 per piece

Transfers: (Minimum Connecting Time):
International to International: 45 min.
International to Domestic: 60 min.
Domestic to International: 60 min.
Domestic to Domestic: 45 min.

Automobile Rentals:
Airport car rental desk
Avis - 305-4273
Europcar Interrent - 305-5325
Hertz - 305-8452

Car rental city office
Avis - 733-3230
Europcar Interrent - 555-9930
Hertz - 542-5805

Hotels:
Ambassador Hotel, Cuesta de Santo Domingo 5, 541-6700
Arosa Hotel, Salud 21, 532-1600
Carlton Hotel, Paseo de la Delocias 26, 539-7100
Castellana Inter-Continental Madrid, Paseo de la Castellana 49,
    310-0200
Convencion Hotel, O"Donnell 53, 574-6800
Emperador Hotel, Gran Via 53, 547-2800
Eurobuilding Hotel, Padre Dominian 23, 345-4500
Golden Tulip Hotel El Coloso, Leganotos 13, 559-7600
Holiday Inn Crowne Plaza Madrid City Centre, Plaza de Espana

s/n, 547-1200
Husa Princesa Hotel, Princesa St. 40, 542-2100
Madrid Hotel, Carretas 10, 521-6520
Melia Confort Los Galgos, Claudio Coello, 139, 562-6600
Melia Madrid, Princesa St. 27, 541-8200
Mindanao Hotel, Peseo san Francisco de Sales 15, 549-5500
Novotel Madrid, Albacete 1, 405-4600
Occidental Miguel Angel, Miguel Angel 29-31, 442-0022
Palace Hotel, Plaza de las Cortes 7, 360-8000
Puerta de Toledo, 4 Puerta de Toledo, 474-7100
Ritz Hotel, Plaza de la Lealtad 5, 521-2857
Sol Inn Alondras, Jose Abascai, 8, 447-4000

Restaurants:
Brasserie de Lista, Ortega y Gasset 6, 435 2818
Cafe Balear, Sagunto 18, 447 9115
Canas y Barro, Amaniel 23, 542 4798
Casa Botin, Cuchileros 17, 366 4217
Casa Paco, Puerta Cerrada 11, 366 3166
Casa Vallejo, San Lorenzo 9, 308 6158
Ciao Madrid, Argensola 7, 308 2519
Cornocopia en Descalzas, Flora 1, 547 6465
El Cenador del Prado, C.del Prado 4, 429 1561
El Cosaco, Plaza del Paja 2, 365 3548
El Pescador, Jose Ortega y Gasset 75, 402 1290
Gure-Etxea, Plaza de Paja 12, 365 6149
Horcher, Alfonso XII 6, 522 0731
La bola, Bola 5, 547 6930
La cacharreria, Moreiria 9, 364 3930
La Pampa, Amparo 16, 528 0449
La trainera, Lagasca 60, 576 8035
Lhardy, Carrera de San Jeronimo 8, 521 3385
Mentidero de la Villa, Santo Tome 6, 308 1285
Viridiana,Juan de Mena 14, 531 5222
Zalacain, Alvarez de Baena 4, 561 5935

Entertainment:
Cafe Central, Plaza de Angel 10, 369 4143
Cafe de Chinitas, Torija 7, 547 1502
Cafe del Foro, San Andres 38, 448 9464
Cafe del Nuncio, Segovia 9, 366 0853
Cafe Gijon, Paseo de Recoletos 24, 521 5425
Cafe Jazz Populart, Huertas 22, 429 8407
Cervantes, Leon 8, 429 6093

Chicote, Gran Via 12, 532 6737
Clamores, Albuquerque 14, 445 7939
Corral de la Moreria, Moreria 17, 364 8446
Corral de la Pacheca, Juan Ramon Jimenez 26, 359 2660
Hard Rock Cafe, Paseo Castellana 2, 435 0200
Hermanos Muniz, Huertas 29, 429 2562
La Champaneria Gala, Moratin 24, 429 2562
La Fidula, Huertas 57, 429 4431
La Scala Melia, Rosario Pino 7, 571 4411
La Venencia, Echegaray 7, 429 7313
Los Gabrieles, Echegaray 17, 429 6261
Palacio de Gaviria, Arenal 9, 526 8089
Teatriz, Hermosilla 15, 577 5379
Torero, Cruz 26, 523 1129

Shops and Stores:

Adolfo Domingues, Serrano 96	Apparel
Del Valle, Conde Xiqueno 2	Apparel
El Corte Ingles, Goya 76	Dept. Store
Galleria del Prado, Plaza de las Cortes 7	Shopping Mall
Marks and Spencer, Serrano 52	Dept. Store
Sesena, De la Cruz 23	Apparel
Sybilla, Jorge Juan 8	Apparel
Zara, Carretas 10	Dept. Store

Places of Interest:

The Prado – an art gallery.
Royal Palace
The Royal Carriage Museum
National Museum Centro de Arte Reina Sofia
Plaza Mayor - cafes, entertainers and market stalls.
Academy of San Fernando – a museum.

SWEDEN

Official Name: The Kingdom of Sweden

Location: Northeast Europe - Scandinavia. Sweden is bordered by Norway and Finland. Its east and south coasts lie on the Baltic Sea.

Government: Constitutional Monarchy

Area: 449,964 sq. km., 173,731 sq. miles.

Population: 8.7 million

Religion(s): Evangelical Lutheran majority. Protestant minorities and Swedish State Church are also present.

Capital City: Stockholm

Major Business Cities: Gothenburg and Malmo.

Time: GMT +1 (GMT +2 from late March to late October)

Currency: Swedish Krona (SEK)=100 ore

Currency Requirements: There are no restrictions on the import and the export of either local or foreign currency.

Business Hours:
- Government: 08.15-17.00 Mon-Fri
- Banks: 09.30-15.00 Mon-Fri (some open longer hours)
- Shops: 09.00-18.00 Mon-Fri; 10.00-17.00 Sat
- Offices: 08.00-17.00 Mon-Fri

Weight and Measures: Metric System

Electric Current: 220 volts AC. Plugs are of the continental 2-pin type.

SWEDEN

Holidays:
New Year's Day - January 1
Epiphany - January 6
Good Friday – April 10*
Easter Monday – April 13*
Labor Day - May 1
Ascension Day - May 21*
Whit Monday – June1*
Mid-summer Holiday - June 21
All Saints' Day – November 1*
Christmas Day - December 25
Boxing Day - December 26*

*Christian Holidays – vary each year.

Holidays falling on a Sunday are not observed on the following Monday.

Suitable Clothing: Bring conservative business clothing, and semi-formal or even black-tie wear for evenings out or dinner parties. In the summer, bring medium weight clothing and raingear. Between November and April, bring winter clothing and a warm coat.

Automobile Driving License: A National Driving License can be used. On the spot fines are imposed for driving offences.

Customs Allowances: Personal items are duty free, but register all valuables upon arrival. Non-E.U. members face more restrictions on tobacco and alcohol: 400 cigarettes, 2 liters of wine and 1 of spirits.

Tipping: A service charge is usually included in the bills of the hotels and the restaurants. Additional tipping is generally left at the guest's discretion. Tips for taxis are normally included in the fare. Cloakroom attendants should receive about SEK10 per coat.

Credit Cards Accepted: Access, American Express, Diner's Club, Eurocard, Master Card, Visa

SWEDEN

Customary Dining Hours:
Breakfast: 07.00-08.00
Lunch: 12.00-13.30
Dinner: 18.00-21.00

Local Customs, Business Protocol and Courtesies: Doing business in Sweden is a mix of tough talk and friendly social activity. It requires a certain level of formality and reserve, but Swedes are also very hospitable and enjoy lots of entertainment. Maintain a cool but sincere professional demeanor. Once rapport is established, business meetings will include casual conversation, but remember that despite the friendlier tone, negotiators here are tough and shrewd. Your counterparts will usually control the pace of a meeting or presentation, and usually quite efficiently. You, too, should avoid wasting time. Presentations should be fact-oriented and well laid out. Be patient when waiting for your proposal to be reviewed and decided upon, generally, by mid-management. However, once contracts are made, they are carried out quickly. Swedes generally take long lunches (keep this in mind when setting appointments) and frequently give formal dinner parties at home for business associates. If invited, bring flowers and a small, tasteful gift (but not something made locally) or fine chocolates, and send a thank-you note the next morning. Remember that as in most European countries, there are certain taboos on the nature of the bouquet; never bring red roses or white bouquets, even numbers of flowers. The host will give a toast to his guests: if you are the guest of honor, give a thank-you toast at the end of the meal to the hostess. Regarding business gifts, it is okay to give your colleague something upon the close of a successful deal or at Christmas- a company item, or any other small, impersonal gift like a book or fine wine.

Health: There is a full Reciprocal Health Agreement with most European countries. The medicines, ambulance travel and the outpatient treatment must be paid by the patient. A medical insurance is recommended.

Language: Swedish. English is widely spoken.

SWEDEN

GOTHENBORG

Country code: 46 - City code: 31

Airport: Landvetter Airport.

Distance from City: 25km (15 miles) east of the city.

Transportation to Center of City:
From International and Domestic Terminals
By Bus (cost) SEK50. Time approx. 30-35 min.
By Taxi (cost) SEK200. Time approx. 25 min.
Tip luggage porters SEK7 per piece

Transfers: (Minimum Connecting Time):
International to International: 30 min.
International to Domestic: 40 min.
Domestic to International: 30 min.
Domestic to Domestic: 30 min.

Automobile Rentals:
Airport car rental desk
Avis - 946030
Europcar Interrent - 805390
Hertz - 946020

Car rental city office
Avis - 805780
Europcar Interrent - 947100
Hertz - 803730

Hotels:
Eggers Hotel, Drottningtorget, 806070
Mornington Hotel, Kungsportsavenyn 6, 176540
Opera Hotel, Norra Hanmgatan 38, 805080
Provobis Hotel Europa, Koepmansgatan 38, 801280
Radisson SAS Park Avenue Hotel Gothenburg, Kungsports-
    avenyn 36-38, 176520
Riverton Hotel, Stora Badhusgatan 26, 101200
Sheraton Gothenburg Hotel & Towers, Sodra Hamngatan
    59-65, 806000

SWEDEN

Restaurants:
A Hereford Beefstouw, Linnegatan 5, 775-0441
Amanda Boman, Saluhallen, 137-676
Belle Avenue, Kungsportsavenyn 36-38, 176-520
Chablis, Aschebergsgatan 22, 203-545
Fiskekrogen, Lilla Torget 1, 711-2184
Gabriel, Feskekorka, 139-051
Rakan, Lorensbergsgatan 16, 169-839
Sjomagasinet, Klipans Kulturreservat, 246-510
The Place, Arkivgatan 7, 160-333
Weise, Linnegatan 54, 426-014

Shops and Stores:

Andreassons, Sodra Hamngatan 49	Apparel
Gillblads, Kungsgatan 42-44	Apparel
Hennes & Mauritz, Kungsgatan 55-57	Apparel
NK, Ostra Hamngatan 42	Dept. Store
Strims, Kungsgatan 27029	Apparel

Places of Interest:
The Kronhuset - a 17th century building.
The Historical Museum
The Maritima Centrum – a museum.
The Domkyrkan – a church.
The Tradsgardsforening – a botanical garden.
The Rohsska Museum of Arts and Crafts
Gotaplatsen – a cultural center
Liseberg – an amusement park.
Nya Elfsborg Fortress - 17th century buildings.

STOCKHOLM

Country code: 46 - City code: 8

Airport: Stockholm-Arlanda International Airport.

Distance from City: 42km (26 miles) north of the city.

SWEDEN

Transportation to Center of City:
From International and Domestic Terminals
By Bus (cost) SEK50. Time approx. 40 min.
By Taxi (cost) SEK300-SEK350. Time approx. 30-40 min.
Tip luggage porters SEK7 per piece
Transfers: (Minimum Connecting Time):
International to International: 30 min.
International to Domestic: 45 min.
Domestic to International: 35 min.
Domestic to Domestic: 15 min.

Automobile Rentals:
Airport car rental desk
Avis - 5951-1500
Europcar Interrent - 5936-0940
Hertz - 797-9900

Car rental city office
Avis - 349910
Europcar Interrent - 210650
Hertz - 240720

Hotels:
Arctia Hotel Hasseloacken, Hazeliusbacken 20, 670-5000
Berns' Hotel Stockholm, Nackstromsgatan 8, 614-0700
Esplanade Hotel, Strandvagen 7a, 663-0740
First Hotel Amaranten, Kingsholmsgatan 31, 654-1060
Grand Hotel, S. Blasieholmshamnen 8, 679-3500
Mornington Hotel, Nybrogatan 53, 663-1240
Oden Hotel, Karlbergsvagen 24, 349340
Provobis Sergel Plaza Hotel, Brunkebergstorg 9, 226600
Radisson SAS Royal Viking Hotel Stockholm, Vasagatan 1,
    141000
Radisson SAS Strand Hotel Stockholm, Nybrokajen 9, 678-7800
Sheraton Stockholm Hotel & Towers, Tagelbacken 6, 142600
Stockholm Plaza Hotel, Birgar Jarlsgatan 29, 145120

Restaurants:
Bakfickan, Opera Huset, Jacobs Torg 2, 207-745
Butler's, Rorstrandsgatan 11, 321-823
Cassi, Narvavagen 30, 661-7461
Clas pa Hornet, Surbrunnsgatan 20, 165-136

SWEDEN

De Fyras Krog, Jarntorgsgatan 5, 240-347
Den Gyldene Freden, Osterlanggatan 51, 249-760
Diana, Brunnsgrand 2, 107-310
Edsbacka Krog, Sollentunavagen 220, 963-300
Gasen, Karlavagen 28, 611-0269
Greitz, Vasagatan 50, 234-820
Hannas Krog, Skanegatan 80, 643-8225
Kallaren Aurora, Munkbron 11, 219-359
KB, Smalandsgatan 7, 679-6032
Nils Emil, Folkungagatan 122, 640-7209
Open Gate, Hogbergsgatan 40, 643-9776
Operakallaren, Opera Huset, Jacobs Torg 2, 676-5801
Paul & Norberg, Strandvagen 9, 663-8183
Prinsen, Master Samuelsgatan 4, 611-1331
Rolfs Kok, Tegnergatan 41, 101-696
Stallmastaregarden, Norrtull, 610-1301
Tranan, Karlbergsvagen 14, 300-765
Ulriksdals Vardshus, Ulriksdals Slottpark, Solna, 850-815
Wasahof, Dalagatan 46, 323-440
Wedholms Fisk, Nybrokajen 17, 611-7874

Entertainment:
Anglais Bar, Humlegardsgatan 23, 614-1600
Café Opera, Opera Huset, 411-0026
Clipper Club, Skeppsbron 1214, 223-260
Daily's Bar, Kungstradgarden, 215-655
Dubliner, Smalandsgatan 8, 679-7707
Fasching, Kungsgatan 63, 216-267
Hannas Krog, Skanegatan 80, 643-8225
King Creole, Kungsgatan 18, 244-700
Limerick, Tegnergatan 10, 673-4398
Mosebacke Establissement, Mosebacke Torg 3, 641-9020
Pelikan Restaurant, Blekingegatan 40, 743-0695
Penny Lane, Birger Jarlsgatan 29, 201411
Stampen, Stora Nygatan 5, 205-793
Sture Compagniet, Sturegatan 4, 611-7800

Shops and Stores:

Ahlens, Klarabergsgatan	Dept. Store
Hannes & Mauritz, Hamngatan 22	Apparel
Hans Allde, Birger Jarlsgatan 58	Apparel
La Chemise, Smalandsgatan 11	Apparel

NK, Hamngatan	Dept. Store
Palarn & Pyret, Hamngatan 10	Apparel
PUB, Drottninggatan 63	Dept. Store
Twilfit, Nymbrogatan	Apparel

Places of Interest:
Kungliga slottet (Royal Palace) - 18th century palace.
Stadshuset - Town hall
Skansen Open-air Museum
Vasa Museum
Historical Museum
Drottningholm Palace - a royal palace and a theatre

SWITZERLAND

Official Name: The Swiss Confederation

Location: Central Europe. Switzerland is bordered by France, Germany, Austria and Italy.

Government: Democracy

Area: 41,284 sq. km., 15,940 sq. miles.

Population: 6.99 million

Religion(s): Roman Catholic and Protestant.

Capital City: Bern

Major Business Cities: Basel, Geneva, Lugano and Zurich.

Time: GMT +1 (GMT +2 from late March to late October)

Currency: Swiss Franc (SFR)=100 centimes

Currency Requirements: There are no restrictions on the import and the export of both local and foreign currencies.

Business Hours:
- Government: 08.00-12.00; 14.00-18.00 Mon-Fri
- Banks: 08.30-17.00 Mon-Fri
- Shops: 08.30-16.00 or 16.30 Mon-Fri
- Offices: 08.30-17.00/18.00 Mon-Fri

Weight and Measures: Metric System

Electric Current: 220 volts AC. Plugs are of the continental 2-pin type.

Holidays:
New Year's Day - January 1

Good Friday – April 10*
Easter Monday – April 13*
Labor Day - May 1
Ascension Day – May 21*
Whit Monday – June 1*
Swiss National Day - August 1
Christmas Eve - December 24 (afternoon only)
Christmas - December 25-26
New Year's Eve - December 31 (afternoon only)

* Christian Holiday - vary each year

Suitable Clothing: Wear a well-cut, conservative business suit or dress. Bring medium weight clothing year round, and a warm coat in winter.

Automobile Driving License: A Full Driving License is required and must be held for at least one year.

Customs Allowances: Personal items are duty free, but register all valuables upon arrival and keep the receipt. Non-E.U. members may bring in, duty free, 400 cigarettes, 2 liters of wine and one of spirits.

Tipping: A service charge of 15% is included in most places. Additional tipping is discretionary.

Credit Cards Accepted: Access, American Express, Diner's Club, Eurocard, Visa

Customary Dining Hours:
Breakfast: 07.00-09.00
Lunch: 12.00-14.00
Dinner:19.00-23.00

Local Customs, Business Protocol and Courtesies: The Swiss take great stock in long-established companies: it will do you much good to put "Since 1880" or "Est'd. 1910" on your business card if your company has been around that long. The belief in long-standing business relationships will carry over to your company if you succeed in signing a first contract with a Swiss company: you can expect this relationship, with multiple contracts, to keep going for years. The flip side of this is that if you blow your presentation or fail to engender interest you may never get another chance. The business day begins early in Switzerland, between 7 and 8 a.m. Since many officials work long hours on full schedules, try to call them at this time to set up appointments. In general, putting on the pressure or appearing over-eager is a bad idea: don't invite your contact to lunch or dinner the first day and keep initial meetings brief and succinct. It's appropriate to invite your Swiss counterparts out to lunch or dinner if relationship progresses, but given the busy nature of Swiss businessmen, do not take refused invitations as a sign of disinterest in doing business with you. Punctuality and eye contact are essential. Upon entering an office give your business card to the receptionist as well as those you are meeting with. Shake hands with women first, and otherwise in order of rank. Decisions tend to be made at the top of the hierarchy, so it's important not to offend by misplacing rank. Use title with last name until indicated otherwise. You will be expected to demonstrate thorough knowledge of your product, its market and any competition. Presentations must be detailed, executed with calm, confident but low-key style. Don't expect a quick resolution of proposals and contracts, as Swiss law puts penalties on unfulfilled contracts. Show patience, too, in waiting for decisions and answering questions about your company and product. But once that contract is signed, the Swiss are most reliable in carrying it out. Regarding gifts, it is okay to give your colleague something upon the close of a successful deal · a tasteful company item, small art object or fine wine.

If you are invited to someone's home (do not refuse), bring chocolate, fine wine or flowers for the hostess but keep in mind that as in many European countries, there are certain taboos on the nature of the bouquet · never bring red (it signifies romantic love), or even numbers of flowers. Table manners are strict, if you want seconds, place your fork and knife apart on the plate, and when finished, place them together on the plate on a diagonal. You should try every dish offered. Wait until toast is offered before drinking·depending on what part of Switzerland you're in, "Prost" (German), "Salute" (Italian) or "A Votre Sante" (French). Give a thank-you toast after dinner. Business and politics are often discussed at meals, but be diplomatic.

Keep in mind, especially when printing business cards and literature, that Swiss cantons have different dominant languages · most often French or German, sometimes Italian. Zurich, which has half the country's main firms, several thousand small ones in its envrirons and many of its banks, is German-speaking.

Health: There are no vaccinations required. The medical facilities in Switzerland are amongst the best in Europe. A medical insurance is recommended.

Language: German is spoken in the central and the eastern parts, French in the west and Italian in the south. English is also spoken.

BASEL

Country code: 41 - City code: 61

Airport: Basel-Mulhausen Airport

Distance from City: 12km (7 miles) northwest of the city.

Transportation to Center of City:
From International and Domestic Terminals
By Bus (cost) SFR3-4. Time approx. 20-30 min.
By Taxi (cost) SFR40.Time approx. 15 min.
Tip luggage porters SFR2 per piece

Transfers: (Minimum Connecting Time):
International to International: 30 min.
International to Domestic: 30 min.
Domestic to International: 30 min.
Domestic to Domestic: 30 min.

SWITZERLAND

Automobile Rentals:
Airport car rental desk
Avis - 325-2840
Europcar Interrent - 325-2903
Hertz - 325-2780

Car rental city office
Avis - 271-2262
Europcar Interrent - 361-6660
Hertz - 271-5822

Hotels:
Basel Hilton, Aeschengraben 31, 275-6600
Basel Hotel, Spalenberg Munzgasse 12, 264-6800
Du Commerce Hotel, Riehenring 91, 691-9666
Europe Hotel, Clarastrasse 43, 690-8080
Krafft am Rhein Hotel, Rheingasse 12, 691-8877
Merian am Rhein Hotel, Rheingasse 2, 681-0000
Metropolitan Hotel, Elisabethenanlage 5, 271-7721
St. Gotthard, Centralbahnstr. 13, 271-5250
Swisshotel Basel, Hotel Le Plaza, Messeplatz 25, 690-3333

Restaurants:
Cafe Pfalz, Munsterbeg 11, 272-6511
Cafe Spalenberg, Spalenberg 16, 261-3205
Chez Donati, St. Johanns-Vorstadt 48, 322-0919
Fischerstube, Rheingasse 45, 692-6635
Lowenzorn, Gemsberg 2, 261-4213
Safran-Zunft, Gerbergasse 11, 261-1959
Schlusselzunft, Freie Strasse 25, 261-2046
St.Alban-Eck, St. Alban-Vorstadt 60, 271-0320
Stuki, Bruderholzallee 42, 261-8222
Teufelhof, Leonhardsgraben 47, 261-1010
Zum Goldenen Sternen, St. Alban-Rheinweg 70, 272-1666
Zum Schnabel, Trillengasslein 2, 261-4909

Entertainment:
Frisco Bar, Untere Rebgasse 3, 681-0990
Hazy-Club, Heuwaage, 239-982
King's Club, Blumenrain 8, 261-3658
Le Plaza Club, Am Messeplatz, 692-3206
Singerhaus, Marktplatz, 261-6466

SWITZERLAND

Zum Sperber, Munzgasse 12, 261-2433

Shops and Stores:

Check-out, Shnabelgasse 4	Apparel
Globus, Marktplatz 2	Dept. Store
Grieder, Freie Strasse 29	Apparel
Jelmoli, Rebgasse 20	Dept. Store
K. Aeschbacher, Shnabelgasse 4	Apparel
La Boutique, Falknerstrasse 33	Apparel
Panterra, Munsterberg 10	Apparel
Pfauen, Freie Strasse 75	Dept. Store
Renz, Freie Strasse 2a, 261-2991	Apparel
Rheinbrucke, Greifengasse 22	Dept. Store
Schatulle, Spalenberg/Rosshofgasse 15	Apparel
Trois Pommes Uomo, Freie Strasse 93	Apparel

Places of Interest:
The Natural History Museum
The Munster – a cathedral
The Kunsthalle – an art gallery.
Kirschgarten House – a museum
Barfusserkirche (Church of the Bare Feet)
Zoologischer Garten – a zoo

BERNE

Country code: 41 - City code: 31

Airport: Berne-Belp International Airport

Distance from City: 10km (6 miles) from the city.

Transportation to Center of City:
From International and Domestic Terminals
By Bus (cost) SFR14. Time approx. 20 min.
By Taxi (cost) SFR35-40. Time approx. 15 min.
Tip luggage porters SFR2 per piece

Transfers: (Minimum Connecting Time):
International to International: 60 min.

SWITZERLAND

International to Domestic: 60 min.
Domestic to International: 60 min.
Domestic to Domestic: 20 min.

Automobile Rentals:
Airport car rental desk
Avis - 372-1313
Hertz - 311-3313

Car rental city office
Avis - 31/372-1313
Europcar Interrent - 381-7555
Hertz - 318-2160

Hotels:
Baren Hotel, Schauplatzgasse 4, 311-3367
Bristol Hotel, Schauplatzgasse 10, 311-0101

Restaurants:
Beaujolais,Aarbergergasse 52, 311 4886
Bellevue-Grill,Kochergasse 3-5, 320 4545
Della Casa, Schauplatzgasse 16, 311 2142
Gfeller, Barenplatz 21, 311 6944
Harmonie, Hotelgasse 3, 311 3840
Klotzlikeller, Gerechtigkeisgasse 62, 311 7456
Kornhauskeller, Kornhausplatz 18, 311 1133
Lorenzini, Marktgass-Passage 3, 311 7850
Rablus, Zeughausgasse 3, 311 5908
Schog-dee, Bollwerk 41, 311 3708
Schultheissenstube, Bahnhofplatz 11, 311 4501
Zimmermania, Brunngasse 19, 311 1542
Zum Rathaus, Rathausplatz 5, 311 6183

Entertainment:
Arlequin, Gerechtigkeitsgrasse 51, 22 3956
Hotel Belle Epoque, Gerechtigkeitsgrasse 18, 311 4336
Hotel Bellevue Palace,Kochergasse 3-5, 320 4545
Kursaal,Schanzlistrasse 71-77, 332 5466
Marian's Jazzroom, Engestrasse 54, 309 6111
Mocambo, Genfergasse 10, 311 5041

Shops and Stores:

ABM, Spitalgasse 3	Dept. Store
Ascher, Gerechtigkeits 59	Souvenirs
EPA, Marktgasse 24	Dept. Store
Globus, Spitalgasse 17-21	Dept. Store
Loeb, Spitalgasse 47-57	Dept. Store
Migros, Marktgasse 46	Dept. Store

Places of Interest:
Kafigturm (Prison Tower)
The Zytgloggeturm (Clock Tower)
The Munster – a cathedral
Bernisches Historisches Museum
Naturhistorisches Museum
Kunstmuseum of Bern – fine arts museum
The Heiliggeistkirche (Church of the Holy Spirit)
Tierpark Dahlholzli - a zoo.

GENEVA

Country code: 41 - City code: 22

Airport: Cointrin International Airport

Distance from City: 5km (3 miles) northwest of the city.

Transportation to Center of City:
From International and Domestic Terminals
By Train (cost) SFR7. Time approx. 7 min.
By Taxi (cost)   SFR30. Time approx. 10-15 min.
Tip luggage porters SFR2 per piece

Transfers: (Minimum Connecting Time):
International to International: 45 min.
International to Domestic: 45 min.
Domestic to International: 45 min.
Domestic to Domestic: 45 min.

Automobile Rentals:
Airport car rental desk
Avis - 798-2300

SWITZERLAND

Europcar Interrent - 798-1110
Hertz - 798-2202

Car rental city office
Avis - 731-9000

Europcar Interrent - 731-5150
Hertz - 731-1200

Hotels:
Bristol Hotel, 10 Rue du Mont-Blanc, 732-3800
D'Anglettere Hotel-Westin Demeure Hotel,17 Quai du
    Mont-Blanc, 906-5555
Eldelweiss Manotel, 2 Pl. de la Navigation, 731-3658
Forum Hotel Geneva, 19 Rue de Zurich, 731-0241
Grand-Pre Hotel, 35 Rue du Grand Pre, 918-1111
Inter-Continental Geneve, 7-9 Chemin du Petit Saconnex,
    919-3939
Metropole Hotel, 34 Quai du General Guisan, 311-1344
Movenpick Hotel Geneva, 20 Route de Pre-Bois, 798-7575
Royal Hotel Geneva, 41-43 Rue de Lausanne, 906-1357
Sofitel Hotel, 18-20 Rue du Cendrier, 731-5200
De Berne Hotel, 26 Rue de Berne, 731-6000
De La Paix Hotel, 11 Quai du Mont-Blanc, 732-6150
Des Bergues Hotel, 33 Quai des Bergues, 731-5050
le Warick Hotel, 14 Rue de Lausanne, 731-6250

Restaurants:
Aux Halles de L'Ile, Pl.de L'Ile 1, 311 5221
Boeuf Rouge, Rue Alfred-Vincent 17, 732 7537
Brasserie Lipp, Rue de la Confederation 8, 311 1011
Buffet Cornavin, Gare Cornavin, 732 4306
Chez Jacky, Rue Jaques-Necker 9-11, 732 8680
Griffin's Cafe, Blvd.Helvetique 36, 735 4206
La Bearn, Quai de la Poste 4, 321 0028
La Cassolette, Rue Jacques-Dalphin 31, 342 0318
La Favola, Rue Jean-Calvin 15, 311 7437
La Mere Royaume, Rue des Corps-Saints 9, 732 7008
La Parle du Lac, Rue de Lausanne 128, 731 7935
Le Cygne, Quai du Mont-Blanc 19, 731 9811
Le Jardin,Rue Adhemar-Fabri 8, 731 1400
Le Lion d'Or, Pl.Gauthier 5, 736 4432

Le Pied-de-Cochon, Pl.du Bourg de Four 4, 310 7497
Les Continents, Petit-Saconnex 7-9, 734 6091
Mirador, Rue du Mont-Blanc 24, 732 9860
Roberto, Rue Pierre-Fatio 10, 311 8033

Entertainment:
Cactus Club, Rue Chaponniere 3, 732 6398
Chez Maxim's, Rue Thalberg 2, 732 9900
Grand Casino, Quai du Mont-Blanc 19, 732 6320
Griffin's Cafe, Blvd.Helvetique 36, 735 1218
Grillon, Rue du Marche 3, 311 2831
La Coupole, Rue Pierre-Fatio 16, 735 6544
Molin Rouge, Av.du Mail 1, 329 3566

Shops and Stores:

Anita Smaga, rue du Rhone 21	Apparel
Au Grand Passage, rue du Rhone 50	Dept. Store
Bon Genie, rue du Marche 34	Dept. Store
Bulgari, rue du Rhone 30	Jewelry
Cactus, rue des Chaudronniers 5	Jewelry
Chacok, rue Verdaine 12	Apparel
Chanel, rue du Rhone 43	Apparel
Christie's, rue Adhemar-Fabri 8-10	Jewelry
Hoffstetter Sports, rue de la Corraterie 12	Apparel
Lanvin, rue du Rhone 62	Apparel
Les Createurs, rue du Rhone 100	Apparel
Ludwig Muller, rue des Chaudronniers 5	Jewelry
Migro, rue des Paquis 41	Dept. Store
Placette, rue Rousseau 27	Dept. Store
Sotheby's, quai du Mont-Blanc 13	Jewelry
Supercentre Coope, rue de la Confederation	Dept. Store

Places of Interest:
Cathedrale St.Pierre – a cathedral
Musee de l'Horlogerie – a museum
The Palais des Nations – European UN headquarters
Carouge - an 18th century town

ZURICH

Country code: 41 - City code: 1

SWITZERLAND

Airport: Zurich-Kloten International Airport

Distance from City: 12km (7 miles) from the city

Transportation to Center of City:
From International and Domestic Terminals
By Train (cost) SFR6. Time approx. 10 min.
By Taxi (cost) SFR45. Time approx. 20-40 min.
Tip luggage porters SFR2 per piece

Transfers: (Minimum Connecting Time):
International to International: 45 min.
International to Domestic: 45 min.
Domestic to International: 45 min.
Domestic to Domestic: 45 min.

Automobile Rentals:
Airport car rental desk
Avis - 813-0084
Europcar Interrent - 813-2044
Hertz - 814-0511

Car rental city office
Avis - 242-2040
Europcar Interrent - 271-5656
Hertz - 242-8484

Hotels:
Ammann Hotel, Kirchgasse 4, 252-7240
Arc en Ville Hotel, Sihlquai 9, 271-5400
Baur au Lac, Talstrasse 1, 220-5020
Central Plaza Hotel, Central 1, 251-5555
Comfort Inn Arc Royal, Leonhardstr. 6, 261-6710
Glarnischhof Hotel, Claridenstr. 30, 286-2222
Glockenhof Hotel, Sihlstr. 31, 211-5650
Krone Unterstrass Hotel, Schaffhauserstr. 1, 361-1688
Leoneck Hotel, Leonhardstr. 1, 261-6070
Rutli Hotel, Zahringerstr. 43, 251-5426
Schweizerhof Zurich, Bahnhofplatz 7, 218-8888
Seiler Hotel Neues Schloss, Stockerstr. 17, 201-6550
Sheraton Atlantis Hotel, Doeltschweg 234, 454-5454
Sofitel Hotel, Stampfenbachstr. 60, 363-3363
Zum Storchen Hotel, Am Weinplatz, 211-5510

SWITZERLAND

Restaurants:
Bierhalle Kropf, In Gassen 16, 221-1805
Blaue Ente, Seefeldstrasse 222, 422-7706
Grill Room, Talstrasse 1, 221-1650
Oepfelchammer, Rindermarkt 12, 251-2336
Petermann's Kunststuben, Seestrasse 160, 910-0715
Piccoli Accademia, Rotwandstrasse 48, 241-6243
Rheifelder Bierhaus, Marktgasse 19, 251-2991
Tubli,Schneggengasse 8, 251-2471
Veltliner Keller, Schlusselgasse 8, 221-3228
Zunfthaus zur Waag, Munsterhof 8, 211-0730

Entertainment:
Bierhalle Kropf, In Gassen 16, 221-1805
Casa Bar, Munstergasse 30, 261-2002
Champagnertreff, Central 1, 251-5555
Diagonal, Talstrasse 1, 211-7396
Jocker, Gotthardstrasse 5, 206-3666
Kronenhalle, Ramistrasse 4, 251-1597
Mascotte, Theaterstrasse 10, 252-1110
Molin Rouge, Muhlegasse 14, 262 0730
Moods, Schlamstrasse 5, 201-8130
Odeon, Am Bellvue, 251-1650
Polygon, Marktgasse 17, 252-1110
Rasputine's, Schutzengasse 16, 211-5058
Terrace, Limmatquai 3, 251-1074

Shops and Stores:

A Propos, Limmatquai 36-38	Apparel
ABM, Bellevueplatz	Dept. Store
Gianni Versace, Storchengasse 23	Apparel
Giorgio Armani, Zinnengasse 4	Apparel
Globus, Bahnhofstrasse	Dept. Store
Jelmoli, Bahnhofstrasse,	Dept. Store
Trois Pommes, Storchengasse 6/7	Apparel
Vilan, Bahnhofstrasse 75	Dept. Store
Weinberg, Bahnhofstrasse 11	Apparel

Places of Interest:
Swiss National Museum
Beyer's Museum of Time
E.G.Burhrle Collection - 19th century paintings.
Rapperswill - a castle.

TAJIKISTAN

Official Name: Republic of Tajikistan

Location: Central Asia. Tajikistan is bordered by China, Pakistan, Afghanistan, Uzbekistan and Kyrgystan.

Government: Parliamentary Republic

Area: 143,100 sq. km., 55,251 sq. mi.

Population: 5.7 million

Religion(s): Islam (Sunni) majority. Russian Orthodox minority.

Capital City: Dushanbe

Major Business Cities: Dushanbe and Khodzhent

Time: GMT +5

Currency: 1 Ruble = 100 Kopecks

Currency Requirements: The Import of foreign currency is unlimited but must be declared. The export is limited to the amount declared upon arrival. The import and the export of local currency are prohibited.

Business Hours:
- Government: 09.00-18.00 Mon-Fri
- Banks: 09.00-18.00 Mon-Fri
- Shops: 09.00-18.00 Mon-Fri
- Offices: 09.00-18.00 Mon-Fri

Weight and Measures: Metric System

Electric Current: 220/127V, 50c

TAJIKISTAN

Suitable Clothing: Dress conservatively and modestly: a light-weight suit in summer, and a warmer one with winter coat in winter. Bring rainwear.

Automobile Driving License: An International driving license is required.

Customs Allowances: As currency and customs requirements have undergone a number of changes in recent years, one should consult your country's Tajiki embassy or consulate when arranging your trip. Valuables, including foreign currency, must be registered upon arrival, otherwise they may be confiscated upon departure. Although you may bring in unlimited amounts of foreign currency, and take out any you initially declare, you may not import or export local currency. Cigarettes are limited to 250, and wine and spirits to one liter and a half liter, respectively. Weaponry, drugs and pornographic material are prohibited.

Tipping: A tip of 10%-15% is expected in most restaurants. Hotels usually include a service charge in the bill.

Credit Cards Accepted: American Express, Carte Blanche, Diner's Club, Visa

Customary Dining Hours:
Breakfast: 07.00-09.00
Lunch: 12.00-14.30
Dinner: 18.30-22.00

Health: It is recommended to consult your doctor before your journey. Drinking water is safe in most major cities. The medical and dental treatment is free, but the medications must be paid. In emergencies you must contact your embassy or hotel receptionist.

Language: Tajik

DUSHANBE

Country code: 7 - City code: 3772

TAJIKISTAN

Airport: Dushanbe
Distance from City: 12 km. (8 mi)

Hotels:
Hotel Dushanbe, Lenin 7, 233661
Hotel Tajikistan, Kommunisticheskaya 22, 274393

Restaurants:
Farogat, Kommunisticheskaya 19
Khisor, Konsumol Lake
Pamir, Kirov 21a
Rokhat Tearoom, Lenin

Shops and Stores:
Central Store, Lenin 83   Dept. Store

Places of Interest:
Aini Memorial Complex
Botanical Gardens
The Fountains
Lenin Park
Shamaisur Mosque

UKRAINE

Official Name: Republic of Ukraine

Location: Central Eastern Europe. Ukraine is bordered by the Russian Federation, Belarus, Poland, The Slovak Republic, Hungary, Romania and Moldova.

Government: Constitutional Republic

Area: 603,700 sq. km., 233,090 sq. miles.

Population: 51.99 million

Religion(s): Ukrainian Orthodox majority

Capital City: Kiev

Major Business Cities: Kiev, Kharkov and Dnepropetrovsk.

Time: GMT +2 (GMT +3 from late March to late September)

Currency: Ukraine Karbovanets (UAK)

Currency Requirements: There are no restrictions on the import and the export of foreign or local currency.

Business Hours:
- Government: 09.00-18.00 Mon-Fri
- Banks: 09.00/09.30-17.30/18.00 Mon-Fri
- Shops: 08.00/09.00-19.00/20.00 Mon-Sat
- Offices: 09.00-18.00 Mon-Fri

Weight and Measures: Metric System

Electric Current: 220 volts

Holidays:
New Year's Day - January 1

UKRAINE

Orthodox Christmas - January 7-8
International Women's Day - March 8
Orthodox Easter - April 27-28*
International Workers' Solidarity Days - May1-2
Victory Day - May 9
Holy Trinity - June 15-16*
Independence Day - August 24
Former Anniversary of the October Revolution - November 7-8

*Christian holidays – vary each year

Suitable Clothing: A conservative suit is required for all occasions (except for those meetings in the bani). Lightweight clothing is fine for summer. Winter months require medium to heavy clothing, warm coat and warm accessories. Best to bring a raincoat or umbrella.

Automobile Driving License: A National License with an authorized translation or an International Driving Permit is required

Customs Allowances: Register valuables upon arrival to avoid confiscation. You are allowed 250 cigarettes or 225g (1/2 lb.) of tobacco and one-half liter of alcohol for personal consumption. Military weapons, drugs, and pornography are prohibited.

Tipping: A service charge is usually added by most first class restaurants and hotels. Small tips are always welcomed.

Credit Cards Accepted: American Express, Carte Blanche, Diner's Card, EuroCard, Visa

Customary Dining Hours:
Breakfast: 07.00-09.00
Lunch: 12.00-14.30
Dinner: 18.30-22.00

Local Customs, Business Protocol and Courtesies: The people of the Ukraine have a strong sense of pride in their national heritage, culture, and independence. Even under Soviet rule, they maintained a distinct identity and are currently eager to expand their trade beyond the borders of the former Soviet countries. Hospitality abounds. As a guest expect to be treated well, but remember · punctuality is a virtue for business meetings and social occasions alike. That goes for the sauna as well. Ukrainians are only slightly less proud of their saunas than Finns, so it's always a good idea to accept an invitation to the <u>bani</u>, the Ukrainian sauna. Leave your clothes at the door, enjoy the vodka, and don't be alarmed if you're swatted on the back with a birch branch (meant to increase circulation). At any gathering, be prepared to shake hands on meeting and on departure (no protocol on who offers the hand first, so don't hesitate). Use titles and surnames unless you're asked to be more informal. When invited to a Ukrainian home, bring a small gift for the hostess. Good ideas include chocolates, flowers, pastry, wine or liquor, a book, or a special souvenir from your country. Are there children? They'll appreciate a gift of candy. Expect your host to offer a toast before the meal. No doubt you'll be offered a second helping, but remember that despite the warm hospitality, shortages exist and food is not wasted. The atmosphere is relaxed, friendly, and generous. To keep it that way avoid any discussion of politics (international and domestic), economic and social conditions, or any reminder of the proud nation's Soviet past. Avoid personal questions.

Health: It is advisable to consult your doctor before your journey. There are no special vaccinations needed. Immunizations against Diphtheria, Hepatitis A, Hepatitis B, Polio, Tetanus and Typhoid are recommended. Drinking water should always be boiled or sterilized and the food should be well cooked. There is a health agreement for urgent medical treatment with some EU countries. A health insurance is recommended.

Language: Ukrainian and Russian.

KIEV

Country code: 380 - City code: 44

Airport: Borispol International Airport

UKRAINE

Distance from City: 35km (21 miles) east of the city center.

Transportation to Center of City:
From International and Domestic Terminals
By Bus (cost) UAK150,000. Time approx. 60 min.
By Taxi (cost) US$40-60. Time approx. 60 min.

Transfers: (Minimum Connecting Time):
International to International: 120 min.
International to Domestic: 240 min.
Domestic to International: 240 min.
Domestic to Domestic: 40 min.

Automobile Rentals: Only cars with drivers can be rented

Hotels:
Bratislava Hotel, vul. Malishka 1, 551-7646
Dnipro Hotel, Kreschatic1, 229-8387
Intourist Hotel, vul. Hospitalna 12, 220-4144
Hotel Kiev, Hrushevskoho 26/1, 293-0155
Hotel Moskva, Zh. Revolutsii 4, 228-2804
Hotel Ukraine, Shevchenko Blvd. 5, 229-4303

Restaurants:
Dinamo, 81 Bvld. M. Grushevskovo, 288 0939
Dybki, Blvd. Stetsenko, 440 5188
Kiev, 26/1 Blvd. M. Grushevskovo, 293 1310
Krakov, 23 Prosp. Peremogi., 274 1908
Kureni, 19 Parkovaya Doroga, 293 4062
Lisova Pisnya, 4 Minkiy Prosp., 432 1887
Melodiya, 36 Blvd. Volodimirskaya, 228 7683
Mlin, Gidropark, 517 0833
Moskva, 4 Blvd. Institutska, 229 1967
Rus, 4 Blvd. Gospitalna, 220 40557
Salute, 11a Blvd. Sichnevovo Povstaniya, 290 5119
Stolichniy, 5 Blvd. Kreshchatik, 229 8188
Vitrak, 11 Prosp. Akedemika Glushkova, 266 7138
Zolotoye, Vorota, 8 Lvivenka Pl., 212 5504

Places of Interest:
The Literature Museum

UKRAINE

Ukrainski Dim (Ukrainian House) - commercial and cultural
    exhibitions.
St.Sophia Monastery Complex
The Museum of Ukrainian History
St.Andrew's Cathedral
Bessarabian Market
Pecherska Lavra Monastery - a museum
Maydan Nezalezhnosti (Independence Square)
Andriyivskiy uzviz

UZBEKISTAN

Official Name: Republic of Uzbekistan

Location: Uzbekistan is bordered by Turkmenistan, Kazakstan, Karakalpakstan, Kyrgyzstan, Tajikistan and Afghanistan.

Government: Constitutional Monarchy

Area: 447,400 sq. km., 172,740 sq. mi.

Population: 22 million

Religion(s): Islam (Sunni)

Capital City: Tashkent

Major Business Cities: Tashkent and Samarkand

Time: GMT +5

Currency Requirements: The Import of foreign currency is unlimited but must be declared. The export is limited to the amount declared upon arrival. The import and the export of local currency are prohibited.

Business Hours:
- Government: 09.00-18.00 Mon-Fri
- Banks: 09.00-18.00 Mon-Fri
- Shops: 09.00-18.00 Mon-Fri
- Offices: 09.00-18.00 Mon-Fri

Weight and Measures: Metric System

Electric Current: 220/127V, 50c

Suitable Clothing: Conservative business attire is appropriate. Lightweight clothing will suffice in summer, but be prepared with very warm clothing (indoor and outdoor) for winter months.

Automobile Driving License: An International driving license is required.

Customs Allowances: Register valuables upon arrival to avoid confiscation. You are allowed 250 cigarettes or 225g (1/2 lb.) of tobacco, one-half liter of liquor and one liter of wine for personal consumption. Weapons and ammunition, drugs, and pornography are prohibited.

Tipping: A tip of 10%-15% is expected in most restaurants. Hotels usually include a service charge in the bill. Taxi drivers expect a 10-15% tip.

Credit Cards Accepted: American Express, Visa, EuroCard, Carte Blanche, Diner's Club.

Customary Dining Hours:
Breakfast: 07.00-09.00
Lunch: 12.00-14.30
Dinner: 18.30-22.00

Health: It is recommended to consult your doctor before your journey. Drinking water is safe in most major cities. The medical and dental treatment is free, but the medications must be paid. In emergencies you must contact your embassy or hotel receptionist.

TASHKENT

Country code: 7 - City code: 3711

Airport: Tashkent

Distance from City: 7 km., (4.3 mi.)

Hotels:
Uzbekistan, Karl Marx 45, 333959
Zarvashan, Akhunbabayeva 15a, 335970
Tashkent, Lenin St. 50
Shark, Pavda Vostoka 16

Rossia, Rustaveli St.
Moskva, Novoi Prospekt

Restaurants:
Anchor Tearoom, Tukayeva 33
Bakhor, Kuibysheva 15
Gulistan, Kalinin Sq.

Shops and Stores:

Almaz, Mukimi 1	Jewelry
Central Store, Rashidov 17	Dept. Store
Benteryozka, Pyervomaiskaya	Gifts

Places of Interest:
Art Gallery
Botanical Garden
Museum of Carpets
Pobeda Park
Theatre Square

LATIN AMERICA
CARIBBEAN

ARGENTINA

Official Name: Argentine Republic

Location: Southern South America. Argentina shares its west border with Chile, the north and northeast with Bolivia, Paraguay, Brazil and Uruguay. On south lies the South Atlantic Ocean.

Government: Federal Republic

Area: 2,766,889 sq. km., 1,068,302 sq. miles

Population: 33.49 million

Religion(s): Roman Catholic. Protestant and Jewish minorities.

Capital City: Buenos Aires

Major Business Cities: Buenos Aires, Cordoba and Rosario

Time: GMT -3

Currency: Nuevo Peso (P)=100 centavos

Currency Requirements: The Import and the export of foreign and local currencies is unlimited.

Business Hours:
- Government: 08.00 or 09.00-17.00 Mon-Fri
- Banks: 10.00-15.00 or 16.00 Mon-Fri
- Shops: 08.00 or 09.00-17.00 Mon-Fri
- Offices: 08.00 or 09.00-17.00 Mon-Fri

Weight and Measures: Metric System

Electric Current:
220 volts AC. Plugs are of the round 2-pin type in older buildings. New buildings use the 3-pin flat type.

ARGENTINA

Holidays:
New Year's Day - January 1
Maundy Thursday - March 27
Good Friday - April 10*
Labor Day - May 1
Revolution Day (1810) - May 25
Malvinas Day** - June 10
National Flag Day** - June 20
Independence Day - July 9
Death of General Jose de San Martin** - August 17
Discovery of America (Columbus Day)** - October 12
Immaculate Conception - December 8
Christmas - December 25

* Christian Holidays - vary each year

** According to a law enacted in 1988, when a holiday falls on a Tuesday or Wednesday, it is observed on the preceding Monday. When it falls on a Thursday or Friday, it is observed on the following Monday.

Suitable Clothing: Winter is June to September, so wear medium weight coat and clothing then; the rest of the year, light clothing is appropriate. Wear a business suit or a conservative dress to meetings. Men should wear a tie even in hot weather. Except for private club functions, don't dress formally, and avoid looking too wealthy, for safety reasons. Bring sungear in summer and rainwear year round.

Automobile Driving License: An International Driving Permit is required.

Customs Allowances: Personal items are duty free, but register valuables, including electronic equipment, and keep receipts or they may face confiscation. If you don't need to declare anything, there are special "express lanes" you may pass through quickly. The number of items you may bring in duty free depends on where they come from: 800 cigarettes from non-contiguous countries and 200 from contiguous countries; 50 and 25 cigars, respectively, and 4 and I liters of spirits, respectively. Prohibited are military weaponry and drugs, with severe penalties for the latter. Inspections tend to be more stringent for arrivals from other South American countries.

Tipping: A service charge of 10-15% is usually included in all restaurant and hotel bills. Most taxi drivers expect a 10% tip.

Credit Cards Accepted: American Express, Diner's Club, Master Card, Visa

Customary Dining Hours:
Breakfast: 07.00 - 10.00
Lunch: 12.30 - 14.30
Dinner: 20.00 - 01.00

Local Customs, Business Protocol and Courtesies: Business and social relationships go hand-in-hand in Argentina, where deals are usually made on the basis of personal contacts. For this reason, the business visitor should be friendly, good-natured, polite and knowledgeable of local customs, and accept invitations for an evening at a cafe as well as to a formal business lunch. Indeed, many business agreements are made over coffee after a leisurely lunch, the main meal of the day, or after dinner. If you are offered "maté," an herbal tea prepared for family, friends and associations, you'll know you've been accepted as a business partner or friend.

Argentina's business and cultural heart is Buenos Aires, although there are several other large cities where much business takes place. Buenos Aires is by appearance and custom the most European city on the continent. The business and social climate are a mix of traditional manners and informal energy. Men and women generally shake hands, or men will offer a slight bow to their female counterparts. At initial meetings, business cards are exchanged, and people will typically address each other using their title and last name. Appointments should be arranged in advance, and be on time, although lateness on the part of your counterpart may not be unusual. Argentineans prefer to conduct all but the most minor business in person rather than over the phone. It helps to speak or understand Spanish, of course, but keep in mind that it may be hard to keep up with as people tend to speak all at once, and very quickly and emotionally. Those engaged in conversation tend to stand very close to one another; moving away would be considered rude. In negotiations, be friendly and polite but firm and confident. Don't be overly critical and offend local sensitivities. Because gift-giving can be easily misconstrued as a bribe, be careful regarding timing when you give a gift. It's best to wait until you have been offered one, and generally, a social setting is the correct context. You might consider a group gift such as office accessories especially if you are a woman presenting a gift to male counterparts. Tasteful souvenirs from your home country are fine, and, so are flowers or chocolate if invited to a home. When the host offers a toast, respond with one as well. And in this hospitable society, you will likely be invited.

Health: It is advisable to consult your doctor before your journey. Vaccinations for hepatitis A, tetanus, typhoid and polio are recommended. There is a risk of malaria in rural areas. It is advisable to drink bottled water. Medical Insurance is recommended.

Language: Spanish. English, French, German and Italian are often spoken as a second language.

BUENOS AIRES

Country code: 54 - City code: 1

Airport: Ministro Pistarini Airport (Ezeiza)

Distance from City: 50km (31 miles) southwest of the city.

Transportation to Center of City:
From International and Domestic Terminals
By Bus (cost) ARS12. Time approx. 40-60 min
By Taxi (cost) ARS40-50. Time approx. 35-55 min.
Tip luggage porters ARS1 per piece

Transfers: (Minimum Connecting Time):

ARGENTINA

International to International: 60 min.
International to Domestic: 60 min.
Domestic to International: 60 min.
Domestic to Domestic: 60 min.

Automobile Rentals:
Avis - 326-5542
Hertz - 312-1317

Hotels:
Aspen Suites, Esmeralda 933, 313-9011
Best Western Embassy All Suites, Ave. Cordoba 860, 322-1228
Bisonte Hotel, Paraguay 1207 Esq. Libertad, 816-5770
Bisonte Palace Hotel, Suipacha 902, 328-4751
Caesar Park Buenos Aires, Prosadas 1232, Recoleta, 819-1100
Comfort Suites Recoleta Plaza, Posadas 1557, 804-3471
Crillon Hotel, Av. Santa Fe 796, 312-8181
Crowne Plaza Panamericano, Carlos Pellegrini 525, 348-5000
Inter-Continental Buenos Aires, 809 Moreno St., 340-7100
Marriott Plaza Hotel Buenos Aires, Florida, 318-3000
Nogaro Hotel, Pte. Julio A. Roca 562, 331-0091
Park Tower, Av. L. N. Alem 1193, 318-9100
Presidente Hotel, Cerrito 850, Ave. 9 de Julio, 816-2222
Regente Palace Hotel, Suipacha 964, 328-6800
Sheraton Buenos Aires Hotel and Towers, San Martin 1225, Plaza Fuerza Aerea, 318-9000

Restaurants:
Broccolino, Esmeralda 776, 322 9848
Cabana las Lilas, R.M.Ortiz 1913, 804 3410
Catalinas, Reconquista 875, 313 0182
Clark's II, Sarmiento 645, 325 1960
Clark's, Junin 1777, 801 9502
El Palacio de la Papa Frita, Lavalle 735, 393 5849
Gato Dumas Cocinero, Junin 1745, 806 5801
Happening, Guido 1931, 805 2633
Harper's, Junin 1763, 801 7140
Henry J.Bean's, Junin 1749, 801 8477
La Burgogne, Ayacucho 2037, 805 3857
La Cabana, Entre Rios 436, 381 2372
La Estancia, Lavalle 941, 326 0330
La Gomeria, Vicente Lopez 2134, 803 6170

ARGENTINA

Las Nazarenas, Reconquista 1132, 312 5559
Lola, R.M.Ortiz 1805, 804 3410
London Grill, Reconquista 455, 311 2223
Mora X, Vicente Lopez 2152, 803 0261
Roma Pizzeria, Lavalle 888,
Sensu, R.M.Ortiz 1815, 804 1214
Tomo I, Carlos Pellegrini 525, 326 6310
Zum Edelweiss, Calle Libertad 431, 382 3351

Entertainment:
Afrika, Avenida Alvear 1885, 804 4031
Bar Baro, Tres Sargentos 415, 311 6856
Cafe Tortoni, Avenida de Mayo 825
Cafe Vienes Mozart, Esmeralda 754, 322 3273
El Verde, Reconquista 878, 315 3693
Hippopotamus, Junin 1787, 804 8310
Mau Mau, Arroyo 866, 393 6131
Newport, Junin 1715, 803 3332
Paladium, Reconquista 945, 312 9819
Satchmo, Aguero 2279
Shampoo, Quintana 362, 42 44 27
Shams, Frederico Lacroze 2121, 773 0721
Tequila, Costanera Norte y La Pampa, 788 0438
Trumps, Bulnes 2772, 801 9866

Shops and Stores:

Adriana Costantini, Avenida Alvear 1892	Apparel
Antoniazzi-Chiappe, Avenida Alvear 1895	Jewelry
Beatriz Jordan, Avenida Rodriguez Saenz Pena 1047	Apparel
Ile de France, Calle Florida 860	Jewelry
Los Cuatro Ases , Calle Florida 519	Apparel
Ricciardi, Plaza Hotel, Calle Florida 1001	Jewelry
Santarelli, Calle Florida 688	Jewelry
Silvia y Mario, M.T. de Alvear 55	Apparel
Supermercado del Disco, Carlos Pellegrini 481	Music

Places of Interest:
The Argentine Museum of Natural Sciences
The City of Buenos Aires Museum
The National Museum of Fine Arts
Basilica de Santisimo Sacramento   - a church
Palermo Park   - zoo and botanical gardens
The Cathedral of San Isidro

BAHAMAS

Official Name: Commonwealth of the Bahamas

Location: Caribbean. The Bahamas consist of 700 islands, that are situated 970km (602 miles) southeast from the Florida Coast.

Area: 13,939 sq. km., 5382 sq. miles.

Population: 263,000

Religion(s): Baptist, Anglican and Roman Catholic.

Capital City: Nassau

Time: GMT -5 (GMT -4 from early April to late October)

Currency: Bahamian Dollar (Ba$)=100 cents

Currency Requirements: The import and the export of foreign currency are unlimited, but the export of more than USD5000 must be declared. The import of local currency is restricted to Ba$100 and export to Ba$70.

Business Hours:
- Banks: 09.30-15.00 Mon-Thur; 09.30-17.00 Fri
- Shops: 09.00-17.00 Mon-Sat
- Offices: 09.00-17.00 Mon-Fri

Weight and Measures: Metric System

Electric Current: 120 volts AC

Holidays:
New Year's Day - January 1
Good Friday – April 10*
Easter Monday – April 13*
Whit Monday – June 1*
Labor Day - June 6

BAHAMAS

Independence Day - July 10
Emancipation Day - August 4
Discovery Day* - October 12
Christmas Day - December 25
Boxing Day - December 26

*Christian Holidays – vary each year
Holidays which fall on a Saturday or Sunday are usually observed on the previous Friday or the following Monday.

Suitable Clothing: Because of the hot weather, business attire is somewhat more casual; light materials can be worn year round and many businessmen forego jackets. Nevertheless, you should wear a lightweight suit for a first meeting, and for all government visits. Wear a dinner jacket for formal occasions. Bring rainwear between June and October, and sungear at all times.

Customs Allowances: Personal items are duty free, but register valuables upon arrival or they may be confiscated upon departure. Although you may bring in unlimited amounts of foreign currency, and take out any you initially declare, you may not import or export local currency. You may bring in 200 cigarettes and one liter each of wine and spirits. Punishment is severe for drugs; military weaponry and pornography are also forbidden.

Tipping: A service charge is usually included by most restaurants and hotels, if not a 15% tip expected. Taxi drivers expect a 15% tip.

Local Customs, Business Protocol and Courtesies: The business world in the Bahamas · with Nassau as its center · is friendly and relaxed but maintains an air of professionalism. Insurance, shipping, banking and tourism are the mainstays of the economy. Schedule meetings in advance and be on time. Shake hands upon introduction, offer business cards and use titles until indicated otherwise. Presentations and contracts should be detailed and well-defined, and your sales approach low-key. Business lunches, dinners or informal meetings over drinks are common, but never breakfasts. Entertaining (sometimes formal) and exchanging business gifts tend to occur only after a deal has

BAHAMAS

been reached. If invited to a home, bring flowers. Sailing is popular and you may be invited for a trip.

Health: It is advisable to consult your doctor before your journey. There are no special vaccinations required. A yellow fever immunization certificate is required if arriving from an infected area. It is recommended to have immunizations against hepatitis A, polio, tetanus and typhoid. The drinking water should be boiled or sterilized.

Language: English.

NASSAU

Country code: 242 - City code: none

Airport: Nassau International Airport.

Distance from City: 16km (9 miles) west of the city center.

Transportation to Center of City:
From International and Domestic Terminals
By Bus (cost) Ba$15-25. Time approx. 15-30 min.

Automobile Rentals:
Airport car rental desk
Avis - 377-7121

Car rental city office
Avis - 326-6380
Hertz - 377-8684

Hotels:
Best Western British Colonial Beach Resort, 1 Bay St.,
    322-3301
Atlantis, Casino Dr., Paradise Island, 363-3000
Nassau Harbor Club Hotel and Marina, East Bay St.,
    369-0771/2
Nassau Marriott Resort and Crystal Palace Casino, Cable Beach,
    327-6200
Ocean Club, Paradise Island Dr. Paradise Island, 363-3000

Paradise Paradise, Paradise Island Dr. Paradise Island,363-3000
Radisson Grand Resort, Casino Dr., Paradise Island, 363-3500

Restaurants:
Buena Vista, b/n W. Hill St. and Delancy St., 322-2811
Cappuccino Café, Royal Palm Mall, Mackey St., 394-6332
Cellar and Garden Patio, 2 Charlotte St., 322-8877
Double Dragon, Bridge Plaza Commons, Mackey St., 393-5718
East Villa Restaurant and Lounge, Box N1461, E. Bay St., 393-3377
Graycliff, W. Hill St. at Cumberland Rd., 322-2796
Green Shutters, 48 Parliament St., 325-5702
Montagu Gardens, E. Bay St., 394-6347
Passin' Jacks, E. Bay St., 394-3245
Pick-a Dilly, 18 Parliament St., 322-2836
Poop Deck, E. Bay St. at Nassao Yacht Haven Marina, 393-8175
Prince George Dockside Restaurant, Bay St., west of Rawson Sq., 322-5854
Shoal Restaurant and Lounge, Nassao St., b/n Meadow St. and Poinciana Dr., 323-4400
Sun And..., Box N3515, Lakeview Rd., 393-1205
Tamarind Hill, Box N233, Village Rd., 393-1306

Entertainment:
Anthony's Caribbean Grill, Paradise Island, 363 3152
Atlantis Showroom, Paradise Island Casino, 363 2518
Bahamen's Culture Club, Nassao and W. Bay St., 356-6266
Buena Vista, Delancy St., 322 2811
Cafe Johnny Canoe Restaurant & Bar, Cable Beach, 327 3373
Cafe Kokomo, 18 Parliament St., 322 2836
Cafe Martinique, Paradise Island, 363 2518
Club Land'or, Paradise Beach Dr., 363 2400
Club Med, Paradise Island Village,Casuarina Dr., 363 2640
Club Paradise, Paradise Island, 363 2518
Club Waterloo, E. Bay St., 394-0163
Courtyard Terrace, Paradise Island, 363 2518
Cudabay, E. Bay St., 393-0771
Drop Off Pub, Bay St., 322 3444
Graycliff, West Hill St., 322 2797
Le Shack, E. Bay St., 325-2148

BAHAMAS

Mama Loo's, Paradise Island, 363 2518
Nasau Marriott Resort & Crystal Palace Casino, Cable Beach,
    327 6200
Paradise Harbour Club & Marina, Paradise Iland Dr., 363 3500
The Boat House, Paradise Island, 363 2518

Shops and Stores:

Balmain Antiques, Bay St.	Antiques
Barry's Limited, Bay St.	Apparel
Bonneville Bones, Bay St.	Apparel
Coin of the Realm, Charlotte St.	Jewelry
Crown Jewelers, Bay St.	Jewelry
Fendi, Bay St.	Dept. Store
Green Lizard, Bay St.,	Gifts Shop
John Bull, Bay St.	Jewelry
Leather Masters Parliament St.	Apparel
Little Switzerland, Bay St.	Jewelry
Nassau Shop, Bay St.,	Dept. Store
The Bay, Bay St.	Apparel
Tick-Tock, Bay St.	Jewelry

Places of Interest:

Straw Market - bazaar
Fort Charlotte
Ardastra Gardens – botanical garden
The Queen's Staircase
Fort Fincastle
The Water Tower
Coral World – underwater observatory.

BOLIVIA

Official Name: Republic de Bolivia

Location: South America. Bolivia is bordered by Chile, Argentina, Paraguay, Brazil and Peru.

Government: Republic

Area: 1,084,391 sq. km., 424,164 sq. miles.

Population: 7.5 million

Religion(s): Roman Catholic majority. Protestant minority.

Capital City: La Paz

Major Business Cities: Santa Cruz., Sucre, Cochabamba, Oruro

Time: GMT -4

Currency: Boliviano (BS)=100 centavos (the Bolivian Peso is no longer in circulation).

Currency Requirements: There are no restrictions on the import and the export of local or foreign currency. Visitors may be asked to prove that they have sufficient funds to support themselves during their stay.

Business Hours:
- Government: 10.00-12.30; 15.00-19.00 Mon-Fri
- Banks: 09.00-12.00; 14.00-17.00 Mon-Fri
- Shops: 09.00/10.00-12.30/13.00; 15.00-19.00 Mon-Fri; 09.30-13.00 Sat
- Offices: 09.00-12.00 & 14.00-17.00 Mon-Fri

Weight and Measures: Metric System, some old Spanish measures

BOLIVIA

Electric Current: 110/220 volts AC. Plugs are of the 2-pin type.

Holidays:
New Year's Day - January 1
Carnival - February 10-11
Good Friday - April 10*
Labor Day - May 1
Corpus Christi - June 11*
Independence Day - August 6
All Saints' Day - November 1
Christmas Day - December 25

*Christian Holidays - vary each year

Suitable Clothing: Dress conservatively - suits for meetings and dark suit or dress for formal occasions. Dressing too flash-ily or too expensively can attract thieves and will not make a good impression. In La Paz, bring medium weight clothing, but lighter material for Santa Cruz.

Automobile Driving License: An International Driving Permit is required. It can also be issued by Federacion Inter-America-na de Touring y Automovil on presentation of a national license. It is recommended to acquire the permit before traveling.

Customs Allowances: Personal items are duty free, but regis-ter valuables such as electronics upon arrival to expedite your way out. There are no currency restrictions. You may bring in 200 cigarettes, 2 liters of wine and one of spirits. Punishment is severe for drug possession.

Tipping: There is a 13% service charge plus local tax included in hotel and restaurant bills, but it is customary to tip another 10%.

Credit Cards Accepted:
American Express, MasterCard, Visa

Customary Dining Hours:
Breakfast: 07.30-09.00
Lunch: 12.00-14.00
Dinner: 19.00-21.30

BOLIVIA

Local Customs, Business Protocol and Courtesies: Business and some customs are heavily European in style, and the La Paz business ties are conservative and go back a long way. The business visitor should be friendly, good-natured, polite and knowledgeable of local customs, and accept invitations for an evening at a cafe as well as to a formal business lunch. Indeed, many business agreements are made over coffee after a leisurely lunch, the main meal of the day, or after dinner. Men and women generally shake hands, or men will offer a slight bow to their female counterparts. At initial meetings, business cards are exchanged providing English/Spanish ones and company literature in Spanish will make a good impression. Present the card Spanish side up. People typically address each other using their title and last name. Appointments should be arranged in advance (avoid Tuesday the 13th, considered a bad luck day). Your contact may be late, but you should never express annoyance or hostility. Your contemporaries are quite sophisticated, and an atmosphere of confident goodwill and courtesy should prevail on both sides. Persistence is important, but pays off only if done with courtesy and with confidence. In meetings or discussions, it is the norm to stand or sit close to one another, and for many people to speak at once. Try to fit into this atmosphere without being too aggressive. You will find that many businessmen in Bolivia are accustomed to serving a multitude of purposes, such as acting as both wholesaler and retailer. Because gift-giving can be easily misconstrued as a bribe, be careful regarding timing when you give a gift. It's best to wait until you have been offered one, and generally, a social setting is the correct context. You might consider a group gift such as office accessories, especially if you are a woman presenting a gift to male counterparts. Tasteful souvenirs from your home country are fine, and, so are flowers or chocolates if invited to a home. Avoid black or lavender, or certain types and colors of flowers which are considered funereal or romantic.

At meals, eat European style with knife and fork. Guests may begin eating even if the others have not yet been served. It is typical to take small portions of each course from a common plate, and to place your utensils across the plate when finished. When the host offers a toast, respond with one as well. You are expected to stay awhile after the meal; business or other subjects are often discussed then. Avoid discussing the longtime border conflict with Chile.

Health: It is advisable to consult your doctor before your journey. Vaccinations for yellow fever, cholera, paratyphoid, typhoid, and polio are recommended. A vaccination is also recommended for travelers visiting risk areas such as Beni, Chuquisaca, Cochabamba, Pando, Santa Cruz, Tarija and parts of La Paz. For people arriving from infected countries it is required to have a yellow fever vaccination certificate. There is a risk of malaria and meningitis in some areas. It is strongly recommended to drink bottled water. Food precautions should be observed at all times. Medical insurance is necessary.

Language: Spanish

LA PAZ

Country code: 591 - City code: 2

Airport: El Alto International Airport

Distance from City: 14km (8 miles) from the city.

Transportation to Center of City:
From International and Domestic Terminals
By Bus (cost) BS3. Time approx. 40-60 min.
By Taxi (cost) BS45-50. Time approx. 35-40 min.
Tip luggage porters BS2 per piece

Transfers: (Minimum Connecting Time):
International to International: 60 min.
International to Domestic: 60 min.
Domestic to International: 60 min.
Domestic to Domestic: 30 min.

BOLIVIA

Automobile Rentals:
Airport car rental desk
National Interrent - 376581
Car rental city office
National Interrent - 37658

Hotels:
Camino Real Royal Suites Hotel, 2123 Capitan Ravelo Ave., 314542
El Rey Palace Hotel, Av. 20 de Octubre 1947, 393016
Eldorado Hotel, Avda. Villazon s/n, Casilla 77, 363355
Gran Hotel Paris, Plaza Murillo esq. Bolivar, 319170
Plaza Hotel, Paseo El Prado, 378311
Presidente Hotel, Calle Potosi 920, 367193
Radisson Plaza Hotel La Paz, Avda. Arce 2177, 316161
Hotel Sagarnaga, Calle Sagarnaga 326, 350252
Europa Hotel, 64 Tiahuanacu St., 315656
Ritz Apart Hotel, Plaza Isabel La Catolica 2478, 433131
Gloria, Potosi 909, 370010
Libertador, Obispo Cardenas 1421, 351792
Nikkei Plaza, Calle Mexico 1555, 326341
Sucre Palace, Avenida 16 de Julio 1636, 363453
Continental, Illampu 626, 378226
Copacabana, Avenida 16 de Julio 1802, 352244
Hosteria Blanquita, Sante Cruz 242, 352933
Hostal Emabajador, Juan de la Riva 1438, 392079
La Joya, Max Parades 541, 324346

Restaurants:
La Cantonata, Av. 6 de Agosto esq. L. Gutierez, 323389
La Trandquera, Capitan Ravelo 2123, 310103
Los Lobos, Tupac Katari #15, Aranhues, 794539
La Suisse, Huan Munoz reyes 1770 – Calacoto, 793160
El Arriero, Av. 6 de Agosto 2535, 322708
Blaskie's House, Canada Stronges 1852, 326816
Viena , federico Zuazo 1905, 391660
Chifa Emy, Los Pinos Calle 7, 795610
Georggisimo, Av. camacho esq. Loayza 1367, 324456
El Vijo Tonel, Av. 6 de Agosto 2604, 324667
Montesano, An. Munoz Reyes Cota Cota, 771112
New Tokyo, Av. 6 de Agosto 2932, 433654
Chez Lacoste, Prolongacion Cordero 123, 322348
El Nuevo galeon, Av. Munoz Reyes 1210, 792536

BOLIVIA

Entertainment:
La Roneria, Av. Ballivian 941, 790831
Rumor's, Av. Ballivian 312, 785890
La Flor de la Canela, Lisimaco Gutierres 589, 413344Forum,
victor sanjines 2908, 325762
Viojotyeca, Barrio Auquisamana Final 21
Sopo's Pub G Y C SRL, PJE> Jauregui Esq. Fernando Guachal-
la, 351443

Shops and Stores:
Joyeria Cosmos, Handal Center, Local 13, Socabaya y Avenida
   16 de Jullio   Jewelry
Joyeria Kings, Loayaza 261   Jewelry
Astesania Sorata, Linares 862   Apparel
Angora Sport, Avenida 16 de Julio   Dept. Store
Javier Nunez de Arco, Av. 6 de Agosto 2255   Antiques
La Casa de Pino, Hermanos Manchego, near av. Arce
                                  Antiques
Tradicional, Salinas 345   Antiques

Places of Interest:
Tiwanaku Archaeological Museum
The National Art Museum
Catedral de Nuestra Senora de La Paz
Casa de Murillo - a museum
Monticulo Observatory
The San Francisco Church
The Galeria Emusa - art and sculpture.

BRAZIL

Official Name: Federative Republic of Brazil

Location: South America. Brazil is bordered by Uruguay, Argentina, Paraguay, Bolivia, Peru, Colombia, Venezuela, Guyana, Suriname and French Guiana . On the east lies the Atlantic Ocean.

Government: Federal Republic

Area: 8,511,996 sq. km., 3,286,500 sq. miles.

Population: 153.9 million

Religion(s): Roman Catholic majority

Capital City: Brasilia

Major Business Cities: Recife, Rio de Janeiro and Sao Paulo.

Time: GMT -3/-5

Currency: Real (BRL)=100 centavos

Currency Requirements: There are no restrictions on the import and the export of local currency. The import of foreign currency must be declared. The export is limited to the amount declared on arrival.

Business Hours:
- Government: 09.00-18.00 Mon-Fri, 09.00-13.00 Sat
- Banks: 10.00-16.30 Mon-Fri
- Shops: 09.00-18.00 Mon-Fri; 09.00-13.00 Sat
- Offices: 09.00-18.00 Mon-Fri; 09.00-13.00 Sat

Weight and Measures: Metric System

Electric Current: 110 or 220v, 60 cycles, AC. Plugs are 2-pin type.

Holidays:
International Peace Day - January 1
Carnival - February 8-11
Good Friday - April 10*
Tirandentes (National Hero Day) - April 21
May Day - May 1
Corpus Christi - June 11*
Independence Day - September 7
Nossa Senhora Aparecida - October 12
   (Patroness Saint of Brazil)
All Souls' Day - November 2*
Day of the Republic - November 15
Christmas Day - December 25

*Christian Holidays - vary each year

Suitable Clothing: Dress conservatively, preferably in a suit. Except for private club functions, don't dress formally, and avoid looking too wealthy, for safety reasons. In Sao Paulo wear medium weight clothing, and dress lighter in Rio de Janeiro.

Automobile Driving License: An International Driving License, a passport and a credit card are required.

Customs Allowances: Personal items are duty free, but register valuables and keep receipts or they may face confiscation. There are no foreign currency limits (but declare how much you have coming in), but Reals may not be imported or exported. You may bring in 250 cigarettes duty free and 2 liters of wine and spirits.

Tipping: A service of 10-15% is usual for restaurants and bars if it is not already included in the bill. Taxi fares are rounded up to the nearest Real.

Credit Cards Accepted: American Express, MasterCard, Visa

Customary Dining Hours:
Breakfast: 07.30-09.00

BRAZIL

Lunch: 12.30-14.30
Dinner: 20.00-22.00

Local Customs, Business Protocol and Courtesies: In general, be friendly and open while still professional. Business is often conducted over long lunches (the main meal) or over many cups of coffee (not to be refused). Personal relationships are important here. Unlike in most other South American countries, businessmen here tend to be punctual. Indeed, Brazilians consider themselves a fully separate culture from the rest of Latin America, and it helps to have a local representative, not a general one for South America. Brazilian businessmen pride themselves on the degree of self-sufficiency in their industry and economy, and they are skilled negotiators. Remember that the language here is Portuguese, and that trying to get by in Spanish is not well-regarded. Men and women generally shake hands, or men will offer a slight bow to their female counterparts. At initial meetings, business cards are exchanged. Use title and last name. Because gift-giving can be easily misconstrued as a bribe, be careful regarding timing when you give a gift. It's best to wait until you have been offered one, and generally, a social setting is the correct context. You might consider a group gift such as office accessories, especially if you are a woman presenting a gift to male counterparts. Tasteful souvenirs from your home country are fine, and, so are flowers or chocolates if invited to a home. Avoid certain types and colors of flowers which are considered funereal or romantic. If visiting a home, bring flowers or send them as a thank-you gesture the next day. Also, send a thank-you note before leaving the country to your associates, hosts and their families.

Health: It is advisable to consult your doctor before your journey. A vaccination certificate for Yellow Fever is necessary if traveling from an infected area. Vaccinations for hepatitis A, tetanus, typhoid and polio are recommended. If visiting outer rural areas vaccinations for yellow fever and malaria prophylaxis are also recommended. It is strongly advisable to drink only boiled or bottled water. Dairy products which may have come from unboiled milk should be avoided. All fruit should be peeled. People requiring special treatment or diets are advised to carry a Portuguese translated description of the nature of their condition, treatment and medicines required. Medical insurance is strongly advised as medical costs are high.

Language: Portuguese

RIO DE JANEIRO

Country code: 55 - City code: 21

Airport: Galeao International Airport

Distance from City: 21km (13 miles) northwest of the city.

Transportation to Center of City:
From International and Domestic Terminals
By Bus (cost) BRL3. Time approx. 35-55 min.
By Taxi (cost) BRL15-20.Time approx. 35-45 min.
Tip luggage porters BRL1 per piece

Transfers: (Minimum Connecting Time):
International to International: 60 min.
International to Domestic: 120 min.
Domestic to International: 75 min.
Domestic to Domestic: 60 min.

Automobile Rentals:
Airport car rental desk
Avis - 398-3357
Hertz - 398-4338

Car rental city office
Avis - 541-2441
Hertz - 275-7440

Hotels:
Caesar Park Hotel Ipanema, Av. Vieira Souto 460, Ipanema, 525-2525
Copacabana Palace Hotel, Av. Atlantica 1702, 255-7070

BRAZIL

Grandville OuroVerde Hotel, Av. Atlantica 1456, Copacabana, 542-1887
Hotel Inter-Conential, Ave. Litoraela 222, Sao Cornado, 322-2200
Hotel Meridien, Ave. Atlantica 1220, 275-9922
Hotel Nacional, Ave. Niemeyer 769, Sao Cornado, 322-1000
Hotel Regente, Ave. Atlantica 1500, Copacabana, 287-4212
Hotel Sol Ipanema, Ave. Viera Souto 320, Ipanema, 267-0095
Lancaster Othon Hotel, Av. Atlantica 1470, 521-6262
Le Meridien Copacabana, Av.Atlantica 1020, 541-0866
Leme Othon Palace Hotel, Av. Atlantica 656, 521-6262
Olinda Othon Hotel, Av. Atlantica 2230, 521-6262
Premier Copacabana Hotel, Rua Tonelero 205, Copacabana, 255-8581
Rio Atlantica Hotel, Av. Atlantica, Copacabana, 255-6332
Rio Internacional Hotel, Av. Atlantica 1500, 295-2323
Rio Othon Palace Hotel, Av. Atlantica 3264, Copacabana, 522-0262
Savoy Othon Hotel, Av. N.S. Copacabana 995, 521-6262
Trocadero Othon Hotel, Av. Atlanica 2064, 521-6262

Restaurants:
A Marisqueira, 232 Rua Barata Ribeiro, 237 3920
Alba Mar, Praca 15 de Novembro, 240 8378
Antonino, 1244 Av.Epitacio Pessoa, 267 6791
Antonio's, 297 Av.Bartolomeu Mitre, 294 2699
Banana Café, 368 Rua Barao da Torre, 521 1460
Carretao, 116 Praca Sao Perpetuo, 399 4055
Del Mare, 37 Rua Paul Redfern, 239 7842
La Tour, 651 Rua Santa Luzia, 240 5493
Les Champs Elysees, 1910 Av.Atlantica 237 9915
Mab's, 1140 Av.Atlantica, 275 7299
Marius, 290 Av.Atlantica, 542 2393
Negresco, 348 Rua Barao da Torre, 287 4842
Nino, 242 Rua Domingos Ferreira, 255 0785
Ouro Verde,1456 Av.Atlantica, 542 1887
Petronius, 460 Av.Vieira Souto, 287 3122
Porcao, 218 Rua Brao da Torre, 521 0999
Rincao Gaucho, 83 Rua Marques de Valensa, 284 5889
Rodeio, 2150 Av.Alvorada, 3256166
Sole E Mar, 11 Av.Nestor Moreira, 295 1997
Tiffany's, 729 Rua Prudente de Morais, 247 0580

Entertainment:
Asa Branca, 17 Av.Mem da Sa, 252 7066
Biblo's Bar, 1484 Av.Epitacio Pessoa, 521 2645
Café Nice, 277 Av.Rio Branco, 240 0490
Caligula, 129 Rua Prudente de Morais, 287 1369
Canecao, 215 Av.Wenceslau Bras, 295 3044
Chiko's Bar, 1560 Av.Epitasio Pessoa, 295 3514
Help, 3432 Av.Atlantica, 521 1296
Hippopotamus, 354 Rua Barao da Torre, 247 0351
Hotel Nacional, 769 Av.Niemeyer,
Ilha Dos Pescadores, 793 Estrada da Barra da Tijuca
    399 0005
Lord Jim, 63 Rua Paul Redfern, 259 3047
Mistura Fina Studio, 1636 Estrada da Barra da Tijuca
    264 0549
Mme.Butterfly, 472 Rua Barao de Torre, 267 4347
New Jirau, 12A Rua Siqueira Campos, 255 5864
New Prive, 28 Rua Jangadeiro, 267 2544
Noites Carioca, 520 Av.Pasteur, 541 3737
Oba Oba, 110 Rua Humaita, 286 9848
People, 370 Av.Bartolomeu Mitre, 294 0547
Plataforma, 32 Rua Adalberto Ferreira, 274 4022
Scala Rio, 296 Av.Afranio de Melo Franco, 239 4448
Texas Club, 974A Av. Atlantica, 275 0246
Zoom, Largo de Sao Corado, 322 4179

Shops and Stores:
Bee, Rua Garsia d'Avilla 83 — Apparel
Centro Commercial, Rua Visconde de Piraja — Apparel
Company , Rua Garsia d'Avilla 56 — Apparel
Copacabana Couros E Artesanatos, Rua Fernando Mendes 45a — Dept. Store
Copacabana, Ave. Nossa Senhora de Copacabana — Mall
H. Stern, Rua Visconde de Piraja 490 — Jewelry
Ipanema, near Rua Visconde de Piraja — Apparel
Krishna, Elle at Lui, Rua Garsia d'Avilla 124 — Apparel
Leblon , near Ave. Artaulfo de Paiva — Shopping Area
Les Griffes, 1702 Ave. Atlantica, Copacabana — Apparel
Minas Souvenir, Rua Fernando Mendes 28-C — Jewelry
Star Jewelry, Rua Duvivier of Ave. de Copacabana — Jewelry

BRAZIL

Places of Interest:
The Gloria Church
The Museum of Fine Arts
The Convent of Santo Antonio
The Botanical Garden
The Museum of the Republic
The Museum Nacional
Jardim Zoologico   - a zoo
Corcovado - the famous statue of Jesus
Sugar Loaf - an impressive rock structure

SAO PAULO

Country code: 55 - City code: 11

Airport: Guarulhos International Airport

Distance from City: 30km (18 miles) northeast of the city.

Transportation to Center of City:
From International and Domestic Terminals
By Bus (cost) BRL5. Time approx. 50-60 min.
By Taxi (cost) USD40. Time approx. 20-30 min.
Tip luggage porters BRL1 per piece

Transfers: (Minimum Connecting Time):
International to International: 60 min.
International to Domestic: 75 min.
Domestic to International: 90 min.
Domestic to Domestic: 45 min.

Automobile Rentals:
Airport car rental desk
Avis - 945-2180
Hertz - 945-2801

Car rental city office
Avis - 257-8255
Hertz - 883-7300

BRAZIL

Hotels:
Augusta Palace, Rua Augusta 467, Consolacau, 256-1277
Best Western Augusta Palace, Rua Augusta 467, 256-1277
Brasilton Sao Paulo, Rua Martins Fontes 330, 258 5811
Caesar Park Hotel Sao Paulo, Rua Augusta 1508, 253-6622
Della Volpe Hotel, Rua Frei Caneca 1199, 285-5388
El Dorado Hotel, R. Marques de Itu 836, 222-3422
Grand Hotel Ca'd'Oro, Rua Augusta 129, 256-8811
Hotel Bourbon, Ave. Vieira de Carvalho 99, Centro, 223-2244
Hotel San Michel, Lgo. do Arouche 200, Centro, 223-4433
Hotel Transamerica, Ave. das Nocoes Unidas 18591, Santo
    Omaro, 523-4511
Maksoud Plaza, Alameda Campinas 150, 253-4411
Metropolitan Plaza Hotel, Ave. Campinas 474, Cerqueira
    Cesar, 287-4855
Mofarrej Sheraton, Ave. Santos, 1437, Cerqueira Cesar,
    284-5544
Nikkey Palace Hotel, Rua Galvao Bueno 425, 270-8511
Othon Palace Hotel, Rua Libero Badaro 190, 521-6262
San Raphael Hotel, Largo do Arouche 150, 250-0333
Sao Paulo Brasilton Hilton, Rua Martins Fontes 330, 258-5811
Sao Paulo Center Hotel, Largo Sta. Ifigenia 40 Centro,
    228-6033
Sao Paulo Hilton, Av. Ipiranga 165, 256-0033
Sheraton Mofarrej Hotel & Towers, Alameda Santos 1437,
    253-5544

Restaurants:
Babbo Giovanni, Rua Bela Cintra 2305, 853 3678
Baby Beef Rubaiyat, Av.Vieira de Carvalho 116, 222 8333
Bassi, Rua 13 de Maio 334, 34 2375
Bongiovanni, Av. 9 de Julho 5505, 280 1355
Butterfly, Azevedo 482, 852 9652
Carlino, Av.Dr.Vieira de Carvalho 154, 223 1603
Chalet Suisse, Rua Libero Badaro 190, 239 3277
Chamonix, Alameda Lorena 1052, 883 4233
Dino's Place, Av.Morumbi 7976, 542 5299
Don Curro, Rua Alves Guimares 230, 852 4712
Eno Moto, Rua Galvao Bueno 54, 279 0198
Famiglia Mancini, Rua Avanhandava 81, 256 4320
Fasano, Rua Haddock Lobo 1644, 852 4000
Gigetto, Rua Avanhandava 63, 256 9804

Le Coq Hardy, Av.Adolfo Pinheiro 2518, 246 6013
Marsel, Rua Epitacio Pessoa 98, 257 6968
O Profeta, Alameda dos Aicas 40, 549 5311
Paddock, Av.Sao Luis 258, 257 4768
Rodeio, Rua Haddock Lobo 1498, 883 2322
Suntory, Alameda Campinas 600, 283 2455
Terraco Italia, Av.Lpiranga 344, 257 6566
Windhuk, Alameda Dos Arapanes 1400, 240 2040

Entertainment:
150 Night Club, Al Campinas 150, 251 2233
A Baiuca, Praca Franklin Roosevelt 256, 255 2233
Big Bar, Rua Avanhandava 16, 258 2674
Clyde's, Rua da Mata 70, 883 0300
L'Ultimo Romantico, Rua Avanhandara 40, 258 6523
Lattitude, Av. 23 de Maio 3001, 212 8698
O Beco, Rua Bela Cintra 306, 259 3377
Palladium, Av.Reboucas 3970, 813 8713
Roof, Av.Cidade Jardim 400, 212 3006
Showdays Saloon, Av.Reboucas 3970, 814 9583
Terraco Italia, Av.Ipiranga 344, 257 3365
Via Brasil, Av. 9 de Julho 5710, 883 2951

Shops and Stores:
Eldorado, Ave. Rbolucas, 3970,   Shopping Center
Iguatemi, Ave. Brivadeiro Faria Lima 1191 Shopping Center
Iqirapuera, Ave. Ibirapuera 3103   Shopping Center
Morumbi, Ave. Roque Petroni Junior 1089   Mall
Paulista, Rua Treze de Maio 1947   Shopping Center
Sterns, Rua Augusta 2340   Dept. Store

Places of Interest:
Ibirapuera Park - exhibition halls and museums.
The Zoological Park
The Jardim Botanico – a botanical garden.
The Museu de Arte de Sao Paulo – an art museum.
The Instituto Butanta – an attraction

CHILE

Official Name: Republic of Chile

Location: West Coast of South America. Chile is bordered by Peru, Bolivia and Argentina. The Pacific Ocean is situated on its west coast. The Antarctic can be found to the south.

Government: Republic

Area: 756,626 sq. km., 292,135 sq. miles.

Population: 13.6 million

Religion(s): Roman Catholic majority with small Protestant minority.

Capital City: Santiago

Major Business Cities: Santiago, Vina del Mar, Concepcion, Valparaiso, Temuco

Time: GMT -4 (GMT -3 from late October to late March)

Currency: Peso (Ch$)=100 centavos

Currency Requirements: There are no restrictions on the import and export of either local or foreign currency.

Business Hours:
- Government: 09.00-17.00 or 18.00 Mon-Fri
- Banks: 09.00-14.00 Mon-Fri
- Shops: 09.30-19.00/20.00 Mon-Fri; 10.00-14.00 Sat (large centers also open 10.00-21.00 Sun)
- Offices: 09.00-18.00 Mon-Fri

Weight and Measures: Metric System

Electric Current: 220 volts AC. Plugs are of the 2-pin type.

Holidays:
New Year's Day - January 1
Easter - April 10-13*
Labor Day - May 1
Navy Day - May 21
Corpus Christi - June 11*
St. Peter's and St. Paul's Day - June 29
Assumption - August 15
Public Holiday - September 11
Independence Day - September 18
Army Day - September 19
Columbus Day - October 12
All Saints' Day - November 1
Immaculate Conception - December 8
Christmas Day - December 25

*Christian Holidays - vary each year

Suitable Clothing: Winter is June to September, so wear medium weight coat and clothing then; the rest of the year, light clothing is appropriate. Wear a business suit or a conservative dress to meetings. Except for private club functions, don't dress formally, and avoid looking too wealthy, for safety reasons.

Automobile Driving License: An International Permit is required.

Customs Allowances: Personal items are duty free, but register valuables and keep receipts or they may face confiscation. There are no foreign or local currency limits (but declare how much you have coming in). You may bring in 450 cigarettes duty free and 2.5 liters of spirits.

Tipping: A service charge of 10% is usually added to the hotel, the restaurant and the bar bills. However, it is customary to leave another 10% in cash for the waiters.

Credit Cards Accepted: American Express, MasterCard, Visa

Customary Dining Hours:
Breakfast: 07.30-09.00
Lunch: 13.00-15.00
Dinner: 20.00-22.00

CHILE

Local Customs, Business Protocol and Courtesies: Business and social customs are heavily European in style; in fact, the environment is far more Teutonic than Latin. Meetings begin on time, conversation and negotiations are low-key, many businessmen speak German and English as well as Spanish, and they work long hours. In general, be friendly but conservative, highly professional and put pressure on your counterparts. Shake hands upon meeting, and exchange business cards. Although English is widely spoken, it makes a good impression to have cards and company literature in Spanish. Use title and last name. Business entertaining is frequently at hotels or restaurants, but if you are invited to someone's home, bring flowers and chocolates for the hostess. Avoid certain types and colors of flowers which are considered funereal or romantic. At meals, eat European style with knife and fork and place your utensils across the plate when finished. When the host offers a toast, respond with one as well. You are expected to stay awhile after the meal; business or other subjects are often discussed then. It's best to wait until you have been offered a business gift before giving one yourself. You might consider a group gift such as office accessories especially if you are a woman presenting a gift to male counterparts. Tasteful souvenirs from your home country are suitable.

Health: It is advisable to consult your doctor before your journey. Vaccinations for typhoid and polio are recommended. It is strongly advisable to drink only bottled water. Food precautions to be observed at all times. Medical insurance is essential.

Language: Spanish.

SANTIAGO

Country code: 56 - City code: 2

Airport: Santiago Comodoro Arturo Merino Benitez International Airport

Distance from City: 20km (12 miles) from the city.
Transportation to Center of City:
From International and Domestic Terminals

By Bus (cost) Ch$1500-1800. Time approx. 30 min. (every 30 min.)
By Taxi (cost) Ch$8000-8500. Time approx. 25-35 min.
Tip luggage porters 100 Pesos per piece

Transfers: (Minimum Connecting Time):
International to International: 60 min.
International to Domestic: 90 min.
Domestic to International: 90 min.
Domestic to Domestic: 30 min.

Automobile Rentals:
Airport car rental desk
Avis - 601-9050
National Interrent - 601-9691
Hertz - 601-9262

Car rental city office
Avis - 331-0121
National Interrent - 517552
Hertz - 235-9666

Hotels:
Hyatt Regency Santiago, Kennedy Ave. 4601, 218-1234
Leonardo da Vinci Hotel, Malaga 194, Las Condes, 206-0591
Quality Hotel El Conquistador, Miguel Cruchaga 920, 696-5599
Radisson Royal Santiago Hotel, Av. Vitacura 2610, 203-6000
Santa Lucia Hotel, 779 Huerfanos, 639-8201

Restaurants:
Bar Central, San Pablo 1063
Bar Nacional #2, Bandera 317
Bar Nacional #1, Huerfanos 1151
Bar-restaurant Ines de Suarez, Morande 558
Cafe Dante, Merced 801
Chez Henry, Alameda 847
Circulo de Periodistas, Amunategui 31
El 27 de Nueva York, Nueva York 27
El Lugar de Don Quijote, Morande y Catedral
Fra Diavolo, Paris 836
Fuente de Soda Orion, O'Higgins y Manuel Rodrigez
Guima, Huerfanos y Teatinos

Guo Fung, Moneda 1549
Kam Thu, Santo Domingo 771
Los Adobes de Argomedo, Agromedo 411
Mermoz, Nuenfanos 1048
Pai Fu, Santa Rosa 101
Silvestre, Huerfanos 956
Torres, O'Higgins 1570
Verdijo, Morande 526

Entertainment:
Baltas, Av.Las Londes 10690
Club Troilo, Cumming 795
El Baile, Lopez de Bello
El Tucano Salsateca, Pedro de Valdivia 1783
Gente, Av. Apoquindo 4900
La Cucaracha,Bombero Nunez 159
Maestra Vida, Pio Nono 380
Pena Nano Parra, San Isidro 57
Varadero, Pio Nono

Shops and Stores:
Arsenal Santa Lucia, Santa Lucia metro, S exit   Apparel
Dauvin Artesania Fina, Pridencia 2169   Jewelry
El Almasen Campensino, Purisima 303   Dept.Store
Los Grandes del Alba, Av.Nueva Apoquindo 9085   Dept. Store

Places of Interest:
Museo Historico Nacional - a museum of history.
The Museo Precolombino - an archaeological museum.
The Fine Arts Museum
Santo Domingo Cathedral
The Church of San Francisco
Santa Lucia Park - fortresses and a museum

COLOMBIA

Official Name: Republic of Colombia

Location: Northwest South America. Colombia is bordered by Panama, Venezuela, Brazil, Ecuador and Peru. To the west lies the Pacific Ocean and to north the Caribbean Sea.

Government: Republic

Area: 1,141,748 sq. km., 440,831 sq. miles.

Population: 33.4 million

Religion(s): Roman Catholic majority.

Capital City: Santa Fe de Bogota

Major Business Cities: Cartagena and Medellin.

Time: GMT -5

Currency: Peso (Col$)=100 centavos

Currency Requirements: The import of foreign currency is limited to the equivalent of USD25,000. The export of foreign currency is limited up to amount declared on import. There are no restrictions on the import of local currency. The export is limited to Col$500. US$ Travelers Checks are recommended.

Business Hours:
- Government: 08.30-17.00 Mon-Fri
- Banks: 08.00-11.30; 14.00-16.00 Mon-Thur, 08.00-11.30; 14.00-16.30 Fri
- Shops: 09.00-12.30 and 14.30-18.30/19.00 Mon-Sat
- Offices: 09.00-17.00 Mon-Fri

Weight and Measures: Metric System

Electric Current: 110/120 volts AC, but some 150 volt supplies still exist. Plugs are American 2-pin type.

Holidays:
New Year's Day - January 1
Epiphany - January 6* **
St. Joseph's Day - March 19 **
Maundy Thursday - March 27
Good Friday - April 10*
Labour Day - May 1
Ascension Day - May 21* **
Corpus Christi - June 11* **
Sacred Heart - June 6**
St. Peter's & St. Paul's Day - June 29**
Independence Day - July 20
Battle of Boyaca - August 7
Assumption - August 15**
Columbus Day - October 12**
All Saints' Day - November 1*
Independence of Cartagena - November 11**
Feast of Immaculate Conception - December 8
Christmas Day - December 25

*Christian Holidays - vary each year

**When these holidays do not fall on Monday, they are usually observed on the following Monday.

Suitable Clothing: Dress conservatively - suits for meetings and dark suit or dress for formal occasions. Bring medium-weight clothing most of the year, and a light coat or jacket. Dressing too expensively is asking for trouble in this country where violent robbery is common.

Automobile Driving License: An International Driving License is recommended but not required. Driving in cities is not recommended.

Customs Allowances: Personal items are duty free, but register valuables and keep receipts or they may face confiscation. Expensive electronics such as video equipment or computers must be in a used condition. Any purchases you make in Colombia of fine jewelery, jewels and gold and platinum must be declared before departure. You may bring in 250 cigarettes duty free and 2 liters of wine and spirits. Prohibited are military weaponry and drugs, with severe penalties for the latter.

Tipping: A service charge of 10% is usually expected in the hotels and the restaurants unless it is already included. Taxi drivers and hotel staff do not expect tips. Bogota's shoeshine boys expect from 50 to 100 pesos.

Credit Cards Accepted: American Express, MasterCard, Visa

Customary Dining Hours:
Breakfast: 07.00-09.00
Lunch: 12.30-14.30
Dinner: 20.00-23.30

Local Customs, Business Protocol and Courtesies: Because of the violent atmosphere caused by the drug cartels, doing legitimate business carries high risks both physically and economically. If you do go, note that sales and other business proposals in Colombia are approached in a circular, low-key way, often after casual talk over the strong black coffee the country is also famous for. Deals are also reached frequently over coffee. The business visitor should be friendly, good-natured, polite and knowledgeable of local customs, and accept invitations for an evening at a cafe as well as a to formal business lunch. You'll find many of the same business and social customs as in the rest of Latin America. Men and women generally shake hands, or men will offer a slight bow to their female counterparts. At initial meetings, business cards are exchanged · providing English/Spanish ones and company literature in Spanish will make a good impression. Present the card Spanish side up. People typically address each other using their title and last name. Appointments should be arranged in advance. Your contact may be late, but you should never express annoyance or hostility. Your contemporaries are quite sophisticated, and an atmosphere of confident goodwill should prevail on both sides. Persistence is important, but pays off only if done with courtesy and confidence. Because gift-giving can be easily misconstrued as a bribe, be careful regarding timing when you give a business gift. It's best to wait until you have been offered one, and generally, a social setting is the correct context. You might consider a group gift such as office accessories, especially if you are a woman presenting a gift to male counterparts. Tasteful souvenirs from your home country are fine for business and social gifts.

At meals, eat European style with knife and fork. Guests may begin eating even if the others have not yet been served. It is typical to take small portions of each course from a common plate, and to place your utensils across the plate when finished. When the host offers a toast, respond with one as well. You are expected to stay awhile after the meal; business or other subjects are often discussed then. Bring flowers to the hostess, in even numbers or send them as a thank-you gesture the next day, and a gift, which will not be immediately opened. You should also send thank-you notes before leaving the country.

Health: It is advisable to consult your doctor before your journey. Vaccinations for hepatitis A, tetanus, typhoid, polio, cholera, yellow fever and malaria are recommended. The use of bottled water is strongly recommended and food precautions should be observed at all times. A medical insurance is advised.

Language: Spanish.

BOGOTA

Country code: 57 - City code: 1

Airport: Bogota El Dorado International Airport

Distance from City: 12km (7 miles) from the city.

Transportation to Center of City:
From International and Domestic Terminals
By Bus (cost) Col$1600-2000. Time approx.30-45 min.

By Taxi (cost) Col$14,000-15,000. Time approx. 20-30 min.
Tip luggage porters 800 pesos per piece

Transfers: (Minimum Connecting Time):
International to International: 60-90 min.
International to Domestic: 60 min.
Domestic to International: 50-60 min.
Domestic to Domestic: 20 min.

Automobile Rentals:
Airport car rental desk
Avis - 266-2147
Hertz - 413-9302

Car rental city office
Avis - 610-4455
Hertz - 211-8060

Hotels:
Dann Hotel, Avda. 19, 5-72, 284-0100
Dann Norte Bogota Hotel, Av.15 No. 114-09, 215-9655
Tequendama Hotel, Carrera 10, 26-21, 286-1111

Restaurants:
Ali Baba Express, Avenida 19 No. 5-94, 3410503
Andreas Terraza, Calle 82, No. 9-09
Andres Carne de Res, Via Chia – Cota Km. 6, 918630122
Bourbon Street, Calle 82 12036, Piso 2, 2570953
Carbon de Palo, Avenida 19 No. 106-12, 2140450
Casa Chaina, Calle 109 No.16-43, 2140517
Casa Medina, Carrera 7a No. 69A-22, 2170288
Casa San Isidro, Cerro de Monserrate, 2819309
Casa Vieja, Avenida Jimenez No. 3-73, 3346171
Clasic de Andrei, Calle 75, No. 4-31
Claustro de San Augustin, Carrera 8a. No.20-50, 2845319
El Patio, Carrera 4A No. 27-86, 2826141
El Portico, Autopista Norte Km. 19, 6760139
Felix, Avenida Jimenez No.4-48
Friday's, Carrera 12 No. 9386
Hatsuhana, Transversal 21 No. 100-43, 6103056
La Cofradia, Carrera 14 No. 84-37
Las Cuarto Estaciones, Carrera 8A No. 98-38, 2569309

Mister Banbilla, Calle 82 No.12-15
O'Sole Mio, Calle 21 No. 84-70, 2362991
Welcome, Carrera 14 No. 80-65, 2564790

Entertainment:
Any Way, Calle 94 No. 11-46, 6167652
Bahia, Kilometro 4.5 Via a La Calera, 3450877
Ciudad zero, Calle 81 No. 11-96, 6163370
Harry's Cantina, Carrera 12A No. 83-21
Kaoba, Calle 82 No. 12-44
Options, Carrera 14 No. 93-14, 2364201
Pipeline, Carrera 13 No. 82-56, 2229220
Ramon Antigua, Carrera 14 No. 85-57, 2566576
Riscos, Km. 4.5 Via A La Calera, 2566100

Shops and Stores:
Andino, Carrera 11 No. 82-71   Shopping Center
Bulevar Niza, Carrera 52 125A-059   Shopping Center
Cedritos, Diagonal 151 No. 32-19   Shopping Center
Centro 93, Carrera 15 Calle 93   Shopping Center
Centro Chia, Avenida Pradilla 900 Este-Chia

                                                                  Shopping Center
El Lago, Carrera 15 calles 77 a 79   Shopping Center
Granahorrar, Calle 72. No. 10-34   Shopping Center
Hacienda Santa Barbara, Avenida 7a No. 115-60   Shopping
Center

Places of Interest:
The Museum of Colonial Art
Santa Clara Church - a church and a museum.
The Planetarium and Museum of Natural History
The San Francisco Church
The National Museum
The Gold Museum

COSTA RICA

Official Name: Republic of Costa Rica

Location: Central America. Costa Rica is bordered by Nicaragua and Panama. The Pacific Ocean lies on its west coast and the Caribbean Sea on its east.

Government: Republic

Area: 51,060 sq. km., 19,720 sq. miles.

Population: 3.23 million

Religion(s): Roman Catholic.

Capital City: San Jose

Major Business Cities: San Jose and Alajuela

Time: GMT -6

Currency: Costa Rican Colon (CRC)=100 centimos

Currency Requirements: There are no restrictions on the import and the export of either local or foreign currency.

Business Hours:
- Government: 08.30-11.30 and 13.00-16.00 Mon-Fri
- Banks: 09.00-15.00/16.00 Mon-Fri
- Shops: 08.00/09.00-18.00/1900 Mon-Sat
- Offices: 08.00-12.00 and 14.00-16.00 Mon-Fri

Weight and Measures: Metric System

Electric Current: 110/220 volts. Plugs of 2-pin type are used.

Holidays:
New Year's Day - January 1

Feast of St. Joseph - March 19
Maundy Thursday - March 27
Good Friday - April 10*
Juan Santamaria - April 11
Labor Day - May 1
Corpus Christi - June 11*
St. Peter & St. Paul - June 29
Guanacaste Annexation Day - July 25
Assumption - Mothers' Day - August 15
Independence Day - September 15
Immaculate Conception - December 8
Christmas Day - December 25

*Christian Holidays - vary each year

Suitable Clothing: Wear light clothing and bring sungear year round; you will need rainwear between June and September. For initial meetings, have a lightweight but conservative suit; beyond that, ask your associates whether dressing more informally is okay (in many cases it is in this hot climate). Generally, dress is relatively casual except for the most formal of occasions. For formal occasions, women wear hats. Don't dress too expensively, or you will draw thieves.

Automobile Driving License: A National Driving License is required and must be held for at least a year. Drivers must be over 21 years of age.

Customs Allowances: Personal items are duty free, but register valuables upon arrival or they may face confiscation later. You may bring in 400 cigarettes and 2 liters of spirits duty free. Punishment is severe for drug possession; weapons and pornography are also prohibited.

Tipping: A 13% service tax and 3% tourist tax is added to the hotel bills, which is required by law. Most restaurants add a service charge. Hotel staff, porters and waiters expect to be tipped. Taxi fares should be negotiated before starting the journey and tipping is not necessary.

Credit Cards Accepted: American Express, MasterCard, Visa

Customary Dining Hours:
Breakfast: 07.30-09.00
Lunch: 12.30-14.00
Dinner: 20.00-22.00

Local Customs, Business Protocol and Courtesies: Unencumbered by war or armed insurgencies, with a strong middle class and huge eco-tourism revenues, Costa Rica has one of the most prosperous, stable economies in South America. It is rapidly becoming industrialized; a point of pride in its business community, which is multinational and cosmopolitan and whose distributors prefer exclusivity. The business visitor should be friendly, good-natured, polite and, when scheduling meetings, mindful of business hours. There is an afternoon siesta after lunch, which is generally eaten at home around noon. Do not schedule meetings for Tuesday the 13th, either, considered a bad luck day. At initial meetings, business cards are exchanged; providing English/Spanish ones and company literature in Spanish will make a good impression. Present the card Spanish side up. People typically address each other using their title and last name. Your contact may be late, but you should never express annoyance or hostility. Your contemporaries are quite sophisticated, and an atmosphere of confident goodwill and courtesy should prevail on both sides. Persistence is important, but pays off only if done with courtesy and confidence. The main hotels are popular spots for business functions in the evenings, and many a deal is agreed upon after dinner. If invited to a home, bring flowers or candy for the hostess and send flowers as a thank-you gesture the next day. It is typical to take small portions of each course from a common plate, and to place your utensils across the plate when finished. When the host offers a toast, respond with one as well. Giving business gifts is appreciated here, so bring plenty along, but do not go overboard on frequency or expense or it may be misconstrued as a bribe or ostentatious. An interesting curio from your home region, art object, or something connected to your area of business would be appropriate. Wait until you have been presented with a gift; this often occurs during leisurely after-dinner discussions, before deals have been cemented.

COSTA RICA

Health: It is advisable to consult your doctor before your journey. Vaccinations for hepatitis A, tetanus, typhoid, polio and malaria are recommended. It is advisable to drink bottled water. Swimming in fresh water should be avoided.

Language: Spanish. English is widely spoken.

SAN JOSE

Country code: 506 - City code: none

Airport: Juan Santamaria International Airport

Distance from City: 18km (11 miles) northwest of the city center.

Transportation to Center of City:
From International and Domestic Terminals
By Bus (cost)   CRC5-20. Time approx. 35 min.
By Taxi (cost)   USD11. Time approx. 30 min.
Tip luggage porters 100 centimos per piece

Transfers: (Minimum Connecting Time):
International to International: 45 min.
International to Domestic: 60 min.
Domestic to International: 60 min.
Domestic to Domestic: 30 min.

Automobile Rentals:
Airport car rental desk
Avis - 442-1321
National Interrent - 441-6533
Hertz - 221-1818

Car rental city office
Avis - 232-9922
National Interrent - 233-4044
Hertz - 223-5959

Hotels:
Balmoral Hotel, 7-9 Central Ave., 222-5022

Best Western San Jose-Downtown, 7th Ave. 6th Street, 255-4766
Corobici Hotel, Autopista General Canas, 232-8122
Gran Hotel Costa Rica, 2nd Ave. and 3rd St., 221-4000
Restaurants:
Ambrosia, Centro Comercial Calle Real, 253-8012
Azafran, Rohrmoser, 220 2008
Bijahua, San Pedro, 225-0613
Didso, near the San Pedro Church, 224 1163
Don Sol, Calle 15,
El Cocorrico Verde, 224 9744
Il Pomodoro, 224 0966
La Cocina de Lena, Centro Comercial El Pueblo,
    255-1360
La Esmeralda, Avenida 2, between Calles 5 and 7,
    221-0530
La Masia de Triguel, Sabana Norte, 296-3528
La Perla, Avenida 2 and Calle Central, 222-7492
La Piazzetta, Paseo Colon, Near Calle 40, 222-7896
Le Chandelier, San Pedro, 225-3980
Machu Pichu Bar and Restaurant, Calle 32, between Av.
    1 and 3, 222-7384
Manolo's Restaurante, Avenida Central, between Calles
    Central and 2, 221-2041
Naturama, Calle 3/5, 257 0907
Pasteleria Imperial, Calle 5,
Pasteria Francesa Boudsocq, Calle 30 at Paseo Colon,
    222-6732
Restaurant Zermatt, b/n 23th St. and 11 Ave, 222-0604
Restaurante Campesino, Calle 7, between Av. 2 and 4,
    255-1356
Soda B y B, Calle 5 and Avenida Central, 222-7316
The Lobster's Inn, b/n Paseo Colon and 24th St., 223-8594
Tin Jo, Calle 11, between Av. 6 and 8, 221-7605

Entertainment:
Baleares, 253 4577
Barlochas, El Pueblo Shop. Center, 21-4514
Casa Matute, Calle 21, 222 6806
Casino Club Colonial, 1 St. Ave., b/n 9th & 11th Sts., 33-0112
Charleston, Avenida 4, between Calles 7 and 9, 255-3993
Club Domino, b/n 7th St. and Ave. Central, 22-1103
Disco Salsa 54, Calle 3 Aven 1st and 3st.

COSTA RICA

El Cuartel De La Boca Del Monte, Avenida 1, between Calles 21 and 23, 221-0327
Key Largo, Calle 7, between Av. 1 and 3, 221-0277
La Villa, north of the Banco Anglo, 225 9612
Nashville South, Calle 5, between Av. 1 and 3, 233-1988
Rio, Avenida Central, Los Yoses, 253-5088
Risa's Bar, Calle 1, between Av. Central and Av.1, 223-2803
Salsa 54, Calle 3, Avenida 1/3
Shakespeare Bar, Calle 28, 257 1288
Shakespeare Bar, Avenida 2 and Calle 28, 257-1288
Soda Palace, Calle 2 and Avenida 2, 221-3441
Taska Al Aldalus, Calle 3, 257 6556

Shops and Stores:

Calle real, San Padro	Shopping Center
Guachipelin, Eskazu	Shopping Center
Guadalupe, Guadalupe	Shopping Center
Maal International Alajuela	Shopping Center
Mall San Pedro	Shopping Center
Multiplaza Santa Ana	Shopping Center
Novacentro, Cartago	Shopping Center
Plaza Los Colegios, Moravia	Shopping Center
Plaza Real Cariari, San Antonio Belen	Shopping Center

Places of Interest:

Museo Nacional - the National Museum
Galeria Nacional de Arte Contemporaneo - an art gallery
Serpentario - live snakes and frogs
Parque Zoologico Simon Bolivar
Plaza de Cultura - cultural exhibits, a museum and a theater
Museo de Ciencias Naturales - the Natural History Museum
Spirogyra Jardin de Mariposas - a butterfly garden

CUBA

Official Name: Republic of Kuba

Government: Socialist Republic

Area: 110,860 sq. km., 42,803 sq. mi.

Population: 10.5 million

Religion(s): Roman Catholic

Capital City: Havana

Major Business Cities: Santiago de Cuba, Camaguey, Holguin, Santa Clara

Time: GMT – 5 hrs.; EST 0

Currency: Cuban Peso = 100 Centavos

Business Hours:
- Government: 08.30-12.30; 13.30-17.30 Mon-Fri, 08.30-12.00 Sat
- Banks: 08.00-12.00; 14.15-16.15 Mon-Fri, 08.30-12.00 Sat
- Shops: 08.30-12.30; 13.30-17.30 Mon-Fri, 08.30-12.00 Sat
- Offices: 08.30-12.30; 13.30-17.30 Mon-Fri, 08.30-12.00 Sat

Weight and Measures: Metric system

Electric Current: A.C. 60c, 110/220V

Suitable Clothing: Wear lightweight clothing most of the year. Dress is relatively informal, but you should bring business attire for initial meetings and social functions, at least. You will need sunglasses, sunhats and sunscreen year round.

Automobile Driving License: International or foreign driving license is required

CUBA

Tipping: Tipping in Cuba is prohibited

Credit Cards Accepted: American Express, Diner's Club, Eurocard, Master Card

Customary Dining Hours:
Breakfast: 07.30-09.00 hrs
Lunch: 12.30-14.00 hrs
Dinner: 20.00-22.00 hrs

Local Customs, Business Protocol and Courtesies: A successful business endeavor in Cuba will require much patience and a long-term view toward the expected freeing up of its political and economic system within the next decade. In the meantime, however one must exercise great caution and patience. You may have to wait many months before getting decisions, which are made by committees. Expect to make several trips to the country before a contract is finalized. Refrain comment on politics, and always ask permission when photographing a person or a place. Discretion is essential: do not discuss other business activities with a contact, but keep only to your dealings with him. Giving business gifts, even small ones, may be interpreted as a bribe and can get you or the official who is the recipient into trouble. People tend to be very friendly and hospitable, but most business and social functions for visitors tend to be in public settings such as restaurants rather than on a more private, individual basis. Cuba's heavily state-run economy means that your first contacts should be with officials of the various agencies under the Ministry of Foreign Trade. Set up your meetings with them well in advance and be punctual. Your contact may be late, but you should never express annoyance or hostility · an atmosphere of confident goodwill and courtesy should prevail on both sides. Persistence is important, but pays off only if done with courtesy and quiet confidence. You'll encounter skilled bargainers, but you yourself should be low key in your approach. They will expect detailed, professional proposals from you, and will likely be very concerned with credit terms and pricing. Cubans often refer to each other as Comanero (Comrade), but foreigners should stick to Senor, Senora or Senorita with title until indicated otherwise. Your effort to provide business cards and company literature in Spanish will make a good impression.

Health: Drink only bottled water except in major hotels. Wash and peel all fruit and vegetables. Imported pharmaceuticals and toiletries are either scarce or unobtainable. All pharmaceuticals are available by prescription only.

Language: Spanish

HAVANA

Country code: 53 - City code: 7

Airport: Jose Marti Intl

Distance from City: 18 km (11 mi.)

Transportation to Center of City:
From International and Domestic Terminals
By Taxi (cost) USD 10-15 Time approx. 25 min.

Transfers: (Minimum Connecting Time):
International to International: 120 min.
International to Domestic: 120 min.
Domestic to International: 120 min.
Domestic to Domestic: 60 min.

Automobile Rentals:
Hvanautos – Capri Htl., 32-50-11
Servicio Especial – 32-00-34; 32-82-43

Hotels:
Capri, Calle 21 & N, Vedado, 320511
Habana Libre, Calles L & 23, Vedado, 305011
Hotel & Bungalous Comodoro, Calles 84 & !ra, 225551
Hotel Plaza, Calle Ignacio Agramonte, Habana Vieja, 622006
Hotel Presidente, Calles Calzada & G, Vedado, 323577
Hotel Colina, Calle L & Javellar, Vedado, 323535
Hotel Deuville, Calle Galiano & Malecon, Centro Habana, 628051

CUBA

Habana Libre, Calles L & 23, Vedado, 328722
Habana Riviera, Avenida Paseo & Malecon, Vedado, 304385
Nacional, Calle 21 7 Malecon, Vedado, 78981
Hotel Inglaterra, Calles Prado 416, Centro Habana, 338254

Restaurants:
El Floridita, Monserrate 557, 631060
La Torre del Mangia, Miramar, Playa, Av. 5, 332450
Tocororo, Miramar, Calle 18, No, 302, 332209
El Pavo Real, Miramar, El Puente de Hierro, Av. 7, No. 205, 332315
Fiesta, Santa Fe, Marina Hemingway, Av. 5 &248th, 228342
La Casa de Quinta y 16, Miramar, Av. 5 & 16th, 294047
La Cecilia, Miramar, Av. 5 & 110th, 331562
La Cova, Santa Fe, Marina Hemingway, Av. 5 & 248th, 331150
La Divina Pastora, Habana del Este, Gran Parque militar Morro-Cabana, 663886
La Torre, Vedado, Altos del edificio Focsa, Calle 17 at M, 324630
Papa's, Santa Fe, Marina Hemingway, Av. 5 at 248th, 331150
El Ranchon, Calle 19 at 140th, 331984
Emperador, Calle 17 at M, 324671
La Bodequita del Medio, La Havana Vieha, Empedrado 256, 624498
La Terraza, Cjimar, Real 161, 653471
Morambon, Av. 5 at 32nd, 233336
Dos Gardenias, Miramar, Calle 26th at 7th, 332353
El Patio, La Habana Vieha, Pl. de la Catedral, 338146

Entertainment:
Tropicana, Marianao, Calle 72 at 41st, 330110
Acros de Cristal, Calle 72 and Av. 41
La Maison, Miramar, Calle 16 at 7th
La Tasca Espanola, Santa Fe, Marina Hemingway, Av. 5 and 248th
La Heladeria, Empedrado esq. Tacon,
La Lambada, Hotel Atlantoco,Santa Maria del Mar, 3307 2553
La Luz, Obispo e/ San Ignasio y Mercaderes
La Mina, Obispo esq. Oficios, Plaza de Armas, 620216
La Pina del Plata, Obispo 557 esq.Monserrate, 631063
La Sevillana, Hotel Inglaterra, 62 7071
Aqua Bar, Complejo Iberostar Neptuno-Triton, 22 6081
Atardeser, Virtudes 813 esq. Galiano, 33 8209

Atlantico, Ave. Las Terrazas e/ 11 y 12, 687 2561
Banana, Tropicoco Beach C., Ave. Sur y Terrazas S.M.M. 687 2531
Buro Bar, Complejo Iberostar Neptuno-Triton, 22 6081

Places of Interest:
The Capitol
Presidential Palace
Plaza de la Revolucion
Church and Convent of San Francisco
The Cathedral
Colonial Museum
Napoleonic Museum
Teatro Garcia Lorca
Palacio de Bellas Artes
Castilla de Punta
Castilo del Morro
Plaza de Armas
Fortaleza de la Cubana
Palace of the Captains-General
Parque Central

ECUADOR

Official Name: Republic of Ecuador

Location: South America. Ecuador is bordered by Colombia to the north and Peru to the south. On the northwest coast lies the Pacific Ocean.

Government: Republic

Area: 272,045 sq. km., 104,506 sq. miles.

Population: 11.02 million

Religion(s): Roman Catholic majority

Capital City: Quito

Major Business Cities: Guayaquil

Time: GMT -5

Currency: Sucre (Su)=100 centavos

Currency Requirements: There are no restrictions on the import and the export of both foreign and local currencies.

Business Hours:
- Government: 09.00-13.00 and 14.00-18.30 Mon-Fri
- Banks: 09.00-13.00 Mon-Fri (some open 09.00-13.30 Sat)
- Shops: 09.00-13.00 and 15.00-19.00 Mon-Fri (some open Sat and Sun)
- Offices: 09.00-13.00 and 15.00-19.00 Mon-Fri; 08.30-12.30 Sat

Weight and Measures: Metric System

Electric Current: 110/240 volts AC. Plugs are of the flat 2-pin type.

ECUADOR

Holidays:
New Year's Day - January 1
Lent Carnival - February 10-11
Good Friday - April 10*
Easter Sunday – April 12*
Labour Day - May 1
Battle of Pichincha - May 24
Festival of St. John the Baptist - June 24
Independence Day - August 10
Guayaquil Day - October 9
All Souls Day - November 2
Cuenca Day - November 3
Christmas Day - December 25

*Christian Holidays - vary each year

Suitable Clothing: In Guayaquil, dress in light clothing; in Quito, medium weight clothing and a jacket or light coat. Rainwear and sungear are important. Wear a lightweight but conservative suit for initial business meetings; beyond that, ask your associates whether going jacket- or tie-less is okay (in many cases it is in this hot climate). Don't dress too expensively, or you will draw thieves.

Automobile Driving License: An International Driving Permit is required

Customs Allowances: Personal items are duty free, but register valuables upon arrival or they may face confiscation later. There are no currency restrictions. You may bring in 300 cigarettes and 1 liter of spirits duty free. Punishment is severe for drug possession, and for bringing in weapons or items that may be used as such.

Tipping: A service charge of 10% is usually added to the bills of most hotels and restaurants. It is usual to tip waiters if the tip is not included. Taxi drivers do not expect a tip.

Credit Cards Accepted: American Express, MasterCard, Visa

ECUADOR

Customary Dining Hours:
Breakfast: 07.30-09.00
Lunch: 12.30-14.00
Dinner: 20.00-22.00

Local Customs, Business Protocol and Courtesies: Despite its small size, Ecuador has two cities which often rival for domestic and international business contracts: its mountain capital, Quito, and the subtropical city of Guayaquil. In Quito, the capital, it will be necessary in many cases to speak Spanish or have an interpreter; in Guayaquil, however, many businessmen speak English. In any case, it makes a good impression to provide cards and company literature in Spanish no matter where you go. For governmental meetings, and with the larger firms, you'll need to schedule appointments ahead. Your contact may be late, but you should never express annoyance or hostility toward the sometimes slower pace of life here. Your contemporaries are quite sophisticated, and an atmosphere of confident goodwill should prevail on both sides. Shake hands upon meeting, and exchange business cards. Use title and last name. Persistence is important in negotiations, as long as it is done in a low-key, relaxed and friendly manner. Giving business gifts is appreciated here, so bring plenty along, but do not go overboard on frequency or expense or it may be construed as a bribe or ostentatious. An interesting curio from your home region, art object, or something connected to your area of business would be appropriate.

Health: It is advisable to consult your doctor in advance of your journey. A yellow fever certificate is compulsory if travelling from an infected area. Vaccinations against polio, typhoid and cholera are recommended. There is a risk of malaria in some regions. It is strongly recommended to boil water since it is considered potentially contaminated. A medical insurance including emergency repatriation is essential.

Language: Spanish. Quichua Indian dialects and some English are also spoken.

ECUADOR

QUITO

Country code: 593 - City code: 2

Airport: Mariscal Sucre International Airport

Distance from City: 8km (4 miles) from the city

Transportation to Center of City:
From International and Domestic Terminals
By Bus (cost) USD1. Time approx. 60 minutes.
By Taxi (cost) USD7-USD10. Time approx. 20-30 min.
Tip luggage porters 50 centavos   per piece

Transfers: (Minimum Connecting Time):
International to International: 60 min.
International to Domestic: 60 min.
Domestic to International: 60 min.
Domestic to Domestic: 45 min.

Automobile Rentals:
Airport car rental desk
Avis - 440270

Car rental city office
Avis - 550243
Hertz - 569130

Hotels:
Hilton Colon International Quito, Av. Amazonas y Patria,
    560-666
Oro Verde Hotel, 12 de Octubre 1820 y Luis, Cordero Casilla
    17, 566-497
Tambo Real Hotel, 12 de Octubre y Patria Esquina, 563-820

Restaurants:
Cafe Bangalo, Carrion 185,
Cafe Cultura, Robles 513, 224 271
Cafe Moka, Calama 247, 520 931
Chifa El Chino, Bolivar 256, 513 435
Columbia Steak House, Colon 1262, 551 857

ECUADOR

El Cafecito, 234 862
El Criollo, Flores 825, 219 811
El Escoces, Amazonas 410, 554 704
Grain de Cafe, 234 340
La Terraza del Tartaro, Veintimilla 1106
Mama Clorinda, Reina Victoria 1144, 544 362
Mona Lisa, Calama 336
Pollos El Rey, 516 373
Puerto Manabi, L.Garcia 1238, 226 206
Restaurant Panoramico, Bolivar 220, 512 711
Restaurante Mare Nostrum, Tamayo 172, 237 236
Trattoria El Chianti, L.Garcia 668, 544 683

Entertainment:
Aleatiay, 238 324
Ana Maria, Liz.Garcia 345
El Huero, Baquedano 188
El Pobre Diablo, 224 982
No Bar, Calama 442, 546 955

Places of Interest:
The Cathedral
La Compania Church
The Monastery and Church of San Francisco
Casa de la Cultura Ecuatoriana - a museum.
The Museum of Colonial Art
Jacinto Tijon y Caamano Museum

MEXICO

Official Name: United Mexican States

Location: Southern North America. Mexico is bordered the USA, the Gulf of California, the Pacific ocean, Guatemala, Belize, the Gulf of Mexico and the Caribbean.

Government: Federal Republic

Area: 1,958,201 sq. km, 756,066 sq. miles.

Population: 89.5 million

Religion(s): Roman Catholic majority.

Capital City: Mexico City

Major Business Cities: Acapulco, Guadalajara and Monterrey.

Time: GMT -6

Currency: Nuevo Peso (MXP) = 100 centavos (Equivalent to 1000 former Pesos)

Currency Requirements: The import of foreign currency is unlimited and must declared. The export of foreign currency is limited to the amount declared upon arrival. Import and export of local currency is limited to MXP5000. The export of gold coins is prohibited.

Business Hours:
- Government: 09.00-15.00 Mon-Fri
- Banks: 09.00-14.00/15.00 Mon-Fri
- Shops: 09.00-20.00 Mon-Sat
- Offices: 09.00-14.00 and 16.00-19.00 Mon-Fri

Weight and Measures: Metric System

Electric Current: 110 volts AC. American 2-pin flat plugs are used.

Holidays:
New Year's Day - January 1
Constitution Day - February 5
Birthday of Benito Juarez - March 21
Maundy Thursday - March 27
Good Friday - April 10*
Labor Day - May 1
Battle of Puebla - May 5
Mother's Day - May 10
State of the Nation Address - September 1
Independence Day** - September 15-16
Columbus Day - October 12
All Souls' Day - November 2*
Revolution Day - November 20
Feast of the Virgin of Guadeloupe - December 12
Christmas Day - December 25

*Christian Holidays - vary each year

** Commences with a cry of 'Viva Mexico' at 23.00 September 15. Holidays falling on a weekend are not celebrated on a previous or following weekday.

Suitable Clothing: Dress in conservative business attire, but you'll need very light materials, sungear and rainwear in summer. Don't dress too expensively, as theft is prevalent.

Automobile Driving License: A National or an International Driving License is required.

Customs Allowances: Due to heavy inspections of luggage for drugs and other contraband, you can expect random searches of luggage and individuals, especially if you are coming in from South America. Valuables must be registered upon arrival, otherwise they may be confiscated upon departure, and keep all receipts and other forms. Duty-free cigarettes are limited to 400 and wine and spirits to two liters. Weaponry, drugs and pornographic material are prohibited. Due to the illegal market in recent years in antique and art objects, there are strong restrictions and duties on bringing out these items, as well as required permits from the Ministry of Culture. Pre-Colombian items may

not be taken out of the country. Prohibited are military weaponry, drugs and pornography.

Tipping: A service charge is usually not included, however 15-20% is expected. Taxi drivers do not expect tips unless they are hired for several hours.

Credit Cards Accepted: American Express, Diner's Club, MasterCard, Visa

Customary Dining Hours:
Breakfast: 07.00-10.00
Lunch: 13.00-16.00
Dinner: 19.00-23.30

Local Customs, Business Protocol and Courtesies: Everyone is breaking down the door to do business in Mexico's enormous market, and this in the face of its slow pace of life. Do not underestimate its businessmen, however, they are very sophisticated and courteous, and will expect you to give strong reasons why they should do business with you. They will likely test you out by giving you smaller initial orders. If you and they perform well, your relationships and contracts will likely grow exponentially. English is widely spoken in the business community but if you walk in speaking good Spanish, or at least make an effort by providing business cards and company literature in Spanish, you will be even more warmly welcomed. If you receive a letter in Spanish, make the effort to have your reply translated into it even if you yourself don't know the language. Even if you do speak Spanish, keep in mind that it may be hard to understand as people tend to speak all at once, and very quickly and emotionally. Those engaged in conversation tend to stand very close to one another; moving away would be considered rude. In negotiations, be friendly and polite but firm and confident. Don't be overly critical and offend local sensitivities.

Business and social relationships go hand-in-hand in Mexico, where deals are usually made on the basis of personal contacts. For this reason, the business visitor should be friendly, good-natured, polite and knowledgeable of local customs, and accept invitations for an evening at a cafe as well as a to formal business lunch. Indeed, many business agreements are made over coffee after a leisurely lunch, the main meal of the day, or after dinner. Men and women generally shake hands, or men will offer a slight bow to their female counterparts. At initial meetings, business cards are exchanged, and people will typically address each other using their title and last name. The elderly are addressed as "Don" and "Dona" with first name. Appointments should be arranged in advance (you should write before your arrival), and be on time, although lateness on the part of your counterpart may not be unusual. Mexicans prefer to conduct all but the most minor business in person rather than over the phone. Because gift-giving can be easily misconstrued as a bribe, be careful regarding timing when you give a gift. It's best to wait until you have been offered one (usually after a deal has been reached), and generally, a social setting is the correct context. You might consider a group gift such as office accessories especially if you are a woman presenting a gift to male counterparts. Tasteful souvenirs from your home country, or other imported items, are fine, and, so are flowers or chocolate if invited to a home. Do not give red or yellow flowers. When the host offers a toast, respond with one as well. And in this hospitable society, you will likely be invited, and you should send thank you notes before leaving the country.

Health: It is advisable to consult your doctor before your journey. Vaccinations for cholera, typhoid, polio, hepatitis A and a course of malaria tablets are recommended. It is strongly advisable to drink only bottled water and food precautions should be observed at all times. Medical insurance is strongly recommended.

Language: Spanish. English is widely spoken.

MEXICO

MEXICO CITY

Country code: 52 - City code: 5

Airport: Benito Juarez International Airport.

Distance from City: 13km (8 miles) south of the city.

Transportation to Center of City:
From International and Domestic Terminals
By Bus (cost) MXP3.
By Taxi (cost) MXP39 (USD7). Time approx. 20-30 min.
Tip luggage porters MXP3 per piece

Automobile Rentals:
Airport car rental desk.
Avis - 762-3688
National Interrent - 762-8250
Hertz - 762-8372

Car rental city office.
Avis - 533-1336
National Interrent - 280-1111
Hertz - 592-8343

Hotels:
Aristos Mexico City Hotel, Paseo de la Reforma 276, 211-0112
Best Western Hotel Majestic, Av. Moderno 73, Col Centro,
    521-8609
Best Western Hotel de Cortes, Cnr. Of Paseo de la Reforma &
    Av. Hidalgo 85, Con Centro, 518-2184
Fiesta Americana Hotel, 80 Paseo de la Reforma, 705-1515
Marquis Reforma Hotel, Paseo de la Reforma 465, 211-3600
Mexico City Airport Marriott Hotel, Benito Juarez Int'l Airport,
    230-0505
Quality Hotel Calinda Geneve, Londres 130, 211-0071
Radisson Plaza Pendregal, Periferico Sur 3487, 681-6855
Sevilla Palace Hotel, Paseo de la Reforma 105, 705-2800
Sheraton Maria Isabel Hotel and Towers, Paseo de la Reforma
    325, 207-3933
Torre Madrid Suites-Hotel, Calle Madrid 5, Col Tabacalera

MEXICO

Restaurants:
Cafe Daiy, Isabela la Catolica 9-11, 521 6203
Cafe el Parnaso, Carrillo Puerto 2
Cafe Tacuba, Tacuba 28, 518 4950
Chucho el Roto, Madero 8
Comedor Vegetariano, Motolinia 315, 512 6575
El Jarocho, on Allende, 554 5418
El Morral, Allende 2, 554 5418
Fonda Santa Anita, Humboldt 48, 518 5723
Kai Lam, Londres 114, 514 4837
La Luna, Oslo 11
La Mesa de Babette, Reforma 408, 208 3775
Paris 16 Cafe, Reforma 368, 511 9911
Restaurant Danubio, Uruguay 3,
Restaurant Zenon, Gante 15, 512 1201
Restaurante Hasti Bhawan,Pl.San Jacinto 9, 616 2208
Restaurante Samy, Ignacio Mariscal 42, 591 1100
Ricocina, Londres 168, 514 0648
Vegetariano Yug,Varsovia 3, 525 5330

Entertainment:
Bar Osiris, Niza 22, 525 6684
Canta Bar, Florencia 56, 208 8600
Celebration, Florencia 56, 541 6415
El Arcano, Division de Norte 2713, 689 8273
El Bar Mata, Filomeno Mata at 5 de Mayo, 518 0237
El Chato, Londres 117, 511 1758
El Numero, Av. de la Republica 9, 703 2318
Harry's Bar and Grill,Liverpool 155, 208 6298
Hosteria del Bohemio, Hidalgo 107, 512 8328
La Opera, 5 de Mayo 10, 512 8959
Museo el Bar,Madero 6, 510 4020
Opulencia, Catolica 26, 512 0417
Papa's Disco, Londres 142, 207 7702
Rock Stock Bar & Disco, Reforma 260, 533 0706
Xcess, Niza 39, 525 5317

Shops and Stores:

Fonart, Patriotismo 691	Jewelry
San Juan, Pl. El Buen Tono	Apparel
Sonora, Teresa de Mier and Cabana	Gift Shop

Places of Interest:
Museo de la Ciudad de Mexico - a museum
Museo Nacional de Arte - a museum
Torre Latinoamericana - an observation deck
Museo Nacional de la Revolution - a museum
Catedral Metropolitana - a cathedral
Templo Mayor and Museum
Castillo de Chapultepec - a castle
Museo Nacional de Antropologia - a museum
Parque Zoologico de Chapultepec - zoo
Palacio de Minera - art exhibits
Palacio de Bellas Artes - a cultural center

PANAMA

Official Name: Republic of Panama

Location: Central America. Panama is bordered by Colombia and Costa Rica. To the north is the Caribbean Sea and to the south is the Pacific Ocean.

Government: Republic

Area: 75,517 sq. km., 29,157 sq. miles

Population: 2.51 million

Religion(s): Roman Catholic.

Capital City: Panama City

Major Business Cities: Panama, Colon, David

Time: GMT -5

Currency: Balboa (PAB)=100 Centesimos

Currency Requirements: There are no restrictions on the import and the export of local and foreign currencies. Visitors must have a minimum of USD300 when entering the country.

Business Hours:
- Government: 08.30-12.30 and 13.30-16.00 Mon-Fri
- Banks: 08.00-13.00 Mon-Fri
- Shops: 08.00-12.00 and 14.00-18.00 Mon-Sat
- Offices: 08.00-12.00 and 14.00-17.00 Mon-Fri; 08.00-12.00 Sat

Weight and Measures: Metric System and Imperial System

Electric Current: 120 volts AC. Plugs are of the flat 2-pin American type.

Holidays:
New Year's Day - January 1
Memorial Day - January 9
Carnival - February 10
Shrove Tuesday/Carnival - February 11
In lieu of Easter Holiday - April 13*
Good Friday - April 10*
Labor Day - May 1
Bank Holiday -May 26
Bank Holiday - August 25
Independence Day - November 3
Anniversary of Separation from Spain - November 28
Mothers' Day - December 8
Privilege Day - December 24
Christmas Day - December 25
Boxing Day - December 26

* Christian Holidays - vary each year

Suitable Clothing: In most business and some social situation, wear a conservative suit or dress. From November to March, bring summer clothing, and medium-weight clothing the rest of the year. A jacket or light coat is necessary between June and September. Don't dress too expensively, or you will draw thieves.

Automobile Driving License: A National or an International Driving License is required. Drivers must be over 23 years of age.

Customs Allowances: Personal items are duty free, but register valuables and keep receipts or they may face confiscation. You may bring in 400 cigarettes or 50 cigars duty free and I liter of spirits. Prohibited are military weaponry and drugs, with severe penalties for the latter.

Tipping: It is customary to leave a 10% tip in the hotels and the restaurants. Taxi drivers do not expect a tip and fares should be negotiated before the trip.

Credit Cards Accepted: American Express, MasterCard, Visa

PANAMA

Customary Dining Hours:
Breakfast: 07.30-09.00
Lunch: 12.30-14.00
Dinner: 20.00-22.00

Local Customs, Business Protocol and Courtesies: Panama is rapidly becoming industrialized, a point of pride in its business community as a result of its membership in the Mercosur Common Market along with its neighboring countries. However, it still takes much effort for foreign sellers to find reliable distributors and representatives but these are essential. Make sure potential distributors are not already overburdened. Also, due to a dearth of mid-level managers, decision making is generally at the top and may take some time. Be friendly, good-natured, polite and, when scheduling meetings, mindful of business hours. There is an afternoon siesta after lunch, which is generally eaten at home around noon. Schedule government and business meetings in advance; do not get annoyed, however, by lateness, which is frequent. You should never express annoyance or hostility. An atmosphere of confident goodwill and courtesy should prevail on both sides. Persistence is important, but pays off only if done with courtesy and confidence. People shake hands when meeting and departing, but it is also customary for men to hug each other and give a slight bow to women. Many business people there speak English, but be prepared to get a good interpreter if necessary. It helps to speak or understand Spanish, of course, but keep in mind that it may be hard to keep up with as people tend to speak all at once, and very quickly and emotionally. Those engaged in conversation tend to stand very close to one another; moving away would be considered rude. Business and social relationships go hand-in-hand in Panama, and deals are usually made on the basis of personal contacts. For this reason, the business visitor should be friendly, good-natured, polite and knowledgeable of local customs, and accept invitations for an evening at a cafe as well as a to formal business lunch. Indeed, many business agreements are made over coffee after a leisurely lunch, the main meal of the day, or after dinner. If you are offered "mate," an herbal tea (served hot or cold) prepared for family, friends and associates, you'll know you've been accepted as a business partner or friend. Because gift-giving can be easily misconstrued as a bribe, be careful regarding timing when you give a gift. It's best to wait until you have been offered one, and generally, a social setting is the correct context. You might consider a group gift such as office accessories, especially if you are a woman presenting a gift to male counterparts. Tasteful souvenirs from your home country are fine, and, so are flowers or chocolate if invited to a home. When the host offers a toast, respond with one as well. At initial meetings, business cards are exchanged - providing English/Spanish ones and company literature in Spanish will make a good impression. Present the card Spanish side up. People typically address each other using their title and last name. The main hotels are popular spots for business functions in the evenings, and many a deal is agreed upon after dinner. If invited to a home, bring flowers or candy for the hostess and send flowers as a thankyou gesture the next day. Giving business gifts is appreciated here, but wait until you have been given one (usually after a business deal is reached) before returning the favor, and do not go overboard on frequency or expense or it may be misconstrued as a bribe or ostentatious. An interesting curio from your home region, art object, or something connected to your area of business would be appropriate.

Health: It is advisable to consult your doctor before your journey. Vaccinations for yellow fever, cholera, polio and typhoid are recommended. A risk of malaria is present. It is advisable to drink bottled water. A medical insurance is essential.

Language: Spanish. English is widely spoken.

PANAMA CITY

Country code: 507 - City code: none

Airport: Panama City-Tocumen International Airport

Distance from City: 27km (16 miles) northeast of the city.

PANAMA

Transportation to Center of City:
From International and Domestic Terminals
By Bus (cost) USD0.25. Time approx. 60 min.
By Taxi (cost) USD25-30.Time approx. 25 min.
Tip luggage porters USD0.50 per piece

Transfers: (Minimum Connecting Time):
International to International: 90 min.
International to Domestic: 45 min.
Domestic to International: 45 min.
Domestic to Domestic: 45 min.

Automobile Rentals:
Airport car rental desk
Avis - 238-4037
Hertz - 238-4106

Car rental city office
Avis - 261-8333 Ext.30
National Interrent - 264-8277
Hertz - 238-4106

Hotels:
Caesar Park Panama, Via Israel and 77th St., 226-4077
Costa del Sol Junior Suites, Via Espana and Federica Boyd,
    223-7111
Europa Hotel, Via Espana 33, 263-6369
Executive Hotel, Cnr St. Aguilino de la Guardia y St. 52,
    264-3333
Gran Hotel Soloy, Ave. Peru and 30th St., 227-1133
Las Vegas Hotel Suite, Apdo. D Balboa, 269-0722
Panama Hotel, Apdo. 1753, 269-8023
Riande Continental City Hotel, Apdo. 8475, 263-9999

Restaurants:
Bon Profit, Via Argentina 5, 263 9667
Cafeteria Manolo, Via Argentina 12
La Casa de las Costillitas, at Via Argentina 6, 269 6670
La Cascada, Av.Balboa and Calle 25, 262 1297
Napoli Ristorante e Pizzeria, Calle 57

PANAMA

Niko's Cafe, Calle 51 Este
Restaurante Alfred, Calle Manuel Maria Icaza

Restaurante Vegetariano Mireya,Calle 50 Este
Tinajas, Calle 51,#22, 269 3840

Entertainment:
Cubares, Calle 52, 264 8905
Dreams, Via Espana, 263 4248
Mabuhay, Calle 50, 225 2755
My Place, Via Venetto, 223 9924
Patatus, Plaza New York, on Calle 50, 264 8467
Rock Cafe, Plaza La Florida, 264 5364

Places of Interest:
San Jose Church
The Museum of Colonial Religious Art
Museo Antropologico Reina Torres de Arranz - a museum
Panama Viejo - ruins
The Panama Canal
Museo de Historia de Panama - a museum

PARAGUAY

Official Name: Republic of Paraguay

Location: South America. Paraguay is bordered by Brazil, Argentina and Bolivia.

Government: Republic

Area: 406,752 sq. km., 157,048 sq. miles

Population: 4.52 million

Religion(s): Roman Catholic

Capital City: Asuncion

Time: GMT -4 (GMT -3 from early October to late March)

Currency: Guarani (G)=10 Centavos

Currency Requirements: There are no restrictions on the import and the export of foreign or local currency.

Business Hours:
- Government: 07.30-12.00 and 14.30-19.00 Mon-Fri
- Banks: 08.30-12.15 Mon-Fri
- Shops: 08.00-12.00 and 15.00-19.00/20.00 Mon-Fri; 07.30-12.00/13.00 Sat
- Offices: 08.00-12.00 and 15.00-17.30/19.00 Mon-Fri; 08.00-12.00 Sat

Weight and Measures: Metric System

Electric Current: 220 volts AC

Holidays:
New Year's Day - January 1
Cerro Cora Battle - March 1

Maundy Thursday - March 27
Good Friday - April 10*
Independence Day - May 15
Labor Day - May 16
Peace Day - June 12
Foundation of the City of Asuncion - August 15
Immaculate Conception - December 8
Christmas Day - December 25

* Christian holidays - vary each year

Suitable Clothing: In most business and some social situation, wear a conservative suit or dress. From November to March, bring summer clothing, and medium-weight clothing the rest of the year. A jacket or light coat is necessary between June and September. Don't dress too expensively, or you will attract thieves.

Automobile Driving License: A National or an International Driving License can be used if it is held for at least one year.

Customs Allowances: Personal items are duty free, but register valuables and keep receipts or they may face confiscation. You may bring in one carton of cigarettes or 50 cigars duty free and I liter of spirits. Prohibited are military weaponry and drugs, with severe penalties for the latter.

Tipping: A service charge of 10-15% is included in most hotel, restaurant and bar bills. Elsewhere a tip of 5-10% is welcomed.

Credit Cards Accepted: American Express, Diner's Club, MasterCard, Visa

Customary Dining Hours:
Breakfast: 07.30-09.30
Lunch: 13.00-15.00
Dinner: 20.00-23.30

Local Customs, Business Protocol and Courtesies: Paraguay is rapidly becoming industrialized, a point of pride in its business community as a result of its membership in the Mercosur Common Market along with its neighboring countries. However, it still takes much effort for foreign sellers to find reliable distributors and representatives; but these are essential. Make sure potential distributors are not already overburdened. Also, due to a dearth of mid-level managers, decisionmaking is generally at the top and may take some time. Be friendly, good-natured, polite and, when scheduling meetings, mindful of business hours. There is an afternoon siesta after lunch, which is generally eaten at home around noon. Schedule government and business meetings in advance; do not get annoyed, however, by lateness, which is frequent. You should never express annoyance or hostility. An atmosphere of confident goodwill and courtesy should prevail on both sides. Persistence is important, but pays off only if done with courtesy and confidence. People shake hands when meeting and departing, but it is also customary for men to hug each other and give a slight bow to women. Many businesspeople there speak English, but be prepared to get a good interpreter if necessary. It helps to speak or understand Spanish, of course, but keep in mind that it may be hard to keep up with as people tend to speak all at once, and very quickly and emotionally. Those engaged in conversation tend to stand very close to one another; moving away would be considered rude. Business and social relationships go hand-in-hand in Paraguay, and deals are usually made on the basis of personal contacts. For this reason, the business visitor should be friendly, good-natured, polite and knowledgeable of local customs, and accept invitations for an evening at a cafe as well as to a formal business lunch. Indeed, many business agreements are made over coffee after a leisurely lunch, the main meal of the day, or after dinner. If you are offered "mate," an herbal tea (served hot or cold) prepared for family, friends and associates, you'll know you've been accepted as a business partner or friend. Because gift-giving can be easily misconstrued as a bribe, be careful regarding timing when you give a gift. It's best to wait until you have been offered one, and generally, a social setting is the correct context. You might consider a group gift such as office accessories; especially if you are a woman presenting a gift to male counterparts. Tasteful souvenirs from your home country are fine, and, so are flowers or chocolate if invited to a home. When the host offers a toast, respond with one as well. At initial meetings, business cards are exchanged; providing English/Spanish ones and company literature in Spanish will make a good impression. Present the card Spanish side up. People typically address each other using their title and last name. The main hotels are popular spots for business functions in the evenings, and many a deal is agreed upon after dinner.

Health: It is advisable to consult your doctor before your journey. A vaccination certificate for yellow fever is mandatory if travelling from an infected area. Vaccinations for typhoid, polio, hepatitis A, tetanus and malaria are recommended. It is advisable to drink bottled water. Food precautions should be observed at all times. A health insurance is recommended.

Language: Spanish. Guarani is also widely spoken.

ASUNCION

Airport: Silvio Pettirassi airport

Distance from City: 16km (9 miles) from the city center.

Transportation to Center of City:
From International and Domestic Terminals
By Bus (cost) G1,000. Time approx. 30 min.
By Taxi (cost) G20,000-G30,000. Time approx. 20 min.
Tip luggage porters G900 per piece

Transfers: (Minimum Connecting Time):
International to International: 60 min.
International to Domestic: 30 min.
Domestic to International: 30 min.
Domestic to Domestic: 30 min.

Automobile Rentals:
Airport car rental desk
Hertz - 22012

Car rental city office
National Interrent - 492157
Hertz - 503921

Hotels:
Cecilia Hotel, Estados Unidos y Mariscal, 210365
Chaco Hotel, Caballero M, Estigarribia, 492066
Excelsior Hotel, Chile 980, 495632
Grand Hotel Armele, Palma y Colon, 444455

Places of Interest:
The Fine Arts Museum
The Ethnological Museum
The Botanical Gardens
La Casa de la Independencia - a monument and a museum.
The National Cathedral
The Pantheon - a monument

PERU

Official Name: Republic of Peru

Location: South America. Peru is bordered by Ecuador, Colombia, Brazil, Bolivia and Chile.

Government: Republic

Area: 1,285,216 sq. km., 496,225 sq. miles.

Population: 23.5 million

Religion(s): Roman Catholic majority.

Capital City: Lima

Time: GMT -5

Currency: Nuevo Sol (PES) = 100 centimos

Currency Requirements: There are no restrictions on the import and the export of local currency. The import of foreign currency must be declared and the export is limited to the amount declared on arrival. Exchange receipts must be kept for reconversion of Nuevo Sol into foreign currency. It is recommended to take US Dollars rather than other foreign currency.

Business Hours:
- Government: 09.00-17.00 Mon-Fri
- Banks: 08.15-11.30 Mon-Fri (Jan -Mar); 09.15-12.45 Mon-Fri (Apr-Dec); Some banks are open 09.30-12.30 Sat.
- Shops: 10.30-13.00 and 15.00/16.00-19.00/20.00 Mon-Sat
- Offices: 09.00-17.00 Mon-Fri

Weight and Measures: Metric System

Electric Current: 220 volts AC. Plugs are of the continental 2-pin type.

Holidays:
New Year's Day - January 1
Maundy Thursday - March 27
Good Friday - April 10*
Labor Day - May 1
St. Peter and St. Paul - June 29
Festival of Independence - July 28-29
St. Rose of Lima - August 30
Battle of Angamos - October 8
All Saints' Day - November 1
Immaculate Conception - December 8
Christmas Day - December 25

* Christian Holidays - vary each year.

Suitable Clothing: Wear a conservative suit and bring in light clothing between January and April, medium weight between June and November and warm clothing for the Andes. Formal clothing isn't necessary. Dressing flashily or expensively can attract thieves and will not make a good impression.

Automobile Driving License: An International Driving License is required. Drivers must be over 25 years of age.

Customs Allowances: Personal items are duty free, but register valuables and keep receipts or they may face confiscation. You may bring in 250 cigarettes duty free and 2 liters of wine and spirits. Prohibited are military weaponry and drugs, with severe penalties for the latter. Also forbidden is the export of wildlife or any items made from indigenous species.

Tipping: A service charge of 18% is added to all bills, but an additional 5% tip is expected. Taxi drivers do not expect a tip.

Credit Cards Accepted: American Express, MasterCard, Visa

Customary Dining Hours:
Breakfast: 07.30-09.00

Lunch: 13.30-15.30
Dinner: 21.30-23.30

PERU

Local Customs, Business Protocol and Courtesies: Although generally an open, friendly people, you will meet with more formal behavior in the business world. The business visitor should be good-natured and polite, and accept all gestures of hospitality. Many business agreements are made over coffee after a leisurely lunch, the main meal of the day, or after dinner. Men and women generally shake hands, or men will offer a slight bow to their female counterparts. At initial meetings, business cards are exchanged; providing English/Spanish ones and company literature in Spanish will make a good impression. Present the card Spanish side up. You will likely need an interpreter at one point or another. People typically address each other using their title and last name. Appointments should be arranged in advance (avoid Tuesday the 13th, considered a bad luck day). Your contact may be late, but you should never express annoyance or hostility. An atmosphere of confident goodwill and courtesy should prevail on both sides. Persistence is important, but pays off only if done with courtesy and confidence. You will find that people here are proud of their beautiful capital, Lima, and of their dual Inca-Spanish ancestry; showing interest will help build a relationship. Because gift-giving can be easily misconstrued as a bribe, be careful regarding timing when you give a gift. It's best to wait until you have been offered one, and generally, a social setting is the correct context. You might consider a group gift such as office accessories, especially if you are a woman presenting a gift to male counterparts. Tasteful souvenirs from your home country are fine, and, so are flowers or chocolates if invited to a home. Avoid black or lavender, or certain types and colors of flowers which are considered funereal or romantic.

Health: It is advisable to consult your doctor before your journey. A vaccination certificate for yellow fever is mandatory if travelling from an infected area. Vaccinations for yellow fever, cholera, hepatitis A, tetanus, typhoid and polio and malaria are recommended. It is advisable to drink bottled water. Food precautions should be observed at all times. A health insurance is strongly recommended.

PERU

Language: Spanish and Quechua. Aymara is spoken in some areas.

LIMA

Country code: 51 - City code: 1

Airport: Jorge Chavez International Airport

Distance from City: 16km (9 miles) west of the city.

Transportation to Center of City:
From International and Domestic Terminals
By Bus (cost) PES1.25-1.50. Time approx. 25-35 min.
By Taxi (cost) USD12-15.
Tip luggage porters PES1.50 per piece

Transfers: (Minimum Connecting Time):
International to International: 60 min.
International to Domestic: 90 min.
Domestic to International: 90 min.
Domestic to Domestic: 30 min.

Automobile Rentals:
Airport car rental desk
Avis - 452-4774
National Interrent - 452-3426
Hertz - 451-8189

Car rental city office
Avis - 437-3530
National Interrent - 444-2333
Hertz - 442-4475

Hotels:
Continental Hotel, Jr. Puno 196, 427-5890
El Condado Miraflores Hotel, Alcanfores 465, 444-3614
Libetador - Lima, Los Eucaliptos 550, 421-6680
Sheraton Lima Hotel and Casino, Paseo de la Republica
    170, 433-3320

PERU

Restaurants:
Bar/Restaurant Machu Piccu, Ancash 312
Bircher Benner, Shell 629
Cafe Cafe, Matir Olaya 250
Cafe Haiti, Diagonal 160
Carlin, Avenida La Paz 646
Centro Naturista, Avenida Nicolas de Pierola 958
Chifa Long, Mauco Capac 483
Chifa Lung Fung, Avenida R. de Panama 3165, 441 8817
Colina, Jiron Berlin 317
Cordano, Jiron Ancash 202
El Cevillano, Avenida Aviacion 3333
El Otro Sitio, Calle Sucre 317
El Senorio de Sulco, Malecon Cisneros 1470, 445 6640
La Casita Azul, Avenida Petit Thouras 5196
La Rosa Nautica, Espigon 4, 447 0057
La Tasca, Avenida Comandante Espinar 300
Las Mesitas, Avenida Grau 323
Natur, Moquequa 132
Oro Verde, Calle Colon 569
Picolo Cafe, Diez Canseco 126

Entertainment:
10 Sesenta, Los Nardos 1060, 441 0744
Bertoloto,Avenida Malecon Bertoloto 770
El Ekeko, Avenida Grau 266, 477 5823
Fiesta Latina,Frederico Villareal 259
Kimbaka, Avenida R. de Panama 1401
La Casona de Barranco, Avenida Grau 329
La Estacion, Avenida Petro de Osma 112
La Pena Poggi, Luna Pizarro 587
Las Brisas del Titicaca, Jiron Wakulski 168
Latin Brothers, Jose Leal 1281
Manos Morenas, Avenida Pedro de Osma 409
Medi Rock, Benavides 420
Muelle Uno Club, Playa Punta Roquitas, 444 1800
Pena Hatuchay,Jiron Lima 228
Pena la Palizada, Avenida del Ejercito 657
Pena Wifala, Cailloma 633
Taberna 1900, Avenida Grau 268

PERU

Shops and Stores:

Casa Wako, Jiron de la Union 841   Apparel
Centro Comercial   Shopping Centre
Collacocha, Calle Colon 534   Apparel
Mercado Artesanal, Avenida Petit Thouras 5321   Jewelry

Places of Interest:

National Museum of History
Peruvian Art Museum
The Cathedral
Bullfighting - a festival
Plaza de Armas - a picture gallery.

PUERTO RICO

Official Name: Commonwealth of Puerto Rico

Location: Caribbean. Puerto Rico is an island situated west of the British Virgin Islands and east of the Dominican Republic. The Atlantic Ocean is to the north and the Caribbean Sea is to the south.

Government: Commonwealth (USA)

Area: 8959 sq. km., 3459 sq. miles.

Population: 3.6 million

Religion(s): Roman Catholic Majority. Christian denominations and Jewish minorities are also present.

Capital City: San Juan

Time: GMT -4

Currency: US Dollar (USD)=100 cents

Currency Requirements: There are no restrictions on the import and the export of foreign or local currency. Transfer of USD10,000 or more should be registered with customs on a declaration form.

Business Hours:
- Government: 08.00-17.00 Mon-Fri
- Banks: 08.30-14.30 Mon-Fri; Banco Popular open 08.30-16.30 Mon-Fri and 08.30-12.00 Sat.
- Shops: 09.00-17.30 Mon-Sat
- Offices: 09.00-18.00 Mon-Fri

Weight and Measures: US System, Metric System, some Spanish weights and measurements

PUERTO RICO

Electric Current: 120 volts

Holidays:
New Year's Day - January 1
Epiphany - January 6
Martin Luther King Jr. Day - January 16
Ponce de Leon Carnival - February 6-11**
George Washington's Birthday - February 22
Emancipation Day - March 22
Palm Sunday - March 23
Good Friday – April 10*
Memorial Day - May 26
San Juan Bautista Day - June 21
USA Independence Day - July 4
Luis Munoz Rivera's Birthday - July 21
Jose Celso Barbosa's Birthday - July 27
Labor Day - September 1
Columbus Day - October 12
Veterans' Day - November 11
Puerto Rico Discovery Day - November 19
Thanksgiving Day - November 28
Christmas Day - December 25
New Year's Eve - December 31

* Christian Holiday – vary each year

** Although not an official holiday, many offices and shops will have their opening hours disrupted by the festivities.

In general if a holiday falls on a Sunday, the following Monday is observed as a holiday; if a holiday falls on a Saturday, the previous Friday is observed as a holiday.

Suitable Clothing: Light materials can be worn year round; wear a conservative summer suit or dress for most meetings. Bring rainwear between June and October, and sungear at all times.

Automobile Driving License: An International Driving Permit or a National License can be used.

Customs Allowances: Personal items are duty free, but register valuables upon arrival or they may be confiscated upon departure. You may bring in 5 cartons of cigarettes duty free; there are no limits on wine or spirits. Punishment is severe for drugs; military weaponry and pornography are also forbidden.

Tipping: If a service charge is not included in the restaurant or in the hotel bill it is expected to leave a tip of 15%. Taxi drivers expect a 15% tip.

Credit Cards Accepted: American Express, MasterCard, Visa

Customary Dining Hours:
Breakfast: 08.00-09.00
Lunch: 12.30-15.00
Dinner: 19.30-23.00

Local Customs, Business Protocol and Courtesies: As an American commonwealth (not a colony), many business practices are similar to the United States' although it has its own cultural heritage and traditions. Its swift economic growth is a source of pride. The business atmosphere is a mix of North and Latin American. Schedule meetings in advance and be on time. Shake hands upon introduction, offer business cards and use titles until indicated otherwise. Presentations and contracts should be detailed and well-defined. Be polite but assertive: otherwise you may be drowned out by many people talking at once. Business lunches, dinners or informal meetings over drinks are common, but never breakfasts. Entertaining (sometimes formal) and exchanging business gifts tend to occur only after a deal has been reached.

Health: It is advisable to consult your doctor before travelling. It is recommended to have immunizations against diphtheria, hepatitis A, hepatitis B, polio, tetanus and typhoid. Bathing in fresh water should be avoided.

Language: Spanish. English is widely spoken.

PUERTO RICO

SAN JUAN

Country code: 1 - City code: 787

Airport: Luis Munoz Marin International Airport

Distance from City: 14km (8 miles) east of the city center.

Transportation to Center of City:
From International and Domestic Terminals
By Bus (cost) USD0.25. Time approx. 35 min.
By Taxi (cost) USD16. Time approx. 20-30 min.
Tip luggage porters USD1 per piece

Transfers: (Minimum Connecting Time):
International to International: 60 min.
International to Domestic: 60 min.
Domestic to International: 60 min.
Domestic to Domestic: 45 min.

Automobile Rentals:
Airport car rental desk
Avis - 791-2500
National Interrent - 791-1805
Hertz - 791-0840

Car rental city office
Avis - 721-4499
Hertz - 725-2072

Hotels:
Best Western Hotel Pierre, 105 De Diego-Santurce, 721-1200
Excelsior Hotel, 801 Ponce de Leon Ave., 721-7400
Radisson Ambassador Plaza Hotel and Casino, 1369 Ashford Ave., Condado, 721-7300
Radisson Normandie Hotel, Ave. Munoz Rivera Esq Rosales, 729-2929
San Juan Marriott Resort and Stellaris Casino, 1309 Ashford Ave., 722-7000

Restaurants:

PUERTO RICO

Al Dente, 309 Recinto Sur, 723 7303
Antonio, 1406 Magdalena, 723 7567
Butterfly People, 152 Fortaleza, 723 2432
Cafe Berlin, 407 San Francisco, 722 5205
Caruso, 1104 Ashford, 723 6876
Chart House, 1214 Ashford 724 0110
Chaumiere, 367 Tetuan, 722 3330
Chef Marisol Cuisine, 202 Cristo, 725 7454
Danza, 56 Fortabeza, 723 1642
Don Pope, 75,67 Luisa, 723 1082
Galeria, 205 San Justo, 725 1092
Hard Rock Cafe, 256 Recinto Sur, 724 7625
Mallorquina, 207 San Justo, 722 3261
Marisqueria Atlantica, 7 Lugo Vina, 722 0890
Ajili Mojili, 1052 Ashford, 725 9195
Panache, 1127 Seaview, 725 8284
Patio de Sam, 102 San Sebastian, 723 1149
Ramiro's, 1106 Magdalena, 721 9049
Yuan, 255 Ponce de leon, 766 0666
Yukiyu, 311 Recinto Sur, 721 0653

Places of Interest:
The Pablo Casals Museum
Casa de los Contrafuertes - a museum
Casa del Callejon - a museum
The San Juan Museum of Art and History
El Morro - a fortress
San Cristobal - a fort
San Juan Cathedral
San Jose Church

URUGUAY

Official Name: Oriental Republic of Uruguay

Location: South America. Uruguay is bordered by Brazil, the Atlantic Ocean and Argentina.

Government: Republic

Area: 176,215 sq. km., 68,037 sq. miles.

Population: 3.13 million

Religion(s): Roman Catholic.

Capital City: Montevideo

Major Business Cities: Montevideo, Salto, Paysandu, Las Piedras

Time: GMT -3

Currency: Uruguayan Peso (UYP)=100 centemos

Currency Requirements: There are no restrictions on the import and the export of either foreign or local currency. It is recommended not to change more than what is needed to avoid losses when changing local currency back into foreign currency.

Business Hours:
- Government: 11.00 or 12.00-17.00 or 18.00 Mon-Fri(Summer); 07.00 or 07.30-13.00 or 13.30 Mon-Fri(Winter)
- Banks: 13.00-17.00 Mon-Fri
- Shops: 09.00-19.00 Mon-Fri; (some are open 09.00-12.30 Sat)
- Offices: 09.00-17.00/18.00 Mon-Fri

Weight and Measures: Metric System

Electric Current: 220 volts AC. Plugs are of the continental flat 2-pin type.

Holidays:
New Year's Day - January 1
Children's/Wise Kings' Day (Epiphany) - January 6
Carnival - February 11-12
Easter - March 28-31
Landing of the 33 Patriots - April 19
Labor Day - May 1
Battle of Las Piedras - May 18
Birth of General Artigas - June 19
Constitution day - July 18
National Independence Day - August 25
Discovery of America - October 12
All Souls' Day - November 2
Family Day - December 25

Suitable Clothing: Between June to September, wear medium weight coat and clothing; the rest of the year, light clothing is appropriate. Wear a business suit or a conservative dress to meetings. Except for private club functions, don't dress formally, and avoid looking too wealthy, for safety reasons.

Automobile Driving License: An International Driving License is recommended. A temporary license must be obtained from the Town Hall, which is valid for 90 days.

Customs Allowances: Personal items are duty free, but register valuables and keep receipts or they may face confiscation. You may bring in 400 cigarettes or 50 cigars duty free and I liter of spirits. Prohibited are military weaponry and drugs, with severe penalties for the latter.

Tipping: When service charge is not included, a 10% tip is expected. Taxi drivers expect a tip.

Credit Cards Accepted: American Express, MasterCard, Visa

Customary Dining Hours:
Breakfast: 07.30-09.00

URUGUAY

Lunch: 12.00-15.00
Dinner: 20.00-24.30

Local Customs, Business Protocol and Courtesies: Business and social customs are heavily European in style, and Montevideo is one of the most cosmopolitan, modern and wealthy cities in the region. Meetings begin on time, conversation and negotiations are low-key and many businessmen speak German, Italian and English as well as Spanish. In general, be friendly but conservative and highly professional. Like in the U.S., businessmen work long hours. The main challenges are finding a reliable distributor who is not overburdened, and overcoming the tendency toward exclusivity in selling contracts. Shake hands upon meeting, and exchange business cards. Although English is widely spoken, it makes a good impression to have cards and company literature in Spanish. Use title and last name. Business entertaining is frequently at hotels or restaurants, but if you are invited to someone's home, bring flowers and chocolates for the hostess. Avoid certain types and colors of flowers which are considered funereal or romantic. At meals, eat European style with knife and fork and place your utensils across the plate when finished. When the host offers a toast, respond with one as well. You are expected to stay awhile after the meal; business or other subjects are often discussed then. It's best to wait until you have been offered a business gift before giving one yourself (this is usually done after an agreement is reached). You might consider a group gift such as office accessories, especially if you are a woman presenting a gift to male counterparts. Tasteful souvenirs from your home country are suitable.

Health: It is advisable to consult your doctor before your journey. Vaccination for typhoid and polio are recommended. It is considered to be safe to drink tap water in the main cities. A health insurance is recommended.

Language: Spanish. Some English may be spoken.

URUGUAY

MONTEVIDEO

Country code: 598 - City code: 2

Airport: Montevideo Carrasco Airport.

Distance from City: 19km (11 miles) from the city.

Transportation to Center of City:
From International and Domestic Terminals
By Bus (cost) UYP5-7. Time approx. 45-55 min. (every 60-90 min)
By Taxi (cost) UYP20-22. Time approx. 35-45 min.
Tip luggage porters 50 Centesimos per piece

Transfers: (Minimum Connecting Time):
International to International: 60 min.
International to Domestic: 60 min.
Domestic to International: 60 min.
Domestic to Domestic: 30 min.

Automobile Rentals:
Airport car rental desk
Avis - 611929
National Interrent - 615267
Hertz - 612857

Car rental city office
Avis - 930303
National Interrent - 615267
Hertz −923920

Hotels:
Klee International Hotel, San Jose 1303 Esq. Yaguaron, 920606
Lafayette Hotel, 1170 Soriano, 924646
Victoria Plaza Hotel, Towers and Casino, 759 Plaza Independencia, 920111

Restaurants:
Danubio Azul, Colonia 835, 901-0354
Dona Flor, Blvar. Artigas 1034, 708-5751

El Fogon, San Jose 1080, 900-0900
El Panoramico, Soriano 1375, 24th Fl., 902-0666
La Genovesa, San Jose 1242, 900-8729
La Posada del Puerto, Perez Castellano-Mercado del Puerto, 915-4270
La Spagneteria, Dr. J. Scoberia, 2504, 711-4986
Los Picapiedras, Arocena y Murillo, 601-3571
Riachuelo, San Jose 1333, 908-5644
Ruffino, San Jose 1166, 908-3384
Verde, Azul y Ajo, Av. De Las Americas 8336, 601-5662
Viejo Sancho, San Jose 1229, 900-4063

Places of Interest:
The Museo Historico Nacional
The Museo de Historia Natural
Galeria Aramayo – an art gallery
The Palacio Taranco
The Cathedral
The Cabildo Building – a museum

VENEZUELA

Official Name: Republic of Venezuela

Location: South America. Venezuela is bordered by Guyana, Brazil and Colombia. To the north lie the Caribbean and to the east the Atlantic Ocean.

Government: Federal Republic

Area: 912,050 sq. km., 352,144 sq. miles.

Population: 20.31 million

Religion(s): Roman Catholic

Capital City: Caracas

Major Business Cities: Caracas, Valencia, Maracay, Barquisimeto, Ciudad Guyana

Time: GMT -4

Currency: Bolivar (B)=100 centimos

Currency Requirements: The import and the export of foreign and local currencies are unlimited.

Business Hours:
- Government: 08.30-11.30; 14.00-16.30 Mon-Fri.
- Banks: 08.30 - 11.30 and 14.00 - 16.30 Mon - Fri.
- Shops: 09.00 - 13.00 and 15.00 - 19.00 Mon - Sat.
- Offices: 08.00 - 18.00 Mon - Fri. (long mid-day break).

Weight and Measures: Metric System

Electric Current: 110 volts AC. Plugs are of the American 2-pin type.

VENEZUELA

Holidays:
New Year's Day - January 1
Carnival Monday - February 10
Carnival Tuesday - February 11
Holy Thursday - March 27
Good Friday - April 10*
Declaration of Independence -April 19
Labor Day - May 1
Carabobo Battle - June 24
Independence Day - July 5
Bolivar's Birthday - July 24
Columbus Day - October 12
Christmas Day - December 25

*Christian Holidays – vary each year.

Suitable Clothing: Dress conservatively in light clothing year round - suits for meetings and dark suit or dress for formal occasions. Dressing too flashily or too expensively can attract thieves and will not make a good impression. Bring rainwear between April and November, and sungear year round.

Automobile Driving License: A National or an International Driving License is required and it must also be held for at least one year. Drivers must be over 21 years of age.

Customs Allowances: Personal items are duty free, but register valuables and keep receipts or they may face confiscation. You may bring in 250 cigarettes duty free, 25 cigars and 2 liters of wine and spirits. Prohibited are military weaponry and drugs, with severe penalties for the latter. Also forbidden is the export of agricultural products such as plants and fruit.

Tipping: A service charge of 10% is included in the bill by the majority of bars and restaurants, but the customer is expected to tip an additional 10% for the waiter. Hotel staff should be tipped. Taxi drivers are only tipped for carrying luggage. Visitors may find that tips are often higher in the capital, Caracas.

Credit Cards Accepted: American Express, MasterCard, Visa

VENEZUELA

Customary Dining Hours:
Breakfast: 07.30-09.00
Lunch: 12.00-14.30
Dinner: 19.00-22.00

Local Customs, Business Protocol and Courtesies: Due to Venezuela's enormous oil wealth, it has a sophisticated, cosmopolitan business community. The business visitor should be friendly, good-natured, polite and knowledgeable of local customs, and accept invitations for an evening at a cafe as well as a to formal business lunch. Indeed, many business agreements are made over coffee after a leisurely lunch, the main meal of the day, or after dinner. If invited out or to a home, you are expected to stick around awhile after dinner; business or other subjects are often discussed then. Shake hands upon meeting. Business cards are exchanged · provide English/Spanish ones and company literature in Spanish. People typically address each other using their title and last name. Appointments should be arranged in advance. Your contact may be late, but you should never express annoyance or hostility. Your contemporaries are quite sophisticated, and an atmosphere of confident goodwill and courtesy should prevail on both sides. Persistence is important, but pays off only if done with courtesy and with confidence. In meetings or discussions, it is the norm to stand or sit close to one another, and for many people to speak at once. Try to fit into this atmosphere without being too aggressive. Keep your discussions and proposals direct. It's best to wait until you have been offered a business gift before giving one in return, and generally, a social setting is the correct context. You might consider a group gift such as office accessories, especially if you are a woman presenting a gift to male counterparts. Tasteful souvenirs from your home country are fine, and, so are flowers or chocolates if invited to a home. Avoid certain types and colors of flowers which are considered funereal or romantic.

Health: Medical advice should be sought before travelling. There is a risk of malaria in rural areas. Vaccinations for yellow fever, typhoid, polio, cholera, hepatitis A and

VENEZUELA

tetanus are recommended. It is advisable to drink bottled water. A medical insurance is advised.

Language: Spanish. Some English, French, German and Portuguese are spoken by some sectors of the community.

CARACAS

Country code: 58 - City code: 2

Airport: Caracas Simon Bolivar International Airport.

Distance from City: 22km (13 miles) from the city.

Transportation to Center of City:
From International and Domestic Terminals
By Bus (cost) B235. Time approx. 60-90 min.
By Taxi (cost) B3000 Time approx. 45 min.
Tip luggage porters 90 Bolivares per piece

Transfers: (Minimum Connecting Time):
International to International: 60 min.
International to Domestic: 120 min.
Domestic to International: 120 min.
Domestic to Domestic: 30 min.

Automobile Rentals:
Airport car rental desk
Avis -551190

Car rental city office
Avis -261-5556
Hertz -952-1603

Hotels:
Caracas Hilton, Av. Libertador Sur 25, 503-5000
Caracas Residencias Anauco Hilton, Parque Central, 573-4111
Eurobuilding Caracas Hotel, Calle la Guairita, 902-1111
Hotel CCT, Centro Ciudad Comercial Tamanaco, 959-0611
Hotel Paseo Las Mercedes, Av. Principal de Las Mercedes,
    910-033

VENEZUELA

Lincoln Suites, Av. Francisco Solano, 762-8575
The Hotel Tamanaco, Ave. Principal de las Mercedes, 909-7111

Restaurants:
Alfi's Centro Comercial Chacaito, 72-3509
Anatole, Av. La Estrella, 52-4353
Aventino, Av. Santa Felipe, 32-2640
Casa Vecchia, Av. Mohedano, 267-1707
Don Sancho, Av. Pichincha, 952-1028
El Caney, Av Pichincha at Av. Casanova, 71-8754
El Carrizo, Av. Blandin, 32-9370
El Porton, Av. Pichincha No. 18. 952-0027
Gazebo, Av. Rio de Janeiro, 92-5568
Il Caminetto, Av. Principal, 92-1231
Il Parino, Teatro Altamira Boulevard, 263-3060
La Belle Epoque, Av. Leonardo da Vinci, 752-1342
La Dolche Vita, Av. Juan Bosco, 261-5763
La Via Emilia, Av. Orinoco, 92-6904
Le Petit Bistro De Jacques, Av. Principal de Las Mercedes,
    91-8108
Los Pilones, Av. Venezuela at Calle Pichincha, 718-8367
Piccolo Mondo, Av. La Trinidad, 91-2357
Posada del Laurel, No. Pastor a Misericordia, 575-1135
Restaurant Lasserre, 3a Av., 283-3079
Rococo, Av. San Felipe con 4a Transversal, 266-1851
Tarzilandia, Final Av. San Juan Bosco, 10a Transversal
    Altamira, 261-8419

Entertainment:
Barrock, 4a Transversal, 266-7841
Brooklyn, Av. Tamanaco 36, 952-2511
Café L'Attico, Av. Luis Roches, 261-2819
Club M-LXXX, Av. Francisco Miranda, 953-6614
Croco's Club, Av. Venezuela, 951-4703
Doors, Calle Madrid, 91-2022
El Sarao, Centro Comercial Bello Campo, 267-4581
Greenwich, 1a Av. Ed. Marvin, 267-1760
Hipocampo, Centro Comercial Chacaito No. 215, 952-0882
La Cantina, Calle Madrid, 993-5548
Le Club, Centro Comercial Chacaito, 951-2084
Liverpool, Av. Principal de Las Mercedes, 993-6165
Madison Pub, Av. Principal Bello Campo, 263-7662

VENEZUELA

Magic, Calle Madrid, 993-6829
Moma, Av Principal de la Castellana, 263-0453
Pal's Club, Centro Comercial Level C-1, 9599-3274
Stage, Av. Luis Roche, 285-7172
The Flower, Av. Principal La Castellana, 393-3013
Xanadu, Av. Blandin, Plaza La Castellana, 263-0415

Shops and Stores:
Charles Jourdan, Centro Cuidad Tamanaco   Shoes
Fascinacion, Centro Cuidad Tamanaco   Leather
Italcambio, Av. Casanova   Jewelry
Joyeria El Arte, Av. Lincoln No. 229   Jewelry
Maria Pia, Centro Cuidad Tamanaco, Nivel C-1   Apparel
Matignon, Centro Cuidad Tamanaco   Shoes
Nardi, Centro Cuidad Tamanaco   Shoes
O'Leary, Av. Lincoln   Apparel
Sylvia S. Denis, Centro Cuidad Tamanaco   Apparel
Tokyo, Centro Cuidad Tamanaco   Apparel

Places of Interest:
Casa Amarilla
Jardin Botanico – a botanical garden.
San Francisco Church
Palacio Municipal – a museum
Galeria de Arte Nacional – an art gallery
Museo de Ciencias Naturales
Caricuao Zoo
Parque Nacional del Este and Planetarium – a park
Capitol – the National Congress building
Panteon Nacional

AFRICA
MIDDLE EAST

ALGERIA

Official Name: Democratic and Popular Republic of Algeria

Location: North Africa. Algeria is surrounded by Tunisia, Libya, Niger, Mali, Mauritania and Morocco. The north coast lies on the Mediterranean.

Government: Democracy

Area: 2,381,741 sq. km., 919,595 sq. miles.

Population: 27.2 million

Religion(s): 90% Muslim, mostly Sunni.

Capital City: Algiers

Major Business Cities: Algiers, Oran

Time: GMT +1

Currency: Dinar (AD)=100 centimes

Currency Requirements: Import of local currency is limited to AD50, export is prohibited. Import of foreign currency is unlimited subject to declaration. A currency declaration form must be filled in at the same time as the disembarkation card and must be stamped by customs on arrival. It is essential that the declaration form is kept in good order at all times and shown on departure with receipts. Each currency exchange should be recorded on the form and receipts retained, the form should also be presented when paying hotel bills to verify the source of exchange. A minimum of AD1,000 has to be changed on arrival and only amounts larger than AD1,000 can be reconverted into foreign currency on departure (however it is very difficult to reconvert).

Business Hours:
- Government: 08.00-12.00; 14.00-17.30 Sat-Wed; 08.00-12.00 Thur
- Banks: 09.00-15.00 Mon-Thur
- Shops: 08.00-12.00/12.30 & 14.00/14.30-18.00 Sat-Thur
- Offices: 08.00-12.00 & 13.00-17.00 Sat-Tue (Wed until 16.00)

Weight and Measures: Metric System

Electric Current: 127/220 volts AC - Continental 2-pin type plug.

Holidays:
New Year's Day - January 1
Eid-ul-fitr* - February 8-10
Eid-ul-adha* - April 18-21
Labour Day - May 1
Al-Hijra (Islamic New Year)* - May 8
Ashura* - May 17
Commemoration Day - June 19
Independence Day - July 5
Birthday of Muhammad* - July 17
Anniversary of the Revolution - November 1

* Muslim holidays are approximate, as they are timed according to local sightings of various phases of the moon.

Suitable Clothing: You will need sunglasses, sunhats and sunscreen year round. Light material is appropriate most of the year (medium-weight between November and March), but men should make sure it covers knees and shoulders, while women should wear skirts or dresses which cover the knees, elbows and neckline as well. A business suit should be worn to all meetings.

Automobile Driving License: International Driving Permit is required and this must be stamped at the offices of the Automobile Club.

Customs Allowances: You will need to show the Currency Declaration form you fill out upon arrival. Throughout your trip: any time you pay for something in hard currency, you will need to show that form along with your passport. Upon leaving, your expenditures and currency you have left must add up to the amount on the form, or you may be held up and even fined. Declare all valuables as well, and be able to account for them upon departure, or they will face confiscation. You may bring in 200 cigarettes, 2 liters of wine and one of spirits duty free. Prohibited are military weaponry, narcotics, and pornography and some food and agricultural products.

Tipping: It is recommended to tip waiters and taxi drivers 10%.

Customary Dining Hours:
Breakfast: 08.00-09.00
Lunch: 12.30-14.30
Dinner: 19.00-22.00

Local Customs, Business Protocol and Courtesies: Visitors should only make essential visits to Algeria as Westerners are vulnerable to attack and kidnapping. You should dress conservatively. Women should respect the traditional Islamic dress code in all public places. In conversation it is customary for people to stand very close together. Photography of military personnel and buildings is prohibited.

Health: Yellow Fever and Cholera certificates are required if traveling from an infected area. Vaccinations recommended for hepatitis A, tetanus, typhoid and polio. Risk of malaria is limited. Bottled water is recommended at all times. Bilharzia is also present · it is advisable not to swim in fresh water. Medical insurance is essential. Health risks can change frequently so it is advisable to consult your doctor well in advance of your journey.

Language: Arabic is the official language. French is widely spoken within business circles.

ALGIERS

Country code: 213 - City code: none

Airport: Houari Boumediene International Airport

Distance from City: 20km (12 miles) east of the city.
Transportation to Center of City:
From International and Domestic Terminals
By Bus (cost) AD10 Time approx. 40 min.
By Taxi (cost) AD400. Time approx. 30 min.
Tip luggage porters AD5 per piece

Transfers: (Minimum Connecting Time):
International to International: 40 min.
International to Domestic: 45 min.
Domestic to International: 45 min.
Domestic to Domestic: 30 min.

Hotels:
Grand Hotel Tripaza, Palace Port Said, 630 040
Grand Hotel des Etrangers, 1 Rue Ali Boumandjel, 633 245
Grand Hotel Regina, Rue Ben Boulaid, 649 900
Hotel d'Angleterre, 11 Rue Ben Boulaid, 636 540
Hotel Safir, Rue Asselah Hocine, 735 040
Hotel Aurassi, Ave Dr Franz Fanon, 748 252
Hotel Albert I, 5 Ave. Pasteur, 630 020
Hotel el-Djazair, Ave. Boudjemaa Souidani, 591 000

Restaurants:
Dar Hizia, Martyr's Monument, Bois des Arcades
El-Boustane, Martyr's Monument, Bois des Arcades
Fast Burger, Bois des Arcades
Royal Burger, 23 Rue Larbi ben M'Hidi

Places of Interest:
The Ketchaoua Mosque
The Museum of Popular Arts and Traditions
Martyrs" Monument
The Sacred Heart Cathedral

BAHRAIN

Official Name: State of Bahrain

Location: Middle East - Gulf Coast. The territory of Bahrain consists of 33 islands situated 25 km (15 miles) off the east coast of Saudi Arabia and 30 km (18 miles) from the Qatar Peninsula.

Government: Constitutional Monarchy

Area: 695 sq. km., 268 sq. miles.

Population: 529,000

Religion(s): Muslim majority. Christian, Bahai and Hindu minorities.

Capital City: Manama

Time: GMT +3

Currency: Dinar (BHD)=1000 fils

Currency Requirements: There are no restrictions to either the import or the export of foreign and local currency.

Business Hours:
- Government:08.00-13.00 Sat-Wed, Thur most offices are closed
- Banks: 08.00-13.00 Sat-Wed, 08.00-11.00 Thursday
- Shops: 08.00/09.00-12.00/13.00 & 15.30/16.00-18.30/20.00 Sat-Thursday
- Offices: 08.00-15.00/15.30 or 08.00-13.00 & 15.00-18.00 Sat-Wed

*Friday is the weekly holiday.

BAHRAIN

Weight and Measures: Metric System

Electric Current: 230 volts AC

Holidays:
New Year's Day - January 1
Eid-ul-fitr* - February 9-11
Eid-ul-adha* - April 18-21
Al-Hijra (Islamic New Year)* - May 8
Ashura* - May 17
Birthday of Muhammad* - July 17
National Day - December 16

* Muslim holidays are approximate, as they are timed according to local sightings of various phases of the moon.

Suitable Clothing: Light material is appropriate, but men should make sure it covers knees and shoulders, while women should wear skirts or dresses which cover the knees, elbows and neckline as well. You will need sunglasses, sunhats and sunscreen year round, especially between June and September. Nights and November to March are cooler, so bring medium-weight clothing and a light jacket then. A business suit should be worn to all meetings, and it is also a polite gesture for Western women to cover their heads, although this is not mandatory. Formal clothing may be needed for some functions.

Automobile Driving License: An International Driving License is required. It must be endorsed by the Traffic Department before it can be used.

Customs Allowances: Declare all valuables, or they may face confiscation upon your departure. Also, you will need a guarantee from your sponsor that you will take out any computers or other electronics you bring in. Antiques may not leave the country; penalties are harsh. Newspapers and videos may be examined for material deemed offensive. No limits exist on foreign currency or Dinars (which are hard currency), as long as what you export was initially declared. You may bring in 400 cigarettes, 2 liters of spirits and 227 ml. of perfume. Prohibited are military weaponry, narcotics, and pornography.

Tipping: A service charge of 10-15% is added to the bill by most restaurants and hotels. Where taxis are metered it is recommended tip 10% of the fare. It is not necessary to leave a tip when a taxi fare has been negotiated in advance. Additional tipping is discretionary. Small change is handy for tipping porters.

Credit Cards Accepted:
American Express, Diner's Club, Visa

Customary Dining Hours:
Breakfast: 07.00-09.00
Lunch: 12.00-14.00
Dinner: 21.30-24.00

Local Customs, Business Protocol and Courtesies: Skilled, tough and ritualized bargaining is the hallmark of the Gulf States' business scene, but the Bahrainis' reputation is the strongest. The 1990s have seen many changes in Bahrain's business laws and environment; its economy is expanding and becoming more diversified.

As in any Persian Gulf country, visitors should, out of courtesy and a practical view towards business, adhere to basic Muslim rules and local etiquette. Schedule appointments in advance, and be on time. Your contact may be late, but you should never express annoyance or hostility. Your contemporaries are quite sophisticated, and an atmosphere of confident goodwill should prevail on both sides. Persistence is important, but pays off only if done with courteous and quiet confidence. Business should be conducted in person as much as possible, and expect lengthy, sociable discussions and careful review of any proposals. Do not expect any instant answers. Even written contracts may be brought up for renegotiation later. It's important to note a tendency toward dealing directly with foreign executives and suppliers; if you are a mid-level or lower-level intermediary or subcontractor, your company's proposals may meet with disdain. Companies prefer to use one importer exclusively.

Although English is widely spoken in the business community, your effort to provide company literature in Arabic will make a good impression. Always use the appropriate titles: Sheik and Sheikha (plus first name) with male and female members, respectively, of the ruling family. Otherwise, Mr., Mrs. or Miss are appropriate. Men shake hands; with a woman, nod your head upon introduction, or shake hands only if she offers hers. Business gifts are not necessary, but a nice gesture on your part, such as an interesting curio from your home region, art object, or something connected to your area of business. Be sincerely patient, for any meeting will be accompanied by the traditional rituals of hospitality. It is considered rude to refuse the coffee and food that will be offered, except at Ramadan, when polite refusal will be appreciated, since your hosts themselves cannot eat until sundown. During this period, don't eat in public during the day. Alcohol is forbidden in any case. If it is important that your discussions not be interrupted by other visitors, try to arrange meeting more privately at a coffeehouse. Entertaining is often done in luxury hotels as well as at a home.

At meals or when socializing, it's best to follow the example of your Saudi host as to whether to eat with one's fingers or use utensils. Southpaws beware: there is a strong taboo against eating or drinking with one's left hand (traditionally, the hand used for toilet activities), although you may use both hands if given a knife and fork. Also, if crossing your legs, make sure your feet and soles are not visibly pointing in anyone's direction. Always ask permission when photographing a person or a place, especially a mosque (non-Muslims are permitted to enter mosques here). It is forbidden to take pictures of military installations and women.

Health: It is advisable to consult your doctor in advance of your journey. typhoid, polio, hepatitis A and tetanus vaccinations as well as an additional medical insurance are recommended. The water in most modern hotels is relatively safe but both food and water precautions should be taken at all times. The quality of medical care is high.

Language: Arabic. English is widely spoken within business and trade circles.

BAHRAIN

MANAMA

Country code: 973 - City code: none

Airport: Bahrain International (Muharraq) Airport

Distance from City: 6.5km (3 miles) from the city.

Transportation to Center of City:
From International and Domestic Terminals
By Bus (cost) BHD0.50. Time approx. 5-10 min.
By Taxi (cost) BHD4. Time approx. 5 min.
Tip luggage porters 200 fils per piece

Transfers: (Minimum Connecting Time):
International to International: 60-90 min.
International to Domestic: 60 min.
Domestic to International: 60-90 min.
Domestic to Domestic: 60 min.

Automobile Rentals:
Airport car rental desk
Avis - 321239
Hertz - 321358

Car rental city office
Avis - 211770
Europcar Interrent - 692999

Hotels:
Bahrain Hilton, P.O. Box 1090, 535000
Forte Grand Diplomat, P.O. Box 5243, 531666
Holiday Inn, P.O. Box 5831, 531122
Ramada Hotel Manama, Gudaibiya Ave., 742000
Regency Inter-Continental Bahrain, King Faisal Hwy., 227777
Sheraton Bahrain Hotel, 6 Palace Ave.,533533
Tylos Hotel, P.O. Box 1086,252600

Restaurants:
Ahmed Abdul Rahim's Coffee House, Covernment Ave.
Al-Aswar Sandwiches, Al-Khalifa Ave.
Al-Osra Restaurant, Government Ave.

BAHRAIN

Cafe Hanan, Government Ave.
Charcoal Grill, Bab Al Bahrain
East Restaurant & Coffee, Government Ave.
Honey Restaurant, Municipality Ave.
Kwality Restaurant, Govenrment Ave.
La Taverna, Government Ave.
Public Coffee House, Isa Al-Kabeer Ave.
Tarbouche, Government Ave.
Upstairs,Downstairs, near the Ramada Hotel

Entertainment:
Bacchus, in the Baisan
Henry's, in the Mansouri Mansions Hotel
Holms Bar, at the Al-Jazira Hotel
Hunter's Lounge, at the Adhari Hotel
Jazz Brunch, at the Diplomat Hotel
Joyce's, at the Tylor Hotel
Layali, at the Sheraton Bahrain
Spats, in the Oasis Hotel
The Warbler, in the Baisan International Hotel

Places of Interest:
The Suk-al-Khamis Mosque
Al Fateh Mosque - a library and a conference hall
Siyadi House - a wood-carved pearl-merchant's house
House of Shaikh Isa
Al Areen Wildlife Park

EGYPT

Official Name: Arab Republic of Egypt

Location: Middle East. Egypt is bordered by Libya to the west, Sudan to the south and Israel to the northeast. On the north border lies the Mediterranean Sea and on the east - the Red Sea.

Government: Republic

Area: 997,739 sq. km., 385,229 sq. miles.

Population: 59.5 million

Religion(s): Islamic majority. All types of Christianity are also present.

Capital City: Cairo

Major Business Cities: Alexandria and Luxor.

Time: GMT +2 (GMT +3 from late April to late September)

Currency: Egyptian Pound (EGP)=100 piastres

Currency Requirements: There are no restrictions on the import of foreign currency, but it has to be declared. The export is limited to the amount declared on arrival. The import and export of local currency is limited to EGP1000.

Business Hours:
- Government: 09.00-14.00 or 21.00 Sun-Thur
- Banks: 09.00-14.00 Sun-Thur (bank hours may vary with some banks opening in the afternoon)
- Shops: 10.00-19.00/20.00 Mon-Sat
- Offices: 08.00/09.00-16.00/17.00 Sun-Thur

EGYPT

Weight and Measures: Metric System; some Egyptian measurment

Electric Current: 220 volts AC - plugs are of the round 2-pin type

Holidays:
Eid-ul-fitr* - February 8-10
Unity Day - February 22
Eid-ul-adha* - April 18-21
Sinai Liberation Day - April 26**
Sham El Nassim - April 28
Labour Day - May 1
Al Hijra (Islamic New Year) - May 8*
Evacuation/Liberation Day - June 18
Revolution Day - July 23
Birthday of Muhammad* - July 17
Armed Forces Day - October 6
Suez Day - October 25**
Victory Day - December 23

*Muslim holidays are approximate, as they are timed according to local sightings of various phases of the moon.

**Public Holidays (excluding any Muslim holidays) falling on a Friday are observed on the following day (Saturday).

Suitable Clothing: Modesty is of the utmost importance.You will need sunglasses, sunhats and sunscreen year round, and a light jacket for evenings, or for the occasional rainy day between December and March. The rest of the year, light material is appropriate, but men should make sure it covers knees and shoulders, while women should wear skirts or dresses which cover the knees, elbows and neckline as well. A business suit should be worn to all meetings. When visiting a mosque, shoes are removed, and long pants or a skirt are required, (and a head covering for women). Sometimes these are provided at the entrance.

Automobile Driving License: An International Driving Permit or National Driving License can be used if it is held for at least one year.

Customs Allowances: Declare all valuables (including electronics, jewelery and cameras), or they may face confiscation upon your departure. Personal items are duty free, with limits to 200 cigarettes and I liter of spirits. Import and export of Egyptian pounds is permitted. No limits exist on foreign currency, as long as what you export was intially declared. Prohibited are guns, cotton (for import) and drugs - with severe punishment for the latter. Bringing most antiquities out is also forbidden.

Tipping: A service charge of 12% is usually added to the bill of most hotels and restaurants, but an extra 5-10% tip is customarily left. Most taxis are not metered and visitors are advised to negotiate the fare in advance. Taxi drivers expect to be tipped 10% of the fare. It is handy to carry small change for tipping cloakroom attendants, porters etc.

Credit Cards Accepted:
American Express, Diner's Club, MasterCard, Visa

Customary Dining Hours:
Breakfast: 08.00-10.00
Lunch: 13.00-15.00
Dinner: 20.00-22.00

Local Customs, Business Protocol and Courtesies: Friendly, casual conversation is the norm when developing a business relationship in Egypt. It is also important that you adhere to basic Muslim rules and local etiquette. Egyptians are justifiably proud of their ancient history, and showing an interest in it will serve you well in business and social situations. It is important, however, that you speak and ask questions intelligently on the suxbject, not resorting to general stereotypes. Much commerce is handled by governmental agencies, which have full jurisdiction over Egypt's main export, cotton, as well as oil, rice and wheat. Although English and French are widely spoken in the business and civil service community, your effort to provide company literature in Arabic will make a good impression. Titles are important, to be used with first name. Men and women do shake hands here upon introduction in a business context. Be sincerely patient, for any meeting will be accompanied by the traditional rituals of hospitality and many interruptions. In the south, which is more conservative, it may be forbidden at times to photograph women. Always ask permission when photographing a person or a place. You may be expected to give "baksheesh"· a tip or bribe·for the privilege. Baksheesh is expected from foreign visitors in other small matters of dealing with day to day life in Egypt, though it is not a problem in a professional environment. Egyptian hospitality is legendary. Invitations are often for lunch, between 2 and 4 pm. Bring flowers for the hostess, and small gifts or candy for the children.

Health: It is advisable to consult your doctor before your journey. Vaccinations for typhoid, polio, hepatitis A and tetanus are recommended. Visitors who intend to travel to the El Faiyoum region are strongly advised to take precautions against Malaria. Bathing in fresh water is not recommended as a risk of bilharzia is present. It is strongly advisable to drink bottled water. If it is purchased on the street, the bottle should always be checked whether the seal has not been tampered. Food precautions should be taken all times and the milk should be boiled. Health insurance is strongly advised.

Language: Arabic. English and French are widely spoken.

CAIRO

Country code: 20 - City code: 2

Airport: Cairo International Airport

Distance from City: 22.5km (13 miles) northeast of the city center.

Transportation to Center of City:
From International and Domestic Terminals
By Bus (cost) PT10-25 Time approx. 45-74 min.
By Taxi (cost) EGP35. Time approx. 20-30 min.
Tip luggage porters 50-75 Piastres per piece

EGYPT

Transfers: (Minimum Connecting Time):
International to International: 90 min.
International to Domestic: 90 min.
Domestic to International: 90 min.

Automobile Rentals:
Airport car rental desk
Avis - 291-4266
Europcar Interrent - 291-4255 Ext. 2212
Hertz - 291-4266 Ext. 2430

Car rental city office
Avis - 354-7400
Europcar Interrent - 345-1022
Hertz - 383-0383

Hotels:
Cairo Marriott Hotel, Saray El Gezira, Zamalek, 340-8888
Cairo Nile Hilton, Tahrir Sq., 578-0444
Cairo Ramses Hilton, 1115 Corniche El Nil, 575-8000
Cairo Sheraton Hotel, Towers and Casino, Galaa Sq., 348-8600
El Gezirah Sheraton Hotel Towers and Casino, Orman, Giza,
 341-1333
Helnan Shepheard Hotel, Garden City, 355-3800
Le Meridien Cairo, Corniche El Nil, Garden City, 362-1717
Pyramisa Suites Hotel and Casino, 60 Giza St., Doki, 336-7000
Semiramis Inter-Continental Cairo, Corniche El Nil, Cairo,
 355-7171
Windsor Hotel, 19 Alfi Bey St., 591-5277

Restaurants:
Alfi Bey, 3 Sharia Alfi Bey
Al-Haty, 3 Sharia Alfi Bey
American Fried Chicken, 8 Sharia Hoda Shaarawi
Arabesque, 6 Sharia Qasr el-Nil, 574-8677
Caroll, 12 Sharia Qasr el-Nil, 574-6434
Coin de Kebab, Talaat Harb
El-Guesh, 32 Midan Falaki
Estoril, 12 Sharia Talaat Harb, 574-3102
Felfela, 15 Sharia Hoda Shaarawi
Fu-Shing, 28 Talaat Harb
Greek Club, Talaat Harb

Kowloon Restaurant, b/n Sharia el-Bustan and Midan Tahrir
La Bistro, 8 Sharia Hoda Shaarawi, 392-7694
La Chesa, 21 Sharia Adly, 393-9360
Paprika, 1129 Corniche el-Nil, 749-227
Peking Restaurant, 14 Sharia Saray el-Azbakiya, 591-2381
Valley of the Kings, Grand Hotel

Entertainment:
After Eight, 6 Sharia Qasr el-Nil
Back to the Moon, Sharia Faisal
El- Samar, El- Gezirah Sheraton, 341-1555
Gowhara, 35 Sharia Qasr el-Nil
Haroun el-Rachid, Semiramis Intercontinental, 355-7171
Longchamp, 21 Sharia Ismail Mohammed Zamalek
Pub 36, Ma'adi

Shops and Stores:

Benetton, 41 Sharia Qasr el-Nil	Apparel
Chelma, 26th July Street	Dept. Store
Cicurel, 26th July Street	Dept. Store
Goldsmiths Bazaar, Sharia allMuizz	Jewelry
Omar Effendi, 2 Talaat Harb	Dept. Store

Places of Interest:
The Egyptian Museum
Gabalaya Park and Aquarium
The Citadel - mosques and museums
Manyal Palace Museum
Convent of St.George
The Great Pyramids of Giza
The Sphinx
Cairo Zoo
Khan-el Khalili Bazaar - shops and stalls

ISRAEL

Official Name: State of Israel

Location: Middle East. Israel is bordered by Lebanon, Syria, Jordan and Egypt. The Mediterranean Sea lies on the west coast and the Red Sea lies on the south coast.

Government: Republic

Area: 21,946 sq. km., 8473 sq. miles.

Population: 5.4 million.

Religion(s): Jewish majority. There are also some Christian minorities and a small Muslim population.

Capital City: Jerusalem

Major Business Cities: Jerusalem, Tel-Aviv, Haifa

Time: GMT +2 (GMT +3 from late March to late October)

Currency: New Israel Shekel (NIS)=100 new agorot (singular, agora)

Currency Requirements: There is no limit on the import of foreign and local currencies. The export of local currency is limited to the value of USD100. Export of foreign currency is limited to the amount imported. The foreign currency exchanged on arrival can be re-converted up to the value US$3000.

Business Hours:
- Government: 08.30-16.00 Sun-Thur
- Banks: 08.30-12.30 Sun-Fri; also open at 16.00-17.30 on Sun, Tue and Thur
- Shops: 09.00-13.00 and 16.00-19.00 Sun-Thur, 09.00-13.00 Fri (Christian shops are closed Sun, Muslim's are closed Fri)

- Offices: 08.00-13.00 and 15.00-18.00 Sun-Thur (Nov-May). 07.30-14.30 Sun-Thur (Jun-Oct)

Weight and Measures: Metric System

Electric Current: 220 volts AC. Most plugs are 3-pin but many sockets accommodate some European 2-pin plugs. Adapters for small appliances can be purchased.

Holidays:
Tu B'Shevat (Arbor Day) - January 23
Purim (Feast of Lots) - March 23
1st Day of Pesah (Passover) - April 22
7th Day of Pesah (Passover) - April 28
Israel Independence Day - May 12
Jerusalem Liberation Day - June 4
Shavu'ot (Pentecost) - June 11
Tisha B'Av - August 12
Rosh Hashana (New Year) - October 2-3
Yom Kippur (Day of Atonement) - October 10
1st Day of Sukkot (Tabernacles) - October 16
Simhat Torah (Rejoicing of the Law) - October 23
1st Day of Hanukkah (Feast of Lights) - December 24

Suitable Clothing: Bring a business suit for government meetings - though in many business situations you will not need it, and ties are rarely worn. Wear light material in summer, and medium-weight between October and April. You will need a coat, though not a very heavy one, in winter. Some areas are chilly at night even in summer, so bring a jacket. When visiting a religious family or synagogue, one should dress modestly; men in long pants, women in skirt or dress. You'll need sun gear most of the year.

Automobile Driving License: A National or an International Driving License required.

Customs Allowances: Personal items are duty free, but register all valuables upon arrival or you may face bureaucratic entanglements or even confiscation later. You may bring in, duty free, 250 cigarettes, 2 liters of wine and 1 of spirits. There are no import limits on foreign currency, and you may take out any amounts previously declared. Drugs, military weaponry and pornography are forbidden, and luggage is examined very carefully going in and out of the country.

Tipping: It is recommended to leave a tip of 10-15%, whenever a service charge has not been included.

Credit Cards Accepted: American Express, MasterCard, Visa

Customary Dining Hours:
Breakfast: 07.30-08.30
Lunch: 13.00-14.00
Dinner: 19.00-21.00

Local Customs, Business Protocol and Courtesies: The Israeli workweek is different from many in that it runs from Sunday to noon on Friday, with some businesses closed entirely and a few open through the afternoon on the latter. Suitable to the hot climate, many start business as early as 7 a.m. and close for an early afternoon siesta. The business atmosphere is very advanced and professional, but also very informal · many forego business suits for sport shirts or simple dresses. Your contact will move quickly to a first-name basis. Conversation is open and friendly; negotiations and sales may take an aggressive tone. Be courteous and positive·but also persistent and confident. Make appointments in advance for all meetings, and be on time. Company literature or business cards in Hebrew and Arabic are a nice gesture, though almost everyone speaks English, and very well. Remember that if your contact is a religious Jew, men and women do not shake hands, that they do not conduct business Friday night and Saturday, and that meat and dairy foods are not eaten together (most restaurants are kosher, though many in Tel Aviv are not). If invited to a home, bring a small gift (candy will do), and send a thank you note and flowers the next day. Regarding photographs, keep in mind that there are strict prohibitions against taking pictures of anything military-related, and that ultra-Orthodox Jews and conservative Arab women object to being photographed.

Health: It is advisable to consult your doctor before travel.

ISRAEL

Vaccination for typhoid, polio, hepatitis A and tetanus are recommended. It is recommended to use bottled water during the first few weeks of the stay or outside the main cities. Medical insurance is advised.

Language: Hebrew and Arabic. English is widely spoken.

TEL AVIV

Country code: 972 - City code: 3]

Airport: Ben Gurion Airport (Tel Aviv) .

Distance from City: 19km (11 miles) from the city.

Transportation to Center of City:
From International and Domestic Terminals
By Bus (cost) NIS5. Time approx. 20 min.
By Taxi (cost) NIS41. Time approx. 20 min
Tip luggage porters NIS2 per piece

Transfers: (Minimum Connecting Time):
International to International: 90 min.
International to Domestic: 120 min.
Domestic to International: 120-180 min.
Domestic to Domestic: 90 min.

Automobile Rentals:
Airport car rental desk .
Europcar Interrent - 972-1097
Hertz - 971-1165

Car rental city office.
Avis - 527-1752
Europcar Interrent - 524-8181
Hertz - 562-2121

Hotels:
Astor Hotel, 105 Hayarkon St., 522-3141
Best Western Regency Suites, 80 Hayarkon St., 517-3939

ISRAEL

Dan Panorama Tel-Aviv, Charles Clore Park, 519-0190
Dan Tel-Aviv, 99 Hayarkon St., 520-2525
Holiday Inn Crowne Plaza, 145 Hayarkon St., 520-1111
Metropolitan Hotel, 11-15 Trumpeldor St., 519-2727
Radisson Moriah Plaza Hotel Tel-Aviv, 155 Hayarkon St., 527-1515
Ramada Continental Hotel, 121 Hayarkon St., 521-5555
Ramat Aviv Hotel, 151 Namir Rd., 699-0777
Sheraton Tel Aviv Hotel and Towers, 115 Hayarkon St., 521-1111
Tel Aviv Hilton, Hayarkon St., Independence Park, 520-2222

Restaurants:
Alexander's, 81 Yehuda Hamaccabi St., 546-3591
Bebale, 177 Ben Yehuda St., 546-7486
Big Mama, 22 Rabbi Akiva St., 517-5096
Cactus, 66 Hayarkon St., 510-5969
Café Cazeh, 19 Sheinkin St., 629-3756
Café Tnuva, 34 Ben-Gurion Blvd., 527-2972
Chicago Pizza Pie Factory, 65 Hayarkon St., 517-7505
Dixie, 120 Yigal Allon St., 696-6123
Forel, 10 Frishman St., 522-3167
Internet Café, 18 Ha'arba'a St., 562-6288
Keren, 12 Eilat St., at Auerbach St., Jaffa, 681-6565
King Solomon Grill, Independence Park, 520-2222
L'Entrecote, 195 Ben Yehuda St., 546-6726
Le Relais Jaffa, 13 Hadolphin St., Jaffa, 681-0637
Little Tel Aviv, 300 Hayarkon St., 605-5539
Mul Yam, Tel Aviv Port, 546-9920
Orna and Ella, 33 Sheinkin St., 620-4753
PastaLina, 16 Elifelet St., Jaffa, 683-6401
Prego, 9 Rothschild Blvd., 510-7319
Shipudei Hatikva, 37 Etzel St., Hatikva, Quarter, 687-8014
Taboon, Main Gate, Jaffa Port, 681-1176
Tandoori, 2 Zamenhoff St., 629-6185
Turquoise, 153/1 St., Jaffa, 658-8320
Twelve Tribes, 115 Hayarkon St., 521-1111
Yin Yang, 64 Rothschild Blvd., 560-6833

Entertainment:
Bar Ganza, 26 Sheinkin St., 528-1053
Bar Mitzvah, 16 Ha'arba'a St., 561-1869

ISRAEL

Camelot, 16 Shalom Aleichem St., 528-5222
Echoes, 14 Twesky St., 562-8250
Fresco, 11 Rambam St., 516-3764
Hakossit, 6 Kikar Malchei Yisrael, 522-3244
Hamisba'a, 344 Dizengoff St., 604-2360
Hard Rock Café, Dizengoff Center, 525-1136
Hashoftim, 39 Ibn Gvirol St., 695-1153
Lemon, 17 Hanagarim St., 681-3313
Logus, 8 Hashomer St., 516-1176
Omar Khayyam, Kikar Kedumin, Old Jaffa, 682-5865
Rose, 147 Yehuda Halevy St., 685-0340
Soweto, 6 Frishman St., 524-0825
Yuazar, 2 Yuazar Ish Habira, 683-9115
Zanzibar, 13 Ibn Gvirol St., 561-9840

Shops and Stores:

Beged-Or, Dizengoff Center, Gate 3	Leather
Dizengoff Center, Dizengoff and King George St.	Mall
Hagara, Dizengoff St.	Apparel
Hamashbir, Dizengoff Center	Dept. Store
Opera Tower, 1 Allenby St.	Jewelry
Tovale, Dizengoff St.	Apparel
Yuval Kaspin, Dizengoff St.	Apparel

Places of Interest:

Land of Israel Museum
The Tel Aviv Museum
The Great Synagogue
The Shalom Tower - a wax museum and an observatory
The Gordon Gallery - art gallery
Safari Park

JORDAN

Official Name: The Hashemite Kingdom of Jordan

Location: Middle East. Jordan is bordered by Syria, Saudi Arabia, Israel and Iraq.

Government: Constitutional Monarchy

Area: 97,740 sq. km., 37,738 sq. miles.

Population: 4.9 million

Religion(s): Sunni Muslim majority. There are also Christian and Shi'ite Muslim minorities.

Capital City: Amman

Major Business Cities: Amman, Irbid

Time: GMT +2 (GMT +3 from early April to late September)

Currency: Dinar (JOD)=1000 fils

Currency Requirements: The Import of local and foreign currencies are unlimited but they have to be declared. The export of foreign currency is limited to the amount declared on arrival. The export of local currency is restricted to JOD300. Israeli currency is prohibited.

Business Hours:
- Government: 08.00-14.00 Sat-Thur
- Banks: 08.30/09.30-12.30/13.30 Sat-Thur (many are open after lunch from 15.30-17.30)
- Shops: 09.00-13.00 and 15.30-18.30 Sat-Thur
- Offices: 08.00/08.30-13.00/14.00 and 15.00/15.30 -18.30/19.00 Sat-Thur

Weight and Measures: Metric System

Electric Current: 220 volts AC. Rounded two prong plugs are used.

Holidays:
New Year's Day - January 1
Start of Ramadan - January 9
Eid-ul-fitr* - February 9-11
Easter - April 10-13**
Eid-ul-adha* - April 18-21
Labor Day - May 1
Al-Hijra (Islamic New Year)* - May 8
Independence Day - May 25
Army Day - June 10
Birthday of Muhammad* - July 17
H.M. King Hussein's Accession - August 11
H.M. King Hussein's Birthday - November 14
Lailat-ul-Isra' Wal Mir'aj* - November 26

* Muslim holidays are approximate, as they are timed according to local sightings of various phases of the moon. During Ramadan, most government offices and businesses work reduced hours.

** Christian Holidays - vary each year

Suitable Clothing: Modesty is of the utmost importance. You will need sunglasses, sunhat and sunscreen year round, and jacket between November and March. Most of the year, light material is appropriate, but men should make sure it covers knees and shoulders, while women should wear skirts or dresses which cover the knees, elbows and neckline as well. A business suit should be worn to all meetings.

Automobile Driving License: An International driving permit is required. Visitors are not allowed to drive vehicles with Jordanian number plates unless a Jordanian license is held.

Customs Allowances: Declare all valuables (including electronics, jewelry and cameras), or they may face confiscation upon your departure. Personal items are duty free, with limits to 200 cigarettes and 1liter of wine or spirits. Up to 300 Jordanian

Dinars may be brought in or out. No limits exist on foreign currency, as long as what you export was intially declared. Prohibited are guns, pornography and drugs.

Tipping: A service charge of 10-12% is usually added to hotel and restaurant bills. Any additional tipping is discretionary. Taxi drivers do not expect to be tipped. If a taxi is not metered, the fare should be agreed in advance.

Credit Cards Accepted: American Express, MasterCard, Visa

Customary Dining Hours:
Breakfast: 07.00-09.00
Lunch: 12.30-14.00
Dinner: 20.00-22.00

Local Customs, Business Protocol and Courtesies: The Jordanian businessmen you will meet are largely a well-educated, pro-Western group, and will give you both a serious and friendly reception. As in any Persian Gulf country, visitors should, out of courtesy and a practical view towards business, adhere to basic Muslim rules and local etiquette. You should investigate carefully the performance of any Jordanian company you are dealing with, and ask for an irrevocable letter of credit. Be prepared for skilled bargainers, who will want to negotiate generous terms of credit. Although English is widely spoken in the business community, your effort to provide company literature and business cards in Arabic will make a good impression. Schedule appointments in advance, and be on time. Your contact may be late, but you should never express annoyance or hostility. An atmosphere of confident goodwill and courtesy should prevail on both sides. Persistence is important, but pays off only if done with courtesy and quiet confidence. Be sincerely patient, for any meeting will be accompanied by the traditional rituals of hospitality. If it is important that your discussions not be interrupted by other visitors, try to arrange meeting more privately at a coffeehouse. It is considered rude to refuse the coffee and food that will be offered, except at Ramadan, when polite refusal will be appreciated, since your hosts themselves cannot eat until sundown. During this period, don't eat in public during the day. Alcohol is forbidden to Muslims, so don't drink in public, or with your host unless he offers. If invited to a home, the proper response is to politely turn down the invitations and accept on the third offer. During the meal, you should turn down seconds until your host has has offered them several times, and offer compliments on the food. Generally, only men will be present. Bring a gift for the host · such as an interesting curio from your home region or art object.

Health: It is advisable to consult your doctor before traveling. Vaccinations for typhoid, polio, hepatitis A and tetanus are recommended. Visitors traveling from an infected area must have a yellow fever certificate. malaria certificate is no longer required by law, but it does pose a threat in Jordan and precautions are recommended. It is advisable to drink only bottled water and food precautions should be observed. Health insurance is recommended.

Language: Arabic. English is also widely spoken.

AMMAN

Country code: 962 - City code: 6

Airport: Queen Alia International Airport

Distance from City: 32km (19 miles) southeast of the city.

Transportation to Center of City:
From International and Domestic Terminals
By Bus (cost) 500-750 fils. Time approx. 50 min.
By Taxi (cost) JOD8. Time approx. 35-50 min.
Tip luggage porters 300 fils per piece

Transfers: (Minimum Connecting Time):
International to International: 45 min.
International to Domestic: 60 min.
Domestic to International: 60 min.
Domestic to Domestic: 30 min.

JORDAN

Automobile Rentals:
Airport car rental desk
Avis - 51555
Europcar Interrent - 601350
Hertz - 68958

Car rental city office
Avis - 99420

Hotels:
Amman Marriott Hotel, Issam Ajluni St., Shmeisani, 607607
Amra Forum Hotel, Jabal Amman, 815071
Carlton, Amman Jabar, 3rd Circle, 654200
City Hotel, Amman Jabar, N. 3rd Circle, 6342251
Jerusalem International Hotel, University Rd., 607121
Regency Palace Hotel, Queen Alya St./ Sport City Rd., 607000
Turino All Suite Hotel, 1 Main Sq., Sweifiyeh, 863944

Restaurants:
Al-Kuds Restaurant, al-Malak al-Hussein St.
Al-Salaam Restaurant, al-Malak al-Feisal St. WS
Noroz Restaurant, Jabal Aman, 3rd Circle

Places of Interest:
Jebel el Qalat (The Citadel) - relics, architectural structures
Jordan Archaeological Museum
Roman Theatre
Jordan National Gallery of Fine Arts
Jordan Folklore Museum
The University of Jordan
Martyr's Memorial

KENYA

Official Name: Republic of Kenya

Location: East Africa. Kenya is bordered by Ethiopia, Sudan, Uganda, Tanzania and Somalia.

Government: Republic

Area: 580,367 sq. km., 224,081 sq. miles.

Population: 27 million

Religion(s): Mostly traditional, 25% Christian and 6% Muslim.

Capital City: Nairobi

Major Business Cities: Nairobi, Mombasa, Kizumu

Time: GMT +3

Currency: Kenyan Shilling (KSh)=100 cents

Currency Requirements:. The export of foreign currency is limited up to the amount declared on arrival. The import and the export of local currency is prohibited. There are no restrictions on traveler's checks and letters of credit.

Business Hours:
- Government: 09.00-13.00; 14.00-17.00 Mon-Fri
- Banks: 09.00-14.00 Mon-Fri; 09.00-11.00 on the first and the last Sat of each month.
- Shops: 08.30-12.30 and 14.00-16.30 Mon-Sat
- Offices: 08.00-13.00 & 14.00-17.00 Mon-Fri; 08.30-12.00 Sat

Weight and Measures: Metric System

Electric Current: 220/240 volts AC. Plugs are round 2 pin UK or flat 3 pin type.

KENYA

Holidays:
New Year's Day - January 1
Eid-ul-fitr** - February 8-10
Good Friday - April 10*
Easter Monday - April 13*
Eid-ul-adha** - April 18-21
Labour Day - May 1
Madaraka Day - June 1
Moi Day - October 10
Kenyatta Day - October 20
Independence Day - December 12
Christmas Day - December 25
Boxing Day - December 26

*Christian Holidays - vary each year

** Muslim holidays are approximate, as they are timed according to local sightings of various phases of the moon.

Suitable Clothing: You will need sunglasses, sunhats and sunscreen year round in most places. Light clothing is best for the warmer coastal areas, generally, and it helps to have a light jacket for evenings and a raincoat. When doing business or dining out, wear a suit and tie. Theft is common so don't make a show of affluence.

Automobile Driving License: Foreign driving licenses can be used for a stay of up to 90 days but they must be endorsed in Kenya at a local police station. An International Driving Permit is recommended for longer stays.

Customs Allowances: Declare all valuables, or they may face confiscation upon your departure. Personal items are duty free, with limits to 250 cigarettes and 1 liter of spirits. Kenyan shillings may not be brought in or out, but no limits exist on foreign currency, as long as what you export was initially declared. Prohibited are weapons (and anything which can be mistaken for them) and narcotics.

Tipping: A service charge is usually added to the bills of most restaurants and hotels. If you are pleased with the service an extra 10% is recommended.

KENYA

Credit Cards Accepted: American Express, Diner's Club, MasterCard, Visa

Customary Dining Hours:
Breakfast: 07.00-09.00
Lunch: 12.00-14.00
Dinner: 19.00-22.00

Local Customs, Business Protocol and Courtesies: Conservative business behavior is the norm in Nairobi, in contrast to the wildlife around the country that Kenya is better known for. Kenya's business atmosphere reflects that of its former colonial rulers: Great Britain. Many of Nairobi's importers and exporters are English or Indian, and though they are less formal than their counterparts in Britain, general Western business protocol does apply: make appointments in advance and be on time, provide business cards, and use titles upon introduction (Bwana and Bibi are Mr. and Mrs., respectively.). Be sincerely patient in the face of Kenya's often slow pace. Any meeting will be accompanied by traditional rituals of hospitality (don't refuse the coffee) and many interruptions. A smile and good manners are important · but don't always believe officials when they say "No problem". Negotiate with calm persistence. Social protocol varies among Kenya's myriad religions and tribes; the best approach is to be polite, conservative and show a positive attitude toward and interest in the country. If invited to a home or giving a business gift, an interesting curio from your home region, an art object, or something connected to your area of business will do.

Health: It is advisable to consult your doctor before traveling. Vaccinations for hepatitis A, tetanus, cholera, typhoid, polio, meningitis and malaria are recommended. A yellow fever vaccination certificate is required if traveling from an infected area. It is advisable to drink bottled water and food precautions should be observed at all times. Health insurance is strongly recommended.

Language: Kiswahill and English.

KENYA

NAIROBI

Country code: 254 - City code: 2

Airport: Jomo Kenyatta Airport.

Distance from City: 13km (8 miles) southeast of the city.

Transportation to Center of City:
From International and Domestic Terminals
By Bus (cost) not recommended.
By Taxi (cost) KSh800-900. Time approx. 15 min.
Tip luggage porters KSh20 per piece

Transfers: (Minimum Connecting Time):
International to International: 60 min.
International to Domestic: 60 min.
Domestic to International: 60 min.
Domestic to Domestic: 30-45 min.

Automobile Rentals:
Airport car rental desk.
Avis - 822186
Europcar Interrent - 822348
Hertz - 822339

Car rental city office.
Avis - 336703
Europcar Interrent - 334722
Hertz - 331960

Hotels:
Ambassadeur Hotel - A Sarova Hotel, P. O. Box 303399, 336803
Boulevard Hotel, P. O. Box 42831, 337221
Inter - continental Nairobi, City Hall Way, 335550
Mayfair Court Hotel, Parklands Rd., 740920-921
Nairobi Hilton, Mama Ngina St., 334000
New Stanley Hotel - A Sarova Hotel, P. O. Box 30680, 333233
Panafric Hotel - A Sarova Hotel, P. O. Box 30486, 720822
Sixeighty Hotel, Kenyatta Ave., 332680

KENYA

Restaurants:
Alan Bobbe's Bistro, Cianda House Arcade, Koinange St., 226 027
Ali Barbour's on Diani Beach, 2033
Branch Office, Sarit Centre, Westlands, 740 434
Carnivore, Langata Road, 501 775
Dawat Restaurant, Shimmers Plaza, Westlands, 749 338
Haandi Restaurant, The Mall in Westland, 448 294
Horsman Restaurant, Lang'ata Road, 882 033
L'ora Blu, Corner House Kimathi St., 218 953
La Malindina, Malindi, 20045
Minar Restaurant, Sarit Centre, Westlands, 748 340
Mombasa Tamarind Restaurant, 474 600
Nairobi Tamarind Restaurant, 220 473
Nawab Tandoori, Muthaiga Shopping Centre, 740 292
Orna's, ABC Place, Westlands, 445 368
Padoga Restaurant, Shankardass House, Moi Ave., 227 036
Rickshaw Chinese Restaurant, Fedha Towers, 223 604
Simba Restaurant, JKI Airport, 210 612
Tamarind Restaurant, National Bank Building,Harambee Ave., 338 958
Trattoria Restaurant,Town House,Wabera St., 211 216
Zephyr, Rank Zerox House,Westlands, 750 055

Entertainment:
Hard Rock Cafe, Barclays Plaza Mezzanine, Loita St., 220 802
International Casino, Westlands Road, 742 600
Nairobi Casino, 742 6000
Resort Kenya Limited, City Hall Way, 335 550
Toona Tree, Nairobi Casino, 742 600

Shops and Stores:
Batiks & Jewelry Ltd., City Hall Way	Jewelry
Biba Ltd, 680 Hotel, Kenyatta Ave., 334 705	Apparel
Jambo Curio Shop, Nairobi-Karatina Road,	Dept.Store
Jevels Corner, Apic Centre, Westlands	Jewelry
Kichaka, Kijabe St.	Apparel
Kumbu Kumbu, Hilton Arcade	Apparel

Places of Interest:
The National Museum
Snake Park

The Railway Museum
All Saints Cathedral
Nairobi National Park
Bomas of Kenya - a cultural center
Karen Blixen Museum

KUWAIT

Official Name: State of Kuwait

Location: Middle East - Persian Gulf. Kuwait is bordered by Iraq to the north and Saudi Arabia to the south.

Government: Constitutional Monarchy

Area: 17,818 sq. km., 6880 sq. miles.

Population: 1.62 million

Religion(s): Muslim majority. Christian and Hindu minorities.

Capital City: Kuwait City

Major Business Cities: Kuwait City, Salmiya, Hawalli

Time: GMT +3

Currency: Kuwait Dinar (KUD)=1000 fils

Currency Requirements: There are no restrictions on the import and the export of foreign or local currency. Gold bullion must be declared.

Business Hours:
- Government: 08.00-14.00 Sat-Wed
- Banks: 08.00/08.30-12.00/12.30 Sun-Thur
- Shops: 08.30-12.30 & 16.30-21.00 Sat-Thur
- Offices: 08.00-13.00 & 16.00-20.00 Sat-Thur

Weight and Measures: Metric System

Electric Current: 240 volts AC. Plugs are flat 3-pin type.

Holidays:
New Year's Day - January 1

KUWAIT

Eid-ul-fitr* - February 8-10
National Day - February 25
Liberation Day - February 26
Mount Arafat Day - April 18
Eid-ul-adha* - April 18-21
Al-Hijra (Islamic New Year)* - May 8
Birthday of Muhammad* - July 17
Lailat-ul-Isra' Wal Mir'aj (Prophet's Ascension to Heaven)
- November 26*

* Muslim holidays are approximate, as they are timed according to local sightings of various phases of the moon.

Suitable Clothing: Although Kuwaitis are more relaxed when it comes to dress codes, visitors should dress modestly. The year-round hot climate requires sunglasses, sunhats and sunscreen. Nights are chilly, so bring along a sweater or light jacket. Otherwise, light material is appropriate, but men should make sure it covers knees and shoulders, while women should wear skirts or dresses which cover the knees, elbows and neckline as well. A business suit should be worn to all meetings.

Automobile Driving License: An International Driving Permit is required. A temporary license can be issued on presentation of a National License.

Customs Allowances: No limits exist on foreign currency or Dinars as long as what you export was initially declared. You may bring in 500 cigarettes. Prohibited are military weaponry, narcotics, alcohol, and pornography.

Tipping: A service charge is usually added to most restaurant, hotel and club bills. An additional tip is discretionary. Elsewhere 10% is usual.

Credit Cards Accepted: American Express, Diner's Club, Visa

Customary Dining Hours:
Breakfast: 07.00-08.30
Lunch: 13.00-14.30
Dinner: 20.00-22.00

KUWAIT

Local Customs, Business Protocol and Courtesies: Kuwait's vast oil-based wealth has allowed it to rebuild its economy and infrastructure at an incredible speed, after both were virtually destroyed by Iraq in the Gulf War. Interest in and discussing the country's recovery, as long as your opinion appears positive, is a good way to build rapport with your contemporaries there. Refrain from comment as much as possible on Middle East politics, and on the subject of women. As in any Persian Gulf country, visitors should, out of courtesy and a practical view towards business, adhere to basic Muslim rules and local etiquette. Schedule appointments in advance, and be on time. Your contact may be late, but you should never express annoyance or hostility. Your contemporaries are quite sophisticated, and an atmosphere of confident goodwill should prevail on both sides. Persistence is important, but pays off only if done with courtesy and quiet confidence. Per capita income is one of the highest in the world, and many modern services and amenities are free. Over 100 Kuwaiti families are active in the economy, and their experienced firms handle myriad functions. Companies prefer to use one importer exclusively. It's important to note a tendency toward dealing directly with foreign executives and suppliers; if you are a mid-level or lower-level intermediary or subcontractor, your company's proposals may meet with disdain. Also, due to sensitivities since the Gulf War, it is advisable to appoint a representative exclusively to Kuwait, rather than have him come from neighboring countries as well. Business should be conducted in person as much as possible, and expect lengthy, sociable discussions and careful review of any proposals. Do not expect any instant answers. Kuwaitis are skilled, stubborn bargainers, and even written contracts may be brought up for renegotiation later. Although English is widely spoken in the business community, your effort to provide company literature in Arabic will make a good impression. Always use the appropriate titles: Sheik and Sheikha (plus first name) with male and female members, respectively, of a ruling family. An emir (prince) may also be referred to as "Your Highness" or "Your Excellency." Otherwise, Mr., Mrs. or Miss are appropriate. Men shake hands; with a woman, shake hands only if she offers hers. Business gifts are not necessary, but a nice gesture on your part, such as an interesting curio from your home region, art object, or something connected to your area of business. Be sincerely patient, for any meeting will be accompanied by the traditional rituals of hospitality. It is considered rude to refuse the coffee and food that will be offered, except at Ramadan, when polite refusal will be appreciated, since your hosts themselves cannot eat until sundown. During this period, don't eat in public during the day. If it is important that your discussions not be interrupted by other visitors, try to arrange meeting more privately at a coffeehouse. Entertaining is often done in luxury hotels as well as at a home.

At meals or when socializing, it's best to follow the example of your Saudi host as to whether to eat with one's fingers or use utensils. Southpaws beware: there is a strong taboo against eating or drinking with one's left hand (traditionally, the hand used for toilet activities), although you may use both hands if given a knife and fork. Also, if crossing your legs, make sure your feet and soles are not visibly pointing in anyone's direction. Always ask permission when photographing a person or a place, especially a mosque. Alcohol is forbidden.

Health: It is advisable to consult your doctor before traveling. Vaccinations for typhoid, polio, hepatitis A and tetanus are recommended. It is advisable to drink bottled water. Medical insurance is recommended.

Language: Arabic. English is widely understood.

KUWAIT CITY

Country code: 965 - City code: none

Airport: Kuwait International Airport

Distance from City: 16km (9 miles) south of the city.

Transportation to Center of City:

From International and Domestic Terminals
By Bus (cost) 500 Fils. Time approx. 30 min.
By Taxi (cost) KUD4. Time approx. 15-20 min.
Tip luggage porters 250 fils per piece

Transfers: (Minimum Connecting Time):
International to International: 60 min.
International to Domestic: 60 min.
Domestic to International: 60 min.

Automobile Rentals:
Airport car rental desk.
Avis - 474-5528
Europcar Interrent - 473-5626
Hertz - 31-9326

Car rental city office.
Avis - 245-2740
Hertz - 472-8114

Hotels:
Carlton Tower Hotel Kuwait, P. O . Box 26950, Safat, 245-2740
Meridien Kuwait, Al Hilali St, Safat, 245-5550
Safir International Kuwait, P. O. Box 5996, Safat, 253-0000
Sheraton Kuwait Hotel & Towers, Fahd al Salem St, Safat, 242-2055

Restaurants:
Abber Al Sharq, 242 7866
Al Ahmadi, 474 2000
Al Andalus Seafood Restaurant, 474 2000
Al Fairooz Golden Restaurant, 391 2130
Al Hambra, 242 2055
Al Hamidi, 572 8000
Al Hayat, 242 2831
Al-Room Restaurant, 565 7000
Baba Taher, 245 6140
Bistretto, 565 7000
Caesar's Restaurant (Indian), 241 1711
Caesar's Restaurant, 243 1100
Chi Chi's, 562 5811
Daavat, 241 1685

Darbar Indian Restaurant, 252 7300
Failaka Restaurant, 253 3000
Fish Market Restaurant, 245 8890
Jeans Grill
Kei Restaurant
Khaldoum Barakat
Khansa Restaurant
Koryokwan Restaurant
L'Orchid Restaurant
La Brasserie
La Palma Restaurant
Mabuhay
Maharaja Palace

Places of Interest:
The National Museum
Sadu House - a museum
The Grand Mosque
Kuwait Towers
The Science and Natural History Museum
Sief Palace
Couered Souk - a market area

LIBYA

Official Name: Socialist People's Libyan Arab Great Jamahiriya

Location: North Africa. Libya is bordered by Egypt, Sudan, Chad, Niger, Algeria and Tunisia. To the north lies the Mediterranean Sea.

Area: 1,775,500 sq. km, 685,520 sq. miles.

Population: 4.87 million

Religion(s): Sunni Muslim

Capital City: Tripoli

Time: GMT +1 (GMT +2 from late March to late September)

Currency: Libyan Dinar (LD)=1000 dirhams

Currency Requirements The import and the export of foreign currency is unlimited but it must be declared. The import and export of local currency is limited to LD20.

Business Hours:
- Government:
- Banks: 07.30/08.00-12.00 Sat-Wed (Winter).   07.30/08.00-12.00 & 16.00-17.00 Sat-Wed (Summer)
- Shops: Hours vary - mainly market type stalls.
- Offices: 07.00-14.00 Sat-Thur.

Weight and Measures: Metric System

Electric Current: 150/220 volts AC.

Holidays:
Eid-ul-fitr* - February 8-10
British Evacuation Day - March 28

LIBYA

Eid-ul-adha - April 18-21*
Al-Hijra (Islamic New Year)* - May 8
Ashura* - May 17
Revolution Day - September 1
Evacuation Day - June 11
Lailat-ul-Isra' Wal Mir'aj - November 26

*Muslim holidays are approximate, as they are timed according to local sightings of various phases of the moon.

Suitable Clothing: A conservative business suit is appropriate. In winter you'll need medium weight clothing and a raincoat. Lightweight clothing is fine for the rest of the year.

Automobile Driving License: A National Driving License valid for at least 1 year.

Customs Allowances: You are allowed 200 cigarettes or 25 cigars or 225g (1/2 lb.) of tobacco. All alcoholic beverages and all goods of Israeli origin are prohibited.

Tipping: A tip of 10-20% is usually included in restaurant and hotel bills. Taxi drivers do not expect a tip.

Local Customs, Business Protocol and Courtesies: Libyan business is governed by strict regulations. All commercial agencies (that is, companies that act as commercial agents or representatives, authorized trade representatives, commission agents, and/or brokerages) must be Libyan-owned, and individual agents must be Libyan nationals. The Ministry of Economy determines the extent of activity that each agency is allowed to engage in. Oil has given a big boost to the Libyan economy.

Although regulations are strict, business contact is not necessarily formal. Coffee houses are popular for an after work drink. Remember, this is an Islamic country · no alcohol. Business cards in English and Arabic or French and Arabic are useful. Don't expect all businessmen to speak English; French and Italian are more prevalent. Business dinners are typically men·only affairs. When invited for dinner you are expected to bring a gift for your host. Plan your busi·

ness schedule around the Islamic holy days, and keep in mind that all business slows down during the holy month of Ramadan. Avoid political discussions, especially as it refers to the Middle East, international oil prices, and Libya's financial aid to dissident groups in other countries.

Health: It is advisable to consult your doctor before your journey. Vaccinations for hepatitis A, yellow fever, cholera, typhoid and polio are recommended. A yellow fever immunization certificate is mandatory if travelling from an infected area. It is advisable to drink only bottled water. Food precautions should be taken any time. Full health insurance is recommended.

Language: Arabic.

TRIPOLI

Country code: 218 - City code: 21

Airport: Tripoli International Airport.

Distance from City: 35km (21 miles) south of the city.

Transportation to Center of City:
From International and Domestic Terminals
By Taxi (cost) US$10. Time approx. 40 min.

Hotels:
Bab – al-Medina Hotel, Sharia al-Kurnish 60805/8
Massif Garnata, Hay al-Andalous
Waddan Hotel, Sharia al-Fatah, 30042/6
Mehari Hotel, Sharia al-Fatah, 34091
Al-Kabir Hotel, Sharia al-Fatah, 45945/9
Bab al-Bahr Hotel, Bab al-Medina, 60805
Libya Palace Hotel, Sharia Sidi Issa, 31180/9

Restaurants:
Bedouin Restaurant, Sharia al-Baladiya
Gazala, Gazelle Fountain, 41078

Safir Restaurant, Sharia al-Baladiya, 47064

Places of Interest:
The Assai al-Hamra – a museum
The Karamanli Mosque
The Arch of Marcus Aurelius - a Roman monument
Italian Cathedral
People's Palace

MOROCCO

Official Name: Kingdom of Morocco

Location: North Africa. Morocco is bordered by Algeria and Mauritania.

Government: Constitutional Monarchy

Area: 710,850 sq. km., 274,461 sq. miles.

Population: 27 million

Religion(s): Muslim majority. Jewish and Christian minorities.

Capital City: Rabat

Major Business Cities: Casablanca, Marrakech and Tangier

Time: GMT

Currency: Moroccan Dirham (MDH)=100 centimes

Currency Requirements: There are no restrictions on the import of foreign currency, but it has to be declared on arrival. The export is limited to the amount declared on arrival. The import and the export of local currency is prohibited.

Business Hours:
- Government: 08.30-12.00; 14.30-18.30 Mon-Thur, 15.00-18.30 Fri
- Banks: 08.15-11.00 and 14.15-16.45 Mon-Fri
- Shops: 09.00-12.30 and 15.00-19.30 Mon-Sat
- Offices: 08.30-12.00 and 14.30-18.30 Mon-Fri

Weight and Measures: Metric System

Electric Current: 110 or 240 volts AC. Plugs are of the Continental 2-pin type.

MOROCCO

Holidays:
New Year's Day - January 1
Manifesto of Independence - January 11
Eid-ul-fitr - February 9-11*
Independence Day - March 2
National Day - March 3
Eid-ul-adha - April 18-21*
Labor Day - May 1
Al Hijra (Islamic New Year) - May 8*
Ashura - May 17*
Prophet's Birthday - July 17*
Anniversary of the Green March - November 6
Independence Day - November 18

* Muslim holidays are approximate, as they are timed according to local sightings of various phases of the moon.

Suitable Clothing: A business suit should be worn to all meetings, but don't appear too affluent, or you may attract pickpockets. Modest dress conveys respect, although Morocco is more liberal than most other countries in the region and sleeveless or short clothing is permitted. You will need lightweight clothing, sunglasses, sunhat and sunscreen except between December and March, when slightly warmer clothing and a light jacket are necessary. Bring raingear as well.

Automobile Driving License: International and National Driving Licenses are accepted.

Customs Allowances: Declare all valuables (including electronics, jewelry and cameras), or they may face confiscation upon your departure. Personal items are duty free, with limits to 200 cigarettes, 3 liters of wine and 1 of spirits. Bringing Moroccan Dirham in or out is prohibited. Foreign currency worth over 15,000 Dinars must be declared coming in. Prohibited are military weaponry and drugs-with severe punishment for the latter, and luggage searches are frequent.

Tipping: Service charges are usually added to restaurant and hotel bills. Tipping is customary.

MOROCCO

Credit Cards Accepted: American express, Diner's Club, MasterCard, Visa

Customary Dining Hours:
Breakfast: 07.00-09.00
Lunch: 12.00-15.00
Dinner: 19.00-21.00

Local Customs, Business Protocol and Courtesies: Morocco has one foot firmly in the Islamic world, the other increasingly steady in the European business world. The past several decades have brought about many changes necessary for modern, international commerce. Even Moroccan women, long barred from business and governmental jobs, are becoming increasingly involved although still usually at a second-class level. Most Moroccan businessmen speak French as a second language, with some fluent in English or Spanish as well. You can expect a positive, friendly attitude toward developing commercial and social ties. Schedule appointments in advance (not for Fridays, the Muslim Sabbath), and be on time. Your contact may be late, but you should never express annoyance or hostility. An atmosphere of confident goodwill and courtesy should prevail on both sides. Persistence is important, but pays off only if done with courtesy and quiet confidence. Bargaining is the name of the game in this culture, which means that it will take time and persistence to get a direct answer. The country's foreign exchange laws acknowledge a weak credit system and therefore encourage a cash-basis policy.

You will be lavishly and frequently entertained. Dinners are sometimes sex-segregated, and it is customary to leave soon after the meal. Don't refuse the traditional drink to friendship: mint tea. Avoid the sensitive subject of Middle East politics, and don't criticize the King. Though business may at times be discussed in Turkish baths, foreigners are usually kept separate. It may be forbidden at times to photograph women, or for non-Muslims to enter mosques. Always ask permission when photographing a person or a place, and you may be asked for a small tip for taking a stranger's photo or gaining access to a tourist site.

MOROCCO

Health: It is advisable to consult your doctor before your journey. Vaccinations for typhoid, polio, hepatitis A and tetanus are recommended. There is a minimal risk of malaria. It is advisable to drink bottled water and food precautions should be observed at all times. Bathing in fresh water should be avoided. Government hospitals provide free or minimal charge for emergency treatment. Medical insurance is recommended.

Language: Arabic. Berber is also spoken by a large minority.

CASABLANCA

Country code: 212 - City code: 2

Airport: Mohamed V International Airport

Distance from City: 30km (18 miles) south of the city.

Transportation to Center of City:
From International and Domestic Terminals
By Bus (cost) MDH20-25 Time approx. 40-50 min.
By Taxi (cost) MDH200. Time approx. 30-35 min.
By Train (cost) MDH20. Time approx. 25 min.
Tip luggage porters 5 Dirhams per piece

Transfers: (Minimum Connecting Time):
International to International: 50 min.
International to Domestic: 50 min.
Domestic to International: 50 min.
Domestic to Domestic: 50 min.

Automobile Rentals:
Airport car rental desk
Avis - 339072
Europcar Interrent - 339161
Hertz - 339181

MOROCCO

Car rental city office
Avis - 312424
Europcar Interrent - 313737
Hertz - 312223

Hotels:
El Kandara Hotel, 44 Blvd. D'Anfa, 261560
Forte Grand Royal Mansour, 27 Ave. de l'Armee Royale, 313011
Holiday Inn Crowne Plaza, 11 Rond Point Hassan, 294949
Hyatt Regency Casablanca, Pl. Mohammed V, 261234
Idou Anfa Hotel, 85 Blvd. D'Anfa, 200136
Sheraton Casablanca Hotel, 100 Ave. des F.A.R., 317878
Toubkal Hotel, 9 Rue Sidi Belyout, 311414

Restaurants:
Al Mounia, 95 rue du Prince Moulay Abdullah
La Cambuse, at Ain Diab
La Corrida, 59 rue Guy Lussac
La Marignan, 63 rue Mohammed Smiha
La Tajine, Centre 2000
Las Delecias, 18 Ave Mohammed V
Le Petit Poucet, 8 Ave Mohammed V
Restaurant Saigon, 40 rue Colbert

Entertainment:
Chirchil Club, rue Pessac
La Cage, by the port
La Fontaine, Blvd Houphuet Boigny
Le Sphinx, Ave Mohammed V

Places of Interest:
The Hassan II Mosque
The Great Mosque
Clock Tower
The Kasbah des Oudaias - palace, museum and gardens
The Archaeology Museum

NIGERIA

Official Name: Federal Republic of Nigeria

Location: West Africa. Nigeria is bordered by Niger, Chad, Cameroon and Benin. On the south coast lies the Gulf of Guinea.

Area: 923,768 sq. km., 356,669 sq. miles.

Population: 101.88 million

Religion(s): Islamic majority. There are also many local religions and a Christian minority.

Capital City: Abuja

Major Business Cities: Lagos

Time: GMT +1

Currency: Naira (N)=100 kobo

Currency Requirements: The import of foreign currency is unlimited, but it must be declared. The export is limited to the amount declared on arrival. The import and export of local currency is restricted to N100.

Business Hours:
- Banks: 08.00-15.00 Mon; 08.00-13.30 Tue-Fri
- Shops: 08.00-17.00 Mon-Fri; 08.00-16.30 Sat
- Offices: 07.30/08.00-15.30/16.30 Mon-Fri

Weight and Measures: Metric System

Electric Current: 210/250 volts.

Holidays:
New Year's Day - January 1
Eid-ul-fitr* - February 8-10
Easter - March 28-31
Eid-ul-adha* - April 18-21
May Day - May 1
Birthday of Muhammad* - July 17
National Day - October 1
Christmas Day - December 25
Boxing Day - December 26

* Muslim Holidays are approximate, as they are timed according to local sighting of various phases of the moon.

Suitable Clothing: There are two types of climate in Nigeria: hot and dry in the North and hot and wet in the South. Needless to say, lightweight, cotton clothing is perfect. No more than a sweater is needed for outerwear, except during the rainy season when raingear is recommended.

Automobile Driving License: An International Driving Permit accompanied by two passport size photos is required. Chauffeur-driven cars are advised since car hire can be difficult.

Customs Allowances: You are allowed 200 cigarettes or 50 cigars or 225g (1/2 lb.) of tobacco, and one bottle of alcohol. Drugs are prohibited, and so are champagne, sparkling wine, and antiques (without clearance permit).

Tipping: It is customary to leave a 10% tip if a service charge has not been included. Airport porters should be tipped per case. Taxi fare including tip should be agreed in advance.

Local Customs, Business Protocol and Courtesies: Not to alarm you, but this is one of the most corrupt countries in the world. You'll need a passport and visa in order to enter the country. No problem, right? Here's the catch. When you arrive at the airport you'll show the official your passport and visa, which may somehow disappear under the desk. The official will inform you that you are in the country illegally · you have no passport and no visa. But don't worry, a mere $50 will solve the problem. As the cash changes hands, the missing documents miraculously appear. This is only the beginning. Expect to pay bribes everywhere. Always keep extra cash in your wallet and always be sure that you know where you wallet is. Caution is a keyword for all dealings.

As for more prosaic matters, Nigerian businessmen are customarily conservative and formal. Always use formal titles. Never make any commitments without checking up on your client's prior performance, but remember your company's past performance is an equal consideration for your Nigerian associates. Punctuality is important here, but not easy. Lagos in particular is difficult to get around. And yes, you can expect to overpay car rentals and taxi drivers. No need to worry about how to act in your host's home. Business entertaining is done in restaurants and clubs, not at home. Robbery and kidnapping are commonplace · always be on your guard and use taxis recommended by your hotel.

Health: It is advisable to consult your doctor before your journey. A vaccination certificate for yellow fever is required if travelling from an infected area. Vaccinations for hepatitis A, cholera, typhoid, polio and malaria are recommended. All water should be regarded as contaminated and food precautions should be observed at all times. It is advisable to take a supply of personal medication, as there are often shortages of medical supplies. A full medical insurance is essential.

Language: English. Various local languages are widely spoken.

LAGOS

Country code: 234 - City code: 1

Airport: Murtala Muhammed Airport.

Distance from City: 22km (13 miles) north of the city.

Transportation to Center of City:
From International and Domestic Terminals
By Taxi (cost) N500-1000. Time approx. 40 min.
Hotels:
Sheraton Lagos Hotel and Towers, 30 Mobolaji Bank, Anthony Way, 497-0311-3

The Sheraton is the only truly safe hotel for Westerners and visitors should only consider staying there to avoid robbery and kidnapping.

Places of Interest:
The National Museum
The National Theatre - a theatre, arts galleries and crafts
The Shitta Mosque
The Taiwo Olowo Tomb
The Oba's Palace
Remembrance Arcade - a memorial monument

OMAN

Official Name: Sultanate of Oman

Location: Arabian Peninsula, Middle East. Oman is bordered by the United Arab Emirates and Yemen. To the east lies the Arabian Sea.

Government: Absolute Monarchy

Area: 212,457 sq. km., 82,030 sq. miles.

Population: 1.73 million

Religion(s): Muslim

Capital City: Muscat

Time: GMT +4

Currency: Omani Rial (RIO)=1000 baiza

Currency Requirements: There are no restrictions on the import and the export of local or foreign currency. Israeli currency is prohibited.

Business Hours:
- Government: 07.30 or 08.00-14.00 Sat-Wed, 07.30 or 08.00-12.00 or 13.00 Thur
- Banks: 08.00-12.00 Sat-Wed; 08.00-11.30 Thur
- Shops: 08.00-13.00 and 16.00-20.00 Sat-Thur
- Offices: 08.00-13.00 and 16.00-18.00/19.00 Sat-Wed

Weight and Measures: Metric System; some Imperial and local systems

Electric Current: 220/240 volts. For round plug fittings you can use either 2 or 3 pin; for flat plug fittings only 3 pin will fit.

OMAN

Holidays:
Eid-ul-fitr* - February 8-10
Eid-ul-adha* - April 18-21
Al-Hijra (Islamic New Year)* - May 8
Birthday of Muhammad* - July 17
National Day - November 18
Lailat-ul-Isra' Wal Miraj* - November 26

* Muslim holidays are approximate, as they are timed according to local sightings of various phases of the moon.

Suitable Clothing: Although foreigners are not expected to, and should not, wear the traditional gowns and veils of Muslim attire, modesty is of the utmost importance. You will need sunglasses, sunhats and sunscreen year round, and a raincoat between June and September. Otherwise, light material is appropriate, but men should make sure it covers knees and shoulders, while women should wear skirts or dresses which cover the knees, elbows and neckline as well. A business suit should be worn to all meetings, and it is also a polite gesture, though not mandatory, for Western women to cover their heads.

Automobile Driving License: A National License is valid for up to seven days if you have a tourist visa. If you are travelling on business or you are intending to stay more than seven days it is necessary to obtain a license from the police.

Customs Allowances: Declare all valuables, or they may face confiscation upon your departure. No limits exist on foreign currency or Omani Rials (which are a hard currency), as long as what you export was initially declared. You may bring in 50 cigarettes and 2 liters of spirits duty free. Prohibited are military weaponry, narcotics, and pornography and some food and agricultural products.

Tipping: A Tip of 10-15% is acceptable everywhere.

Credit Cards Accepted: American Express, Diner's Club, Visa

Customary Dining Hours:
Breakfast: 07.30-09.00

Lunch: 13.00-15.00
Dinner: 20.00-22.30

Local Customs, Business Protocol and Courtesies: Omanis are very proud of their distinct, well-preserved cultural arts, and expressing interest in them is a good way to build rapport. Do not, however, ask to visit a mosque (non-Muslims are forbidden here), and refrain comment as much as possible on Middle East politics and on the subject of women. Visitors should, out of courtesy and a practical view towards business, adhere to basic Muslim rules and local etiquette. Schedule appointments in advance, and be on time. Your contact may be late, but you should never express annoyance or hostility. Your contemporaries are quite sophisticated, and an atmosphere of confident goodwill should prevail on both sides. Persistence is important, but pays off only if done with courtesy and quiet confidence. Business should be conducted in person as much as possible, and expect lengthy, sociable discussions and careful review of any proposals. Do not expect any instant answers. Omani's are skilled bargainers, and even written contracts may be brought up for renegotiation later. It is advisable to sell on letter of credit. Although English is widely spoken in the business community, your effort to provide company literature in Arabic will make a good impression. Always rise when someone (except a servant or secretary) enters the room. Use the appropriate titles: Sheik and Sheikha (plus first name) with male and female members, respectively, of a ruling family. Otherwise, Mr., Mrs. or Miss are appropriate. Men and women do shake hands here; it is also customary to touch your right palm to your heart after each handshake. Business gifts are not necessary, but a nice gesture on your part, such as an interesting curio from your home region, art object, or something connected to your area of business.

Be sincerely patient, for any meeting will be accompanied by the traditional rituals of hospitality. It is considered rude to refuse the coffee and food that will be offered, except at Ramadan, when polite refusal will be appreciated, since your hosts themselves cannot eat until sundown. During this period, don't eat in public during the day. At meals or

OMAN

when socializing, it's best to follow the example of your Saudi host as to whether to eat with one's fingers or use utensils. Southpaws beware: there is a strong taboo against eating or drinking with one's left hand (traditionally, the hand used for toilet activities), although you may use both hands if given a knife and fork. Also, if crossing your legs, make sure your feet are not visibly pointing in anyone's direction. Always ask permission when photographing a person or a place.

Health: It is advisable to consult your doctor before your journey. Yellow fever certificate is required if you are arriving from or via an infected area. Immunizations against diphtheria, hepatitis A, hepatitis B, malaria, polio, tetanus and typhoid are recommended. There is a risk of malaria throughout the country. Bathing in fresh water should be avoided. All drinking water and milk should be boiled or sterilized, especially outside the main towns. The food should be well cooked.

Language: Arabic and English

MUSCAT

Country code: 968 - City code: none

Airport: Muscat Seeb International Airport

Distance from City: 40km (24 miles) west of the city center

Transportation to Center of City:
From International and Domestic Terminals
By Bus (cost) 200 Baiza. Time approx. 60-90 min.
By Taxi (cost) RIO5-6. Time approx. 45 min.
Tip luggage porters 50 Biaza per piece

Transfers: (Minimum Connecting Time):
International to International: 60 min.
International to Domestic: 60 min.
Domestic to International: 60 min.
Domestic to Domestic: 60 min.

OMAN

Automobile Rentals:
Airport car rental desk
Hertz - 521187

Car rental city office
Avis - 799666 Ext.4287
Europcar Interrent - 694093
Hertz - 566046

Hotels:
Mercury Al-Falaj Hotel, Saif Bin Sultan St., Ruwi, 702311
Ruwi Novotel Hotel, P.O. Box 2195, Ruwi, 704244
Sheraton Oman Hotel, P.O. Box 3260, Ruwi, 799899

Restaurants:
Al Khiran Terrace, Al Bustan Palace Hotel, P.O. Box 1998, Muttrah 114, 799666
Al Marjan, Al Bustan Palace Hotel, P.O. Box 1998, Muttrah 114, 799666
Blue Marlin, Al Bustan Palace Hotel, P.O. Box 1998, Muttrah 114, 799666
BlueCactus. P.O. Box 1142, Muttrah 114, 605907
Corc's Bistro, Al Falaj Hotel Mercure, P.O. Box 2031, Ruwi 112, 702311
Cote Jardin Restaurant, Seeb Novotel, P.O. Box 69, Seeb 111, 510300
Green Mountain Restaurant, Sheraton Oman hotel, P.O.Box 3260, Ruwi 112, 799899
Just Jass Restaurant, Muscat Holiday Inn, P.O. Box 1185, Seeb 111, 697123
La Mamma, Sheraton Oman Hotel, P.O.Box 3260, Ruwi 112, 799899
Lo Amigos, Muscat Holiday Inn, P.O. Box 1185, Seeb 111, 697123
Mumtaz Mahal, P.O. Box 1142, Muttrah 114, 605907
Oasis By The Sea, P.O. Box 3779, Ruwi 112, 602757
OK Corral, Muscat Intercontinental, P.O. Box 398, Muttrah 114, 600500
Pavo Real, The Mexican Restaurant, P.O. Box 19, Muscat 113, 602603
Shirchill's, Muscat Holiday Inn, P.O. Box 1185, Seeb 111, 697123
Sole Mio, P.O. Box 3390, Ruwi 112, 601343

The Far Eastern Restaurant, Sheraton Oman Hotel, P.O.Box 3260, Ruwi 112, 605945

Tokyo Taro, Al Falaj Hotel Mercure, P.O. Box 2031, Ruwi 112, 702311

Tropicana, Gulf Forum Hotel, P.O.Box 1455, Ruwi 112, 560100

Tuscany, Hyatt Regency, P.O. Box 951, Shatti Al Qurum 133, 602888

Entertainment:

Al Hamra, Al Bustan Palace Hotel, P.O. Box 1998, Muttrah 114, 799666

Par 19, Seeb Novotel, P.O. Box 69, Seeb 111, 510300

Saba NightClub, Sheraton Oman hotel, P.O.Box 3260, Ruwi 112, 799899

Sometime Piano Bar, Muscat Holiday Inn, P.O. Box 1185, Seeb, 111, 697123

Sur Nightclub, Muscat Intercontinental, P.O. Box 398, Muttrah 114, 600500

The Lounge Bar, Sheraton Oman hotel, P.O.Box 3260, Ruwi 112, 799899

Places of Interest:

Jalali, Mirani and Mutrah Forts
The Medinat Qaboos Oman Museum
The Natural History Museum
Ruwi Sultan's Armed Forces Museum
The Clock Tower

QATAR

Official Name: State of Qatar

Location: Middle East - Gulf Coast. Quatar is bordered by the United Arab Emirates and Saudi Arabia.

Government: Absolute Monarchy

Area: 11,437 sq. km., 4416 sq. miles.

Population: 524,000

Religion(s): Muslim.

Capital City: Doha

Time: GMT +3

Currency: Qatar Riyal (QRI)=100 dirhams

Currency Requirements: There are no restrictions on the import and export of foreign or local currency. Israeli currency is prohibited.

Business Hours:
- Government: 07.30-12.3; 14.00-18.00 Sun-Wed
- Banks: 07.30-12.30; 14.00-18.00 Sat-Thur
- Shops: 07.30/08.00-12.00/12.30 and 15.00/16.00-20.00 Sat-Thur
- Offices: 07.30-12.30; 14.00-18.00 Sat-Thur

Weight and Measures: Metric System and some Imperial measures

Electric Current: 240/415 volts AC. Plugs are of the 3-pin type.

Holidays:
Eid-ul-fitr - February 8-10*

QATAR

Eid-ul-adha - April 18-21*
Al-Hijra (Islamic New Year) - May 8*
The Amir's Ascension Day - June 27
Independence Day - September 3

* Muslim holidays are approximate, as they are timed according to local sightings of various phases of the moon. The official day of rest is Friday.

Suitable Clothing: Although foreigners are not expected to, and should not, wear the traditional gowns and veils of Arab attire, modesty is of the utmost importance. You will need sunglasses, sunhats and sunscreen year round, and a raincoat between June and September. Nights and November to March are cooler, so bring medium-weight clothing and a light jacket then. Otherwise, light material is appropriate, but men should make sure it covers knees and shoulders, while women should wear skirts or dresses which cover the knees, elbows and neckline as well. A business suit should be worn to all meetings, and it is also a polite gesture for Western women to cover their heads, although this is not mandatory.

Automobile Driving License: An International Driving Permit is recommended. A 90 day Temporary Driving Permit can be issued on presentation of a National License. Applicants will be required to pass an oral highway code test and should be accompanied by someone who knows the procedure. Europcar Interrent helps visitors to obtain a temporary license on presentation of a valid National License.

Customs Allowances: Declare all valuables, or they may face confiscation upon your departure. No limits exist on foreign currency or Qatar Riyals, as long as what you export was initially declared. You may bring in 450 cigarettes, but no alcohol. Also prohibited are military weaponry, narcotics, and pornography. Antiques may not leave the country.

Tipping: A service charge is added to most hotel and restaurant bills. Elsewhere a tip of 10% is appreciated. Taxi drivers do not expect a tip.

QATAR

Credit Cards Accepted: American Express, Diner's Club, Visa

Customary Dining Hours:
Breakfast: 07.30-09.00
Lunch: 13.00-15.00
Dinner: 20.00-23.00

Local Customs, Business Protocol and Courtesies: Contrary to its history and image as a big major oil state, Qatar is actually running out of its oil reserves but does, however, have one of the largest natural gas reserves in the world. Interest in and discussing its expanding economy as long as your view appears positive is a good way to build rapport with your contemporaries there. Refrain from comment as much as possible on Middle East politics, and on the subject of women. As in any Persian Gulf country, visitors should, out of courtesy and a practical view towards business, adhere to basic Muslim rules and local etiquette. Schedule appointments in advance, and be on time. Your contact may be late, but you should never express annoyance or hostility. Your contemporaries are quite sophisticated, and an atmosphere of confident goodwill and courtesy should prevail on both sides. Persistence is important, but pays off only if done courteously and with quiet confidence. Business should be conducted in person as much as possible, and expect lengthy, sociable discussions and careful review of any proposals. Do not expect any instant answers. Even written contracts may be brought up for renegotiation later. It's important to note a tendency toward dealing directly with foreign executives and suppliers; if you are a mid-level or lower-level intermediary or subcontractor, your company's proposals may meet with disdain. Companies prefer to use one importer exclusively. Although English is widely spoken in the business community, your effort to provide company literature in Arabic will make a good impression. Always use the appropriate titles: Sheik and Sheikha (plus first name) with male and female members, respectively, of a ruling family. An emir (prince) may also be referred to as "Your Highness" or "Your Excellency." Otherwise, Mr., Mrs. or Miss are appropriate. Men shake hands; with a woman, nod your head upon introduction, or shake hands only if she offers hers. Business gifts are not necessary, but a nice gesture on your part, such as an interesting curio from your home region, art object, or something connected to your area of business.

Be sincerely patient, for any meeting will be accompanied by the traditional rituals of hospitality. It is considered rude to refuse the coffee and food that will be offered, except at Ramadan, when polite refusal will be appreciated, since your hosts themselves cannot eat until sundown. During this period, don't eat in public during the day. Alcohol is forbidden in any case. If it is important that your discussions not be interrupted by other visitors, try to arrange meeting more privately at a coffeehouse. Entertaining is often done in luxury hotels as well as at a home. At meals or when socializing, it's best to follow the example of your Saudi host as to whether to eat with one's fingers or use utensils. Southpaws beware: there is a strong taboo against eating or drinking with one's left hand (traditionally, the hand used for toilet activities), although you may use both hands if given a knife and fork. Also, if crossing your legs, make sure your feet and soles are not visibly pointing in anyone's direction. Always ask permission when photographing a person or a place, especially a mosque.

Health: It is advisable to consult your doctor before your journey. A certificate for yellow fever is required from visitors travelling from an infected area. Vaccinations for typhoid, polio, hepatitis A and tetanus are recommended. Bottled water should be used at all times. Food should be well cooked and milk should be boiled. Visitors should maintain a high salt and fluid intake due to the intense climatic conditions. Health insurance is advised due to the high charges for medical treatment. Visitors will be asked to provide certificates to prove they are HIV-negative and free of tuberculosis, syphilis, leprosy, cholera, typhoid and hepatitis B.

Language: Arabic.

DOHA

Country code: 974 - City code: none

Airport: Doha International Airport

Distance from City: 8km (4 miles) southeast of the city.

Transportation to Center of City:
From International and Domestic Terminals
By Taxi (cost) QRI15-20. Time approx. 10-15 min.
Tip luggage porters 3 Riyals per piece

Transfers: (Minimum Connecting Time):
International to International: 60 min.
International to Domestic: 60 min.
Domestic to International: 60 min.
Domestic to Domestic: 60 min.

Automobile Rentals:
Airport car rental desk
Avis - 416880
Europcar Interrent - 351550
Hertz - 424063

Car rental city office
Avis - 447766
Europcar Interrent - 435222
Hertz - 416891

Hotels:
Ramada Hotel Doha, C Ring Rd., 417417
Sheraton Gulf Hotel Doha, Ras Avu Abboud, 432432
Sofitel Doha Palace, P.O. Box 7566, 435222

Restaurants:
Al Banuche, Sheraton Gulf Hotel, 432432
Al Magilis, Al Saadd St., 447417
Al Mina, Sheraton Gulf Hotel, 432432
Al Mudiaf, C Ring Rd., 363700
Al Shahee, Sheraton Doha Hotel, 854444
Al Shoka, C Ring Rd., 444106
Bangkok Thai, C Ring Rd., 365423

Bukhara, Khalifa & Squash Complex, 833345
Caravan, C Ring Rd., 320320
Chingari, Ramada Hotel, 417417
Clubhouse, Khalifa Tennis & Squash Complex, 409666
Doha Club, Doha Club, 418822
Far East Al Mirquab St., 411669
Flamingo's Nest, Sheraton Gulf Hotel, 432432
Hyde Park, Ramada Hotel, 417417
La Braserie, Sofitel Hotel, 435222
Maharadja, Qatar Palace Hotel, 421642
Maxim, Ramada Hotel, 417417
Qurtoubah, Hitteen St., 438683
Rouf Top Lounge, Ramada Hotel, 417417
Shebestan, Al Sadd St., 321555
Thai Kitchen, Al Miraclub St., 414067
Venice, Al Sadd St., 441750
Ya Mali Sham, Airport Rd., 414364

Places of Interest:
The Grand Mosque
The Abu Bakir al-Siddiq Mosque
The National Museum
The New Amir's Palace
The Ethnographic Museum
Doha Fort
Doha Zoo

SAUDI ARABIA

Official Name: Kingdom of Saudi Arabia

Location: Middle East - Arabian Peninsula. Saudi Arabia is bordered by Jordan, Iraq, Kuwait, the Gulf of Oman, Qatar, United Arab Emirates, Oman and Yemen. The west coast lies on the Red Sea.

Government: Absolute Monarchy

Area: 2,240,000 sq. km.

Population: 17 million

Religion(s): Sunni Muslim majority.

Capital City: Riyadh

Major Business Cities: Dhahran and Jeddah.

Time: GMT +3

Currency: Saudi Arabian Riyal (ARI) = 100 Halalah.

Currency Requirements: There are no restrictions on the import and the export of local or foreign currency. Israeli currency is prohibited.

Business Hours:
- Government: 07.30-14.30 Sat-Wed
- Banks: 08.30-12.00 and 17.00-19.00 Sat-Thur
- Shops: 10.00-13.00 and 17.00-22.30 Sat-Wed
- Offices: 08.00-17.00 or 09.00-14.00 and 17.00-20.00 Sat-Wed

Weight and Measures: Metric System

Electric Current: 110/220 volts AC. Plugs are of the 2-pin widespread type.

Holidays:
Eid-ul-fitr - February 8-10*
Eid-ul-adha - April 18-21*
Al-Hijra (Islamic New Year) - May 8*
Birth of the Prophet Muhammad - July 17*
National Day -September 23
Lailat-ul-Isra' Wal Mir'aj - November 26*

* Muslim holidays are approximate, as they are timed according to local sightings of various phases of the moon. Depending on the region, celebrations can last between two and ten days.

Suitable Clothing: Although foreigners are not expected to, and should not, wear the traditional gowns and veils of Saudi attire, modesty is of the utmost importance. The year-round desert climate requires sunglasses, sunhats and sunscreen. Light material is appropriate, but men should make sure it covers knees and shoulders, while women should wear skirts or dresses which cover the knees, elbows and neckline as well. Foreign women of Arab descent, however, are expected to adhere to stricter Muslim dress, veil included.

Automobile Driving License: A valid International or National Driving License accompanied by officially sanctioned translation in English or Arabic is required.

Customs Allowances: No limits exist on foreign currency or Riyals (which are hard currency), as long as what you export was initially declared. Upon entering and exiting Saudi Arabia, you and your luggage will probably face a lengthy, thorough search. Alcohol and pork products will be automatically confiscated, although you may bring in 600 cigarettes duty free. Also prohibited are military weaponry, narcotics and pornography, and foreign magazines may even be scissored up, if not taken away entirely. As drug trafficking gets the death penalty, make sure all prescription drugs are well-labeled and include your name and those of your doctor and pharmacy.

Tipping: There is no rule for tipping although the custom is becoming more common. A tip of 10% is appropriate for waiters and taxi drivers. Porters may also be tipped.

SAUDI ARABIA

Credit Cards Accepted: Access, American Express, Diner's Club, Eurocard, MasterCard, Visa

Customary Dining Hours:
Breakfast: 07.30-09.00
Lunch: 12.30-14.30
Dinner: 20.00-22.00

Local Customs, Business Protocol and Courtesies:
There is a long list of rules and customs visiting business-men must adhere to in Saudi Arabia, and violating them is, at best in poor taste, at worst, illegal. Saudi Arabia is the most conservative of the Persian Gulf States when it comes to religious customs and protocol. Prohibitions include alcohol, photographing women or religious rituals and build-ings, nightclubs. There is heavy censorship of foreign pub-lications and films. During the monthlong holiday of Ra-madan, it is advised against eating or drinking on the streets before sundown, as Muslims must fast during the day. Sau-di women are heavily veiled and usually off the street; even Western women are prohibited from driving, and must al-ways be with a male relative in the car or while outside. Even if a businessman is invited to dine in a Saudi home, no women will be present, and he should bring a gift for the host, not his wife. The view and treatment of women in Saudi society makes it extremely difficult for foreign busi-nesswomen to function there. Respect for Muslim customs includes a knowledge and willingness to keep one's dis-tance: not only are non-Muslims prohibited from entering within 30 miles of the city of Mecca, the center of Islam, but also from even entering mosques, unlike in more open societies like Egypt. Openly celebrating non-Muslim holi-days is forbidden. The only respite may be on a U.S. mili-tary base, where some, though not all, rules are relaxed. In any case, not adhering to the basic societal rules and eti-quette will get you nowhere in business with the Saudis. Be well-versed in Saudi business habits, laws and procedure as well. Schedule appointments in advance, and be on time. Your contact may be late, but you should never ex-press annoyance or hostility. An atmosphere of confident goodwill and courtesy should prevail on both sides. Be sin-

cerely patient, for any meeting will be accompanied by the rituals of hospitality. It is considered rude to refuse the coffee and food that will be offered (except at Ramadan, where polite refusal will be appreciated, since your hosts cannot eat until sundown).

Although English is widely spoken in the business community, your effort to provide company literature in Arabic will make a good impression. Always use the appropriate titles: "Sheik" with first name for a prince or any other member of a ruling family. A prince may also be referred to as "Your Highness" or "Your Excellency." For non-royalty, Mr. is appropriate. Men shake hands; with a woman, shake hands only if she offers hers. Business gifts are not necessary, but a nice gesture on your part, such as an interesting curio from your home region, art object, or something connected to your area of business. Only Saudi citizens may conduct Saudi business. There is a tendency to prefer direct access to executives and suppliers; if you are a mid-level or lower-level intermediary or subcontractor, your company's proposals may meet with disdain. Persistence is important, but pays off only if done with courteous and quiet confidence. If a dispute arises between Saudi and foreign businessman, the case must come before the Saudi government even if the contract was made outside the country. Resolution is determined by two committees within the Ministry of Commerce, and the foreign representative is barred from leaving the country until the dispute is settled.

At meals or when socializing, it's best to follow the example of your Saudi host as to whether to eat with one's fingers or use utensils. Southpaws beware: there is a strong taboo against eating or drinking with one's left hand (traditionally, the hand used for toilet activities), although you may use both hands if given a knife and fork. Also, if crossing your legs, make sure your feet are not visibly pointing in anyone's direction. Refrain from comment as much as possible on Middle East politics, and don't mention women, even from your host's family, at all. Always ask permission when photographing a person or object.

SAUDI ARABIA

Health: It is advisable to consult your doctor before your journey. Vaccinations for typhoid, polio, hepatitis A and tetanus are recommended. It is advisable to drink only bottled water. The milk should be boiled, the food should be well cooked and the vegetables and the fruits must be peeled. It is essential to maintain a good fluid and salt intake. The medical facilities are of a high standard, but treatment is expensive and insurance is recommended.

Language: Arabic. English is also spoken.

JEDDAH

Country code: 966 - City code: 2

Airport: King Abdul Aziz International Airport

Distance from City: 30km (18 miles) north of the city.

Transportation to Center of City:
From International and Domestic Terminals
Taxi (cost) ARI50. Time approx. 30-40 min.

Transfers: (Minimum Connecting Time):
International to International: 90 min.
International to Domestic: 150 min.
Domestic to International: 150 min.
Domestic to Domestic: 75 min.

Automobile Rentals:
Airport car rental desk
Avis - South Terminal 685-5544
     - North Terminal 651-1779
Hertz - 2/857-5622

Car rental city office
Avis - 661-0925
Hertz - 699-2562

SAUDI ARABIA

Hotels:
Al Fau Holiday Inn, P. O. Box 10924, 661-1000
Al Salam Hotel, King Khaled St. & Mekkah Rd., 631-4000
Alhamra Sofitel Hotel, Jeddah, Palestine Rd., 660-2000
Jeddah Inter-Continental, Corniche Rd., 661-1800
Jeddah Kaki Hotel, P. O. Box 2559, 631-2201
Jeddah Marriott Hotel, P. O. Box 6448, 671-4000
Jeddah Trident Hotel, Mina St., 647-4444

Restaurants:
Al – Baghouli, Bangladeshi Market
Al – Joraif, Prince Fahd St., 631 7901
Al – Zehra, Amir Majid St.
Asian Delights, Alhamra Sofitel, 660 2000
Boukhari, Sary St.
Ghina Dragon, Sitten St.
Indonesian Padang, Macarona Rd., 676 2958
Jakarta Restaurant, Red Sea Compound
Koreana, Palestine Rd.
Mongolian Grill, Red Sea Palace, 642 8555
Oriental, Main St., Salama District
Shanghai, Herra St.
Shawli, Corniche Commercial Center, 2 Fl.
Sumatra Restaurant, Khalid Ibot Walid St.
Taj Mahal, Amir Majid St. abd Makarona St.
The Singapore Hawker, City Center complex, Medina Rd.
Tropical Restaurant, Mahmal Center downtown
Tropicana, Tahlia St.

Places of Interest:
The Municipality Museum
The Naseef House
Al-Shafee Mosque
The Corniche Sculptures

RIYADH

Country code: 966 - City code: 1

Airport: Riyadh-King Khalid International Airport.

SAUDI ARABIA

Distance from City: 35km (21 miles) north of the city.

Transportation to Center of City:
From International and Domestic Terminals
By Taxi (cost) ARI55-75. Time approx. 30-40 min.

Transfers: (Minimum Connecting Time):
International to International: 90 min.
International to Domestic: 90 min.
Domestic to International: 90 min.
Domestic to Domestic: 60 min.

Automobile Rentals:
Airport car rental desk
Avis -220-2634
Hertz -220-2678

Car rental city office
Avis - 463-2252
Hertz - 476-2110

Hotels:
Hyatt Regency Riyadh, King Abdulaziz St., 479-1234
Riyadh Inter- Continental Hotel, Mazzar St., 465-5000
Salahedin Hotel, King Abdulaziz Rd., 454-4888
White Palace Hotel, Airport St., 478-7800
Zahret Al Shark Hotel, King Abdulaziz Rd., 403-8800

Places of Interest:
The Riyadh Museum
Masmak Fortress
Murabba Palace
King Faisal Center for Research and Islamic Studies
King Saud University Museum
Dir'aiyah - archaeological ruins.

SOUTH AFRICA

Official Name: Republic of South Africa

Location: Southern Africa. Republic of South Africa is bordered by the Indian Ocean, the Atlantic Ocean, Namibia, Botswana, Zimbabwe, Mozambique, Swaziland and Lesotho.

Government: Republic

Area: 1,221,037 sq. km., 471,445 sq. miles.

Population: 41.7 million

Religion(s): Dutch Reform Church, Church of England, Roman Catholic, Methodist, Lutheran and other Christian groups. There are also Jews, independent black church movements, Hindus and Muslims.

Capital City: Pretoria

Major Business Cities: Cape Town, Durban, East London and Johannesburg.

Time: GMT +2

Currency: Rand (SAR)=100 cents

Currency Requirements: There are no restrictions on the import or export of foreign currency, but it has to be declared. The import or export of SA Reserve Bank notes is limited to SAR500.

Business Hours:
- Government: 08.30-17.00 Mon-Fri
- Banks: 08.30-15.30 Mon-Fri; 08.30-11.30 Sat
- Shops: 08.30-17.00 Mon Fri, 09.00-12.00 Sat
- Offices: 08.30-16.30/17.00 Mon-Fri

Weight and Measures: Metric System

Electric Current: 220/230 volts AC. Plugs are of the square 3-pin type. A special adapter is required.

Holidays:
New Year's Day - January 1
Human Rights Day - March 21
Good Friday - April 10*
Family Day - March 31
Constitution Day - April 27
Day in lieu of Sunday April 27 - April 28
Workers' Day - May 1
Youth Day - June 16
National Women's Day - August 9
Heritage Day - September 24
Day of Reconciliation - December 16
Christmas Day - December 25
Day of Goodwill - December 26

* Christian holidays vary each year.

Suitable Clothing: A business suit should be worn to all meetings. Bring a more formal suit or dress for evening functions. Theft is common, however, so in general don't make a show of affluence. Weather is warmest between March and November, but long sleeves help against insects - generally, lightweight clothing, sunglasses, sunhat and sunscreen are useful. Bring raingear as well.

Automobile Driving License: An International Driving License is required. Drivers must be at least 23 years of age and must have a valid license that is held for at least 3 years.

Customs Allowances: Declare all valuables (including electronics, jewelry and cameras), or they may face confiscation upon your departure. Personal items are duty free, with limits to 400 cigarettes, 2 liters of wine and 1 of spirits. Up to 500 Rand may be brought in or out, while no restrictions exist on foreign currency.

Tipping: If a service charge is not included, a 10% tip is customary to be left. Room service is usually given SAR2. Waiters, taxi drivers and caddies usually expect a 10% tip.

Credit Cards Accepted: American Express, MasterCard, Visa

Customary Dining Hours:
Breakfast: 07.00-09.00
Lunch: 12.00-14.00
Dinner: 19.00-22.00

Local Customs, Business Protocol and Courtesies: The combination of its extraordinary industrial prowess and natural resources · including the world's largest reserves of diamonds, gold and platinum · and the end of apartheid make the Republic of South Africa an increasingly attractive place to do business. At the same time, visitors should keep in mind that the transition to an integrated society and socioeconomic equity is a sensitive issue. Rather, focus on the country's stunning natural offerings. The business atmosphere retains a formal, British flavor. It's best to cultivate relationships with managing directors, as they make most decisions. Schedule meetings in advance, and be on time, for punctuality is a strong point here. Exchange business cards, using title with last name until indicated otherwise by your associates. Once a deal is completed, business gifts are typical, such as an interesting curio from your home region, art object, or something connected to your area of business. You will almost certainly be invited to business/social functions, some of them formal and lavish.

Health: It is advisable to consult your doctor before your journey. The medical facilities are excellent. Vaccinations for hepatitis A, tetanus, cholera, typhoid, polio and malaria are recommended. Although it is considered to be safe to drink water in urban areas, bottled water is advised. Food precautions should be observed at all times. Health insurance is recommended.

Language: Afrikaans, English. Various African languages including Zulu and Sesotho are also spoken.

SOUTH AFRICA

JOHANNESBURG

Country code: 27 - City code: 11

Airport: Johannesburg (Jan Smuts) International Airport.

Distance from City: 20km (12 miles) east of the city.

Transportation to Center of City:
From International and Domestic Terminals
By Bus (cost) SAR25. Time approx.30 min.
By Taxi (cost) SAR85-95. Time approx. 30 min.
Tip luggage porters SAR3   per piece

Transfers: (Minimum Connecting Time):
International to International: 60 min.
International to Domestic: 60 min.
Domestic to International: 60 min.
Domestic to Domestic: 30 min.

Automobile Rentals:
Airport car rental desk
Avis - 975-3354
Hertz - 394-4020

Car rental city office
Avis - 331-8631
Hertz - 680-5496

Hotels:
Carlton, Main St., 331-8911
Parktonian All Suite Hotel, 120 De Korte St., Braamfontein, 403-5740
Holiday Inn Garden Court-Airport, 2 Hulley Rd., Kempton Park, 392-1062

Restaurants:
Chon Hing, 26 Alexander St., 83 3206
Ciro at the Ritz, 17 3rd St., 880 2470
Franco's Pizzeria & Trattoria, 54 Tyrone Ave., 646 5449
Ile de France, 26 Cramerview Centre, 706 2837
Leipoldt's, 94 Juta St., 339 2765

Liger Longer, 58 Wierda Rd., 884 0465
Ma Cuisine, 40 7th Ave., 880 1946
O Fado, Hutton Ct.,291 Jan Smuts Ave., 880 4410
Osteria Tre Nonni, 9 Grafton Ave., 327 0095
Pescador Restaurant, Grayston Centre, 884 4429
Plaka Taverna, 3a Corlett Dr., 788 8777
Red Chamber Mandarin Restaurant, Rosebank Mews,Rosebank, 788 5536
Shamiyana, 71 Corlett Dr., 786 8810
Turtle Creek Winery, 58 Wierda Rd., 884 0466
Widgeons Bistro, 60 Tyrone Ave., 486 2053

Entertainment:
Hooters, corner of Bolton Rd. and Bath Ave. 442 7320
House of Tandoor, 26 Rockey St., 487 1569
Jagger's, Mutual Sq., Rosebank, 788 1718
Krypton, Constantia Centre,Tyrwhitt Ave., 442 7372
Picasso Bistro, 169 Oxford Rd., 788 1213
The Fairway Cafe, 76 Op Den Bergen St., 624 1894
The Yard of Ale, Market Theatre complex, Bree St., 836 6611

Shops and Stores:
Badia Clothing, Carlton Center, Commissioner St.   Apparel
Carlton Center, Commissioner/Weilligh Sts.   Shopping Mall
Hyde Park Mall, Jan Smuts Ave.   Shopping Mall
Sandton City, Sandton Dr.   Shopping Mall
Sandton Square, 5th St.   Shopping Mall

Places of Interest:
The Africana Museum
Market Theatre - shops, bars and an art gallery
The Planetarium

SUDAN

Official Name: Republic of Sudan

Location: Northeast Africa. Sudan is bordered by Egypt, the Red Sea, Ethiopia, Eritrea, Kenya, Uganda, Zaire, the Central African Republic, Chad and Libya.

Government: Republic

Area: 2,505,810 sq. km., 967,500 sq. miles.

Population: 27.47 million

Religion(s): Muslim majority. Christian and traditional Animist religious minorities are also present.

Capital City: Khartoum

Time: GMT +2

Currency: Sudanese Dinar (SD)=10 Sudanese Pounds=100 piastres

Currency Requirements: The import and the export of foreign currency are unlimited but they must be declared. The import and the export of local currency are prohibited.

Business Hours:
- Government: 07.30 or 08.00-14.30 Sat-Thur
- Banks: 08.00-14;.00; 17.00-20.00 Sat-Thur
- Shops: 08.00-14.30; 17.30-20.00 Sat-Thur
- Offices: 08.00-14.30 Sat-Thur

Weight and Measures: Metric System and some traditional weights and measures.

Electric Current: 240 volts AC. Plugs are of the 2-pin type.

Holidays:
Independence Day - January 1
Coptic Church's Christmas Day - January 7
Ramadan Bairam (Eid-ul-fitr) - February 9-12*
Easter Day - March 30
Eladhia Bairam (Eid-ul-adha) - April 18-22*
Al-Hijra (Islamic New Year) - May 8*
National Salvation Revolution's Day - June 30
Birthday of Prophet Muhammad - July 18*
Anniversary of October Revolution - October 21
Lailat-ul-Isra' Wal Mir'aj - November 26*
Christmas Day - December 25

* Muslim holidays are approximate, as they are timed according to local sightings of various phases of the moon.

Suitable Clothing: A business suit should be worn to all meetings, and a good suit or dress for formal occasions. Modesty is of the utmost importance. You will need sunglasses, sunhat and sunscreen year round, and a light jacket for evenings, or for the occasional rainy day between December and March. The rest of the year, light material is appropriate, but men should make sure it covers knees and shoulders, while women should wear skirts or dresses which cover the knees, elbows and neckline as well.

Automobile Driving License: An International Driving Permit is recommended although a temporary license is available from the local authorities on presentation of a National Driving License.

Customs Allowances: Declare all valuables or they may face confiscation upon your departure. Personal items are duty free. Import and export of Sudanese Dinars is prohibited, but no limits exist on foreign currency, as long as what you export was initially declared. Prohibited are guns, drugs and pornography. Alcohol is forbidden, but up to 200 cigarettes may be brought in.

Tipping: Tipping in Sudan is not customary.

Credit Cards Accepted: American Express, Diner's Club, Visa

SUDAN

Customary Dining Hours:
Breakfast: 09.00-10.00
Lunch: 14.00-17.00
Dinner: 21.00-23.00

Local Customs, Business Protocol and Courtesies: Ongoing civil war, grinding poverty and a reputation for harboring terrorists make the Sudan rather inhospitable regarding international commerce. If you do venture there, however, most government officials and businessmen do speak English. Schedule appointments in advance, and shake hands upon introduction and leaving. Be persistent, but not pushy, when it comes to sales. You should never express annoyance or hostility. An atmosphere of uncritical and confident goodwill and courtesy should prevail on both sides. Persistence pays off only if done with courtesy and quiet confidence. Unless your host offers to drink alcohol with you, do not accept alcohol, which is forbidden to Muslims, as is drinking in public. During the monthlong holiday of Ramadan, eat only in private. Do not take pictures of women or military installations. In any case, photographing, for official or unofficial purposes, often requires a permit.

Health: It is advisable to consult your doctor before your journey. A yellow fever vaccination certificate is required if you are coming from an infected area. Vaccinations for yellow fever, typhoid, polio, cholera and visceral leishmaniasis are recommended. Bottled water should be used and food precautions observed at all times. The milk should always be boiled. Bathing in fresh water should be avoided. Health insurance is strongly advised and it should cover for repatriation.

Language: Arabic. English and various local dialects are widely spoken.

KHARTOUM

Country code: 249 - City code: 11

SUDAN

Airport: Khartoum Airport.
Distance from City: 4km (2 miles) southeast of the city.

Transportation to Center of City:
From International and Domestic Terminals
By Bus (cost) SD8-12. Time approx. 25-35 min.
By Taxi (cost) SD75-100. Time approx. 20 min.
Tip luggage porters SD50-75 Piastres per piece

Transfers: (Minimum Connecting Time):
International to International: 60 min.
International to Domestic: 60 min.
Domestic to International: 60 min.
Domestic to Domestic: 30 min.

Hotels:
Khartoum Hilton, P. O. Box 1010, Morgran, 774100

Restaurants:
American Club, 770114
Apollo, 462577
Chinese Restaurant, Palace Hotel, 336222
Coptic Club, 463502
German Club, 462438
Italian Restaurant, Palace Hotel, 336222
Ivory Club, Khartoum Hilton, 774100
Morgran Coffee Shop, Khartoum Hilton, 774100
Officers Club, 463566
Sudan Club, 772044
Syrian Club, 464110

Entertainment:
Pool Bar, Khartoum Hilton, 774100
Sunset Lounge, Khartoum Hilton, 774100

Places of Interest:
The National Museum
Khalifa's House Museum
The Omdurman Souq – a temple
The Old Zoo
The Natural History Museum
Omdurman Camel Market

SYRIA

Official Name: Syrian Arab Republic

Location: Middle East. Syria is bordered by Turkey, Iraq, Jordan, Israel and Lebanon. A part of its coastline lies on the Mediterranean Sea.

Government: Socialist Democracy

Area: 185,180 sq. km., 71,498 sq. miles.

Population: 15 million

Religion(s): Muslim majority. Christian and other minorities including Jews are also present.

Capital City: Damascus

Major Business Cities: Aleppo

Time: GMT +2 (GMT +3 from end of March to end of September)

Currency: Syrian Pound (SYP)=100 piastres

Currency Requirements: The import of foreign currency is unlimited, but amounts over USD5000 must be declared on arrival. The export is limited to USD5000 or up to the amount declared on arrival. Import of local currency is unlimited, but the export is prohibited.

Business Hours:
- Government: 08.00-14.00 Sat-Thur
- Banks: 08.00/09.00-14.00 Sat-Thur
- Shops: 09.30-20.00 Sat-Thur
- Offices: 09.00-14.00; 16.00-20.00 Sat-Thur

Weight and Measures: Metric System

SYRIA

Electric Current: 220 volts AC. Plugs are of the flat 2-pin type.

Holidays:
New Year's Day - January 1
Eid-ul-fitr - February 8-10*
Revolution Day - March 8
Mother's Day - March 21
National Day - April 17
Eid-ul-adha - April 18-21*
Labor Day - May 1
Martyr's Day - May 6
Al-Hijra (Islamic New Year) - May 8*
Birthday of Muhammad - July 17*
Christmas Day - December 25

* Muslim holidays are approximate, as they are timed according to local sightings of various phases of the moon.

Suitable Clothing: Modesty is of the utmost importance. You will need sunglasses, sunhat and sunscreen year round, and jacket between November and March. Most of the year, light material is appropriate, but men should make sure it covers knees and shoulders, while women should wear skirts or dresses which cover the knees, elbows and neckline as well. A business suit should be worn to all meetings.

Automobile Driving License: An International Driving Permit is required.

Customs Allowances: Declare all valuables (including electronics, jewelry and cameras), or they may face confiscation upon your departure. Personal items are duty free, with limits to 200 cigarettes and 1 liter of wine or spirits. Prohibited are guns, pornography and drugs.

Tipping: Tipping is discretionary but a tip of 10% is acceptable for most services. It is advisable to negotiate taxi fares in advance if vehicles are unmetered.

Credit Cards Accepted:
American Express, MasterCard, Visa

SYRIA

Customary Dining Hours:
Breakfast: 07.00-09.00
Lunch: 14.00-16.00
Dinner: 21.00-23.00

Local Customs, Business Protocol and Courtesies: Western businessmen may get a chilly reception and it may take a great deal of time and effort to build a relationship. Otherwise, it's the same business atmosphere as in other Middle Eastern countries. As in any Persian Gulf country, visitors should, out of courtesy and a practical view towards business, adhere to basic Muslim rules and local etiquette. Although English is widely spoken in the business community, your effort to provide company literature and business cards in Arabic will make a good impression. Business cards are immediately exchanged.

Syrian women do sometimes shake hands, but one should wait for them to initiate. Schedule appointments in advance, and be on time. Your contact may be late, but you should never express annoyance or hostility. An atmosphere of confident goodwill and courtesy should prevail on both sides. Persistence is important, but pays off only if done with courtesy and quiet confidence. You should investigate carefully the performance of any company you are dealing with, and ask for an irrevocable letter of credit. Be prepared for skilled bargainers, who will want to negotiate generous terms of credit. Be sincerely patient, for any meeting will be accompanied by the traditional rituals of hospitality. Though business may at times be discussed in Turkish baths, foreigners are usually kept separate.

It is considered rude to refuse the coffee and food that will be offered, except at Ramadan, when polite refusal will be appreciated, since your hosts themselves cannot eat until sundown. During this period, don't eat in public during the day. Alcohol is forbidden to Muslims, so don't drink in public, or with your host unless he offers. Follow his example as to whether or not to use utensils, and never eat with your left hand only. If invited to a home, bring a gift for the host such as an interesting curio from your home region or art object.

SYRIA

Health: It is advisable to consult your doctor before your journey. A yellow fever certificate is required if you are travelling from infected areas. Vaccinations for typhoid, polio, hepatitis A and tetanus are recommended. Visitors are advised to drink bottled water and to take necessary food precautions. A medical insurance is recommended.

Language: Arabic. English and French are spoken within business circles.

DAMASCUS

Country code: 963 - City code: 11

Airport: Damascus International Airport.

Distance from City: 30km (18 miles) southeast of the city.

Transportation to Center of City:
From International and Domestic Terminals
By Bus (cost) SYP5. Time approx. 45 min.
By Taxi (cost) SYR60-75. Time approx. 30 min.

Transfers: (Minimum Connecting Time):
International to International: 45 min.
International to Domestic: 45 min.
Domestic to International: 45 min.
Domestic to Domestic: 45 min.

Automobile Rentals:
Airport car rental desk
Europcar Interrent - 543-1536

Car rental city office
Avis - 223-0880
Europcar Interrent - 222-9300 Ext.418

Hotels:
Cham Palace Damascus, Rue Maysaloun, 223-2300
Le Meridien Damascus, Ave. Choukry Kouatly, 371-8730

Omayad Hotel, 4 Bresil St., 221-7700

Restaurants:
Abu Kemal, 29 May Street,
Al Fares,Abdel Malek bin Marwan St., 333 3574
Al Fursan, Al Mahdi ibn Barakeh Street, 333 0017
Al Koh, 333 8883
Al Motaa, Abdel Malek bin Marwan St., 333 5696
L'Etoile d'Or, Cham Palace, 223 2320
Old Damascus Restaurant, Al Amwi St., 222 9662
Omayyad Palace Restaurant, 222 0826
Palais des Nobles, Al Quwatli St., 221 6397
Piano Bar, Hamenia St., 543 0375
The Orient Club, Al Najmeh Square, 221 3004

Entertainment:
British Council, Abdul Makle bin Marwan St., 333 3109
Casino Al Jawhara, Port Said St., 221 4945
Crazy Horse, 223 0988
French Institute, Bahsa, 246 1812
Les Nuits de L'Oasis, 371 8730
Moulin Rouge, 29 May St., 442 7227
Russian Cultural Centre, 29 May St., 442 7353
Sahrieh Supper Club and English Pub, 222 9300

Shops and Stores:

Azem School, Azem Palace	Antiques
Souk al Haiyatin,	Bazaar
Souk al Hamidiye	Bazaar
Souk Al Silah	Bazaar

Places of Interest:
The Ummayyad Mosque
The Tomb of St. John the Baptist
The Tikiyeh Mosque
Al-Azem Palace – a museum
House of Hanania

TUNISIA

Official Name: Republic of Tunisia

Location: North Africa. Tunisia is bordered by Algeria and Libya. Its northern border lies on the Mediterranean Sea.

Government: Republic

Area: 164,000 sq. km., 63,320 sq. miles.

Population: 8.74 million

Religion(s): Islam majority. Some Roman Catholic and Protestant minorities are also present.

Capital City: Tunis

Time: GMT +1

Currency: Tunisian Dinar (TUD)=1000 millimes

Currency Requirements: The import and the export of local currency are strictly prohibited. The import of foreign currency is unlimited but the amount must be declared if it exceeds TUD500. The export of foreign currency is limited to the amount imported on arrival. All currency documentation must be retained. Local currency may be reconverted into foreign currency for up to 30% of the amount imported or TUD100 - whichever is the largest.

Business Hours:
- Government: 07.30-13.30 Mon-Fri
- Banks: 08.00-11.00/12.00; 14.00-16.00/17.00 Mon-Fri
- Shops: 09.00-12.30; 15.00-19.00 Mon-Sat
- Offices: 08.30-12.30; 14.30-19.30 Mon-Thur; 08.30-13.00 Fri-Sat

TUNISIA

Weight and Measures: Metric System

Electric Current: 220 volts AC. Plugs are of the Continental 2-pin type.

Holidays:
New Year's Day - January 1
Eid-ul-fitr (end of Ramadan) - February 8-10*
Independence Day - March 20
Youth Day - March 21
Martyrs' Day - April 9
Eid-ul-adha - April 18-21*
Labor Day - May 1
Al-Hijra (Islamic New Year) - May 7*
Birthday of the Prophet Muhammad - July 17*
Republic Day - July 25
Women's Day - August 13
New Era Day - November 7
Lailat-ul-Isra' Wal Mir'aj - November 26*

* Muslim holidays are approximate, as they are timed according to local sightings of various phases of the moon.

Suitable Clothing: A business suit should be worn to all meetings. Modesty is of the utmost importance. You will need sunglasses, sunhat and sunscreen year round, and a light jacket for evenings, or for the occasional rainy day between November and April. The rest of the year, light material is appropriate, but men should make sure it covers knees and shoulders, while women should wear skirts or dresses which cover the knees, elbows and neckline as well.

Automobile Driving License: A National Driving License is required.

Customs Allowances: Declare all valuables or they may face confiscation upon your departure. Personal items are duty free. You may bring in up to 400 cigarettes, 2 liters of wine, 1 of spirits and a quarter liter of perfume. Camera film is limited to 20 rolls. Import and export of Tunisian Dinars is prohibited, but no limits exist on foreign currency, as long as what you export was initially declared. Prohibited are weaponry, drugs and pornography, and the export of antiquities.

Tipping: A tip of 10-15% is expected for all services.

Credit Cards Accepted: American Express, Diner's club, MasterCard, Visa

Customary Dining Hours:
Breakfast: 07.30-09.00
Lunch: 12.00-14.00
Dinner: 20.00-22.00

Local Customs, Business Protocol and Courtesies: Sensibility is the hallmark of Tunisian businessmen. This characteristic makes Tunisians more open to Western habits, although it will help you to adhere to local Muslim customs, such as not drinking alcohol in public and dressing modestly. Businesswomen, or a companion of a businessman, should cover up when invited to a home or function. Nevertheless, even though the local women rarely participate in business, female business travelers are accepted. French is the most widely spoken second language, but many businessmen also speak English. Schedule appointments in advance, and once in a meeting, move things along or things may never get off the ground. Do be patient, however. You should never express annoyance or hostility. An atmosphere of uncritical and confident goodwill and courtesy should prevail on both sides. Persistence is important, but pays off only if done with courtesy and quiet confidence. Business gifts are appropriate · just don't go overboard on expense or it may be interpreted as a bribe. An interesting curio from your home region, art object, or something connected to your area of business will do. Don't praise an object you see in someone's home: tradition dictates that the owner give it to you. Traditional signs of hospitality and acceptance · not to be refused are mint tea, a visit to a Turkish bath (sex segregated) and trying a water pipe (men only).

Health: It is advisable to consult your doctor before your journey. A yellow fever vaccination certificate is required from

TUNISIA

visitors who are travelling from an infected area. Vaccinations for cholera, typhoid and polio are recommended. It is recommended to drink only bottled water. It is advisable to follow all food precautions and to boil the milk. Medical insurance is advised.

Language: Arabic

TUNIS

Country code: 216 - City code: 1

Airport: Carthage International Airport.

Distance from City: 8km (4 miles) northeast of the city.

Transportation to Center of City:
From International and Domestic Terminals
By Bus (cost) TUD1. Time approx. 30 min.
By Taxi (cost) TUD5. Time approx. 15-20 min.
Tip luggage porters 300 millimes per piece

Transfers: (Minimum Connecting Time):
International to International: 45 min.
International to Domestic: 45 min.
Domestic to International: 45 min.
Domestic to Domestic: 45 min.

Automobile Rentals:
Airport car rental desk
Avis - 750299
Europcar Interrent - 233411
Hertz - 236000

Car rental city office
Avis - 798710
Europcar Interrent - 340303
Hertz - 248559

TUNISIA

Hotels:
El Hana International Tunisia, 49 Ave. Habib Bourguiba, 331144
IBN Khaldoun Hotel, 30 Rue du Koweit, 833211
L'Africa Meridien, 50 Ave. Habib Bourguiba, 347477
Les Ambassadeurs, 75 Ave. Taieb Mhiri, 288011
Majestic Hotel, 36 Ave. de Paris, 332666
Oriental Palace Hotel, Ave. Jean Jaures 29, 348846
Tunis Hilton, Ave. Ligue Arabe, Mutuellevile, 782800

Restaurants:
Chez Nous, 5 Rue de Marseille, 243043
Gaston's, 73 Rue de Yougoslavie, 340417
Istanbul, Rue Pierre Coubertin
La Mamma, 11 Rue de Marseille, 241256
Le Strasbourg, Rue de Serbie, 241139
Mac-Doly, Ave du Ghana
Restaurant Baghdad, 29 Ave Habib Bourguiba
Restaurant Carcassone, 8 Ave de Carthage
Restaurant Dar el-Jeld, 260916
Restaurant Le Cosmos, 241610
Restaurant Neptun, 3 Rue du Caire
Restaurant Saidouna, Rue Charles de Gaulle

Entertainment:
Bar Coquille, Ave de Carthage
Cabaret Protiniere, Place Barcelone, Rue de Hollande
Café de Paris, Ave Habib Bourguiba and Ave de Carthage
Gaston's, 73 Rue de Yougoslavie, 340417

Places of Interest:
The Medina – a medieval city
Djamaa Ez-Zitouna (Grand Mosque)
The Bardo Museum
The Carthage Museum
Belvedere Park
Carthage

TURKEY

Official Name: The Republic of Turkey

Location: Southeastern Europe/Southwestern Asia. Turkey is bordered by Georgia, Armenia, Iraq, Syria, Bulgaria and Greece. To the north lies the Black Sea, to the south the Mediterranean Sea and to the west the Aegean Sea.

Government: Republic

Area: 779,452 sq. km., 300,948 sq. miles.

Population: 58.5 million

Religion(s): Muslim majority with a Christian minority.

Capital City: Ankara

Major Business Cities: Istanbul, Izmir.

Time: GMT +2 (GMT +3 from late March to late October)

Currency: Turkish Lira (TRL)

Currency Requirements: There are no restrictions on the import of foreign currency although, for large amounts, a written declaration from the Turkish authorities should be obtained. No more than USD5,000 in local currency may be imported or exported.

Business Hours:
- Government: 08.30-12.00; 13.30-17.00 Mon-Fri
- Banks: 08.30-12.00 and 13.30-17.00 Mon-Fri
- Shops: 09.30-13.00 and 14.00-17.00 Mon-Sat
- Offices: 08.30-12.30 and 13.30-17.00 Mon-Fri

Weight and Measures: Metric System

Electric Current: 220 volts AC. Plugs are of the continental round 2-pin type.

Holidays:
New Year's Day - January 1
Ramazan Bayrami - February 8 (half day)-11*
National Independence Day - April 23
Kurban Bayrami - April 17 (half day)-21*
Ataturk's Commemoration Day - May 19
Victory Day - August 30
Republic Day - October 28 (half day)-29

* Muslim Bayrams are approximate, as they are timed according to local sightings of various phases of the moon.

Suitable Clothing: Modesty is important, especially for women, who should cover their shoulders and knees at all times. Wear conservative business attire. Bring sungear and light clothing in summer, and medium weight clothing, umbrella and a coat in winter. You will need sunglasses, sunhats and sunscreen year round, and a light jacket for evenings, or for the occasional rainy day between December and March. The rest of the year, light material is appropriate. When visiting a mosque, shoes are removed, and long pants or a skirt are required, (and a head covering for women). Sometimes these are provided at the entrance.

Automobile Driving License: A National License or an International Driving Permit is required.

Customs Allowances: Declare all valuables (including electronics, jewelry and cameras) and keep receipts, or they may face confiscation upon your departure. Personal items are duty free, with limits to 400 cigarettes and 5 liters of spirits. You must obtain an export license to bring out antiques. Prohibited are military weaponry and drugs with the death penalty for smuggling the latter.

Tipping: The hotels and the restaurants include a service charge in their bills. A 10-20% tip is always appreciated by waiters. Taxi drivers always appreciate a small tip.

TURKEY

Credit Cards Accepted: Access, American Express, Eurocard, Master Card, Visa

Customary Dining Hours:
Breakfast: 07.00-08.30
Lunch: 12.30-14.30
Dinner: 19.30-22.30

Local Customs, Business Protocol and Courtesies: Turkey is officially part of Europe (and ruled over much of it for centuries) and it is insulting to refer to it as part of the Middle East. It is the only Islamic country which is a secular state. Since almost everyone is Muslim (with varying degrees of observance), it is helpful to adhere to certain etiquette, such as dressing modestly and not giving alcohol as a gift. Shake hands when meeting people, and expect any meeting to begin with cups of the famous coffee. Friendly, casual conversation is the norm when developing a business relationship in Turkey. Turks are proud of their history, and showing an interest in it will serve you well in business and social situations. It is important, however, that you speak and ask questions intelligently on the subject. Much of the country's commerce is handled by governmental agencies, and you will need a local representative to deal with the bidding process. The focus in negotiations will be on credit and pricing. Use title with last name until indicated otherwise. With elders or other superiors, people use first followed by "bey" (Sir) or "Hanim" (Madam). Headings on correspondence should be "Sayin" followed by first and last name.

Turks are very hospitable. You'll frequently be invited for lunch and dinner out; meals last a long time and offer a variety of dishes that will leave you stuffed. If invited to a home, be on time and bring flowers for the hostess. Shake hands with children and bring them candy or small gifts as well. Shoes are removed in the home, and guests are served first. Follow your host's example as to when to use or not use utensils, and don't leave food on your plate or leave the table during the meal. It is important to compliment the hostess. When you're done, leave utensils across the plate on a diagonal. Don't point your feet in anyone's direction.

TURKEY

Business gifts are customary upon completing an agreement and at the New Year, such as such as an interesting curio from your home region, art object, crystal piece, or something connected to your area of business.

Health: It is advisable to consult your doctor before your journey. Vaccinations for hepatitis A, polio and typhoid are recommended. It is advisable to drink bottled water and to follow all necessary food precautions. Private health insurance is recommended.

Language: Turkish. English, French and German are widely spoken.

ANKARA

Country code: 90 - City code: 312

Airport: Esenboga Airport.

Distance from City: 28km (17 miles) northeast of the city.

Transportation to Center of City:
From International and Domestic Terminals
By Bus (cost) TRL250,000.Time approx. 30-45 min.(every 30 min)
By Taxi (cost) TRL1,000,000.
Tip luggage porters TRL5000 per piece

Transfers: (Minimum Connecting Time):
International to International: 90 min.
International to Domestic: 90 min.
Domestic to International: 90 min.
Domestic to Domestic: 30 min.

Automobile Rentals:
Airport car rental desk
Avis - 398-0315
Europcar Interrent - 398-0503
Hertz - 398-0535

Car rental city office
Avis - 467-2313
Europcar Interrent - 417-8444

Hotels:
Ankara Hilton,Tahran Cad. 12, Kavaklidere, 468-2888
Grand Hotel Ankara, Ataturk Bulvari 183, 425-6655
Ickale Hotel, Gazi Mustafa Kemal Bulvari 89, 231-7710
Kent Hotel, Mitahat Pasa Cad. 4, Yenisehir, 435-5050
Mega Residence, Tahran Cad. 5, Kavaklidere, 468-5400
Mercure Inn Ankara, Ataturk Bulvari 80, Kizilay, 417-8585
Sheraton Ankara Hotel, Noktali Sokak, Kavaklidere, 468-5454

Restaurants:
Akman Boza ve Pasta Salonu, Ulus Ishani G, Blok. 1,
     311 8755
Goksu, Bayindir Sok.22\a, 431 2219
Kale Washington, Doyran Sok.5, 311 4344
Mest, Attar Sok. 10, 468 0743
Nenehatun Washington, Nenehatun Cad. 97, 445 0212
RV, Ilbank Blok.243, Ataturk Bul., 427 4344
Zenger Pasa Konagi, Doyran Sok. 13, 311 7070

Places of Interest:
The Museum of Anatolian Civilisations
Ataturk Mausoleum

ISTANBUL

Country code: 90 - City code: 212

Airport: Ataturk International Airport (formerly Yesilkoy).

Distance from City: 25km (15 miles) west of the city.

Transportation to Center of City:
From International and Domestic Terminals
By Bus (cost) TRL200,000. Time approx. 30-45 min.

TURKEY

By Taxi (cost) TRL1,000,000. Time approx. 35 min.
Tip luggage porters TRL5000 per piece

Transfers: (Minimum Connecting Time):
International to International: 60 min.
International to Domestic: 75 min.
Domestic to International: 90 min.
Domestic to Domestic: 30 min.

Automobile Rentals:
Airport car rental desk
Avis - 663-0646
Europcar Interrent - 663-0746
Hertz - 0663-0807

Car rental city office
Avis - 257-7670
Europcar Interrent - 360-3333
Hertz - 246-2794

Hotels:
Bale Oteli Hotel, Refikasydam Cad, 62, 253-0700
Seylan Inter-Continental Istanbul, Asker Ocagi Cad, No. 1, Taksim, 231-2121
Ciregan Palace Hotel Kempinski Istanbul, Ciragan Cad. 84, Besiktas, 258-3377
Conrad International Istanbul, Yildiz Cad, Besiktas, 227-3000
Dilson Hotel, Siraseliviler Cad, 49, 252-9600
Divan Hotel, Cumhuriyet Cad, 2, Sisli, 231-4100
Erboy Hotel, Ebusuud Cad, 32, Sirkeci, 513-3750
Fuar Hotel, Namik Kemal Cad, 26, Aksaray, 589-1440
Hyatt Regency Istanbul, Taskisla Cad, Taksim, 225-7000
Istanbul Hilton, Cumhuriyet Cad, Harbiye, 231-4650
Kalyon Hotel, Sahil Yolu, Sultanahmed, 517-4400
Merit Antique Hotel Istanbul, Ordu Cad. 226, Laleli, 513-9300
Pera Palace Hotel, Mersrutiyet Cad, 98-100, 251-4560
President Hotel, Tiyatro Cad, 25, Beyazit, 516-6980
Swissotel Istanbul, The Bosphorus, Bayildim Cad, 2 Maska, 259-0101

Restaurants:
Cati, Orhan Apaydin Sok. 20\7, 251-0000

TURKEY

Club 29, Nispetiye Cad. 29, 263-5411
Develi Restaurant, Balikpazari,Gumusyuzuk Sok. 7, 585-1189
Dort Mevsim, Istiklal Cad. 509, 293-3941
Doy-Doy, Sifa Hamami Sok.13, 517-1588
Firat, Cakmaktas Sok. 11, 517-2308
Gelik, Sahilyolu 68-70, 560-7284
Haci Salih, Anadolu Han 201, 243-4528
Hacibaba, Istiklal Cad.49, 244-1886
Hanedan, Gigdem Sok. 27, 260-4854
Korfez, Korfez Cad. 78, 413-4314
Osmancik, Mesrutiyet Cad., 251-5074
Rehans, Emir Nevrut Sok. 17, 244-1610
Resat Pasa Konagi, Sinan Ercan Cad.34\1, 361-4311
Sarnic, Sogukcesme Sok., Sultanahmet, 512-4291
Tugra, Ciragan Cad. 84, 258-3377
Yakup 2, Asmali Mescit Cad. 35-37, 249-2925
Ziya, Mualim Naci Cad. 109, 261-6005

Entertainment:
2019, Talimbane 19, Taksim, 235-6197
Beyoglu Pub, Istiklal Cad. 140\17, 252-3842
Club 29, Pasabahce Yolu, Cubuklu, 322-2829
Cuba Bar, Vapur Iskelesi Sok. 20, 260-0550
Galata Tower, Kuledibi, 245-1160
Juliana's, Bayildim Cad. 2, Maca, 259-0940
Kervansaray, Cumhuriyet Cad. 30, 247-1630
Memo's, Salhane Sok. 10, 260-8491
Orient House, Tiyatro Cad. 25, 251-4560
Regine's, Cumhuriyet Cad. 16, 247-1630
Zihni, Bronz Sok. 1A, 246 -9043

Shops and Stores:
Angel Leather, Nuruosmaniye Cad. 67   Apparel
Beymen Club, Rumeli Cad. 81   Apparel
Beymen, Halaskargazi Cad. 230   Apparel
Georges Basoglu, Cevahir Bedestan 36-37   Jewelry
Nasit, Arasta Bazaar 111   Jewelry
Urart, Abdi Ipekci Cad. 181   Jewelry
Venus, Kalpakcilar Cad. 160   Jewelry
Zeki Triko, Valikonagi Cad.   Apparel

Places of Interest:
Topkapi – a palace
The Blue Mosque
St.Sophia – a museum
Rumeli Hisar
The National Park of Mount Uludag
The Ruins of Troy
The Dolmabahce Palace

IZMIR

Country code: 90 - City code: 232

Airport: Adnan Menderes Airport.

Distance from City: 25km (15 miles) south of the city.

Transportation to Center of City:
From International and Domestic Terminals
By Bus (cost) TRL150,000. Time approx. 45 min.
By Taxi (cost) TRL150,000.
Tip luggage porters TRL4000 per piece

Transfers: (Minimum Connecting Time):
International to International: 60 min.
International to Domestic: 60 min.
Domestic to International: 60 min.
Domestic to Domestic: 30 min.

Automobile Rentals:
Airport car rental desk
Avis - 251-1211
Europcar Interrent - 274-2163
Hertz - 251-3481

Car rental city office
Avis - 892226
Europcar Interrent - 425-4698
Hertz - 463-6966

TURKEY

Hotels:
Buyuk Efes Hotel, Gazi Osmanpasa Bulvari 1, 484-4300
Grand Hotel Merqure Izmir, Cumhuriyet Bulvari 138, 489-4090
Izmir Hilton, Gazi Osmanpasa Bulvari 7, 441-6060
Izmir Palas Hotel, Ataturk Blvd., 421-5583
Kismet Hotel, 1377 Sokak 9, 463-3850

Restaurants:
Altinkapi, 1444 Sok. 9, 422-5687
Deniz, Ataturk Cad. 188, 422-0601
Ilif Iskender, Gumhuriyet Bul. 194
Omur Balik Lokantasi, 902 Sok. 44, 425-6839

Entertainment:
Charlie's Cocktail Bar, 1386 Sok. 8B, 421-4981
Kubana, Kultur Park, 425-4773
Mogambo, Kultur Park, 425-5488

Places of Interest:
Kadifekale – a fortress
Cesme - a resort
Teos – ruins
Ephesus – 13th century Hellenistic and Roman city

UNITED ARAB EMIRATES

Official Name: United Arab Emirates

Location: Middle East - Persian Gulf. United Arab Emirates are bordered by the Gulf, the Musandam Peninsula, Oman, Saudi Arabia and Qatar.

Government: Federation of Emirates

Area: 77,700 sq. km., 30,000 sq. miles.

Population: 2.08 million

Religion(s): Sunni Muslim majority.

Capital City: Abu Dhabi

Major Business Cities: The Emirates are made up of seven small former Sheikhdoms formed in 1971. The largest is Abu Dhabi. The others are known as the Northern States and include Dubai, Sharjah, Ajman, Fujairah, Umm Al Qaiwain and Ras Al-Khaimah.

Time: GMT +4

Currency: UAE Dirham (ADH)=100 fils

Currency Requirements: The import and the export of both foreign and local currencies are unrestricted. Israeli currency is prohibited.

Business Hours:
- Government: 07.00 or 07.30-13.00 or 14.00 Sat-Wed, 07.00 or 07.30-12.00Thur
- Banks: 08.00-12.00/13.00 Sat-Wed, 08.00-11.00 Thur
- Shops: 09.00-13.00 and 16.30-22.00 Sat-Thur (hours vary greatly and some shops close Thur afternoons)

- Offices: 08.00-13.30 & 16.30-19.00 Sat-Thur (some close Fri and Sat)

Weight and Measures: Imperial System, Metric System and local systems

Electric Current: 220/240 volts AC. Plugs are of the square 3-pin widespread type.

Holidays:
New Year's Day - January 1
Eid-ul-fitr - February 7-9*
Eid-ul-adha - April 17-20*
Al-Hijra (Islamic New Year) - May 6*
Birthday of Muhammad - July 16*
Accession of H.H. Sheik Zayed - August 6
Lailat-ul-Isra' Wal Mir'aj - November 25*
UAE National Day - December 2-3
Christmas Day - December 25

* Muslim holidays are approximate, as they are timed according to local sightings of various phases of the moon.

Suitable Clothing: Although foreigners are not expected to, and should not, wear the traditional gowns and veils of Arab attire, modesty is of the utmost importance. The year-round desert climate requires sunglasses, sunhats and sunscreen, though you might need a raincoat between January and March. Nights are chilly, so bring along a sweater or light jacket. Otherwise, light material is appropriate, but men should make sure it covers knees and shoulders, while women should wear skirts or dresses which cover the knees, elbows and neckline as well. A business suit should be worn to all meetings.

Automobile Driving License: An International Driving Permit is recommended. Local license can be issued on presentation of a valid National Driving License. A letter from the visitor's sponsor is also required.

Customs Allowances: No limits exist on foreign currency or Dirham, as long as what you export was initially declared. Note customs differences between Abu Dhabi, Dubai and Sharjah;

you may bring unrestricted amounts into Sharjah, 200 cigarettes into Abu Dhabi, and 100 into Dubai. Check alcohol limits, which often change, but generally speaking, 1 liter is the limit, though it is prohibited outright in Sharjah. Prohibited are military weaponry, narcotics, and pornography.

Tipping: Service charges of 15% are added to most restaurant and hotel bills and tipping in this case is unnecessary. Metered cabs might warrant a rounding up of the fare. A small change is sufficient for porters etc.

Credit Cards Accepted: American Express, Diner's Club, Eurocard, MasterCard, Visa

Customary Dining Hours:
Breakfast: 07.30-09.00
Lunch: 12.30-14.30
Dinner: 20.00-22.00

Local Customs, Business Protocol and Courtesies: Although it is more liberal that its huge neighbor Saudi Arabia, one should, out of courtesy and a practical view towards business, adhere to basic Muslim rules and local etiquette. This tiny Persian Gulf principality has a booming business climate, investing heavily abroad in high technology as well as its native oil industry. Schedule appointments in advance, and be on time. Your contact may be late, but you should never express annoyance or hostility. Your contemporaries are quite sophisticated, and an atmosphere of confident goodwill and courtesy should prevail on both sides. Persistence is important, but pays off only if done courteously and with quiet confidence. Business should be conducted in person as much as possible, and expect lengthy, sociable discussions and careful review of any proposals. Do not expect any instant answers. Even written contracts may be brought up for renegotiation later. It's important to note a tendency toward dealing directly with foreign executives and suppliers; if you are a mid-level or lower-level intermediary or subcontractor, your company's proposals may meet with disdain. Companies tend to use one importer exclusively. Although English is widely spoken in the business community, your effort to provide company literature in Arabic will make a good impression. Always use the appropriate titles: Sheik and Sheikha (plus first name) with male and female members, respectively, of a ruling family. An emir (prince) may also be referred to as "Your Highness" or "Your Excellency." Otherwise, Mr., Mrs. or Miss are appropriate. Men shake hands; with a woman, nod your head upon introduction, or shake hands only if she offers hers. Business gifts are not necessary, but a nice gesture on your part, such as an interesting curio from your home region, art object, or something connected to your area of business. Be sincerely patient, for any meeting will be accompanied by the traditional rituals of hospitality. It is considered rude to refuse the coffee and food that will be offered, except at Ramadan, when polite refusal will be appreciated, since your hosts themselves cannot eat until sundown. During this period, don't eat in public during the day. If it is important that your discussions not be interrupted by other visitors, try to arrange meeting more privately at a coffeehouse.

At meals or when socializing, it's best to follow the example of your host as to whether to eat with one's fingers or use utensils. Southpaws beware: there is a strong taboo against eating or drinking with one's left hand (traditionally, the hand used for toilet activities), although you may use both hands if given a knife and fork. Also, if crossing your legs, make sure your feet or soles are not visibly pointing in anyone's direction. Refrain from comment as much as possible on Middle East politics, and don't mention women, even from your host's family, at all. Always ask permission when photographing a person or a place, especially a mosque.

Health: It is advisable to consult your doctor before your journey. Vaccinations for typhoid, polio, hepatitis A and tetanus are recommended. It should be safe to drink tap water, but a caution is recommended especially outside the major cities. The facilities are of a very high standard, but they are also extremely expensive. Medical insurance is advised.

Language: Arabic. English is widely spoken.

UNITED ARAB EMIRATES

ABU DHABI

Country code: 971 - City code: 2

Airport: Abu Dhabi (Nadia) International Airport.

Distance from City: 37km (22 miles) southeast of the city.

Transportation to Center of City:
From International and Domestic Terminals
By Bus (cost) ADH3. Time approx. 45-60 min.
By Taxi (cost) ADH 45-55. Time approx. 30 min.
Tip luggage porters 1.5 Dirhams per piece

Transfers: (Minimum Connecting Time):
International to International: 60 min.
International to Domestic: 60 min.
Domestic to International: 60 min.
Domestic to Domestic: 60 min.

Automobile Rentals:
Airport car rental desk
Avis - 757180
Europcar Interrent - 757183

Car rental city office
Avis - 323760
Europcar Interrent - 319922

Hotels:
Abu Dhabi Gulf Hotel, P.O.Box 3766, 414777
Abu Dhabi International Hotel, Hamdan St., 779900
Al Ain Palace Hotel, P.O.Box33, 794777
Baynunah Hilton Tower, Corniche Rd., 327777
Corniche Residence, P.O.Box6677, 211200
Dana Hotel, P.O.Box 47300, 761000
Delma Centre, Hamdan St., 332100
Emirates Plaza Hotel, P.O.Box 5295, 722000
Federal Hotel, Khalifa St., 789000
Forte Grand Abu Dhabi, P. O. Box 45505, 742020
Habara House , P.O.Box 47173, 431010

UNITED ARAB EMIRATES

Hilton International, P.O.Box 877, 661900
Holiday Inn Abu Dhabi, Zayed the Second St., 335335
Khalida Palace Hotel, P.O.Box 4010, 662470
Le Meridien Abu Dhabi, P. O. Box 46066, 776666
Mina Hotel, P.O.Box 44421, 781000
Novotel Centre Hotel Abu Dhabi, Hamdan St., 333555
Oasis Residence, P.O.Box 46336, 351000
Sheraton Abu Dhabi Resort & Towers, Corniche Rd., 773333
Zakher Hotel, Umm Al Naar St., 341940

Restaurants:
Siraj Restaurant, Zayed the Second St.
Talk of the Town, Shaikh Khalifa Bin Zayed St.
Bhavna Restaurant, Zayed the Second St.
Tarbouche, Shaikh Hamdan Bin Mohammed St. Maroosh
Shaikh Hamdan Bin Mohammed & As-Salam St.
Sarawan Restaurant, Zayed the Second St.
La Brioche, Shaikh Hamdan Bin Mohammed St.
Mandarin Restaurant, Zayed The First St.
Foodlands, Zayed the Second St.
Al-Dhafra, Dhow Wharf near the fish market
El Sombrero, Sheraton Hotel

Entertainment:
Al Finjan, Le Meridien, 776666
Al Karya, Sheraton Hotel, 7030240
Al Sahara Night Club International Hotel, 779900
Bounty, Jazira Beach Resort, 5629100
Cozy Corner, Jazira Beach Resort, 5629100
Diwan Nightclub Emirates Plaza, 722000
Jhankar, Emirates Plaza, 722000
Manila Bay Disco, Emirates Plaza, 722000
Monbasa, Emirates Plaza, 722000
Talk of the Town Khalidia Palace, 622470
Tiffany Bar, Khalidia Palace, 662470

Shops and Stores:
Al Ahlia Prisunic, P.O Box 4033   Shoping Center
Ayoun Al Reem, Centre and Salon, P.O Box 15155   Apparel
Zakher Shopping Center, P.O.Box 932   Shopping Center
Ajman, Ajman Souk, P.O.Box 2585   Market

Places of Interest:
The Diwan Amiri (White Fort)
The Blue Mosque
The Cultural Foundation – exhibits, a library and a gallery.
The Eastern Fort
Hili Gardens – a park and an archaeological site.
Hili Fun City and Ice Rink – an amusement park.
Al-Ain - camel market, a zoo and museum
Um al Nar
Deep Sea Fishing Safari Tours
Dhow Trips

DUBAI

Country code: 971 - City code: 4

Airport: Dubai International Airport.

Distance from City: 4km (2 miles) southeast of the city.

Transportation to Center of City:
From International and Domestic Terminals
By Bus (cost) ADH1. Approx. time 20-30 min.
By Taxi (cost) ADH 30-45. Time approx. 10-15 min.
Tip luggage porters 1.5 Dirhams per piece

Transfers: (Minimum Connecting Time):
International to International: 60 min.
International to Domestic: 60 min.
Domestic to International: 60 min.
Domestic to Domestic: 60 min.

Automobile Rentals:
Airportcar rental desk
Avis - 245219
Europcar Interrent - 245240
Hertz - 245222

Car rental city office
Avis - 282121

Europcar Interrent - 835632
Hertz - 824422

Hotels:
Al Ahrar Hotel, P.O.Box 12978, 271000
Al Aman Hotel, P.O.Box 8187 265188
Al Butien Plaza, P.O.Box 8384, 263888
Ambassador Hotel, Al Falah St., 531000
Astoria Hotel, P. O. Box 457, 534300
Avon Hotel, P.O.Box 1041, 258877
Carlton Tower Hotel, Beniyas St., 227111
Claridge Hotel, P. O. Box 1833, 716666
Concord Palace, P.O.Box 7052, 512555
Dubai Marine Hotel & Beach Resort, Khalid Bin Walid St., 520900
Forte Grand Dubai, P. O. Box 10001, 824040
Four Points Hotel Dubai, P. O. Box 5772, 688888
Golden Tulip Maredias Hotel, Salahdin Rd., 289393
Hyatt Regency Hotel, P. O. Box 5588, 221234
Inter-Continental Dubai, Beniyas St., 227171
Novotel Dubai, Al Mateena St., 720000
Palm Beach Hotel, Khalid Bin Waleed St., 525550
Princeton, Al Garhoud, 827777
Ramada Hotel Dubai, Adj. Rais Ctre, Bur Dubai, 521010
Riviera Hotel, Beniyas St., 222131
Royal Abjar Hotel, P. O. Box 8668, 625555
Sheraton Dubai Hotel, Beniyas St.(Creek Rd.), 281111

Restaurants:
Golden Fork, Beniyas Square, between Phoenicia & Rex hotels
Hatam Restaurant, Beniyas Square
Pizza Corner, Beniyas Rd.
Cafeteria Al-Abra, Al-Sabkha & Beniyas Rd.
Popeye, Al-Sabkha & Beniyas Rd
Pillars, Phoenicia Hotel, Beniyas Square
Gulf Restaurant & Cafeteria, Al-Sabkha Rd. & Diera St.
Sadaf, Al-Maktoum Rd.
The pub, Intercontinental Hotel
Villa Veduta, Intercontinental Hotel
Da Pino , Al-Khaleej Hotel

Entertainment:
Al-Nakheel, Carlton Tower, 227111

Al-Sayyad, Claridge Hotel, 227141
Alamo, The Dubai Marine Beach Club, 441221
Amy's Key Club, Airport Hotel, 823464
Atlantic, Nihal, 278800
Bangkok Cellat, Highland Lodge, 824040
Baron's Table, Peninsula, 533000
Boardwalk, The Dubai Creek and Yacht Club, 825777
Butterfly Night Club, Carlton Tower, 227111
Carlton Pub, The Carlton Tower, 227111
Cheers Bar, Highland Lodge, 379470
Constellation Bar, Aviation Club, 824122
Crazy Horse Regent Palace, 535555

Shops and Stores:

Abu Hail, P.O.Box 5005	Shopping Center
Al Dhiyafah, Centre,	Shopping Center
Al Ghurair, P.O.Box 69999	Shopping Center
Al Manal Centre, P.O.Box 4455	Shopping Center
Al Mulla Plaza, P.O.Box 59	Mall
Beach Centre, P.O.Box 53500	Shopping Center
Bur Jumain, P.O.Box 8022	Shopping Center
The Centre, P.O.Box 1714	Shopping Center
City Centre, P.O.Box 60811	Shopping Center
Magrudy's Shopping Mall, P.O.Box 1155	Mall
Wafi Shopping Mall, P.O.Box 721	Mall
Jumaira Plaza, P.O.Box9287	Shopping Mall

Places of Interest:

Sikket-El-Kheil Souk - a market and a museum
Hatta – an ancient village
Dubai Creek Golf Club
The Dubai Museum
Shaikh Saeed's House – a museum
Bur Dubai

ASIA

CHINA

Official Name: Zhonghua Renmin (People's Republic of China)

Location: Far East. China is bordered by Vietnam, Laos, Myanmar, Bhutan, Nepal, India, Pakistan, Afghanistan, CIS, Mongolia, and North Korea. The China Sea and the Yellow Sea lie on its East Coast.

Government: Socialist Republic

Area: 9,571,300 sq. km., 3,695,500 sq. miles.

Population: 1.188 billion

Religion(s): Buddhism, Daoism and Confucianism. There are also Muslim, Protestant and Roman Catholic minorities.

Capital City: Beijing (Peking)

Major Business Cities: Guangzhou (Canton), Macau and Shanghai.

Time: GMT +8

Currency: 1 Yuan (Remninbi CNY)=10 chiao/jiao or 100 fen

Currency Requirements: The import and the export of local currency is prohibited. The import and the export of foreign currency is unlimited and must be declared. The exchange of foreign currency must be done only at the Bank of China or its currency exchange offices. It is recommended that a record of all transaction details is retained.

Business Hours:
- Government: 08.00-12.00; 13.30-17.00 Mon-Sat
- Banks: 09.30-12.00; 13.30-17.00 Mon-Sat

- Shops: 09.00-17.00 Mon-Sat
- Offices: 08.00/08.30-11.30/12.00; 13.30/14.00-17.00/18.00 Mon-Sat

Weight and Measures: Metric System and some Chinese units.

Electric Current: 220-240 volts AC. Most hotel rooms have 2-pin sockets.

Holidays:
Founding of the Republic of China - January 1
Chinese Lunar New Year - February 6-9
Youth Day - March 29
Children's Day - April 4
Tomb-Sweeping Day and Death of President Chiang Kai-shek (1975) - April 5
Dragon Boat Festival - June 9
Mid-Autumn (Moon) Festival - September 16
Teacher's Day (Confucius' Birthday) - September 28
Double Tenth National Day - October 10
Taiwan Retrocession Day - October 25
Birthday of President Chiang Kai-shek (1887) - October 31
Dr. Sun Yat-sen's Birthday - November 12
Constitution Day - December 25

Suitable Clothing: Due to China's geographical diversity, it's best to check the climate of the individual regions you will be traveling to. In much of the country, however, light to medium-weight material will do, except for winter, when you should bring warm clothes and a coat. Raingear is useful in most areas and times of year. A conservative, neat appearance is of the utmost importance. A business suit or business-like dress should be worn to all meetings and functions.

Customs Allowances: Declare all valuables or they may face confiscation upon your departure. Personal items are duty free. You may bring in, duty free, up to 600 cigarettes and a liter of spirits. Film is restricted to 72 rolls or 3000 feet. Import and export of local currency is prohibited, but no limits exist on foreign currency, as long as what you export was initially declared. If you purchase antiquities, you must obtain official permits to bring them home. Strict censorship in China means that most material against the regime will be confiscated. Also prohibited are weaponry, drugs, pornography and agricultural products.

Tipping: Tipping is well established and a service charge is usually included in the bills.

Credit Cards Accepted: American Express, Diner's Club, JCB, MasterCard, Visa

Customary Dining Hours:
Breakfast: 07.00-08.30
Lunch: 12.00-13.30
Dinner: 18.30-22.30

Local Customs, Business Protocol and Courtesies: A successful business endeavor in China will require two elements in particular: finding helpful officials and maintaining patience over the long term. Since the economy is tightly state-controlled, any contacts you make should be done through the various ministries handling business. In Beijing, the Ministry of Foreign Trade controls all import/export firms and organizations. For contacts in specific regions or free-enterprise zones, you can get information from the local offices of the Ministries of Commerce, Foreign Affairs or Foreign Trade and Economic Cooperation. Your Chinese counterparts will expect you to have thorough knowledge of your product and any competition; bring along experts to vouch for your product and whether its market is lucrative. Presentations must be detailed, executed with calm, confident but low-key style. Negotiations will invariably focus on credit terms and pricing. Be warned, too, that it is much harder to sell to China than to buy its products. However, once agreement is reached, the word of a Chinese businessman or official is as good as his signature or stamp on a contract.

In this red-taped-up country, patience is most important. You may have to wait many months before getting decisions, which are made by committees. Expect to make several trips to the country before a contract is finalized. When visiting, schedule appointments in advance and be punctual. If you are in a group meeting, the person with highest rank is introduced first. Do not shake hands (unless a hand is offered) or make any other physical contact; rather, bow your head slightly. You should have business cards in English and Mandarin; present it with both hands, Mandarin side up. Use Mr., Mrs. or Miss with the family name. If applauded by a group, join in, and give a thank you with a smile. In general, polite persistence pays off. On your part, smiling is important in the face of bureaucracy and to maintain general goodwill, but keep in mind that your Chinese counterparts will keep smiling even in a negative or apologetic situation-such as failure or embarrassment. Be warned, too, that any gesture on your part which causes your contact to "lose face," will hurt the relationship. Avoid discussing political subjects (which could offend officials or hurt civilians), and keep in mind that the Chinese do not look kindly upon Western men becoming friendly with Chinese women. Also, do not photograph military or major infrastructure, museums and archeological sites.

In this society which honors gift-giving, it is important to remember the rules and taboos that go with it. When visiting a home (an honor that should not be refused), wrap your gift in red which means celebration, not white, which means death. English-language books, art books, or good liqueur, chocolates or tobacco will do, but don't give bad-luck gifts like knives, clocks, or anything grouped by four. White flowers are for funerals. Also, don't take seriously the "oh, you shouldn't have' response; keep offering until the gift is accepted. You will most certainly be presented with gifts as well during your trip, but do not open them. Business gifts are customary upon first meeting and upon completion of a successful deal. If you have a company gift, present it to the highest-ranking member of the company in a group situation.

Business/social functions in restaurants are frequent and will leave you stuffed. A ten-course meal is typical; after the first appetizer, the host will offer a toast. It is customary to empty your cup then; with any subsequent toasts (you should make a thank-you toast toward the end of the meal), a sip will suffice. Wait until your host begins eating before you begin. Most Western restaurants will provide forks and

CHINA

knives, if requested. Western visitors are not expected to eat with chopsticks, but it will look good to your counter-parts if you are able to. To eat properly from a rice bowl, raise it to your chin. Spoons are used for soup. For most other dishes, chopsticks are used. Do not cross them, rath-er, lay them side by side by your plate or across the rim. Your host will likely criticize the food and service, which is the customary way of saying that nothing is good enough for the guest. Agreeing with him would be offensive. No matter how excellent the food is, leave a little food on your plate; eating every bite is considered bad manners. Don't be offended if your companions burp; it is a sign of satis-faction. The Chinese rarely drink without food, and they drink beer and soda straight out of the bottle. Tea is served after the meal, and most leave right afterwards.

Health: It is advisable to consult your doctor before your journey. Vaccinations for hepatitis A, tetanus, typhoid, polio and malaria are recommended. It is necessary to have a vaccination certificate for Yellow Fever if traveling from an infected area. Medical insurance is recommended.

Language: Mandarin Chinese and other dialects.

BEIJING

Country code: 86 - City code: 10

Airport: Beijing Capital International Central Airport

Distance from City: 28km (17 miles) northeast of the city.

Transportation to Center of City:
From International and Domestic Terminals
By Bus (cost) CNY8-12. Time approx. 50-75 min.
By Taxi (cost) CNY15-22. Time approx. 35-45 min.
Tip luggage porters CNY1 per piece

Transfers: (Minimum Connecting Time):
International to International: 90 min.

CHINA

International to Domestic: 90 min.
Domestic to International: 90 min.
Domestic to Domestic: 90 min.

Hotels:
Asia Jin Jiang Hotel, 8 Xinzhong Xi Jie, 6500-7788
Beijing International Hotel, 9 Jianguomen Nei Dajie, 6512-6688
Capital Hotel Beijing, 3 Qian Men East St., 6512-9988
China World Hotel, 1 Jianguomen Wai Ave., 6505-2266
Gloria Plaza Hotel Beijing, 2 Jianguomennan Ave., 6515-8855
Grand Hotel, East Chang An Ave. 35, 6513-7788
Holiday Inn Crowne Plaza Beijing, 6513-3388
Jianguo Hotel Beijing, 5 Jianguomen Wai Dajie, 6500-2233
Jing Guang New World Hotel, Hu Jia Lou, Chao Yang Qu,
    6501-8888
New Otani Chang Fu Gong Hotel, 26 Jianguomen Wai Dajie,
6512-5555
Overseas Chinese Prime Hotel, 2 Wangfujing Ave., 6513-6666
Palace Hotel Beijing, 8 Goldfish Lane, Wangfujing, 6512-8899
Swisshotel Beijing, Hong Kong Macau Center, 6501-2288
Traders Hotel, 1 Jianguomen Wai Ave., 6505-2277
Zhaolong Hotel, 2 Worker's Stadium Rd. N., 6500-2299

Restaurants:
Beijing Quangude Roast Duck Restaurant, Xinhua Nan Street,
334422
Bianyifang Roast Duck Restaurant, 2 Chongwenmen Avenue,
750505
Cui Hua Lou, 60 Wangfujing, 554581
Donglaishin Restaurant, 16 Jinyu Hutung, 550069
Fang Shan, Qiong Hua Island in Bei Hai Lake, 441184
Feng Ze Yuan, 83 Zhushikou Street, 332828
Hongbinlou Restaurant, 82 Changan Boulevard West 656404
Huai Yang Fan Zhuang, 217 Xdan Bei Road, 660521
Jin Yang, 241 Zhu Shi Kou Road, 334361
Kang Le, 259 Andingmen Nei Road, 442015
Kou Rou Ji, 14 Qianhai Dongyan, 445921
Lili Restaurant, 30 Oianmen Road, 752310
Sha Guo Ju 60 Xisinandajie, 661126
Sichuan Restaurant, 51 West Rong Xian Lane, 656348
Tong He Ju, 3 Xisi Nan Road, 666357

CHINA

Entertainment:
Berena's Bistro, 6 Gongren Tiyuchang Donglu, 592-2628
Café Café, Dongdaqiaoxie Jie, 507-1331 ext. 5127
Frank's Place, Gongren Tiyuchang Donglu, 507-2617
Hard Rock Café, 8 Dongsanhuan Beilu, 501-6688
Jazz Ya, 18 Sanlitun Beilu, 415-1227
JJ's Disco, 74 Xinjiekou Bei Dajie, 607-9691
Local Joint, Yong'anxili, 595-7687
NASA Disco, b/n Xitucheng Lu & Xueyuan Lu, 201-6622
Rasput Inn, 1 Sanlitun Lu, 507-1331 ext. 5050
Schiller's Bar & Restaurant, Liangmahe Nanlu, 461-9276
Sophia's Choice, 40 Liangmaqiao Lu, 500-4466
Underground Club, 1A Jianguomenwai, 506-4466 ext. 6196
Water Hole, 3 Guanghuaxili, 507-4761

Shops and Stores:

Beijing Department Store, Wangfujing	Dept. Store
Beijing Hunxia Arts , 249 Dongsi Nan str.	Theatre Shop
Dong Feng, Wangfujing	Dept. Store
Friendship Store, Chang An Jie	Jewelry
Jianhua Fur Shop, 192 Wangfujing	Furs
Xidan Emporium, 120 North Xidan Road	Dept. Store

Places of Interest:
The Museums of the Chinese Revolution and Chinese History
Tiananmen Gate - a monument.
The Forbidden City - towers, palaces, the Imperial Library
The Temple of Heaven
The Ming Tombs
Summer Palace - palaces, pavilions, a lake and a restaurant
The Ancient Observatory (Guguanxiangtai)
The National Art Gallery
Beijing Zoo
The Great Wall - a monument

HONG KONG

Official Name: Hong Kong.

Location: Far East. Hong Kong is located in the South China Sea, joining the southeast coast of China.

Area: 1084 sq. km., 419 sq. miles.

Population: 6.3 million

Religion(s): Buddhism, Confucianism and Taoism. There are also Muslim and Christian minorities.

Major Business Cities: Victoria, Kowloon, Tsuen Wan

Time: GMT +8

Currency: Hong Kong Dollar HKD=100 Cents

Currency Requirements: There are no restrictions on the import and the export of local or foreign currency.

Business Hours:
- Government: 09.00-17.00 Mon-Fri, 09.00-13.00 Sat
- Banks: 09.00-17.00 Mon-Fri; 09.00-13.00 Sat
- Shops: 09.00-17.00 Mon-Fri, 09.00-13.00 Sat
- Offices: 09.00-17.00 Mon-Fri, 09.00-13.00 Sat

Weight and Measures: Metric System

Electric Current: 200/220 volts AC 50 cycles. Plugs are of the round 3-pin type, but most hotels provide adapters.

Holidays:
Western New Year's Day - January 1
Lunar New Year - February 6-8
Easter - April 10-13*
Ching Ming Festival - April 5

HONG KONG

Tuen Ng Festival - June 9
Her Majesty the Queen's Birthday - June 28
Monday following the Queen's Birthday - June 30
Hong Kong Returning to China, SAR Establishment Day
- July 1
Day following SAR Establishment Day - July 2
Sino-Japanese War Victory Day - August 18
Day following Chinese Mid-Autumn Fest. - September 17
National Day - October 1
Day following National Day - October 2
Chung Yeung Festival - October 10
Christmas Day - December 25
First week-day after Christmas Day - December 26

*Christian Holidays - vary each year

Suitable Clothing: Light to medium-weight material will do year round, and bring rainwear and sungear. A conservative, neat appearance is of the utmost importance. A business suit or business-like dress should be worn to all meetings and functions.

Automobile Driving License: An International Driving License is recommended.

Customs Allowances: Declare all valuables or they may face confiscation upon your departure. Personal items are duty free. You may bring in, duty free, up to 600 cigarettes and a liter of spirits. Film is restricted to 72 rolls or 3000 feet. Import and export of local currency is prohibited, but no limits exist on foreign currency, as long as what you export was intially declared. If you purchase antiquities, you must obtain official permits to bring them home. Strict censorship in China means that most material against the regime will be confiscated. Also prohibited are weaponry, drugs, pornography and agricultural products.

Tipping: Most hotels and restaurants add a 10% service charge (hotels levy 5% tax). A tip of 10% is accepted if it is not already included in the bill.

Credit Cards Accepted: American Express, Diner's Club, JCB, MasterCard, Visa

HONG KONG

Customary Dining Hours:
Breakfast: 07.30-09.00
Lunch: 13.00-14.30
Dinner: 19.00-23.00

Local Customs, Business Protocol and Courtesies: Although Hong Kong is very cosmopolitan, with businessmen from all over the world and very sophisticated, sticking to certain Chinese traditions and customary behavior is helpful in most situations. In any case, you should have a local representative to break you into Hong Kong business circles. Schedule in advance for business and official meetings. Use the title of your contact with family name until told otherwise; if the business card you receive doesn't give you the title, use Mr. or Madame with family name. Shake hands or nod head to everyone present, in order of rank. In general, persistence pays off, but be polite and good-natured. Be warned, too, that any gesture on your part which causes your contact to "lose face," will hurt the relationship. Avoid discussing political subjects (which could offend officials or hurt civilians). Be ready for intense bargaining, and although written contracts are important, the Hong Kong businessman is usually as good as his word. Since Hong Kong is considered Asia's godown, (warehouse), you should deliver early or on time if importing, since your partner will likely have a long list of deliveries to or from other companies. Get local advice about labeling and take it seriously. For example, don't package in blue or white, which are traditional mourning colors. Use green, gold or red. Same as when wrapping a gift. When visiting a home (an honor that should not be refused), appropriate gifts are English-language books, art books, good liqueur (unless the recipient is Muslim), chocolates or tobacco, don't give bad-luck items like knives, clocks, or anything grouped by four. White flowers are for funerals. In some homes, shoes are removed. Send a thank you note before you leave Hong Kong.

Business/social functions in restaurants are frequent but women are often excluded. A ten-course meal is typical; after the first appetizer, the host will offer a toast. It is customary to empty your cup then; with any subsequent toasts

HONG KONG

(you should make a thank-you toast toward the end of the meal), a sip will suffice. Wait until your host begins eating before you begin. Your host will likely criticize the food and service, which is the customary way of saying that nothing is good enough for the guest. Agreeing with him would be offensive. Most restaurants provide forks and knives, if requested. Western visitors are not expected to eat with chopsticks, but it will look good to your counterparts if you are able to. To eat properly from a rice bowl, raise it to your chin. Spoons are used for soup. For most other dishes, chopsticks are used. Do not cross them, rather, use the chopstick rests that are provided.

Health: It is advisable to consult your doctor before traveling. Vaccinations for tetanus, typhoid and polio are recommended, but not essential. There is a reciprocal Health Agreement with the UK on presentation of a valid passport and an NHS card, for free emergency treatment at certain hospitals and clinics. There is a small charge for other treatments. A Medical insurance is recommended.

Language: Chinese

HONG KONG

Country code: 852 - City code: none

Airport: Hong Kong-Kai Tak International Airport

Distance from City: 7.5km (4 miles) northeast of Hong Kong Island.

Transportation to Center of City:
From International and Domestic Terminals
By Bus (cost) HKD12.30-19. Time approx. 25-35 min.
By Taxi (cost) HKD70-90. Time approx.30-40 min.
Tip luggage porters HKD10 per piece

Automobile Rentals:
Avis - 25766831

Hotels:

Century Hong Kong Hotel, 238 Jaffe Rd., Wanchai, 2598-8888

Charterhouse Hotel, 209-219 Wanchai Rd, Wanchai, 2833-5566

Conrad International Hong Kong, 88 Queensway, Pacific Pl., 2521-3838

Empire Hotel, 33 Hennessy Rd., Wanchai, 2866-9111

Excelsior Hotel, 281 Gloucester Rd., Causeway Bay, 2894-8888

Furama Kempinski Hotel Hong Kong, 1 Cannaught Rd, Central, 2525-5111

Island Shangri-La Hong Kong, Pacific Pl., Supreme Court Rd, Central, 2877-3838

JW Marriott Hotel Hong Kong, 88 Queensway, Pacific Pl., 2810-8366

Luk Kwok Hotel, 72 Gloucester Rd, Wanchai, 2866-2166

Mandarin Oriental Hotel, 5 Connaught Rd, 2522-0111

New World Harbour View Hotel, 1 Harbour Rd, 2802-8888

Park Lane Hong Kong, 310 Gloucester Rd., 2890-3355

Regal Hong Kong Hotel, 88 Yee Wo St., Causeway Bay, 2890-6633

Ritz-Carlton Hong Kong, 3 Connaught Rd, Central, 2877-6666

Wharney Hotel Hong Kong, 57-73 Lockhart Rd, Wanchai, 2861-1000

Restaurants:

Ah Lee Leng Tong Restaurant, 503-505 Lockhart Road, Causeway Bay, 2834 3480

Broadway Seafood, Hay Wah Building, 73-85B Hennessy Rd., Wan Chai, 2529 9233

Canton Room, 1/f, Luk Kwok Hotel, 72 Gloucester Rd., Wan Chai, 2866 2166

Chee Kee Wonton Noodles Shop, 50-52 Russell St., Causeway Bay, 2575 6522

Chang Fa Kong Seafood, 6Fl., Causeway Bay, Plaza II, 463 Lockhart Rd., Causeway Bay, 2572 6288

Cityplaza Harbour Restaurant, Unit 255, City Plaza II, Taikoo Shing, 1111 Kings Road, Quarry Bay, 2884 4188

Diamond Restaurant, 267-275 Des Voeux Road, Central, 2544 4708

East Ocean Seafood, 3 Fl., Harbour Centre, 25 Harbour Rd., Wan Chai, 2827 8887

Fook Lam Moon Restaurant, 35-45 Johnston Rd., Wan Chai, 2866 0663

Guangzhou Garden, 2Fl.,Two Exchange Sq., 8 Connaught Place, Central, 2525 1163

Jade Garden, Swire House, 11 Chater Rd., Central, 2526 3031

Jumbo Floating Restaurant, Shum Wan, Wong Chuk Hang, Aberdeen, 2553 9111

Luk Yu Tea House and Restaurant, 26 Stanley St., Central, 2523 5464

New Cathay Seafood, 9 Tung Lo Wan Road, Causeway Bay, 2577 4838

North Point Fung Shing, 62-6568 Java Road, North Point, 2578 4898

Ser Wong Fun, 30 Cochrane St., Central, 2543 1032

Tai Woo Restaurant, 15-19 Wellington St., Central, 2524 5618

Yung Kee Restaurant, 32-40 Wellington Street, Central, 2522 1624

Bamboo Village, Shoop Nos. 3-10, G/F, Tonnochy Towers, 2827 1188

Entertainment:

Brewery Tap Pub and Restaurant, Shop A-D, Vogue Alley, 66-72 Paterson St., Causeway, 2576 2075

Bull & Bear, Hutchinson House, 10 Harcourt Rd., Central, 2525 7436

China City Night Club, 4/F Peninsula Centre, 67 Mody Rd., Tsim Sha Tsui East, 2723-3278

Club 1997, G/F Cosmos Building 9-11 Lan Kwai Fong, Central, 2810-933]

Club Celebrity, 1/F 175-191 Lockhart Rd, Wan Chai, 2575-7161

Club Bottoms Up, Basement, 14016 Hankow Rd, Tsim Sha Tsui, 2721-4509

Club Cabaret, 1st Basement, New World Centre, 18 Salisbury Rd., Tsim Sha Tsui, 2369-8431

Delaney's – The Irish Pub, 2/F One Capitan Place, 18 Luard Rd., Wan Chai, 2804-2880

Joe Bananas, G/F Shiu Lam Building, 23 Luard Rd., Wan Chai, 2529-1811

La Dolce Vita 97, G/F Cosmos Building, 9-11 Lan Kwai Fong, Central, 2810-9333

Latino Bar, Shop B-2-22B, Basement 2, New World Centre, 18 Salisbury Rd., Tsim Sha Tsui, 2369-8571

Lord Stanley's Bistro & Bar, 92A Stanley Main St., Stanley, 2813-8562

Mad Dogs Kowloon, Basement, 32 Nathan Rd., Tsim Sha Tsui, 2301-2222

Mandarin Palace Night Club, 24-28 Marsh Rd., Wan Chai, 2575-6551

Ned Kelly's Last Stand, 11A Ashley Rd., Tsim Sha Tsui, 2376-0562

New Tonnochy Night Club, 105 Tonnochy Rd., Wan Chai, 2511-1383

Rick's Café, G/F 78-82 Jaffe Rd., Wan Chai, 2528-1812

Shops and Stores:

Aberdeen Jewelry Factory Ltd., Flat G, 1/F, Block 2, 33 Yip Kan St., Wong Hang   Jewelry

Alered Dunhill Ltd., 5 Ice House St., Central   Apparel

Boutique Bazaar, G/F Swire House, Chater Rd, Central   Apparel

Boutique Bazaar, Shop 110, 1/F The Landmark, 16 Des Voeux Rd C., Central   Apparel

Boutique Cristian Dior, G/F, St. George's Building, 2 Ice House St., Central   Apparel

Chanel Boutique, 6 & 6A,, G/F, Prince's Building, 3 Des Voeux Rd., Central   Apparel

Dabera Ltd., 28/F Admiralty Centre, Tower 1, 18 Harcourt Rd., Central   Jewelry

Favorite Jewellers, 140A, 1/F, Prince's Bldg., 10 Chater Rd, Central

Gentlemen Givenchi, Gloucester Tower, The Landmark, 11 Pedder St., Central   Apparel

Hong Kong Daimaru Department Store, 1/F Paterson St., Causeway Bay   Dept. Store

Hugo, Basement, the Landmark, Centrall   Apparel

International Pearl Centre Ltd., G/F, Hankow Centre, 49 Peking Rd., Tsim Sha Tsui   Jewelry

Kitty Ivory & Jewelry Shop, B1-8, New World Centre, 18-24 Salisbury Road   Jewelry

Pink Box, Shop 2, Level 1, The Peak Galleria, 118 Peak Rd. The Peak   Jewelry

Seibu Department Store, Two Pacific Place, 88 Queensway, Central   Dept. Store

Wan Hing Jewelry & Arts Co, AR216, 1/F, 130 Nathan Rd., Tsim Sha Tsui   Jewelry

HONG KONG

Places of Interest:
Space Museum
Museum of History
Kowloon Mosque
Hong Kong Science Museum
Sung (Song) Dynasty Village
Hong Kong Museum of Art
Zoological and Botanical Gardens
Ocean Park
Water World - water park
Museum of Chinese Historical Relics

INDIA

Official Name: Union of India

Location: Southern Asia. India is bordered by Pakistan, China, Nepal, Bhutan, Bangladesh and Myanmar.

Government: Federal Republic

Area: 3,287,262 sq. km., 1,269,218 sq. miles.

Population: 882.95 million

Religion(s): Hindu majority. Muslim, Sikhs, Buddhists, Christians, Jains, Parsees and other minorities are present.

Capital City: New Delhi

Major Business Cities: Bombay, New Delhi, Calcutta, Madras

Time: GMT +5.30

Currency: Rupee (INR)=100 paise

Currency Requirements: The import of foreign currency must be declared if the value exceeds USD10,000 and a form will be endorsed or a certificate issued. The export of foreign currency is limited to the amount declared on the arrival and the form or the certificate issued will be required. The import and the export of local currency is prohibited except for Rupee Travelers Cheques.

Business Hours:
- Government: 10.00-17.00 Mon-Fri
- Banks: 10.00-14.00 Mon-Fri; 10.00-12.00/12.30 Sat
- Shops: 09.30-18.00 Mon-Sat
- Offices: 09.30-17.30 Mon-Fri

Weight and Measures: Metric System, British Imperial System and traditional Indian weights and measures

Electric Current: 220 volts AC. Plugs are of the round 2 and 3-pin type.

Holidays:
Republic Day - January 26
Eid-ul-fitr** - February 8-10
Mahashivratri** - March 7
Good Friday - April 10*
Eid-ul-adha** - April 18-21
Mahavir Jayanti** - April 20
Buddha Purnima/Vaisakha Puja/Wesak** - May 22
Birthday of Mohammad** - July 17
Independence Day - August 15
Mahatma Gandhi's Birthday - October 2
Vijaya Dasami/Dusserah/Ramila** - October 11
Divali(Deepavali)** - October 30-November 3
Guru Nanak's Birthday - November 14
Christmas Day - December 25

*Christian Holidays - vary each year

** Hindu and Muslim holidays are approximate, as they are timed according to local sightings of various phases of the moon.

Suitable Clothing: Dress modestly and conservatively. Light clothing year round, except for the north, when you will need medium clothing and a jacket or light coat in the winter. Sungear and raingear. On any first meeting with an official or business-man, wear a suit coat. Avoid wearing leather, as cows are sacred. Cover arms, legs and shoulders, remove shoes and cover head when entering a temple. Informal dress, light clothing is the norm.

Automobile Driving License: An International Driving License is recommended. A temporary license can be issued by the local authorities on presentation of a valid National Driving License. Most rental cars are chauffeur driven.

Customs Allowances: Declare all valuables (including electronics, which must be listed on the Tourist Baggage Re-export Form), or they may face confiscation upon your departure. Personal items are duty free, with limits to 200 cigarettes and I liter of wine or spirits. If you are staying for more than six months, you must fill out an income tax clearance form. Check the current restrictions on bringing in foreign currency. Any amounts over $1,000 must be indicated on the Currency Declaration Form. Importing or exporting rupees is forbidden. Prohibited are guns, gold, pornography, some agricultural products, and drugs-with severe punishment for the latter. Bringing most antiquities out is also strictly forbidden, and may meet with imprisonment.

Tipping: It is customary to leave a 10-15% tip when service charge is not included. Taxi drivers do not expect a tip.

Credit Cards Accepted:
Access, American Express, Diner's Club, Eurocard, MasterCard, Visa

Customary Dining Hours:
Breakfast: 07.30-09.00
Lunch: 12.30-14.30
Dinner: 20.00-22.00

Local Customs, Business Protocol and Courtesies: India is diverse enough to encounter many customs, some of them Western and some unfamiliar to the visitor. For example, upon meeting, some shake hands, and others greet by clasping their hands at the chest and offering a slight bow · this latter gesture is called Namaste. A visiting woman should shake hands only with other women, or with a man only if he offers his hand first. Schedule business and governmental meetings in advance, and be on time. Small talk is customary before getting down to business. It is considered polite to take interest in a guest's personal life, so don't be offended by inquiries about your family and health. You should never express annoyance or hostility. An atmosphere of uncritical and confident goodwill and courtesy should prevail on both sides. Persistence is important, but pays off only if done with courtesy and quiet confidence. You may have to make several trips to the country before finalizing a contract. Do not expect quick decisions; they are weighed seriously and made at the top. It helps to have contacts in high places, and to have a local representative or relative who is well-connected. Indian businessmen largely speak English and contracts can be made in both English and the local language. Women will encounter difficulties in being taken seriously, and may initially face exclusion from important meetings or social functions. The best way to deal with this is to act fully professional and politely make one's credentials known · while at the same time adhering to local customs. Since business cards are presented upon acquaintance, you can make your title known immediately, and use title until indicated otherwise. Present cards or gifts with both hands. Gifts are often presented after a first meeting and once a relationship has become better established · such as an interesting curio from your home region, art object, or something connected to your area of business. It is customary to wrap gifts green, red or yellow and open them immediately.

Entertaining is extensive. Your Indian counterparts may invite you to a private club (usually men only) or a restaurant, in which case the host pays. You should invite them in turn to a restaurant or function of equal value during your stay. It is okay to be fifteen minutes late or so, and wait to be seated, and for the host to serve you. Wash out your mouth, as well as your hands, before the meal. It's best to follow the others' example as to whether to use utensils, how to hold food with your fingers, or scoop it up with bread. The meal may be vegetarian, or close to it. The cow is sacred to Hindus and pork is also forbidden to many. Sikhs and Parsees do not smoke, and one should drink alcohol only if offered. Gestures to avoid: Do not stand close when speaking to someone, and don't touch your head, point with your hands, or point your feet at anyone. Avoid getting enmeshed in discussions concerning politics, poverty in the country, military expenditures, foreign aid and conflicts with neighboring countries.

Health: It is advisable to consult your doctor before your journey. A Vaccination for yellow fever is required. Vaccinations for typhoid, polio, hepatitis A and tetanus are recommended, as well as a course of anti-malaria pills. It is strongly advised to drink bottled water. The milk should be boiled and food precautions should be observed. Medical insurance is strongly recommended.

Language: The regional language is Hindi. English is also widely spoken.

BOMBAY

Country code: 91 - City code: 22

Airport: Bombay International Airport .

Distance from City: 32km (19 miles) north of the city.

Transportation to Center of City:
From International and Domestic Terminals
By Bus (cost) INR50. Time approx. 90 min (every hour)
By Taxi (cost) INR200. Time approx. 60-75 min.
Tip luggage porters INR7.

Transfers: (Minimum Connecting Time):
International to International: 90-120 min.
International to Domestic: 180 min.
Domestic to International: 120-180 min.
Domestic to Domestic: 30 min.

Automobile Rentals:
Europcar Interrent - 645-2796
Hertz - 494-5405

Hotels:
Ambassador Hotel, Churchgate, 204-1131
Kempiski Hotel The Leela Bombay, Sahar, 836-3636
Taj Mahal Hotel-Old Wing, Apollo Bunder, 202-3366

Restaurants:
Brittania and Co., Sprott Rd., 261 5264
Cafe Naaz, B.G.Kher Rd., 367 2969
Delhi Darbar, Holand House, 202 0235

Edward VIII, 113/A Colaba Causeway, 283 3975
Gaylord's, V.N.Rd., 282 1259
Kardeel Juice Stand, 95 M.G.Rd.
Khyber Restaurant, 145 Mahatma Gandhi Rd., 267 3227
Leopold's, Colaba Causeway
Madras Lunch and Coffee House, 56 Dr.V.B.Gandhi Marg.
Mondegar's, Metro House, Colaba Causeway
Pizzeria, 143 Marine Dr., 285 6115
Samrat, J.Tata Rd., 282 0942
Strand Coffee House, Strand Rd., 283 3418
Trishna, 7 Rope Walk Lane, 267 2176
Under the Over, 36 Altamount Rd., 386 1393

Entertainment:
Earthquake, 38 Sarvodaya Compound, 495 2038
Leopold Cafe, Colaba Causeway, 202 0131
London Pub, 8 Dariya Vihar, 363 0274
The Cellar, Marine Drive, 202 4343
The Ghetto, 30 Bhulabhai Desai Rd., 492 1556
The Pub at Rasna, J.Tata Rd., 283 6243

Places of Interest:
The Gateway of India - a monument
The Prince of Wales Museum and Jehangir Art Gallery
St.Thomas' Cathedral
The Mani Bhavan Mahatma Gandhi Museum
The Cave
The Veermata Jeejamata (Victoria and Albert) Museum
The Tarporevala Aquarium

DELHI

Country code: 91 - City code: 11

Airport: Indira Gandhi International Airport.

Distance from City: 21km (13 miles) south of the city.

Transportation to Center of City:
From International and Domestic Terminals
By Bus (cost) INR30. Time approx 45 min.

By Taxi (cost) INR120-130.
Tip luggage porters INR7 per piece

Transfers: (Minimum Connecting Time):
International to International: 60-180 min.
International to Domestic: 180 min.
Domestic to International: 180 min.
Domestic to Domestic: 90 min.

Automobile Rentals:
Europcar Interrent - 301-0101

Hotels:
Le Meridien Delhi, Windsor Pl., Janpath, 371-0101
New Delhi Hilton, Barakhamba Ave., Connaught Pl., 332-0101
Surya Hotel, New Friends Colony, 683-5070
Taj Mahal Hotel, One Mansingh Rd., 301-6162

Restaurants:
Appetite Restaurant, 753 2079
Cafe 100, B-block, 332 0663
Don,t Pass Me By, 79 Scindia House, 335 2942
El Arab, 13 Regal Bldg.
Embassy Restaurant, D-block, 332 0480
Laght Restaurant, Main Bazaar, 520 687
Mahavir Sweets, 26/2 Inner Circle, 373 1762
Malhotra Restaurant, 1833 Chuna Mandi, 731 1849
Moti Mahal Restaurant,Netaji Subhash Marg., 327 3611
Nurila's, L-Block, 332 2419
Zen Restaurant, B-block, 372 4444

Entertainment:
Dances of India, Anjuman Hall, 331 7831
Duke's Place, Village Bistro building
Village Bistro, Hauz Khas Village

Places of Interest:
Lal Qila - palaces, halls and a museum
The National Museum
The National Gallery of Modern Art
The Indira Gandhi Memorial
Delhi Zoo
The National Museum of Natural History

INDONESIA

Official Name: Republic of Indonesia

Location: Southeast Asia. The territory of Indonesia consists of 13,500 islands. The main ones are Sumatra, Java, Sulawesi, Bali, Kalimantan and Irian Jaya. They are situated between the Pacific and the Indian Oceans.

Government: Republic

Area: 1,904,569 sq. km., 735,358 sq. miles.

Population: 189.7 million

Religion(s): Muslim majority. Christian, Hindu and Buddhist minorities.

Capital City: Jakarta

Major Business Cities: Jakarta, Surabaya, Bundung, Medan, Semarang

Time: GMT +7/+9

Currency: Rupiah (Rp) = 100 sen

Currency Requirements: There are no restrictions on the import or the export of foreign currency. The import and export of local currency is restricted to Rp50,000, and has to be declared. Local currency can be exchanged on departure.

Business Hours:
- Government: 08.00-15.00 Mon-Thur, 08.00-11.00 or 11.30 Fri, 08.30-14.00 Sat
- Banks: 08.00-12.00/14.30 Mon-Sat
- Shops: 09.00-21.00 Mon-Sun
- Offices: 08.00/09.00-16.00/17.00 Mon-Fri; 08.00-13.00 Sat

INDONESIA

Weight and Measures: Metric System

Electric Current: 220 volts AC. 2 pin round plugs are used.

Holidays:
New Year's Day - January 1
Eid-ul-fitr** - February 9-10
Good Friday - April 10*
Nyepi (Balinese Saka New Year) - April 9
Eid-ul-adha** - April 18
Ascension Day - May 21*
Al-Hijra (Muslim New Year)** - May 8
Wesak - May 22
Birthday of Muhammad** - July 17
Indonesian National Day   - August 17
Lailat-ul-Isra' Wal Mir'aj** - November 28
Christmas Day - December 25

*Christian Holidays - vary each year

** Muslim holidays are approximate, as they are timed according to local sightings of various phases of the moon.

Suitable Clothing: The climate is warm all year round, no overcoats needed, but be sure to pack a raincoat or umbrella. Jackets and ties are essential items, though in this sultry environment the jacket is not always required. Lightweight cotton is the fabric of choice.

Automobile Driving License: An International Driving Permit required.

Customs Allowances: Declare all valuables upon arrival. You are allowed one carton of cigarettes or 50 cigars (cigar smokers - there are some good Indonesian brands) or 32 oz. of tobacco, one opened and one unopened bottle of alcohol (a good way to bring in two bottles!). In addition to the usual military weapons, ammunition, drugs, and pornography, there are some unexpected prohibited items: radios, tape devices, Chinese language literature, and Chinese medicines. Protected species stay in their habitat - no exporting these exotic creatures. There is strict punishment (including death) for selling, possessing, or using drugs.

Tipping: A service charge of 10% is usually included in the bill. In case it is not included, it is customary to leave a 10% tip. A 10% tip is expected by taxi drivers.

Credit Cards Accepted: American Express, MasterCard, Visa

Customary Dining Hours:
Breakfast: 06.30-08.30
Lunch: 12.00-13.00
Dinner: 19.00-22.00

Local Customs, Business Protocol and Courtesies: This is definitely an environment where courtesy counts! Your business here may involve encounters with both government and private trading, and you'll find public and private associates alike to be hospitable, courteous, and cordial. Confidence and persistence are a plus, but be sure they are clothed in good manners and not marred by arrogance or impatience. Exchanging small gifts is a way of showing good will, so it's a good idea to pack a few small but significant items. Upon introduction, offer your hand. After that, greetings are less formal, which means a brief nod of the head or a slight bow. Be sure to have business cards handy. Use surnames preceded by Bapek (sir) or Ibu (madam). Your host will let you know if he or she prefers informality. Be patient. If negotiations seem to proceed at a slow pace (for Westerners), it's not a snag or a snub. That's simply the way business is done.

Indonesia is largely Islamic, and visitors are expected to show respect for Islamic law and custom. When dining with Muslim associates, lefties take caution. If your host eats with the fingers do likewise, but be sure to use your right hand, and never, ever accept food with the left hand. If you are offered silverware, the fork goes in the left hand and the spoon in the right. You may be used to crossing your legs at the dining table but Indonesians are not. It's best to keep your feet flat on the floor where your shoes (especially soles) are discreetly kept out of sight. Your host may or may not drink alcohol. If your host drinks, then fine, accept by all means. If not, stick to coffee or tea · which it is impolite to refuse. In short, when dining with Indonesians, take your cues from your host. In all dealings, manners are of the utmost importance and it is not good manners to discuss politics, religion, and economics · that goes for local and international stuff.

Health: It is advisable to consult your doctor before your journey. It is recommended to have vaccinations for hepatitis A, tetanus, cholera, typhoid and polio. A vaccination certificate for yellow fever and cholera is mandatory if traveling from an infected area. There is a risk of Malaria outside the main cities. Only bottled water should be used and food precautions should be observed. Medical insurance is recommended.

Language: Bahasa Indonesian. Dutch and English are also spoken as a second language.

JAKARTA

Country code: 62 - City code: 21

Airport: Soekarno Hatta International Airport.

Distance from City: 20km (12 miles) northwest of the city.

Transportation to Center of City:
From International and Domestic Terminals
By Bus (cost) Rp3,000. Time approx. 60 min.(every 30 min.)
By Taxi (cost) Rp30,000. Time approx. 50 min.
Tip luggage porters Rp800 per piece

Transfers: (Minimum Connecting Time):
International to International: 60 min.
International to Domestic: 120 min.
Domestic to International: 60 min.
Domestic to Domestic: 60 min.

Automobile Rentals:
Airport car rental desk.
Avis - 314200

Car rental city office.
National Interrent - 325493
Hertz - 252-3333

Hotels:
Aryaduta Hotel, Jakarta, Jln. Prapatan 44-48, 231-1234
Borobudur Inter-Continental Jakarta, Jln. Lapangan Banteng
Selatan, 380-5555
Ciputra Hotel, Jln. S Parman, 566-0640
Golden Tulip Hotel Jayakarta-Jakarta, Jln. Hayam Wuruk 126,
629-4408
Gran Melia Jakarta, Jln. H.R.Rasuna Said Kav X-O, 526-8080
Grand Hyatt Jakarta, Jln. M.H. Thamrin, 390-1234
Indonesia Hotel, Jln. M.H. Thamrin, 390-6262
Jakarta Hilton Garden Tower, Jln. Jend Gatot Subroto, 570-3600
Jakarta Hilton International, Jln. Jend Gatot Subroro, 570-3600
Logoon Tower Jakarta Hilton International, Jln. Jend Gatot
Subroto, 570-3600
Le Meridien Jakarta, Jln. Jend Sudirman Kav 18-20, 251-3131
Mandarin Oriental Jakarta, Jln. M.H. Thamrin, 314-1307
Millennium Sirih - Jakarta , Jln. Fachrudin 3, 230-3636
Radisson Jakarta, Jln. Pecenongan, 350-0077
Sari Pan Pacific Hotel, Jln. M.H. Thamrin, 390-2707
Sheraton Bandara, Bandara Soekarno - Hatta, 559-7777

Restaurants:
Asiatique, Jln. H.R. Rasuna Said, 252-3456
George and Dragon, Jln. Teluk Betung 32, 325-625
George's Curry House, Jln. Teluk Betung 32, 325-625
Green Pub, Jakarta Theatre Bldg., Jln. M.H. Thamrin 9,
359-332
Handayani, Jln. Abdul Muis 35E, 373-614
La Bistro, Jln. K.H. Wahid Hasyim 75, 364-272
Manari, Jln. Jend. Gatot Subroto 14, 516-102
Mira Sati, Jln. Patiunus 15, 771-621
Natrabu, Jln. H.A. Salim, 335-668
Oasis, Jln. Raden Saleh 47, 326-397
Omar Khayyam, Jln. Antara 5-7, 356-719

Pageru, Jln. Sudan Cholagogue 64, 774-892
Pandok Laguna, Jln. Batu Tulis Raya 45, 359-994
Sari Kuring, Jln. Silang Monas Timur 88, 352-972
Tora-Ya, Jln. Gereja Theresia 1, 310-0149

Entertainment:
Blue Ocean Restaurant and Night Club, Jln. Hayam Wuruk 5, 366-650
Captain's Bar, Jln. M.H. Thamrin, 321-307
Ebony Videotheque, Kuningam Plaza, Jln. Rasuna Said C11, 513-700
Fire Discotheque, Plaza Indonezia L3-003, Jln. M.H. Thamrin, 330-639
Hard Rock Café, Sarinah Bldg., Jln. M.H Tamhrin 11, 390-3565
Jaya Pub, Jln. M.H. Thamrin 12, 327-508
Tanamur, Jln. Tanah Abang Timur 14, 353-947
The Star Dust, Jln. Hayam Wuruk 126, 629-4408

Shops and Stores:

Pasaraya, Jln. Iskandarsyah 1	Dept. Store
Plaza Indonesia, Jln. M.H. Thamrin	Dept. Store
Plaza Senoyan, Jln. Asia-Africa 8	Dept. Store
PT. Ramacraft, Jln. Panarukan 25	Apparel
Sarinah, Jln. M.H. Thamrin 11	Dept. Store

Places of Interest:
Sunda Kelapa - a seaport
Museum Bahari (Maritime Museum)
The Old Batavia Museum
Taman Impian Jaya Ancol -an amusement park
The National History Museum
Istiqlal Mosque
The Indonesian National Museum
Jakarta Ragunan Zoo

JAPAN

Official Name: Japan

Location: Far East. The territory of Japan consists of a group of islands situated in the Pacific Ocean, east of China and Korea.

Government: Constitutional Monarchy

Area: 377,815 sq. km., 145,875 sq. miles.

Population: 125 million

Religion(s): Shintoist and Buddhist majority. There is also a Christian minority.

Capital City: Tokyo

Major Business Cities: Fukuoka, Kyoto, Nagoya and Osaka.

Time: GMT +9

Currency: Japanese Yen (JYE)=100 sen

Currency Requirements: There are no restrictions on the import and the export of foreign currencies. The Import of local currency is unlimited. The export is limited to YE5,000,000.

Business Hours:
- Government: 09.00-17.00 Mon-Fri
- Banks: 09.00-15.00 Mon-Fri
- Shops: 10.00-19.00 Mon-Sat (many are closed on Wed or Thur)
- Offices: 09.00-17.00 Mon-Fri

Weight and Measures: Metric System

Electric Current: 110 volts AC. Flat 2-pin plugs are used.

Holidays:
New Year's Day - January 1
Coming of Age Day - January 15
National Foundation Day - February 11
Vernal Equinox Day - March 21
Greenery Day - April 29
Constitution Memorial Day - May 3
National Holiday - May 4
Children's Day - May 5
Respect the Aged Day - September 15
Autumnal Equinox Day - September 23
Health Sports Day - October 10
Culture Day - November 3
Labor Thanksgiving Day - November 23*
Day in lieu of Labor Thanksgiving Day -   November 24
Birthday of the Emperor - December 23

* When a national holiday falls on Sunday, the following Monday is a holiday. When a day (except for Sundays and the above) is between two national holidays, it is also a holiday. This rule applies on May 4.

Suitable Clothing: Always wear conservative, well-tailored business attire and appear absolutely neat. Bring light materials for summer, and medium weight the rest of the year.

Automobile Driving License: A National or International Driving License is required. Be aware that some road signs may be written in Japanese only.

Customs Allowances: Personal items are duty free, but register valuables and keep receipts or they may face confiscation. You may bring in 400 cigarettes or 100 cigars duty free and 3 liters of spirits. Prohibited are military weaponry and drugs, with severe penalties for the latter.

Tipping: Tipping is not customary and not expected. For appreciation of service, a financial gift is given rather than a loose change. Special envelopes for gifts can be purchased specifically for this. Hotels and restaurants include service charge of 20% to the bill. Taxi drivers do not expect a tip.

Credit Cards Accepted: American Express, Diner's Club, JCB, MasterCard, Visa

Customary Dining Hours:
Breakfast: 07.30-09.00
Lunch: 12.00-13.30
Dinner: 19.00-21.30

Local Customs, Business Protocol and Courtesies: Business and social relationships in Japan are marked by rank, conformity and traditional industrial and social structures which may appear overwhelming and impenetrable to Western visitors. This is not a cold country, however: you will encounter much friendliness and hospitality. As long as you too are sincerely friendly, professional and well-behaved, you will likely succeed at building amicable business relationships there. Patience and good verbal and social skills are important. Business subjects and proposals, at least initially, tend to be approached indirectly, so don't be too pushy or expect your contacts to directly propose a deal either. With formal presentations, of course, you must be absolutely thorough and professional. Keep in mind that the seemingly endless parade of business functions lets your Japanese counterparts observe you and see if your character and behavior measure up. Although they are used to and understand the Western behavior, if you appear rude, loud or offensive, or embarrass anyone in anyway, you will be met with a wall of politely disinterested smiles.

Japan's tradition-worshipping attitude carries over into its very strong, unique industrial frameworks: Commercial and industrial might have been traditionally clustered in groupings. Although seemingly impenetrable, it can also make it easier for you if you have a good relationship with one executive or company, to get introductions to others. These groupings have trading companies · the largest of them called general trading companies, or sogo shosha which are another good way of making contact if you do not know any key officials. Punctuality is a must here. When meeting with a group of professionals, shake hands in order of rank. Decisions tend to be made at the top of the hierarchy, so it's important not to offend by misplacing rank. Japanese greet each other with a slight bow, but are used to shaking hands with foreign visitors. Print your business cards in English and Japanese; this can be done easily at the big hotels or print shops in the cities. Most officials speak English, but you may want to provide an interpreter to help with the details of deal-making. Even once a contract is signed, you'll still be expected to be sociable. When eating in a restaurant or home, the traditional way of sitting is to kneel on the floor. If kneeling is too uncomfortable for you, at least try to keep your feet tucked out of sight, or not pointing in anyone's direction.

There is a ritual of pouring sake, in which no one pours for himself. The host pours first and then the guest pours for the host, and so on down the line. The guest is expected to begin eating first, after saying, "Thank you very much, I will begin to eat. As temptingly arranged as Japanese food is, it is considered bad manners to stuff yourself. Drink soup directly from the bowl, not with spoon, and don't cross chopsticks. Unless you insist beforehand, your host and associates will insist on paying the bill. If invited to a home, remove your shoes at the door even if your host tells you it's okay to keep them on. Quality, though not ostentatious, gifts are appreciated, such as nice imported accessories or fine wine or liqueur. Your gift may initially be politely refused, but continue to offer it until it is accepted. Gifts are not immediately opened.

Health: The International Association for Medical Assistance to Travelers provides English speaking doctors. It is recommended to have vaccinations for hepatitis A, tetanus, typhoid and polio. A health insurance is also strongly recommended.

Language: Japanese

JAPAN

OSAKA

Country code: 81 - City code: 6

Airport: Osaka Itami Airport

Distance from City: 20km (12 miles) northwest of the city.

Transportation to Center of City:
From International and Domestic Terminals
By Bus (cost) JYE450-550. Time approx. 20 min.
By Taxi (cost) JYE7500-10000. Time approx. 20 min.
Tip luggage porters JYE150-300 per piece

Transfers: (Minimum Connecting Time):
International to International: 45 min.
International to Domestic: 90 min.
Domestic to International: 90 min.
Domestic to Domestic: 30 min.

Automobile Rentals:
Airport car rental desk
Nippon Interrent - 841-8175

Airport: Kansai Airport

Distance from City: 5km (3 miles) off coast of Osaka Bay and 48km (29 miles) from Osaka's main rail terminus.

Transportation to Center of City:
From International and Domestic Terminals
By Bus (cost) JYE1300.
By Taxi (cost) JYE15000.
Tip luggage porters JYE150-300 per piece

Transfers: (Minimum Connecting Time):
International to International: 45 min.
International to Domestic: 90 min.
Domestic to International: 90 min.
Domestic to Domestic: 30 min.

Automobile Rentals:
Airport car rental desk
Hertz - 2469-0561
Car rental city office
Nippon Interrent - 371-9354
Hertz - 974-0802

Hotels:
ANA Hotel Osaka, 1-3-1 Dojimahama Kita-ku, 347-1112
Imperial Hotel, 8-50 Tenmabshi 1 - Chrome, 881-1111
Mayako Hotel Osaka, 6-1-55 Uehommachi, Tennoji-ku, 773-1111
Nankai South Tower Hotel, 1-60 Namba 5-chome, Chuo-ku, 646-1111
New Otani Hotel, 1-4-1 Shiromi, Chuo-ku, 941-1111
Nikko Hotel Osaka, 1-3-3 Nishi-Shinsaibashi, 244-1111
Osaka Hilton, 8-8 Umeda 1-chome, Kita-ku, 347-7111
Royal Hotel, 5-3-68 Nakonoshima, Kita-ku, 448-1121
Westin Hotel Osaka, 1-1-20 Oyodo-naka, Kita-ku 440-1111

Restaurants:
Fuguhisa, 3-14-24 Higashi-Ohashi, Higashinari-ku, 972-5029
Kani Doraku, 1-6-18 Dotonbori, Chuo-ku, 211-8975
Kanki, 1-3-11 Shibatacho Kita-ku, 374-0057
Kobe Misono, Star Bldg. 3F, 11-19 Sonezak-ishinchi,
Kushitaru, Sander Bldg., 13-5 Nishi-Shin-Saibashi 1-chome, Unagidani, Chou-ku, 281-0365
La Bamba, Shiko Grown Bldg, 10-7 Doyamacho, Kita-ku, 367-0192
Le Rendezvous, 2-2-49 Oyodo-minami, Oyodu-ku, 453-1111
Little Carnival, Umeda Center Bldg. B1F, 2-4-12 Nakazaki-Nishi, Kita-ku, 373-9828
Mimui, 6-18 Hiranomachi 4-chome, Chuo-ku, 231-5770
Osaka Joe's, IM Excellence Bldg. 2nd Floor, 1-11-20 Sonezak-ishinchi, Kita-ku, 344-0124
Ron, 1-10-2 Sonezakishinchi, Kita-ku, 344-6664
Tako-ume, 1-1-8 Dotonbori, Chuo-ku, 211-0321

Entertainment:
Karma, Eiraku Biru, Sonezaki Shinchi, Chuo-ku, 344-6181
Kirin City, 2F Kirin Plaza Bldg., 7-2 Soemoncho, Chuo-ku, 212-6572
Pig & Whistle, 2F IS Bldg., 1-32 Shin-Saibashi-suji 2-chome,

Chuo-ku, 213-6911
Pig & Whistle, B1 Ohatsutenjin Bldg., 2-5 Sonezaki, Kita-ku, 361-3198
Yasubei, Dai-ichi Blvd., BF2, 1-3 Umeda, Kita-ku, 344-4545

Shops and Stores:

Daimaru, 1-7-1 Shin-Saibashi-suji, Chou-ku — Dept. Store
Sogo, 1-8-3 Shin-Saibashi-suji, Chou-ku — Dept. Store
Takashimaya, 5-1-5 Nanba, Chou-ku — Dept. Store
Kintetsu, 1-1-43 Abeno-suji, Abeno-ku — Dept. Store
Matsuzakaya, 1-1 Tenmabashi Kyomachi, Chou-ku — Dept. Store
Mitsukoshi, 7-5 Koraibashi 1-chome, Chuo-ku — Dept. Store
Hankyu, 8-7 Kakutacho, Kita-ku — Dept. Store
Hanshin, 1-13-13 Umeda, Kita-ku — Dept. Store

Places of Interest:
Osaka Castle
Nara National Museum
Todaiji Temple

TOKYO

Country code: 81 - City code: 3

Airport: Tokyo New International Airport at Narita

Distance from City: 60km (37 miles) east of the city.

Transportation to Center of City:
From International and Domestic Terminals
By Bus (cost) JYE2,700. Time approx. 2hrs (every 20-50 min.)
By Taxi (cost) JYE24,000-30,000.Time approx. 1.5-2.5 hours
Tip luggage porters JYE300 per piece

Transfers: (Minimum Connecting Time):
International to International: 1.0 - 3.5 hrs
International to Domestic: 2.0-3.5 hrs
Domestic to International: 2.0-3.5 hrs

Automobile Rentals:
Airport car rental desk
Nippon Interrent - 320601
Hertz - 3272-8200

Car rental city office
Europcar Interrent - 601350
Hertz - 5401-7656

Hotels:
ANA Hotel Tokyo, 1-12-33 Akasaka, Minato-ku, 3505-1111
Century Hyatt Tokyo, 2-7-2 Nishi-Shinjuku, 3348-1234
Dai-ichi Hotel Annex, 1-5-2 Uchisaiwai-cho, 3503-5611
Dai-ichi Hotel Tokyo, 1-2-6 Shimbashi, Minato-ku, 3501-4411
Golden Tulip Grand Palace Hotel, 1-1-1 Chome Chiyoda-Ku
    3264-1111
Holiday Inn Crowne Plaza Metropolitan, 1-6-1 Nishi-Ikebukuro,
    3980-1111
Imperial Hotel, 1-1 Uchisaiwai-cho, 1-chome, 3504-1111
Inter-Continental Tokyo Bay, 1-16-2 Kaigan, Minato-ku,
    5404-2222
Keio Plaza Inter-Continental Tokyo, 2-1 Nishi-Shinjuku, 2-chome,
    3344-0111
New Otani Hotel Tokyo, 4-1 Kioi-Cho, Chiyoda-ku, 3265-1111
Okura Hotel 2-10-4 Toranomon, Minato-ku, 3582-0111
Park Hyatt Tokyo, 3-7-1-2 Nishi Shinjuku, 5322-1234
Radisson Miyako Hotel Tokyo, 1-50 Shirokanedai 1-chome,
    3447-3111
Richmond Hotel Tokyo, 3-5-14 Mejiro, Toshima-ku, 3565-4111
Royal Park Hotel, 2-1-1 Nihonbashi-Kakigara-cho, 3667-1111
Westin Hotel Tokyo, 1-4-1 Mita, Meguro-ku, 5423-7000

Restaurants:
Ashoka, Pearl Bldg. 2F, 7-9-18 Ginza, Chuo-ku, 3572-2377
Chez Inno, 3-2-11 Kyobashi, 3274-2020
Edo-Gin, 4-5-1 Tsukiji, Chuo-ku, 3543-4401
Farm Grill, Ginza Nine 3 Gokan 2F, 8-5 Ginza, Chuo-ku,
    5568-6156
Ganchan, 6-8-23 Roppongi, Minato-ku, 3478-0092
Hakkaku, Ginza Ins 2, 2-2 Nishi-Ginza, Chuo-ku, 3561-0539
Heichinrou, Fukoku Seimei Bldg. 28F, 2-2-2 Uchisaiwaicho,
    Chioda-ku, 3508-0555

Higo Batten, AG Bldg. 1F, 3-18-17 Ninami-Aoyama, Minato-ku, 3423-4462

Inakaya, Reine Bldg. 1F, 5-3-4 Roppongi, Minato-ku, 3408-5040

L'Orangerie, Hanae Mori Bldg. 5F, 3-6-1 Kita-Aoyama, Minato-ku, 3407-7461

La Tour d'Argent, 4-1 Kioicho, Chioda-ku, 3239-3111

Le Trianon, 1-2 Kioicho, Chioda-ku, 3234-1111

Moti, Kimpa Bldg. 3F, 2-14-31 Akasaka, Minato-ku, 3584-6640

Robata, 3-8 Yurakucho 1-chome,Chioda-ku, 3591-1905

Sasashin, 20-3 Nihonbashi, Ningyocho 2-chome, Chuo-ku, 3668-2456

Sasashu, 2-2-6 Ikebukuro, Toshima-ku, 3971-6796

South China, Co-op Olympia Bldg. B1-3, 6-35-3 Jingo-mae, Shibuya-ku, 3400-0031

Spago, 5-7-8 Roppongi, Minato-ku, 3423-4025

Takeno, 6-21-2 Tsukiji, Chuo-ku, 3541-8698

Tatsumiya, 1-33-5 Asakusa, Taito-ku, 38-42-7373

Tenmatsu, 1-6-1 Dodenzaka, Shibuya-ku, 3462-2815

Tokyo Joe's, Akasaka Eight-One Bldg. B1, 2-13-5 Nagatacho, Chioda-ku, 3508-0325

Tonki, 1-1-2 Shimo-Meguro, Meguro-ku, 3491-9928

Victoria Station, 4-9 Roppongi 2-chome, Minato-ku, 3479-4601

Entertainment:

Ari's Lamplight, Odakyu Building, 7-8-1 Minami-Aoyama, Minato-ku, 3499-1573

Blue Note Tokyo, 5-13-3 Minami—Aoyama, Minato-ku, 3407-5781

Body and Soul, Senme Bldg. 1F, 3-12-3 Kita Aoyama, Minato-ku, 5466-3525

Charleston, 3-8-11 Roppongi, Minato-ku, 3402-0372

Den, DST Bldg. 1F 4-2-3 Akasaka, Minato-ku, 3584-1899

Garbus Cine Café, Hibiya Chanter 1F, 1-2-2 Yarakucho, Chioda-ku, 3501-3185

Hall, 2-8-7 Yurakucho, Chiyoda-ku, 3201-2661

Hard Rock Café, 5-4-20 Roppongi, Minato-ku, 3408-7018

Henry Africa, 3-15-23 Roppongi, Minato-ku, 3403-9751

Lexington Queen, Daisan Goto Bldg. B1, 3-13-14 Roppongi, Minato-ku, 3401-1661

Sappori Lion,6-10-12 Ginza, Chuo-ku, 3571-2590

Stonefield's, Sunlight Akasaka Bldg. 4F, 3-21-4 Akasaka, Minato-ku, 3583-5690

The Square Building Discos, Roppongi Square Bldg., 3-10-3 Roppongi, Minato-ku, Giza, 3403-6538

Wine Bar, 3-21-3 Akasaka, Minato-ku, 3586-7186

Yaraku Food Center, , 2-2 Nishi-Ginza, Chuo-ku, Americana, 3564-1971

Shops and Stores:
Comme des Darcons, 5-11-5 Minami-Aoyama, Minato-ku Apparel
Isetan, 3-14-1 Shinjuku, Shinjuku-ku   Dept. Store
Keio, 1-1-4 Nishi-Shinjuku, Shinjuku-ku   Dept. Store
Koshino Junko, 6-5-36 Minami-Aoyama, Minato-ku   Apparel
Marui, 3-30-16 Shinjuku, Shinjuku-ku   Dept. Store
Matsuya, 3-6-1 Ginza, Chuo-ku   Dept. Store
Matsuzakaya, 6-10-1 Ginza   Dept. Store
Mitsukoshi, 1-41 Nihonbashi Muromach, Chuo-ku   Dept. Store
Odakyu, 1-1-3 Nishi- Shinjuku, Shinjuku-ku   Dept. Store
Parco, 15-1 Udagawa-cho, Shibuya-ku   Dept. Store
Seibu, 21-1 Udagawa-cho, Shibuya-ku   Dept. Store
Takashimaya, 2-4-1 Nihonbashi, Chuo-ku   Dept. Store
Tokyu Hands, 12-18 Udagawa-cho, Shibuya-ku Dept. Store
Tokyu, 2-24-1 Dogenzaka, Shibuya-ku   Dept. Store
Waco, 4-5-11 Ginza, Chuo-ku   Dept. Store

Places of Interest:
Asakusa Kannon Temple (Senso-Ji)
Idemitsu Museum of Arts
Imperial Palace
Tokyo National Museum
Japan Folk Crafts Museum
Meijo Jingo (Shrine)

KOREA

Official Name: Taehan Minkuk (Republic of Korea)

Location: Far East. Projecting into the East China Sea, bordered to the north by North Korea which separates it from China.

Government: Republic

Area: 120,538 sq. km., 46,540 sq. miles.

Population: 43.65 million

Religion(s): Mahayana Buddhism majority. There are also Christian, Confucianism, Daoism and Chundo Kyo minorities.

Capital City: Seoul

Major Business Cities: Seoul, Pusan, Teagu, Inchon

Time: GMT +9

Currency: Won (SKW) = 100 chon. A larger denomination, the Chon (jeon) is valued at SKW 1,000. The Chon is for use only on checks, banker's orders etc.

Currency Requirements: The import of foreign currency above USD10,000 must be entered on a Foreign Exchange Record. The export of foreign currency is limited to the amount declared on arrival. The export of local currency is limited to SKW 3,000,000. Allowances may vary and it is recommended to check with the embassy for current allowances.

Business Hours:
- Government: 09.00-17.00/18.00 Mon-Fri; 09.00-13.00 Sat
- Banks: 09.30-16.30 Mon-Fri; 09.30-13.30 Sat
- Shops: 10.30-19.30 Mon-Fri (smaller shops open earlier)
- Offices: 08.30/09.00-18.00 Mon-Fri; 09.00-13.00 Sat

KOREA

Weight and Measures: Metric System

Electric Current: 110 and 220 volts AC. Plugs are of the flat 2-pin type. It is recommended to always check the power supply before using the equipment.

Holidays:
New Year - January 1-2
Lunar New Year - February 6-8
Independence Day - March 1
Arbor Day - April 5
Children's Day - May 5
Buddha's Birthday - May 14
Memorial Day - June 6
Constitution Day - July 17
Liberation Day - August 15
Thanksgiving - September 15-17
National Foundation Day - October 3
Christmas Day - December 25

Suitable Clothing: Wear a conservative business suit for all meetings. At more informal business meetings after you and your associates have gotten to know each other, you can probably forego a jacket and tie, but ask your host. Bring rainwear and sungear. When visiting a home, bring an extra pair of clean socks to change into - this is regarded as very considerate.

Automobile Driving License: An International Driving License is required.

Customs Allowances: Declare all valuables or they may face confiscation upon your departure. Personal items are duty free. You may bring in, duty free, up to 400 cigarettes, 50 cigars, 2 ounces of perfume and 2 liters of spirits. Film is restricted to 72 rolls or 3000 feet. Taking out antiques is prohibited in most cases, as is carrying weaponry, drugs, pornography and literature considered treasonous.

Tipping: Tipping is not a custom in Korea. A 10% service charge is added to your hotel bill. There is also a 10% tax (VAT) added to the price of rooms, meals and other services. Tipping a taxi driver is not necessary unless he assists you with your luggage or provides some extra service.

Credit Cards Accepted: American Express, Diner's Club, JCB, MasterCard, Visa

Customary Dining Hours:
Breakfast: 07.00-09.00
Lunch: 12.00-14.30
Dinner: 18.00-21.30

Local Customs, Business Protocol and Courtesies: Your first business meetings with a potential Korean associate will probably have nothing to do with business, rather, there will be a period in which your contact can get to know you as a human being before he decides whether he wants to get to know you as a businessman. Friendliness, sincerity and courtesy, all with a smile, are essential. Present, with both hands, your business card printed in Korean as well as English. Your contact will probably ask you personal questions. Be forthright (without going overboard) in your answers, and don't act overly familiar at this stage, such as using first names (unless otherwise indicated by him). Use Mr. Mrs. or Miss. Koreans go by last name first, and women keep their names after they marry. This does not mean, however, that women are on equal status in Korean society · in fact, it is just the opposite (men and women often eat and entertain separately). A visiting businesswoman will probably encounter difficulties in this process of becoming business-friends.

If your contacts do get to know you and trust you, they will welcome you into a solid, long lasting and warm business and social relationship, for loyalty is one of the most valued traits of Korean society. But don't blow your first meeting or you will probably never get another chance. There is a long list of don'ts: bad manners (such as blowing your nose in front of people) and lack of courtesy (especially disrespect to elders or superiors), unfriendliness, insincerity and showing up without making an appointment. Being introduced by someone he or she doesn't like or trust, using an incompetent interpreter, or bringing a lawyer to a first meeting will also ruin chances at subsequent dealings. The second part of the getting to know you stage, if all goes well in the first, involves going out for drinks. Never pour your own drink but wait for your host to pour it for you. Drink it all, then hand it back to him and pour his drink. Eat a lot, because you will be often be invited to drink, and it is rude to refuse. If you get through all this and establish a friend-ship, your new friend will invite you to drop in-anytime, un-announced, at his home. When visiting, remove your shoes at the door, but do not go barefoot. Bring candy or small gifts for the children, and wine or a nice quality book or art object for your hosts. Don't wrap your gifts in blue or white, or give objects in groups of four (Korean's tend to be very superstitious associating blue, white, or objects grouped by four, with death.) Gifts are not opened immediately. The var-ious kinds of food are served all at once; eat everything on your plate. The hostess may not be present at dinner, in fact, women often eat separately. Dining out with your associates may be frequent and lavish (for men, anyway). Initially, let your host pay for dinner or drinks out; you should recipro-cate sometime later during your stay. Finally, the desire to create a comfortable environment extends to language; even if your associate speaks English, bring an interpreter to the actual negotiations so that all the details of an agreement can easily be worked out.

Health: It is advisable to consult your doctor before travel-ing. A vaccination certificate for yellow fever is mandatory if traveling from an infected area. Vaccinations for hepatitis A, tetanus, cholera, typhoid and polio are recommended. A vac-cination for Japanese encephalitis is also recommended since it is transmitted by mosquitoes between June and the end of October in rural areas. An AIDS free certificate is required for visits of longer than 3 months. It is advisable to drink bottled water and food precautions should be observed at all times. Medical insurance is recommended.

Language: Korean.

KOREA

SEOUL

Country code: 82 - City code: 2

Airport: Kimpo International Airport .

Distance from City: 20km (12 miles) west of the city.

Transportation to Center of City:
From International and Domestic Terminals
By Bus (cost) SKW3,500. Time approx. 60-80 min. (every 15-20 min.)
By Taxi (cost) SKW20,000. Time approx. 30-40 min.
Tip luggage porters SKW800 per piece

Transfers: (Minimum Connecting Time):
International to International: 60 min.
International to Domestic: 100 min.
Domestic to International: 80 min.
Domestic to Domestic: 40 min.

Automobile Rentals:
Airport car rental desk.
Avis - 666-1121
National Interrent - 665-5711
Hertz - 665-9105

Car rental city office
Avis - 838-0018
National Interrent - 552-5711
Hertz - 796-0525

Hotels:
Amiga, 248-7Nonhyon-dong, Kangnam-gu, 3440-8000
Grand Hyatt, 747-7 Hannam-dong, Yongsan-gu,797-1234
Hamilton Hotel, 119-25 Itaewon-dong, 794-0171
Hilton International, 395 Namdaemunno 5-gu , Chug-gu, 753-7788
Inter-continental, 159-8 Samsong-dong, Kangnam-gu, 555-5656
Koreana Hotel, 61 1-Ka, Taepyung Rd, Chung-ku, 730-9911
Lotte Hotel, 1 Sogong-dong, Chung-ku, 771-1000

Plaza, 23, T'aer'yongno 2-ga, Chung-gu, 771-2200
Ritz-Carlton, 602 Yoksam-dong, Kangnam-gu, 3451-8000
Seoul Hilton, 395 5-ka, Namdaemun-ko, 753-7788
Sheraton Walker Hill, San-21, Kwangjang-dong, Kwangjin-gu, 233-3131
Sofitel Ambassador, 186-54, 2-ka, Changchung, 275-1101
Swiss Grand, 201-1 Hong-dong, Sodaemun-gu, 356-5656
Shilla, 202, Changch'ung-dong 2-ga, Chung-gu, 233-3131
Capital, 22-76, It'aewon-dong, yongsan-gu, 792-1122
Garden, 169-1, Tohwa-dong, Map'o-gu, 717-9441

Restaurants:
Amsa Haemult'ang, 58-18 Songp'a-dong, Songp'a-gu, 421-2044
Athene, 1362-26, Yangjae-dong, Sch'o-gu, 554-3200
Bennigan's, 164-1, Hyehwa-dong, Chongno-gu, 766-9800
Coco's, 163-14, Hyehwa-dong, Chongno-gu, 742-1031
Dae Won Gak, 323, Songbuk-dong, Songbuk-gu, 762-0161
Denny's, 3, Chongdam-dong, Kangnam-gu, 316-0101
Gold Rush, 1-93, Tongsung-dong, Chongno-gu, 741-1020
Gues, 132-2, It'aeon-dong, Yongsan-gu, 749-0316
Ha Dong Kwan, 26, Suha-dong, Chung-gu, 776-5656
Ham Hung Myon Ok, 1-12, Ogum-dong, Songp'a-gu, 404-1919
Han Woo Ri, 91-18 Nonhyon-dong, Kangnam-gu, 545-9933
La Cantina, 50, Ulchiro 1-ga, Chung-gu, 777-2579
La Palroma, 40-1, Chamshil-dong, Songp'a-gu, 411-3658
Old Germany, 683-132, Hannam-dong, Kangnam-gu, 795-8780
Patio, 664-1, Shinsa-dong, Kangnam-gu, 3442-3293
Rio Valley, 1316-28 Soch'o-dong, Soch'o-gu, 783-7701

Entertainment:
It'aemon, It'aemon-ro, It'aemon-dong, Yongsan-gu, 797-7319
Kayagum Hall, San 21, Kwangjan-dong, Kwangjin-gu, 453-0121
Korea House, 80-2, P'il-dong, Chongno-gu, 266-9101
Kuk Il Kwan, 20, Kwanhun-dong, Chongno-gu, 275-0560
London Pub, 16-2, youido-dong, Yongdungp'o-gu, 783-7701
Pan Korea, 101-1.Ulchiro 2-ga, Chung-gu,267-6105
Sanchon, 2-2, Kwanhun-dong, Chongno-gu, 735-0312
Sheraton Walker Hill - Casino, San 21, Kwangjan-dong, Kwangjin-gu, 453-0121

Shops and Stores:

KOREA

Acris Dept. Store, 1445-15, Soch'o dong, Soch'o-gu   Dept.Store
Galeria 515, Arkujong-dong, Kangnam-gu   Dept. Store
Grace, 30-33, Ch'angch'on-dong, Sodaemun-gu   Dept. Store
Grand Dept. Store 936-21, Taecg'I-dong, Kangnam-gu   Dept. Store
Hamilton Store, 119-25, It'aewon-dong, Yongsan-gu   Dept. Store
Hanshin Core, 284, Hagye-dong, Nowon-gu   Dept. Store
Kunyoung Omni., 506-1 Chunggye-dong, Nowon-gu Dept. Store
New Core, 58-24, Chamwon-dong, Soch'o-gu   Shopping Center
Printemps,1, Changgyo-dong, Chung-gu   Dept. Store
Shinsegae, 52-5, Ch'ungmuro 1-ga, Chung-gu   Dept. Store

Places of Interest:
Kyongbok Palace
The National Museum
Chongmyo Royal Ancestral Shrines
Pagoda Park
Chogye-Sa Temple
Namsan Tower
Seoul Grand Park
National Museum of Contemporary Art

MALAYSIA

Official Name: Malaysia

Location: South-East Asia. Malaysia is composed of East Malaysia and West Malaysia. South China Sea separates them by 400 miles. West Malaysia is bordered by Thailand and Singapore. East Malaysia is bordered by Borneo and the Philippines.

Government: Constitutional Monarchy

Area: 329,758 sq. km., 127,320 sq. miles.

Population: 18.61 million

Religion(s): Muslim and Buddhist majority.

Capital City: Kuala Lumpur

Major Business Cities: Johor Bahru, Kota Kinabulu and Penang.

Time: GMT +8

Currency: Ringitt or Malaysian Dollar (RGT)=100 sen

Currency Requirements: There are no restrictions on the import and export of either local or foreign currency, except on Israeli currency.

Business Hours:
- Government: 08.00-16.30 Mon-Fri; 08.00-12.45 Sat
- Banks: 10.00-15.00 Mon-Fri; 09.30-11.00 Sat
- Shops: 09.00/10.00-22.00 Mon-Fri
- Offices: 08.30-12.00; 14.00-17.30 Mon-Fri; 08.30-12.00 Sat

Weight and Measures: Metric System and local system

Electric Current: 220-240 volts AC. Plugs are square 3-pin type.

Holidays:
New Year's Day - January 1
Chinese New Year - February 7-8
Hari Raya Puasa (Eid-ul-fitr)** - February 10-11
Hari Raya Haji (Eid-ul-adha)** - April 18-21
Labor Day - May 1
Muharram/Al-Hijra (Islamic New Year)** - May 8
Wesak Day** - May 22
Birthday of HM Yang di Pertuan Agong*** - June 7
Birthday of the Prophet Muhammad** - July 17
Independence Day - September 1
Deepavali (Divali)** - October 30-November 3
Christmas Day - December 25
Boxing Day - December 26*

* Christian Holidays - vary each year

** Muslim and Hindu holidays are approximate, as they are timed according to local sightings of various phases of the moon.

*** If a holiday falls on a weekend it is often celebrated on the following Monday.

Suitable Clothing: Dress modestly. You can wear light to medium-weight clothing most of the year, and raingear is useful between July and October. Bring a sweater or light jacket. For men, wear a conservative suit for government meetings, and a white shirt, tie and slacks for business meetings. Women should wear a conservative dress or suit.

Automobile Driving License: An International Driving License is required. A UK driving license is sufficient, but it must be endorsed by the Registrar of Motor Vehicles in Malaysia.

Customs Allowances: Declare all valuables or they may face confiscation upon your departure. Personal items are duty free, but you may have to put down a deposit when bringing in video equipment, computers or other expensive electronics, to be refunded upon your departure. You may bring in, duty free, up to

200 cigarettes and a liter of spirits and wine. No limits exist on foreign currency, as long as what you export was initially declared; limits on Ringitt are 10,000 import and 5,000 export. If you purchase antiquities, you must obtain official permits from the museums authority to bring them home. Prohibited are weaponry, drugs (which get the death penalty) and pornography.

Tipping: A service charge of 10% and 5% government tax are usually included in all bills. Taxi drivers do not expect a tip. A 10% tip is always welcome although not expected.

Credit Cards Accepted: American Express, Diner's Club, MasterCard, Visa

Customary Dining Hours:
Breakfast: 07.00-08.00
Lunch: 12.00-14.00
Dinner: 19.00-21.00

Local Customs, Business Protocol and Courtesies: Breaking into Malaysian business circles is best done through personal, governmental or banking contacts. Although Malaysia is Muslim country, and you should therefore adhere to basic Muslim customs, sticking to certain Chinese traditions and customary behavior can also be helpful as many of the upper echelon of the business world in Malaysia are Chinese. In any case, your behavior will be carefully observed. Do not cause shame or loss of face, or be confrontational; this will be met with vague politeness and careful diplomacy designed to keep you out of the loop. Schedule appointments in advance, and be on time. Your contact may be late, but you should never express annoyance or hostility. Your contemporaries are quite sophisticated, and an atmosphere of confident goodwill and courtesy should prevail on both sides. Persistence is important, but pays off only if done courteously and with quiet confidence. Men shake hands, traditionally, by touching the right palm and then one's heart, or by bowing slightly and touching the forehead with right hand. Do not, however, attempt to imitate this, and shake hands with a woman only if she offers first. Use the title of your contact with family name until told otherwise; if the business card you receive doesn't give you the title, use "Bin" (Son of) or "Binti" (Daughter of) with given name. Never present a business card, gift or eat with your left hand; using both hands is considered polite. Avoid discussing political subjects. Giving toasts is uncommon, especially since those who are strictly Muslim may not drink alcohol. At meetings or in social situations, do not refuse tea or coffee.

Dining out often follows a business meeting, and don't refuse invitations to them, or to a home. Be on time. Malaysians remove their shoes in the house. Seating may be on floormats. Bring a small, tasteful but inexpensive gift such as fine chocolates, art book or something interesting from your native country. Use red or green, not yellow, black or white wrapping paper. and send flowers the next day. At meals or when socializing, it's best to follow the example of your host as to whether to eat with one's fingers or use utensils. Southpaws beware: there is a strong taboo against eating or drinking with one's left hand (traditionally, the hand used for toilet activities), although you may use both hands if given a knife and fork. Also, if crossing your legs, make sure your feet and soles are not visibly pointing in anyone's direction. In Chinese restaurants, Western visitors are not expected to eat with chopsticks, but it will look good to your counterparts if you are able to. To eat properly from a rice bowl, raise it to your chin. Spoons are used for soup. For most other dishes, chopsticks are used. Do not cross them, rather, use the chopstick rests that are provided.

Health: It is advisable to consult your doctor before your journey. Vaccinations for cholera, hepatitis A, tetanus, typhoid, polio and malaria are recommended. Drinking water is generally considered potentially contaminated and visitors who are unaccustomed to the Malaysian way of life should be cautious. A Health insurance is recommended.

Language: Bahasa Malaysia. English and Chinese (Mandarin) are widely spoken.

MALAYSIA

KUALA LUMPUR

Country code: 60 - City code: 3

Airport: Subang International Airport.

Distance from City: 25km (15 miles) southwest of the city.

Transportation to Center of City:
From International and Domestic Terminals
By Bus (cost) RGT2 Time approx.30-60 min.
By Taxi (cost) RGT16-25. Time approx. 40 min.
Tip luggage porters 2 Ringitts per piece

Transfers: (Minimum Connecting Time):
International to International: 60 min.
International to Domestic: 90 min.
Domestic to International: 90 min.
Domestic to Domestic: 60 min.

Automobile Rentals:
Airport car rental desk.
Avis - 746-3950
National Interrent - 746-2025
Hertz - 746-2091

Car rental city office.
Avis - 241-7144
National Interrent -248-0522
Hertz - 242-1014

Hotels:
Concorde Hotel, 2 Jln. Sultan Ismail, 244-2200
Dynasty Hotel, 218 Jln. Lpoh, 443-7777
Grand Continental Hotel, Jln. Belia/Jln.Raja Laut, 293-9333
Holiday Inn City Centre, 12 Jln. Raja Laut, 293-9233
Holiday Inn on the Park, Jln.Pinang, 248-1066
Istana Hotel, 73 Jln. Raja Chulan, 241-9988
JV Marriott Hotel Kuala Lumpur, 183 Jln. Bukit Bintang,
    245-9000
Kuala Lumpur Parkroyal, Jln. Sultan Ismail, 242-5588

Kuala Lumpur Travelodge Apartment Hotel, 161-d Jln. Ampang, 264-8000
Melia Kuala Lumpur, 16 Jln. Imbi, 242-8333
Ming Court Hotel, Kuala Lumpur, Jln. Ampang, 261-8888
New Worl Hotel Kuala Lumpur, 128 Jln. Ampang, 263-6888
Pan Pacific Hotel, Kuala Lumpur, Jln. Putra, 442-5555
Regent, Kuala Lumpur, 160 Jln. Bukit Bintang, 241-8000
Renaissance Kuala Lumpur Hotel, Cnr. Of Jln. Sultan Ismail & Jln. Ampang, 262-2233
Shangri-La Hotel, Kuala Lumpur, 11 Jln. Sultan Ismail, 232-2388
Swiss-Garden Hotel, 117 Jln. Pudu, 241-3333
Swiss-Inn, 62 Jln.Sultan, 232-3333
Wenworth Hotel, Kuala Lumpur, Jln. Yew, 983-3888

Restaurants:
Bon Ton, 7 Jln. Kia Peng, 341-3611
Chikuyo Tei, Jln. Raja Chulan, 230-0729
Coliseum Café, 98 Jln. Tuanku Abdul Rahman, 292-6270
Kedai Makanan Yut Kee, 35 Jln. Dang Wangi, 298-8108
Lafite Restaurant, 11 Jln. Sultan Ismail, 232-2388
Lai Ching Yuen, 126 Jln. Bukit Bintang, 241-8000
Lotus Restaurant, 15 Jln. Gasing, Petaling Jaya, 792-8795
Melaka Grill, Jln. Sultan Ismail, 242-2122
Noya Heritage, 44-4 Jln. Sultan Ismail, 243-3520
Regent Grill, 160 Jln. Bukit Bintang, 341-8000
Satay Anika, Jln. Bukit Bintang, 248-3113
Teochew Restaurant, 270-272 Jln. Changkat Thamby Dollah, 241-5851
Terrace Garden, 308 Jln. Ampang, 457-2378
Yazmir, 6 Jln. Kia Peng, 341-5655

Entertainment:
Anglers Pub, 22 Jln. SS2/67, Petaling Jaya
Carlos Hacienda, 364 Jln. Tun Razak, 242-8470
Club Oz, Jln. Sultan Ismail, 232-2388
Damn Yankees, East Block, Wisma Selangor, Jln. Ampang, 264-9159
DJ Pub, 37 Jln. SS22/19, Damansara Jaya, 717-0966
Hard Rock Café, Wisma Condore, 2 Jln. Sultan Ismail, 244-4062
Hip-E Club, Damansara Utama, 719-6569

Pub, 11 Jln. Sultan Ismail, 232-2388
Riverbank, Central Market, 274-6651
Shark Club, Jln. Sultan Ismail, 241-7878
Spuds, Ground floor, Annex. Bldg., Jln. Raja Chulan, 248-5097
Tin Mine, Jln. Sultan Ismail, 242-2222
Uncle Chili's, Jln. Barat, 75-9122

Shops and Stores:

Central Market, Jln, Cheng Lock,	Jewelry
Jade House, KL Paza	Jewelry
Karyaneka Handicrafts Center, Jln. Raja Chulan	Jewelry
Metrojaya, Jln. Bukit	Dept. Store
Parkson, Jln. Bukit	Dept. Store
Yaohan, Jalan Putra	Dept. Store

Places of Interest:
Masjid Negara - a mosque
Muzium Negara - National Museum
The National Art Gallery
Railway Station
Masjid Jame - a mosque
Central Market

PAKISTAN

Official Name: Islamic Republic of Pakistan

Location: Southern Asia. Pakistan consists of the province Sind, Baluchistan, Punjab and the North-West Frontier Province (NWFP). It is bordered by Afghanistan, India, and Iran. To the south lies the Arabian Sea.

Government: Republic

Area: 803,950 sq. km., 310,405 sq. miles.

Population: 122.80 million

Religion(s): Muslim majority. There are also very small Hindu and Christian minorities.

Capital City: Islamabad

Major Business Cities: Karachi, Lahore, Faisalabad, Hydera-bad and Peshawar.

Time: GMT +5

Currency: Pakistani Rupee (Re - singular; Rs - plural)=100 paisa

Currency Requirements: The import of foreign currency is unlimited and has to be declared. The export is limited to the amount declared on arrival. The import and the export of local currency is restricted to Rs500. All transactions must be made through authorized dealers.

Business Hours:
- Government: 09.00-15.00 Sun-Thur
- Banks: 09.00-13.00 and 15.00-20.00 Sun-Thur
- Shops: 09.00/10.30-20.00 Sat-Thur
- Offices: 09.00-17.00 Sat-Thur

Weight and Measures: Metric System; British Imperial System and local weights

Electric Current: 220 volts AC. Plug is of the 2 or 3 round pin type.

Holidays:
Eid-ul-fitr* - February 8-10
Pakistan Day - March 23
Eid-ul-adha* - April 18-21
May Day - May 1
Ashura* - May 17
Birthday of Muhammad* - July 17
Independence Day - August 14
Defence of Pakistan Day - September 6
Anniversary of the Death of Quaid-i-Azam - September 11
Iqbal Day - November 9
Birth of Quaid-i-Azam/Christmas - December 25

* Muslim holidays are approximate, as they are timed according to local sightings of various phases of the moon. Businesses are usually closed on Fridays.

Suitable Clothing: Dress modestly and conservatively. You should wear a suit for government or business meetings, although in the hot summer months a shirt and tie without jacket, or a lighter-weight (but well-covering) dress, is acceptable. No head cover for women. You may need a jacket in northern Pakistan, and long sleeves to keep bugs away. In general, have light clothing year round and medium weight clothing, with raingear and a light coat, between November and March.

Automobile Driving License: An International Driving Permit is required. It can be issued on presentation of a National Driving License.

Customs Allowances: Declare all valuables (including electronics, which must be listed on the Tourist Baggage Re-export Form), or they may face confiscation upon your departure. Personal items are duty free, with limits to one carton of cigarettes and five rolls of film. There is an import limit of 100 Rupees, but foreign currency may be brought in and out freely as long as you declare it when you enter the country. Permits are required to take home a carpet, and bringing most antiquities out is strictly forbidden. Prohibited are weaponry, alcohol, pornography, agricultural products, and drugs-with careful airport searches and severe punishment for the latter.

Tipping: Tipping is discretionary. When a service charge is included in the bills, a tip of 10% is appropriate.

Credit Cards Accepted:
American Express, MasterCard, Visa

Customary Dining Hours:
Breakfast: 07.00-09.30
Lunch: 13.00-14.30
Dinner: 20.00-22.00

Local Customs, Business Protocol and Courtesies: Any business relationships and contracts you make will likely involve the Pakistani Government, with its myriad public and semi-public companies. As the country is Islamic, it is important for visitors, in building business and personal relationships, to adhere to local customs and dress modestly. Schedule meetings in advance, and be on time · although your contact may be late. Rather than shaking hands upon meeting and departing, people grasp wrists, as the hand is considered "unclean." A visiting woman should shake hands only with other women, or with a man only if he offers his wrist first. Regarding titles, "Sahib" or "Jenab" denote Mister, but are used after one's name. Madame is "Begum"; use it alone or after a name. In negotiations, you should never express annoyance or hostility. Your contemporaries can be quite sophisticated, and an atmosphere of confident goodwill should prevail on both sides. Persistence is important, but pays off only if done with courtesy and quiet confidence and a smile. People are reserved and formal in their business dealings, but also very hospitable, and you will most likely be invited to a home. Usually, there is a specific section of a Pakistani house reserved for entertaining, and it would be rude to ask to see any other part of the house. Remove your shoes at the door, but keep your feet hidden during the meal and never point then in anyone's direction. At meals, it's best to follow the example of your host · as to whether to eat with one's fingers or use utensils, or whether alcohol will be allowed. Southpaws beware: there is a strong taboo against eating or drinking with one's left hand (traditionally, the hand used for toilet activities), although you may use both hands if given a knife and fork. Don't refuse offers of food or coffee, whether in a meeting or socially. Conversation about family is fine, but don't get personal about women. Avoid getting enmeshed in discussions concerning politics, poverty in the country, military expenditures, foreign aid and conflicts with neighboring countries. Giftgiving-such as an tasteful souvenir or curio from your home region, an art object, or something connected to your area of business-is not unusual, but the appropriate response is to politely turn down a gift until it is offered a second time. Do accept, however, if he offers again.

Health: It is advisable to consult your doctor before your journey. A vaccination certificate for yellow fever is required for visitors travelling from an infected area. A cholera certificate is no longer required by law, but visitors are advised to take precautions as cholera still poses a serious threat in Pakistan. Vaccinations for typhoid, polio, hepatitis A and tetanus are recommended. In areas below 2000m there is a risk of malaria. It is strongly advisable to drink only bottled water. The milk should always be boiled or sterilized. Food precautions should be observed at all times. Medical insurance is recommended.

Language: Urdu. English and various regional languages including Punjabi, Baluchi, Pashtu and Sindhi are widely spoken.

KARACHI

Country code: 92 - City code: 21

Airport: Karachi International Airport

Distance from City: 16km (9 miles) northeast of the city

Transportation to Center of City:
From International and Domestic Terminals
By Bus (cost) Rs15-20. Time approx.30-40 min.
By Taxi (cost) Rs200. Time approx. 25 min.
Tip luggage porters Rs10 per piece

Transfers: (Minimum Connecting Time):
International to International: 90 min.
International to Domestic: 90 min.
Domestic to International: 90 min.
Domestic to Domestic: 30 min.

Automobile Rentals:
Airport car rental desk
Avis - 526295

Car rental city office
Avis - 526985

Hotels:
Avari Towers, Fatima Jinnah Rd., 566-0100
Karachi Marriott Hotel, 9 Abdullah Harron Rd., 568-0111

Restaurants:
Golden Dragon, Roung Market, F-7/3, 827333
Jaltarang, Rawal Dam, 821216
Kashmir Wala's, Daman-e-Koh, 829585
Mei Hua Chinese, 20-D, Western Half, Al-Asghar Plaza 212697
Mr. Chips, 13-0 Markaz F-7, 821922
Omer Khayyam Iranian, Blue Area, Plot 46, Shop No. 11, 812847
Pappa Salis, Shop No. 2, Block 13/E, F-7 Markaz, 818287
Rawal, Islamabag Int. Airport, 591071
Shifang, Jinnah Super Market, 217564
Szechuan Food, Flat 12, St.16 Raha Market, F-7/2, 810673
Tabaq Tai Kong, 16-D, West Blue Area, 812744
Taj Mahal, Markaz F-7, School Rd., 812932
The Great Wall, 41-Blue Area, Attaturk Av., Shalimar-6, 815111
Tuaam, 75, Ajaib & Sons Plaza, Jinnah Av., 825719
Usmania, 13 West Blue Area, 811345
Valentine, 24/D Rashid Plaza, Blue Area, 828602

Village, Feroze Centre, Fazal-e-Hag Rd., Blue Area, 821853

Shops and Stores:
Aabpara Market, Ramna-6   Shopping Center
Civic Centre   Shopping Center
Covered Bazar, Ramna-6   Shopping Center
Fine Art Jewellers, 4-F, Super Market   Jewelry
Islamabad Jewellers, Civic Centre   Jewelry
Jewelery's, Shop No. 2-A, Block 12-F, Jinnah Super Market
Jewelry
Jinnah Super Market, Shalimar-7   Shopping Center
Jumma Bazar, Aabpara, Ramna-6   Shopping Center
Super Market, Shalimar06   Shopping Center

Places of Interest:
The Tomb of Quaid-i-Azam - a monument
The National Museum
The Faysee Rahman Art Gallery
The Defence Society Mosque
Karachi Zoo
Memon Mosque
Old City - bazaars

SINGAPORE

Official Name: Republic of Singapore

Location: South East Asia. Singapore is an island in the South China Sea. It is situated to the south of the Malay Peninsula.

Area: 641 sq. km., 247 sq. miles.

Population: 2.87 million

Religion(s): The major religions are Buddhism, Islam, Hinduism, Confucianism, Christianity and Taoism.

Capital City: Singapore

Time: GMT +8

Currency: Singapore Dollar (SID) = 100 cents

Currency Requirements: There are no restrictions on the import and the export of foreign or local currency.

Business Hours:
- Banks: 09.30-15.00 Mon-Fri; 09.30-11.30 Sat
- Shops: 09.30-21.00 Mon-Sun
- Offices: 09.00-16.30/17.00 Mon-Fri; 09.00-13.00 Sat

Weight and Measures: Metric

Electric Current: 220/240 volts AC. Plugs are of the square 3-pin type.

Holidays:
New Year's Day - January 1
Chinese New Year - February 7-8
Hari Raya Puasa - February 9*
Good Friday – April 10*
Hari Raya Haji - April 18*

Labor Day - May 1
Vesak Day - May 21*
National Day - August 9
Deepavali (Diwali) - October 30-November 3*
Christmas Day - December 25

* Muslim and Hindu holidays are approximate, as they are timed according to local sightings of various phases of the moon.

Suitable Clothing: Dress as neatly as possible, preferably in a business suit, although the hot weather may allow just a shirt and tie for more informal business meetings. Women should always dress modestly. Bring white or black dinner jacket or long dress for formal occasions. Generally, light materials, sungear and rainwear are important.

Automobile Driving License: An International Driving License is required. Drivers must be over 23 years of age and must have any valid license that is held for at least 2 years.

Customs Allowances: Register valuables upon arrival or they may be confiscated upon departure. Although you may bring in unlimited amounts of foreign currency, and take out any you initially declare, you may not import or export Singapore Dollars. One liter of wine, spirits and beer is duty free-but all cigarettes are taxed. Brunei dollars may circulate here, but Malaysian currency may not. Corporal punishment and imprisonment applies to foreigners as well for serious crimes. Drug smuggling often gets the death penalty. Other prohibited items are military weaponry or items that resemble weapons, pornography, agricultural products and animals.

Tipping: Tipping is not encouraged in restaurants and hotels. A service charge of 10% is usually added to the restaurant bills. It is not necessary to tip taxi drivers.

Local Customs, Business Protocol and Courtesies: Big Brother appears so benign that it's hard to believe the extent to which Government exerts its influence over life in Singapore · but the visitor should never forget its presence. Businessmen are supposed to value state and society above individual gain, and act accordingly. Life is very orderly here

· to the point where a particular fruit is forbidden to be eaten in public because it is so messy. Littering, jaywalking, chewing gum in public and violating no-smoking rules all meet with heavy fines. Crime, needless to say, is virtually nonexistent. Though Singapore is a multicultural society-mainly ethnic Chinese, Malay and Tamil-Chinese businessmen dominate, so it's important to be knowledgeable to their customs (see sections on China and Hong Kong). If you are in a group meeting, the person with highest rank is introduced first. Shake hands with a slight bow, and present business cards (English-only is acceptable) with both hands. Use Mr., Mrs. or Miss with the family name. With Malay or Tamil contacts, use title with given name. Expect tough negotiators, but greater efficiency in decision making than in the rest of the region.

Not that this is a cold country. Food and friendly conversation will break the ice in most business situations. Your behavior will be watched-be friendly, but also professional and discrete. Business/social functions in restaurants are frequent and will leave you stuffed. If invited to one, let the host seat you. He will order all the courses, which are served all at the same time. If you are the host at a function, make sure an even number is present, and that the guest of honor sits facing the door. Most restaurants will provide forks and knives, if requested. Western visitors are not expected to eat with chopsticks, but it will look good to your counterparts if you are able to. To eat properly from a rice bowl, raise it to your chin. Spoons are used for soup. For most other dishes, chopsticks are used. Do not cross them, rather, lay them side by side by your plate or across the rim or chopstick rests. Your host will likely criticize the food and service, which is the customary way of saying that nothing is good enough for the guest. Agreeing with him would be offensive.

Dining rules are different for Tamils or Malays. The latter are Muslim, so do not drink alcohol (unless your associates indicate that it's all right) or order pork or, if with Buddhist Tamils, avoid beef. A bowl of water and towel is given to each person, useful since some foods are eaten with hands. It's best to follow the others' example, as to whether to use utensils, how to hold food with your fingers, or scoop it up with bread. Gestures to avoid: don't touch your head or point with hands or feet. When visiting a home (an honor that should not be refused), wrap your gift (a fine book, chocolate or tasteful souvenir from your country will do) in the celebratory colors red, yellow or green, not blue, black or white, which can be associated with death. Business gifts are rare, and any gift to an official may be interpreted as a bribe.

Health: It is advisable to consult your doctor before your journey. It is mandatory to have certificates for cholera and yellow fever if you are travelling from an infected area. Vaccinations for hepatitis A, hepatitis B, tetanus, polio and typhoid are recommended. It is advisable to drink bottled water for the first few weeks. Drinking water from the tap is considered to be safe, but may cause mild abdominal upset. Emergency treatment can be received at the Singapore General Hospital. A health insurance is advised.

Language: English. Malay, Mandarin and Tamil are also spoken

SINGAPORE

Country code: 65 - City code: none

Airport: Changi International Airport

Distance from City: 20km (12 miles) northeast of the city

Transportation to Center of City:
From International and Domestic Terminals
By Bus (cost) SID5. Time approx. 20 min
By Taxi (cost) SID15.

Automobile Rentals:
Airport car rental desk
Avis - 543-2331

SINGAPORE

Car rental city office
Avis - 287-8877
National Interrent - 338-8444
Hertz - 447-3388

Hotels:
ANA Hotel Singapore, 16 Nassim Hill, 732-1222
Amara Hotel Singapore, 165 Tanjong Pagar Rd., 224-4488
Asia Hotel, 37 Scotts Rd., 737-8388
Carlton Hotel Singapore, 76 Bras Basah Rd., 338-8333
Elisabeth Singapore, 24 Mount Elizabeth, 738-1188
Equatorial Hotel, 429 Bukit Timah Rd., 732-0431
Furama Hotel Singapore, 10 Eu Tong Sen St., 533-3888
Garden Hotel Singapore, 14 Balmoral Rd., 235-3344
Goodwood Park Hotel, 22 Scotts Rd., 737-7411
Hilton International Singapore, 581 Orchard Rd., 737-2233
Holiday Inn Park View Singapore, 11 Cavenagh/Orchard
    Rd., 733-8333
Hyatt Regency Singapore, 10-12 Scotts Rd., 738-1234
Inter-Continental Singapore, 80 Middle Rd., 338-7600
King's Hotel, 304 Havelock Rd., 733-0011
Le Meridien Orchard, 100 Orchard Rd., 733-8855
Mandarin Hotel, 333 Orchard Rd., 737-4411
Marco Polo Hotel Singapore, 247 Tanglin Rd., 474-7141
Melia at Scotts, 45 Scotts Rd., 732-5885
Miramar Hotel, Singapore, 401 Havelock Rd., 733-0222
Negara Hotel, Singapore, 10 Claymore Rd., 737-0811

Restaurants:
Aziza's, 36 Amerald Hill Rd., 235-1130
Banana Leaf Apollo, 56/58 Race Course Rd., 293-8682
Bastiani's, Bastiani's Clarke Quay, 433-0156
Beng Hiang, 112-116 Amoy St., 221-6695
Dragon City, 214, Dunearn Rd., 250-3322
Imperial Herbal Restaurant, 41 Seah St., 3rd floor, 337-0491
La Brasserie, The Marco Polo, Tanglin Rd., 474-7141
Lei Garden, 200 Orchard Blvd., Basement 2, 235-8122
Li Bay, 39 Scotts Rd., 737-6888
Nadaman, 22 Orange Grove Rd., 24th FL., 737-3644
Noya and Baba, 262 River Valley Rd., 734-1382/6
Palm Beach Seafood, Leisure Park, 5 Stadium Walk,
    344-3088

Pete's Place, 10/12 Scotts Rd., 738-1234
Prego Restaurant, Westin Plaza, 2 Stamford Rd., 338-8585
Raffles Tiffin Room, Raffles Hotel, 1 Beach Rd., 337-1886
Sukmainda, 25 Scotts Rd., 737-7966
Sushi Nagawa, 270 Orcard Rd., 732-1111
Thanying, 165 Tanjong Pagar Rd., 222-4688
UDMC Seafood Center, East Coast Pkwy., 442-3112
Xin Cousine, 317 Outram Rd., 733-0188

Entertainment:
Brannigans, 10-12 Scotts Rd., 733-1188
Caesars, 02-36 Orchard Towers, 400 Orchard Rd., 235-2840
Captain's Bar, Marina Sq., 338-0066
Celebrities, 400 Orchard Rd., 734-5221
Dickens Tavern, 04-01 Parkway Parade, 80 Marina Parade Rd.,
    440-0215
Fire, 150 Orchard Rd., 235-0155
Flag & Whistle, 10 Duxton Hill, 233-1126
Hard Rock Café, 02-01, 50 Cuscaden, 235-5232
Harry's Quayside, 28 Boat Quay, 538-3029
Rumours, 03-08 Forum Galleria, 483 Orchard Rd., 732-8181
The Warehouse, 332 Havelock Rd., 732-9922
Wild West Tavern, 12 Clark Quay, 334-4180
Xanadu, 22 Orange Grove Rd., 737-3644

Shops and Stores:

Daimaru, Liang Court	Dept. Store	
Delfi Orchard, 402 Orchard St.	Jewelry	
Hermes, Liat Towers	Apparel	
Isetan, Wisma Astria, 435 Orchard St.	Dept. Store	
Larry's, Orchard Towers	Jewelry	
Lucky Plaza, 304 Orchard St.	Jewelry	
Mario Valentino, Marina Sq.	Apparel	
Metro, Marina Sq.	Dept. Store	
Overseas Emporium, People's Park Complex	Dept. Store	
Tan Yoong, Lucky Plaza	Apparel	
Tokyu, Funan Center	Dept. Store	
Yaohan, Plaza Singapura	Dept. Store	

Places of Interest:
The National Museum
The Singapore Science Center

SINGAPORE

The Church of St. Gregory The Illuminator
Thian Hock Keng Temple
The Temple of 1000 Lights
The Zoological Gardens
The Van Kleef Aquarium
Jurong Bird Park
Sentosa Island
The Singapore Crocodilarium
Raffles Hotel - a shopping arcade and a museum

TAIWAN

Official Name: Taiwan, Republic of China

Location: China. Taiwan is located between the south and east China Seas, off the southeast coast of China.

Government: Democracy

Area: 36,000 sq. km., 13,900 sq. miles.

Population: 20.93 million

Religion(s): Buddhism, Christianity, Taoism and Islam.

Capital City: Taipei

Major Business Cities: Tainan, Taipei.

Time: GMT +8

Currency: New Taiwan Dollar (NTD)=100 cents

Currency Requirements: The import of foreign currency is unlimited but must be declared on arrival. The export is limited to the equivalent of USD5,000 for visitors leaving within six months of arrival, or up to the amount imported and declared. All exchange receipts must be kept. The import and the export of local currency is limited to NTD40,000.

Business Hours:
- Government: 8.30-12.00 Mon-Fri; 8.30-12.00 Sat
- Banks: 09.00-15.30 Mon-Fri; 09.00-12.30 Sat
- Shops: 09.00-21.30 Mon-Sat
- Offices: 08.00/09.00-17.30 Mon-Fri; 08.30/09.00-12.00 Sat

Weight and Measures: Metric System, some traditional Chinese units

TAIWAN

Electric Current: 110 volts 60 cycles AC. Plugs are of the flat 2-pin type.

Holidays:
National Holiday and Founding Day - January 1
Chinese Lunar New Year - February 6-9
Youth Day - March 29
Children's Day - April 4
Tomb-Sweeping Day and Death of
    President Chiang Kai-shek (1975) - April 5
Labor Day - May 1
Dragon Boat Festival - June 9
Mid-Autumn Moon Festival - September 16
Birthday of Confucius/Teacher's Day - September 28
Double Tenth National Day - October 10
Retrocession Day - October 25
Birthday of President Chiang Kai-shek - October 31
Dr Sun Yat-sen's Birthday - November 12
Constitution Day - December 25

Suitable Clothing: Wear light clothing year round, although you should bring a sweater or light jacket, and raingear as well. For more casual business meetings, it's best to get advice from your Chinese counterparts as to whether to forego a suit jacket or tie, but in general for a meeting, a lightweight conservative suit or dress will do. Be absolutely neat.

Automobile Driving License: A National or an International Driving License can be used if it is held for at least one year. Drivers must be over 21 years of age.

Customs Allowances: Declare all valuables or they may face confiscation upon your departure. Personal items are duty free. You may bring in, duty free, up to 200 cigarettes and a liter of spirits and wine. Import and export of Taiwanese dollars is limited to 40,000. The import value limit on gold and silver is $5,000; greater amounts can be kept safely until your departure. No limits exist on importing foreign currency, but you may bring out only $5,000 or equivalent. Prohibited are weaponry, items resembling weapons, drugs, pornography, pro-Communist literature and products of mainland China.

TAIWAN

Tipping: Tipping is not customary. A 10% service charge is usually included in hotel and restaurant bills; extra tipping is not required. Most people leave taxi drivers their small change. Any other tipping is optional.

Credit Cards Accepted: American Express, MasterCard, Visa

Customary Dining Hours:
Breakfast: 07.30-09.00
Lunch: 12.00-12.30
Dinner: 19.00-22.30

Local Customs, Business Protocol and Courtesies: When visiting, schedule appointments in advance and be punctual. If you are in a group meeting, the person with highest rank is introduced first. People generally bow slightly rather than shake hands. You should have business cards in English and Mandarin; present it with both hands, Mandarin side up. Use Mr., Mrs. or Miss with the family name. In general, persistence pays off, but be polite and good-natured. In any case, your behavior will be carefully observed. Do not cause shame or loss of face, or be confrontational; this will be met with vague politeness and careful diplomacy designed to keep you out of the loop. Keep in mind too that a smile doesn't always convey the positive, but politely masks the negative, such as embarrassment. Avoid discussing political subjects, referring to Taiwan as "the Republic of China" and do not photograph military or major infrastructure, museums and archeological sites. Your counterparts will expect you to have thorough knowledge of your product and any competition. Presentations must be detailed, executed with calm, confident but low-key style. Once agreement is reached, the word of a Taiwanese businessman or official is as good as his signature or stamp (a Chinese character in red ink called a "chop") on a contract or other document. In this society which honors gift-giving, it is important to remember the rules and taboos that go with it. When visiting a home (an honor that should not be refused), wrap your gift in red which means celebration, not white, which means death. English-language books, art books, or good liqueur or fine chocolates will do, but don't give bad-luck gifts like knives, clocks, or anything grouped by four. White flowers are for funerals. Also, don't take seriously the "oh, you shouldn't have' response; keep offering until the gift is accepted. You will most certainly be presented with gifts as well during your trip, but do not open them immediately upon receipt. Business gifts are customary upon first meeting and upon the completion of a successful deal.

Business/social functions in restaurants are frequent and will leave you stuffed. A ten-course meal is typical; after the first appetizer, the host will offer a toast. It is customary to empty your cup then; with any subsequent toasts (you should make a thank-you toast toward the end of the meal), a sip will suffice. Wait until your host begins eating before you begin. Your host will likely criticize the food and service, which is the customary way of saying that nothing is good enough for the guest. Agreeing with him would be offensive. Most restaurants will provide forks and knives, if requested. Western visitors are not expected to eat with chopsticks, but it will look good to your counterparts if you are able to. To eat properly from a rice bowl, raise it to your chin. Spoons are used for soup. For most other dishes, chopsticks are used. Do not cross them, rather, lay then side by side by your plate or across the rim. No matter how excellent the food is, leave a little food on your plate; eating every bite is considered bad manners. Don't be offended if your companions burp; it is a sign of satisfaction. Tea is served after the meal, and most leave right afterwards.

Health: It is advisable to consult your doctor before your journey. A vaccination certificate for yellow fever is mandatory if you are travelling from an infected area. Precautions for typhoid, polio, hepatitis A, tetanus and cholera are recommended. Drinking only bottled water is strongly recommended. Food precautions should be observed at all times. Medical insurance is essential.

Language: Chinese (Mandarin). English and Japanese are also spoken.

TAIWAN

TAIPEI

Country code: 886 - City code: 2

Airport: Taipei-Chiang Kai-shek International Airport.

Distance from City: 40km (24 miles) southwest of the city.

Transportation to Center of City:
From International and Domestic Terminals
By Bus (cost) NTD40. Time approx. 60-90 min.
By Taxi (cost) NTD1000-1500. Time approx. 40 min.
Tip luggage porters NTD20 per piece

Transfers: (Minimum Connecting Time):
International to International: 60 min.
International to Domestic: 60 min.
Domestic to International: 60 min.

Automobile Rentals:
National Interrent - 517-5677

Hotels:
Ambassador Hotel, 63 Chung Shan N. Rd, Sec. 2, 551-1111
Grand Formosa Regent, Taipei, 41 Chung Shan N. Rd, Sec 2, 523-8000
Grand Hyatt Taipei, 2 Sung Shou Rd., 720-1234
Howard Plaza Hotel, 160 Jen-Ai Rd, sec 3, 700-2323
Lai Lai Sheraton Hotel Taipei, 12 Chung Hsiao E. Rd, Sec.1, 321-5511
Magnolia Hotel, 166 Tun Hwa N. Rd., 712-1201
President Hotel, 9 The Hwei St., 595-1251
Rebar Holiday Inn Crowne Plaza, 32 Nanking E. Rd, Sec 5, 763-5656
Ritz Hotel, 41 Min Chuan East Rd, Sec. 2, 597-1234
Royal Hotel, Taipei, 37-1 Chung Shan N. Rd, Sec. 2, 542-3266
Shangri-La's Far Eastern Plaza Hotel, 201 Tun Hwa S. Rd, Sec. 2, 378-8888
Taipei Fortuna Hotel, 122 Chung Shan N. Rd, Sec. 2, 563-1111
Taipei Hilton, 38 Chung Hsiao W. Rd, Sec 1, 311-5151

Restaurants:
Tao Hsiang Village, 84 Patch Rd., 2578-6271
Kubla Khan, 263 Hsinyi Rd.., 2356-0097
The Oriental King, 105 Tienmu W. Rd., 2871-2000
Genghis Kahn, 176 Nanking E. Rd., 2711-4412
Charming Garden, 2-3F/ 16 Nanking E. Rd., 2521-4131
Opus, 58, Lane 122, Jenai Rd., Sec. 4, 2705-9974
Chalet Swiss, 1/F, 47 Nanking E. Rd., Sec. 4, 2715-2051
Hugo, 31 Chungshan N. Rd., Sec 7, 2871-0074
La Lune Vague, 7, Alley 7, Lane 290, Chungshan, 2837-2214
La Maison 5, 2F, 182 Sungchiang Rd., 2562-5659
Zum Fass, B1, 55, Lane 119, Linsen N. Rd., 2531-3815
Taj Palace, 2/F, 270 Sungching Rd., 2567-2976
Cantina, 15, Lane 25, Chungcheng St., 2592-3355
Fukui, 60 Fuhsing N. Rd., 2772-7738
Soul, 4, Lane 33, Chungshan N. Rd., 2551-2326
Tequila Sunrise, 42 Hsinsheng S. Rd., Sec. 3, 2362-7563
Lanka, 48 Chungyi St. Shihlin, 2832-0153
Ruth's Chris, 2F, 135 Minsheng E. Rd., Sec 3, 2545-8888
Kevin, 119 Minsheng E. Rd., Sec. 3, 2712-1733
Kenneth, 130 Tunhua S. Rd., Sec 2, 2703-2222
Royal, 49 Jenai Rd., Sec 2, 2351-0979
Jimmy's Kitchen, B1, 73 Jenai Rd., Sec 4, 2711-3793
Friday's, 150 Tunhua N. Rd, 2713-3579

Shops and Stores:
Asiaworld Dept. Store, 50 Chunghsiao W. Rd, Sec. 1
        Dept. Store
Durban's Dept. Store, 180 Chungkung Rd. Sec 4.,
        Dept. Store
Evergreen Tokyu Dept. Store, 6 Nanking E. Rd., 2,
        Dept Store
Shin Shin Co., 247 Linsen N. Rd.   Dept. Store
Sunrise Dept. Store, 15, Fuhsing N. Rd.,   Dept Store.

Places of Interest:
The National Museum of History
The Taipei Fine Arts Museum
Chung Cheng (Chiang Kai-shek) Memorial Hall
The Chinese Culture and Movie Center
The Lungshan (Dragon Mountain) Temple

THAILAND

Official Name: The Kingdom of Thailand

Location: South East Asia. Thailand is bordered by Myanmar, the Indian Ocean, Malaysia, the Gulf of Thailand, Cambodia and Laos.

Government: Constitutional Monarchy

Area: 513,115 sq. km., 198,115 sq. miles.

Population: 57.96 million

Religion(s): Buddhist majority.

Capital City: Bangkok

Major Business Cities: Chiang Mai and Phuket.

Time: GMT +7

Currency: Baht (BHT)=100 satang

Currency Requirements: There are no restrictions on the import of foreign and local currencies but they should be declared. The export of local currency is limited to BHT 50,000.

Business Hours:
- Government: 08.30-12.00; 13.00-16.30 Mon-Fri, 08.00-12.00 Sat
- Banks: 08.30-15.30 Mon -Fri
- Shops: 08.30-19.00 Mon-Sun (some shops may vary)
- Offices: 08.30-16.30/17.00 Mon-Fri

Weight and Measures: Metric System and several traditional measures

Electric Current: 220 volts AC. A variety of plugs are used. It is advisable to have international adapters.

Holidays:
New Year - January 1
Magha Puja - February 21
Chakri Day - April 6
Songkran - April 12-14
Family Day - April 14
Labor Day - May 1
Coronation Day - May 5
Royal Ploughing Ceremony - May 9
Visakha Puja - May 20
Asalha Puja - July 19
Khao Phansa - July 20
H.M. The Queen's Birthday - August 12
Chulalongkorn Day - October 23
H.M. The King's Birthday - December 5
Constitution Day - December 10
New Year's Eve - December 31

Suitable Clothing: Generally, wear a business suit in all government business appointments, although in the summer months a shirt and tie with good pants is acceptable. Dress modestly in most situations - avoid shorts, short dresses or bare shoulders.

Automobile Driving License: An International Driving Permit is required. Drivers must be over 23 years of age.

Customs Allowances: Declare all valuables or they may face confiscation upon your departure. Personal items are duty free. You may bring in, duty free, up to 200 cigarettes, a liter of wine or spirits, and three and five rolls of video and still film, respectively. Computer and other large electronics are taxed. Bringing out antiquities is forbidden, with harsh penalties. Also prohibited are military weaponry, pornography and gold bullion and drug. Penalties for the latter are imprisonment or death; refuse to carry anyone else's luggage, as it may carry drugs.

Tipping: A 10% service charge and an 11% government tax are added to the bill by most hotels. Taxi drivers usually do not

expect a tip. Taxi fares should be negotiated in advance.
Credit Cards Accepted: American Express, Diner's Club, MasterCard, Visa

Customary Dining Hours:
Breakfast: 07.00-09.00
Lunch: 12.00-14.00
Dinner: 20.00-22.00

Local Customs, Business Protocol and Courtesies: Thai society is very tolerant and unprejudiced, and welcoming of visitors, and as long as you try to adhere to certain behaviors and customs, you will be warmly received. Showing tolerance, patience, sensibility and good humor yourself is essential to building business and social relationships. Smiling in general is important · as a greeting, expression of thanks, or apology. Cynicism, sarcasm and impatience have no place here; calmness, generosity, fun and a desire to please do. Since most Thais practice Buddhism, you should be respectful of its customs: for example, remove shoes when entering a temple, do not touch a priest's robes or anyone's head or hair (the head is considered the repository of the soul). Do not ever say anything negative about the royal family. Men go first in many situations, from entering an elevator to being served at a meal to getting a taxi. In preparation for your first trip, get a list of representatives or agents from your country's Thai embassy. Once you arrive, you'll find that business meetings tend to shift from one mood to another, from an intense atmosphere of negotiations to an unwinding period of relaxed conversation. Use first names, with "Kun" first. In any case, you will have to make several visits, in case of superstition · induced slowness. Decisions and the signing of contracts are timed according to astrological clocks, or after consulting spirits and watching for omens.

Business lunches are preferred, or dinners, as long as they don't run late in the evening. In this "sanuk" (fun-loving) country, casual buffet dinners, picnics and boat trips are preferred over formal affairs. At meals, eat less and less as you go through the many courses, and sit facing the door. The person who invites, or most senior associate present, pays. Some of your contacts and events may be ethnic Chinese, and one should observe their customs. At any social event, your associates, and you too, will invariably play at "guessing status" of those present. Whoever is or appears to be of highest social or professional status (and it might be you, the honored guest) must act as host · giving toasts and being at your most charming. If you don't measure up, it may deal a death blow to your business relationships. Your physical gestures and demeanor are important, too, in this obsession over status. Keep one's head lower than a superior's or elders'. Do not cross your legs or show the soles of your shoes, or point feet · and especially do not put feet up on a chair or desk. "Wai" is an important hello or goodbye custom: palms carefully pressed together, as if in prayer, serve as the Western equivalent of a handshake, although your counterparts may do it Western-style. The higher the hands are raised, the greater respect shown. Only Thais do this gesture, and for those they consider a superior based on age, rank and corporate level. If someone greets you with a "Wai," acknowledge it with a smile and brief nod. Family is important here, and when invited to a Thai home, be sure to bring a nicely wrapped gift, but don't expect it to be opened immediately. If given a gift, do not open it immediately unless the giver insists. Take off your shoes in a home, and bring flowers, chocolates and/or a tasteful souvenir from your country.

Health: It is advisable to consult your doctor before your journey. A vaccination certificate for yellow fever is mandatory if you are travelling from an infected area. Vaccinations for cholera, typhoid, polio, hepatitis A and tetanus are required. There is a risk of malaria in the rural areas. Bottled water should be used and food precautions should be observed at all times. The medical facilities are good, but a health insurance is recommended.

Language: Thai. Chinese and English are also spoken.

THAILAND

BANGKOK

Country code: 66 - City code: 2

Airport: Bangkok Don Muang International Airport

Distance from City: 30km (18 miles) north of the city.

Transportation to Center of City:
From International and Domestic Terminals
By Bus (cost) BHT80. Time approx. 45-60 min. (every 30 min.)
By Taxi (cost) BHT400-500. Time approx. 30-60 min.
Tip luggage porters 20BHT per piece

Transfers: (Minimum Connecting Time):
International to International: 75 min.
International to Domestic: 120 min.
Domestic to International: 120 min.
Domestic to Domestic: 30 min.

Automobile Rentals:
Airport car rental desk
Avis - 25553000-4
Hertz - 391-0461

Car rental city office
Avis - 2870222
National Interrent - 216-8020
Hertz - 382-0293

Hotels:
Amari Atrium Hotel, 1880 Petchburi Rd, Bangkapi, 718-2000
Amari Boulevard Hotel, 2 Soi 5, Sukhumvit Rd, 255-2940
Amari Watergate Hotel, 847 Petchburi Rd, Rajthevi, 653-9000
Bel-Aire Princess Hotel, 16 Sukhumvit Rd, Soi 5, 253-4300
Century Park Hotel Bangkok, 9 Ratchaprarop Rd, 246-7800
Dusit Thani, Rama IV Rd., 236-0450-9
Golden Tulip Asia Hotel Bangkok, 296 Phayathai Rd., 215-0808
Golden Tulip the Mandarin Hotel, 662 Rama IV Rd.,
    238-0230-58
Grand Hyatt Erawan Bangkok, 494 Rajdamri Rd., 254-1234

Hilton International Bangkok, 2 Wireless Rd., 253-0123
Holiday Inn Crowne Plaza, 981 Silom Rd., 238-4300
Indra Regent Hotel, 120-126 Rajaprarop Rd., 208-0022
Jade Pavilion Hotel, 30 Sukhumvit Soi 22, 259-4675
Kempinski Hotel Mansion Bangkok, 75-23 Sukhumvit Soi
   11, 255-7200
Landmark Bangkok, 138 Sukhumvit Rd., 254-0404
Le Meridien Bangkok, 971 Ploenchit Rd., 253-0444
Manhattan Hotel Bangkok, 13 Soi, 15 Sukhumvit Rd., 255-0166

Restaurants:
Ban Chiang, 14 Srivieng Rd., 236-7045
Ban Khun Phor, 458/7-9, Soi 8, Siam Sq., 250-1733
Banana Leaf, Silom Complex, Silom Rd., 231-3124
Cabbages & Condoms, 10 Sukhumvit Soi 12
Coca Noodles, Siam Square Shopping Center, 251-3538
Genji, 2 Wireless Rd., 253-0123
Himali Cha Cha, 1229/11 New Rd., 235-1569
Hok Thean Lauo, 762 Ladya Rd. Klongsam, 437-1121
Le Dalat, 51 Sukhumvit Soi 23, 258-4129
Lemongrass, 5/1 Sukhumvit Soi 24, 258-8637
Mandalay, 77/5 Soi Ruamrudee Sukhumvit, 250-1220
My Choice, Soi 36 Sumkhumvit, 258-6174
Nai Sow, 3/1 Maitrichit Rd., 222-1539
Old Dragon, 81 Royal City Ave., 203-0972
River City Bar B-Q, 5 FL., River City Shopping Center,
   237-0077
Royal Kitchen, N. Sathorn, 234-3063
Salathip, 89 Soi Wat Suan Phu, New Rd., 236-7777
Sanuknuk, 411/6 Sukhumvit Soi 55, 390-0166
Seafood Market, 388 Sukhumvit Rd., 258-0218
Soi Polo Fried Chicken, Soi Polo
Sweet Basil, 23 Soi 62, 176-5490
The Atlanta, Sukhumvit 78 Soi 2, 252-1650
Thong Lee, Sukhumvit Soi 20
Ton Po, Phra Atit Rd.
Tumnak Thai, 131 Rajadapisek Rd., 274-6420

Entertainment:
Bobbies Arms, Car Park Blvd., Patpong 2 Rd., 233-6828
Brown Sugar, 231/20 Soi Sarasin, 250-0103
Drunken Duck Pub, 59/4 Soi 31 Sukhumvit Road, 258-4500

THAILAND

Hard Rock Café, Siam Sq., 251-0792
Rang Phah, 16 Sukhumvit 23 Soi, 258-4321
September, 120/1 Sukhumvit 23, 258-5785
Silom Plaza, 320/14 Silom Rd., 234-2657
Trail Dust, 43/2 Sukhumvit 31, 258-4590

Shops and Stores:
A. A. Company, Siam Center   Jewelry
Choisy, 9/25 Suriwongse Rd.   Apparel
Design Thai, 304 Silom Rd.   Apparel
Indra Garment Export Centre, Rajaprarop Road   Apparel
Marco Tailor, 430/33 Siam Sq., Soi 7   Apparel
Narayana-Phand, 295/2 Rajaprop, Payatai   Jewelry
Polin, 860 Rama IV Rd., 234-8176   Jewelry
The Jim Thompson Thai Silk Co., 9 Suriwongse Rd.   Apparel

Places of Interest:
Wat Phra Kaew and Grand Palace
Royal Barges
Wat Benchamabophit Marble Temple
Wat Arun Temple of Dawn
Jim Thompson Tai House
National Art Gallery
Wat Pho The Temple of the Reclining Buddha
Floating Market

VIETNAM

Official Name: Socialist Republic of Vietnam

Location: South East Asia. Vietnam is bordered by China, Laos and Cambodia. The South China Sea lies to the east and south.

Government: Socialist Republic

Area: 331,114 sq. km., 127,844 sq. miles.

Population: 70 million

Religion(s): Buddhist majority. Taoist, Confucian, Hoa Hao, Caodaist and Roman Catholic minorities.

Capital City: Hanoi

Major Business Cities: Ho Chi Minh City

Time: GMT +7

Currency: New Dong (VND)= 10 hao = 100 xu

Currency Requirements: The import and the export of local currency is prohibited. The import and export of foreign currency is unlimited but must be declared for sums over USD3,000.

Business Hours:
- Banks: 07.30/08.00-16.30 Mon-Sun
- Shops: 09.00-14.00 Mon-Fri
- Offices: 07.30/08.00-16.30 Mon-Fri

Weight and Measures: Metric System

Electric Current: 110/220 volts AC.

VIETNAM

Holidays:
New Year's Day - January 1
Tet, Lunar New Year - February 6-11
Liberation of Saigon - April 30
International Labour Day - May 1
National Day - September 2
Christmas - December 25-26

Automobile Driving License:, It is required to obtain an International Driving Permit and take a test in order to hire a car.

Tipping: Tipping is officially prohibited but widely practiced.

Health: It is advisable to consult your doctor before your journey. There is a risk of malaria. Vaccinations for hepatitis A, tetanus, cholera, typhoid and polio are recommended. It is highly advised to drink only bottled water and to take food precautions at any time. Medical insurance is highly recommended and should cover emergency repatriation by air.

Language: Vietnamese.

HANOI

Country code: 84 - City code: 4

Airport: Hano-Thu Do International Airport at Noi Bai.

Distance from City: 40km (24 miles) from the city.

Transportation to Center of City:
From International and Domestic Terminals
By Taxi (cost) USD30-35 Time approx. 40 min.

Hotels:
Dan Chu Hotel, 29 Trang Tien St., 53323
Giang Vo Hotel, SwedishEmbassy Area, 53407
Hanoi Daewoo Hotel, Ngoc Khanh, Liau Giai St., 831-5555
Hoa Binh Hotel, Ly Thuong Kiet St., 53315
Hoan Kiem Hotel, 25 Tran Hung Dao St., 54204

VIETNAM

Hotel Sofitel Metropole, 15 Ngo Queyen St., 26919
Thang Loi Hotel, Yen Phu St., West Lake Area, 52211
Thang Long Hotel, Swedish Embassy Area, 57796
The Sophia Hotel, 6 Hang Bay St., 55069
Thong Nhat Hotel, 15 Ngo Quyen St., 58221

Restaurants:
Al Fresco's, 23L Hai Ba Trung St., 8267782
Alittle Italian, The Pear Tree, 78 Tho Nhuom, 8258167
Baan Thai, 3B Cha Ca St., 8281120
Bistrot, 34 Tran Hung Dao, 8266136
Bo Ho Restaurant, corner of Hang Khay St. & Ba Trieu St., 56418
Club Opera, 59 Ly Thai To St., 8268802
Dafano, 10 Hang Hanh St., 8285581
Gustave, 17 Tran Tien St., 8250625
Huong Sen Restaurant, 52 Le Duan St., 52805
Indochine, 16, Nam Ngu St., 8246097
Khazana, 27 Quoc To Giam, 8433477
La Vong, 107 Nguyen Truong To St., 8239875
Piano Restaurant, 50 Hang Vai St., 23 2423
Sophia Restaurant, 6 Hang Bai St., 55069
The Little Italian, 81 Tho Nhuom St., 258167

Entertainment:
Apocalypse Now, 46 Hang Vai St.
Hanoy Roxy, 8 B Ta Hien St.
Lan Anh Bar, 9A Da Tuong St., 267552
New Sunset Pub, 31 Cao Ba Quat St., 8230173
No Noodles, 51 Luond Van Can St., 8257721
Polite Pub, 5 Bao Khanh St.
Queen Bee, Lang Ha St.
The Emerald, 53 Hang Luoc, 8259285
Tin Tin Pub, 14 Hang Mon St.

Shops and Stores:

Shop, 11 Hang Son St.,	Souvenirs
State General Department Store, Hang Bai St.,	Dept. Store
The Calabash, 1 Hang Be St.	Apparel

Places of Interest:

VIETNAM

The History Museum
The Army Museum
Ho Chi Minh's Mausoleum
Chua Mot Cot Street - Ho Chi Minh's place
The Ho Chi Minh Museum
St.Joseph's Cathedral
Temple of Literature
The Ambassadors Pagoda

PACIFIC

AUSTRALIA

Official Name: Commonwealth of Australia

Location: Indian/Pacific Ocean. Australia is the largest island but the smallest continent in the world. To the south is the Southern Ocean and to the north are the Arafura and Timor Seas. The Indian Ocean lies to the west of Australia while the Coral and Tasman Seas of the South Pacific lie to the east.

Government: Parliamentary State (Monarchy)

Area: 7,682,300 sq. km., 2,966,151 sq. miles.

Population: 17.57 million

Religion(s): Protestant majority. Roman Catholic and other smaller minorities.

Capital City: Canberra

Major Business Cities: Adelaide, Brisbane, Cairns, Darwin, Hobart, Melbourne, Perth and Sydney.

Time: GMT +10.30/+11 (GMT +8/+10 from late March to late October)

Currency: Australian Dollar (AUD) = 100 cents

Currency Requirements: The export and the import of foreign and local currency for amounts exceeding AUD5000 must be declared.

Business Hours:
- Government: 09.00-17.30 Mon-Fri, 09.00-12.00 Sat
- Banks: 09.30-16.00 Mon-Thur, 09.30-17.00 Fri
- Shops: 09.00-17.30 Mon-Fri, 09.00-12.00 Sat
- Offices: 09.00-17.00 Mon-Fri

AUSTRALIA

Weight and Measures: Metric System

Electric Current: 240/250 volts AC. Plugs are 3 pin type. However, sockets are different so an adapter may be needed.

Holidays:
New Year's Day - January 1
Australia Day - January 26
In lieu of Australia Day - January 27
Good Friday - April 10*
Easter Monday - April 13*
Anzac Day - April 25
Christmas Day - December 25

*Christian Holidays - vary each year

Suitable Clothing: Australians tend to dress informally, but you should stick with a conservative suit or dress. In winter (May through September), bring medium weight clothing and a coat; in summer (year round in the Northern Territory), wear light clothing. Be prepared to layer in the country's varied climate. Rainwear and sungear are absolutely essential.

Automobile Driving License: In addition to a valid passport, a National Driving License with English translation must be carried while driving. Drivers must be over 21 years of age.

Customs Allowances: Personal items are duty free, but register valuables upon arrival and keep receipts. You may bring in 200 cigarettes and 1 liter of wine and spirits. Prohibited are military weaponry, items resembling a weapon, and drugs, with harsh penalties.

Tipping: A service charge is usually not added to the bill in restaurants. A tip of 10% is welcomed by waiters and bar attendants at top hotels. Tipping at anytime is discretionary. Taxi drivers do not expect a tip. However, rounding the fare up to the nearest dollar is appreciated.

Credit Cards Accepted: American Express, Diner's Club, Master Card, Visa

AUSTRALIA

Customary Dining Hours:
Breakfast: 07.00 - 10.00
Lunch: 11.30 - 14.30
Dinner: 18.00 - 22.00

Local Customs, Business Protocol and Courtesies: Even in a business context, a good sense of humor is always appreciated among Australians. Although business is handled quite professionally, there is a comfortable air of informality. Much business is conducted over drinks; the visitor will rarely be expected to cover the bill, but if it's "your shout" it's your turn to pay. Offering to pay when it's not your turn is considered rude. Don't mistake the local friendly humor for unprofessionalism, however; you'll find that people work hard and expect presentations and contracts to be fully professional. Honesty is well-regarded, which means you should not try to hide potential problems your partnership may encounter. Plan appointments in advance for any official meeting, and don't be late. Upon acquaintance, take the cue from your Australian counterparts on the level of formality concerning dress and behavior. Suits are customary in New South Wales, but businessmen frequently go about in shorts in subtropical Brisbane. Although fancy business luncheons are rare, senior management sometimes entertains more formally, in the evening especially upon completion of a big business deal. If invited to someone's home, be sure to bring flowers, but keep in mind that, other than small token gifts from your home country, gift giving is rare.

Health: Visitors travelling within six days of a visit to a country that has an instance of yellow fever will require a vaccination certificate. There is a Reciprocal Health Agreement with the UK, New Zealand, Italy, Malta and Sweden for emergencies only. Visitors from these countries who wish to benefit from this Agreement should enroll either before or after treatment. Health insurance is recommended.

Language: English

AUSTRALIA

BRISBANE

Country code: 61 - City code: 73

Airport: Brisbane International Airport

Distance from City: 13km (8 miles) northeast of the city

Transportation to Center of City:
From International and Domestic Terminals
By Bus (cost)   AUD7. Time approx. 35 min.
By Taxi (cost) AUD20. Time approx. 20 min.
Tip luggage porters AUD1 per piece

Transfers: (Minimum Connecting Time):
International to International: 60 min.
International to Domestic: 90 min.
Domestic to International: 90 min.
Domestic to Domestic: 30 min.

Automobile Rentals:
Airport car rental desk
Avis - 38604200
Hertz - 38604522

Car rental city office
Avis - 32527111
National Interrent - 38571499
Hertz - 32216166

Hotels:
All Seasons Abbey Hotel, 160 Roma St., 32361444
Brisbane City Travelodge, Roma St., 32382222
Brisbane Hilton, 190 Elizabeth St., 32313131
Brisbane Parkroyal, Cnr. Alice and Albert Sts., 32213411
Carlton Crest Hotel Brisbane, Cnr. Ann and Roma Sts.,
    32299111
Comfort Inn Buranda, Tottenham and Wolseley Sts., 33910081
Conrad International Treasury Casino Brisbane, William St.,
    33068888
Gazebo Hotel Brisbane, 345 Wickham Terr., 38316177

Heritage Hotel, Cnr. Edward and Margaret Sts., 32211999
Metro Inn Tower Mill, 239 Wickham Terr., 38321421
Quay West, 132 Alice St., 3856 6000
Royal Albert Botique Hotel, Elizabeth and Albert Sts., 32918888
Sheraton Brisbane Hotel and Towers, 249 Tubot St., 38353535

Restaurants:
About Face, 252 Kelvin Grove Rd., 3356-8605
Baguette Bar Cafe, 150 Racecourse Rd., 3268-6168
Brasserie Indochine, 307 Queen St., 3229-4033
Fiasco's, 640 Stanley St., 3391-1413
Grape Wine & Food Bar, 308 Wickham St., 3852-1301
Il Centro, 1 Eagle Street Pier, 3221-6090
Indigo, 695 Brunswick St., 3254-0275
Malaysian Experience, 80 Jepherson St., 3870-2624
Michael's Riverside Restaurant, 123 Eagle St. 3832-5522
Oriental Bangkok Restaurant, 454 Upper Edward St., 3832-6010
Oxley,s on the River, 330 Coronation Dr., 3368-1866
Peperinas Restaurant and Tapas Bar, 140 Sylvan Rd.,
    3870-9981
Pier 9 Oyster Bar and Seafood Grill, 1 Eagle Street Pier,
    3229-2194
Sirocco Mediterranean Cafe, South Bank Parklands, 3846-1803
Summit Restaurant, Sir Samuel Griffith Dr., 3369-9922
Tables of Toowong, 85 Miskin St., 3371-4558
Victoria's,Queen St.Mall, 3231-3131

Entertainment:
Breakfast Greek Hotel, 2 Kingsford-Smith Dr., 3262-5988
Conrad Treasury Casino, William and Elizabeth Sts., 3306-8888
Friday's, 123 Eagle St., 3832-2122
Hogie's Pool Bar & Nightclub, 127 Charlotte St., 3221-5555

Shops and Stores:
Chopstix, 249 Brunswick Str., Fortitude Valley   Shopping Area
Cotton Wool, Brisbane Arcade, Queen St. Mall   Apparel
David Jones, Queen St., downtown   Dept. Store
Greg Grant Country Clothing, Myer Center, Queen St.   Apparel
Myer, Queen St., downtown   Dept. Store
Rowes Arcade, 235 Edward St.   Shopping Area
Savoir Faire, 20 Park Road., Milton   Shopping Area
T&G Arcade, 141 Queen St.   Shopping Arcade

The Pavilion, b/n Queen and Albert Sts.   Mall
Places of Interest:
St.John's Anglican Cathedral
Anzac Square and the Shrine of Remembrance -monuments
The Old Windmill - an old convict building.
Parliament House
Queensland Cultural Centre - art galleries and a museum
Lone Pine Koala Sanctuary
The Treasury Building - a casino
The Old Commissariat Store
Surfers Paradise - beaches

CANBERRA

Country code: 61 - City code: 262

Airport: Canberra Airport

Distance from City: 8km (4 miles) from the city.

Transportation to Center of City:
From International and Domestic Terminals
By Bus (cost) AUD5. Time approx. 25 min.
By Taxi (cost) AUD10-15. Time approx. 10 min.
Tip luggage porters AUD1 per piece

Automobile Rentals:
Airport car rental desk
Avis - 62491601
Hertz - 62496211

Car rental city office
Avis - 62496088
Hertz - 62574877

Hotels:
Hyatt Hotel Canberra, Commonwealth Ave., Yarralumla, 270-1234
Parkroyal Canberra, 1 Binara St., 247-8999

AUSTRALIA

Restaurants:
Barocca Cafe, 60 Marcus Clarke St., 6248 0253
Cafe Lella, Jardine St., Green Sq., 6239 6383
Cavalier Carousel Restaurant, Red Hill Lookout, 6273 1808
Charcoal Restaurant, 61 London Circuit, 6248 8015
Green Square Deli, Jardine Sq., 6295 7845
Gus' Coffee Lounge, Bunda St., and Garema Pl., 6248 8118
Tang Dynasty, 27 Kennedy St., 6295 0122
The Oak Room, Commonwealth Ave., 6270 8977
The Republic, 20 Allara St., 6247 1717
Tosolini's, East Row and London Circuit, 6247 4317
Vivaldi, University Ave., 6257 2718

Entertainment:
Bobby McGee's, London Circuit, 6257 7999
Casino Canberra, 21 Binara St., 6257 7074
Pandora's at Night & Wally's Bar, Mort and Alinga Sts.
   6248 7405
The Private Bin, 50 Northbourne Ave., 6247 3030

Shops and Stores:
Federation Square, O'Hanlon Pl., Gold Greek Village,
   Gungahlim   Mall

Places of Interest:
National Film and Sound Archive - a museum
The National Science and Technology Center
The Australian National Gallery - an art gallery
St. John the Baptist Church and Schoolhouse
The National Botanic Gardens
The Royal Australian Mint - an observation gallery
The National Aquarium and Australian Wildlife Sanctuary
The Telecom Tower
The National Capital Planning Exhibition
The Australian War Memorial - monuments and a museum
Sheep Station - sheep shearing and boomerang throwing
   demonstrations

MELBOURNE

Country code: 61 - City code: 39

AUSTRALIA

Airport: Tullamarine International Airport.

Distance from City: 22km (13 miles) from the city.

Transportation to Center of City:
From International and Domestic Terminals
By Bus (cost) AUD9. Time approx. 35 min.
By Taxi (cost) AUD25-30. Time approx. 23-30 min.
Tip luggage porters AUD1 per piece

Transfers: (Minimum Connecting Time):
International to International: 60 min.
International to Domestic: 60 min.
Domestic to International: 45 min.
Domestic to Domestic: 45 min.

Automobile Rentals:
Airport car rental desk.
Avis - 93381800
Hertz - 93384044

Car rental city office.
Avis - 96636366
National Interrent - 93295000
Hertz - 96636244

Hotels:
All Seasons Crossley Hotel, 51 Little Bourke St., 96391639
All Seasons Swanston Hotel, 195 Swanston St., 96634711
All Seasons Welcome Hotel, Melbourne, 265-281 Little Bourke St., 96390555
Centra Melbourne, Cnr. Flinders and Spencer Sts., 96295111
Como Hotel, 630 Chapel St, S. Yarra, 98240400
Elizabeth Tower Hotel, 792 Elizabeth St., 93497211
Grand Hyatt Melbourne, 123 Collins St., 96571234
Le Meridien at Rialto, 495 Collins St., 96209111
Melbourne Hilton on the Park, 192 Wellington Parade, 94192000
Metro Inn Apartement Hotel Melbourne, 133 Jolimont Rd., 96542844
Parkroyal on St. Kilda Road, 562 St. Kilda, 95298888
Sheraton Tower Southgate, One Brown St., 96963100
Sofitel Melbourne Hotel, 25 Collins St., 96530000

St. Kilda Road Travelodge, Cnr. St. Kilda & Park St., 96994833
Stamford Plaza Melbourne, 111 Little Collins St., 96591000
Windsor Hotel, 103 Spring St., 96336000

Restaurants:
Akita, Courtney and Blackwood Sts., 9326 5766
Bistro 1, 126 Little Collins St., 9654 3343
Cafe Di Stasio, 31 Fitzroy St., 9525 3999
Caffe e Cucina, 581 Chapel St., 9827 4139
Continental Cafe, 132A Greville St., 9510 2788
Est Est Est, 440 Clarendon St., 9682 5688
Flower Drum, 17 Market La., 9662 3655
France-Soir, 11 Toorak Rd., 9866 8569
Guernica, 257 Brunswick St., 9416 0969
Il Bacaro, 168-170 Little Collins St., 9654 6778
Jacques Reymond, 78 Williams Rd., 9525 2178
Madam Fang, 27-29 Grossley St., 9663 3199
Madame Joe Joe, 9 Fitzroy St., 9534 0000
Marchetti's Latin, 55 Lonsdale St., 9662 1985
Melbourne Wine Room, 25 Fitzroy St., 9525 5599
Milan, 44 Cotham Rd., 9853 5379
O'Connell's, Montague and Coventry Sts., 9699 9600
Paul Bocuse Restaurant, 211 La Trobe St., 9660 6600
Ristorante Roberto, 31 Russell St., 9650 3399
Shark Fin House, 131 Little Bourke St., 9663 1555
Stella, 159 Spring St., 9639 1555

Entertainment:
Bell's Hotel, Moray and Coventry Sts., 9690 4511
Cha Cha's, 20 Chapel St., 9525 1077
Chasers, 386 Chapel St., 9827 6615
Comedy Club, 380 Lygon St., 9348 1622
Continental Cafe, 132A Greville St., 9510 2788
Downstairs at Eric's, Darling Sr. and Toorak Rd.,
    9820 3804
Dog's Bar, 54 Acland St., 9525 3599
Florentino Cellar Bar, 80 Bourke St., 9662 1811
Hyatt on Collins, 123 Collins St., 9657 1234
Limerick Arms Hotel, 364 Clarendon St., 9690 4511
Metro, 20-30 Bourke St., 9663 4288
The Last Laugh, 64 Smith St., 9419 8600

AUSTRALIA

Shops and Stores:

Altmann and Cherny, 120 Exhibition St.	Jewelry
Australia on Collins, 260 Collins St.	Shopping Center
Block Arcade, 260 Copllins St.	Arcade
Daimaru, 211 LaTrobe St.	Dept. Store
David Jones, 310 Bourke St.	Dept. Store
Makers Mark Gallery, 85 Collins St.	Jewelry
Myer, 314 Bourke St.	Dept. Store
Royal Arcade, 355 Bourke St.	Shopping Arcade
Sam Bear, 255 Russell St.	Apparel
Sportsgirl Center, 254 Collins St.	Apparel

The Jam Factory, 500 Chapel St., South Yarra Shopping Center

Place of Interest:
The State Library and Museum of Victoria
The Old Melbourne Gaol - a museum
The National Gallery of Victoria
The Old Treasury Building - a museum
St.Paul's Cathedral
Luna Park - an amusement park
Melbourne Zoological Gardens
Cook's Cottage
The Polly Woodside Maritime Museum
The Australia Gate Sensor Vision Theatre - a film-show
Philip Island - an attraction

PERTH

Country code: 61 - City code: 89

Airport: Perth International Airport.

Distance from City: 10km (6 miles) from the city.

Transportation to Center of City:
From International and Domestic Terminals
By Bus (cost) AUD7-10. Time approx. 20-30 min.
By Taxi (cost) AUD20-25. Time approx. 20-50 min.
Tip luggage porters AUD1 per piece

Transfers: (Minimum Connecting Time):
International to International: 60 min.
International to Domestic: 120 min.
Domestic to International: 90 min.
Domestic to Domestic: 30 min.
Automobile Rentals:
Airport car rental desk.
Avis - 92771177
Hertz - 94794788

Car rental city office.
Avis - 93257677
Hertz - 93217777

Hotels:
Hyatt Regency Perth, 99 Adelaide Terrace, 225-1234
Novotel Langley Perth, 221 Adelaide Terrace, 221-1200
Perth Parkroyal, 54 Terrace Rd., 325-3811
Perth Parmelia Hilton, Mill St., 322-3622
Perth Travelodge, 778 Hay St., 321-9141
Sheraton Perth Hotel, 207 Adelaide Terrace, 325-0501
Parmelia Hilton, Mill St., 93223622
Chateau Commodore, 417 Hay St., 93250461
Sebel of Perth, 37 Pier St., 93257655
New Esplanade, 18 The Esplanade, 93252000
The Adelphi, 130A Mountains Bay Rd., 93224666

Restaurants:
Botticelli, 147 James St., 9328 4322
Chanterelle, 210 Rokeby Rd., 9381 4637
Coco's, 85 The Esplande, 9474 3030
Emperor's Court, 66 Lake St., 9328 1628
Fraser's, Fraser Ave., 9481 7100
Frost Bites, 397 Murray St., 9321 3258
Mead's Fish Gallery, 15 Johnson Parade, 9383 3388
Minty's, 309 Hay St., 9325 5299
Oriel, 483 Hay St., 9382 1886
Oriental Joe's Diner, 99 Adelaide Terr., 9225 1268
Perugino, 77 Outram St., 9321 5420
Pierre's, 8 Outram St., 9322 7648
Princess Court, 326 Hay St, 9325 1230
San Lorenzo, 23 Victoria Ave., 9384 0870

Universal, 221 William St., 9227 6771
Witch's Cauldron, 89 Rokeby Rd., 9381 2508
Yen Do, 416 William St., 9227 8833

Entertainment:
Adelphi, 130A Mounts Bay Rd., 9322 3622
Astoria, 37 Bay View Terr., 9384 1372
Brass Monkey Pub and Brasserie, 209 William St., 9227 9596
Chicago's, 707 Wellington St., 9327 7000
Club Bay View, 20 St.Quentin's Ave., 9385 1331
Exit, 187 Stirling St., 9227 8200
Hyde Park Hotel, 331 Bulwer St., 9328 6166
Orsini's, 207 Adelaide Terr., 9325 0501
Queen's Tavern, 520 Beaufort St., 9328 7267
The Globe, 393 Murray St., 9481 2521
Vic, 226 Hay St., 9380 0868

Shops and Stores:

Aherns, Murray Street	Dept. Store
Charles Edward Jewelers, 45 King St.	Jewelry
Citiplace, Post Office	Mall
Forrest Chase, Post Office	Mall
Linneys, 37 Rokeby Rd., Subiaco	Jewelry
Myer, Murray Street	Dept. Store
Opal Center, 47 London Ct.	Jewelry

Place of Interest:
The Old Fire Station - a museum
St.Mary's Cathedral
The Museum of Childhood
It's a Small World - a museum
Underwater World - an aquarium
Cohunu Wildlife Park
Swan River Cruise - a cruise of vineyards
Adventureworld - rides, animals, waterways and gardens
Freemantle

SYDNEY

Country code: 61 - City code: 29

AUSTRALIA

Airport: Sydney (Kingsford Smith) International Airport.

Distance from City: 12km (7 miles) from the city.

Transportation to Center of City:
From International and Domestic Terminals
By Bus (cost) AUD5. Time approx. 30-60 min (every 30 min.)
By Taxi (cost) AUD20-25. Time approx. 20-40 min.
Tip luggage porters AUD1 per piece

Transfers: (Minimum Connecting Time):
International to International: 60 min.
International to Domestic: 75 min.
Domestic to International: 60 min.
Domestic to Domestic: 30 min.

Automobile Rentals:
Airport car rental desk.
Avis - 96670667
Hertz - 96692444

Car rental city office.
Avis - 94393733
Hertz - 93606621

Hotels:
ANA Hotel Sydney, 176 Cumberland St., The Rocks, 92506000
All Seasons Premier Menzies Hotel, 14 Carrington St., 92991000
Centra North Sydney, 17 Blue St., 99550499
Gazebo Hotel, 2 Elizabeth Bay Rd., 93581999
Hyde Park Plaza Hotel, 38 College St., 93316933
Inter-Continental Sydney, 117 Macquarie St., 92300200
International Top Of The Town Hotel, 227 Victoria St., Kings
     Cross, 93610911
Landmark Parkroyal, Sydney, 81 Macleay St, Potts Point,
     93683000
Metro Inn Apartments, Beehive Tower, 132-136 Sussex St.,
     92909200
Metro Inn Apartments, Kingsleigh Tower, 27-29 King St.,
     92991388
Nikko Darling Harbour, 161 Sussex St., 92991231
Observatory Hotel, 89-113 Kent St., 92562222

Old Sydney Parkroyal, 55 George St., 92520524
Park Hyatt Sydney, 7 Hickson Rd, The Rocks, 92411234
Parkroyal at Darling Harbour, 150 Day St., 92611188

Restaurants:
Bayswater Brasserie, 32 Bayswater Rd., 9357 2177
Bel Mondo, 18-24 Argyle St., 9241 3700
Bill's, 433 Liverpool St., 9360 9631
Bilson's, Overseas Passenger Terminal, 9251 5600
Cosmos, 185A Bourke St., 9331 5306
Darley Street Thai, 28-30 Bayswater Rd., 9358 6530
Fez, 247 Victoria St., 9360 9581
Fishface, 132 Darlinghurst Rd., 9332 4803
Forty-One, 2 Chifley Sq., 9221 2500
Golden Century, 393-399 Sussex St., 9212 3901
Kables, 199 George St., 9238 0000
Mario's, 38 Yurong St., 9331 4945
Mohr's, 527 Crown St., 9319 5682
Pavilion on the Park, 1 Art Gallery Rd., 9232 1322
Prasit's Northside on Crown, 415 Crown St., 9319 4803
Restaurant CBD, 75 York St., 9299 8911
Rockpool, 107 George St., 9252 1888
Star Grill, Panasonic Imax Theatre, 9211 9888
The Wharf, Pier 4,Hickson Rd., 9250 1761
Unkai, 176 Cumberland St., 9250 6123

Entertainment:
Harbourside Brasserie, Pier 1, Hickson Rd., 9252 3000
Kinselas, Bourke and Campbell Sts., Taylor Sq.,9331 3100
Rose,Shamrock and Thistle, 193 Evans St., 9555 7755
Sky, Level 3, Skygarden, 77 Castlereagh St., 402 138
Soho Bar, 171 Victoria St., 9358 6511
Sydney Dance Company, Pier 4,Hickson Rd., 9221 4811
Sydney Harbour Casino, Wharves 12 and 13, 9777 9000
The Basement, 29 Reiby Pl., 9251 2797
The Cauldron, 207 Darlinghurst Rd., 9331 1523
The Craig Brewery, 225 Harbourside, 9281 3922

Shops and Stores:
Aboriginal Art. Centres, 117 George St., L1, The Rocks
                                                      Souvenirs
Angus and Coote, 496 George St.,   Jewelry

David Jones, Elizabeth and Market Sts.	Dept. Store
Grace Bros, George and Market Sts.	Dept. Store
Harbourside, Darling Harbour	Shopping Center
Pitt Street Mall, b/n King and Market St.	Mall
Queen Victoria Building, George St.	Dept. Store

Places of Interest:
The Australian Museum
Sydney Opera House
Darling Harbour - a museum and an aquarium
Taronga Park Zoo
Australia's Wonderland - an amusement park
Koala Park Sanctuary
The Art Gallery of New South Wales
The Museum of Sydney
Sydney Tower - an observation deck and a restaurant
Sydney Harbour Cruise
Bondi Beach
Manly - a traditional seaside resort suburb

NEW ZEALAND

Official Name: New Zealand

Location: South Pacific. New Zealand consists of two major islands. They are separated by the Cook Strait and are lying 1,920km (1,193 miles) southeast of Australia.

Government: Parliamentary State (Monarchy)

Area: 270,534 sq. km., 104,454 sq. miles.

Population: 3.5 million

Religion(s): Anglican, Roman Catholic and other Christian denominations.

Capital City: Wellington

Major Business Cities: Auckland and Christchurch

Time: GMT +12 (GMT +13 from early October to mid March)

Currency: New Zealand Dollar (NZD)=100 cents

Currency Requirements: There are no restrictions on the import and the export of foreign or local currency.

Business Hours:
- Government: 09.00-17.00 Mon-Fri
- Banks: 09.30-16.00 Mon-Fri
- Shops: 09.00-17.30 Mon-Fri; 09.00/10.00-13.00 Sat (late night shopping on Thur/Fri)
- Offices: 09.00-17.00 Mon-Fri

Weight and Measures: Metric System

Electric Current: 230 volts AC. Most hotels provide 110-volt AC sockets for electric razors only. The 3-pin power outlet is different from that in some countries and an adapter socket may be required.

Holidays:
New Year - January 1-2
Waitangi Day - February 6
Good Friday - April 10*
Easter Monday - April 13*
Anzac Day - April 25
Queen's Birthday - June 2
Labor Day - October 27
Christmas - December 25

*Christian Holidays - vary each year

Suitable Clothing: Wear a conservative suit or dress to meetings, and in better restaurants. In winter (May through September), bring medium weight clothing and a coat; in summer, wear light clothing. Be prepared to layer in the country's varied climate. Rainwear and sungear are absolutely essential.

Automobile Driving License: An International Driving License can be used if it is held for at least 1 year. Drivers must be over 21 years of age. UK, Australian, Canadian and U.S. licenses are also accepted.

Customs Allowances: Personal items are duty free, but register valuables upon arrival and keep receipts, or they may be confiscated upon departure. You may bring in 200 cigarettes and l liter of wine and spirits. There are no currency restrictions. Prohibited are military weaponry and drugs, with harsh punishment for the latter.

Tipping: Service charges are not added to the hotel and the restaurant bills. Tipping is not the general custom in New Zealand and it is left to your discretion. Porters and taxi drivers do not expect a tip.

Credit Cards Accepted: American Express, Diner's Club, MasterCard, Visa

Customary Dining Hours:
Breakfast: 07.00-09.00
Lunch: 12.30-14.30
Dinner: 17.30-19.30

Local Customs, Business Protocol and Courtesies: New Zealanders have an informal society, and a good sense of humor is always appreciated, but the business atmosphere is more British · that is, more formal, in style than Australian. Trade protectionism is high here, and an import license a highly valued commodity. Schedule meetings in advance, and be on time. Friendly, informal conversation will usually open a meeting-good topics to cover are New Zealand's sights, culture and water sports. A good nature is appreciated, as well as a smile and thank you. Be persistent in negotiations, but not at the expense of politeness. All presentations and contracts should be thorough and well-defined. If invited to a home, you should accept, and bring flowers and be on time. Send thank you note next day. Business is also often conducted over drinks. Business gifts are rare.

Health: There are no vaccinations required. Medical insurance is advised.

Language: English and Maori

AUCKLAND

Country code: 64 - City code: 9

Airport: Auckland Mangere International Airport.

Distance from City: 22km (13 miles) south of the city.

Transportation to Center of City:
From International and Domestic Terminals
By Bus (cost) NZD10. Time approx. 40 min. (every 30 min.)
By Taxi (cost) NZD40. Time approx. 30-40 min.
Tip luggage porters NZD1 per piece

NEW ZEALAND

Transfers: (Minimum Connecting Time):
International to International: 55 min.
International to Domestic: 90 min.
Domestic to International: 75 min.
Domestic to Domestic: 20 min.

Automobile Rentals:
Airport car rental desk
Avis - 275-7239
National Interrent - 275-9953

Car rental city office
Avis - 379-2650
National Interrent - 275-0066
Hertz - 309-0989

Hotels:
Centra Auckland, 128 Albert St., 302-1111
Hyatt Auckland, Cnr Waterloo Quadrant & Princes St., 366-1234
Quality Hotel Anzac Avenue, 150 Anzac Ave., 379-8509
Sheraton Auckland Hotel & Towers, 83 Symonds St., 379-5132
Stamford Plaza, Auckland, Albert St., 309-8888
Auckland Airport Travelodge, Cnr. Kirkbride & Askot Rds.,
    275-1059
Grand Chancelor Hotel, Auckland Airport, Cnr. Kirkbride & Askot
    Rds., 275-7029
Carlton Hotel Auckland, Mayoral Drive, 366-3000
Auckland City Travelodge, 96-100 Quay St., 377-0349
White Heron, end of Auckland's St., 379-6860
Hotel de Brett, corner of High & Shortland St., 303-2389
Abby's, Albert St., 303-4799
Barry Court Motor Inn, 10 Gladstone Rd., 303-3789
The Boulevard, 13 Alpers Av., 522-0160
The Parlell Inn, 320 Parnell Rd., 358-0642
Ascot Parnel, 36 St. Stephens Av., 309-9012

Restaurants:
A Little Italy, 309 Karangahape Rd., 379 58130
Antoine's, 333 Parnell Rd., 379 8756
Bronze Goat, 108 Ponsonby Rd., 378 4193
Cin Cins, Quay St., 307 6966
Da Vinci's, 508 Queen St., 377 5428

El Inca, 373 Karangahape Rd., 308 9985
Harbourside Seafood and Grill Restaurant, 307 0556
Hong Kong Seafood Restaurant, 164 Great South Rd.,
   524 4756
Iguacu, 269 Parnell Rd., 309 4124
Imperial Garden, 100 Albert St., 303 4141
Mekong, 295 Queen St., 379 7591
Metropole, 223 Parnell Rd., 379 9300
New Orient, Queen St., 379 7793
Penguins Nest, 174 Hurstmere Rd., 489 9574
Plusone, 13 St.Mary's Bay Rd., 376 5112
The French Cafe, 210B Symonds St., 377 1911
Tony's Lord Nelson, 37 Victoria St., 379 4564
Tony's, 27 Wellesley St., 307 4196
Topo Gigio, 278 Dominion Rd., 630 2296
Union Fish Company, 16 Quay St., 379 6745
Varick's Restaurant and Wine Bar, 70 Jervois Rd., 376 2049

Entertainment:
Burgundys of Parnell, 309 5112
Iguacu, 269 Parnell Rd.,
Lio Karaoke Bar, 379 3833
Nag's Head, 117 St.Georges Bay Rd.
Power Station, 377 3488
Stanley's Night Club and Cocktail Bar, 390 201
The Key Club, 358 1736
The Las Vegas Theatre Restaurant, 379 0938
Windsor Castle Tavern, 144 Parnell Rd.

Shops and Stores:

Bonz, 30 Queen St.	Apparel	
CML Mall, b/n Queen St. and Wyndham St.	Mall	
Compendium, Lorne St.	Jewelry	
Deka, 48 Queen St.	Dept. Store	
Fingers, 2 Kitchener St.	Jewelry	
Jason's, 101 Karangahape Rd.	Apparel	
Opal and Jade Vault, Lorne St.	Jewelry	
Queens Arcade, Queens St. Sh.	Arcade	
Smith and Caughey, 253-261 Queen St.	Dept. Store	
Strand Arcade, Queen St. and Elliot Street	Arcade	

NEW ZEALAND

Places of Interest:
Auckland City Art Gallery
Auckland Institute and Museum
Cathedral Church of St.Mary
Hobson Wharf - a museum
Kelly Tarlton's Underwater World and Antarctic Encounter - an aquarium
Museum of Transport and Technology

WELLINGTON

Country code: 64 - City code: 4

Airport: Wellington-Rongotai International Airport.

Distance from City: 8km (4 miles) southeast of the city.

Transportation to Center of City:
From International and Domestic Terminals
By Bus (cost) NZD8. Time approx. 20 min.(every 30 min.)
By Taxi (cost) NZD25-30. Time approx. 15 min.
Tip luggage porters NZD1 per piece

Transfers: (Minimum Connecting Time):
International to International: 90 min.
International to Domestic: 90 min.
Domestic to International: 75 min.
Domestic to Domestic: 30 min.

Automobile Rentals:
Airport car rental desk
Avis - 802-1088
Hertz - 388-7070

Car rental city office
Avis - 801-8108
National Interrent - 473-6600
Hertz - 384-3809

Hotels:
Bay Plaza, 40-44Oriental Parade, 385-7799
James Cook Central Hotel, 147 The Terrace, 499-9500
Parkroyal, cnr. Grey and Featherson Sts., 472-2722
Quality Hotel Oriental Bay, 73 Roxburgh St., 385-0279
Quality Hotel Plimmer Towers, Cnr. Boulcott & Gilmer Sts.
   473-3750
Quality Hotel Willis Street, 355 Willis St., 385-9819
Sharella Motor Inn, 20 Glenmore St., 472-3823
Terrace Regency, 345 The Terrace, 385-9829
Wellington Parkroyal, Cnr. Grey & Featherston Sts., 472-2722
West Plaza Hotel, 110-116 Wakefield St., 473-1440

Restaurants:
Angkor, 41 Dixon St., 384 9423
Armadillo, 129Willis St., 384 1444
Bengal Tiger, 385 1304
Bodrum, 384 4338
Boulcott Brasserie, 499 4199
Brasserie Flipp, 385 9493
Brer Fox, 10 Murphy St., 471 2477
Feruccio's, 38 Cambridge Terrace, 384 6582
Gah Wah, 283 6646
Il Casino, 385 7496
Las Casa Pasta House, 385 9657
Little Itali, 801 5151
Marbles Restaurant, 87 Upland Rd., 475 8490
Mexican Cantina, 19 Edward St., 385 9711
Orient Express Restaurant and Bar, 29 Brandon St., 499 4833
Paleros Greek Tavern, 388 4776
Petit Lyon, 8 Courtenay, 384 9402
Satay Malaysia, 385 7709
Scorpio's, 383 7563
Shanghai Cafe, 384 4953
The Grain of Salt, 232 Oriental Parade, 384 8642
Uncle Changs, 801 9565

Entertainment:
Barrett's, 26 Allen St.
Diva Bar and Cafe, Dixon St., 385 2987
Downstage Theatre, 801 7992
Ecstasy, b/n Courtenay Pl. and Tory St.,384 9495

NEW ZEALAND

Encore Cafe and Bar, Cortenay St., 801 8891
Mid City Tavern, 385 6839
Thorndon Tavern, Moles Woth St., 472 5006

Shops and Stores:

BNZ Center, Bank of New Zealand Bldg.	Mall
City Market, 150 Willis St.	Gifts
Farmar's, 94-102 Cuba Mall	Dept. Store
Gresham Plaza, Lambton Quay	Apparel
Kircaldie and Stain's, Lambton Quay	Dept. Store

Places of Interest:
The Maritime Museum
Southward Museum
The Parliament Buildings
The National Library
Old St.Paul's Cathedral
The Botanic Garden

PHILIPPINES

Official Name: Republic of the Philippines

Location: South-East Asia. The Philippines consist of more than 7000 islands and islets that are lying off the southeast coast of Asia between Taiwan and Borneo in the Pacific Ocean and the South China Sea. There are two major islands - Luzon in the north and Mindanao in the south.

Government: Republic

Area: 300,000 sq. km., 115,830 sq. miles.

Population: 64.08 million

Religion(s): Roman Catholic majority.

Capital City: Manila

Major Business Cities: Manila, Quezon, Davao City, Caloocan City, Cebu City

Time: GMT +8

Currency: Philippine Peso (PP)=100 centavos

Currency Requirements: There is no limit on the import of foreign currency, but the sum has to be declared. The export is limited to the amount declared on arrival. The import and the export of local currency is restricted to PP5,000. An authorization from the Central Bank is required for larger amounts.

Business Hours:
- Government: 07.30-18.00 Mon-Fri
- Banks: 9.00-15.00/16.00 Mon-Fri
- Shops: 09.00/09.30-12.00; 14.00-19.30/20.00 Mon-Sat
- Offices: 08.00/09.00-12.00 and 13.00-17.00 Mon-Fri

PHILIPPINES

Weight and Measures: Metric System

Electric Current: 220 volts AC (110 in most hotels). Plugs are of the flat and the round 2-pin and 3-pin type.

Holidays:
New Year's Day - January 1
Maundy Thursday - March 27
Good Friday - April 10*
Day of Valour (Araw Ng Kagitingan) - April 9
Labor Day - May 1
Independence Day - June 12
Manila Day (Araw ng Maynila) - June 24
National Heroes' Day - August 31
All Saints' Day - November 1
Bonifacio Day - November 30
Christmas Day - December 25
Rizal Day - December 30
New Year's Eve - December 31

*Christian Holidays - vary each year.

Suitable Clothing: You can wear light to medium-weight clothing most of the year, and raingear is useful between July and October. Wear a conservative suit for government or business meetings, and a light jacket and tie, or dress for formal occasions. Do not wear shorts.

Automobile Driving License: A National or an International Driving License can be used if it is held for at least 1 year.

Customs Allowances: Personal items are duty free, but register valuables upon arrival or they may be confiscated upon departure. You may bring in or take out unlimited amounts of foreign currency - declare amounts over $300. You may bring in 400 cigarettes, 2 liters of wine or spirits. Drug smuggling meets with prison or execution. Also prohibited are military weaponry and pornography.

Tipping: Waiters at restaurants expect approximately a 10% tip of the bill. Tipping taxi drivers is not customary, but it is advisable to make sure that the taximeter is turned on before starting the ride.

Credit Cards Accepted: American Express, Diner's Club, MasterCard, Visa

Customary Dining Hours:
Breakfast: 07.30.09.00
Lunch: 12.30-14.00
Dinner: 19.00-22.00

Local Customs, Business Protocol and Courtesies: Friendliness is essential to building business relationships in the Philippines. If your company is not known, a good way to get into the Philippine business door is with letters of introduction from mutual acquaintances; you, too, should research the performance of potential partners. You'll find a business environment not unlike the American one: some of the big companies are American-run and many executives were educated in the U.S. and have a good reputation as joint venture partners. Many Chinese business men operate here, so be mindful of their traditions (see the sections on China and Hong Kong). Schedule meetings in advance, but don't be surprised or angry if your contact is late. Shake hands upon meeting, and use your contact's title until otherwise indicated. Western businesswomen should encounter few problems here, as Filipino businesswomen tend to be taken seriously as well. Be brief, discrete and succinct in presentations and negotiations. Do not cause shame or loss of face, or be confrontational; this will be met with vague politeness and careful diplomacy designed to keep you out of the loop. Laughing or giggling from your counterpart may simply disguise embarassment or discomfort. If invited to a home, arrive around an hour late, and follow your host's example as when to sit and begin eating. Send a thank you note the next day, or flowers to the hostess. If you do the inviting, you yourself will be expected to pay for the meal or entertainment. Small designer-label gifts are highly appreciated, appropriate if invited home for dinner or as a business gift.

PHILIPPINES

Health: It is advisable to consult your doctor before your journey. A vaccination certificate for yellow fever is mandatory if travelling from an infected area. Vaccinations for hepatitis A, tetanus, cholera, typhoid, polio and malaria (tablets) are recommended. It is advisable to drink only bottled water. Food precautions should be observed at all times. Health insurance is essential.

Language: Filipino. English is also widely spoken.

MANILA

Country code: 63 - City code: 2

Airport: Manila-Ninoy Aquino International Airport.

Distance from City: 12km (7 miles) south-east of the city.

Transportation to Center of City:
From International and Domestic Terminals
By Bus (cost) PP5-10. Time approx.30-90 min.
By Taxi (cost) PP350-570. Time approx.25-35 min.
Tip luggage porters 15 Pesos per piece

Transfers: (Minimum Connecting Time):
International to International: 60 min.
International to Domestic: 120 min.
Domestic to International: 120 min.
Domestic to Domestic: 45 min.

Automobile Rentals:
Airport car rental desk
Avis - 832-2088
National Interrent - 833-0648
Hertz - 831-9827

Car rental city office
Avis - 521-0062
National Interrent - 818-8667
Hertz - 832-5325

Hotels:
Bayview Park Hotel, 1118 Roxas Blvd, Cnr. United, 526-1555
Century Park Hotel Manila, Pablo Ocampo Sr. St., 522-1011
Dusit Hotel Nikko, Ayala Center, Makati, 810-4101
Heritage Hotel Manila, Edsa Cnr. Roxas Blvd., 891-8888
Holiday Inn Manila Pavilion, United Nations Ave., Ermita,
  522-2911
Inter-Continental Manila, 1 Ayala Ave., Makati, 815-9711
Mandarin Oriental Manila, Makati Ave., Makati, 750-8888
New World Hotel, Esperanza St., Cnr. Makati Ave., 811-6888
Palm Plaza Hotel, Pedro Gil/Cnr M Adriatico Sts., 521-3502
Peninsula Manila, Cnr. Ayala and Makati Aves., 810-3456
Shangri-La Hotel Manila, Ayala Ave., Cnr. Makati Ave. 813-8888
Shangri-La's Edsa Plaza Hotel, 1 Garden Way, Ortigas Center,
633-8888

Restaurants:
Aristocrat Restaurant, 432 San Andres, 524 7671
Bistro Remedios, 1903 Adriatico St., 521 8097
Blue Bacon & Green Eggs, 27 Lantana St., 721 7666
Cafe Ysabel, 455 P.Guevarra St., 722 0349
City Garden Seafood Restaurant, Bank Dr.,St. Francis Sq.,
  635 3006
Flavours and Spices, Garden Sq., 815 3029
Kamayan Restaurant, 47 Pasay Rd., 815 1463
La Primavera, Garden Square Bldg., 818 1945
La Tasca, Legazpi St., Greenbelt Park, 819 8435
Le Souffle Restaurant and Wine Bar, 2F Josephine Bldg.,
  Greenbelt Dr. at Makati Ave. 812 3287
SM Megamall Food Court, SM Megamall Bldg., 633 5012
Sugi, Greenbelt Mall, 816 3886

Entertainment:
Blue Cafe, Nakpil St. at Bocobo St., 581 725
Cafe Adriatico, 1790 Adriatico St., 584 059
Cafe Mondial, Adriatico St. at Pedro Gil St., 598 946
Chatterbox, 41 West Ave., 997 539
Cine Cafe, 76-C Roces Ave., 969 421
Club Dredd, 570 EDSA, at Tuason St., 912 8464
Guernica's, 1856 Bocobo St., 521 4415
Hobbit House, 1801 A.Mabini St., 521 7604
Lost Horizon, Philipine Plaza, 832 0701

PHILIPPINES

Mayric's, 1320 Espana St., 732 3021
Oar House, A.Mabini St., 595 864
Penguin Cafe, 604 Remedios St., 631 2088
Remembrances, 1795 A.Mabini St., 521 6705
Sirena, Manila Peninsula, Ayala Ave., 819 3456
Zamboanga, 1619 Adriatico St., 572 835

Shops and Stores:

Harrison Plaza	Shopping District
Makati Commercial Center, Makati Ave	Shopping District
Robinson's, b/n Shaw Blvd/Ortigas Ave, EDSA	Dept. Store
Shangri-La, b/n Shaw Blvd/Ortigas Ave, EDSA	Dept. Store
SM, b/n Shaw Blvd/Ortigas Ave, EDSA	Dept. Store

Places of Interest:
San Agustin -a church and a monastery
The Cathedral
Fort Santiago - ruins
Rizal Shrine Museum
The National Museum
The Museum of Arts and Science
The Ayala Museum
Malacanang Palace - a museum
Intramuros

U.S.A.

U.S.A.

Official Name: United States of America

Location: North America. The United States of America consists of 50 states and the District of Columbia. They are bordered by Canada and Mexico. To the east lies the Atlantic Ocean and to the west the Pacific Ocean.

Government: Federal Republic

Area: 9,809,155 sq. km., 3,787,318 sq. miles.

Population: 260,341,000

Religion(s): Protestant majority. Roman Catholic, Jewish and many ethnic minorities are also present.

Capital City: Washington, D.C.

Major Business Cities: Atlanta, Baltimore, Boston, Chicago, Cincinnati, Cleveland, Dallas, Denver, Detroit, Houston, Kansas City, Los Angeles, Miami, Milwaukee, Minneapolis, New Orleans, New York, Philadelphia, Phoenix, Pittsburgh, San Francisco and Seattle.

Time: GMT -5/-10 (GMT -4/-9 from April to late October)

Currency: US Dollar (USD) = 100 cents.

Currency Requirements: There are no restrictions on the import and the export of foreign or local currency. Movement of USD10,000 or more should be registered with customs on a declaration form.

Business Hours:
- Government: 08.30-16.30 Mon-Fri
- Banks: 09.00-15.00 Mon-Fri (some close later)

- Shops: 8.00-18.00 Mon-Sat, some open 12.00-17.00 Sun
- Offices: 09.00-17.00/17.30 Mon-Fri

Weight and Measures: British Imperial System

Electric Current: 110/120 volts AC. Plugs are of the flat 2-pin type with dual voltage. It is advisable to purchase an adapter before the arrival in USA.

Holidays:
New Year's Day - January 1
Martin Luther King Jr.'s Birthday - January 20
Lincoln's Birthday - February 12
Presidents' Day/Washington's Birthday - February 17
Memorial Day Weekend - May 24-26
Independence Day Weekend - July 4-6
Labor Day Weekend - August 30-September 1
Columbus Day - October 12
Veterans' Day - November 11
Thanksgiving Weekend - November 27-30
Christmas Day - December 25

In general, if a holiday falls on a Sunday, the following Monday is observed as a holiday; if a holiday falls on a Saturday, the previous Friday is observed as a holiday.

Suitable Clothing: As the U.S. climate varies greatly, your wardrobe should fit the area traveled to. In the north, wear light to medium clothing in summer and winter clothes and coat in winter. In the southern states, wear light clothing in summer and medium weight clothing and a jacket in winter. If visiting mountainous areas, dress more warmly. A business suit should be worn to all meetings, though take your cue from your host as to what to wear on other occasions.

Automobile Driving License: Foreign driver's licenses are accepted at most car rental companies and locations. Foreign international permits are acceptable only when presented with a valid license and a valid passport with photo. Most companies require renters to be at least 25 years old, although some may rent to drivers of 21 years. Payment is normally by major credit cards.

U.S.A.

Customs Allowances: You may bring in, duty free, 200 cigarettes, 100 cigars (but not Cuban) and about 5 liters of spirits. If you are coming from a South American country, you may be searched for drugs.

Tipping: Tipping is widespread in the service industry and gratuities are heavily relied upon. Service charges are not usually included in the bill. A tip of 10-15% is generally regarded the norm for waiters and taxi drivers. A tip of US$1 per taxi is appropriate for doormen.

Credit Cards Accepted: American Express, Diner's Club, MasterCard, Visa

Customary Dining Hours:
Breakfast: 06.00-11.00
Lunch: 11.00-14.00
Dinner: 17.00-22.00

Local Customs, Business Protocol and Courtesies: The United States business behavior includes a certain degree of friendliness; being formal and overly reserved may be interpreted as cold. At the same time, professionalism is expected, particularly a demonstration of competence and industriousness. Presentations should be direct, thorough and convincing, and not waste time, for American businessmen have a lot on their plate and work long hours. One should write and call to set appointments before arriving in the country, and be absolutely punctual. Upon introduction, people rise and shake hands, but not necessarily at subsequent meetings. Although business cards are important, they are generally exchanged only if you and the other person plan to meet again, or at least would consider contacting each other again. Generally, they are offered before leaving a meeting. Your American counterpart will probably immediately offer his or her first name. Otherwise, Mr. or Ms. are almost always appropriate, although those with Ph.d.'s sometimes go by Dr. Keep in mind that the American women are far ahead of women in most other countries when it comes to the business world, and perceived condescension or overly personal behavior will not be tolerated. People do not stand close to one another when talking.

U.S.A.

Entertaining is frequent, as are business breakfasts and lunches, although the level of hospitality varies greatly. Large corporations often have caterered lunchtime spreads in the office. If you are invited to a home, bring flowers, wine or chocolates, and send a thank-you note the next day. Business gifts are rare, but you might give or send a nice office accessory, fine wine, or something unique to your country, at the end of your trip, after an agreement has been reached, or at Christmas. As for language, bear in mind that the English taught in most European and some other regions is British English, and that some idioms, terms and pronunciation are different from American English. Nevertheless, Americans are very tolerant of grammatical errors from non-native speakers although they tend to have little patience if they have trouble understanding you. Friendly humor, within the bounds of professional behavior, is always appreciated. It is considered the norm for people to talk about their jobs and careers since they take up so much of their lives though never salary. Your host may or may not be very interested in or knowledgeable about the culture or history of your country or region, so take your cue from him or her in casual discussions.

Health: There are no special precautions necessary. Although medical treatment is excellent the cost is extremely high. It is strongly advisable to have medical insurance with coverage up to at least US$1.5 million.

Language: English.

ATLANTA

Country code: 1 - Area code: 404

Airport: Hartsfield Atlanta International Airport.

Distance from City: 15km (9 miles) south of the city.

Transportation to Center of City:
From International and Domestic Terminals

By Bus (cost) USD8. Time approx. 30-40 min.

By Taxi (cost) USD17 Time approx. 20-30 min.
Tip luggage porters USD1 per piece

Transfers: (Minimum Connecting Time):
International to International: 90 min.
International to Domestic: 90 min.
Domestic to International: 60 min.
Domestic to Domestic: 55 min.

Automobile Rentals:
Airport car rental desk
Avis - 530-2700
National - 530-2800
Hertz - 530-2925

Car rental city office
Avis - 659-4814
National - 816-3169
Hertz - 394-6500

Hotels:
Atlanta Hilton & Towers, 255 Courtland St. N.E., 659-2000
Atlanta Marriott Marquis, 265 Peachtree Center Ave., 521-0000
Atlanta Marriott Suites Midtown, 35 14th St., 876-8888
Comfort Inn Downtown, 101 International Blvd., 524-5555
Courtyard Atlanta Downtown, 175 Piedmont Ave. N.E.,
   659-2727
Courtyard Atlanta/Peachtree Dunwoody, 5601 Peachtree-Dun-
woody Rd., 843-2300
Fairfield Inn Atlanta/Downtown, 175 Piedmont Ave. N.E.,
   659-7777
Fairfield Inn Atlanta/Midtown, 1470 Spring St, N. W., 872-5821
Grand Hotel Atlanta, 75 Fourteen St., 881-9898
Hyatt Regency Atlanta, On Peachtree St., 577-1234
Radisson Hotel Atlanta, 165 Courtland & Int'l Blvd., 659-6500
Radisson Inn at Executive Park Atlanta, 2061 N. Druid Hills Rd.,
   321-4174
Renaissance Atlanta Hotel – Downtown, 590 W. Peachtree St.,
   881-6000
Residence Inn Atlanta/Midtown, 1041 W. Peachtree St.,

872-8885
Ritz Carlton Atlanta, 181 Peachtree St. N. E., 659-0400
Wyndham Midtown Hotel, 125 Tenth St. N.E., 872-4800

Restaurants:
Abruzzi Ristorante, 2355 Peachtree Rd., 261 8186
Bacchanalia, 3125 Piedmont Rd., 365 0410
Buckhead Diner, 3073 Piedmont Rd., 262 3336
Cafe Tu Tu Tango, 220 Pharr Road, 841 8222
Canoe, 4199 Paces Ferry Road, 432 2663
Cascade Java, 2345 Cascade Road, 752 5282
Cheyenne Grille, 2391 Peachtree Road, 842 1010
Ciboulette, 1529 Piedmont Ave., 874 7600
City Grill, 50 Hurt Plaza, 524 2489
Colonnade Restaurant, 1927.1879 Cheshire Bridge Rd.,
    874 5642
Dining Room,in the Ritz-Carlton,Buckhead, 3434
    Peachtree Rd., 237 2700
Fisherman's Cove, 201 Courtland St., 659 3610
Fronteras Mex-Mex Grill, 5060 N. Royal Atlanta Road,
    414 5026
Hong Kong Delight, 5920 Roswell Road, 255 3388
Luna Si, 1931 Peachtree St., 355 5993
Pricci, 500 Pharr Rd., 237 2941
South City Kitchen, 1144 Crescent Ave., 873 7358
The 1848 House, 780 South Cobb Dr., 428 1848
The Cabin, 2878 Buford Highway, 315 7676
The Industry, 1789 Cheshire Bridge Road, 817 3722

Entertainment:
Atkins Park Bar & Grill, 794 N.Highland Ave., 876 7249
Atlanta Live Nite Club, 3330 Pledmont Road, 869 0003
Axys, 1150B Peachtree St., 607 0922
Ball Bottoms, 225 Pharr Road, 816 9669
Blind Willie's, 828 N.Highland Ave., 873 2583
Cotton Club, 1021 Peachtree St., 874 9524
Eddie's Attic, 515B N.McDonough St., 377 4976
Kaya, 1068 Peachtree St., 874 4460
Have A Nice Day Cafe, 857 Cottler Rd., 351 1401
One Ninety One Club, 191 Peachtree St., 222 0191
Otto's, 265 E.Paces Ferry, 233 1133
Park Bench, 256 E.Paces Ferry, 264 1334

Point, 420 Moreland Ave., 659 3522
Ruperts, 3330 Piedmont Rd., 266 9834
Taverna at Phipps, 3500 Peachtree Rd., 814 9640
The Martini Club, 1140 Crescent Ave., 873 0784
Tongue & Groove, 963 Peachtree Rd., 261 2325

Shops and Stores:

Abbadabba's, 421-B Moreland Ave., N.E.	Apparel
Bally Inc., Lenox Square, 3393 Peachtree St.	Shoes
Casual Corner, 210 Peachtree St.	Apparel
Eventz Over Georgia, 1229 Oakdale Rd.	Souvenirs
Lenox Square, 3393 Peachtree St.,	Mall
Papillon, 231 Peachtree St., N.E.	Apparel
Phipps Plaza, 3500 Peachtree Rd.	Mall
Tiffany & Co., Phipps Plaza, 3500 Peachtree Rd.	Jewelry

Places of Interest:
The World of Coca-Cola - a museum of memorabilia
The High Museum of Art, Folk Art and Photography Galleries
Atlanta International Museum of Art and Design
Atlanta History Center
The Center for Puppetry Arts Museum
Fernbank Science Center – a planetarium
Atlanta Botanical Garden
SciTrek - a science museum
Stone Mountain Park – museums and memorials to war heroes.
Underground Atlanta - entertainment and shopping center
King Center – a museum and a library

BOSTON

Country code: 1 - Area code: 617

Airport: Logan International Airport.

Distance from City: 4km (2 miles) northeast of the city.

Transportation to Center of City:
From International and Domestic Terminals
By Bus (cost) USD7.50 Time approx. 30 min. (every 8-12min.)

U.S.A.

By Taxi (cost) USD15 Time approx. 20-30 min.)
Tip luggage porters USD1   per piece

Transfers: (Minimum Connecting Time):
International to International: 75 min.
International to Domestic: 90 min.
Domestic to International: 60 min.
Domestic to Domestic: 40 min.

Automobile Rentals:
Airport car rental desk
Avis - 561-3500
National - 569-6700
Hertz - 569-7272

Car rental city office
Avis - 534-1400
Hertz - 338-1500

Hotels:
Boston Back Bay Hilton, 40 Dalton St., 236-1100
Boston Harbor Hotel, 70 Rowes Wharf, 439-7000
Boston Marriott Copley Place, 110 Huntington Ave., 236-5800
Boston Marriott Long Wharf, 296 State St., 227-0800
Boston Marriott Peabody, 8a Centennial Dr., Peabody, 977-9700
Boston Park Plaza Hotel & Towers, 64 Arlington St., 426-0000
Bostonian Hotel, At Faneuil Hall Market Pl., 523-3600
Colonnade, 120 Huntington Ave., 424-7000
Copley Plaza Hotel, 138 St. James Ave., 267-5300
Copley Square Hotel, 47 Huntington Ave., 536-9000
Doubletree Guest Suits Cambridge, 400 Soldiers Field Rd.,
    783-0897
Farrington Inn, 23 Farrington Ave., 787-1860
Le Meridien Boston, 250 Franklin St., 451-1900
Lenox Hotel, 710 Boylston St., 536-5300
Residence Inn Boston/North Shore, 51 Newbury St., Rte.1,
    Danvers, 777-7171
Sheraton Inn Lowell, 50 Warren St., Lowell, 452-1200
Sheraton Inn Plymouth, 180 Water St., Plymouth, 747-4900

Restaurants:
Bay Tower, 60 State St., 723 1666

U.S.A.

Bertucci's, 21 Brattle St., 864 4748
Biba, 272 Boylston St., 426 7878
Bombay Club, 57 John F.Kennedy St., 661 8100
Daily Catch, 441 Harvard St., 734 5696
Dali, 415 Washington St., 661 3254
Durgin-Park, 340 Faneuil Hall Marketplace, 227 2038
East Coast Grill, 1271 Cambridge St., 491 6568
Golden Palace, 14 Tyler St., 423 4565
Hamersley's Bistro, 553 Tremont St., 423 2700
Ho Yuen Ting, 13A Hudson St., 426 2316
Iruna, 56 John F.Kennedy St., 868 5633
Jasper, 240 Commercial St., 523 1126
Julien, 250 Franklin St., 451 1900
L'Espalier, 30 Gloucester St., 262 3023
Legal Sea Foods, 35 Columbas Ave., 426 4444
Ristorante Lucia, 415 Hanover St., 523 9148
Seasons, North and Blackstone Sts., 523 3600
The Harvest, 44 Brattle St., 492 1115
Union Oyster House, 41 Union St., 227 2750

Entertainment:
Avalon, 15 Lansdowne St., 262 2424
Bill's Bar, 5 Lansdowne St., 421 9678
Blacksmith House, 56 Brattle St., 354 30036
Boston Jazz Line, 787 9700
Bull & Finch Pub, 84 Beacon St., 227 9605
Catch a Rising Star, 4 John F.Kennedy St., 661 9887
Custom House Lounge, 60 State St., 723 1666
Green Street Grill, 280 Green St., 876 1655
Hard Rock Café, 131 Clarendon St., 353 1400
House of Blues, 96 Winthrop St., 497 2229
Lizard Lounge, 1667 Massachusetts Ave., 547 0759
Middle East, 472-480 Massachusetts Ave., 864-EAST
Paradise, 967 Commonwealth Ave., 254 3939
Passim's, 47 Palmer St., 492 7679
Quest, 1270 Boylston St., 424 7747
Regattabar, Bennett and Eliot Sts., 864 1200
Ryles Jazz Club, 212 Hampshire St., 876 9330
Scullers Jazz Club, 400 Soldiers Field Rd., 562 4111
Top of the Hub, Prudential Center, 536 1775
Wally's, 427 Massachusetts Ave., 424 1408

U.S.A.

Shops and Stores:

Boston Antique Center, 54 Canal St., 742 1400	Antiques
Bromfield Pen Shop, 5 Bromfield St., 482 9053	Antiques
Brooks Brothers, 46 Newbury St.	Apparel
Filene's, 426 Washington St.	Dept. Store
Fine Time Time Museum, 279 Newbury St.	Jewelry
Giorgio Armani, 22 Newbury St.	Apparel
John Lewis,Inc., 97 Newbury St.	Jewelry
Macy's, 450 Washington St.	Dept. Store
NEXT, 208 Newbury St.	Apparel
The Harvard Coop, 1400 Massachusetts Ave.	Dept. Store

Places of interest:
Museum of Science
The New England Aquarium
Paul Revere House
Freedom Trail
The Harvard University Museums of Cultural and Natural
    History
USS Constitution
Old Statehouse
Faneuil Hall
Boston Tea Party
Bunker Hill Monument
Beaver II

CHICAGO

Country code: 1 - Area codes: 312; 708; 773; 847
(All listings are 312 unless noted otherwise)

Airport: O'Hare International Airport.

Distance from City: 28km (17 miles) northwest of the city.

Transportation to Center of City:
From International and Domestic Terminals
By Bus (cost) USD14.75 Time approx. 45-60 min. (every 5-10 min.)
By Taxi (cost) USD25-30 Time approx. 40 min.
Tip luggage porters USD1 per piece

U.S.A.

Transfers: (Minimum Connecting Time):
International to International: 90 min.
International to Domestic: 90 min.
Domestic to International: 75 min.
Domestic to Domestic: 50 min.

Automobile Rentals:
Airport car rental desk
Avis - 694-5600
National - 694-4640
Hertz - 686-7272

Car rental city office
Avis - 782-6827
National - 471-3450
Hertz - 372-7600

Hotels:
Best Western Inn Of Chicago, 162 E. Ohio at N. Michigan Ave., 787-3100
Chicago Hilton & Towers, 720 S. Michigan Ave., 922-4400
Chicago Marriott Downtown, 540-Michigan Ave., 836-0100
Chicago, The Drake, 240 E. Walton Place, 787-2200
Courtyard Chicago/Downtown 30 E. Hubbard at State St, 329-2500
Doubletree Guest Suites Downtown, 198 E. Delaware, 664-1100
Holiday Inn – City Center, 300 E. Ohio St., 787-6100
Hyatt Regency Chicago, In Illinois Center, 565-1234
Hyatt at University Village, 625 S. Ashland Ave., 243-7200
Hyatt on Printers Row, 500 South Dearborn, 986-1234
Midland Hotel, 172 W. Adams at LaSalle, 332-1200
Palmer House Hilton, 17 East Monroe St., 726-7500
Quality Inn Downtown, 1 Midcity Plaza, 829-5000
Radisson Hotel & Suites Chicago, 160 E. Huron St., 787-2900
Regal Knickerbocker Hotel, 163 E. Walton Place, 751-8100
Renaissance Chicago Hotel, One W. Wacker Dr., 372-7200
Sheraton Chicago Hotel & Towers, 301 E. North Water St., 464-1000
Swissotel Chicago, 323 E. Wacker Dr., 565-0565

Restaurants:
Ambria, 2300 N.Lincoln Park, (773) 472 5959

Arun's, 4156 N.Kedzie Ave., (773) 539 1909
Everest, 440 S.La Salle St., 663 8920
Frontera Grill, 445 N.Clark St., 661 1434
Klay Oven, 414 N.Orleans St., 527 3999
Le Francais, 269 S.Milwaukee Ave., 541 7470
Le Titi de Paris, 1015 W.Dundee Rd., (847) 506 0222
Morton's of Chicago, 1050 N.State St., 266 4820
Pizzeria Uno/Pizzeria Due, 29 E.Ohio St., 321 1000
Printer's Row, 550 S.Dearborn St., 461 0780
Reza's, 5255 N.Clark St., (773) 561 1898
Rosebud, 1500 W.Taylor St., 942 1117
Spiaggina, 980 N.Michigan Ave., 280 2750
The Berghoff, 17 W.Adams St., 427 3170
Three Happiness, 2130 S.Wentworth Ave., 791 1228
Trio, 1625 Hinman, 733 8746
Tuttaposto, 646 N.Franklin St., 943 6262
Yoshi's Cafe, 3257 N.Halsted St., (773) 248 6160

Entertainment:
Blue Chicago, 937 N.State St., 642 6261
Buddy Guy's Legends, 754 S.Wabash Ave., 427 0333
Cabaret Metro, 3730 N.Clark St., (773) 549 0203
Cubby Bear Lounge, 1059 W.Addison St., (773) 327 1662
Double Door, 1572 N.Milwaukee Ave., (773) 489 3160
Green Mill Cocktail Lounge, 4802 N.Broadway, (773) 878 5552
Improv, 504 N.Wells St., 782 6387
Kingston Mines, 2548 N.Halsted St., (773) 477 4646
Lounge Ax, 2438 N.Lincoln Ave., (773) 525 6620
New Checkerboard Lounge, 423E. 43rd St., (773) 624 3240
No Exit, 6970 N.Glenwood Ave., (773) 743 3355
Pops for Champagne, 2934 N.Sheffield Ave., (773) 472 1000
Second City, 1616 N.Wells St., 337 3992
Wild Hare, 3530 N.Clark St., (773) 327 4273
Zanies, 1548 N.Wells St., 337 4027

Shops and Stores:

Avenue Atrium, 900 N. Michigan Ave.	Mall
Bloomingdale's, 900 N. Michigan Ave.	Dept. Store
Brooks Brothers, 209 S. LaSalle St.	Apparel
Burberry's, 633 Michigan Ave.	Apparel
Carson Pirie Scott & Co., 1 S. State St.	Dept. Store
Lester Lampert Inc., 57 E. Oak St.	Jewelry

Lincoln Park Neighborhood, Clark St.	Mall
Marshall Field's & Co, 111 N. State St.	Dept. Store
Nieman Marcus, 737 N. Michigan Ave.	Dept. Store
Oak Street, 25 E. Oak St.	Mall
S.A. Peck and Company, 55 E. Washington St., Ste. 539	
	Jewelry
Saks Fifth Avenue, 700 N Michigan Ave.	Dept. Store
The Goldsmith Ltd., 835 N. Michigan Ave.	Jewelry
Tiffany & Company, 730 N. Michigan Ave.	Jewelry
Water Tower Place, 835 N.Michigan Ave.	Mall

Places of Interest:
Chicago Public Library Cultural Center
Sears Tower
Art Institute of Chicago – a museum
Michigan Avenue - shops
The Loop
The Field Museum of Natural History
Lincoln Park Zoo
Lincoln Park Conservatory
The Museum of Science and Industry
The Wrigley Building
Chicago City Hall/Cook County Building

CLEVELAND

Country code: 1 - Area code: 216

Airport: Cleveland Hopkins International Airport.

Distance from City: 16km (9 miles) southwest of the city.

Transportation to Center of City:
From International and Domestic Terminals
By Train (cost) USD1.50. Time approx. 25 min.
By Taxi (cost) USD20. Time approx. 30 min.
Tip luggage porters USD1 per piece
Transfers: (Minimum Connecting Time):
International to International: 30 min.

U.S.A.

International to Domestic: 30 min.
Domestic to International: 30 min.
Domestic to Domestic: 30 min.

Automobile Rentals:
Airport car rental desk
Avis - 265-3700
National - 267-4693
Hertz - 267-8900

Car rental city office
Avis - 623-0801
Hertz - 831-3836

Hotels:
Marriott Cleveland Society Center, 127 Public Sq., 696-9200
Renaissance Cleveland Hotel, 24 Public Sq., 696-5600
Sheraton Cleveland Centre Hotel, 777 St. Clair Ave., 771-7600
Wyndham Cleveland Hotel, 1260 Euclid Ave., 615-7500
Radisson Suite Hotel, 1706 E., 12th St., 523-8000
Ritz-Carlton, Stouffer Renaissance Cleveland Plaza Hotel, 24
    Public Sq., 696-5600

Restaurants:
Bohemia, 900 Literary Rd., 566 8800
Luchita's, 3456 W. 117th St., 252 1169
Nate's Deli and Restaurant, 1923 W. 25th St., 696 7529
Sammy's, 1400 W.10th St., 523 5560
Sweetwater's Cafe Sausalito, 1301 E. 9th St., 696 2233
The Palazzo, 10031 Detroit Ave., 651 3900
Tommy's, 1824 Coventry Rd., 321 7757
Wilbert's Bar and Grill, 1360 W. 9th St., 771 2583

Entertainment:
Harbor Inn, 1219 Main Ave., 241 3232
Improv Comedy Club, 696 4677
Shooter's on the Water, 1148 Main Ave., 861 6900
Smart Bar, Merwin Ave., 522 1575

Shops and Stores:

Avenue, Tower City Center	Mall
Galleria, 1301 E. 9th St.	Mall

U.S.A.

West Side Market, 25th and Lorian Rd.   Dept. Store

Places of Interest:
University Circle – a cultural center
Western Reserve Historical Society – a museum
The Cleveland Metroparks Zoo
Cedar Point Amusement Park
Geauga Lake – an amusement park
Sea World

DALLAS

Country code: 1 - Area code: 214

Airport: Dallas/Fort Worth International Airport.

Distance from City: 20km (12 miles) northwest of the city.

Transportation to Center of City:
From International and Domestic Terminals
By Bus (cost) USD10-15. Time approx. 40-60 min.
By Taxi (cost) USD25-30. Time approx. 30 min.
Tip luggage porters USD1   per piece

Transfers: (Minimum Connecting Time):
International to International: 70 min.
International to Domestic: 70 min.
Domestic to International: 50 min.
Domestic to Domestic: 50 min.

Automobile Rentals:
Airport car rental desk
Avis - 574-4130
National - 574-3400
Hertz - 453-0370

Car rental city office
Avis - 869-2400
National - 357-0478

Hotels:

Adolphus, 1321 Commerce St., 742-8200

Best Western Market Center, 2023 Market Center Blvd., 741-9000

Best Western Windsor Suites Hotel, 2363 Stemmons Trail, 350-2300

Courtyard Dallas – Market Center, 2150 Market Center Blvd. at Stemmons, 653-1166

Hyatt Regency Dallas, At Reunion, 651-1234

Le Meridien Dallas, 650 N. Pearl St., 979-9000

Renaissance Dallas Hotel, 2222 Stemmons Fwy., 631-2222

Sheraton Suites Market Center, 2101 Stemmons Fwy., 747-3000

Wyndham Anatole Hotel, 2201 Stemmons Fwy., 748-1200

Wyndham Garden Hotel, Dallas Market Center, 2915 Market Center Blvd., 741-7481

Restaurants:

Bailey's Barbeque, 826 Taylor St., 335 7469

Benito's, 1450 W. Magnolia Ave., 332 8633

Calle Doce, 415 W. 12th St., 941 4304

French Room, 1321 Commerce St., 742 8200

Hoffbrau, 3205 Knox St, 559 2680

Jennivine, 3605 McKinney Ave., 528 6010

Joe T.Garcia's, 2201 N. Commerce St., 626 4356

Mia's, 4322 Lemmon Ave., 526 1020

Saint-Emilion, 3617 W. 7th St., 737 2781

Entertainment:

Billy Bob's Texas, 2520 Rodeo Plaza, 624 7117

Caravan Dreams, 312 Houston St., 877 3000

Cowboy's, 7331 Gaston Ave., 321 0115

Flip's, 1520 Greenville Ave., 824 9944

Louie's, 1839 N. Henderson St., 826 0505

Poor David's Pub, 1924 Greenville Ave., 821 9891

San Francisco Rose, 3024 Greenville Ave., 826 2020

White Elephant Saloon, 100 E. Exchange Ave., 624 8241

Shops and Stores:

Crescent, 500 Crescent St.,	Apparel
Galleria, LBJ Fwy.	Mall
Mariposa, 2817 Routh St.	Jewelry

U.S.A.

McKinney Avenue, Crescent St.	Apparel
Neiman Marcus, 1618 Main St.	Dept. Store
NorthPark Center, Central Expressway	Mall

Places of Interest:
Texas School Book Depository
The Dallas Art Museum
Fair Park - museums
Fire Station No.1 – a museum
West End Historic District and West End Market Place
Six Flags Over Texas – a theme park
Old Red Courthouse
Reunion Tower
Fort Worth Stockyards Historic District

DENVER

Country code: 1 - Area code: 303

Airport: Denver International Airport.

Distance from City: 37km (22 miles) northeast of the city.

Transportation to Center of City:
From International and Domestic Terminals
By Bus (cost) USD6. Time approx. 50 min. (every 10 min.)
By Taxi (cost) USD30. Time approx.45 min.
Tip luggage porters USD1   per piece

Transfers: (Minimum Connecting Time):
International to International: 60 min.
International to Domestic: 60 min.
Domestic to International: 60 min.
Domestic to Domestic: 50 min.

Automobile Rentals:
Airport car rental desk
Avis -342-5500
National -342-0717
Hertz - 342-3800

Car rental city office
Avis - 839-1280
National - 321-7990
Hertz - 342-3800

Hotels:
Adam's Mark Denver Hotel, 1550 Court Pl., 893-3333
Best Western Landmark Hotel, 455 S. Colorado Blvd., 388-5561
Comfort Inn Downtown, 401 17th St., 296-0400
Denver Marriott City Center, 1701 California, 297-1300
Hyatt Regency Denver, 1750 Welton St., 295-1234
Residence Inn Denver/Downtown, 2777 Zuni St., 458-5318
Warwick Hotel, 1776 Grants St., 861-2000
Westin Hotel, Tabor Center, 1672 Lawrence St., 572-9100

Restaurants:
Avenue Grill, 630 E. 17th Av., 861 2820
Bandera Restaurant, 184 Steele St., 377 9673
Barolo Grill, 3030 E. 6th Ave., 393 1040
Blake Street Baseball Club, '901 Blake St., 298 0133
Boulevard Bistro, 600 S.Colorado Blvd., 757 3341
Brasserie Z, 815 17th St., 293 2322
Brittany Hill Restaurant, 9350 Grant St., 451 5151
Broker DTC Restaurant, 5111 DTC Pkwy., 770 5111
Broker Restaurant, 821 17th St., 292 5065
Buckhorn Exchange, 1000 Osage St., 534 9505
California Cafe Bar & Grill, 8505 Park Meadows Center Dr.,
    649 1111
Cliff Young's, 700 E. 17th Ave., 831 8900
Dick's Last Resort Restaurant, 1909 Blake St., 292 1212
Dixon's Downtown Grill, 1610 16th St., 573 6100
Govnr's Park, 672 Logan St., 831 8605
imperial Chinese Seafood Restaurant, 1 Broadway,   698 2800
Le Central, 112 E. 8th Ave., 863 8094
Strings, 1700 Humboldt St., 831 7310
T-WA Inn, 555 S.Federal Blvd., 922 4584
Wynkoop Brewing Company, 1634 18th St., 297 2700
Zenith American Grill, 1750 Lawrence St., 820 2800

Entertainment:
Bullwackers Casino, 101 Gregory St., 716 5500

Canyon Casino, 131 Main St., 777 1111
Colorado Central Station Casino, 340 Main St., 582 3000
Comedy Works, 1226 15th St., 595 3637
El Chapultepec, 20th St. at Market St., 295 9126
Famous Bonanza, 107 Main St., 526 7212
Fitzerald's Casino, 101 Main St., 538 5825
Grizzly Rose, I-25 Exit 215, 295 1330
Harveys Wagon Wheel Hotel & Casino, 321 Gregory St.,
   HAR VEYS
Herman's Hideaway, 1578 S.Broadway, 778 9916
Jazz Alley Casino, 321 Main St., 426 1125
Rock Island, Wazee and 15th Sts., 572 7625
The Glory Hole Saloon & Gaming Hall, 131 Main St., 582 1171
The Gold Mine Casino, 119 Black Hawk, 428 0711

Shops and Stores:

Atlantis Gems Inc., 718 16th St.	Jewelry
B. Jammin', 512 Larimer St., #24R	Apparel
Burberrys Limited, 3000 E. First Ave.	Apparel
Cherry Greek Shopping Mall, 1st Avenue and Milwaukee St.,	Mall
Denver Buffalo Company Trading Post, 1109 Lincoln St.,	Aparel
Hyde Park Inc, 7777 E. Hampden Ave.	Jewelry
Laminer Square, 14th and Laminer Sts.,	Apparel
St. Croix Shop, 3000 E., First Ave.	Apparel

Places of Interest:

Larimer Square – a shopping area
The Colorado History Museum
Denver Art Museum
Denver Mint
Molly Brown House
Denver Zoo
Denver Museum of Natural History
Denver Children's Museum
Denver Botanic Gardens
Pike's Peak

DETROIT

U.S.A.

Country code: 1 - Area code: 313

Airport: Detroit Metropolitan International Airport.

Distance from City: 32km (19 miles) southwest of the city.

Transportation to Center of City:
From International and Domestic Terminals
By Bus (cost) USD13 (every 15 min.)
By Taxi (cost) USD25-32 Time approx. 40 min.
Tip luggage porters USD1   per piece

Transfers: (Minimum Connecting Time):
International to International: 60 min.
International to Domestic: 90 min.
Domestic to International: 60 min.
Domestic to Domestic: 45 min.

Automobile Rentals:
Airport car rental desk
Avis - 942-3453
National - 941-7000
Hertz - 941-4747

Car rental city office
Avis - 942-0494

Hotels:
Atheneum Suite Hotel & Conference Center, 1000 Brush Ave.,
962-2323
Doubletree Hotel Detroit, 333 E. Jefferson Ave., 222-7700
Hyatt Regency Dearborn, Fairlane Town Center, 593-1234
Omni International, 333 E. Jefferson Ave., 222-7700
St. Regis Hotel, 3071 W. Grand Blvd., 873-3000
Westin Hotel Renaissance Center, Renaissance Center,
   568-8000

Restaurants:
Blue Nile, 508 Monroe St., 964 6699
Durango Grill, 222 Sherman Dr., 544 2887
Elwood Bar & Grill, 2100 Woodward Ave., 961 7485

Fishbone's Rhythm Kitchen Cafe, 400 Monroe St., 965 4600
Lelli's Inn, 7618 Woodward Ave., 871 1590
Pegasus Taverna, 558 Monroe St., 964 6800
The Caucus Club, 150 W.Congress St., 956 4970
The Rattlesnake Club, 300 River Pl., 567 4000
The Summit, Renaissance Center, 568 8600
The Whitney, 4421 Woodward Ave., 832 5700
Traffic Jam & Snug, 511 W. Canfield St., 831 9470
Under the Eagle, 9000 Joseph Campau St., 875 5905
Van Dyke Place, 649 Van Dyke Ave., 821 2620
Wah Court, 2037 Wyandotte Ave., 254 1388

Entertainment:
Alvin's, 5756 Cass St., 832 2355
Baker's, Keyboard Lounge, 20510 Livernois Ave., 864 1200
Bouzouki Lounge, 432 E. Lafayette St., 964 5744
Rhinoceros Restaurant, 265 Riopelle St., 259 2208
Soup Kitchen Saloon, 1585 Franklin St., 259 2643
Woodbridge Tavern, 289 St., 259 0578

Shops and Stores:

Crowley's	Apparel
J.L.Hudson's	Dept. Store
Millender Center,	Jewelers
New Center One Mall, University Cultural Center	Mall
World of Shops, Renaissance Center	Mall

Places of Interest:
The Detroit Historical Museum
The Children's Museum
The Detroit Institute of Arts
Henry Ford Museum and Greenfield Village
Detroit Zoological Park
Belle Isle – a park with a zoo and an aquarium
Pewabic Pottery
University Cultural Center
International Institute of Metropolitan Detroit – a museum
Renaissance Center
Greektown

U.S.A.

HONOLULU

Country code: 1 - Area code: 808

Airport: Honolulu International Airport.

Distance from City: 8km (4 miles) northwest of the city.

Transportation to Center of City:
From International and Domestic Terminals
By Bus (cost) USD6.00. Time approx. 30 min. (every 30 min.)
By Taxi (cost)USD18.00-20.00. Time approx. 20 min.
Tip luggage porters USD1   per piece

Transfers: (Minimum Connecting Time):
International to International: 120 min.
International to Domestic: 120 min.
Domestic to International: 60 min.
Domestic to Domestic: 75 min.

Automobile Rentals:
Airport car rental desk
Avis - 834-5564
National - 831-3800
Hertz - 831-3500

Car rental city office
Avis - 973-2622
National - 922-3331

Hotels:
Hawaii Maritime Center, Pier 7, 536-6373
Hilton Hawaiian Village, 2005 Kalia Rd., 949-4321
Kawaiahao Church, 957 Punchbowl St., 522-1333
New Otani Kaimana Beach Hotel, 2863 Kalakaua Ave.,
    923-1555
Sheraton Moana Surfrider, 2365 Kalakaua Ave., 922-3111
Sheraton Waikiki Hotel, 2255 Kalakaua Ave., 922-4422

Restaurants:
Bali by the Sea, 2005 Kalia Rd., 941 2254

California Pizza Kitchen, 4211 Waialae Ave., 737 9446
Compadres Mexican Bar and Grill, 1200 Ala Moana Blvd., 591 8307
Golden Dragon, 2005 Kalia Rd., 946 5336
Hau Tree Lanai, 2863 Kalakaua Ave., 921 7066
Hy's Steak House, 2440 Kuhio Ave., 922 5555
Keo's Thai Cuisine, 625 Kapahulu Ave., 737 8240
La Mer, 2199 Kalia Rd., 923 2311
Maile, 5000 Kahala Ave., 734 2211
Maple Garden, 909 Isenberg, 941 6641
Michel's at the Colony Surf, 2895 Kalakaua Ave., 923 6552
Restaurant Suntory, 2233 Kalakaua Ave., 922 5511
The Secret, 2552 Kalakaua Ave., 922 6611
Tripton's American Cafe, 449 Kapahulu Ave., 737 3819

Entertainment:
Alii Kai Catamaran's, Pier 8, street level, 524 6694
Anna Bannana's, 2440 S.Beretania St., 946 5190
Maile Louge, 5000 Kahala Ave., 734 2211
Royal Luau, 2259 Kalakaua Ave., 923 7311
Rumours, 410 Atkinson St., 955 4811
Windjammer Cruises, 2222 Kalakaua Ave., 922 1200

Shops and Stores:
Ala Moana Shopping Center, 1450 Ala Moana Blvd., 946 2811 Mall
Royal Hawaiian Shopping Center, 2201 Kalakaua Ave.,922 0588 Mall
Ward Centre, 1200 Ala Moana Blvd.,   Apparel
Ward Waterhouse, 1050 Ala Moana Blvd.,   Mall

Places of Interest:
Hawaii Maritime Center
Iolani Palace
Aliiolani Hale – an old building
Kawaiahao Church
Mission Houses Museum
Honolulu Zoo
The Waikiki Aquarium
Diamond Head – a mountain
USS Arizona Memorial

U.S.A.

HOUSTON

Country code: 1 - Area code: 281

Airport: Houston/Intercontinental Airport.

Distance from City: 32km (19 miles) north of the city.

Transportation to Center of City:
From International and Domestic Terminals
By Bus (cost) USD1.25. Time approx. 45 min.
By Taxi (cost) USD30-35 Time approx. 30-45 min.
Tip luggage porters USD1 per piece

Transfers: (Minimum Connecting Time):
International to International: 60 min.
International to Domestic: 60 min.
Domestic to International: 45 min.
Domestic to Domestic: 10 min.

Automobile Rentals:
Airport car rental desk
Avis - 443-5800
National - 641-0533
Hertz - 443-0800

Car rental city office
Avis - 659-6537
National - 443-8850
Hertz - 531-5491

Hotels:
Doubletree Hotel at Allen Center, 400 Dallas St., 759-0202
Four Seasons Hotel, 1300 Lamar St., 650-1300
Houston Marriott Medical Center, 6580 Fannin St., 796-0080
Houston Plaza Hilton, 6633 Travis St., 313-4000
Hyatt Regency Houston, In the Center of Downtown, 654-1234
Renaissance Houston Hotel, 6 Greenway Plaza E., 629-1200
Wyndham Warwick Hotel, 5701 Main St., 526-1991

U.S.A.

Restaurants:
Anago, 65 Exeter St., 421 4909
Anthony's, 4007 Westheimer Blvd., 961 0552
Armani Cafe, 214 Newbury St., 437 0909
Athens Bar & Grill, 8037 Clinton Dr., 675 1644
Bello Mondo, Copley Place, 236 5800
Benno's on the Beach, 1200 Seawall Blvd., 762 4621
Cafe Annie, 1728 Post Oak Blvd., 840 1111
Cafe Budapest, 90 Exeter St., 266 1979
Ciao Bella, 240A Newbury St., 536 2626
Davio's Ristorante and Cafe, 269 Newbury St., 262 4810
Dick's Last Resort, 55 Huntington Av., 267 8080
DuBarry Restaurant Francais, 159 Newbury St., 262 2445
Famous Atlantic Fish Company, 777 Boylston St., 267 4000
Gaido's, 39th and Seawall Blvd., 762 9625
Grill & Bar, 161 Berkeley St., 542 2255
Shrimp N'Stuff, 3901 Ave.O., 765 5708
Spanish Flower, 4701 N.Main St., 869 1706
The Capital Grille, 359 Newbury St., 262 8900
This is It, 239 W.Gray St., 523 5319
Wentletrap, 2301 Strand, 765 5545

Entertainment:
Alley Cat Lounge, 1 Boylston Place, 451 6200
Avalon, 15 Lansdowne St., 262 2424
Bill's Bar & Lounge, 5 Lansdowne St., 421 9678
Bishop's Pub, 1-3 Boylston Place, 351 2510
Brandwin,Inn, 304 Newbury St., 438 4848
Comedy Theater Productions, 264 Washington St., 320 0040
Dick Doherty Comedy Production, 750 Main St., 729 2565
Fitzgerald's, 2706 White Oaks Dr., 862 7580
Good Time Emporium, 30 Sturtevant St., 628 5559
IBA/ETC, 405 Shawmut Av., 927 1781
Jake Ivory's, 1 Lansdowne St., 262 2605
Karma Club, 11 Lansdowne St., 262 2605
La Carafe, 813 Congress Ave., 229 9399
Longy School of Music, One Follen St., 876 0956
M-80, 969 Commonwealth Av., 562 8800
Regattabar, One Bennett St., 661 5050
Roxy's, 279 Tremont St., 338 7699
Sticky Mike's, 5 Boylston Place, 262 2605
The Charles Playhouse, 74 Warrenton St., 426 6912

U.S.A.

Shops and Stores:
Galleria, Post Oak Blvd.,   Jewelry
Old Peanut Butter Warehouse, 100 20th St., 762 8358
                                                                        Antiques
Parks Shops in Houston Center, 1200 McKinney St.,   Mall
Post Oak Boulevard   Apparel
River Oaks Shopping Center, Shepherd.,   Mall

Places of Interest:
The Museum of Fine Arts
The Contemporary Arts Museum
Houston Zoo
Museum of Natural Science
Astroworld and Waterworld – an amusement complex
Texas Commerce Tower
Orange Show
Houston Fire Museum

INDIANAPOLIS

Country code: 1 - Area code: 317

Airport: Indianapolis International Airport

Distance from City: 11km (6 miles) southwest of the city.

Transportation to Center of City:
From International and Domestic Terminals
By Bus (cost) USD1. Time approx. 15-20 min.
By Taxi (cost) USD16. Time approx. 10-15 min.
Tip luggage porters USD1 per piece

Transfers: (Minimum Connecting Time):
Domestic to Domestic: 40 min.

Automobile Rentals:
Airport car rental desk
Avis - 244-3307

National - 243-1151
Hertz - 243-9321

Car rental city office
Avis - 243-3711
National - 844-9011

Hotels:
Canterbury Hotel, 123 S. Illinois St., 634-3000
Courtyard Downtown, 501 W. Washington St., 635-4443
Embassy Suites Downtown, 110W Washington St. 236-1800
Hyatt Regency Indianapolis, At State Capitol, 632-1234
Omni Severin Hotel, 40 W. Jackson Pl., 634-6664
Westin Hotel, Indianapolis, 50 S. Capitol Ave., 262-8100

Restaurants:
Arni's, 3443 W. 86th St., 875 7034
Benvenuti, 36 S. Pennsylvania St., 633 4915
Chanteclair, 2501 High School Rd., 243 1040
Charlie & Barney's Bar and Grill, 1130 W. 86th St., 844 2399
Eller House, 7050 E. 116th St., 849 2299
Marker, 2544 Executive Dr., 248 2481
MCL Cafeterias, 6110 E. 10th St., 356 1587
Pesto, 303 N.Alabama St., 269 0715
Peter's Restaurant & Bar, 8505 Keystone Crossing, 465 1165
Shapiro's Delicatessen & Cafeteria, 808 S. Meridian St., 631 4041
Snax/Something Different, 2411 E. 65th St., 257 7115

Entertainment:
Chatterbox Tavern, 435 Massachusetts Ave., 636 0584
Crackers, 8702 Keystone Crossing, 846 2500
Rick's Cafe American, 39 Jackson Pl., 634 6666
Slippery Noodle Inn, 372 S.Meridian St., 631 6968
Shops and Stores:
Broad Ripple Village, 62nd St. and College Ave.,   Antiques
Circle Centre Mall, 115 W. Washington St.,   Mall
Fashion Mall, 9000 Keyston Crossing, 574 4000   Apparel
Jacobson's   Dept.Store
Parisian   Dept.Store

Places of interest:

U.S.A.

Indiana State Museum
Eiteljorg Museum of American Indian and Western Art
National Track and Field Hall of Fame
The Children's Museum
The Indianapolis Museum of Art
The Indianapolis Motor Speedway Hall of Fame Museum
Indianapolis Zoo
Indiana Soldiers' and Sailors' Monument
Scottish Rite Cathedral
Eagle Creek Park
Canal Walk

KANSAS CITY

Country code: 1 - Area code: 913

Airport: Kansas City International Airport

Distance from City: 30km (18 miles) northwest of the city.

Transportation to Center of City:
From International and Domestic Terminals
By Bus (cost) USD1. Time approx. 55 min.
By Taxi (cost) USD25-USD30. Time approx. 25-40 min.
Tip luggage porters USD1   per piece

Transfers: (Minimum Connecting Time):
International to Domestic: 90 min.
Domestic to International: 45 min.
Domestic to Domestic: 45 min.

Automobile Rentals:
Airport car rental desk
Avis - 243-5760
National - 243-5770
Hertz - 243-5765

Car rental city office
Avis - 471-3006

Hotels:
Best Western Seville Plaza Hotel, 4309 Main St., 561-9600

Courtyard Kansas City Airport, 7901 N. Tiffany Springs Pky., 891-7500
Hyatt Regency Crown Center, 2345 McGee St., 421-1235
Kansas City Airport Marriott, 775 Brasilia, 464-2200
Kansas City Marriott Downtown, 200 W. 12th St., 421-6800
Radisson Suite Hotel Kansas City, 106W 12th St., 221-7000
Residence Inn Kansas City Airport, 9900 M.W. Prairie View Rd., 891-9009
Ritz-Carlton, 401 Ward Parkway, 756-1500
Sheraton Suites Country Club Plaza, 770 West 47th St., 931-4400
The Raphael, 325 Ward Parkway, 756-3800
Westin Crown Center, One Pershing Rd., 747-4400

Restaurants:
Cafe Allegro, 1815 W. 39th St., 561 3663
Golden Ox, 1600 Genesse St., 842 2866
Ponak's, 2856 Southwest Blvd., 753 0775
Savoy Grill, 219 W. 9th St., 842 3890
West Side Cafe, 723 Southwest Blvd., 472 0010

Entertainment:
Grand Emporium, 3832 Main St., 531 1504
Jazz Hotline, 763 1052

Shops and Stores:
Country Club Plaza   Apparel
Crown Center   Jewerly
Westport   Apparel

Places of Interest:
The Nelson-Atkins Museum of Art
Liberty Memorial
The Treasures of the Steamboat Arabia – a museum
The Harry S.Truman Library and Museum
Fleming Park
Hallmark Visitor's Center
Country Club Plaza – a shopping center

U.S.A.

LOS ANGELES

**Country code: 1 - Area codes: 213; 310
(All listings are 213 unless noted otherwise)**

Airport: Los Angeles International Airport.

Distance from City: 27km (16 miles) southeast of the city.

Transportation to Center of City:
From International and Domestic Terminals
By Bus (cost) USD1.50. Time approx. 60-90 min.
By Taxi (cost) USD25-30. Time approx. 35-40 min.
Tip luggage porters USD1 per piece

Transfers: (Minimum Connecting Time):
International to International: 120 min.
International to Domestic: 120 min.

Domestic to International: 90 min.
Domestic to Domestic: 70 min.

Automobile Rentals:
Airport car rental desk
Avis - 646-5600
National - 338-8200
Hertz - 568-3400

Car rental city office
Avis - 977-1450

Hotels:
Best Western Hotel By The Casino, 7330 Eastern Ave.,
    Bell Gardens, (562) 928-3452
Century Plaza Hotel & Tower, 2025 Ave. of the Stars
    (310) 277-2000
Hyatt Regency Los Angeles, At Broadway Plaza, 683-1234
Inter-Continental Los Angeles, 251 S. Olive St., 617-3300
New Otani Hotel & Garden, 120 S. Los Angeles St., 629-1200
Park Hyatt Los Angeles, 2151 Ave. of the Stars, 277-2777
Radisson Wilshire Plaza Hotel, 3515 Wilshire Blvd, 381-7411

U.S.A.

Regal Baltimore Hotel, 506 South Grand Ave., 624-1011
Sheraton Grande Hotel, 333 S. Figueroa St., 617-1133
Westin Bonaventure Hotel & Suites, 404 S. Figueroa St.,
    624-1000
Wyndham Checkers Hotel Los Angeles, 535 S. Grande Ave.,
    624-0000
Wyndham Garden Hotel, 5757 Telegraph Rd., Commerce,
    887-8100

Restaurants:
Ca'Brea, 346 S. La Brea Ave., 938 2863
Chan Dara, 310 N.Larchmont Blvd., 467 1052
El Cholo, 1121 S.Western Ave., 734 2773
Hotel Bel-Air, 401 Stone Canyon Rd., 472 1211
L'Orangerie, 903 N. La Cienega Blvd., (310) 652 9770
Mon Kee Seafood Restaurant, 679 N.Spring St., 628 6717
Pacific Dining Car, 1310 W. 6th St., 483 6000
Remi, 1451 3rd St., 393 6545
Restaurant Katsu, 1972 N.Hilburst Ave., 665 1891
Spago, 1114 Horn Ave., 652 4025
Tavola Calda, 7371 Melrose Ave., 658 6340

Entertainment:
Bar One, 9229 Sunset Blvd., (310) 271 8355
Checca, 7323 Santa Monica Blvd., 850 7471
Chez Jay, 1657 Ocean Ave., (310) 395 1741
Cocunut Teaszer, 8117 Sunset Blvd., 654 4773
Comedy Store, 8433 Sunset Blvd., 656 6225
Dan Tana's, 9071 Santa Monica Blvd., 275 9444
Improvisation, 8162 Melrose Ave., 651 2583
Le Dome, 8720 W. Sunset Blvd., (310) 659 6919
Marla's Jazz Supper Club, 2323 W. M.L.King Jr.Blvd.,
    294 8430
Roxy, 9009 Sunset Blvd., 276 2222
Viper Room, 8852 Sunset Blvd., 358 1880

Shops and Stores:

Ann Taylor, 357 N.Camden Dr.	Apparel
Barneys New York, 9570 Wilshire	Apparel
Battaglia, 306 N.Rodeo Dr.,	Apparel
Bernini, 362 N.Rodeo Dr.,	Apparel
Beverly Connection, 100 N.La Cienaga St.	Mall

U.S.A.

Cartier, 370 N.Rodeo Dr.	Jewelry
Celine, 460 N.Rodeo Dr.	Apparel
Freehand, 8413 W. 3rd St.	Jewelry
Off the Wall, 7325 Melrose Ave.	Antiques
Rodeo Collection, 421 N. Rodeo Dr.	Apparel
Tiffany and Company, 210 N. Rodeo Dr.	Jewelry
Van Cleef and Arpels, 300 N. Rodeo Dr.	Jewelry

Places of Interest:
El Pueblo de Los Angeles Historical Monument
The California Museum of Science and Industry and The
    Natural History Museum
Hollywood and Hollywood Walk of Fame
Exposition Park
Universal Studios and City Walk
Huntington Library, Art Gallery and Botanical Gardens
Burbank Studios

MEMPHIS

Country code: 1 - Area code: 901
Airport: Memphis International Airport.

Distance from City: 14km. (9 miles) south of the city.

Transportation to Center of City:
From International and Domestic Terminals
By Bus (cost) USD1. Time approx. 20 min.
By Taxi (cost) USD17. Time approx. 15 min.
Tip luggage porters USD1 per piece

Hotels:
Courtyard Memphis Airport, 1780 Nonconnah Blvd., 396-3600
Four Points Hotel Memphis Airport, 2240 Democrat Rd.,
    332-1130
French Quarter Suites, 2144 Madison Ave., 843-0353
Holiday Inn Crowne Plaza, 250 N. Main St., 527-7300
Peabody Hotel, 149 Union Ave., 529-4000
Radisson Hotel Memphis, 185 Union Ave., 528-1800
Sleep Inn, 40 N. Front St., 522-9700

U.S.A.

Restaurants:
Cafe Max, 6161 Poplar Ave., 767 3633
Cafe Ole, 959 S.Cooper St., 274 1504
Charlie Vergos'Rendezvous, 52 S. 2nd St., 523 2746
Chez Philippe, 149 Union Ave., 529 4188
Corky's, 5259 Poplar Ave., 685 9744
Justine's, 919 Coward, 527 3815
La Tourelle, 2146 Monroe Ave., 726 5771
Landry's Seafood House, 263 Wagner Pl., 526 1966
Marena's, 11545 Overton Park, 278 9774
Paulette's, 2110 Madison Ave., 726 5128

Entertainment:
B.B.King's Blues Club, 147 Beale St., 524 5464
Blues Hall/Rum Boogie Cafe, 182 Beale St., 528 0150

Shops and Stores:

Belz Factory Outlet Mall, 3536 Canada Rd.	Mall
Hickory Ridge Mall, 6076 Winchester at Hickory Hill	Mall
Mall, 4457 Americanway at Perkins St.	Dept. Store
Oak Court Mall, 4465 Poplar Ave.	Mall

Places of Interest:
Memphis Botanic Garden
Memphis Brooks Museum of Art
Memphis Zoo and Aquarium
National Civil Rights Museum
W.C. Handy Memphis Home and Museum

MIAMI

Country code: 1 - Area code: 305
Airport: Miami International Airport

Distance from City: . 11km (6 miles) northwest of the city.

Transportation to Center of City:
From International and Domestic Terminals
By Bus (cost) USD1.25 Time approx. 30 min.

U.S.A.

By Taxi (cost) USD15-20 Time approx. 15 min.
Tip luggage porters USD1   per piece

Transfers: (Minimum Connecting Time):
International to International: 90 min.
International to Domestic: 90 min.
Domestic to International: 60 min.
Domestic to Domestic: 55 min.

Automobile Rentals:
Airport car rental desk
Avis - 637-4900
National - 638-1026
Hertz - 871-0300

Car rental city office
Avis - 670-2847
Hertz - 354-3477
Hotels:
Best Western Marina Park Hotel, 340 Biscayne Blvd., 371-4400
Biscayne Bay Marriott Hotel & Marina, 1633 N. Bayshore Dr.,
Biscayne, 374-3900
Carlton Hotel, 1433 Collins St., Miami Beach, 538-5741
Clarion Hotel, 5301 NW 36th St., 871-1000
Crowne Plaza Miami, 1601 Biscayne Blvd. at 16th St., 374-0000
Doubletree Grand Hotel on Biscayne Bay, 1717 N. Bayshore
    Dr., 372-0313
Doubletree Hotel at Coconut Grove, 2649 S. Bayshore Dr.,
    858-2500
Everglades Hotel, 244 Biscayne Blvd., 379-5461
Hyatt Regency Miami, At Miami Convention Center, 358-1234
Inter-Continental Miami, 100 Chopin Plaza, 577-1000
Mayfair House Hotel, 3000 Florida Ave., 441-0000
Miami Airport Courtyard South, 1201 NW LeJeune Rd.,
    642-8200
Occidental S.E. 4th Street, 374-5100
Sheraton Biscayne Bay Hotel, 495 Brickell Ave., 373-6000
Wellesley Inn Miami Airport, 8436 NW 36th St., 592-4799

Restaurants:
94TH Aero Squadron, 1395 NW 11th St., 261 4220
Casa Rolandi, 1930 Ponce de Leon Blvd., 444 2187

Charade Restaurant, 1850 NW LeJeune Rd., 871 4350
Chef Allen's, 19088 N.E. 29th Ave., 935 2900
Chez Moy, 1 N.W. 54th St., 757 5056
Choice Picks Food Court, 5301 NW 36th St., 871 8000
Coral Cafe, 5101 Blue Lagoon Dr., 256 3845
Dinier's, 2530 Ponce de leon Blvd., 567 2444
Dominique's, 5225 Collins Ave., 865 6500
Grand Cafe, 2669 S. Bayshore Dr., 858 9600
Hy Vong Vietnamese Cuisine, 3458 S.W. 8th St., 446 3674
Las Tapas, 401 Biscayne Blvd., 372 2737
Le Cafe Royal, 5800 Blue Lagoon Dr., 264 4888
Los Ranchos, 401 Biscayne Blvd., 375 8188
Mark's Place, 2286 N.E. 123rd St., 893 6888
News Cafe, 800 Ocean Dr., 538 6397
Shorty's Bar-B-Q, 9200 S.Dixie Hwy., 670 7732
The Atrium at the SPA, 8755 NW 36th Av., 523 6030
The Cove, 5101 Blue Lagoon Dr., 256 3845
Tony Chan's Water Club, 1717 N.Bayshore Dr., 374 8888
Un Bon Bakery Cafe, 1101 NW 57th Av., 266 0000
Unicorn Village Restaurant & Marketplace, 3565 N.E. 207th St.,
    933 8829
Windows, 4400 NW 87th Av., 592 2000
Yuca, 177 Giralda Ave., 444 4448

Entertainment:
Baja Beach Club, 3015 Grand Ave., 445 0278
Banana Bar, 1260 Collins Ave., 538 1951
Bash, 655 Washington Ave., 538 2274
Brassie's Lounge, 2201 Collins Ave., 534 1511
Club Tropigala at La Ronde, 4441 Collins Ave., 672 7469
Deco Lounge, 1677 Collins Ave., 532 2311
Escuelita, 220 21th St., 534 5599
Harry's Bistro, 1701 Collins Ave., 534 3500
Les Deux Fontaines, 1230-38 Ocean Dr., 672 7878
Les Violins Supper Club, 1751 Biscayne Blvd., 371 8668
Mac's Club Deuce, 222 14th St., 673 9537
Marlin Bar, 1200 Collins Ave., 604 5000
Moe's Cantina, 616 Collins Ave., 532 1087
Oceanside Promenade, 1052-1060 Ocean Dr.,538 0007
Official All Star Cafe, 960 Ocean Dr., 304 1999
Rezurection Hall, 245 22nd St., 672 0702
Shore Club Cafe, 1901 Collins Ave., 672 0303

The Hemisphere Lounge, 1601 Collins Ave., 604 1601
The Penguin Lounge, 1418 Ocean Dr., 534 9334
Tobacco Road, 626 S. Miami Ave., 374 1198

Shops and Stores:
Bayside To-Go, Bayside Market Place, 401 N. Biscayne Blvd.,
    #P-107   Souvenirs
Bloomingdale's, 8778 SW 136th St.   Dept. Store
Burdines, 22 E. Flagler St.   Dept. Store
Bvlgari, 9700 Collins Ave., Suite 118, Bal Harbour   Jewelry
Da Vinci, 401 N. Biscayne Blvd. #S145   Jewelry
Galtrucco, 9700 Collins Ave., Bal Harbour   Apparel
Giordano's Petite Shoes, 3125 NE 163rd St.   Shoes
Kirk Jewelers, 132 E. Flagler St.   Jewelry
Miami Free Zone, 2305 N.W. 107th Ave., 591 4300   Mall
New Man, 9700 Collins Ave., Bal Harbour   Apparel
Rainbow Jewelry, 101 NE 1st St.   Jewelry
Sears, International Mall, 1625 NW 107th Ave.   Dept. Store

Places of Interest:
Bayside Market Place
Coconut Grove Convention Center – antique and home furnish-
    ing shows.
Everglades National Park
Fashion District
Metro-Dade Center – an art center
Miamarina
Miami Free Zone –duty free shopping center
Miami Seaquarium
Parrot Jungle – bird shows
The Cuban Museum of Art and Culture

MILWAUKEE

Country code: 1 - Area code: 414

Airport: General Mitchell International Airport .

Distance from City: 10km (6 miles) south of the city

Transportation to Center of City:
From International and Domestic Terminals
By Bus (cost) USD1.25 Time approx. 30 min.(every 20 min)
By Taxi (cost) USD15-17 Time approx. 15-20 min.
Tip luggage porters USD1   per piece

Transfers: (Minimum Connecting Time):
Domestic to International: 60 min.
Domestic to Domestic: 40 min.

Automobile Rentals:
Airport car rental desk
Avis - 744-2266
Hertz - 747-5200

Car rental city office
Avis - 272-0892
National - 483-9800

Hotels:
Ambassador Hotel, 2308 W. Wisconsin Ave., 342-8400
Astor Hotel, 924 E. Juneau Ave., 271-4220
County Clare, 1234 N. Astor St., 27-CLARE
Hostelling International, 6750 W. Loomis Rd., Greendale,
    961-2525
Hotel Wisconsin, 720 N. Old World 3th St., 271-4900
Hyatt Regency Hotel, 333 W. Kilbourn Ave., 276-6338
Knickerbocker on the Lake, 1028 E. Juneau Ave., 276-8500
Milwaukee Hilton, 509 W Wisconsin Ave., 271-7250
Park East Hotel, 916 E. State St., 276-8800
Pfister Hotel, 424 E. Wisconsin Ave., 273-8222
Plaza Hotel and Apartments, 1007 N. Cass St., 276-2101
Ramada Inn Downtown, 633 W. Michigan St., 272-8410
Wyndham Milwaukee Center Hotel, 139 E. Kilbourn Ave.,
    276-8686

Restaurants:
African Hut Restaurant, 1107 N.Old World Third St.,
    764 1110

Benjamin Briggs Pub, 2501 W.Greenfield Av., 383 2337
Boder's on the River, 11919 N.River Rd., 242 0335
Chip and Py's, 1340 W. Town Square Rd., 241 9589
Crocus Restaurant and Cocktail Lounge, 1801 S. Muskego
    Ave., 643 6383
Elsa's on the Park, 833 N. Jefferson St., 765 0615
English Room, 424 E. Wisconsin Ave., 273 8222
Giovanni's, 1683 N. Van Buren St., 291 5600
Grenadier's, 747 N. Broadway St., 276 0747
Harold's, 4747 S. Howel Ave., 481 8000
Izumi's, 2178 N.Prospect Ave., 271 5278
Jake's, 3030 W. North Ave., 771 0550
Karl Ratzsch's Old World Restaurant, 320 E. Mason St.,
    276 2720
La Fuente Restaurant, 625 S. 5th Ave., 271 8595
Mike and Anna's, 2000 S. 8th St., 643 0072
Nistoric Turner Restaurant, 1034 N. 4th St., 276 4844
Omega V, 3473 S. 27th St., 645 6595
Steven Wade's Cafe, 17001 W. Greenfield Ave., 784 0774
Three Brothers Bar & Restaurant, 2414 S. St.Clair St.,
    481 7530
Watts Tea Shop, 761 N. Jefferson St., 276 6352

Entertainment:
Bombay Bicycle Club Estate, 509 W. Wisconsin Ave.,
    271 7250
Brew City BBQ, 1114 N. Water, 278 7033
Brooklyn's, 1135 N.Water, 289 8696
Buffalo Wild Wings & Weck, 1123 N. Water, 277 0293
ComedySportz, 126 N. Jefferson St., 272 8888
Eagan's, 1030 N. Water, 271 6900
Estate, 2423 N. Murray Ave., 964 9923
La Playa, 424 E. Wisconsin Ave., 273 8222
Luke's Sports Spectacular, 1225 N.Water, 223 3210
Major Goolsby's, 340 W. Kilbourn Ave., 271 3414
McGillycuddy's, 1247 N. Water, 278 8888
Mel's Corner Tap, 158, E. Juneau, 274 7201
Milwaukee River Club, 134 E. Juneau, 223 4822
O'Danny's, 1213 N.Water, 223 3422
Oak Barrel, 1211 N. Water, 224 0535
Rosie's Waterworks, 1111 N. Water, 274 7213
Safe House, 779 N.Front Sr., 271 2007

Sweetwater, 1127 N. Water, 278 8847
The Harp, 113 E. Juneau, 289 0700
Water Street Brewery, 1101 N. Water, 272 1195

Shops and Stores:

Capitol Court 5500 W.Capitol Dr.	Mall
Grand Avenue Mall, 275 W. Wisconsin Ave.,	Mall
House of Harley-Davidson, 6221 W. Layton Ave., Greenfield	
	Apparel
Jim's Cheese Pantry, Inc., 410 Portland Rd.	Souvenirs
Mayfair, 2500 N. Mayfair Rd.,	Apparel
Mitchell Leather Goods Outlet, 226 N. Water St.	Leather
Northridge Shopping Center, 7700 W.Brown Deer Rd.	Dept. Store
Premaman, The Grand Ave., 275 E. Wisconsin Ave.	Apparel
Southgate Mall, 3333 S. 27th St.	Mall
Southridge Mall, 5300 S. 76th St.	Mall
Terminal Hobby Shop, 5619 W. Florist Ave.	Toys
Usinger's Famous Sausages, 1030 N. Old World 3rd St.	Food
Zita's Inc., 1122 N. Astor St.	Apparel

Places of interest:

The Milwaukee Art Museum
The Milwaukee County Historical Society – a museum
Milwaukee Public Museum
Discovery World - Museum of Science, Economics and Technology
Milwaukee County Zoo
The American Geographical Society Collection – a museum
Pabst Mansion – a museum
The Schlitz Audubon Center
St. Joan of Arc Chapel

MINNEAPOLIS

Country code: 1 - Area code: 612

Airport: Minneapolis/St. Paul International Airport.

Distance from City: 15km (9 miles) southeast of the city.

Transportation to Center of City:
From International and Domestic Terminals
By Bus (cost) USD1.25. Time approx. 40 min.
By Taxi (cost) USD20 Time approx. 20 min.
Tip luggage porters USD1   per piece

Transfers: (Minimum Connecting Time):
International to International: 60 min.
International to Domestic: 60 min.
Domestic to International: 40 min.
Domestic to Domestic: 40 min.

Automobile Rentals:
Airport car rental desk
Avis - 726-5220
National - 726-5600
Hertz - 726-1600
Car rental city office
Avis - 332-6322
National - 835-6656

Hotels:
Best Western Normandy Inn, Cnr. 4th Ave. & S. 8th St., 370-1400
Courtyard Minneapolis/St. Paul Airport, 1352 Northland Dr., 452-2000
Hyatt Regency Minneapolis, On Nicollet Mall, 370-1234
Luxeford Suites, 1101 La Salle Ave., 332-6800
Minneapolis Hilton & Towers, 1001 Marquette Ave. S., 376-1000
Minneapolis Marriott City Center, 30 S. Seventh St., 349-4000
Minneapolis, the Marquette, 710 Marquette Ave., 333-4545
Radisson Hotel Metrodome, 615 Washington Ave. S. E., 379-8888
Radisson Hotel St. Paul, 11 E. Kellog Blvd., 292-1900
Radisson Inn St. Paul, 411 Minnesota St., 291-8800
Radisson Plaza Hotel Minneapolis, 35 S. 7th St., 339-4900
Regal Minneapolis Hotel, 1313 Nicollet Mall, 332-6000
Whitney Hotel, 150 Portland, 339-9300

Restaurants:
Black Forest Inn, 1 E. 26th St., 872 0812

U.S.A.

Bryant Lake Bowl, 810 W. Lake St., 825 3737
Cafe Latte, 850 Grand Ave., 224 5687
Cafe Un Deux Trois, 114 S. 9th St., 673 0686
Chez Bananas, 129 N. 4th St., 340 0032
D'Amico Cucina, 100 N. 6th St., 338 2401
Dakota Bar and Grill, 1021 E. Bandana Blvd., 642 1442
Goodfellow's, 800 Nicollet Mall, 332 4800
Khyber Pass Cafe, 1399 St.Clair Ave., 698 5403
Kincaid's Steak, Chop and Fish House, 8400 Normandale Lake
    Blvd., 921 2255
Loring Cafe, 1624 Harmon Pl., 332 1617
Mickey's Diner, 36 W. 7th St., 222 5633
Saint Paul Grill, 350 Market St., 292 9292
Whitney Grille, 150 Portland Ave., 339 9300

Entertainment:
Dakota Bar and Grill, 1021 E. Bandana Blvd., 642 1442
Fine Line Music Cafe, 318 1st Ave., 338 8100
First Avenue, 29 N. 7th St., 332 1775
Gallivan's, 354 Wabasha St., 227 6688
Heartthrob Cafe, 30 E. 7th St., 224 2783

Shops and Stores:
Calhoun Square, Lake and Hennepin Aves.	Mall
City Center, 7th St. and Hennepin Ave.,	Jewelry
Gaviidae Common, 651 Nicollet Mall,	Apparels
Nicollet Mall, 700 Nocollet Mall	Dept.Store
The Conservatory, 800 Nicollet Mall	Apparel

Places of Interest:
James Ford Bell Museum of Natural History
Minneapolis Institute of Arts – a museum
The American Swedish Institute – a museum
Walker Art Center
Minnesota Zoo
Historic Fort Snelling – a history center
Landmark Center - museums
Bloomington – a shopping mall
The Science Museum of Minnesota
Minnehaha Park

U.S.A.

NEW ORLEANS

Country code: 1 - Area code: 504

Airport: New Orleans International Airport.

Distance from City: 19km (11 miles) northwest of the city.

Transportation to Center of City:
From International and Domestic Terminals
By Bus (cost) USD1.10. Time approx. 50 min. (every 30 min.)
By Taxi (cost) USD21. Time approx. 20-30 min.
Tip luggage porters USD1   per piece

Transfers: (Minimum Connecting Time):
International to Domestic: 60-90 min.
Domestic to International: 60 min.
Domestic to Domestic: 30 min.
Automobile Rentals:
Airport car rental desk
Avis - 464-9511
National - 466-4335
Hertz - 468-3695

Car rental city office
Avis - 523-4317
National - 525-0416
Hertz - 568-1645

Hotels:
Best Western The Inn Bourbon, 541 Bourbon St., 524-7611
Comfort Inn Downtown, 1315 Gravier St., 586-0100
Dauphine Orleans Hotel, 415 Dauphine St., 586-1800
Doubletree Hotel, 300 Canal St., 581-1300

Doubletree Hotel New Orleans Lakeside/Metairie, 3838 North
    Causeway Blvd., 836-5253
Hyatt Regency New Orleans, Poydras Plaza & Loyola Ave.,
    561-1234
Le Meridien New Orleans, 614 Canal St., 525-6500
Le Pavillon Hotel, 833 Poydras St., 581-3111
New Orleans Hilton Riverside, Two Poydras St., 561-0500

U.S.A.

New Orleans Marriott, 555 Canal St., 581-1000
Radisson Hotel New Orleans, 1500 Canal St., 522-4500
Sheraton New Orleans Hotel, 500 Canal St., 525-2500
Westin Canal Place, 100 Rue Iberville, 566-7006
Windsor Court Hotel, 300 Gravier St., 523-6000
Windham Riverfront Hotel, 701 Convention Center Blvd.,
    524-8200

Restaurants:
Allegro Bistro & Cocktails, 1100 Poydras St., 582 2350
Antoine's, 713 St.Louis St., 581 4422
Arnaud's, 813 Bienville St., 523 5433
Camellia Grill, 626 S.Carrollton Ave., 866 9573
Cannon's Uptown Inc., 4141 St.Charles Ave., 891 3200
Commander's Palace, 1403 Washington Ave., 899 8221
Days Inn Canal, 1630 Canal St., 586 0110
Galatoire's, 209 Bourbon St., 525 2021
Gautreau's, 1728 Soniat St., 899 7397
Grill Room, 300 Gravier St., 522 1992
House of Blues, 225 Decatur St., 529 2624
K-Paul's Louisiana Kitchen, 416 Chartres St., 524 7394
Napoleon House, 500 Chartres St., 524 9752
Palace Cafe, 605 Canal St., 523 1661
Poppy's Grill, 717 St.Peter, 525 7624
Praline Connection, 542 Frenchmen St., 943 3934
Remoulade, 309 Bourbon St., 523 0611
T.G.I.Friday's Restaurant, 132 Royal St., 523 4401
Top of the Mart, 2 Canal St., 523 3181
Tropical Isle, 721 Bourbon St., 529 4109

Entertainment:
Bally's Casino Lakeshore Resort, 1 Stars & Stripes Blvd.,
    248 3200
City Lights, 310 Howard Av., 568 1700
Creole Queen, Poydras St., 529 4567
Crescent City Brewhouse, 527 Decatur St., 522 0571
Famous Door, 339 Bourbon St., 522 7626
Fitze'l, 733 Bourbon St., 561 0432
Funky Pirate, 727 Bourbon St., 523 1960
Gazebo Restaurant, 1016 - 1018 Decatur St., 522 0862
Hard Rock Cafe, 440 N.Peters St., 529 8617
House of Blues, 225 Decatur St., 529 2583

Jimmy's Music Club, 8200 Willow St., 861 8200
Lafitte's Blacksmith Shop, 941 Bourbon St., 523 0066
Maple Leaf Bar, 8316 Oak St., 866 9359
Margaritaville Cafe, 1104 Decatur St., 592 2565
Michael's, 840 St. Charles St., 522 5517
Mulate's, 201 Julia St., 522 1492
Napoleon House, 500 Chartres St., 524 9752
Palm Court Jazz Cafe, 1204 Decatur St., 525 0200
Pat O'Brien's, 718 St.Peter St., 525 4823
Pete Fountain's, 2 Poydras St., 523 4374
Preservation Hall, 726 St.Peter St., 523 8939
Tipitina's, 501 Napoleon Ave., 897 3943

Shops and Stores:

Canal Place Shopping Center, 333 Canal St.	Mall
Canal Place, 1 Canal Pl.	Apparel
Centry, 200 Broadway #108	Shoes
French Quarter's	Antiques
Magazine Street	Antiques
Maison Blanche, 901 Canal St.	Dept.Store
New Orleans Center, 600 Poydras St.	Dept.Store
Quarter Moon Designs, 918 Royal St.	Jewelry
Royal Street	Antiques

Places of Interest:
The Louisiana State Museum
The Old US Mint
The New Orleans Pharmacy Museum
Musee Conti Wax Museum
French Quarter (known as Vieux Carre) – jazz clubs
Jackson Square – a pedestrian mall
Canal Street
Bourbon Street – jazz clubs
St. Louis Cathedral

NEW YORK

Country code: 1 - Area code: 212 or 718

Airport: John F. Kennedy International Airport.

Distance from City: 24km (14 miles) southeast of the city.

Transportation to Center of City:
From International and Domestic Terminals
By Bus (cost) USD1.50. Time approx. 60 min.
By Taxi (cost) USD30 plus tolls. Time approx. 50-60 min.
Tip luggage porters USD1   per piece
Transfers: (Minimum Connecting Time):
International to International: 120 min.
International to Domestic: 100 min.
Domestic to International: 75 min.
Domestic to Domestic: 60 min.

Automobile Rentals:
Airport car rental desk
Avis -244-5400
National - 632-8300
Hertz - 656-7600
Airport: La Guardia Airport.

Distance from City: 13km (8 miles) east of central Manhattan.

Transportation to Center of City:
From International and Domestic Terminals
By Bus (cost) USD8.50-10 Time approx. 40 min. (every 30 min)
By Taxi (cost) USD20 plus tolls. Time approx. 30 min.
Tip luggage porters USD1   per piece

Transfers: (Minimum Connecting Time):
International to International: 120 min.
International to Domestic: 60 min.
Domestic to International: 60 min.
Domestic to Domestic: 45 min.

Automobile Rentals:
Airport car rental desk
Avis - 507-3600
National - 429-5893
Hertz - 478-5300

Airport: Newark International Airport.

Distance from City: 26km (16 miles) southwest of central Manhattan.

Transportation to Center of City:
From International and Domestic Terminals
By Bus (cost) USD7 Time approx. 40-60 min.
By Taxi (cost) USD35 Time approx. 45 min.
Tip luggage porters USD1   per piece

Transfers: (Minimum Connecting Time):
International to International: 120 min.
International to Domestic: 150 min.
Domestic to International: 60 min.
Domestic to Domestic: 60 min.

Automobile Rentals:
Car rental city office
Avis - 593-8375
National - 875-1255
Hertz - 486-5060

Hotels:
Algonquin Hotel, 59 West 44th St., 840-6800
Beekman Tower Suite Hotel, 3 Mitchell Pl., 355-7300
Best Western President Hotel, 234 West 48th St., 246-8800
Best Western Seaport Inn, 33 Peck Slip & Front St., 766-6600
Best Western Woodward, 210 West 55th St., 247-2000
Comfort Inn Manhattan, 42 W 35th St., 947-0200
Doral Court, 130 East 39th St., 685-1100
Doral Inn, 541 Lexington & 49th St., 755-1200
Doral Park Ave. E. 38th St., 687-7050
Doral Tuscany, 120 East 39th St., 686-1600
Doubletree Guest Suites, 1568 Broadway, 719-1600
Dumont Plaza Suite Hotel, 150 East 34th St., 481-7600
Eastgate Tower Suite Hotel, 22 East 39th St., 687-8000
Essex House Hotel Nikko New York, 160 Central Park South, 247-0300
Grand Hyatt new York, Park Ave. & Grand Central, 883-1234
Helmsley Middletowne, 148 E 48th St., 755- 3000
Plaza, 5th Avenue at 59th Street, 759-3000
Waldorf-Astoria, 301 Park Avenue, 355-3000

U.S.A.

Restaurants:
98 Mott Street, 98 Mott St., 226 6603
American Renaissance, 260 West Broadway, 343 0049
Aquavit, 13 W. 54th St., 307 7311
Arizona 206, 206 E. 60th St., 838 0440
Balthazar, 80 Spring St, 965-1785
Boca Chica, 13 1st Ave., 473 0108
Carmine's, 200 W. 44th St., 221 3800
Chanterelle, 2 Harrison St., 966 6960
Daniel, 20 E. 76th St., 288-0033
Dawat, 210 E. 58th St., 355 7555
Four Seasons, 99 E. 52nd St., 754 9494
Gramercy Tavern, 42 E. 20th St., 477 0777
Kin Khao, 171 Spring St., 966 3939
La Grenouille, 3 E. 52nd St. 752-1495
Le Cirque, 455 Madison Ave., 303-7788
Le Madri, 168 W. 18th St., 727 8022
Le Perigord, 405 E. 52nd Street, 755-6244
Lespinasse, 2 E. 55th St., 339 6719
Ludlow Street Cafe, 165 Ludlow St., 353 0536
Lusardis, 1494 2nd Ave, 249-2020
Markham, 59 5th Ave., 647 9391
Mid-City Café, 575 5th Ave. 682-1000
San Domenico, 240 Central Park, 265 5959
Smith & Wollensky, 201 E. 49th St., 753 1530
Symphony Cafe, 950 8th Ave., 397 9595
Zoe, 90 Prince St., 966 6722

Entertainment:
Au Bar. 41 E. 58th St., 308-9455
Ballroom, 253 W. 28th St., 244 3005
Bitter End, 147 Bleecker St., 673 7030
Blue Note, 131 W. 3rd St., 475 8592
Bottom Line, 15 W. 4th St., 228 7880
Dan Lynch's Blues Bar, 221 2nd Ave., 677 0911
Fashion Café, 51 Rockefeller Plaza, 765 3131
Hard Rock Café, 221 W. 57th St., 459 9320
Harglo's, 974 2nd Ave., 759 9820
Michael's Pub, 211 E. 55th St., 758 2272
Original Improvisation, 433 W. 34th St., 279 3446
Palladium, 126 E. 14th St., 473 7171
Rainbow & Stars, 30 Rockefeller Plaza, 632 5000

Rainbow Room, 30 Rockefeller Plaza, 632 5000
Roseland, 239 W. 52nd St., 247 0200
Sardi's, 234 W. 44th St., 221 8440
Shark Bar, 307 Amsterdam Ave., 874 8500
Tattoo, 151 E. 50th St., 753-1144
Tunnel, 220 12th Ave., 695-7292
The Whiskey, 235 W. 46th St., 764 5500
Twins, 1712 2nd Ave., 987 1111
Village Vanguard, 178 7th Ave., 255 4037
Water Club, 500 E. 30th St., 683 3333

Shops and Stores:

Ann Taylor, 133 Beekman St.	Apparel
Bloomingdale's, 1000 3rd Ave. at 59th St.	Dept. Store
Bulgari, 730 5th Ave.	Jewelry
Burberrys, 9 E. 57th St.	Apparel
Calvin Klein, 654 Madison Ave.	Apparel
Cartier, 653 5th Ave.	Jewelry
Diesel Super Store, 770 Lexington Ave.	Apparel
Disney Store, 711 5th Ave.	Toys
F.A.O. Schwarz, 767 5th Ave.	Toys
Fortunoff, 681 5th Ave.	Jewelry
Giorgio Armani, 760 Madison Ave.	Apparel
H. Stern, 645 5th Ave.	Jewelry
J. Crew, 99 Prince St.	Apparel
Lord & Taylor, 424 5th Ave.	Dept. Store
Macy's, Herald Sq., Broadway at 34th St.	Dept. Store
Moschino, 803 Madison Ave.	Apparel
Polo, 867 Madison Ave.	Apparel
Saks Fifth Ave, 611 5th Ave.	Dept. Store
Stern's, 33rd St. and 6th Ave.	Dept. Store
Takashimaya New York, 693 5th Ave	Dept. Store
The Pop Shop, 292 Lafayette St.	Souvenirs
Tiffany & Co., 727 5th Ave.	Jewelry
Valentino, 747 Madison Ave.	Apparel
Versace, 647 5th Ave.	Apparel

Places of Interest:
Bronx Zoo
Central Park
Fifth Avenue
Lincoln Center

U.S.A.

Museum of Modern Art
Radio City Music Hall
Rockefeller Center
The American Museum of Natural History
The Empire State Building
The Metropolitan Museum of Art
The Museum of the City of New York
The Statue of Liberty and Ellis Island
The World Trade Center
Times Square
Wall Street

PHILADELPHIA

Country code: 1 - Area code: 215

Airport: Philadelphia International Airport.
Distance from City: 11km (6 miles) southwest of the city.

Transportation to Center of City:
From International and Domestic Terminals
By Bus (cost) USD8 Time approx. 15 min.
By Taxi (cost) USD20 Time approx. 10 min.
Tip luggage porters USD1   per piece

Transfers: (Minimum Connecting Time):
International to International: 90 min.
International to Domestic: 90 min.
Domestic to International: 90 min.
Domestic to Domestic: 40 min.

Automobile Rentals:
Airport car rental desk
Avis - 492-0900
National - 492-2750
Hertz - 492-7205

Car rental city office
Avis - 563-8976
National - 567-1760
Hertz - 492-2951

Hotels:
Best Western Center City Hotel, 501 N. 22nd St. 557-0259
Days Inn at Philadelphia Airport, 4101 Island Ave., 492- 0400
Doubletree Hotel, Broad St., at Locust, 893-1600
Holiday Inn Independence Mall, 400 Arch St., 923-8660
Independence Park Inn, 235 Chestnut St, 922-4443
Latham Hotel, 17th & Walnut St., 563-7474
Park Hyatt Philadelphia, Broad & Walnut St., 893-1776
Penn's View Hotel, Front and Market Sts, 922-7600
Philadelphia Airport Hilton, 4509 Island Ave., 365-4150
Philadelphia Marriott, 1201 Market St., 625-2900
Philadephia Airport Marriott, Arrivals Rd., 492-9000
Sheraton Society Hill Hotel, 2nd & Walnut St., 238-6000
Sheraton University City Hotel, 36th & Chestnut St., 387-8000
Warwick Hotel, 1701 Locust St., 735-6000
Wyndham Franklin Plaza Hotel, 17th & Race St., 448-2000

Restaurants:
Cafe Nola, 328 South St., 627 2590
City Tavern, 138 S. 2nd St., 413 1449
Downey's, Front and South Sts., 625 9500
Famous Delicatessen, 4th and Bainbridge Sts., 922 3274
Hikaru, 607 S. 2nd St., 627 7110
Irish Pub, 2007 Walnut St., 568 5603
Joe's Peking Duck House, 925 Race St., 922 3277
Le Bec-Fin, 1523 Walnut St., 567 1000
Lee's, 44 S. 17th St., 564 1264
Magnolia Cafe, 1602 Locust St., 546 4180
Pat's, 1237 E. Passyunk, 468 1546
Pizzeria Uno, 1721 Locust St., 790 9669
Reading Terminal Market, 12th and Arch Sts., 922 2317
Restaurant School, 4207 Walnut St., 222 4200
Sansom Street Oyster House, 1516 Sansom St., 567 7683
Susanna Foo, 1512 Walnut St., 545 2666
Tequila's,1511 Locust St., 546 0181
The Fountain, 1 Logan Sq., 963 1500
Tiramisu, 528 S. 5th St., 925 3335
Victor Cafe, 1303 Dickinson St., 468 3040

Entertainment:
Cherry Tree Music Co-op, 3916 Locust Walk, 386 1640

U.S.A.

Comedy Cabaret, 126 Chestnut St., 625 5653
Dave and Buster's, Pier 19, 325 N. Columbus Blvd., 413-1951
Dirty Frank's, 347 S. 13th St., 732 5010
Egypt, 520 N. Christopher Columbus Blvd., 922-6500
Hepburn's 254 S. 12th St., 545 8088
Katmandu, Pier 25, 629 1101
Khyber Pass, 56 S. 2nd St., 440 9683
Painted Bride Art Center, 230 Wine St., 925 9914
River Deck, Café and Dance Club, 4100 Main St., 483-4100
Rock Lobster, Pier 13-14 on Christopher Columbus Blvd.,
    627-ROCK
Trocadero, 1003 Arch St., 922 0194
Warmdaddy's, 4 S. Front St., 627 2500
Woody's, 202 S. 13th St., 545 1893
Zanzibar Blue, 301 S. 11th St., 829 1990

Shops and Stores:

Barsky Diamonds, 724 Sansom St.	Jewelry
Beautiful Beads, 110 S. 18th St.	Apparel
Boyds, 1818 Chestnut St.	Apparel
Daffy's, 17th & Chestnut Sts.	Apparel
Dan's Shoes, 1204 Chestnut St.	Apparel
JCPenney Co., Inc., 1035 Market St.	Dept. Store
Lord and Taylor, 13th and Market Sts.	Dept. Store
Neiman Marcus, 170 N. Guelph Rd., King of Prussia	Dept. Store
Polo, 200 S. Broad St.	Apparel
Strawbridge and Clothier, 8th and Market Sts.	Dept.Store
Sydney Rosen Company, 714 Sansom St.	Jewelry
Tiffany and Co., 1414 Wallnut St.	Jewelry

Places of Interest:

The United States Mint
Academy of Natural Sciences
The Philadelphia Museum of Art
The Pennsylvania Academy of the Fine Arts
Cathedral of Saints Peter and Paul
Philosophical Hall
Independence Hall
The Philadelphia Zoological Gardens
Sesame Place and Twiddlebug Land – an amusement park.
Penn's Landing – a memorial park
Independence National Historical Park

U.S.A.

Liberty Bell

PITTSBURGH

Country code: 1 - Area code: 412

Airport: Pittsburgh International Airport.

Distance from City: 25km (15 miles) north of the city.

Transportation to Center of City:
From International and Domestic Terminals
By Bus (cost) USD12 Time approx. 40 min.
By Taxi (cost) USD30 Time approx. 25-30 min.
Tip luggage porters USD1   per piece

Transfers: (Minimum Connecting Time):
International to International: 90 min.
International to Domestic: 90 min.
Domestic to International: 60 min.
Domestic to Domestic: 40 min.

Automobile Rentals:
Airport car rental desk
Avis - 472-5200
National - 472-5094
Hertz - 472-5955

Car rental city office
Avis - 261-0540

Hotels:
Four Points Hotel Greensburg, 100 Sheraton Dr. Rte. 30 E.,
    836-6060
Pittsburgh Hilton & Towers, 600 Commonwealth Pl., 391-4600
Sheraton Station Square Hotel, 7 Station Square Dr., 261-2000
Pittsburgh Vista Hotel, 1000 Penn Ave., 281-3700
Westin Willian Penn, 530 William Penn Pl., Mellon Sq.,
    281-7100

U.S.A.

Restaurants:
Common Plea, 310 Ross St., 281 5140
The Grand Concourse, 1 Station Sq., 261 1717
Georgetowne Inn, 1230 Grandview Ave., 481 4424
Gallagher's Pub, 2 S. Market Sq., 261 5554
Richest's Restaurant, 140 6th St., 471 7799

Entertainment:
Chauncy's, 232 0601
FunnyBone Comedy Club, 281 3130
Jellyrolls, 391 7464

Shops and Stores:

Saks Fifth Avenue, 513 Smithfield St.	Dept.Store
Lazarus, 200 Stanwix St.	Dept.Store
Kaufmann's, 5th Ave. and Smithfield St.	Dept.Store
Shops at Station Square	Mall
Fifth Avenue Place	Mall
1 Oxford Centre	Mall

Places of Interest:
The Carnegie - museums
The Frick Art and Historical Center
The Buhl Science Center
Allegheny Center – an amusement park
Point State Park
Allegheny County Courthouse and Jail

PORTLAND

Country code: 1 - Area code: 503

Airport: Portland International Airport

Distance from City: 15 km. (9 miles) Northeast from the city center.

Transportation to Center of City:
From International and Domestic Terminals
By Bus (cost) USD1. Time approx. 45 min. (every 15-30 min.)

U.S.A.

By Taxi (cost) USD 19-25. Time approx. 20 min.
Tip luggage porters USD1   per piece

Transfers: (Minimum Connecting Time):
International to International: 70 min.
International to Domestic: 70 min.
Domestic to International: 45 min.
Domestic to Domestic: 40 min.

Automobile Rentals:
Avis – 1-800-3311212
Hertz – 1-800-6543131
National – 1-800-2277368

Hotels:
5th Ave Suites Hotel, 506 SW Washington St., 222-0001
Caeavan Motor Hotel, 2401 SW Fourth Ave., 226-1121
Governor Hotel, S.W. 10th @ Alder, 224-3400
Heathman Hotel, 1001 S.W. Broadway @ Salmon, 241-4100
Hotel Vintage Plaza, 422 SW Broadway, 228-1212
Imperial Hotel, 400 SW Broadway, 228-7221
Mallory Hotel, 729 SW 15th Ave., 223-6311
Portland Hilton, 921 S.W. Sixth Ave., 226-1611
Portland Marriott, 1401 S.W. Front Ave., 226-7600
Quality Inn Portland Airport, 8247 N.E. Sandy Blvd., 256-4111
Red Lion, 1000 N. E. Multnomah St., 281-6111
Sheraton Portland Airport Hotel, 8235 N.E. Airport Way,
    281-2500
The Benson, 309 S. W. Broadway, 228-2000
The Mark Spencer Hotel, 409 SW 11th Ave., 224-3293
The Riverside, 50 SW Morrison St., 221-0711

Restaurants:
Alexis, 215 W Burnside St., 224-8577
B.Moloch Heatman Bakery and Pub, 901 S.W.Salmon St.,
    227 5700
Bankok Kitchen, 2534 S.E. Belmont St., 236 7349
Bridgeport Brew Pub, 1313 N.W. Marshall St., 241 7179
Cozze, 1205 SE Morrison St., 232 3275
Esparza's Tex-Mex Cafe, 2725 S.E. Ankeny St., 234 7909
Genoa, 2832 S.E. Belmont St., 238 1464
Indigine, 3725 S.E. Division St., 238 1470

U.S.A.

Jake's Famous Crawfish, 401 S.W. 12th Ave., 226 1419
L'Auberge, 2601 N.W. Vaughn St., 223 3302
Le Bistro Montage, 301 SE Morrison St., 234-1324
Marco Polo Garden, 19 NW Fifth, Portland, 222-1090
McMenamins Edgefield, 2126 S.W.Halsey St., 492 4686
Pilsner Room, 309 S.W. Montgomery St., 220 1865
Santana's, 1110 SW Third Ave., 222 5461
Yen Ha, 8640 S.W. Canyon Rd., 292 0616

Entertainment:
Brasserie Monmartre, 626 S.W. Park Ave., 224 5552
Buddy McGraw's Irish Pub, 3518 SE Hawthorne Blvd., 233 1178
Dublin Pub, 6821 Beaverton-Hillsdale Hwy, 297 2889
Embers, 110 N.W. Broadway, 222 3082
Galway's Pub, 3728 NE Sandy Blvd., 281 5464
Harvey's Comedy Club, 436 N.W. 6th Ave., 241 0338
Horse Brass Pub, 4534 SE Belmont, 232 2202
Jazz de Opus, 33 N.W. 2nd Ave., 222 6077
Rigler's, 1332 W Burnside, 225 0543
Rock'N'Rodeo, 220 S.E. Spokane St., 235 2417

Shops and Stores:

Pioneer Place, 700 S.W. 5th Ave.	Jewelry
Saks Fifth Avenue	Mall
Meier & Frank, 621 S.W. 5th Ave.	Dept. Store
Nordstrom, 701 S.W.Broadway	Dept. Store
Nike Town, 930 S.W. 6th Ave.	Dept. Store
Portland Pendleton Shop, 900 S.W. 4th Ave.	Apparel

Places of Interest:
Portland Art Museum
Old Church
World Trade Center
Maritime Center and Museum

SAINT LOUIS

Country code: 1 - Area code: 314

Airport: Lambert - St. Louis International Airport

Distance from City: 16 km. (10 miles) northwest from the city center.

Transportation to Center of City:
From International and Domestic Terminals
By Bus (cost) USD1. Time approx. 35 min.
By Taxi (cost) USD20. Time approx. 20 min.
Tip luggage porters USD1   per piece
Hotels:
Adam's Mark Hotel, 4th and Chestnut Sts, 241-7400
Budgetel Inn - Hazelwood, 318 Taulor Rd, 731-4200
Congress Airport Inn, 3433 N. Lindbergh Blvd., 739-5100
Courtyard By Marriott, 2340 Market St., 241-9111
Drury Inn - Convention Center, 711 N. Broadway, 231-8100
Drury Inn-Union Station, 201 S. 20th St., 231-3900
Embassy Suites Hotel, 901 N. 1st Street, 241-4200
Hampton Inn Union Station, 2211 Market St., 621-8200
Holiday Inn Airport Oakland Park, 4505 Woodson Rd., 427-4700
Holiday Inn Select, 811 N. Ninth St., 421-4000
Hotel Majestic, 1019 Pine St., 436-2355
Hyatt Regency St. Louis, 1 St. Louis Union Stadium, 231-1234
Mayfair Grand Heritage Hotel, 806 St. Charles St., 421-2500
Ramada Inn at the Arch, 333 Washington Ave., 621-7900
Regal Riverfront Hotel, 200 S. Fourth St., 241-9500
St. Louis Airport Hilton, 10330 Natural Bridge Rd., 429-1100
St. Louis Marriott Pavilion Hotel, 1 Broadway, 421-1776

Restaurants:
Al's Restaurant, 1200 N.First St., 421 6399
Backstage Bistro, 3536 Washington Ave., 534 3663
BB's Jazz,Blues & Soups, 700 S.Broadway, 436 5222
Blue Water Grill, 2607 Hampton Ave., 645 0707
Blueberry Hill, 6504 Delmar Blvd., 727 0880
Broadway Oyster Bar, 736 S.Broadway, 621 8811
Cafe de France, 410 Olive St., 231 2204
Caleco's Bar & Grill, 101 N.Broadway, 421 0708
Cardwell's, 8100 Maryland St., 726 5055
Casa Gallardo Mexican, 1821 Market St., 421 6766
Charlie Gitto's, 207 N.Sixth St., 436 2828
Chick-fil-A, 515 N.Sixth St., 231 3361
Cunetto's House Pasta, 5453 Magnolia Ave., 781 1135

Dierdorf & Hart's, 1820 Market St., 421 1772
Harry's Restaurant, 2144 Market St., 421 6969
Hooters, 1820 Market St., 436 8888
Hot Locust Cantina, 2005 Locust St., 231 3636
Rigazzi's, 4945 Daggett St., 772 4900
Sidney Street Cafe, 2000 Sidney St., 771 5777
Tony's, 410 Market St., 231 7007

Entertainment:
Alton Belle Riverboat Casino, 219 Piasa St., 474 7500
Backstage Bistro, 3536 Washington Ave., 534 3663
BB's Jazz,Blues & Soups, 700 S.Broadway, 436 5222
Blueberry Hill, 6504 Delmar, 727 0880
Boomer's, 707 Clamorgan Alley, 621 8155
Broadway Oyster Bar, 736 S.Broadway, 621 8811
Cabool, 1521 Washington Ave., 231 8784
Club Viva!, 408 N.Euclid, 361 0322
Hannengan's, 719 North Second St., 241 8877
I.E.C., 1401A Mississippi Ave., 271 9420
Indigo Room, 1204 Washington Ave., 436 9941
Kicks Nightclub, 660 Maryville Centre Dr., 878 2747
Mike & Min's, 925 Geyer, 421 1655
Mississipi Nights, 914 N.First St., 421 3853
President Riverboat Casino, 800 N. 1st, St., 622 3000
St. Louis' Casa Loma Ballroom, 3354 Iowa Ave., 664 8000
The Summit, 200 N.Broadway, 436 2770

Shops and Stores:

Central West End	Apparel
Famous-Barr, 601 Olive St.	Dept. Store
Hamilton Jewelers, 750 Locust St.	Jewelry
Jamestown Mall, Lindbergh and Old Jamestown Rd.	Mall
Neiman Marcus, Plaza Frontenac	Dept. Store
Plaza Frontenac, Clayton Rd.	Mall
Saint Louis Center, b/n 6th and 7th Sts.	Mall
Union Station, 18th and Market Sts.	Apparel

Places of Interest:
Gateway Arch - observation deck
Museum of Westward Expansion

U.S.A.

Basilica of St. Louis
Old Courthouse
St. Louis Zoo
St. Louis Art Museum
Cathedral of St. Louis

SAN FRANCISCO

Country code: 1 - Area code: 415

Airport: San Francisco International Airport.

Distance from City: 25km (15 miles) south of the city.

Transportation to Center of City:
From International and Domestic Terminals
By Bus (cost) USD9-13 Time approx. 30-50 min.
By Taxi (cost) USD28-30 Time approx. 30 min.
Tip luggage porters USD1   per piece

Transfers: (Minimum Connecting Time):
International to International: 105 min.
International to Domestic: 105 min.
Domestic to International: 60 min.
Domestic to Domestic: 50 min.

Automobile Rentals:
Airport car rental desk
Avis - 877-6780
National - 877-4745
Hertz - 635-6683

Car rental city office
Avis - 259-1169
National - 474-5300
Hertz - 771-2200

Hotels:
ANA Hotel San Francisco, 50 Third St., 974-6400
Abigail Hotel, 246 McAllister St., 861-9728
Best Western Miyako Inn, Cnr. Sutter & Buchanan St.,

921-4000
Californian Hotel, 405 Taylor St., 885-2500
Campton Place Hotel San Francisco, 340 Stockton St.,
    781-5555
Carlton Hotel, 1075 Sutter St., 673-0242
Grand Hyatt San Francisco, On Union Sq. 345 Stockton St.,
398-1234
Hyatt Regency San Francisco, 5 Embarcadero Center, 788-1234
Hyatt at Fisherman's Wharf, 555 N. Point St., 563-1234
Palace Hotel, 2 New Montgomery St., 392-8600
Pan Pacific Hotel San Francisco, 500 Post St., 771-8600
Park Hyatt San Francisco, At Embarcadero Center, 392-1234
Radisson Miyako Hotel San Francisco, 1625 Post St., 922-3200
Renaissance Stanford Court Hotel/San Francisco, 905 Califor-
    nia St., Nob Hill, 989-3500
Ritz-Carlton, 600 Stockton & California St., 296-7465
Rodeway Inn Civic Center, 860 Eddy St., 474-4374
San Francisco Hilton & Towers, 333 O'Farrell St., 771-1400
San Francisco Marriott Moscone Center, 55 Fourth St.,
    896-1600

Restaurants:
American Bistro, 2373 Chestnut St., 440 2373
Annie's Restaurant, 20 Annie St., 777 1102
Buena Vista Cafe, 2765 Hyde St., 474 5044
Cafe Freddy's, 901 Columbus Ave., 922 0151
Cafe Venue, 721 Market St., 546 1144
Campton Place Restaurant, 340 Stockton St., 955 555
Canvas Cafe, 761 Post St., 673 6040
Capp's Corner, 1600 Powell St., 989 2589
Carnelian Room, 555 California St., 433 7500
Chevy's, 4th and Howard Sts., 543 8060
Ernie's, 847 Montgomery St., 397 5969
Fog City Diner, 1300 Battery St., 982 2000
Garden Court, Market and Montgomery Sts., 546 5000
Harbor Village, 4 Embarcadero Center, 781 8833
Hayes Street Grill, 320 Hayes St., 863 5545
Lulu, 816 Folsom St., 495 5775
Masa's, 648 Bush St., 989 7154
Mifune, 1737 Post St., 922 2728
Postrio, 545 Post St., 776 7825
Stars, 150 Redwood Alley, 861 7827

Entertainment:
13 Views Bar, 5 Embarcadero Center, 788 1234
Bottom of the Hill, 1233 17th St., 626 4455
Cobb's Comedy Club, 2801 Leavenworth St., 928 4320
DNA Lounge, 375 11th St., 626 1409
Great American Music Hall, 859 O'Farrell St., 885 0750
Jazz at Pearl's, 256 Columbus Ave., 291 8255
La Rocca's Corner, 957 Columbus Ave., 674 1266
London Wine Bar, 415 Samsone St., 788 4811
Metronom Ballroom, 1830 17th St., 252 9000
Pacific Bar, 500 Post St., 929 2087
Park Grill Bar, 333 Battery St., 296 2933
Pat O'Shea Mad Hatter, 3848 Geary Blvd., 752 3148
Piazza, 55 Cyril Margin, 392 8000
Punch Line, 444A Battery St., 397 7573
Redwood Room, 495 Geary St., 775 4700
Slim's, 333 11th St., 621 3330
The Lobby Lounge, 1250 Columbus Ave., 775 7555
The Ritz-Carlton Bar, 600 Stockton St., 296 7465
Top of the Mark, California and Mason Sts., 392 3434
View Lounge, 55 Fourth St., 896 1600

Shops and Stores:

American Rag Cie, 1305 Van Ness Ave.	Apparel
Bally, 238 Stockton St.	Shoes
Cannery, 2801 Leavenworth St.	Dept. Store
Courtoue, 459 Geary St.	Apparel
Diesel, 101 Post St.	Apparel
Eileen West, 2915 Sacramento St.	Apparel
Embarcadero Center, One Embarcadero Center	Dept. Store
Episode, 150 Post Street	Apparel
First Step, 216 Powell St.	Shoes
Gianni Versace, Post and Kearny Sts.	Apparel
Macy's West, Stockton and O'Farrell Sts.	Dept. Store
Patagonia, 770 N. Point St.	Apparel
Payless Shoe Source Inc., 45 Kearny St.	Shoes
Polo, 90 Post Street	Apparel

Places of interest:
Fisherman's Wharf
The National Maritime Museum

U.S.A.

The Museum of the City of San Francisco
Underwater World at Pier 39
Palace of Fine Arts - museums
The Steinhart Aquarium
Chinatown
Golden Gate Bridge
San Francisco Zoo

Alcatraz
Coit Tower

SEATTLE

Country code: 1 - Area code: 206

Airport: Tacoma International Airport.

Distance from City: 20km (12 miles) south of the city.

Transportation to Center of City:
From International and Domestic Terminals
By Bus (cost) USD7.50 Time approx. 25-30 min.
By Taxi (cost) USD30-USD35 Time approx. 25-30 min.
Tip luggage porters USD1   per piece

Transfers: (Minimum Connecting Time):
International to International: 90 min.
International to Domestic: 90 min.
Domestic to International: 70 min.
Domestic to Domestic: 70 min.

Automobile Rentals:
Airport car rental desk
Avis - 433-5231
National - 433-5501
Hertz - 248-1300

Car rental city office
Avis - 448-1700
National - 448-7368
Hertz - 682-5050

Hotels:
Best Western Executive Inn, 200 Taylor Ave. North, 448-9444
Edgewater Hotel, 2411 Alaskan Way, Pier 67, 728-7000
Renaissance Madison Hotel/Seattle, 515 Madison St., 583-0300
Residence Inn Seattle Downtown/Lake Union, 800 Fairview Ave.
     N., 624-6000
Seattle Hilton, 1301 Sixth Ave., 624-0500
Sheraton Seattle Hotel & Towers, 1400 Sixth Ave., 621-9000

Sheraton Tacoma Hotel, 1320 Broadway Plaza, Tacoma,
     572-3200
Westin Hotel, Seattle, 1900 Fifth Ave.,728-1000

Restaurants:
Alfi's Food & Deli, 1510 Seventh Ave., 623 8196
Andaluca Restaurant & Bar, 407 Olive Way, 382 6999
Andiamo, 1400 Sixth Ave., 389 5769
Bombore 89 University St., 624 8233
Briazz,Inc., 1400 Fifth Ave., 343 3099
Campagne, 86 Pine St., 728 2800
Canlis, 2576 Aurora Ave., 283 3313
Crepe de Paris, 1333 Fifth Ave., 623 4111
D'Amico's Cafe, 6001 Union St., 682 8617
Dahlia Lounge Restaurant, 1904 4th Ave., 682 4142
Emmet Watson's Oyster Bar, 1916 Pike Pl., 448 7721
Isabella Ristorante, 1909 Third Ave., 441 8281
LeoMelina, 96 Union St., 623 3783
Menu Guide Puget Sound, 2000 Fairview Ave., 726 2819
Nikko Restaurant, 1900 Fifth Ave., 322 4641
ObaChine, 1518 Sixth Ave., 749 9653
Place Pigalle, Pike Place Market, 624 1756
Salvatore Ristorante Italiano, 6100 Roosevelt Way NE, 527 9301
Seattle Dining on CD Rom, 9932 Rainier Ave., 721 5325
The Hunt Club, 900 Madison St., 343 6156
Wild Ginger, 1400 Western Ave., 623 4450

Entertainment:
Adriatica, 1107 Dexter Ave., 285 5000
Arnie's Northshore Restaurant, 1900 N. Northlake Way, 547 3242
Ballard Firehouse, 5429 Russell St., 784 3516
Bohemia Cafe, 111 Yesler Way, 447 1514

Central Saloon, 207 1st Ave., 622 0209
Comedy Underground, 222 Main St., 628 0303
Crocodile Cafe, 2200 2nd Ave., 448 2114
Dimitriou's Jazz Alley, 2033 6th Ave., 441 9729
Emerald Queen Casino, 2102 Alexander Ave., 831 ROLL
Fenix, 315 2nd Ave., 467 1111
Harrah's Skagit Valley Casino, 590 Darrk Lane, 724 777
Off Ramp Cafe, 109 Eastlake Ave., 628 0232
Ok Hotel, 212 Alaskan Way S, 621 7903
Pescatore, 5300 34th Ave., 784 1733
Ray's Boathouse, 6049 Seaview Ave., 789 3770
Suquamish Clearwater Casino, 15347 Suquamish Way,
    598 6889
Swinomish Casino & Bingo, 837 Casino Dr., 293 2691

Shops and Stores:

Antique Importers, 640 Alaskan Way	Antiques
Aramark, 800 Convention Place	Gifts
Ben Bridge Jeweler, 4th and Pike	Jewelry
Boutique Europa, 1015 1th Ave.	Apparel
Brooks Brothers, 1516 4th Ave.	Apparel
Church's English Shoes Ltd., 520 Pike St.	Shoes
City Centre, 1420 5th Ave.	Mall
Eddie Bauer, 1330 Fifth Ave.	Apparel
Fox's Gem Shop, 1341 Fifth Ave.	Jewelry
Mario's, 1513 6th Ave.	Apparel
Patagonia, 2100 First Ave.	Apparel
The Bon Marche, 3rd and Pine Sts.	Dept. Store
Westlake Center, 1601 5th Ave.	Mall

Places of Interest:
The Seattle Art Museum
The Seattle Aquarium
The Klondike Gold Rush National Historical Park
The Space Needle – an observation deck
Woodland Park Zoo
The Thomas Burke Memorial Washington State Museum
Museum of History and Industry
The Seattle Center - museums, exhibition hall, theaters, etc.
Pike Place Market

U.S.A.

TULSA

Country code: 1 - Area code: 918

Airport: Tulsa International Airport

Distance from City: 6 km. (10 mi.) northeast from the city center.

Hotels:
Doubletree Hotel Downtown, 616 W. Seventh St., 587-8000
Econo Lodge Airport, 11620 E. Skelly Dr., 437-9200
Radisson Inn Tulsa Airport, 2201 N. 77th East Ave., 835-9911
Adam's Mark Hotel, 100E. 2nd St., 582-9000
Southern Hills Marriott, 1902 E. 71st St., 493-7000
Hawthorn Suites Hotel, 3509 South 79th E. Ave., 663-3900

Restaurants:
Bravo Ristorante, Adam's Mark Hotel, 100 E. End St., 582-9000
Jamils, 2833 E. 51 St, 742-9097
Metro Diner, 3001 E. 11th St., Rte. 66, 592-2616
Nelson's Buffeteria, 514 S. Boston St., 584-9969

Shops and Stores:
Lion's Indian Store, 401 E. 11th St.   Souvenirs
Mister Indian's, 1000 S. Main St.   Souvenirs

Places of Interest:
Gilcrease Museum - art museum
Woolaroc - wildlife preserve
Bartlesville Museum
Will Rogers Memorial - museum
Cherokee National Museum

WASHINGTON D.C.

Country code: 1 - Area code: 202

Airport: Dulles International Airport.

Distance from City: 41km (25 miles) west of the city.

Transportation to Center of City:
From International and Domestic Terminals
By Bus (cost) USD16 Time approx. 45-60 min.
By Taxi (cost) USD35-40 Time approx. 40 min.
Tip luggage porters USD1   per piece

Transfers: (Minimum Connecting Time):
International to International: 90 min.
International to Domestic: 90 min.
Domestic to International: 45 min.
Domestic to Domestic: 45 min.

Automobile Rentals:
Airport car rental desk
Avis - 661-3500
National -471-5278
Hertz - 471-6020

Airport: Baltimore/Washington International Airport Maryland.

Distance from City: 48km (29 miles) northeast of Washington

Transportation to Center of City:
From International and Domestic Terminals
By Bus (cost) USD19. Time approx. 45 min.
By Taxi (cost) USD40. Time approx. 30-40 min.
Tip luggage porters USD1   per piece

Transfers: (Minimum Connecting Time):
International to International: 90 min.
International to Domestic: 90 min.
Domestic to International: 45 min.
Domestic to Domestic: 45 min.

Airport: National Airport in Virginia.

Distance from City: 6km (3 miles) south of downtown Washington.

U.S.A.

Transportation to Center of City:
From International and Domestic Terminals
By Bus (cost) USD 8. Time approx. 15 min.
By Taxi (cost) USD 15. Time approx. 10-15 min.
Tip luggage porters USD1   per piece

Automobile Rentals:
Airport car rental desk
Avis - 419-5815
National - 419-1032
Hertz - 419-6300

Car rental city office
Avis - 467-6585

National - 842-7454
Hertz - 628-6174

Hotels:
ANA Hotel, Washington D.C., 2401 M. St., N. W., 429-2400
Bellevue Hotel, 15 E. Street N. W., 638-0900
Best Western Capitol Skyline Hotel, 10 "I" Street S. W.,
    488-7500
Best Western New Hampshire Suites Hotel, 1121 New Hamp-
    shire Ave. N. W., 457-0565
Canterbury Hotel, 1733 N. Street N. W., 393-3000
Capitol Hilton, 16th & K. St., N. W., 393-1000
Carton, 923 16th & K. St., N. W., 638-2626
Courtyard Washington/Northwest, 1900 Connecticut Ave.,
    N. W., 332-9300
Doubletree Guest Suites, 801 New Hampshire Ave., 785-2000
Doubletree Guest Suites, 2500 Pennsylvania Ave., N. W.,
    333-8060
Doubletree Hotel Park Terrace, 1515 Rhode Island Ave., N. W.,
    232-7000
Embassy Row Hotel, 2015 Massachusetts Ave. N. W., 265-1600
Grand Hyatt Washington, At Washington Center, 582-1234
Howard Johnson Hotel & Suites, 1430 Rhode Island Ave.,
    N. W., 462-7777
Hyatt Regency Washington, On Capitol Hill, 737-1234
JW Marriott Hotel on Pennsylvania Avenue, 1331Pennsylvania
    Ave. N. W., 393-2000

Marriott at Metro Center, 775 12th Street N. W., 737-2200
Park Hyatt Washington, At the West End, 789-1234
Phoenix Park Hotel, 520 N. Capitol St., N. W., 638-6900
Quality Hotel Downtown, 1315 16th St. N. W., 232-8000
Radisson Barcelo Hotel Washington, 2121 P. St., N. W.,
    293-3100

Restaurants:
Art Gallery Grill, 1712 I St., 298 6658
Asia Nora, 2213 M St., 797 4360
Blackie's House of Beef, 1217 22nd St., 333 1100
Bombay Place, 2020 K St., 331 4200
Bread & Chocolate, 2301 M St., 833 8360
Donatello Restaurant, 2514 L St., 333 1485
Galileo, 1110 21st St., 293 7191
Georgia Brown's, 950 15th St., 393 4499
Gerard's Place, 915 15th St., 737 4445
Le Lion D'or, 1150 Connecticut Ave., 297 7972
Luigi's, 1132 19th St., 331 7574
Maison Blanche, 1725 F St., 842 0070
Primi Piatti, 2013 I St., 223 3600
Occidental Grill, 1475 Pennsylvania Ave., 783 1475
Old Ebbitt Grill, 675 15th St., 347 4801
Prime Rib, 2020 K St., 466 8811
Provence, 2401 Pennsylvania Ave., 296 1166
Star of Siam, 1136 19th St., 785 2838
Taberna del Alabardero, 1776 I St., 429 2200
Thai Kingdom, 2021 K St., 835 1700

Entertainment:
9:30 Club, 815 V St., 393 0930
Ben's Chili Bowl, 1213 U St., 667 0909
Bombay Club, 815 Connecticut Ave., 659 3727
Brickskeller, 1523 22nd St., 293 1885
Capitol City Brewing Company, 1100 New York Ave.,
    628 CCBC
State of the Union, 1357 U St., 588 8810
Coco Loco, 810 Seventh St. 289 2626
Crow Bar, 1006 20th St., 223 2972
Hard Rock Cafe, 999 E St., 737 7625
Improvisation, 1140 Connecticut Ave., 296 7008
Jaleo, 380 Seventh St., 628 7949

Los Atlantis, 289 1779
Marrakesh, 617 New York Ave., 393 9393
One Step Down, 2517 Pennsylvania Ave., 331 8863
Planet Fred, 1221 Connecticut Ave., 466 2336
Planet Hollywood, 1101 Pennsylvania Ave., 783 7827
Ritz Nightclub, 919 E St., 638 2582
Rumors, 1900 M St., 466 7378
The Bank, 915 F St., 737 3250
The Irish Times, 14 F St., 543 5433
West End Cafe, 1 Washington Circle, 293 5390

Shops and Stores:

Barami, 1730 K St.	Apparel
Beadazzled, 1522 Connecticut Ave.,	Dept.Store
Betsy Fisher, 1224 Connecticut Ave.	Dept.Store
Brooks Brothers, 1840 L St.	Apparel
Connecticut Connection, 1101 Connecticut Ave.	Mall
Ginza, 1721 Connecticut Ave.	Dept.Store
International Square, 1851 K St.	Mall
Millennium, 1528 U St.	Dept. Store
Tiny Jewel Box, 1147 Connecticut Ave.	Jewelry
Watergate 600 Office Building	Apparel

Places of Interest:
Capitol Hill
Ford's Theater
Georgetown
Jefferson Memorial
The J.Edgar Hoover Federal Bureau of Investigation Building
The Lincoln Memorial
The National Air and Space Museum
The National Museum of American Art
The National Museum of American History
The National Museum of Natural History
The Washington Monument
The White House

CANADA

CANADA

Official Name: Dominion of Canada

Location: North America. Canada is bordered by the USA. The Atlantic Ocean lies to the east and the Pacific Ocean lies to the west. Alaska lies to the northwest, Greenland to the northeast and to the north is the Polar ice-cap.

Government: Federal Parliamentary State (Monarchy)

Area: 9,970,610 sq. km., 3,849,674 sq. miles.

Population: 27.46 million

Religion(s): Roman Catholic majority. United Church of Canada. Anglican and other religions are also present.

Capital City: Ottawa

Major Business Cities: Edmonton, Montreal, Quebec, Toronto, Vancouver and Winnipeg.

Time: GMT -3.30/-8 (GMT -2.30/-7 from March to end of October).

Currency: Canadian Dollar (CAD)=100 cents

Currency Requirements: There are no restrictions on the import and the export of either foreign or local currency but the amount has to be declared.

Business Hours:
- Government: 09.00-17.00 Mon-Fri
- Banks: 08.00/09.00-15.00/17.00 Mon-Fri (some open Sat mornings)
- Shops: 09.00-17.00 Mon-Fri
- Offices: 09.00-17.00 Mon-Fri

CANADA

Weight and Measures: Metric System

Electric Current: 110 volts AC. Plugs are of the American flat 2-pin type. Universal adapters are available at electrical stores.

Holidays:
New Year's Day - January 1
Good Friday - April 10*
Easter Monday - April 13*
Victoria Day - May 19
Canada Day - July 1
Labor Day - September 1
Thanksgiving - October 13
Remembrance Day** - November 11
Christmas Day - December 25
Boxing Day - December 26

*Christian Holidays – vary each year.
** Mainly only banks and government offices take this day as a Holiday

Suitable Clothing: In summer, bring medium-weight clothing, and for winter, medium-weight clothing and a heavy coat. Particularly in Vancouver, you will need rainwear year round.

Automobile Driving License: A Full National Driving License is required. An International Driving Permit is recommended but it is valid only if it is accompanied by a National License.

Customs Allowances: You may bring in, duty free, 200 cigarettes, 50 cigars and 1 liter of spirits.

Tipping: It is accepted to tip waiters and taxi drivers 15% of the bill. Doormen, cloakroom attendants, porters and bell hops are tipped CAD1 per item. Tipping in clubs and bars is a standard practice.

Credit Cards Accepted: American Express, Diner's Club, MasterCard, Visa,

CANADA

Customary Dining Hours:
Breakfast: 07.00-09.00
Lunch: 12.00-14.00
Dinner: 19.00-21.30

Local Customs, Business Protocol and Courtesies: The Canadian business atmosphere is more European than American; your approach should be formal and conservative. Make your proposals thorough and fully professional, and be on time to appointments. If you are doing business in Quebec, it is best to speak French with French-speaking associates if you can, and to avoid the subject of the conflict with English-speaking Canada. Also, don't treat the country as the USA's "51st state;" rather, show interest in history and customs that are specifically Canadian. Business entertaining is usually in restaurants. Mealtime manners are European.

Health: There are no special precautions necessary. Although the medical facilities are excellent they can be very expensive. A medical insurance is strongly recommended.

Language: English.

CALGARY

Country code: 1 - Area code: 403

Airport: Calgary International Airport

Distance from City: 14.5 km. (9 miles) from the city center

Transportation to Center of City:
From International and Domestic Terminals
By Bus (cost) CAD10-12 Time approx. 30-40 min.
By Taxi (cost) CAD20-30 Time approx. 15-20 min.
Tip luggage porters CAD1 per piece

Transfers: (Minimum Connecting Time):
International to International: 90 min.
International to Domestic: 90 min.

Domestic to International: 45 min.
Domestic to Domestic: 45 min.

Hotels:
Best Western Airport Inn, 1947 18th Ave. N.E., 250-5015
Best Western Port O'Call Inn, 1935 McKnight Blvd. N.E., 291-4600
Best Western Suites Calgary Center, 1330 8th Street S.W., 228-6900
Calgary Airport Hotel, 2001 Airport Rd. N.E., 291-2600
International Hotel of Calgary, 220 4th Ave. S.W., 265-9600
Palliser Calgary, 9th Ave. and 1st Street S.W., 262-1234
Quality Hotel Westward, 119 12th Ave. S.W., 266-4611
Sheraton Cavalier Hotel, 2620 32nd Ave. N.E., 291-0107
Westin Hotel, 320 4th Ave. S.W., 266-1611
Delta Bow Valley, 209 4th Av., 266-1980
Radisson Plaza Hotel, 110 9th Av., 266-7331

Restaurants:
Billy MacIntyre's Cattle Company, No. 500, 3630 Brentwood Rd. NW, 282-6614
Bumper's The Beef House, 672 2622
Buon Giorno Ristorante Italiano, 823 - 17 Ave., 244 5522
Buzzards Café, 140 10th Ave. SW, 264-6959
Cedars Deli, 1009A - 1 St., 264 2532
Chianti Cafe & Restaurant, 438 - 17 Ave., 229 1600
Grand Isle Seafood Restaurant, 128 2nd Ave. SE, 269-7783
Hard Rock Cafe, 108, 7710- 5 St., 255 7117
Hy's Steak House, 316 4th Ave. SW, 263-2222
Kabin Restaurant, 1712 Bow Valley Tr., 678 4878
Kaos Café, 718 17 Ave. SW, 228-9997
Luciano's, 9223 Macleod Tr., 253 4266
Mescalero, 1315 1st St. SW, 266-3339
Owl's Nest Dining Room, Westin Hotel, 320 4th Ave. SW, 266-1611
River Cafe, 200 - 8 Ave., 233 2666
Senor Frogs, 739- 2 Ave., 264 5100
Silver Dragon Restaurant, 211 Banff Ave., 762 3939
Sukiyaki House, 517 - 10 Ave., 263 3003
Teatro, 200 - 8 Ave., 290 1012
TICINO Swiss, 762 3848
Unicorn Restaurant and Pub, 304- 8 Ave., 233 2666

Entertainment:
Cash Casino Place, 4040B Blackfoot Trail SE, 287-1635
Crazy Horse, 1315 - 1 St., 266 3339
Dusty's Saloon, 1088 Olympic Way, 263 5343
Gargoyle's , 1213 1st St. SW, 263-4810
Glenn's Cafe & Memories Nightclub, 3745 Memorial Dr.,   272 5590
Longhorn Dance Hall, 9631 Macleod Trail S, 258-0528
Ranchman's Restaurant, 9615 Macleod Tr., 253 1100
Ranchman's, 9615 Macleod Trail S, 253-1100
Republik, 219-17th Ave. SW, 244-1884
River Park Casino, 1919 Macleod Trail S, 269-6771
Rocking Horse Saloon, 24 7400 Macleod Trail S, 255-4646
Senor Frog's, 739 2nd Ave. SW, 264-5100
Sole Luna, 739 2nd Ave. SW, 264-5100

Shops and Stores:
4th Street Business Revitalization Zone, 1711- 4 St.,
Shopping Centre
Calgary Downtown Association, 304- 8 Ave.
Shopping Centre
Calgary Eaton Centre, 333 - 7 Ave.   Shopping Centre
Classy Formal Wear, 6455 MacLeod Tr.,   Apparel
Deerfoot Mall, 901 - 64 Ave., 274 7024   Mall
Don Forster Mens Wear, 1818- 2 St., 228 5159   Apparel
Kactus Western Wear, 226 0175   Apparel
Kensington, Kensington Rd.   Shopping District
Smithbilt Hats Ltd., 1235 - 10 Ave.,   Dept.Store
Stephen Avenue Mall, b/n 8th Ave. SW
    and 3rd St. SW   Mall
Uptown 17, 10th Street   Shopping District

Places of Interest:
Museum of the Regiments
Naval Museum of Alberta
Science Centre and Planetarium
Calaway Amusement Park
Calgary Zoo
Botanical Gardens
Canada Olympic Park
Fort Calgary Interpretive Centre

CANADA

EDMONTON

Country code: 1 - Area code: 403

Airport: Edmonton International Airport.

Distance from City: 29km (18 miles) south of the city.

Transportation to Center of City:
From International and Domestic Terminals
By Bus (cost) CAD11 Time approx. 60 min.
By Taxi (cost) CAD30 Time approx. 30-40 min.
Tip luggage porters CAD1 per piece

Transfers: (Minimum Connecting Time):
International to International: 60 min.
International to Domestic: 90 min.
Domestic to International: 45 min.
Domestic to Domestic: 45 min.

Automobile Rentals:
Airport car rental desk
Avis - 890-7596
Hertz - 890-4435

Car rental city office
Avis - 448-9025
Tilden Interrent - 422-6097
Hertz - 423-3431

Hotels:
Best Western Cedar Park Inn, 5116 Calgary Trail N., 434-7411
Best Western City Center Inn, 11310-109 Street, 478-2042
Delta Edmonton Centre Suite Hotel, Edmonton Eaton Centre,
   429-3900
Edmonton Hilton, 10235 101st St., 428-7111
Inn On 7th, 10001 107th St., 429-2861
Macdonald Hotel, Edmonton, 10065 100th St., 424-5181
Quality Hotel Executive Suites, 10815 Jasper Ave., 423-1650
Renaissance Edmonton Hotel, 10155 105th St., 423-4811
Westin Hotel, 10135 100th St., 426-3636

Restaurants:
Bistro Praha, 10168 100A St., 424-4218
Bourbon Street, West Edmonton Mall, 8770 170st St.,
Chianti Cafe & restaurant, 10501- 82 Ave., 439 9829
Harvest Room, 10222 - 102 St., 424 5181
Hy's Steak Loft, 10013 - 101A Ave., 424 4444
Joey Tomato's Kitchen, 222 Baseline Rd., 449 1161
La Boheme, 6327 112th Av., 474-5693
La Casa Ticino, 8327 - 112 St., 432 7275
La Spiga, 10133 125 St. & 102nd Av., 482-3100
Mikado, 10651 - 116 St., 425 8096
Pacific Fish Company, 10020 101A Av., 422-0282
Pradera, 10135 - 100 St., 493 8994
Royal Pizza, 222 Baseline Rd., 417 3000
Sawmill, 9504 - 170 St., 486 5866
Shogun Japanese Restaurant, 10125 - 121 St., 488 9757
The Old Spaghetti Factory, 10220 - 103 St., 432 7275
The Olive Garden, 10121 - 171 St., 484 0700
Unheardof Dining Lounge, 9602 82nd Av., 432-0480
Vi's By The River, 9712 - 111 St., 482 6402

Entertainment:
Casino ABS Downtown, 10549 102 St., 424-9461
Casino ABS South, 7055 Argyll Rd., 466-0199
Don Johnston's Under The Boardwalk, 10220 - 103 St.,
    414 0261
Elephant & Castle Pubs, Edmonton Eaton Centre, 424-4555
Elephant & Castle Pubs, West Edmonton Mall, 444-3555
Gas Pump Nightclub & Bar, 10166 - 114 St., 488 4841
Mustang Saloon & Bar, 16648 - 109 Ave., 444 7474
Palace Casino, West Edmonton Mall, 444-2112
Red's Edmonton, 8770 - 170 St., 481 6420
Rose & Crown, 10235 101st. St., 428-7111
The Sherlock Holmes, 5004 - 98 Ave., 463 7788
The Sidetrack Cafe, 10333 - 112 St., 421 1326
Wild West Saloon, 12912 - 50 St., 476 3388
Yuk Yuk's, 8770 - 170 St., 481 9857

Shops and Stores:
As Time Goes By, 10015 - 82 Ave.,   Antiques
Eaton Centre, 102nd Av.   Shopping Center
Edmonton Centre, 100 St. and 102 A Ave.,   Shopping Center

Kingsway Garden Mall, 109 St. and Princess
Elizabeth Ave.   Shopping Center
ManuLife Place, 102nd Av.   Shopping Center
Old Strathcona Historic Area, Whyte Av. & 104th St.   Apparels
Southgate, 111 St. and 51 Ave.   Shopping Center
West Edmonton Mall, 87th Av. & 170th St.   Mall

Places of Interest:
The Provincial Museum of Alberta
Edmonton Space and Science Centre
Old Strathcona Model and Toy Museum
The Canadian Country Music Hall of Honour
Edmonton Art Gallery
Valley Zoo
Whitemud Drive Amusement Park
Wild Waters Waterslide Park
Fort Edmonton Park
The Telephone Historical Centre – a museum

HALIFAX

Country code: 1 - Area code: 902

Airport: Halifax International

Distance from City: 40 km. (25 miles) from the city center.

Transportation to Center of City:
From International and Domestic Terminals
By Bus (cost) CAD20-30. Time approx. 40 min.
By Taxi (cost) CAD30-35. Time approx. 35-45 min.
Tip luggage porters CAD1 per piece

Transfers: (Minimum Connecting Time):
International to International: 75 min.
International to Domestic: 75 min.
Domestic to International: 45 min.
Domestic to Domestic: 45 min.

Hotels:
Econo Lodge, 560 Bedford Hwy., 443-0303

CANADA

Golden Tulip Prince George Hotel, 1725 Market St., 425-1986
Halifax Hotel, 1990 Barrington St., Scotia Sq., 425-6700
Radisson Suite Hotel Halifax, 1649 Hollins St., 429-7233
Sheraton Halifax Hotel, 1919 Upper Water St., 421-1700
Westin Nova Scotian Halifax, 1181 Hollis St., 421-1000
Prince George Hotel, 1725 Market St., 425-1986

Restaurants:
Alfredo,Welnstein and Ho, 1739 Grafton St., 421 1977
Birmingham Bar and Grill, Spring Garden Rd., 420 9622
Cafe Mokka, 1588 Granville St., 492 4036
China Classic, 6311 Quinpool Rd., 429 2828
China Town, 381 Bedford Hwy., 443 2444
Cheelin, 1496 Lower Water St., 422 2252
Chef Klaus Understatement, 5218 Prince St., 420 9923
Da Maurizio, 1496 Lower Water St., 423-0859
Fong's Restaurant, 451 Windmill Rd., 469 9165
Great Wall, 1649 Bedford Row. 422 6153
House of Hum, 316 Prince Albert Rd., 469 2502
King's Palace, 6140 Quinpool Rd., 423 1247
Le Bistro, 1333 South Park St., 423 8428
Lyn D's, 1520 Queen St., 492 8100
MacAskill's Restaurant, 88 Alberney Dr., 466-3100
Old Man Morias, 1150 Barrington St., 422-7960
Privateer's Warehouse, 422-1289
Salty's on the Waterfront, 1869 Upper Water St., 423-6818
Satisfaction Feast, 1581 Grafton St., 422-3540
The Cellar's Backroom, 5677 Brenton Place, 492 DINE
The Fireside, 1500 Brunswick St., 423 5995

Entertainment:
Cheers, 1743 Grafton St., 421-1655
Little Nashville Cabaret, 169 Wyse Rd., 461 0991
Lowrence of Oregano, 1725 Argyle St., 425 8077
Market Street Jazz Cafe, 1770 Market St., 492 CAFE
Maxwell's Plum, 1600 Grafton St., 425 5249
Mexicali Rosa's, 5680 Spring Garden Rd., 422 7672
Midtown Tavern, 1684 Grafton St., 422 5213
Neighbour's Pub, 352 Portland St., 465 4713
Neon Armadillo, 1741 Grafton St., 423 0909
New Palace Cabaret, 1721 Brunswick St., 429 5959
O'Carroll's, 1860 Upper Water St., 423-4405
Pacifico Bar and Grill, 1505 Barrington St., 422 3633

Peddler's Pub, Granville Mall, 423 5033
Peddler's Too, 900 Windmill Rd., 468 4449
Privateer's Warehouse, 422-1289
Reilly's, 313 Prince Albert Rd., 469 5850
Split Crow, 1855 Granville St., 422 4366
The Left Bank, 1496 Lower Water St., 492 3049
The Promenade, 1181 Nollis St., 421 1000

Shops and Stores:

Barrington Place Shops, 1903 Barrington St.,	Shopping Centre
City Center Atlantic, 5523 Spring Garden Rd.,	Shopping Centre
Jennifer Of Nova Scotia, 5635 Spring Gardan Rd.	Jewelry
K-Mart Mall, 50 Tacoma Dr.,	Dept. Store
Mic Mac Mall, 21 Mic Mac Boulevard,	Mall
Pewter House, 1875 Granville St.	Crafts
Plaid Place, 1903 Barrington Pl.	Accessories
Real Atlantic Superstore, 650 Portland St.	Dept. Store
Scotia Square, 5201 Duke Street,	Shopping Centre
South Centre Mall, 16 Dentith Rd.	Mall
Stornoway, 1873 Granville St.	Crafts
Wool Sweater Outlet, 1870 Hollis St.	Outlet

MONTREAL

Country code: 1 - Area code: 514

Airport: Mirabel International Airport

Distance from City: . 55km (34 miles) from the city.

Transportation to Center of City:
From International and Domestic Terminals
By Bus (cost) CAD14.50 Time approx. 55 min.
By Taxi (cost) CAD60 Time approx. 40 min.
Tip luggage porters CAD1 per piece

Transfers: (Minimum Connecting Time):
International to International: 60 min.

CANADA

International to Domestic: 90 min.
Domestic to International: 60 min.
Domestic to Domestic: 45 min.

Automobile Rentals:
Airport car rental desk
Avis - 476-3481
Tilden Interrent - 476-3460
Hertz - 476-3385

Car rental city office
Avis - 866-7906
Tilden Interrent - 636-9030
Hertz - 842-8537

Hotels:
Best Western Europa-Downtown, 1240 Drummond St., 866-6492
Best Western Ville-Marie Hotel & Suites, 3407 Peel St.,
    288-4141
Courtyard By Marriott, 410 rue Sherbrooke West, 844-8851
Inter-Continental Montreal, 360 rue St. Antoine Quest, 987-9900
Le Centre Sheraton, 1201 Rene-Levesque Blvd. W., 878-2000
Maritime Hotel, 1155 Guy St., 932-1411
Montreal Bonaventure Hilton, 1 Place Bonaventure, 878-2332
Montreal Marriott Chateau Champlain, 1 Place du Canada,
    878-9000
Queen Elizabeth, Montreal, 900 Rene Levesque Blvd. W.,
    861-35111
Radisson Hotel des Gouverneurs, 777 University St., 879-1370
Ritz-Carlton Kempinski Montreal, 1228 Sherbrooke St. W.,
    842-4212
Westin Mont-Royal Hotel, 1052 Sherbrooke St. W., 284-1110
Du Fort, 1390 rue du Fort, 938-8333

Restaurants:
Bers, 990 Blvd. de Maisonneuve Ouest, 844-1000
Bocca d'Oro, 1448 rue St-Mathieu, 933-8414
Bonaparte, 443 rue St-Francois-Xavier, 844-4368
Café Stash, 200 rue St-Paul Ouest, 845-6611
Gibby's, 298 Pl. d'Youville, 282-1837
Guy and Dodo Morali, Les Cours Mont-Royal, 1444 rue
    Metcalfe, 842-3636

Helene de Champlain, Ile Ste-Helene, 395-2424
Katsura, 2170 rue de la Montagne, 849-1172
L'Express, 3927 rue St-Denis, 845-5333

Le Café de Paris, Ritz-Carlton, 1228 rue Sherbrooke Ouest, 842-4212
Le Passe-Partout. 3857 Blvd. Decarie, 487-7750
Le Taj, 2077 rue Stanley, 845-9015
Les Halles, 1450 rue Crescent, 844-2328
Les Trois Tilleuls, 290 rue Richelieu, Saint Marc sur Richelieu, 584-2231
Maison Kam Fung, 1008 rue Clark, 878-2888
Milos, 5357 Av. du Parc, 272-3522
Nuances, 1 Av. de Casino, 392-2708
Pizzaiole, 1446-A rue Crescent, 845-4158
Schwartz's Delicatessen, 3895 Blvd. St-Laurent, 842-4813
Shes Clo, 3199 rue Ontario Est, 522-5348
Toque, 3842 rue St-Denis, 499-2084
Wilensky's Light Lunch, 34 rue Fairmount Ouest, 271-0247
Zen, Le Westin Mont-Royal, 1050 rue Sherbrooke Ouest, 499-0801

Entertainment:
Biddle's, 2060 rue Aylmer, 842-8656
Club Soda, 5240 Av. du Parc, 270-7848
Déjà vu. 1224 rue Bishop, 866-0512
Deux Pierrots Boite aux Chansons, 104 rue St-Paul Est, 861-1270
Hard Rock Café, 1458 rue Crescent, 987-1420
Hurley's Irish Pub, 1225 rue Crescent, 861-4111
L'Air du Temps, 191 rue St-Paul Ouest, 842-2003
L'Ours Qui Fume, 2019 rue St-Denis, 845-6998
Metropolis, 59 rue Ste-Catherine Est, 288-2020
Quai des Brumes Dancing, 4481 rue St-Denis, 499-0467
Thursday's, 1449 rue Crescent, 288-5656
Zoo, 3556 Blvd. St-Laurent, 848-6398

Shops and Stores:
Antiquites Landry, 1726 rue Notre-Dame Ouest — Antiques
Complexe Desjardins, Sainte Catherine and Saint Urbain Sts. — Shopping Centre

CANADA

Eaton Centre, 705 Sainte Catherine St.,	Shopping Complex
Eaton, 677 rue Ste-Catherine Ouest	Dept. Store
Holt Renfrew, 1300 rue Sherbrooke Ouest,	Dept. Store
La Baie, 585 rue Ste-Catherine Ouest	Dept. Store
Ogilvy, 1307 rue Ste-Catherine Ouest	Dept. Store
Place Montreal Trust, Sainte Catherine St. and McGill College Ave.,	Shopping Centre
The Bay, 585 Sainte Catherine St.,	Dept.Store
Viva Gallery, 1970 rue Notre-Dame Ouest	Antiques

Places of Interest:
Basilique Notre-Dame de Montreal – a church
Centre d'Histoire de Montreal
McCord Museum of Canadian History
The Botanical Garden
La Ronde – an amusement park.
The Museum of Fine Arts
Mary Queen of the World Cathedral
The Dow Planetarium
Images du Futur – a museum
Olympic Park

OTTAWA

Country code: 1 - Area code: 613

Airport: MacDonald-Cartier International Airport.

Distance from City: 15km (9 miles) from city center.

Transportation to Center of City:
From International and Domestic Terminals
By Bus (cost) CAD2. Time approx.60 min.(every 15 min.)
By Taxi (cost) CAD15-20 Time approx. 20 min.
Tip luggage porters CAD1 per piece

Transfers: (Minimum Connecting Time):
International to International: 90 min.
International to Domestic: 90 min.
Domestic to International: 30 min.
Domestic to Domestic: 30 min.

CANADA

Automobile Rentals:
Airport car rental desk
Avis - 739-3334
Tilden Interrent - 737-7023
Hertz - 521-3332
Car rental city office
Avis - 238-3421
Tilden Interrent - 232-3536
Hertz - 241-7681

Hotels:
Best Western Victoria Park Suites, 377 O'Connor, 567-7275
Chateau Laurier, Ottawa, 1 Rideau St., 241-1414
Les Suites Hotel Ottawa, 130 Besserer St., 232-2000
Lord Elgin Hotel, 100 Elgin Blvd., 235-3333
Radisson Hotel Ottawa Centre, 100 Kent St., 238-1122
Sheraton Ottawa Hotel & Towers, 150 Albert St., 238-1500
Westin Hotel, Ottawa, 11 Colonel By Drive, 560-7000

Restaurants:
Boko Restaurant, 87 George St., 241-9848
Bravo Bravo, 292 Elgin St., 233-7525
Café Wim & Restaurant, 537 Sussex Dr., 241-1771
Cathay Restaurant, 228 Albert St., 233-7705
Chequers, 816 Hazeldean Rd., Stittsville, 836-1665
Chez Jean Pierre, 210 Somerset St., 235-9711
Courtyard Restaurant, 21 George St., 241-1516
Dragon Buffet Restaurant, 1620 Scott St., 728-2826
Flippers, 823 Bank St., 232-2703
Fresco, 354 Elgin St., 235-7541
Fuliwah Restaurant, 691 Somerset St., 233-2552
Greek Souvlaki House Inc., 1200 Prince of Wales Dr.,
    225-1144
Le Café, 53 Elgin St., 943-1403
Les Muses, 100 rue Laurier, Hull, 776-7009
Maplelawn Café, 529 Richmond Rd., 722-5118
Nate's Deli, 316 Rideau St., 789-9191
New Dubrovnik Dining Lounge, 1170 Carling Av., 722-1490
Noah's, 407 Laurier Av., 782-2422
Oscar's 123 Queen St., 234-9699
Savana Café, 431 Gilmour St., 233-9159

CANADA

Entertainment:
Cachet Club, 96 George St., 562 0433
Cajun Attic, 594 Rideau St., 789 1185
Casino de Hull, 772 2100
Diamond Gaming Services Inc., 727 8081
Earl of Sussex Pub, 431 Sussex Dr., 565-5544
Glue Pot Pub, 340 Queen St., 594 8222
Mayflower II Restaurant and Pub, 201 Queen St., 238-1138
RJ'S Boom Boom Saloon, 200 Rideau St., 562 2512
The Rainbow Bistro, 76 Murray St., 241 5123
Topaz Entertainment Palace, 2335 St., 733 7100
Tucson's Roadhouse, 2440 Bank St., 738 7596
Upstairs Club, 207 Rideau St., 241 7044
Zuma's Rodeo Texas Grill and Dance Hall, 742 W St. Laurent at
    Hwy.417, 741-9046

Shops and Stores:

Alyea's Jewellers Limited, 52 Sparks St.	Jewelry
Canada's Four Corners, 93 Sparks St.	Gifts
Canadian Geographic, 39 McArthur Av.	Gifts
Holt Renfrew, 240 Sparks St.	Apparel
Inuit Artists' Shop, 2081 Merivale Rd.	Jewelry
Jubilee Fine Jewellers, Rideau Centre	Jewelry
Oh Yes Ottawa!, Rideau Centre	Souvenirs
Pat Flesher Furs, 437 Cooper St.	Apparel
The Snow Goose, 83 Sparks St.	Crafts

Places of Interest:
The Canadian Museum of Civilization
The National Museum of Science and Technology
The National Gallery of Canada – an art gallery
The National Archives of Canada
The National Aviation Museum
The Parliament Buildings
The National War Memorial

QUEBEC

Country code: 1 - Area code: 418

CANADA

Airport: Jean Lesage International Airport.

Distance from City: 15km (9 miles) from Old Quebec City.

Transportation to Center of City:
From International and Domestic Terminals
By Bus (cost) CAD6.75-CAD9 Time approx. 60 min.
By Taxi (cost) CAD20 Time approx. 20 min.
Tip luggage porters CAD1 per piece

Transfers: (Minimum Connecting Time):
International to International: 90 min.
International to Domestic: 90 min.
Domestic to International: 30 min.
Domestic to Domestic: 30 min.

Automobile Rentals:
Airport car rental desk
Avis - 872-0409
Tilden Interrent - 871-1224
Hertz - 871-1571

Car rental city office
Avis - 872-9831
Tilden Interrent - 694-1727
Hertz - 694-1224

Hotels:
Le Chateau Frontenac, Quebec, 1 rue des Carrieres, 692-3861
Loews Le Concorde, 1225 pl. Montcalm, 647-2222
Quebec Hilton, 1100 Rene-Levesque Blvd., 647-2411
Radisson Hotel des Gouverneurs, , 690 Rene-Levesque Blvd.,
    647-1717
Ramada Hotel Quebec Centre Ville, 395 rue de la Couronne,
    647-2611

Restaurants:
A la Petit Table, 1200 rue St-Jean, 694-0618
Aux Anciens Canadiens, 34 rue St-Louis, 692-1627
Café de la Paix, 44 rue des Jardins, 692-1430
Café Suisse, 32 rue Ste-Anne, 694-1320
Casse-Crepe Breton, 1136 rue St-Jean, 692-0438

Chez Temporel, 25 rue Couillard, 694-1813
Gambrinus, 15 rue du Fort, 692-5144
L'Apsara, 71 rue d'Auteuil, 694-0232
L'Astral, 1225 Pl. Montcalm, 647-2222
L'Echaude, 73 Sault-au-Matelot, 692-1299
Le Café de la Terrasse, Chateau Frontenac, 1 rue Carrieres,
   692-3861
Le Cochon Dingue, 46 Blvd. Rene Levesque, 523-2013
Le Commensal, 860 rue St-Jean, 647-3733
Le Graffiti, 1191 Av. Cartier, 529-4949
Le Marie Clarisse, 12 rue du Petit-Champlain, 692-0857
Le Paris Brest, 590 Grande Allee Est, 529-2243
Le Saint-Amour, 48 rue Ste-Ursule, 694-0667
Les Freres de la Cote, 1190 rue St-Jean, 692-5445
Paparazzi, 1365 Av. Maguire, Sillery, 683-8111
Portofino Bistri Italiano, 54 rue Couillard, 692-8888

Entertainment:
Chez Dagobert, 600 Grande Allee Est, 522-0393
Chez Son Pere, 24 St-Stanislas, 692-5308
L'Emprise at Hotel Clarendon, 75 rue Ste-Anne, 692-2480
Le d'Auteuil, 35 rue d'Auteuil, 692-2263
Le Pab Saint-Alexandre, 1087 rue St-Jean, 694-0015
Maison de la Chanson, 78 rue Petit Champlain, 692-2613
Merlin, 1179 Av Cartier, 529-9567
Vogue and Lock Holmes, 1170 d'Artigny, 529-9973

Shops and Stores:

Antiquites Zaor, 112 rue St. Paul	Antiques
Collection Lazuli, 774 rue St-Jean	Gifts
Francois Cote Collections, 35 rue Buade	Apparel
Holt Renfrew & Co., Ltd, Pl Ste-Foy, Ste Foy	Dept. Store
Joaillier Louis Perrier, 48 rue du Petit-Chamolain	Jewelry
L'Heritage Antiquites, 110 rue St. Paul	Antiques
La Baie, Pl. Laurier, Ste Foy	Dept. Store
La Maison Darlington, 7 rue Buade	Apparel
Les Trois Colobes Inc., 46 rue St-Louis	Crafts
Louis Laflamme, 1192 rue St-Jean	Apparel
Simons, 20 cote de la Fabrique	Dept. Store
Zimmermman, 46 cote de la Fabrique	Jewelry

Places of Interest:

CANADA

Holy Trinity Anglican Cathedral
Basilique Notre-Dame-de-Quebec
Musee de L'Amerique Francaise – a museum
The Civilization Museum
Vieux-Port de Quebec (Old Port of Quebec) - parks
Quebec Aquarium
Quebec Zoological Gardens

VANCOUVER

Country code: 1 - Area code: 604

Airport: Vancouver International Airport.

Distance from City: 15km (9 miles) southwest of the city.

Transportation to Center of City:
From International and Domestic Terminals
By Bus (cost) CAD9 Time approx. 30-40 min.
By Taxi (cost) CAD22-CAD26 Time approx. 20-25 min.
Tip luggage porters CAD 1per piece

Transfers: (Minimum Connecting Time):
International to International: 90 min.
International to Domestic: 60 min.
Domestic to International: 50 min.
Domestic to Domestic: 45 min.

Automobile Rentals:
Airport car rental desk
Avis - 273-4577
Tilden Interrent - 273-3121
Hertz - 606-3782

Car rental city office
Avis - 736-5583
Tilden Interrent - 685-6111
Hertz - 688-2411

CANADA

Hotels:

Best Western Capilano Inn & Suites, 1634 Capilano Rd., N. Vancouver, 987-8185

Best Western Exibition Park Vancouver, 3475 E. Hastings St., 294-4751

Best Western King Inn & Conference Centre, 5411 Kingsway, Burnaby, 438-1383

Best Western Listel O'Doul's Hotel, 1300 Robson St., 684-8461

Best Western Motor Inn, 3075 Kingsway, 430-3441

Best Western Sends, 1755 Davie St., 682-1831

Chateau Granville, 1100 Granville St., 669-7070

Hyatt Regency Vancouver, 655 Burrard St., 683-1234

Landis Hotel & Suites, 1234 Hornby St., 688-1234

Pacific Palisades Hotel, 1277 Robson St., 688-0461

Pan Pacific Hotel, Vancouver, 300-999 Canada Pl., 662-8111

Quality Hotel Downtown, 1335 Howe St., 682-0229

Renaissance Vancouver Hotel-Harbourside, 1133 W. Hastings St., 689-9211

Sheraton Wall Centre Hotel, 1088 Burrard St., 331-1000

Vancouver Hotel, 900 W. Georgia St., 684-3131

Waterfront Centre Hotel, Vancouver, 900 Canada Place Way, 691-1991

Wedgewood Hotel, 845 Hornbu St., 689-7777

Westin Bayshore, 1601 W. Georgia St., 682-3377

Restaurants:

Caffe de Medici, 1025 Robson St., 669-9322

Chartwell, W. Georgia St., 844-6715

Chiyoda, 1050 Alberni St., 688-5050

Griffin's, 900 W.Georgia St., 662-1900

Imperial Chinese Seafood, 355 Burrard St., 688-8191

Isadora's, 1540 Old Bridge St., Granville Island, 681-8816

Japanese Deli House, 381 Powell St., 681-6484

Kirin Mandarin Restaurant, 1166 Alberni St., 102, 682-8833

Le Crocodile, 100-909 Burrand St., 669-4298

Le Gavroche, 1616 Alberni St., 685-3924

Naam Restaurant, 2724 W. 4th Av., 738-7151

Pink Pearl, 1132 E. Hastings St., 253-4316

Quattro on Fourth, 2611 W. 4th Ave., 734-4444

Rubina Tandoori, 1962 Kingsway, 874-3621

Seasons in the Park, Queen Elizabeth Park at 33 and Cambie St., 874-8008

Shijo Japanese Restaurant, 1926 W. 4th St., 732-4676
Szechuan Changqing, 1668 W. Broadway, 734-1668
Tojo's, 777 W. Broadway, 872-8050
Vassili's Taverna, 2884 W Broadway, 733-3231
Villa de Lupo, 869 Hamilton St., 688-7436
William Tell, 765 Beatty St., 688-3504

Entertainment:
86th Street Music Hall, 750 Pacific Blvd., 683-8687
Alma Street Café, 2505 Alma St., 222-2244
Automotive Billiards Club, 1095 Homer, 682-0040
Bacchus Lounge, 845 Hornby St., 689-7777
Commodore Ballroom, 870 Granville St., 681-7838
Garden Terrace, 791 W. Georgia St., 689-9333
Gerard Lounge, 845-Burrard St., 682-5511
Glass Slipper, 185 E 11th Av. 877-0066
Graceland, 1250 Richards St., 688-2648
Great Canadian Casino, 2477 Heather St., 872-5543
Hard Rock Café, 686 W. Hastings , 687-7625
Joe Fortes, 777 Thurlow St., 669-1940
Mars, 1320 Richards St., 662-7707
Richard's on Richards, 1036 Richards St., 687-6794
Roof Lounge, 900 W. Georgia St., 684-3131
Royal Diamond Casino, 535 Davie St., 685-2340
Soho Café and Billiards, 1144 Homer, 688-1180
Steam Works, 375 Water St., 689-2739
Town Pump, 66 Water St., 683-6695
Yaletown Brewing Company, 1111 Mainland St., 681-2739

Shops and Stores:

Altus Mountain Gear, 137 West Broadway,	Apparel
Bay Downtown Vancouver, 674 Granville St.,	Dept.Store
Boutique Zole, 763 Hornby St.	Apparel
Eaton's, 701 Granville St.,	Dept.Store
Four Continents, 2475 Bayswater,	Antiques
Hermes Canada, 633 Granville St.,	Apparel
Instante, 773 Hornby St.	Apparel
Scandinavia Arts Ltd., 648 Hornby St.,	Jewelry
Tilley Endurables Western Inc., 2401 Granville St.	Apparel
Versus, 1008 W.Georgia St.	Apparel

CANADA

Places of Interest:
The Vancouver Museum
Sports Hall of Fame Museum
The Museum of Anthropology
The Granville Island Brewery
Vancouver Aquarium
Vancouver Art Gallery
Christ Church Cathedral
Van Dusen Botanical Garden
Splashdown Park – a water park
Science World – a museum

WINNIPEG

Country code: 1 - Area code: 204

Airport: Winnipeg International Airport.

Distance from City: 7km (4 miles) from the city center.

Transportation to Center of City:
From International and Domestic Terminals
By Bus (cost) CAD1.50 Time approx. 30-35 min.
By Taxi (cost) CAD10-CAD15 Time approx. 20 min.
Tip luggage porters CAD1per piece

Transfers: (Minimum Connecting Time):
International to International: 90 min.
International to Domestic: 60 min.
Domestic to International: 45 min.
Domestic to Domestic: 30 min.

Automobile Rentals:
Airport car rental desk
Avis - 956-2847
Tilden Interrent - 925-3531
Hertz - 925-6625

Car rental city office
Avis - 956-2847

CANADA

Tilden Interrent - 925-3525
Hertz - 925-6600

Hotels:
Best Western Carlton Inn, 942-0881
Crowne Plaza Winnipeg Downtown, 350 St. Mary Ave.,
942-0551
Fort Garry Hotel, 222 Broadway, 942-8251
Holiday Inn Airport, 2520 Portage Ave., 885-4478
Lombard Hotel, 2 Lombard Place, 957-1350
Place Louis Riel, 190 Smith St., 947-6961
Travelodge Hotel Downtown Winnipeg, 360 Colony St.,
786-7011

Restaurants:
Amici, 326 Broadway, 943-4997
Bistro Dansk, 63 Sherbrook St., 775-5662
Cafe Carlo, 243 Lilac St., 477 5544
Civita, 691B Corydon Ave., 453 4616
D'8 Schtove, 1842 Rembina Rte., 275-2294
Deen's, 205 Marion St., 233 2208
Green Gates, 6945 Roblin Blvd., 897 0990
Henry's Diner & Pour House, G-1033 Hwy.26, 864 2395
Homer's 520 Ellice Av., 788-4858
Kelekis, 1100 Main St., 582-1786
King's Palace, 260 King St., 943 1077
Le Beaujolais, 131 Provencher Blvd., 237-6306
Mandarin, 613 Sargent Av., 775-7819
Medicine Rock Cafe, 990 Hwy 26, 864 2451
Oceana, 1910 Pembina Hwy., 261 0494
Peppoli, 454 River Ave., 284 3996
Picasso's, 615 Sargent Av., 775-2469
Pockets Bar & Grill, 171 McDermont Ave., 957 7665
Prairie Oyster, The Forks Market, 942 0918
Restaurant Dubrovnik, 390 Assiniboine Av., 944-0594
Tiamo, 729 Corydon Ave., 475 2233
Victor's, 331 Smith St., 947-2751

Entertainment:
Celebrations Dinner Theatre, 1808 Wellington Ave., 982 8282
Centre Culturel Franco Manitobain, 340 Provencher Blvd.,

233 8972
Cristal Casino, 222 Broadway Av., 957-2600
Grapes, 1747 Ellice Ave., 783 3485
Hy's Steak Loft, 216 Kennedy St., 942-1000
Ice Works Cabaret, 165 McDermont Ave., 947 2582
Manitoba Centennial Centre, 555 Main St., 956-1360
McPhilips Street Station, 484 McPhilips St., 957-3900
Mustang Sally's, 114 Market Ave., 944 1117
Palomino Club, 1133 Portage Ave., 772 0454
Pockets, 171 McDermont Ave., 957 7665
Regent, 1425 Regent Av., 957-2700
Rumor's Restaurant & Comedy Club, 2025 Corydon Ave.,
    488 4520
S.O.S. Comedy Island, 2520 Portage Ave., 885 4478
The King's Head, 120 King St., 957-1479
Shops and Stores:

Boulet Boots, 128 Adelaide St.	Outlet
Bra Bra & Panterie, 554A Des Meurons	Apparel
Danali Casual Mens Wear, 1883 Grant Ave.,	Apparel
Dream Weaver, 661 Corydon Ave.	Apparel
Eaton Place, Graham Av.	Mall
Grafts Guild of Manitoba, 183 Kennedy St.	Jewelers
Grat Canadian Print Company, 75 Albert St.	Crafts
Holidaze, 2631 Portage Ave.	Dept.Store
Osborene Village, Osborne St.	Shopping Area
The Upstairs Gallery, 266 Edmonton St.	Crafts

Places of Interest:
The Winnipeg Art Gallery
The Centennial Centre – a museum and a planetarium
St. Boniface Cathedral
Assiniboine Zoo
Mennonite Heritage Village – a museum
Lower Fort Garry – an old stone fort
Fun Mountain Water Slide Park
Manitoba Children's Museum
The Commonwealth Air Training Plan Museum